Oct 15, 1985

The Bible
and
Liberation

The Bible and Liberation

POLITICAL AND SOCIAL HERMENEUTICS

Edited
by
Norman K. Gottwald

REVISED EDITION
OF
A **RADICAL RELIGION** READER

ORBIS  BOOKS
Maryknoll, New York 10545

Second Printing, November 1984

The Catholic Foreign Mission Society of America (Maryknoll) recruits and trains people for overseas missionary service. Through Orbis Books Maryknoll aims to foster the international dialogue that is essential to mission. The books published, however, reflect the opinions of their authors and are not meant to represent the official position of the society.

The Index of Scriptural References and the Index of Names were prepared by James Sullivan; the Index of Subjects was prepared by Norman K. Gottwald

Library of Congress Cataloging in Publication Data
Main entry under title:

The Bible and liberation.

  Includes bibliographies and indexes.
  1. Bible—Hermeneutics—Addresses, essays,
lectures. 2. Bible—Criticism, interpretation,
etc.—Addresses, essays, lectures. 3. Christianity
and politics—Biblical teaching—Addresses, essays, lectures. 4. Sociology, Biblical—Addresses,
essays, lectures. 5. Liberation theology—Ad-
resses, essays, lectures. I. Gottwald, Norman K.
(Norman Karol), 1926–
BS476.B49 1983   220.6'01   82-22242
ISBN 0-88344-043-1
ISBN 0-88344-044-X (pbk.)

Contents

Part III
SOCIOLOGICAL READINGS OF THE OLD TESTAMENT

Part IV
SOCIOLOGICAL READINGS OF THE NEW TESTAMENT

Part V
THE BIBLE IN POLITICAL THEOLOGY AND MARXIST THOUGHT

List of Contributors

Phyllis A. Bird, Professor of Old Testament, Perkins School of Theology, Southern Methodist University, Dallas, Texas.

John Pairman Brown, Director, Northern California Ecumenical Council, San Francisco, California.

Walter Brueggemann, Professor of Old Testament, Eden Theological Seminary, Webster Groves, Missouri.

Alfredo Fierro, Director of the Instituto Universitario de Teología, Madrid, an institute for lay theological education.

Elisabeth Schüssler Fiorenza, Professor of Theology, University of Notre Dame, Notre Dame, Indiana.

Frank S. Frick, Professor of Religious Studies, Albion College, Albion, Michigan.

Kuno Füssel, Assistant Professor of Systematic Theology, University of Münster, Münster, West Germany.

John G. Gager, Professor of Religion, Princeton University, Princeton, New Jersey.

Norman K. Gottwald, W. W. White Professor of Biblical Studies, New York Theological Seminary, New York City.

Joseph L. Hardegree, Jr., instructor in Human Relations and Organizational Behavior Program, University of San Francisco, San Francisco, California.

Lucien Legrand, Professor of Sacred Scripture, St. Peter's Pontifical Institute of Theology, Bangalore, India.

David Lochhead, Professor of Theology, Vancouver School of Theology, Vancouver, British Columbia.

Bruce J. Malina, Professor of New Testament, Creighton University, Omaha, Nebraska.

Arthur F. McGovern, Professor of Philosophy, University of Detroit, Detroit, Michigan.

Carlos Mesters, Centro de Estudos Bíblicos, Rio de Janeiro, Brazil, working with base communities of lay Bible study.

Carol L. Meyers, Associate Professor, Department of Religion, Duke University, Durham, North Carolina.

ix

Henri Mottu, Director, Centre de Recontres, Cartigny, Switzerland, an institute for adult theological education and pastoral training.

Allen Myers, Biblical Studies Editor, Wm. B. Eerdmans Publishing Company, Grand Rapids, Michigan.

George V. Pixley, Professor of Old Testament, Seminario Bautista, Mexico City, Mexico.

Sergio Rostagno, pastor, Waldensian Church, Pomaretto, Italy.

Luise Schottroff, Professor of New Testament, Johannes Gutenberg University, Mainz, West Germany.

Robin Scroggs, Professor of New Testament, Chicago Theological Seminary, Chicago, Illinois.

Juan Luis Segundo, Director, Peter Faber Pastoral Center, Montevideo, Uruguay.

Rudolf J. Siebert, Professor of Religion, Western Michigan University, Kalamazoo, Michigan.

Robert H. Smith, Associate Professor of Exegetical Theology, Christ Seminary-Seminex, St. Louis, Missouri.

Gerd Theissen, Professor of New Testament, University of Heidelberg, Heidelberg, West Germany.

Robert R. Wilson, Associate Professor of Old Testament, Yale Divinity School, New Haven, Connecticut.

Franklin J. Woo, Director, China Program, Committee for East Asia and the Pacific, National Council of the Churches of Christ in the U.S.A., New York City.

Abbreviations

AA	*American Anthropologist*
AAWG.PH	Abhandlungen der Akademie der Wissenschaften in Göttingen—Philologisch—historische Klasse
AcOr	*Acta Orientalia*
ANET	*Ancient Near Eastern Texts,* ed. J. B. Pritchard
ASOR	American School of Oriental Research
ASR	*American Sociological Review*
ATANT	Abhandlungen zur Theologie des Alten und Neuen Testaments
AThR	*Anglican Theological Review*
BA	*Biblical Archeologist*
BAR	*Biblical Archeologist Reader*
BT	*The Bible Translator*
BTB	*Biblical Theology Bulletin*
BZAW	Beihefte zur *Zeitschrift für die alttestamentliche Wissenschaft*
CBQ	*Catholic Biblical Quarterly*
CurTM	*Currents in Theology and Mission*
DBSup	*Dictionnaire de la Bible, Supplément*
EvTh	*Evangelische Theologie*
HR	*History of Religions*
HSM	Harvard Semitic Monographs
HTR	*Harvard Theological Review*
HUCA	*Hebrew Union College Annual*
HZ	*Historische Zeitschrift*
IB	*Interpreter's Bible*
IDB	*Interpreter's Dictionary of the Bible*
IDBSup	Supplementary Volume to *Interpreter's Dictionary of the Bible*
IEJ	*Israel Exploration Journal*
Int	*Interpretation*
JAAR	*Journal of the American Academy of Religion*
JBAC	*Jahrbuch für Antike und Christentum*
JBL	*Journal of Biblical Literature*
JNES	*Journal of Near Eastern Studies*

JR	*Journal of Religion*
JRAI	*Journal of the Royal Anthropological Institute*
JRT	*Journal of Religious Thought*
JSOT	*Journal for the Study of the Old Testament*
JSS	*Journal of Semitic Studies*
JThSt	*Journal of Theological Studies*
KuD	*Kerygma und Dogma*
NT or *NovT*	*Novum Testamentum*
NTS	*New Testament Studies*
NTSMS	New Testament Studies Monograph Series
NZSTR	*Neue Zeitschrift für systematische Theologie und Religions philosophie*
Or	*Orientalia*
PEQ	*Palestine Exploration Quarterly*
PG	*Patrologia Graeca*
PL	*Patrologia Latina*
RAC	*Reallexikon für Antike und Christentum*
RelSRev	*Religious Studies Review*
RevExp	*Review and Expositor*
RHPR	*Revue d'histoire et de philosophie religieuses*
SBLDS	Society of Biblical Literature Dissertation Series
SBLMS	Society of Biblical Literature Monograph Series
SBLSP	Society of Biblical Literature Seminar Papers
SBT	Studies in Biblical Theology
SJA	*Southwestern Journal of Anthropology*
SNTS	Society for New Testament Studies
TRu	*Theologische Rundschau*
ThSt	*Theological Studies*
ThZ	*Theologische Zeitschrift*
TLZ	*Theologische Literaturzeitung*
TTS	Tübinger Theologische Studien
USQR	*Union Seminary Quarterly Review*
VT	*Vetus Testamentum*
VTSup	Vetus Testamentum, Supplements
WMANT	Wissenschaftliche Monographien zum Alten und Neuen Testament
ZAW	*Zeitschrift für die alttestamentliche Wissenschaft*
ZNW	*Zeitschrift für die neutestamentliche Wissenschaft*
ZTK	*Zeitschrift für Theologie und Kirche*
ZwTh	*Zeitschrift für Wissenchaftliche Theologie*

INTRODUCTION

The Bible and Liberation: Deeper Roots and Wider Horizons

In 1975 the *Radical Religion* collective published a special issue of the journal on "Class Origins and Class Readings of the Bible" (Vol. II, Nos. 2–3) and in 1976 expanded it into a Reader entitled *The Bible and Liberation: Political and Social Hermeneutics* (edited by Norman K. Gottwald and Antoinette C. Wire). There was an immediate demand that quickly exhausted all copies. The decision of the *Radical Religion* board and of Orbis Books to publish a revised and expanded edition of the Reader is based on continuing requests for an anthology of this type for use in both academic and church study circles. In the meanwhile, although articles and books have multiplied, no comparable anthology of materials on the same scale and with the same focus has appeared.

It is a timely moment for a fundamental revision of the Reader because liberative understandings and uses of the Bible have extended ever more widely into ecclesial and theological circles, on the one hand, while the serious sociological study of the Bible in its original context has begun to penetrate academic curricula and scholarly research projects, on the other hand. When the original Reader was composed in 1976, it was difficult to find the desired range and depth of English-language materials. Today "the Bible and liberation" is a many-sided theme increasingly recognized in the English-speaking world, as elsewhere, as a valid subject of academic study, theological reflection, and ecclesial practice which has stimulated fresh studies as well as translations of key works from other languages. The revised Reader is able to select from a far larger pool of resources than could have been imagined five years ago.

1

AIMS AND RATIONALE OF THE REVISED READER

The Foreword of the original Reader explained its aims in the following terms:

> The Reader attempts both to describe and to illustrate ways of studying the Bible that have two primary aims in view:
> 1. To bring to light the actual social struggles of our biblical ancestors and to locate the human and religious resources they drew upon in the midst of those struggles.
> 2. To tap the biblical social struggles and religious understandings as important resources for directing us in the social struggles we are presently engaged in [p.v].

The revised Reader maintains that two-fold focus in a fundamental effort to interconnect aspects of Bible study that have been split apart and treated as unrelated, even antagonistic, in academia and in the churches. It is the journal's belief that many yawning chasms presently separating the several integral aspects of political and social hermeneutics must and can be soundly bridged by critical reflection and practice.

The original Foreword went on to characterize some of these frustrating and destructive chasms in terms that retain their cogency:

> 1. The chasm *between religion and the rest of life*, which we try to bridge by showing the precise relations between religion and social practice in biblical communities and among those who study the Bible today.
> 2. The chasm *between the past as "dead history" and the present as "real life,"* which we try to bridge by showing how the biblical past was once a live present and how the present is formed by a history which absolutely demands to be understood if we are to live intelligibly and creatively today.
> 3. The chasm *between thought and practice*, which we try to bridge by showing that thought as sterile "head-tripping" and practice as mindless activities can only be overcome by practice that is based on critical thought and by thought that is informed by critical practice, thereby producing an ever-renewed totality which gives human existence its distinctive meaning and promise.
> 4. The chasm *between biblical academics and popular lay Bible study*, which we try to bridge by clarifying what biblical specialists have to offer lay users of the Bible who have developed a clear sense of their own purposes in Bible study and of their basic right and competence to decide which biblical contents and which tools of biblical study are appropriate for them [pp. v–vi].

Such a program of "bridge-building" over traditional chasms is admittedly audacious in raising expectations that require hard work and that are bound to be disappointed in one respect or another. It is obvious that the Reader could have been tightened and focused by addressing only *one* of the above chasms, by limiting itself, for example, to the social location of religion in biblical and contemporary settings or by concentrating on how the results of academic biblical studies are to be appropriated in ecclesial instruction. To isolate the aspects of a political and social hermeneutics of the Bible in that way, however, would be to duplicate a common practice already well represented in published literature. More seriously, to take up parts of the task without considering the whole would be to make a much too hasty prejudgment about how we are to deal with all the factors that must be considered in bringing biblical social data and models into our social struggle situations. In particular, it would fail to address the need for the collaboration of scholarship and church practice in any effective political and social interpretation of the Bible.

In reviewing the many written and spoken evaluations passed on by users of the original Reader, it is evident that the broad spectrum of articles allowed readers to find different points of entrance into the problems and possibilities of sociopolitical Bible study. By and large, there is a consistency of appraisal that an assembly of problems and approaches of the sort presented in the Reader defines the extraordinary range and complexity of factors that committed Bible users must eventually address no matter where they begin the process of sociopolitical interpretation.

It is our intention in the revision to retain, and even to enlarge, the breadth of the original Reader so that readers can engage the issues of political and social hermeneutics at points of immediate interest to them and, in that very process of choice, be lured to think about the interconnecting factors that they might otherwise be inclined to overlook or downgrade in importance. In this way, it is our hope that theorists will be nudged toward practice and activists toward reflection, Old Testament devotees will be drawn toward the New Testament as well (and vice versa), lovers of history will sense the need for social theory, and social theorists will attend to social history, while text-oriented Bible readers will be driven to consider their presuppositions in interpreting texts as they do, just as the fanciers of hermeneutics will have to check their theories against the texts as socially-generated documents.

As a result, conversations and collaborations among people dealing with the Bible in various functional roles in our society may be encouraged. We are beginning to recognize that "the liberated/liberating Bible" seen only by the scholar, or only by the academic teacher, or only by the pastor, or only by the church teacher, or only by the community organizer, or only by the social analyst—or only by any number of other roles we care to name—is far from the complete Bible that will be adequate for liberation. Our very functional specializations constitute at the start both a strength and a limit to interpretation, as well as a way of specifying our bondage within a highly instrumental and people-separating capitalist culture. Not only must we question both the intellectually dismembered Bible and the spiritually unified Bible that scholarship and church now respectively present us, but we must also question our own scattered and stereotyped religious and academic roles that separate us from one another and that incline us to be structurally unable to receive the liberating insights and energies that we desire.

ORGANIZATION

The revised Reader is divided into five parts.

Part I. Social Scientific Method in Biblical Studies

What is "biblical sociology" all about? The three articles in this section provide the general orientation widely requested by readers who have never been exposed to formal study in the social sciences or to ways of applying sociological methods to the Bible.

Bruce J. Malina presents an overview of sociological method in biblical studies, with particular reference to theories of textual meaning partially testable by experimental psychology. Norman K. Gottwald reviews the tasks and limits of a sociological criticism of ancient Israel indebted to macrosociological and anthropological theory. Gerd Theissen explains and illustrates a number of sociological approaches to the New Testament that draw on sociological role theory.

Part II. Social Class as a Hermeneutical Factor

Does the class position of biblical writers and biblical readers have something critical to do with how the Bible is interpreted? Sergio Rostagno opens up the issue by arguing that the assumption in most Christian Bible study of a "universal" or class-neutral meaning to the Bible is belied by the overwhelmingly bourgeois stance of most biblical interpretation, whether orthodox or liberal, against the plain reality that the Bible as a whole demonstrates a decided bias toward the poor. The following essays show in greater detail how social-class factors, always implicit in biblical studies, can be raised to the level of consciousness so that informed choices can be made concerning presuppositions and methods of study.

David Lochhead and Joseph L. Hardegree, Jr., the latter with reference to the Book of Hosea, illustrate how the social (ideological) presuppositions both of biblical writers and of biblical interpreters interact in complicated ways, and they go on to describe specific steps that can be taken to identify and facilitate this process in group Bible study. Both these articles are oriented to the North American scene.

George V. Pixley argues strongly for a new form of biblical study that makes a critical strategic assessment of the adequacy of our faith and its biblical sources as a contribution to liberation from sociopolitical oppression, particularly in his own Latin America. Carlos Mesters pungently reports on the "grass-roots" biblical study process among base communities of politically disprivileged Christians in Brazil, while Kuno Füssel lucidly explains "the materialist reading of the Bible" (advanced by Belo, Clévenot, and Casalis) that is now widely followed among lay and university-based Bible study circles in Europe.

Part III. Sociological Readings of the Old Testament

What are some of the current applications of political and social hermeneutics to the Old Testament, and how is the traditional map of Old Testament studies altered by the results? A survey of the history of sociological criticism of the Old Testament is given by Frank S. Frick and Norman K. Gottwald. The following articles illustrate particular applications of social scientific method to the Old Testament, varying in their emphases on social description or sociological explanation, and in their appropriation of the results of biblical sociological study for a present-day political and social hermeneutics.

Four reviewers of Norman K. Gottwald's *The Tribes of Yahweh*, a sociological study of premonarchic Israel, raise questions about the book's implications for contemporary theological method which the author addresses by reflecting further on his sociological and theological conclusions concerning early Israel.

Israelite prophecy is treated by two contributors. Robert R. Wilson illuminates current confused thinking about the social location and function of Israelite prophecy by recourse to anthropological sources on prophet-like "intermediaries" who are common in many observed societies. Henri Mottu analyzes the encounter of Jeremiah and Hananiah, and more broadly the true-false prophecy issue, by a description of the antagonistic prophetic understandings of their times and by a careful search for the criteria by which truth can be found within prophetic ideology.

The social status of women in ancient Israel has been a lively topic in sociological criticism. Phyllis A. Bird distills a range of socioreligious roles and evaluations of Israelite women with a view to assessing the scope and quality of their societal participation. Carol L. Meyers proposes underpopulation due to famine and plague in earliest Israel as the occasion for channeling women into child-bearing and agricultural labor, a restriction that was ideologically maintained throughout biblical history after the original necessity had passed.

Walter Brueggemann uses the results of literary and sociological studies of ancient Israel to suggest that the course of Israel's internal history can be characterized as a struggle between a "Mosaic liberation" trajectory and a "royal consolidation" trajectory. Although incomplete in detail and problematic in structure, this study gives a foretaste of what a fuller socioreligious history of ancient Israel may one day look like.

Part IV. Sociological Readings of the New Testament

Since the New Testament is often conceived as more "individualistic" or "nonpolitical" than the Old Testament, what have been the results of sociological criticism of the New Testament, and does this supposed "privatization" of early Christian faith stand up to social scientific scrutiny? Robin Scroggs surveys the main forms of sociological criticism of the New Testament currently practiced. The assembled articles, as in the case of the Old Testament, display a range of methods on the spectrum of social history/description and sociological analysis/explanation, as well as different degrees of explicitness in tackling sociopolitical hermeneutical issues.

The politics of Jesus has been a central issue in sociological criticism of the New Testament. John Pairman Brown and George V. Pixley document the "political" concreteness of Jesus' confrontation with authorities and social systems, the former focusing on the Roman imperial system and the latter on the temple economy of the Jews. Pixley hypothesizes that Jesus' historical project to realize the Kingdom of God was a movement to overthrow the temple economy through a consciously chosen strategy that included organizing the common people.

The role of women in the New Testament has prompted even more inquiry and discussion than the corresponding issue in the Old Testament. Elisabeth Schüssler Fiorenza and Luise Schottroff use critical tools to uncover the co-equality of women and men in the circle of Jesus' followers and in the early spread of the Christian mission into the Gentile world, a revolutionary social upthrust that was eclipsed before long as the church accommodated itself to the male-dominated Roman world. Schottroff gives us vivid portraits of Mary of Magdala and Priscilla, while Fiorenza calls for a retrieval of the primal Christian legitimation of sexual co-equality in order to unmask and reverse the patriarchal-hierarchic "power play" that still dominates the Christian church.

The class composition of the early church has become the center of extensive sociological study. John G. Gager reviews three recent social histories of early Christianity, assessing their methods in relation to the social advantage/disadvantage of early Christians and their attitudes toward the state. Robert H. Smith gives a markedly "middle class" reading of the much-disputed status of early Christians, but he sharply questions how our contemporary social position as interpreters affects our reading of the evidence and to what solacing or challenging purposes we are likely to put the evidence we uncover from biblical times.

Part V. The Bible in Political Theology and Marxist Thought

How is the Bible viewed in current radical theology and political thought? What are the key issues in a contemporary political and social hermeneutics of the Bible?

Arthur F. McGovern sums up the pivotal dimensions of Scripture that inform Latin American liberation theology and rebuts the criticisms of its "unbiblical" character as largely due to deliberate misunderstanding by critics. Alfredo Fierro reviews the way the Exodus motif has functioned in three exemplars of secular theology, theology of hope, and liberation theology. After replying to "depoliticizing" interpretations of the Exodus, he argues that the emerging political disclosure of biblical testimonies frees Christians to participate in all immediately relevant and necessary forms of political action, including revolution.

Juan Luis Segundo uses communication theory about first and second level learning to distinguish two separate but related ways of reading the many ideological concretions of faith in the Bible. We read them for "simple learning" about the many ways that faith has been and can be materialized, but we also read them in a process of "learning to learn" in which we have to choose the ideological form of analysis/action most appropriate for our situation. Rudolf J. Siebert reports on the biblical interpretations of the Czech Marxists Vitězslav Gardavsky and Milan Machoveč, viewing them as pointers toward "a political proof of God" through "the Christian practice of qualitative social change."

READER AIDS

Certain aids for the reader have been included to enhance this volume as a text book, reference resource, or collection of supplementary readings.

Each of the articles and excerpts from books is prefaced with an abstract that will help the general reader, academic instructor, or Bible study leader to ascertain quickly which selections are most germane to the purposes at hand.

The volume is supplied with indexes according to authors, biblical citations, and subjects. Within the subject index, there is a notation system for designating pages in the text where definitions or explanations of terms occur.

NONSEXIST LANGUAGE

Unfortunately, nonsexist language is not yet fully accepted among those who write on the subject of the Bible and liberation.

In the original Reader, a concerted effort was made to use nonsexist language. We avoided "man" as a false generic for men and women, and "he/ him" where the context called for a feminine or an indefinite pronoun. In biblical and historical argumentation we tried to be alert for cases where either the original language or later interpreters overlooked or distorted the presence or activity of women because of masculine mindsets or forms of expression. In this edition, Elisabeth Schüssler Fiorenza's and Luise Schottroff's articles forcefully document many instances of sexist language (sometimes by New Testament writers and more often by biblical translators and commentators). As they demonstrate, far from being mere peccadillos, these "small" instances combine to obscure the creative role of women in Christian origins.

Because this edition of the Reader draws upon materials from many independent sources, the editor has not attempted a thoroughgoing nonsexist correction of all the articles. The inconsistencies in practice among the writers serve to remind us that one of the *major* incomplete tasks of liberation is a re-working of normal language (including the language of scholars) to eliminate the unintended perpetuation of sexual stereotypes. To carry forward this refashioning of language, it will be necessary to know practical nonsexist alternatives to expressing matters in a traditional sexist way. Every writer committed to the co-equality of men and women is well advised to make regular use of a nonsexist style book such as Casey Miller and Kate Swift, *The Handbook of Nonsexist Writing for Writers, Editors and Speakers* (New York: Barnes and Noble Books, 1981).

Liberation perspectives call us to align theory and practice. If we really mean that women are co-equal with men, our practice of language must accord with the intention of our theory.

Norman K. Gottwald

Part I

SOCIAL SCIENTIFIC METHOD
IN BIBLICAL STUDIES

1

BRUCE J. MALINA

The Social Sciences
and Biblical Interpretation

Biblical texts, in common with all writing, communicate meanings according to assumptions shared in common by writers and readers. Texts may be read by means of a conceptual approach that envisions a series of enclosed sentence propositions, or they may be read through a social contextual approach that recognizes evocations of a scenario progressively enacted and modified in the course of reading. Experimental psychology inclines to the latter view, which also accords with human reliance on "simplifying" models that process things, persons, events, and ideas by breaking and grouping them into manageable "chunks" for purposes of understanding.

In the social sciences there are three primary models that "chunk" how the social world works: (1) the structural-functional model that posits social order and harmony; (2) the conflict model that posits social struggle and change; (3) the symbolic interaction model that posits social behavior on the basis of shared sociocultural meanings and values. Each model is arguably relevant for reading biblical texts, but in each case the cross-cultural leap to the biblical social world must be made with critical consciousness. Imposed theological "shortcuts" to meaning do not validly replace good social science models for interpreting the Bible.

Reprinted in a slightly expanded version from *Interpretation. A Journal of Bible and Theology* 37/3 (1982): 229–42.

The Bible is a collection of texts, "meaningful configurations of language intended to communicate."[1] Generally speaking, the task of contemporary biblical scholarship is to investigate and discover what was in fact communicated by those meaningful configurations of language. Language inevitably imparts meanings which are rooted in a social system.[2] Consequently, the thrust of biblical scholarship is to find out what an author communicated to his contemporaries within their common social context.

Understanding linguistic communication from a different time and social context obviously requires some set of interpretative tools to carry off the task of cross-temporal and cross-cultural inquiry. The twin pitfalls of ethnocentrism and anachronism have to be avoided if only in fairness to the persons of the past whom we seek to understand. In order to deal with their interpretative task, biblical scholars for the most part utilize models of language based upon and derived from sentence grammars along with a smattering of literary theory equally rooted in sentence grammars. Here the basic unit of language is the sentence—a linguistic unit expressing a complete thought. The problem with sentences, however, is that they are intuitively understandable, but not interpretable (e.g., "He did so"); they yield complete but isolated thoughts, not complete meanings. Further, the problem with sentence-based literary theory is that the patterns or literary forms that it uncovers, while undoubtedly encoding meaning, bear meanings from some larger social system, and literary theory does not deal with the larger frame.[3]

In order to deal with anachronism, biblical scholars as a rule adopt an historical perspective. Like historians, they collect information and place it along a time line. And like historians, they inevitably furnish answers, if only implicitly, to such questions as: why did things happen this way rather than that; how did it all come out in the end; what is the point of it all; and what should we do about it.[4] The answers to these largely latent questions are generally based on the present social location of the interpreter-historian. The reason for this is that biblical scholars, like most historians, are generally unaware of the social system that endows their role with meaning and therefore do not perform their task in a consciously cross-cultural way.[5] But if our texts derive from cultures other than our own,[6] then biblical interpretation will always be a process of cross-cultural interpretation. Such interpretation would entail situating the texts at some distance from ourselves with the aid of cross-cultural models, initially to determine our respective cultural scripts in general, and subsequently to point up the respective meanings of given items of behavior in some comparative way. What is necessary for this task, then, is a set of models that might account quite explicitly for the interpreter as well as leave room for the communication from the past and the social world in which it was rooted, in some comparative framework.

In other words, if biblical interpretation is the investigation of linguistic communications from the past, then at least two sets of tools would be required: one set of a linguistic sort that can deal with texts as texts, and not as words or sentences or supersentences, and another set of an historical sort that can deal with the past in some cross-cultural way. Now the value of the social sciences for biblical interpretation is that they can provide some of the important tools for both the linguistic and the historical dimensions of biblical scholarship. To further clarify this thesis, consider reading theory for a moment.

Biblical scholarship is ultimately rooted in the reading of ancient written texts; biblical interpretation is the interpretation of written language. Now written language clearly does not live in scrolls or books. Rather the markings on a page stand for or represent wordings that represent meanings that can come alive only through the agency of the minds of readers.[7] How does a reader get to understand the meanings through the wordings in the writings? While our acquaintance with writing systems (orthography) and wording systems (lexico-grammar) has afforded us many interesting data, I should like to focus upon the meanings that get imparted in the process of reading. There are currently two major models of reading comprehension in vogue in experimental psychology.[8]

The first model might be called the propositional model. This model considers the text to be a sort of supersentence—a logical perspective for those whose training in language focused on wording, i.e., the sentence and word level. In this view, the text being read evokes mental representations in the mind of the reader which consist of a chain or series of propositions which derive directly from the sentences that constitute the text. The text is made up of sentences, which in turn are made up of words. The reader basically performs two tasks: s/he has to parse the text into propositional units, and then s/he has to connect the resulting propositions in some way. This connection takes place by means of some superstructure—a deep structure, story grammar, narrative grammar, or something of the sort. As most will recognize, this sort of model undergirds contemporary structuralist exegesis.[9] The difficulty with the model is that it cannot be verified experimentally. Rather the research of experimental psychologists indicates that this is not what goes on in the mind of a reader at all.[10] Presumably, then, this is not what goes on in the mind of an observer of some phenomenon either.

We might call this propositional model of reading comprehension the conceptual approach. It seems to be rooted in presuppositions about the nature and function of language that derive from the reification of highly abstract entities like words and sentences. For words and sentences are not the end products of language. Rather the end products of language are spoken and/or written texts—meaningful occurrences of language intended to communicate. And as noted above, what texts invariably communicate is information from a social system. Words and sentences are the means for realizing text, ways of conceptualizing the means of linguistic communication at an analytic level. The human ability to communicate is the ability to mean. The language is to mean (although not all meaning is languaging). And the unit of meaning (not of thought) is text. Now if a text does not present a chain or series of propositions, what does it evoke in the mind of a reader?

The second model of reading comprehension might be called a scenario model. This model considers the text as a succession of explicit and implicit scenes or schemes in which the mental representation evoked in the mind of the reader consists of a series of settings, episodes, or models deriving directly from the mind of the reader, coupled with appropriate alterations to these settings, episodes, or models as directed by the text. Here too, the reader must perform two tasks: s/he has to use the text to identify an appropriate "domain of reference," i.e., call to mind an appropriate scene, scheme, or model suggested by the text, and then s/he must use the identified "domain of reference" as the larger frame within which to situate the meanings proposed in the text as far as this is possible. This model of reading comprehension does have some validation from contemporary experimental psychology.[11] And the social science approach to biblical interpretation is based on such a model.[12] We might call this the social context approach, based on presuppositions about linguistics rooted in a belief in text as the basic unit of meaning.

If this is the way readers comprehend, it would seem that the best a contemporary biblical scholar can offer his/her public is a set of domains of reference deriving from and appropriate to the social world from which the texts derive and thus facilitate biblical understanding. For the understanding and interpretation of any sort of text is ultimately rooted in a social world, in a set of models sketching how the world works. All interpretation, it would seem, requires such models and ultimately rests on such models. And if the focus of interpretation is a piece of language, then along with social world models, the interpreter would need appropriate linguistic tools to tie in with his/her overall project, a form of sociolinguistics.[13]

Perhaps at this point it might be of use to say a word about models. A model is an abstract, simplified representation of some real world object, event, or interaction, constructed for the purpose of understanding, control, or prediction.[14] A model is a scheme or pattern that derives from the process of abstracting similarities from a range of instances in order to comprehend. It seems, again from experimental psychology, that human beings make such abstract models in order to deal with the huge variety of sensations and resulting perceptions that are part and parcel of human experience. Human beings cannot keep more than 7±2 disparate items in mind at once.[15] To handle complexity, human beings "chunk" or abstract similarities and thus reduce the number of items being dealt with. For example, a concrete batch of assorted apples can be chunked into categories like Winesap apples, Delicious apples, Jonathan apples, etc.; then the various varieties can be chunked on the basis of similarity into the category of apple. Then at the same level of abstraction, apples, pears, peaches, etc. can be grouped and then chunked into fruit; and at that level of abstraction, fruit, vegetables, meat, and fish can be grouped and chunked into food. This chunking process results in mini-models as soon as it takes its departure from the concrete, unique, individual item presented to the senses. Human beings, it seems, cannot make sense of their experiences and their world without making models of it, without thinking in terms of abstract representations of it.

The difference between models of the nonhuman and the human is that modelled nonhuman items cannot and do not interject themselves into human affairs; the sun and the planets have not protested about a geocentric or solarcentric scheme of things and seem to remain unaffected by it. On the other hand, models of human behavior that serve living humans often tend to be self-fulfilling; such models ascribe statuses and roles and expectations to humans which tend to be lived out. Now the social system of any human group is a sort of model that offers categories of human experience and behavior that serve to help understand, control, and predict the flow of human interaction. Such models of human interactions are social science models— sociological, anthropological, political, economic, educational, religious, cross-cultural, psychological. Social science models are models of the systems of development, structure, and function of human groups conceived as processes of interaction or as organized patterns of collective behavior. The understanding and interpretation of human behavior is always based on models of how the social world works, whether the person understanding and interpreting is aware of the model (explicit models) or unaware (implicit models), since human beings chunk in order to understand.

In sum, biblical interpretation, like the interpretation of any written language, will be based upon and derive from models of how the world of people works (social sciences) and models of the nature and function of language (linguistics). However, most interpreters will agree that the texts which they are to interpret are texts from the past, texts not only from a socially different group of people (like the newspapers *Al Ahram* or *Die Zeit*), but texts from a noncontemporary social group. Hence some sort of historical models are equally required. What then is the relationship between history and the social sciences?[16]

Social sciences are based upon models of how the world of human interaction works and why it works that way. Specifically, the social sciences look to how meanings are imposed on men and women to seek to explain human behavior in terms of typicalities. They underscore generalities, the common elements of meaning typical of a given social group. On the border line between the social sciences and the humanities is that set of models called history. History focuses upon the "that," "how," and "why" men created meanings in the past that affect our present with a view to our future. History, with its roots in the present and a set of working images of the past, seeks to explain events in terms of the distinctiveness of agents and agencies, in terms of particularities and differences. The other social sciences, rooted in the present, prescind from the past for the most part to seek out generalities, commonalities, samenesses.

The problem with history as a model of interpretation of alien meaning is that in order to ferret out distinctiveness, all the commonalities of the area under study have to be known and articulated. Until rather recently, historians have relied upon disciplined intuition (often sophisticated ethnocentrism) alone to account for commonalities. The social sciences indicate how and why meanings get imposed on and in the present. The social sciences with history would presume that meanings must have been imposed on persons in the past as well, since they seem to be imposed on everyone on the planet at present, not only on our own social group members. Now for the interpretation of texts from the past, some sets of models of the social-science-with-history sort are necessary to deal with imposed meanings in the past so that the distinctive, particular, and different might emerge in some validatable, testable, and articulate way.

In other words, to interpret texts (units of meaning) from the past, the interpreter has to imagine how meanings functioned, how they operated, how they related to each other, in terms of the persons, things, and events of the past that embodied meanings. Models of such operations and relations are, at bottom, models of society, social science models. The point to be underscored is that if interpretation of written language of any sort takes place, some domain of reference will be used by the reader. This domain of reference will be rooted in some model of society and of social interaction.

At a rather high level of abstraction, there are three main types of social science models that one might use to understand social interaction.[17] These three are called the structural functionalist, the conflict, and the symbolic models. These models derive from certain presuppositions, just as all models do, whether those of chemistry, physics, biology, or anything else. The presuppositions that underpin the models revolve around the quality or sort of activity that social interaction is. Thus we might assume that a social system is embodied in a group of interacting persons whose interactions follow certain mutually understood and expected patterns (structures) that are oriented around mutually shared purposes or concerns (functions). Meaningful human behavior is behavior according to socially shared patterns (structures) performed for socially meaningful purposes (functions). If we were to take a photograph of our entire society, freeze all activity for a moment, so to say, and then analyze what is going on in terms of what relationships and for what purposes, we would end up with a general image of the main outline of the structures of the society along with their functions. This sort of still picture, when verbalized as a social science model, is called structural functionalism. The still picture that we get to see is one of a society that is cohesive and integrated by consensus on meanings, values, and norms. The society is held together by core values, the ends of society. And these core values get realized in human living by means of social arrangements or smaller but interrelated systems called social institutions. Thus society is in equilibrium, in good balance, and the social system tends to persist over time with major or minor amounts of adaptive change. Changes in one institution lead to changes in others, since all are interrelated means to societal ends. Consequently, the structural functionalist model presupposes that every society is a relatively persistent, stable structure of elements, as well as a well-integrated structure of elements. Every element in society has a function, a purpose; it renders a contribution to the maintenance of society as a whole, integral system. Every functioning social structure is based on a consensus of values among its members. In this still picture type of model, any nonadaptive social change is deviance. The picture tends to be static.[18]

Photographs are useful to situate and interrelate the elements found in it. And structural functionalism is useful for discovering what sort of structures or patterns of behavior are typical of a society, what norms express the "oughts" for that behavior, and how such behavior supports and fulfills useful social functions. However, to view society as the outcome of consensus, a sort of consensual obligation in which people freely choose to oblige themselves in certain ways, is not to see the whole picture. For as with human behavior in general, so too social systems reveal constraints as well as freedom. Thus while structural functionalist models emphasize consensus or freedom in the formation and endurance of social systems (the still-photo approach), the flip-side theory would emphasize the constraints human groups put on themselves as well as on the individuals that comprise them. This flip-side theory is called the conflict model (or the coercion, power, or interest model).

Conflict models are like slow-motion films. They would have us explain social systems in terms of various groups which have differing goals and interests, and therefore use coercive tactics on each other to get their own goals realized. Each of the various groups protects the distinctive interest of its members, and relations between various groups include disagreement, strain, conflict, and force—as well as consensus and cooperation. If dissent and conflict are part of the normal social process, then any social system must also protect and assert its members' interests in relations with other systems, even by challenging the established order. No system can perdure if it fails to maintain a favorable balance between its members' personal needs and the demands of the broader society.

Consequently, conflict models presuppose that all units of social organization, i.e., persons and groups in a society, are continuously changing unless some force intervenes to thwart the change. Change is all around us, ubiquitous. Wherever there is social life, there is conflict. What holds social systems and their subsystems together is not consensus but constraint, the coercion of some by others, and not universal agreement. While value systems can generate change, constraint generates conflict. Conflict is everywhere because constraint is to be found wherever human beings set up social organizations.

From this perspective and in terms of this sort of model, a good way to understand biblical texts is to find out what elements or factors interfere with the normal process of change. Absence of conflict would be surprising and abnormal. What sorts of conflict typify the behavior described in various biblical books? In this slow-motion type of model, there is an unending process of change in society—as in the individual him/herself. Social change, deviance, is normal. Social pressures toward obligatory consent lead to reactions that result in changes of various sorts.[19]

Both the structural functionalist and conflict models presuppose that a social system is a group of interacting persons whose interactions are structured and oriented around common purposes. These presuppositions at a high level of abstraction define what the models will enable one to see and describe, and how they will explain behavior. However, what if we define a social system as a system of symbols that acts to establish powerful and long-lasting perceptions and motivations in human beings, formulating conceptions of value objects and clothing these conceptions with such an aura of factuality that the perceptions and motivations are held to be uniquely real. In this definition the social system is a system of symbols, i.e., meanings, values, and feelings about the meanings and values that are attached to and embodied by persons, things, and events.

The social system, as a system of symbols, consists of persons (self, others), things (nature, time, and space), and events (activities of persons and things) that have unique reality because of their perceived symbolic meaning. People do not simply respond to situations; they respond to the way they read and define situations, in terms of what they expect in and from situations. The range of meanings within a situation gets interpreted symbolically by persons defining the situation. However, no symbol can mean everything and anything. The symbol gets its range of meanings from shared social definitions and expectations, from the shared social symbol system, much like words get their meanings from the shared social speech system. This sort of model that would analyze social systems in terms of the symbols that comprise them is called the symbolic model (and to some extent, the symbolic interactionist model).

The symbolic model presupposes that human individual and group behavior is organized around the symbolic meanings and expectations that are attached to objects that are socially valued. Such socially valued objects include, at a high level of abstraction, the self, others, nature, time, space, and the All (gods, God). Any existing person or group embodies a complex of symbolic patterns that temporarily at least maintains both personal and social equilibrium (as in the structural functionalist model) but which requires continual readjustments in new and shifting situations (as in the conflict model). These readjustments include slight to great alterations of ideas, values, moods, attitudes, roles, and social organization. Thus the symbolic model presupposes that for the most part, human interactions are symbolic interactions. People are always wrapped in social roles, sets of social rights and obligations relative to each other. These symbolic roles situate people relative to others, give them social definition and status. The social system then turns out to be a patterned arrangement of role sets, status sets, and status sequences consciously recognized and regularly at work in a given society. Social structure thus keeps people apart, brings them together, defines differences, points up similarities, and both constrains and facilitates action. In terms of this model, biblical interpreters would do well to seek out what roles, significant symbols, gestures, and definitions of situations are expressed or implied in the texts. What symbols embody the cultural cues of perception? What sorts of interaction take place between persons of lesser or higher rank, and how do people define themselves in their various rankings?[20]

Of the three approaches, which is the best? As mentioned previously, human beings generate models in order to understand their experiences. No model that we know of is useful for every conceivable purpose. There is no model to help understand all models, just as there is no language that one could learn to get to understand all languages. The use of models is like the use of tools; in this sense models are question-specific or area-specific constructs. The appropriate model depends on the type of information one seeks to generate and comprehend. Nevertheless, for the biblical interpreter's task, the task of understanding a piece of alien, written communication, the social sciences along with sociolinguistics in some form are useful and necessary. For it seems one cannot interpret without some model of how the world of human interactions works, and a comparative set of models of how the social world works would be required to understand alien meaning.

There are generally three criticisms levelled against the use of social science models in biblical interpretation. Theologians of various stripes see the utilization of the social sciences as reductionistic, hence eminently useless. Some social scientists see such an approach useful, but impossible given the paucity of data in our body of texts. Finally for many historians and theologians, the social sciences are simply too deterministic to adequately explain anything as distinctive and personal as change in human history. I would like to deal with these objections one by one.

Reductionism refers to the procedure of subsuming one model into another when both of the models are at the same level of abstraction.[21] For example, to explain biology as simply one form of physics, economics as one form of psychology, or theology as one form of sociology, would be reductionistic. However, to explain sets of data—and not models—from the perspectives of biology, sociology, political science, economics, and the like is not reductionistic. Rather such varied explanations pushed to their limit simply reveal how much can be known and explained by using a given model. The data set, the range of information, remains intact. On the other hand, to equate biblical interpretation (a task requiring the explanation of past, textual meanings) with theology as some systematic theologians do is reductionistic; the same holds for those theologians who use a model called "the analogy of faith" to explain (away) the results of biblical interpretation. The analogy of faith approach, like theological hermeneutics, is a model of doing theology. To subsume biblical interpretation and its models under the analogy of faith or hermeneutics would be reductionistic.

The use of the social sciences for uncovering and explaining the imposed meanings of the past in our texts is often accused of being invalid because our sampling is insufficient. In other words, our sources of information are data poor for the social sciences approach. Now this objection would be perfectly valid were our task one of sociology of the mathematical sort, the task of which is largely one of prediction strategies. The use of the social sciences in biblical interpretation is essentially one of retrodiction, not prediction; we have some idea about how the story turned out, and this important datum acts as a control that is lacking in prediction. Applying social science models to biblical texts is heavily oriented toward efficient causality (why = how). Sociology, on the other hand, requires a larger data set because of its predictive goals; sociology is heavily oriented toward final causality (why = for what reason). Finally, social sciences applied to biblical texts have the quality of a "who-dun-it," seeking the probabilities in the past that made the story make social sense and turn out as it did. Sociology, in turn, has the quality of science fiction, seeking the range of possibilities in the future as indicated by the present to see where the story might be going. In other words, given the purpose of biblical interpretation, the fact of its being relatively poor in data might preclude sociological "number crunching" (statistical analysis, systems analysis), but it does not preclude using social science models for determining how meanings were imposed on people in the past and what those meanings might be, with some high degree of probability.

The third objection to the use of the social sciences in biblical interpretation is often implicit in the charge of reductionism. This is the charge that the social sciences are deterministic, hence leave little room for God's creative activity or the creative activity of men. Now it should be quite clear that the social sciences are indeed deterministic, but only in the sense that they are sets of models that seek out the "that," "how," and "why" of meanings imposed on human beings. Models, sets of tools for understanding, predicting or both, are designed with a view to limited purposes. Social science models seek out generalities, typicalities, and samenesses within human groups. From the social science point of view, human beings are socially determined. Yet unless used reductionistically, the social sciences do not preclude other avenues of approach to our data set. We can indeed seek out the distinctiveness of the God of Israel and of his Messiah Jesus, but that distinctiveness cannot be adequately discerned until all the commonalities of the time and place have been duly accounted for. I think it would be a fault in method to claim distinctiveness before commonalities have been duly discerned and accounted for.

Furthermore, perhaps the most significant feature of the use of social science models in biblical interpretation is the way social science models of the cross-cultural sort constantly require the interpreter to articulate and account for his/her own social location. This procedure can greatly reduce the high-level ethnocentrism that often plagues even the most "scientific" biblical interpretation. Take, for example, the text segment about paying taxes to Caesar, Mark 12:13–17. German scholarship labels the text segment as a *Streitgespräch* (conflict story) in which a presumably Germanic Jesus is greatly concerned about truth as he is embroiled in controversy with his adversaries over his message. English-speaking scholarship would see Jesus as a professor at a graduate seminar best remembered for his pithy, insightful pronouncements on life in general and on religion in particular; thus the literary scheme of the text segment would be that of a pronouncement story. Structuralist approaches of the French variety would have us analyze the deep structure of the passage to underscore how nicely and neatly Jesus or the evangelist handled a typical language scheme; the literary scheme of this text segment would articulate deep structural, binary opposition of some sort, probably between politics and religion; with his concluding remark Jesus overcomes the opposition and restores the world to equilibrium. Finally, the use of social science models from Mediterranean cultural anthropology would have us see first-century Mediterranean Jesus in a challenge-riposte situation in which he is challenged by equals in the usual contests for honor typical of the cultural area from time immemorial.[22] Jesus, once again, defends his honor, even increases it as his opponents are shamed and fended off. In this perspective, the teller of the story shows us how Jesus is truly an honorable person in whom one's commitment would not be misplaced.

Now which of these interpretations better mirrors what a first-century Mediterranean author would tend to communicate within his social context? If only because it is both totally irrelevant to our cultural context *and* yet also makes eminent first-century Mediterranean sense, I would opt for the last interpretation. It derives from a social science model that makes explicit what is implicit in the text segment, a social science model that makes the interpreter aware of his/her own implicit presuppositions, a social science model that can be tested, checked out by others, and validated in a way that most other approaches to interpretation cannot.[23]

By way of conclusion, I should like to offer one observation and several caveats. The observation is this: many of the conclusions derived from social science methods and their explicit articulations can be and often are reached by means of scholarly intuition using the prevailing canons of the historical-critical method. Then why bother with social science methods? An answer to this question can be found in the many commentaries listing the range of scholarly interpretative conclusions on specific text segments. How can one determine which interpretation has a higher degree of probability? How can one tell whether the meanings suggested by interpreters are ethnocentric anachronisms of a high order of abstraction, or whether they in fact mirror the concerns of those to whom the texts were originally directed? The intuitive methods now in vogue do not allow for such a determination; at most they allow for a sort of hand count or poll more indicative of the social world of interpreters than of the social world of the authors of our texts. On the other hand, social science methods do allow for some such determination. And aside from that, social science methods offer broader frames of interpretation that allow for new questions and the assimilation of new information, like historical geography and archaeology (itself woefully in need of interpretative models). In sum, social science methods can offer biblical interpretation adequate sophistication in determining and articulating the social systems behind the texts under investigation. Instead of spelling out meanings on an intuitive basis, often in terms of sophisticated ethnocentrism, social science methods can put some testable control on meanings thus intuited as well as provide a fruitful framework for further study.

Now some caveats. Models borrowed from the social sciences have to be good social science models.[24] For purposes of biblical scholarship, the assessment of social science models would have to follow the criticisms of social scientists as well as the degree of fit with the area under consideration. For example, Festinger's cognitive dissonance model[25] cannot be validated as it stands, hence it would be inappropriate as an explanatory tool to clarify biblical texts.[26] Furthermore, those who have used it do not outfit it with a cross-cultural matrix, hence they would filter out elements distinctive to cultures other than ours from where the model derives.

This lack of cross-cultural adjustment seems to be the great drawback to using models derived from contemporary sociology of religion. The reason for this is that modern sociology of religion is based on the contemporary experience of religion. In our society, religion is a formal, independent, un-embedded social institution. It was not such in the world of the Bible.[27] The same holds for models from formal economics. To use experiences of economics post-dating the eighteenth century as analogues for the first-century Mediterranean, for example, is simply inappropriate. A better place to look for social science models in these areas is in religious and economic anthropology that accounts for societies in which religion and economics are substantive rather than formal (as in the contemporary world).[28]

Finally, I would like to point out the lack of precision developing in the terminology used in social science approaches to biblical interpretation. In French and German, there is little if any difference between "social" and "sociological," while in English the difference is notable. "Social description" and "social history" are no more "sociology" than "policy" and "politics" are identical, although the same word refers to both in French and German.[29] It would be unfortunate if these imprecisions in terminology would be imported into the lexicon of biblical scholarship, if only because our colleagues in the social sciences do not understand them. I would think that any use of the social sciences in biblical interpretation would at least be recognizable and acceptable by our peers who happen to be social scientists.

What then would characterize a good social science model for biblical interpretation? Minimally, the model should have the following features:

1. It should be a cross-cultural model, accounting for the interpreter as well as those interpreted in some comparative perspective.

2. It should be of a sufficient level of abstraction to allow for the surfacing of similarities that facilitates comparison.

3. The model should be able to fit a larger sociolinguistic frame for interpreting texts.

4. It should derive from experiences that match what we know of the time-and-place-conditioned biblical world as closely as possible.

5. The meanings it generates should be irrelevant but understandable to us and our twentieth-century, U.S. society.

6. The application of the model should be acceptable to social scientists (even if they disagree with the validity of the enterprise).

The outcome of such an approach to the Bible should be increased understanding of the behavior described in the texts—the behavior of the persons who people the text as well as the behavior ascribed to God by analogy with human behavior. Instead of biblical dogmas, we would get to know and appreciate the personages who embodied biblical faith. Instead of moral guidelines and theological propositions, we would discover social persons and the underpinnings of their interpersonal relations. Instead of the Bible as a source of the "religion of the book," we would find the Bible as a record of the "religion of persons" and their theocentric and christocentric successes and failures that lie at the source of our Judeo-Christian tradition. Instead of theology, we would make the acquaintance of our flesh-and-blood ancestors in faith and the dimensions of their quest for an adequately meaningful human existence. If such be the hoped-for outcomes, the approach is certainly worth a try.

NOTES

1. Robert de Beaugrande, *Text, Discourse and Process: Toward a Multidisciplinary Science of Texts*, Advances in Discourse Processes, Vol. 4 (Norwood, N.J.: Ablex Publ. Co., 1980), p. 1.

2. "If we ask of any form of communication the simple question, What is being communicated?, the answer is: information from the social system. The exchanges which are being communicated constitute the social system," from Mary Douglas, "Do Dogs Laugh? A Cross-cultural Approach to Body Symbolism," in *Implicit Meanings: Essays in Anthropology* (London: Routledge & Kegan Paul, 1975), p. 87.

3. For a sampling of essays illustrating this point, see John Maier and Vincent Tollers, eds., *The Bible in Its Literary Milieu: Contemporary Essays* (Grand Rapids: Eerdmans, 1979).

4. See Hayden White, *Metahistory: The Historical Imagination in Nineteenth-Century Europe* (Baltimore: Johns Hopkins University Press, 1973), pp. 5–38.

5. This has perhaps been most clearly articulated by Norman K. Gottwald, *The Tribes of Yahweh: A Sociology of the Religion of Liberated Israel, 1250–1050 B.C.E.* (Maryknoll, N.Y.: Orbis Books, 1979), pp. 8–17, 602–07.

6. Ethnocentrism of any variety (e.g., U.S. fundamentalism) presumes that the range of meanings available to persons in the various cultures of biblical times are identical with the range of meanings available today; culture thus gets identified with universal human nature.

7. On the tri-level nature of language (spelling/speaking—wording—meaning), see Michael A. K. Halliday, *Language as Social Semiotic: The Social Interpretation of Language and Meaning* (Baltimore: University Park Press, 1978).

8. See A. J. Sanford and S. C. Garrod, *Understanding Written Language: Explorations of Comprehension Beyond the Sentence* (New York: John Wiley and Sons, 1981).

9. See, for example, *Int* 28 (1974): 133–220; Daniel Patte, *What is Structural Exegesis?* (Philadelphia: Fortress Press, 1976); or Daniel Patte and Aline Patte, *Structural Exegesis: From Theory to Practice: Exegesis of Mark 15 and 16, Hermeneutical Implications* (Philadelphia: Fortress Press, 1978).

10. Sanford and Garrod, *Understanding Written Language*, pp. 63–85; and George Miller and Philip Johnson-Laird, *Language and Perception* (Cambridge, Eng.: Belknap Press, 1976).

11. Sanford and Garrod, *Understanding Written Language*, pp. 109–54.

12. De Beaugrande, *Text, Discourse*, p. 14, notes: "To utilize sentences, language users rely on grammatical knowledge as a general, virtual system. To utilize texts, people need experiential knowledge of specific, actual occurrences." For the most part, social science models derive from "experiential knowledge of specific, actual occurrences," from actual human behavior.

13. Of the three applications of general linguistics (language as system), namely, language as art (aesthetic linguistics), language as knowledge (psycholinguistics), and language as behavior (sociolinguistics), perhaps language as behavior is the most appropriate to the biblical scholar's task; see Halliday, *Language as Social Semiotic*, pp. 8–35; De Beaugrande, *Text, Discourse;* and R. A. Hudson, *Sociolinguistics* (Cambridge, Eng.: Cambridge University Press, 1980).

14. See T. F. Carney, *The Shape of the Past: Models and Antiquity* (Lawrence, Kans.: Coronado Press, 1975), pp. 1–43.

15. George Miller, "The Magical Number Seven, Plus or Minus Two," *Psychological Review* 63 (1956): 81–97; this limitation explains why long charts of comparison used to study, e.g., the interrelationship of the Synoptic Gospels, become tedious and "unconvincing"—unless one lives with them over a span of time and works out a chunking process to handle the material.

16. Peter Burke, *Sociology and History* (London: Allen & Unwin, 1980), offers an excellent, brief overview along with valuable suggestions.

17. For an excellent survey, see Jonathan H. Turner, *The Structure of Sociological Theory*, rev. ed. (Homewood, Ill.: Dorsey Press, 1978).

18. For structural functionalist approaches to biblical texts, see, e.g., Robert R. Wilson, *Prophecy and Society in Ancient Israel* (Philadelphia: Fortress Press, 1980); Bruce J. Malina, "The Apostle Paul and Law: Prolegomena for an Hermeneutic," *Creighton Law Review* 14 (1981): 1305–1339, with a critique of Bengt Holmberg, *Paul and Power: The Structure of Authority in the Primitive Church as Reflected in the Pauline Epistles* (Philadelphia: Fortress Press, 1980); and Gottwald, *Tribes of Yahweh,* passim.

19. For the conflict approach, see John G. Gager, *Kingdom and Community: The Social World of Early Christianity* (Englewood Cliffs, N.J.: Prentice-Hall, 1975), pp. 79–88.

20. For the symbolic approach, see Bruce J. Malina, "The Social World Implied in the Letters of the Christian Bishop-Martyr (Named Ignatius of Antioch)," in Paul J. Achtemeier, ed., SBL 1978 Seminar Papers, II (Missoula, Mont.: Scholars Press, 1978), pp. 71–119; idem, *The New Testament World: Insights from Cultural Anthropology* (Atlanta: John Knox Press, 1981), chap. 6; Gillian Feeley-Harnik, *The Lord's Table: Eucharist and Passover in Early Christianity* (Philadelphia: University of Pennsylvania Press, 1981); John Pilch, "Biblical Leprosy and Body Symbolism," *BTB* 11 (1981): 108–13.

21. See H. H. Penner and E. A. Yonan, "Is a Science of Religion Possible?," *JR* 52 (1972): 107–133, esp. pp. 118–19.

22. See Malina, in *The New Testament World*, chap. 2.

23. J. Duncan M. Derrett has collected much useful social data in his works *Law in the New Testament* (London: Darton, Longman & Todd, 1970); *Jesus's Audience:*

The Social and Psychological Environment in Which He Worked (New York: Seabury, 1973); *Studies in the New Testament*, 2 vols. (Leiden: Brill, 1977 and 1978), but his interpretation is often intuitive or biased by Indian models; he fails to show whether and how Indian social forms relate to the first-century Mediterranean context; however, as ethnographical description, Derrett makes a valuable contribution.

24. It would seem that psychological models of a psychoanalytic, clinical, or psychotherapeutic sort are useless to the task either because they tend to be either too culturally specific and untestable or of doubtful value when tested. For example, Gerd Theissen's use of Freudian models, in *Sociology of Early Palestinian Christianity* (Philadelphia: Fortress Press, 1978), pp. 99–110, is simply inappropriate and useless in the light of criticisms like those of David E. Stannard, *Shrinking History: On Freud and the Failure of Psychohistory* (New York: Oxford University Press, 1980); and Joachim Jeremias's explanation of Jesus' healing technique in terms of *Überwältigungstherapie* (in English: "overpowering therapy," a form of emotional flooding therapy) in his *New Testament Theology: The Proclamation of Jesus*, trans. John Bowden (New York: Scribner's, 1971), p. 92, is simply ludicrous in that clinical use of this sort of therapy invariably leads to a worsening of the condition of the patient; see James O. Prochaska, *Systems of Psychotherapy: A Transtheoretical Analysis* (Homewood, Ill.: Dorsey Press, 1979), pp. 265–304.

25. Leon Festinger, Henry W. Riecken, and Stanley Schachter, *When Prophecy Fails: A Social and Psychological Study of a Modern Group that Predicted the Destruction of the World* (New York: Harper & Row Torchbooks, 1964; original, 1956).

26. For a balanced approach to the model, see Robert P. Carroll, *When Prophecy Failed: Cognitive Dissonance in the Prophetic Traditions of the Old Testament* (New York: Seabury, 1979), and notably the critical sociological literature cited on pp. 234–235. For a larger frame that includes dissonance in cross-cultural perspective, see Everett M. Rogers with F. Floyd Shoemaker, *Communication of Innovations: A Cross-Cultural Approach*, 2nd ed. (New York: Free Press, 1971).

27. Perhaps the first attempt at a distinct and differentiated religious institution that might be like religion in our experience can be traced to Mani (A.D. 216–277); see Wilfred C. Smith, *The Meaning and End of Religion: A New Approach to the Religious Traditions of Mankind* (New York: Mentor Books, 1964), pp. 86–90.

28. For the substantive/formal distinction, with explanations and illustrations, see George Dalton, "Economic Theory and Primitive Society," *AA* 63 (1961): 1–25; S. Todd Lowry, "Recent Literature on Ancient Greek Economic Thought," *Journal of Economic Literature* 17 (1979): 65–86.

29. I see no reason for calling the social science approach to biblical interpretation "materialist" (the binary opposite of "idealist") as the French do, e.g., Fernando Belo, *Lecture materialiste de l'evangile de Marc: Recit-Pratique-Ideologie*, 3rd ed. (Paris: Du Cerf, 1976); Eng., *A Materialist Reading of the Gospel of Mark*, trans. Matthew J. O'Connell (Maryknoll, N.Y.: Orbis Books, 1981); the "materialist" model leaves much to be desired; see the critique by Joel S. Kahn and Joseph R. Llobera, "French Marxist Anthropology: Twenty Years After," *Journal of Peasant Studies* 8 (1980): 81–100.

2

NORMAN K. GOTTWALD

Sociological Method in the Study of Ancient Israel

Sociological method in Old Testament studies supplements and enriches historical method by providing a complementary grid of understanding for viewing biblical communities as social entities in process. The biblical communities arose, developed, and declined according to regularities known from a wide range of studies in comparative anthropology and social history.

The fruitfulness of sociological method for understanding the origins of Israel as a social revolutionary movement primarily of peasants; for delineating Israel in relation to Canaanites, 'apiru, pastoral nomads, and Philistines; and for assessing the social organization presupposed in the patriarchal narratives is illustrated. The necessity of carefully applied sociological theory and method in order to avoid arbitrary and unsupportable comparisons between Israel and other peoples is underscored by these examples.

The article explains the methodological framework that informs the author's The Tribes of Yahweh: A Sociology of the Religion of Liberated Israel, 1250–1050 B.C.E. *(Maryknoll, N.Y.: Orbis Books, 1979).*

Reprinted from *Encounter with the Text: Form and History in the Hebrew Bible,* ed. M. J. Buss (Philadelphia: Fortress Press, and Missoula: Scholars Press, 1979), pp. 69–81.

Historical method and sociological method are different but compatible methods for reconstructing ancient Israelite life and thought. Historical study of ancient Israel aims at grasping the sequential articulation of Israel's experience and the rich variety of its cultural products, outstandingly its literature and religion. Sociological study of ancient Israel aims at grasping the typical patterns of human relations in their structure and function, both at a given moment or stage (synchronics) and in their trajectories of change over specified time spans (diachronics). The hypothetically "typical" in collective human behavior is sought by comparative study of societies and expressed theoretically in "laws," "regularities," or "tendencies" that attempt to abstract translocal and transtemporal structural or processual realities within the great mass of spatiotemporal particularities. In such terms, the tribal phase of Israel's social history is greatly illuminated by a theoretical design of social organization (as developed by Sahlins and Fried, among others).[1]

Historical method embraces all the methods of inquiry drawn from the humanities (e.g., literary criticism, form criticism, tradition history, rhetorical criticism, redaction criticism, history, history of religion, biblical theology). Sociological method includes all the methods of inquiry proper to the social sciences (e.g., anthropology, sociology, political science, economics). Sociological method in data collection and theory building enables us to analyze, synthesize, abstract, and interpret Israelite life and thought along different axes and with different tools and constructs from those familiar to us from historical method. Sociological inquiry recognizes people as social actors and symbolizers who "perform" according to interconnecting regularities and within boundaries or limits (social systems).

If we wish to reconstruct ancient Israel as a lived totality, historical method and sociological method are requisite complementary disciplines. Historical method has long recognized the need for collaboration with archaeology, which as a discipline does not fit immediately or comfortably into the molds of the humanities. It is increasingly clear that the need of historical method for sociological inquiry into ancient Israel is just as urgent as its need for archaeology.

The social system of ancient Israel signifies the whole complex of communal interactions embracing functions, roles, institutions, customs, norms, symbols, and the processes and networks distinctive to the sub-systems of social organization (economic production, political order, military defense, judicatory procedure, religious organization, etc.). This social system must be grasped in its activity both in the communal production of goods, services, and ideas and in the communal control of their distribution and use.

We must resist the tendency to objectify Israel's social system into a static and monolithic hypostasis. It developed unevenly, underwent change, and incorporated tension and conflict. It was a framework for human interaction in which stability struggled against change and change eroded away stability. To call this complex of human interaction a social system is meaningful in that it was something more than an aggregation of discrete interhuman relations. There were regularities in the ways that Israelites organized their actions and thoughts, cooperated and contended with one another and with outside groups. These regularities form an analyzable system in the additional sense that they placed Israelite behavior and valuing under impulses and pressures toward normativeness or standardization. The social system tended to validate particular uses and distributions of natural and human resources and to delimit the exercises and distributions of personal and public power. The social system supplied the constraints of physical coercion and symbolic persuasion. By carefully noting the regularities and normative tendencies, it is possible to identify deviations and idiosyncrasies, both those that appear to have been "social waste" and those that augured "social innovation."

The materials for sociological study of ancient Israel are the biblical text and all available extrabiblical evidence, written and material. In addition, the contents, structures, and developmental trajectories of other social systems—whether in Israel's immediate milieu or far beyond in time and space—are potentially relevant for comparative study. What is vital is that those contents, structures, and trajectories be examined in their total contexts and that they be compared with Israel in its total context. Alleged comparison of isolated social data torn out of systemic context is not comparison at all, but superficial juxtaposition lacking criteria for evaluation.

Sociological method works as a totality with its own analytic tools and theoretical perspectives quite as much as does historical method. Since historical method has already "staked out" the field of biblical study, sociological method tends to arrive on the scene as a "tacked on" adjunct to the customary privileged methods. As long as it performs in the role of supplying addenda or trying to do "rescue work" on texts and historical problems that are momentarily resistant to historical methods, sociological method in biblical study will appear tangential and quixotic, as a problematic interloper.[2]

In any given text the sociological data may be no more than traces or shattered torsos. What are we to make, for example, of the kinship and marriage patterns attested in the patriarchal accounts? When sociological method is called in to assist on this problem, it must try to contextualize the fragments within their larger complexes. So far, what is loosely called "sociological" inquiry in this instance is a ransacking of ancient Near Eastern societies for parallel social phenomena. As in the appeal to Nuzi parallels to patriarchal kinship and marriage practices, insufficient attention is paid to the nature of the compared texts and to the social systems presupposed by the texts.

We are becoming freshly aware of the scandalous imprecision of such "sociological" dabbling in the patriarchal traditions. The historical and social loci of the patriarchal traditions are simply not specifiable with any degree of confidence, and, in fact, there is every reason to believe that the historical and social horizons of the separate units and cycles of tradition are highly diverse.[3] In this stalemated situation, sociological inquiry can be most helpful when it extends the examination of how biblical texts with similar social data function in relation to texts or traditions of a similar nature among other peoples, whether literate or preliterate. Working on its own ground, sociological method will try to build up a body of knowledge about types or families of texts and traditions containing social data of certain kinds. How do these tradition types reflect or refract social reality in various types of social systems? How, for example, do genealogies function in oral and written traditions, as separate pieces and as elements within larger compositions, in tribal and in statist societies, etc.?[4]

In other words, a sociology of ancient Israel can be a proper complement to literary and historical inquiry only as it pursues its own proper object of reconstructing the Israelite social system as a totality, without prejudging which of its results are likely to be germane to understanding specific texts or historical problems and without diverting too much energy at the start to narrowly or obscurely framed "social puzzles" in idiosyncratic literary and historical contexts.

In order to approximate comprehensive reconstruction of the Israelite social system, sociological method depends upon literary and historical criticism to undertake their tasks in a similarly comprehensive and systemic way. It also relies upon archaeology to break loose from the domination of historically framed orientations and to become an instrument for recovering the total material life of ancient Israelites irrespective of immediate applications to texts or to historical and sociological problems.

We may illustrate the way the integral projects of sociological method intersect with historical methods by noting the impact of the introduction of a new model for understanding the origins of Israel within its Canaanite matrix. The proposal that earliest Israel was not an invading or infiltrating people but a social revolutionary peasant movement within Canaan is at least a quasi-sociological model.[5] This heuristic model gives a new way of looking at all the old texts, biblical and extrabiblical, and the material remains.[6] Its effect has been to shift attention away from the precise historical circumstances of Israel's occupation of Canaan and toward the social processes by which Israel came to dominance. The effort to reconstruct a history of the occupation has long been deadended by the sparse historical data. A sociological model in this case provides a way of re-viewing the fragmentary historical data and in the end may help us to understand why the historical data are as obscure as they are. Finally, the specifically historical project of identifying the agents and spatiotemporal course of the emergent dominion of Israel in Canaan may be freshly facilitated by the working out of a different conception of the process at work in that achievement.

The effect of the peasant-revolt model of the origins of Israel has been to replace uncritical cultural assumptions about Israel's alleged pastoral nomadism with sharper sociological inquiry into the internal composition of early Israel, demographically and socioeconomically.[7] What exactly was this formation of people called Israel which took control in Canaan and whose social system took form as it gained the upper hand in the land? From what social spaces in Syro-Palestine did these people derive? What brought them together, enabled them to collaborate and to succeed? What were the goals these people shared and what social instrumentalities and material conditions contributed to their accomplishment? How does this social system of earliest Israel relate to those that preceded it and those against which it was counterposed? In other words, a proper model of the Israelite emergence in Canaan is not attainable apart from a proper model of the social system of the people who gained dominion in the land.[8] And of course neither the historical course of Israel's coming to power nor its emergent social system can be grasped without an understanding of the cultic-ideological process of tradition formation.

Up to the present, biblical studies have grappled with a model of the settlement and with a model of the cultic production of traditions, but there has been no adequate mediation between these two forms of inquiry within a larger analytic model of the social system involved in the twin process of taking power in the land and of building its own traditions. Martin Noth and George Mendenhall have made suggestive, incomplete, and at times mistaken attempts at an encompassing societal model. By drawing together the seminal contributions of Noth and Mendenhall, while weeding out their errors and false starts, we have the beginnings of a comprehensive social model for early Israel—or, more precisely, we have an inventory of the questions to be pursued and a general sense of the appropriate range of model options.[9]

A theoretical model of the origins and operations of early Israelite society will entail two axes of investigation: (1) the analysis of Israel's internal composition and structure at its several organizational levels and in its sectoral subsystems; (2) the characterization of Israel's social system as an operational and developing totality in comparison and contrast with other social systems. Both types of inquiry have synchronic and diachronic dimensions, and both types of inquiry will proceed dialectically in movement back and forth between concrete data about specific social systems and more abstract heuristic models, such as a theoretical design of "tribalism."[10]

As for the first task, evidence of the internal composition and eclectic structure of early Israel is largely biblical, but there are significant checkpoints in the Ugaritic, Alalakh, and Amarna texts, as well as rich resources concerning the material culture which have yet to be sufficiently mined. These immediate social data must be reflected upon against the backdrop of the large body of information and theory we now possess as a consequence of anthropological field studies, work in pre-history, and theorizing about social organization.

To what levels, ranges, and functions of social organization do the designations *shēveṭ, mishpaḥāh,* and *beth-'āv* refer? To date it has seemed sufficient to give them the native meanings of "tribe," "clan," and "household" or "extended family," without further ado. If early Israel is conceivable as a form of "retribalization," what were the bonding organizational elements for holding together the segmented "tribes" of diverse origin? Noth provided the summary answer of "a sacral league," but his analogy between the Greek amphictyony and the intertribal league of Israel holds good at such an abstract level that it is of doubtful value in illuminating the crucial features of Israel's retribalization process. If Israel was a revolutionary movement within Canaanite society, how did matters develop from the uncoordinated restiveness of peasants and *'apiru* in Amarna days into the coalition of Israelite tribes? So far only Alt has offered a bare sketch of diachronic possibilities.[11] Merely appealing to Mosaic traditions and Yahwistic faith as "explanations" for this coalescing process does not clarify and reconstruct the arduous struggle by which Israel put itself together in Canaan.

As for the second task, what was the over-all character of Israel's social system in comparison with other preceding and contemporary social systems? Such a comparison depends upon prior analysis of the social systems compared, and this analysis must follow an inventory of social desiderata so that we do not simply accept at face value either the form or the preponderance of specific social data as they happen to appear to us in texts. The comparison of social systems must constantly contextualize social systems and subsystems within the systems as a whole and in terms of the direction of their movement (e.g., expansion, differentiation, decline, transition to new systems, etc.).

Whether two different social complexes can be meaningfully compared is of course a matter of much discussion.[12] In biblical studies there has been an abundance of hasty and superficial cross-cultural comparisons. With each new discovery in the ancient Near East—such as the Amarna, Mari, Ugaritic, or Ebla texts—there has been a rush of claims for direct correlations between them and the biblical text, or for wholesale borrowings of systems or institutions or offices by Israel. On more careful analysis these "parallels" either vanish or are greatly scaled down and nuanced. Such defaults establish the urgency of developing more reliable ways of comparing and contrasting social data and systems. If we wish, for example, to compare early Israelite society with its Canaanite counterpart and matrix, we face serious gaps in our knowledge of aspects of both entities, but these difficulties need to be brought out more systematically so that we will be clearer about the explanatory strength or weakness of our theory and thereby more aware of the kinds of research needed to test and improve theory.

It is evident that comparison of early Israel with other contemporary social systems entails diachronic and synchronic approaches. The social systems under comparison were not static, isolated entities; they developed internally and stood in varying relations to one another over spans of time and in different regions. A great deal of nuancing in treating these societal interfaces is required, often dismally lacking, for example, in the way "Canaan" and "Israel" are counterposed by biblical scholars, like characters in a morality play. According to all known analogies of revolutionary movements, we should expect that by no means all of the people of Canaan will have been "polarized" by the nascent Israelite movement. It should be expected that as the Canaanite and rising Israelite social systems collided and conflicted, there will have been many people—probably a majority at first—who were conflicted in their own feelings and stances toward the two options. We should expect to find those who strove for neutrality, by choice or necessity, some who were half-hearted converts and those who switched sides, others who were secret supporters and yet others who were opportunist in their allegiances.[13] A re-examination of Israel's early traditions in terms of these dynamics of social revolutionary movements will reveal unexpected results toward a clearer conception of how Israel arose. The result is likely to be that the initially simplistic-appearing peasant revolt model will turn out to be even more complex and nuanced than the previous conquest and immigration models of Israel's origins.

In pursuing the comparative approach to Israelite society a major issue is how we are to decide which social systems should be compared with Israel's. Here we encounter the vexed problem of determining the boundaries of social systems in relation to the boundaries of the various historic state, tribal, and cultural formations which appear under various, vaguely depicted proper names and gentilics in the biblical and extrabiblical texts. No doubt we should identify the Canaanite city-state system as the dominant and definitive social system within earliest Israel's horizon.[14] But do the *'apiru* of the Amarna period form another such system? Here the time trajectory enters into consideration. The *'apiru* appear as a sub-set within Amarna "feudalism" or "Asiatic mode of production,"[15] but insofar as the *'apiru* are seen as forerunners and one of the contributors to early Israel, they may indeed merit attention as another social system in embryo or as one trajectory along which the Canaanite social system declined and the Israelite social system rose. And it would be a grave methodological error to assume that early Israel arose along only one such trajectory. More often than not, the relation of the *'apiru* to early Israel has been examined as though it was the only or the primary pertinent relationship and that, if the *'apiru* data could not account for all or most of the features of early Israel, then they were irrelevant.

Pastoral nomadism as the supposed socioeconomic condition of early Israel might be viewed as another social system, but we now see how doubtful it is that we can locate an autonomous pastoral nomadic system in the immediate environment of Canaan contemporary with early Israel. The transhuman, village-based pastoral nomadism of Israel's environment was a minor sub-set of village tribalism subordinated socioeconomically and politically to sedentary Canaan. This pastoral nomadism was at most a minor contributor to early Israel. Nonetheless, it is necessary that this pastoral nomadic sub-specialization of village tribalism be carefully analyzed in order to reassess properly its vastly overstated role in Israelite origins.[16]

Other possible social systems in Israel's milieu come to mind. Do the Philistines constitute a new social system or are they merely heirs of the Canaanite system with new organizational twists, mostly of a political and military nature?[17] And what are we to make of the Ammonites, Moabites, and Edomites, whose origins were roughly contemporary with Israel and yet who did not become a part of Israel? Did these people feel the tug of Israel's social mutation, did some of them actually engage in social revolution, and if so, why did they accept kingship earlier than did Israel itself?[18]

Against this methodological sketch, we can see why the patriarchal traditions are particularly resistant to sociological analysis. From all appearances, those traditions belong to any number of peoples moving along various trajectories toward their convergence in early Israel. The patriarchal groups are proto-Israelites. Just as Noth recognized that the patriarchal traditions can only be approached backwards, working out of the congealing traditions of united Israel in Canaan, so the sociological analysis of the patriarchal communities must be approached backwards from the coalescing peoples of the intertribal community in Israelite Canaan. No sociological wonders will be workable on the patriarchal traditions until much more is known of their literary form and function, of their temporal horizons, and of their rootage in one or another of the social trajectories along which sectors of the Syro-Palestinian peoples converged toward their unity in Israel.[19]

An instance of the great difficulties in precise sociological analysis of the groups represented in the patriarchal traditions of Genesis 25–35 is the practice of using the connubium reported in Genesis 34 between Shechemites and Israelites as evidence for clan exogamy, a habit that goes back at least to the nineteenth-century anthropologist E. B. Tylor.

Genesis 34 tells us only that the two parties began to reach agreement on an alliance that was to include the exchange of wives. It does *not* tell us that a presupposition for the proposed wife-exchange was that Israelites or Shechemites could not marry among themselves and thus were obliged to get wives from outside. It does *not* tell us that the wives to be exchanged between the group constituted all or most of the marriage arrangements to be made by Israelites and Shechemites, thereby sharply reducing or excluding intragroup marriages or intermarriage with other groups. In other words, since we do not know the actual scope demographically or the internal social structure of the two contracting entities in Genesis 34, we have to try out various hypotheses to see how clan-exogamous they look on close examination. The results are not reassuring.

If, for example, "Israel" in Genesis 34 was actually only a relatively small social group (still proto-Israelite), the connubium formula might be read—especially noting the phrase "we will become one people" (v. 16)—as alluding to an early endeavor to meld together two groups of people into one tribal formation as complementary moieties. We might in that case be witnessing an initial act by which a member of later Israel (Manasseh or a section of Manasseh?) was formed from two originally separate groups that become segments practicing exogamy and thus exchanging wives within the newly shaped tribe. Granted that the formation was not carried through according to Genesis 34, it could at least be construed that connubium covenant was a means by which some peoples did come together as tribal entities within Israel, the tribes being built up by exogamous clans.

If, on the other hand, we imagine (as the final state of the text certainly does), that many Israelite tribes are present and that this is an "external" arrangement between autonomous entities, a matter of intertribal "foreign policy," we could say that Israel developed, or sought to develop, peaceful relations with some surrounding peoples by connubium covenant. But would a tribal organization (Israel) and a city organization (Shechem) be likely to enter into such an exogamous connubium? Would a large assemblage of tribes be able to get enough wives from one city for an exclusive connubium if exogamy forbade marriage of Israelites to fellow Israelites? The anthropological evidence is that whole tribes are not exogamous; it is clans within a tribe that are exogamous and that take wives from and give wives to other exogamous clans, the tribe as a whole remaining endogamous (although marriages may be allowed or prescribed outside the tribe in certain cases). The more large-scale the Israelite partner in the proposed connubium is conceived to have been, the more likely it becomes that the group already would have worked out marriage patterns, exogamous or otherwise (that cannot be known from the text), among its member units, and thus the more peripheral the connubium with Shechem would become as a wife-exchange mechanism and the more it would look like an alliance sealed with limited intermarriage bearing no correlation whatsoever with exogamy rules. Maybe the difficulties can be eased by conceiving the proposed connubium as an arrangement involving only a single clan or group of clans (of Manasseh?) located in the vicinity of Shechem. In that way a possible symmetrical, exogamously-based exchange of wives could be made plausible, but that hypothesis still fails to deal with the issue of whether a city would be interested in, or capable of, wholesale exogamy.

The farther our analysis and speculation about alternatives runs, the more evident it becomes that even if Genesis 34 goes back to early times, the obstacles to perceiving its exact sociohistoric context, the parties involved, and the mechanisms posited, are insuperably opposed to any reasonable confidence that this tradition shows the existence of exogamous clans in early Israel. A careful examination of other early biblical traditions thought to attest to clan exogamy yields similarly doubtful or flatly negative results.[20]

A main sociological task in the study of early Israel is the development of an adequate socioeconomic and cultural material inventory. This will require further historicoterritorial and topological studies (of the sort begun by Alt and carried on by Rowton). Archaeology will have to attend not only to fortified cities but to the agricultural village/neighborhood complexes that included settlements, roads, fields, springs, irrigation, terrace systems, etc. Renewed attention will have to be given to population size, density, and distribution. The role of technological factors taken in combination will have to be explored more thoroughly: the introduction of iron, waterproof cisterns, improved terracing, and irrigation works. The archaeology of biblical Israel, previously overwhelmingly oriented to direct synchronizations with biblical literature and history (e.g., who were the kings of Genesis 14:1?), will increasingly offer a wider spectrum of data for the social and cultural reconstruction of the early Israelite movement. More and more we can hope for the collaboration of all methodologies in clarifying the material and socioreligious processes by which the Israelites came into dominance in the hill country of Canaan.[21]

The sociological inquiry which I have here illustrated in the instance of Israel's origins will equally apply to the major social transition to the monarchy and the resulting tensions and conflicts between state, empire, and tribe, as well as to the later period of the disintegration of the Israelite states and the survival and reconstruction of social forms into the postexilic age. It is obvious that in this task it will be necessary to call upon a host of specialists so far only sporadically enlisted in the task of reconstructing ancient Israel, e.g., agronomists, botanists, hydrologists, geologists, demographers, etc. The reconstructed cultural-material complexes will bear important indicators for social, military, and religious organization, especially when contextually compared with agrarian complexes and urban center/rural periphery complexes of similar sorts that can be studied at first hand by contemporary ethnologists.

In sum, it is essential that we devise a constructive model of the Israelite social system in its own right, firmly rooted in its material conditions, a model which delineates the major subsystems and segmented organization, as well as a model that grasps the integrating mechanisms and the solidifying ideology of the social whole.[22] This model will necessarily be viewed genetically in order to show how Israel arose, achieved its first cohesive form, and then passed over into other forms in the course of time through a combination of internal and external pressures. Synchronics and diachronics, internal dynamics and external interfaces and interpenetrations will be drawn together under the principle or law of internal relations whereby an alteration in any element of the whole will be seen to bring about alterations in the entire system.

A model of the Israelite social system will incorporate the highly centralized and richly articulated religion of Yahweh. But it must do so sociologically by understanding the religion as a social phenomenon (institutionally and symbolically) and therefore related to all the other social phenomena within the system by the law of internal relations. This socioreligious inquiry must proceed without simplistic recourse to the tautological, philosophically idealist claim that because religion was central to the social system, it can be posited as the unmoved mover of the Israelite mutation.[23]

The sociological contribution to biblical hermeneutics is that the Israelite traditions must not only be interpreted within their original matrices, but must be interpreted from out of the social matrix of the interpreter. In the end it will be learned that an adequate biblical hermeneutics will require the investigation of the evolution of social forms and systems from biblical times until the present![24] Any interpreter who claims continuity with the biblical texts must also assume the continuity of the history of social forms as an indispensable precondition of the hermeneutical task.

NOTES

1. Marshall Sahlins, *Tribesmen* (Englewood Cliffs, N.J.: Prentice-Hall, 1968); Morton H. Fried, *The Evolution of Political Society: An Evolutionary View* (New York: Random House, 1968).

2. Frank S. Frick and Norman K. Gottwald, "The Social World of Ancient Israel," *SBL 1975 Seminar Papers* I (1975), pp. 165–78. See also Article 10 in this volume.

3. The precariousness of attaching patriarchal tradition to Bronze Age historical and social settings is independently demonstrated by Thomas L. Thompson, *The Historicity of the Patriarchal Narratives: The Quest for the Historical Abraham* (Berlin: de Gruyter, 1974) and John Van Seters, *Abraham in History and Tradition* (New Haven: Yale University Press, 1975).

4. Renger, working with Amorite texts in which he finds exogamous clan organizations, posits patriarchal exogamy for the biblical patriarchs, but can only succeed by capriciously regarding the biblical genealogies as actual descent lineages and sometimes as fictitious or eponymous constructs (J. Renger, "*mārat ilim:* Exogamie bei den semitischen Nomaden des 2 Jahrtausends," *Archiv für Orientforschung* 14 [1973]: 103–7). Much more sophisticated in using comparative methods and thus advancing our comprehension of biblical genealogies are Abraham Malamat, "Tribal Societies: Biblical Genealogies and African Lineage Systems," *Archives Européennes de Sociologie* 14 (1973): 126–36, and Robert R. Wilson, *Genealogy and History in the Biblical World,* Yale Near Eastern Researches, 7 (New Haven: Yale University Press, 1977). See also Norman K. Gottwald, *The Tribes of Yahweh: A Sociology of the Religion of Liberated Israel, 1250–1050 B.C.E.* (Maryknoll, N.Y.: Orbis Books, 1979), pp. 308–10, 334–37.

5. See George E. Mendenhall, "The Hebrew Conquest of Palestine," *BA* 25 (1962): 66–87, and *The Tenth Generation: The Origins of the Biblical Tradition* (Baltimore: Johns Hopkins University Press, 1973). The same broad conclusion that early Israel was "the *first* ideologically based socio-political revolution in the history of the world" was reached independently by Jan Dus, "Moses or Joshua? On the Problem of the Founder of the Israelite Religion," *Radical Religion* 2, nos. 2 and 3 (1975): 26–41. See also the discussions in the May 1978 issue of *JSOT:* by Alan J. Hauser, "Israel's Conquest of Palestine: A Peasants' Rebellion?," pp. 2–19; Thomas L. Thompson, "Historical Notes on 'Israel's Conquest of Palestine: A Peasants' Rebellion?,'" pp. 20–27; and Norman K. Gottwald, "The Hypothesis of the Revolutionary Origins of Ancient Israel: A Response to Hauser and Thompson," pp. 37–52.

6. A striking example of heuristic value of a sociological model for textual criticism and historical reconstruction is Marvin L. Chaney, "HDL-II and the 'Song of Deborah': Textual, Philological, and Sociological Studies in Judges 5, with Special

Reference to the Occurrences of ḤDL in Biblical Hebrew" (Ph.D. diss., Harvard University, 1976).

7. Norman K. Gottwald, "Were the Early Israelites Pastoral Nomads?" *Rhetorical Criticism: Essays in Honor of James Muilenburg,* ed. J. J. Jackson and M. Kessler (Pittsburgh: Pickwick, 1974), pp. 223-55; idem, "Nomadism," *IDBSup* (1976), pp. 629-31; idem, *The Tribes of Yahweh,* pp. 464-92.

8. Gottwald, *Tribes of Yahweh,* pp. 493-587.

9. My critiques of Noth's and Mendenhall's models for early Israel will be found in *Tribes of Yahweh,* pp. 220-33, 345-57, 376-86, 599-602. See Note 5 above for Mendenhall, and Martin Noth, *A History of the Pentateuchal Traditions* (1948) (Englewood Cliffs, N.J.: Prentice-Hall, 1972).

10. For an elaboration of this programmatic statement, see *Tribes of Yahweh,* pp. 228-33, and for provisional conclusions on the content see pp. 237-587.

11. Albrecht Alt, "The Settlement of the Israelites in Palestine," *Essays in Old Testament History and Religion* (1925) (Oxford: Blackwell, 1966), pp. 175-204.

12. Walter R. Goldschmidt, *Comparative Functionalism: An Essay in Anthropological Theory* (Berkeley: University of California Press, 1966).

13. For an analysis of Israel's Canaanite converts, allies, and neutrals, see *Tribes of Yahweh,* pp. 555-583.

14. W. Helck, *Die Beziehungen Aegyptens zu Vorderasien im 3. und 2. Jahrtausend v. Chr.* (Wiesbaden: Harrassowitz, 1962); M. A. K. Mohammad, "The Administration of Syro-Palestine during the New Kingdom," *Annales du Service des Antiquités de l'Egypte* (Cairo) 56 (1959): 105-37; Giorgio Buccellati, *Cities and Nations of Ancient Syria,* Studi Semitici, 26 (Rome: Università di Roma, 1967).

15. Norman K. Gottwald, "Early Israel and 'The Asiatic Mode of Production' in Canaan," *SBL 1976 Seminar Papers* (1976), pp. 145-54.

16. On classificatory typology of pastoral nomadism, see Douglas L. Johnson, *The Nature of Nomadism* (Chicago: University of Chicago Press, 1969), and for ancient Near East pastoral nomadism, see M. B. Rowton, "Autonomy and Nomadism in Western Asia," *Orientalia* 42 (1973): 247-58, and "Urban Autonomy in a Nomadic Environment," *JNES* 32 (1973): 201-15.

17. Cf. Albrecht Alt, "Aegyptische Tempel in Palaestina und die Landnahme der Philister," in *Kleine Scriften,* I (1944) (Munich: Beck, 1953), pp. 216-30; Hanna E. Kassis, "Gath and the Structure of the 'Philistine' Society," *JBL* 84 (1965): 259-71.

18. Cf. S. H. Horn, "Ammon, Ammonites," *IDBSup* (1976): 20; J. R. Bartlett, "The Rise and Fall of the Kingdom of Edom," *PEQ* (1972), pp. 26-37, and "The Moabites and the Edomites," in *Peoples of Old Testament Times,* ed. D. J. Wiseman (Oxford: Clarendon, 1973), pp. 229-58.

19. Gottwald, *Tribes of Yahweh,* pp. 32-44, 105-10.

20. Ibid., pp. 301-15.

21. Ibid., pp. 642-63.

22. Ibid., pp. 191-663.

23. Ibid., pp. 591-691.

24. Ibid., pp. 692-709.

3

GERD THEISSEN

The Sociological Interpretation of Religious Traditions: Its Methodological Problems as Exemplified in Early Christianity

The New Testament contains some direct statements that describe groups, organizations, and institutions (sociographic statements), as well as some direct statements that describe individuals in terms of their origins, statuses, and roles within social settings (prosopographic statements). In addition, inferences about typical and recurring social behaviors and structures may be cautiously drawn from accounts of historical incidents, descriptions of social norms, and even from religious symbols.

Social groups in the New Testament period may be compared and contrasted with one another and with social groups in other historic situations according to controlled comparative methods. Specific illustrations from New Testament texts are given for each type of method introduced. Awareness of the strengths and limits of each method allows for judicious hypotheses that can be further evaluated, modified, refined, or replaced.

This essay is Chapter 5 of Gerd Theissen, *The Social Setting of Pauline Christianity*, ed. and trans. and with an Introduction by John H. Schütz, copyright © 1982 by Fortress Press, Philadelphia. Reprinted by permission of Fortress Press.

Every age has its preferred intellectual procedures for grappling with the irritating and fascinating phenomenon of religion. It may do so systematically or normatively through philosophy of religion and criticism of religion, historically through analysis of the multiplicity of religions, or phenomenologically through the isolation of that which is most "essential" from the ebb and flow of the history of religions.

By all indications, questions from the sociology of religion are in the forefront today. This is certainly true for inquiry into contemporary religious phenomena; but it is also increasingly, if hesitantly, the case in connection with specific topics of historical research.[1] Hesitation on the part of historical research is understandable and justified. Contemporary sociology of religion which conducts empirical research can avail itself of the methods of interview, questionnaire, observation, field investigation, and sometimes even laboratory investigation in order to arrange its material from the outset with an eye to statistical evaluation. The historian, however, is entirely dependent on chance sources which have survived. Moreover, these have been shaped by interests quite different from that of providing information about their social background.[2] In fact, it is a characteristic trait of religious tradition that it masks its mooring in human activity, preferring to speak of the gods' activity or to testify to an experienced reality lying beyond the world of human sense perception. The problematic nature of sociological research in the field of the history of religion is, therefore, problematic first of all in terms of methodology. To phrase this as a question, How does one obtain information about sociological circumstances from religious expressions in our sources? In what follows this question is discussed with reference to early Christianity. But first the material problem of a sociology of early Christianity should be sketched out at least in brief. Methodological reflections without application to a concrete case are fruitless.

The sociology of primitive Christianity is the sociology of an emerging ancient Christianity and its radical transformation. It began as a renewal movement within Judaism and became an independent religion. It took root in rural areas but spread primarily through the cities of the Hellenistic Mediterranean. It was at first a movement of those who were socially unintegrated; but it soon developed a new pattern of integration which later could be taken over by the larger society. The basic problem in a sociology of primitive Christianity is this: How could this marginal, subcultural current conquer and transform an entire culture? A sociology of *primitive* Christianity investigates only a part of this process, namely the period prior to the institutional consolidation of ancient Christianity by means of canon, episcopal office, and *regula fidei* and before the transformation of Hellenistic-Roman culture through the crisis of the third century C.E., that is, the period up to the close of the enlightened monarchy of the Antonines in the second century C.E.

Primitive Christian sources contain no sociological statements and only a few prescientific sociological references contain paranetic, poetic, ecclesiological, and mythical statements. We thus face a methodological problem. How does one derive sociological statements from these nonsociological

forms of expression? What, indeed, is a sociological statement? The following working definition may suffice for our investigation: A sociological statement seeks to describe and explain interpersonal behavior with reference to
those characteristics which transcend the personal. First of all, then, a sociological question is less concerned with what is individual than with what is
typical, recurrent, general. Second, it is less concerned with the singular conditions of a specific situation than with structural relationships which apply
to several situations.[3] Therefore, a sociology of primitive Christianity has the
task of describing and analyzing the interpersonal behavior of members of
primitive Christian groups.

A discussion of available procedures can begin with the form-critical analysis of texts, which construes a text's *Sitz im Leben* in three ways: construc-
tively, analytically, and comparatively.[4] In form criticism the "constructive"
approach is that which rests on direct disclosure of the *Sitz im Leben,* that is,
on expressions which intend to describe the social situation to which we owe
the transmission and formulation of the texts. We can generalize by saying
that "constructive" refers to the interpretation of all texts with (prescientific)
sociological elements. The "analytic" approach infers from the form of a
text the underlying *Sitz im Leben.* Here too it is possible to generalize. Analytic refers to every inference *from* poetic, ethical, ecclesiological, and historical expressions *to* the underlying social reality. It is characteristic of this
process of inference that it puts to the texts questions which are independent
of the intention which originally shaped those texts. Finally, "comparative"
refers to that procedure which considers texts which neither deal with, nor
come from, early Christian groups. These must in turn be investigated con-
structively and analytically in their own right, while their use for shedding
light on primitive Christianity raises special methodological problems.

CONSTRUCTIVE METHODS

Constructive methods can be applied to sociographic or prosopographic
statements. All descriptions of groups, institutions, organizations, and so
forth, may be termed "sociographic," while all statements about individuals, their background, status, and roles are "prosopographic." Unfortunately, there are but few statements with sociographic intent about early
Christian groups. In Acts 4:32-37, Luke depicts a communism and fellowship of the primitive community which is based on agape. From a Roman
official in Bithynia we learn that Christianity there has spread through all
levels of society, both in the cities and in the countryside (Pliny, *Epist.* X, 96).
For the milieu of primitive Christianity we have Josephus's descriptions of
the Pharisees, Essenes, and Zealots (*War* II, 18; *Ant.* XVIII, 1:1-6). It goes
without saying that these sociographic sketches are to be read critically. Luke
and Josephus both write for the Hellenistic reader. Josephus portrays the
religious currents of Judaism as philosophical schools; Luke sees the ancient
ideal of *panta koina,* "everything in common," realized in the primitive com-

munity. Both idealize or negatively distort, as Josephus does in the case of the Zealots—he makes them responsible for the Jewish War—or as Christian authors do in the case of the Pharisees.

Prosopographic statements about individuals are more numerous. We learn, for example, that the first disciples were fishermen (Mark 1:16ff.); that fishermen could recruit day laborers (Mark 1:20); that some of the first Christians owned houses (Peter, Matt. 8:14; Mary, Acts 12:12ff.); and that others owned land (Barnabas, Acts 4:36-37; Ananias and Sapphira, Acts 5:1ff.). The sociological assessment of these bits of information presents the same basic problems to be found in any social-scientific assessment of empirical data: problems of reliability, validity, and representativeness. This can be illustrated by the example of Manaen in Acts 13:1, a *syntrophos* [foster brother; RSV "member of the court"] of the Roman client prince Herod Antipas.

The Problem of Reliability

The first question is whether this note is historical. Does every investigator, after repeated examination of the same sources, conclude that according to everything we can know, Manaen was actually raised as a youth with the young prince Herod? We must be clear about whether the text is reliably transmitted—this piece of information is missing, for example, in St. Gall Codex 133, but that is easily explained[5]—or whether anything points to a legendary tradition. Luke is happy to report on Herod Antipas and his circle in order to bring Christianity into contact with the larger world and to synchronize the two. But even if this note were unhistorical and an unwarranted supposition, sociologically it would not be without value inasmuch as it gives information about what a later generation thought possible with reference to earliest Christianity or what seemed plausible within the frame of reference of its own experience: *that* members of the higher classes also belonged to the primitive Christian fellowship. Thus, while it is the case that within historical research the question of reliability is identical with that of historicity, the concept of historicity can also be taken in a wider sense. From historical sources we get insight not only about what is reported but also about those who report it and hand it on. Since those who hand on such material do so within a framework of social groups, even the "unhistorical" is relevant for a sociological analysis of primitive Christian sources, so long as it originates from these groups and permits inferences about them.

The Problem of Validity

Validity presupposes or implies reliability. Here the specific question is, Can an elevated social standing be inferred from the status of *syntrophos*? We know from contemporary witnesses about *syntrophoi*[6] that the term refers not just to childhood "playmates" but also to confidants who often exercised influence as mature adults. Nevertheless, it cannot simply be concluded that Manaen belonged to the upper circles in Antioch. Herod Antipas had in the meantime lost his holdings and principality and been exiled to Lyons (*Ant.* XVIII, 7, 2). Manaen could have become entangled in this fate, so that with equal justification we might look on him as a failure who now found in a position of control and influence within the Christian community a substitute for what he had lost. We don't know which was the case. It is only certain that at one time he belonged to the upper classes. This conclusion is valid, but not the unqualified conclusion of current elevated social status based on wealth and influence.

The Problem of Representativeness

For sociological analysis what is interesting is not the biography of Manaen but the question of whether or not, on the basis of these statements, we can learn something about the class membership of Christians. This can never be done directly. It can be assumed that the (possibly former) status of Manaen is emphasized precisely because it represents something unusual. We must utilize further clues. In that regard, it is scarcely accidental that an elevated social status seems probable for three of the five "prophets and teachers" of the Antioch community (Acts 13:1). Barnabas is known for his gift to the Jerusalem community (Acts 4:36f.). Later he also organized relief efforts for it (Acts 11:30). Paul was only a cloth worker, but he possessed Tarsian and Roman citizenship (Acts 21:39; 22:25ff.). Since we know from Dio Chrysostom (*Or.* 30, 21–23) that at a later time the civil rights of cloth workers were in some dispute, we must accord Paul a particularly privileged status. We learn nothing further about the other two members of this "leadership" group in Antioch. In any event, people with a relatively elevated social status predominate in this group. Further, it is interesting that almost all come from outside: Barnabas from Cyprus (Acts 4:36), Paul from Tarsus, Lucius from Cyrenaica. Furthermore, Manaen probably was not raised in Antioch, and Simeon's epithet "Niger," while it certainly could refer to his Negroid appearance, also might serve as a designation of origin. Therefore Manaen, while certainly not representative of all Christians, does represent the leadership group in the community in Antioch. It is also true of other Hellenistic Christian communities that they display an internal social stratification (cf. 1 Cor. 1:26ff.; Pliny, *Epist.* X, 96) and that the higher strata dominate, not in numbers, but in influence.

In any event, discrete statements must be evaluated very cautiously. For example, it is not permissible to assume, on the basis of the few Christians who are specifically named and their often rather high social status, to have refuted the view that the rise of primitive Christianity had something to do with social contradictions.[7] The very assumption that those few who are specifically named are typical of early Christianity is itself problematic, not to mention the fact that whether early Christianity is class-specific or not says little about whether its origins are linked with social tensions. It is well known that most lower-class movements articulating protest had leaders from the upper classes.

ANALYTIC METHODS

Since there is available but a limited number of statements containing express sociographic elements, we usually rely on analytic methods, that is, inferences drawn from historical events, social norms, or religious symbols.

Inferences from Events

Above all, historiographic texts from the past preserve for posterity that which is unusual. The normal situation is not worth mentioning. Sociological interest, however, is geared to the normal case, that which is typical and recurrent. For that reason we learn from historiographic traditions—it makes no difference whether we are speaking about the popular religious traditions of the New Testament or the literary traditions of Josephus—only incidentally about the social relationships which interest us. Nevertheless, we do learn something. Focusing attention on that which is unusual often allows us to look more carefully as well at the background, that is, the usual. For example, the unusual fact is that Christians were given the name "Christians" in Antioch (Acts 11:26); it follows, therefore, that they were not ordinarily distinguished from Jews by a special designation (or set apart within Judaism). The execution of James by the high priest Ananus II was exceptional, arousing indignation (*Ant.* XX, 9, 1). Thus the normal relationship between Jewish Christians and Jews was scarcely characterized by routine persecution. A second way of deducing the typical from discrete historical events is to search for events which reoccur in relation to a particular feature. For example, Jesus frequently touches on the territory belonging to cities without entering the cities themselves (Mark 5:1; 7:24, 31; 8:27). From this it may be concluded that his movement was at home in the rural districts. Initially, it had no success in cities (Matt. 11:20–24).

What is most instructive, however, is the analysis of conflicts. To be sure, conflicts are also atypical events, but in most cases they expose to view the structures which transcend individuals. Personal animosities are more likely to be their occasion than their real cause. In most cases entire groups are partners to the conflicts, individual protagonists serving as representatives of institutions and authorities. Their cause often lies in various, but typical, behavior of social groups, in differing attitudes, customs, and social assumptions. In such cases the extraordinary makes directly visible the ordinary; beyond the dramatic we can see the banal. Such is the case in the conflict between the weak and the strong in Corinth (1 Cor. 8:1–11:1) where the different customs of eating emerge, customs probably determined by class attitudes.[8] The problem of the ritual character of meat purchased in the market

(1 Cor. 10:25) is no problem for those who have little money with which to buy meat. Other conflicts are similarly illuminating, such as those between Christians and Pharisees, between Hellenistic and "Hebraic" Christians in Jerusalem (Acts 6:1ff.), between Jewish and Gentile Christianity (Gal. 2:1-14), between Paul and his Corinthian opponents (2 Cor. 10-13). Conflicts also characterize the transition from primitive Christianity to the established, institutionalized church, as in the case of Gnosticism or Montanism. The analysis of such conflicts is one of the most fruitful analytic approaches of a sociology of primitive Christianity. Conversely, every sociology of primitive Christianity must seek to determine to what extent it can make such conflicts comprehensible.

Inferences from Norms

Norms are social regulations and as such are social facts regardless of the extent to which they are observed. Primitive Christian norms (in the broadest sense) come to us in two ways. Either they are explicit (that is, ethical norms) or can be inferred from the regularity of some well-attested behavior, as in the case of norms governing speaking and literary activity.

An initial group of explicitly formulated norms are practical norms, general rules by means of which every social world orders and governs the impressions, experiences, and certitudes of its members.[9] One such practical norm is the (very pessimistic) recognition that those who have will receive more while from those who have not even what they have will be taken (Mark 4:25). One can scarcely imagine such a piece of wisdom at home in the social circles of those in society who earn a profit. Numerous such "insights" are transmitted in the New Testament through aphorisms, wisdom sayings, and maxims. In them we have fragments from that world of certitudes and truisms by which any group or society orders the experience of its members.

Such practical norms are not expressly sanctioned. They belong to the everyday certitudes which suggest themselves automatically. Nobody commands that the world must be seen as it is in such norms, but anyone entertaining other opinions will soon feel the pressure of social control. With ethical and juridical norms it is quite different. Here nonobservance will be deliberately punished. These norms appear as commands, which is particularly clear in the case of legal norms. Usually these are formulated in some express statute, while sanctions are provided and institutional mechanisms are devised to govern the interpretation, application, and sanctioning of the norms. It is precisely these institutional regulations which make legal norms so very instructive.[10] In early Christianity, however, we have only a few legal norms with such regulating devices. Perhaps one such is the excommunication procedure in Matthew 18:15-17 in which the *ecclesia* as institution comes to the fore. Further instances are perhaps to be found in other community rules and ordinances with legal characteristics (e.g., *Didache*). Many community rules, however, are instances of sacred law *(heiliges Recht),* which means that the sanctioning of the norm rests with God, so that it is often difficult to say whether there as yet stands behind these an earthly court. For example, was an affront to a member of the community punished by an assembly (*synhedrion,* Matt. 5:22), or did one leave the punishment to God (Rom. 12:19)?

The majority of norms coming down to us are doubtless of the ethical sort. Here too institutional features of life are involved insofar as these build up a framework within which such social regulations become meaningful and practicable.[11] The precept that wives, children, and slaves should respect the head of the household, *paterfamilias,* as well as his obligation to be concerned for those who are dependent on him (Col. 3:18–4:1), presupposes the setting of the Christian house. By contrast, the precept that to follow Jesus requires hating one's relatives, including wife and children (Luke 14:26ff.), has a quite different social mooring. This is a norm at home among itinerant charismatics, a standard for those apostles and prophets and missionaries who are without home, family, or possessions.

When inferring from prosopographic and historical statements to typical social behavior and its conditions, the methodological problem consists in deriving a generalization from the singular instance. What is given is a statement about an individual social action; the typical is then reached by inference, making problematical the representativeness of the singular. When we infer from explicitly formulated norms, however, the very opposite holds true. What is asserted is a generalization, even if it is asserted as an imperative rather than an indicative. By paying attention to the practical norms, we learn what kind of general behavior is wanted. Here the question becomes how far the norms are really followed and whether discrepancies between reality and norm can be determined retrospectively with any methodological reliability. Some typical discrepancies can doubtless still be recognized. First, it must be determined whether a norm is considered of general applicability and whether it is possibly meant allegorically. For example, the dictum that one should, if the occasion arises, part with a hand or foot or eye in order to enter the kingdom of God (Mark 9:42ff.) is prescribed in a qualified form with reference to scandal, and is scarcely to be taken literally. Nevertheless, it points without question to an extreme ascetic disposition in early Christianity. Therefore, it is not beyond the realm of possibility that some "disciples," like Origen at a later time, had themselves castrated in literal obedience to Matthew 19:11–12.[12] In general we ought not to be too hasty to relativize a norm as allegorical or of limited application.

Even when it has been determined that we are dealing with a norm which is designed to be taken literally and applied generally, it must be kept in mind that commands are always more radical than actual behavior. For example, the disciples are enjoined to break with their families (Luke 14:26). We learn from 1 Cor. 9:4–5, however, that some traveled with their wives. The commandment indicates only a certain trend in behavior. In particular instances we must even assume that a command—for example when formulated negatively—runs *counter* to the trend of behavior. Whatever must be forbidden is usually being done somewhere. Thus from the prohibition of a mission among the Samaritans and Gentiles (Matt. 10:5-6) we can infer the existence of such a mission (cf. Acts 8:1-5). Different forms of discrepancy between actual behavior and the norm can certainly still be recognized, especially when historiographic and sociographic data yield more direct information about actual behavior.

With regard to norms disclosed by linguistic and literary behavior, the methodological procedure is rather different. Here the norm itself is derived from concrete behavior as evidenced in many examples. Because the examples are numerous, decisions about their representativeness are easier. In this case what interests us are language, style, arrangement of material, and genre *(Gattung)* as norms of social interaction. From these we learn something of the educational level of the authors or the brokers of the tradition. To be sure, here too we must have reservations about the representativeness and validity of our inferences. What has been retained for us is only the written form of linguistic behavior. Whoever expresses himself primarily in writing, or puts into writing what was once oral tradition, must possess a certain minimum of education, to wit, at least a familiarity with the written medium. The New Testament authors certainly belong to those of above average education within Christian groups, so that from them we do not learn the daily speech habits of the lower class. To be sure, in antiquity even ordinary people could write, as papyri and ostraca show. Nevertheless, we have only a very limited insight into the speech conventions of lower classes. A. Deissmann's confidence in uncovering these with the help of epigraphy, papyrus discoveries, and ostraca, and in using the results to assess the New Testament sociologically, requires some correction.[13] Thus we cannot simply identify the literary language of poetry and philosophy with the speech habits of the upper class; and many alleged vulgarisms or Semitisms of the New Testament can be demonstrated to be at home in the less pretentious technical prose of medicine.[14] Nevertheless, it is instructive that within the New Testament we can observe various levels of language. The authors of Luke's Gospel and Hebrews are examples of two who can be considered relatively educated people on the basis of their good Greek. Unfortunately, poor Greek does not necessarily indicate lower social status, as is indicated by Josephus, who belongs to the upper strata of Aramaic-speaking Palestinian society but confesses to be not the best master of Greek (Ant. XX, 12, 1). Semitizing Greek is not in itself vulgar Greek, however attractive the idea might be that the author of the Apocalypse, with its aggressive imagery, came from the lower classes since he writes the worst Greek in the New Testament. Beyond that it must be kept in mind that education is not an absolutely certain criterion of elevated social status. Wealth and ignorance sometimes go beautifully hand in hand.

The idea that literary forms, as genre-specific norms for the shaping of texts, express social relationships is one of the basic perceptions of classical form criticism. Hymns, for example, serve to confirm collectively a mythically interpreted world which was created and inhabited by early Christian groups. Letters provide communication for those who are separated. If the letter was capable of becoming one of the most important "literary" forms of early Hellenistic Christianity, it did so because this form corresponded to the diaspora setting of a small group with a great cohesive strength. Thus from literary forms we learn something basic about the forms of interaction among the individuals involved in the literature, whether it is a matter of polemic, consensus, apologetic, instruction, or whatever. The boundaries of literary forms are the boundaries of social communication. Only in the second half of the second century, for example, did Christianity begin to use the "elevated" literary forms of antiquity (apology, protreptic writing, and so forth), at which point primitive Christian literature came to an end and patristic literature began.[15] Thus even a history of its literature shows that primitive Christianity was a subcultural current at some remove from the general culture. This "general" culture, however, is predominantly a culture of the upper class.

While ethical and juridical norms (often practical norms as well) directly express typical social behavior, the social background of linguistic and literary norms must be traced more patiently. The starting point is relatively broad, to be sure, but what can be determined is also relatively general, at least insofar as it is *not* the case with a particular literary genre—as it is the case with the parables—that themes specific to a genre themselves reveal something more precise about the social milieu of that genre.

Inferences from Symbols

Symbols are the result of a metaphorical process: images from life are transferred to other themes. In such instances it is usually no longer possible to decide if the image has attracted the object, the object the image, or if both were originally yoked.[16] Since the concept *metaphor* could involve a prior judgment, we use the term *symbol*.

In the case of ecclesiological symbols we are interested in the image and what it expresses. The image of the body of Christ says something about the great cohesion of Christian groups which understood themselves to be bound together as closely as members of a body, as if the personal boundaries of human individuality had been left behind (1 Cor. 12:12–27). At the same time this image contains an unmistakable demand for the realization of its content. The wish and the reality cannot be separated; the imperative is concealed within the indicative. The same thing is true of other ecclesiological symbols. Now and then Paul refers to the Jerusalem Christians as the "poor" (Gal. 2:10; Rom. 15:26). Later Jewish Christian groups call themselves Ebionites ("the poor"), a self-description used by the Qumran community as well. The "poor" certainly are poor in a literal sense. It is real need which leads to the support of the Jerusalem community (Acts 11:27ff.; Gal. 2:10; 2 Cor. 8:9). Nonetheless, this is not a purely sociographic characterization.

The poor, as for example in the Psalms, have a claim on divine help of a very particular sort, so that the term is also a self-description within the framework of a "piety of poverty" widespread in the Orient.[17]

Next to the ecclesiastical, the poetic symbols of the parables are the most instructive. To be sure, they do not express a social condition. The theme of the parables is the kingdom of God, his grace, responsibility before him, and so forth. The images of the parables, however, convey to us a great deal about the social milieu of the Jesus movement: kings, landowners, and moneylenders make their appearance here alongside farmers, workers, and slaves. We learn something of the rebellious cry of tenant farmers against absentee landowners (Mark 12:1-9), or the problem of indebtedness (Matt. 5:25-26; 18:23-25). Precisely because the parables are not narratives of real events they are particularly rich for sociological interpretation.[18] They compress normal experience into penetrating scenes of social life. They have a way of distilling that which is typical, even if at times they heighten this beyond the bounds of probability. For example, the situation of being in debt may be typical, but the size of the debt is doubtlessly exaggerated in Matthew 18:23-25.

It is more difficult to get beyond this general social milieu and determine the specific social location of the authors, the brokers of the tradition, and those who are being addressed. For example, a certain identification of the narrator with the socially powerful is unmistakable in many (not all) of the parables: the decent vineyard owner rather than the dissatisfied laborers (Matt. 20:1-16); the unloved nobleman about to receive kingly power rather than his refractory subjects (Luke 19:12-27); the great landholder rather than the rebellious tenant farmers (Mark 12:1-9). At the very least, whoever wishes to reconstruct the Jesus movement as a social revolutionary movement ought not to overlook such things. But is it therefore justified to conclude from this, among other things, that those who heard Jesus, and possibly he himself, belonged to the upper social strata?[19]

In assessing the parables we must first of all pay attention to the logic imminent in the genre itself. They have as their theme God's surprising, gracious, and challenging activity. To that extent they must emphasize in their imagery the socially powerful. Only a relationship to something superior can serve to make transparent the relationship to God. It could further be argued that in the parables the socially powerful by no means always support the socially weak. In the case of the parable of the unjust judge (Luke 18:1-8), that is expressly related to the conclusion *a minori ad maius:* If the unjust judge helps, how much more will God help? In this case the sociological interpretation of social symbols in poetic creations poses a fundamental problem endemic to the interpretation of symbols itself: Is the relationship between symbol and social reality symmetrical or asymmetrical? When the poetic fantasy turns to kings, landowners, and the rich, is that the fantasy of kings, landowners, and the rich, or of those who are excluded from these upper social brackets? Fairy tales and the sensational press in our own day show that the latter is also a possibility.

The same problem is encountered with mythical symbols. Unlike poetic images, these do not offer a social reality which then as a whole stands transparently for something else. Instead, they more directly make something "other" their theme, such as the actions of gods, angels, and demons. To be sure, they do this by using images from the familiar social world: God may be represented as a king, the angels as his court; the less comprehensible the old king's actions, the more will hopes focus on his son; rebels, such as Satan and his troops, are made responsible for evil. Whereas in poetic symbols earthly reality is focused in compressed and concentrated form, in mythical symbols it is expanded to the point of transcending reality as experienced.[20] Thus, for example, the mythic symbolism of the domination of demons can be the symbolic intensification of the negative experience of earthly rule, including political rule, as a New Testament demon naively indicates when it calls itself "legion" and expresses the wish to remain in the territory (Mark 5:9–10)— which was precisely what the Romans wanted too.

Experienced reality, however, is not merely interpreted in symbolic intensification. This intensification is also set over *against* the experienced reality. Without question the expectation of a new world and a divine kingdom is a rejection of this world and its kingdoms.[21] Two possibilities exist in the concept of "symbolic intensification." Reality can be heightened, *via eminentiae,* or denied, *via negativa.* Thus is demonstrated the problem of symmetry versus asymmetry between symbol and reality.

Apart from that, the sociological interpretation of mythical symbolism can choose from among various perspectives: the semantic, the syntagmatic, and the paradigmatic view of myth. The semantic perspective starts with the metaphorical image which is the content of the myth. E. Topitsch has drawn the distinction between biomorphic, sociomorphic, and technomorphic interpretations of the world, depending on which model of the known and familiar is projected onto the unknown and unfamiliar.[22] All these models reveal something about the familiar social world. Nevertheless, it should be noted that mythical symbolism is frequently "residual," that is, that it reflects relationships of earlier times. Thus God is still a king even after monarchy ceases to exist. The Son of God is sacrificed even after human sacrifice has long since been forbidden. Heavenly gods indulge in polygamy long after it has been abandoned in human affairs. Such historical relics are eagerly construed by the psychoanalytic interpretation of myth as psychic regression.[23] Once a polygamous divine family has been established, however, it is scarcely necessary to assume that all members of a society continue to use it to control their polygamous tendencies through projection. Once they have arisen, images quickly attain their own independent value and become available for new uses and interpretations, something which also argues for a certain skepticism in the face of any overly hasty inferences from mythical images to their social basis.[24]

A second mode of interpretation turns less on a correspondence of content than on structural homologies between social reality and religious imagery, frequently observable even when content differs. Here the syntagma of the myth, the relationships among the sequential units, may stand in the foreground. A myth does not consist of static symbols but is based on dramatic events.[25] To the syntagma of the myth, for example, would belong any reference back to prototypic origins.[26] A frequently repeated syntagmatic scheme is the genealogy, by means of which rival primal powers are "reconciled" in a kinship system while at the same time their conflict is understood as a degeneration contrasting with the origin itself.[27] It is sociologically significant that primitive Christianity, as it entered the Hellenistic world of sociocultural pluralism, did not travel this path of integrating competing cosmic-numinous powers even in the defense against Christian Gnosticism (cf. 1 Tim. 1:4). The integration of numinous powers takes place in primitive Christianity in the form of a suffering *pantokrator* in a much more radical fashion than in any such genealogical system (Col. 1:15ff.). Correspondingly, the social integration of various socio-cultural and ethnic groups moved forward much more decisively in primitive Christianity than elsewhere (Gal. 3:28; Eph. 2:11–14).[28]

Alternatively one can start with the paradigmatic quality of the myth, that is, from the actual relationships and oppositions between its elements independent of their syntagmatic sequence. God and the devil, heaven and hell are such "oppositions." C. Lévi-Strauss has put forward the thesis that in the paradigmatic structure of the myth can be seen the basic conflicts of a society.[29]

On balance, drawing inferences from mythical symbols must be considered the most problematic way to attain a sociological analysis of religious traditions. Every other means should be attempted first.[30] On the other hand, it is precisely this investigation of the relationship between mythical symbols and social situations which is one of the most interesting tasks on the agenda of research in the sociology of religion.[31]

In the case of all analytic procedures, drawing inferences from historical, normative, and symbolic statements about sociologically relevant matters runs counter to the intention of religious texts, which speak about something else. Such inferences, although contrary to the intention of the texts, are neither illegitimate nor impossible. Every historian works with them. He proceeds not only to "understand," if by that is meant the disclosure of the intentions immanent in the text's expressions, but also puts these intentions into contexts of which the original authors and subsequent conveyors were not conscious. He is always uncovering processes which were operative behind their intentions. At its heart, the procedure of drawing sociological inferences cannot be distinguished from historical source analysis. Nor is there anything novel in the observation that the results of a critical analysis diverge significantly from a text's self-understanding, that there exists a "hermeneutical conflict" (P. Ricoeur).[32] Furthermore, this hermeneutical conflict, which arises from dealing with texts in a scientific and methodical fashion, has nothing to do with a history-of-religions reductionism which regards religious intentions as masking some kind of nonreligious (socio-economic or psychic) reality. Such a reductionism, instead of explaining the conflict, would only unilaterally dissolve it. This kind of interpretation, however, no longer belongs to the methodology proper.

COMPARATIVE PROCEDURES

It is true that in order to describe an individual instance of social behavior a scant single source may suffice, while that which is typical only becomes apparent when social behavior is attested in several circumstances by several sources. This raises an evident query about the methodological feasibility of any sociology of primitive Christianity, since the earliest Christian sources are too fragmentary to offer a satisfactory basis for sociological conclusions. Many of the phenomena of primitive Christianity, however, we find reflected in non-Christian sources, and broadening our analysis to include these non-Christian sources is as essential for a sociology of primitive Christianity as it is for any other scholarly, scientific investigation of primitive Christianity. On the basis of the evidence in the New Testament, for example, one can assume with good reason that the synagogue ruler Crispus, mentioned in Acts 18:8, was a man of some standing. This assumption becomes all the more probable, however, when the inscriptions are studied in which such synagogue rulers boast of their expenditures for synagogue buildings,[33] for these indicate beyond doubt that prudence suggested seeking out wealthy men for that office.

Comparative procedures can take one of two directions. Either we can use them to help establish what is typical for primitive Christianity by analyzing the differences in comparison with the surrounding culture, or we can look for those characteristics which early Christianity shares with comparable movements, groups, or phenomena of whatever era. In the first instance the procedure turns primarily on contrast, in the second on analogy—but only *primarily* in either case, for a comparison marked by absolute divergence or identity would make no sense. It follows that procedures which turn on contrast and analogy themselves presuppose analogies and differences. But the distinction is a significant one. In the one case the analogous factors are less problematic, and methodological interest concentrates on the contrasts, while in the other it is the differences which are obvious and the analogies which must be drawn out.

Common elements shared among different religious groups or movements which are rooted in the same historical and social situation present no problem. One need not analyze these in detail but can start from the heuristic assumption that different religious movements offer different answers to a comparable social situation—for example, Pharisees, Essenes, and Zealots to the social situation of Palestine at that time. In this case the social situation is constant while the corresponding religious movements are variable. Then the task becomes one of correlating the differences among the independently emerging religious movements with the differences within the common social situation.

In this fashion P. Alfaric analyzes the religious movements in Palestinian society in the first century after Christ.[34] Sadduceeism is an association of the privileged strata with religious and political conservatism. Pharisaism represents the aspiring, achievement-oriented middle class. Zealots articulate the protest of the middle and lower strata while Essenes are viewed as a quietistic reaction from the same groups. It would be methodologically consistent to ask also about specific social and religious factors within the Jesus movement. The wish, however, to deny insofar as possible anything unique to the status of early Christianity leads Alfaric to view the Jesus movement as an insignificant variant of the Essene community. Since, however, there can be no doubt that this movement emerged independently of the Essenes, as it clearly distinguished itself from the latter in social behavior—for example, in its attitude toward "sinners," toward "the people," toward the law—this is methodologically inconsistent.

The comparative procedure moves in a different direction when substantively related religious movements in differing historical situations are chosen for comparison. In the case of primitive Christianity the point of comparison would be all messianic-chiliastic movements, where again and again we find comparable characteristics: the expectation of the near end of the world, messianic prophets and leaders, miraculous and ecstatic phenomena (for example, exorcisms), and unfulfilled hopes of a Parousia.[35] Granted the assumption that such movements can, within limits, be compared, sociology of religion's chief comparative task is to inquire into corresponding related structures in the underlying social situation. Thus, messianic-chiliastic movements are frequently reactions of an oppressed people to a politically imposed foreign culture in which the injured sense of self-esteem within the dominated culture seeks to assert itself. No doubt these are structural features which are relevant for the messianic movements in Roman-occupied Palestine including, among others, the primitive Christian movement.

The disadvantage of any such procedure relying on analogies is its relative lack of precision. No phenomenon corresponds entirely to another. It would be a gross contradiction of historical sensibility, for example, to reduce all too quickly to a common denominator the Mau Mau movement in Kenya and early Christianity. On the other hand, the advantage is that we are relatively well informed about some of these messianic-chiliastic movements, particularly through investigations which have been methodically carried out. Thus at the very least we have access to a series of interesting hypotheses worthy of investigation.

Finally, contrasting and analogizing comparisons are distinguished only by a matter of accent. In the one case historical proximity provides the background for the emergence of differences; in the other, historical distance provides the background for structurally related characteristics. The background, and the configuration *(Gestalt)* which stands out in relief from it, can obviously alternate. Methodologically, both procedures are complementary. In a contrasting comparison the overall social situation is perceived as relatively constant, the corresponding religious movements seen as the variable.

In an analogizing comparison the structural marks of religious movements are held as relatively constant, the corresponding social situations as variable. In the first example sociology of religion's analysis must look above all for further variables within the static social situation; in the second example, for possible constants within the fluctuating social situation. It is true that historical sociology of religion does not have access to quantities of empirical data; but when it investigates the material provided by history it proceeds in a fashion which logically speaking is not fundamentally different from the way sociology works when dealing with the present.

Using the example of primitive Christianity, we have looked at various methodological approaches for securing sociologically relevant data from religious traditions. It is not necessary to emphasize that the prospect of achieving an approximate comprehension of the matter to be investigated, by means of adequate statements about it, depends on the plurality, and methodological independence, of various procedures for drawing inferences. Only competing methods offer the possibility of reciprocal control and correction. That is no less true for the methods of sociology of religion than it is with reference to the study of religion *(Religionswissenschaft)* in general, where by necessity different perspectives must compete. The sociological perspective itself is but one among others.[36]

NOTES

1. Still unexcelled in the historical sphere are Max Weber's works in the sociology of religion. Cf. his *Gesammelte Aufsätze zur Religionssoziologie,* 3 vols., 5th ed. (Tübingen, 1963), and *The Sociology of Religion,* trans. Ephraim Fischoff (New York, 1963 and Boston: Beacon, 1974).

2. Ernst von Dobschütz, *Christian Life in the Primitive Church,* trans. George Bremner, ed. W. D. Morrison (New York: Putnam, 1904), p. xxxiv: "How, too, were the communities composed? From what social strata did they acquire members? We have nothing but indications and unsafe conjectures. According to modern views, housing arrangements, rate of wages, and other questions of the same kind are of great significance for the development of morality. In that period which resembles our own so much, this must also have been the case to some extent. No such question is even once touched upon in our Christian sources; even secular works give us no adequate account of these circumstances."

3. Establishing what is typical and what is determined is also considered a specific characteristic of the sociological point of view by M. Scheler, *Die Wissensformen und die Gesellschaft,* 2nd ed. (Munich/Bern, 1960), p. 17.

4. Cf. Rudolf Bultmann, *History of the Synoptic Traditions,* 2nd ed., trans. J. Marsh (New York: Harper & Row, 1968), pp. 2–7.

5. Cf. Ernst Haenchen, *The Acts of the Apostles: A Commentary,* trans. B. Noble and G. Shinn (Philadelphia: Westminster, 1971), p. 394, Note 5.

6. Joachim Jeremias, *Jerusalem in the Time of Jesus,* trans. F. H. and C. H. Cave (Philadelphia: Fortress Press, 1969), p. 88, and the evidence cited in *A Greek Lexicon of the New Testament and Other Early Christian Literature,* 2nd ed., trans. W. F.

Arndt and F. W. Gingrich, rev. and augmented by F. W. Gingrich and F. W. Danker from Walter Bauer's 5th ed. (Chicago: University of Chicago Press, 1979), p. 793.

7. Against R. Schumacher, *Die soziale Lage der Christen im apostolischen Zeitalter* (Paderborn, 1924), p. 40.

8. Cf. C. K. Barrett, "Things Sacrificed to Idols," *NTS* 11 (1964/65): 138-153, specifically p. 146.

9. Cf. Peter Berger and Thomas Luckmann, *The Social Construction of Reality: A Treatise in the Sociology of Religion* (Garden City, N.Y.: Doubleday, 1966); Peter Berger, *The Sacred Canopy: Elements of a Sociological Theory of Religion* (Garden City, N.Y.: Doubleday Anchor, 1967).

10. Roman law is certainly one of the most important sources for the sociology of the Roman Empire. A. N. Sherwin-White, *Roman Society and Roman Law in the New Testament* (New York: Oxford University Press, 1963), has utilized it in the sociological analysis of early Christianity.

11. E. A. Judge, *The Social Pattern of the Christian Groups in the First Century* (London: Tyndale, 1960); in the German edition of his book (*Christliche Gruppen in nichtchristlicher Gesellschaft* [Wuppertal, 1964]), he takes ethical and other norms as his point of departure: "I try . . . to describe a range of social forms of the age to which Christians, as members of earthly society, would consider themselves obligated." In addition, many ethical norms refer so directly to typical social behavior that their analysis can also be considered at least in part to belong to the constructive method.

12. A different interpretation can be found in J. Blinzler, "*Eisen eunouchoi:* Zur Auslegung von Mt. 18, 12," *ZNW* 48 (1957): 254-70. That the New Testament norms were not intended to be situationally conditioned (whether de facto they are is another matter) has been demonstrated by W. Schrage, *Die konkreten Einzelgebote in der paulinischen Paränese* (Gutersloh, 1961).

13. Adolf Deissmann, *Das Urchristentum und die untern Schichten,* 2nd ed. (Gottingen, 1908); idem, *Light from the Ancient East: The New Testament Illustrated by Recently Discovered Texts of the Graeco-Roman World,* trans. Lionel Strachen (London, 1927; repr. Grand Rapids: Baker Books, 1965).

14. Lars Rydbeck, *Fachprosa, vermeintliche Volkssprache und Neues Testament* (Uppsala University) (Stockholm: Almquist and Wiksell, 1967).

15. F. Overbeck, "Uber die Anfänge der patristischen Literatur," *HZ* 48 (1882): 417-72 (Darmstadt, 1966).

16. On the problem of the concept of "metaphor," cf. P. Wheelwright, "The Semantic Approach to Myth," in *Myth: A Symposium,* ed. T. A. Seboek (Bloomington: Indiana University Press, 1958), pp. 95-103; repr. (Magnolia, Miss.: Peter Smith).

17. On the self-designation "poor," cf. L. E. Keck, "The Poor among the Saints in the New Testament," *ZNW* 56 (1965): 100-137; idem, "The Poor among the Saints in Jewish Christianity and Qumran," *ZNW* 57 (1966): 54-78. On the Oriental piety of poverty, cf. Hendrick Bolkestein, *Wohltätigkeit und Armenpflege im vorchristlichen Altertum* (Utrecht: Oosthoek, 1939). An interesting contribution to the sociological analysis of religious symbolism inspired by the sociology of knowledge is Wayne A. Meeks, "The Image of the Androgyne: Some Uses of a Symbol in Earliest Christianity," *HR* 13 (1974): 165-208.

18. On the legal background of the parables, cf. J. D. M. Derrett, *Law in the New Testament* (New York: Fernhill-Humanities Press, 1970). An evaluation of socio-

ecological data can be found in M. D. Goulder, "Characteristics of the Parables in Several Gospels" *JTS* 19 (1968): 51–69. Martin Hengel, "Das Gleichnis von den Weingärtnern Mc 12, 1–12 im Lichte der Zenon-papyri und der rabbinischen Gleichnisse," *ZNW* 59 (1968): 1–39, illuminates in exemplary fashion the socio-economic background of this parable.

19. See G. W. Buchanan, "Jesus and the Upper Class," *NT* 7 (1964/1965): 195–209.

20. On the symbolic intensification of reality, cf. W. E. Mühlmann, "Umrisse und Probleme einer Kulturanthropologie," in W. E. Mühlmann and E. W. Müller, *Kulturanthropologie* (Cologne: Kapenheuer, 1966), pp. 15–49.

21. That eschatology in every form was rejected by the Sadducees, the rich Jewish aristocracy (Josephus, *Wars* II, 8, 14), is understandable. Those who profit from the status quo have no reason to look forward to a day when it will be changed. There is a certain affinity between specific mythical symbols and social agents. It is not permissible, however, to infer elevated social status solely on the basis of the eschatological denial; this must be independently confirmed. On the Sadducees, cf. Josephus, *Ant.,* XVIII, 8, 14.

22. Cf. Ernst Topitsch, *Vom Ursprung und Ende der Metaphysik: eine Studie zur Weltanschauungs Kritik* (Vienna: Shringer, 1958).

23. From the wealth of literature I cite only W. Schmidbauer, *Mythos und Psychologie: Methodische Probleme aufgezeigt an der Ödipus-Sage* (Munich/Basel, 1970).

24. This holds for all inferential methods. Texts are determined as much by the past as by the present; tradition-history and sociological analysis supplement each other. Social situations are repeatedly interpreted in the light of certain traditions, while the traditions are handed on if they illuminate social situations. *Topoi* cast in historical-traditional modes make possible inferences back to a social situation in various ways: 1. The recurrence of the *topoi* can point to the recurrence of underlying experiences. The traditions about the persecuting of the newborn king (Matt. 2:16) would not have survived in early Christianity but for the extirpative policy of Herod over against all rival competitors for the throne, including his own children. 2. Traditions become modified in actual practice. Both the Old and the New Testaments speak of someone's being called at the work place (1 Kings 19:19–21; Amos 7:15; Mark 1:16–20). That in the New Testament fishermen and tax collectors take the place of farmers corresponds to new circumstances. 3. Tradition and situation appear to be incongruent. Contrary to the *topos* of creation *ex nihilo,* Paul writes in 1 Cor. 1:26–29 of "not many" wise, powerful, and wellborn. These people must have been very important, therefore, for the social structure of the Corinthian community.

25. Cf. S. Holm, "Mythos und Symbol," *TLZ* 93 (1968): 561–72, and Paul Ricouer, *The Conflict of Interpretations: Essays in Hermeneutics,* ed. Don Ihde (Evanston, Ill.: Northwestern University Press, 1974), Part 4, "The Symbolism of Evil Interpreted," pp. 267–86.

26. See M. Eliade in several publications, among which one in particular might be mentioned: "Signification du Mythe," in *Le Langage II: Actes du XIIIe Congrès de Philosophie de Langage Française* (Neuchâtel, 1967), pp. 165–79, where he distinguishes between two states of origin.

27. Cf. K. Heinrich, "Die Funktion der Genealogie im Mythos," in *Parmenides und Jona* (Frankfurt, 1966), pp. 9–28.

28. There is in Colossians and Ephesians a structural homologue between the integration of (pagan) powers in the cosmic body of Christ and the integration of Gentiles

and Jews in his ecclesiastical body. The alien character of the Logos in this world is structurally homologous to the alien character of the Johannine community in this world (cf. the important essay for the sociology of New Testament literature by Wayne A. Meeks, "The Man from Heaven in Johannine Sectarianism," *JBL* 91 [1972]: 44–72). Structural homologies between "foundation" and "superstructure" have become the occasion for research into the sociology of literature, especially within "genetic structuralism." Cf. L. Goldmann, "Die Soziologie der Literatur: Stand und Methodenprobleme," in *Literatursoziologie I,* ed. J. Bark (Stuttgart, 1974), pp. 85–113. There are here points of contact with E. Köhler, "Uber die Möglichkeiten historisch-soziologischer Interpretation," in idem, *Espirit und arkadische Freiheit* (Frankfurt, 1966), pp. 83–103 (also in *Methoden der deutschen Literaturwissenschaft,* ed. V. Zmegac [Frankfurt, 1972], pp. 227–48). The materialistic point of departure for Goldmann and Köhler, so far as they themselves do not already modify it, cannot be appropriated uncritically. The phenomenology of religion also regards the homologous correspondence between man and the universe to be a basic characteristic of religion: cf. M. Eliade, *The Sacred and the Profane: The Nature of Religion,* trans. Willard Trask (New York: Harcourt, Brace, 1959), pp. 165 ff.

29. Claude Lévi-Strauss, "The Story of Asdiwal," in *The Structural Study of Myth and Totemism,* ed. E. Leach (London: Tavistock and New York: Barnes and Noble, 1967), pp. 1–47; idem, "The Structural Study of Myth," in *Structural Anthropology* (Garden City, N.Y.: Doubleday, 1967), pp. 207–31. For a critique, cf. E. Leach, ed., *The Structural Study of Myth and Totemism,* especially the essay of M. Douglas, "The Meaning of Myth," pp. 49–69 in that volume.

30. This is missing, for example, in the very interesting essay of H. G. Kippenberg, "Versuch einer soziologischen Verortung des antiken Gnostizismus," *Numen* 17 (1970): 211–31. He relies too one-sidedly upon an inference drawn from mythical symbols, regarding the rebellion against the ruler of creation, visible in the devaluation of the monotheistic creator-god to the status of satanic demiurge, as secretly a rebellion against the world's political ruler. For the correspondence between mythical projections and social reality he appeals especially to E. Topitsch's theory of myth, which is criticized by P. Munz, "The Problem of 'Die soziologische Verortung des antiken Gnostizismus,' " *Numen* 19 (1972): 41–51—although, to be sure, Kippenberg's theses are not thereby refuted. In particular, it remains that Gnosticism had its social location in the higher strata of society; cf. Adolf von Harnack, *Die Mission und Ausbreitung des Christentums in den ersten drei Jahrhunderten,* 4th ed. (Leipzig, 1924), pp. 103–4; Eng., *Mission and Expansion of Christianity in the First Three Centuries,* 2 vols., trans and ed. James Moffat, repr. (Freeport, N.Y.: Books for Libraries, 1962), Vol. 1, pp. 93–96; C. Andresen, *Die Kirchen der alten Christenheit* (Stuttgart/Berlin; Kohlhammer, 1971), pp. 103–4; P. Alfaric, *Die sozialen Ursprunge des Christentums* (Darmstadt, 1963), pp. 363 ff., orig., *Les origines sociales du Christianisme,* Sorbonne Conference, Dec. 17, 1946 (Paris: Cahiers rationalistes, 1947, repr. 1959); A. B. Ranowitsch, "Das Urchristentum und seine historische Rolle," in *Aufsätze zur Alten Geschichte* (Berlin: 1961), pp. 135–65; M. Robbe, *Der Ursprung des Christentums* (Leipzig: Uranis-Verlag, 1967), pp. 202 ff. Proof for this assumption, which is usually simply stated in passing, would have to be passed on as many modes of inference as possible, including: 1. Sociographic data. A Valentinian can place seven stenographers at Origen's disposal (Eusebius, *Hist. eccl.* VI, 18, 1; 23, 1 f). 2. Conflicts. For example, those in the Roman community; cf. H. Langerbeck, "Zur

Auseinandersetzung von Theologie und Gemeindeglauben in der römischen Gemeinde in den Jahren 135-64," in *Aufsätze zur Gnosis,* AAWG.PH 3, 96 (Gottingen, 1967), pp. 167-79. 3. The linguistic and literary level of Gnostic writings must be evaluated. The astounding production of books by the Gnostics presupposes a certain prosperity. 4. The Gnostic ethos is frequently "liberal." Things like meat sacrificed to idols, entertainment, and sexuality are not denigrated. 5. Ecclesiastical symbols, in particular the distinction between *gnostikoi* and *pistikoi,* betray an elitist self-understanding. 6. A soteriology of knowledge may be a characteristic of higher social circles. Where an interior process yields salvation, the fundamental need underlying the quest for salvation is less likely to be grounded in external, material circumstances. 7. By way of analogy, other radical and mystical currents in the history of religions must be canvassed. By way of contrast, other formulations of Christian faith within the upper social strata at that time must be investigated, for we also find members of the upper strata as leaders of the orthodox communities.

31. That would constitute a new stage of investigation. Basic sociological data must first be in hand before social situations and texts can be correlated. There are three possibilities for doing this: 1. Chronological correlation. Most apocalyptic texts come from the period between 200 B.C. and 100 A.D., in the very time when Judaism strove for political independence without any lasting success. Chronological relationships of that sort point to substantive relationships. 2. Quantitative correlation. The higher Christianity climbed into the upper classes, the more it took over "elevated" literary forms. For the most part, the realm of history allows only relative assessments ("more/less"), since precise statistics are usually missing. In every case it should be noted that not everything which can be quantitatively correlated actually belongs together. 3. The material correlation, which is the stipulation of every chronological and quantitative correlation. For an example, see the structural homologies sketched out in Note 28, above.

32. Ricoeur, *Conflict of Interpretations,* pp. 27ff., 62 ff.

33. Cf. J. B. Frey, *Corpus Inscriptionum Iudaicarum* (Rome, 1936), Nos. 265, 548, 722, 766, 781, 1404.

34. Alfaric, *Ursprünge,* pp. 43-75. The same methodological objections can be raised against attempts to reduce Jesus and the Zealots to a common denominator—even against the more discriminating essay by S. G. F. Brandon, *Jesus and the Zealots* (Manchester, 1965, New York: Scribner's, 1968).

35. Cf. among others, W. E. Mühlmann, *Chiliasmus und Nativismus* (Berlin, 1961); A. F. C. Wallace, "Revitalization Movements," *AA* 58 (1956): 264-81. On early Christianity see esp. C. Colpe, "Der Begriff 'Menschensohn' und die Methode der Erforschung messianischer Prototypen," *Kairos* 14 (1972): 241-57.

36. This essay has concerned itself only with the question of how sociologically relevant data can be derived from our texts. Only when this data is in hand does the further question arise of just how far historical-sociological study is hermeneutically relevant for the interpretation of early Christian texts. The sociology of religion is hermeneutically relevant at least to the extent (1) that the texts from time to time express the theme of social conditions, even if only in this manner, that such themes appear as the imaginative realities of religious parabolic discourse and metaphor; (2) that the form and content of texts stand in a materially illuminating correlation to social conditions; and (3) that all texts are forms of social interaction between their authors, those who convey them, and their recipients.

This essay was the theme of a discussion in a seminar of my colleague Dr. K. Berger in Heidelberg on May 30, 1975. I would like to thank my discussion partners, particularly Dr. Berger, for numerous suggestions and arguments which have left their mark especially in Notes 24 and 36. I have discussed the question of the integration of data from the sociology of religion within a sociology of early Christianity in my 1974 essay, "Theoretische Probleme religionssoziologischer Forschung and die Analyse des Urchristentums," *NZSTR* 16 (1974): 35–56.

Part II

SOCIAL CLASS AS A HERMENEUTICAL FACTOR

4

SERGIO ROSTAGNO

The Bible:
Is an Interclass Reading Legitimate?

The dominant social class position of Protestantism has been bourgeois, largely omitting the specific interests and viewpoints of workers, while at the same time pretending to preach a gospel that overrides class and unites all Christians equally. This illusion is not supported by the class struggle features of the Old and New Testaments, in which Yahweh takes the side of the poor and in which to be in Christ is to confront one's riches or poverty as a field of concrete action. The "dialectic" of Paul toward poverty and wealth gives way in the later New Testament to an outright interclass ethical perspective: rich and poor, masters and slaves should be at peace irrespective of justice.

The Bible does not itself give an historical material analysis of justice and injustice in terms of production relationships. However, the Bible clearly reflects the impact of production relationships on justice and pictures God's decisive acts as acts impinging on the structure of production. The actual "worldliness" of the gospel, recovered in the class dimensions of Scripture, can free and motivate us to face the class divisions of today which require our recognition and intelligent intervention.

Reprinted from *The Bible and Liberation: Political and Social Hermeneutics,* 1st ed., ed. N. K. Gottwald and A. C. Wire (Berkeley: Community for Religious Research and Education [Radical Religion], 1976), pp. 19–25.

Historically speaking, the church has always been a church of the bourgeoisie, even when it claimed to transcend class barriers or labored under the illusion that it pervaded all classes in the same way. Indeed, it has been a truly bourgeois church, if the notion of interclassism is taken as part of bourgeois ideology. We are referring here to the history of Protestantism. The church has been the church of the class which has identified itself with the history of the West, in which Christianity may be considered to have been a major force. Only those members of the working class who accepted this view of history attended church. But most of the working people never accepted this view and only gave the church the kind of formal allegiance subjects give to the claims of their rulers. They could not really belong to the church of another class.

It was only when Christian Socialism arrived on the scene that an effort was made to interpret Christianity from the point of view of the labor movement. The resulting changes in perspective also affected biblical studies. But the exegetical tradition of Protestantism, with its claims to being scientific, developed against the background of the great historiographical presuppositions of the bourgeoisie, even though this criticism should be modified to some extent. For one thing, the ranks of the best and most important of the biblical exegetes include leftists. Nevertheless, the main point is that, both regarding methods and results, scholarship at the university level has undoubtedly highlighted facts and relationships which are of value for an objective reading of the texts.

It was this scholarly work which undermined the cultural and ideological presuppositions of the eighteenth century by enabling readers to adopt a more direct approach to the text itself (though the limits affecting all interpretation remained). The real text, taken objectively, embodied or could become an element of critical confrontation for the church. What is more important, however, is that the research that was undertaken is centered on conclusions which are existentialist rather than Marxist. It claims to consider humanity in certain typical existential situations which provide analogies for all historical situations resulting from the human condition. It deals, therefore, with *humanity,* rather than with *workers* as they try to wrest from the dominant class its hold on the means of production and its hold over the vital spheres of human life. In this sense, it could be said that exegesis was an interclass affair. It never succeeded in explaining, in an *integral* way, the two elements of materialism. It interpreted the revolutionary element as *hubris.* The Marxist belief that the mode of production in material matters governs the development of social, political, and intellectual life was regarded as merely a heretical way of thinking. This was an indication that biblical exegesis had been effectively estranged from the labor movement.

Exegesis has worked and still works in accordance with such generalized and contradictory principles that anything and everything can in fact be found in the text. To say that the biblical message is not timeless but historical (*geschichtlich*), not individualistic but community-oriented, not traditionalist but open to the future and so on, is meaningless unless completed by precise definitions. But the whole of exegesis was overshadowed by a universe of dogmatic discourse that should have been attentively analyzed—that man is continuously in need of salvation, that all his paths are ultimately false paths and that he could never free himself from his burden on his own. This line of thought placed the exploited and the exploiter, the revolutionary and the imperialist, who were all in need of pardon, under the same heading. If this is what happened in the "domain of scholarship" we can well imagine the state of affairs in the traditional parish. Here the interclass approach was underpinned by a form of religious individualism which did not violate the principle that there is only one God for all, a God who bestows grace on all. Each human being was regarded as the personal consumer of a standard piece of goods, which the institutionalized church supplies and ought to supply in absolutely equal measure to all.

The intellectuals may have condemned this very real "Platonism of the people" but they rarely did any better in their own exegeses. The interclass nature of their theology merely highlighted the fact that they were in an intermediate position between those who had the power of decision-making and those who did not. They resembled the latter insofar as their decisions had little weight, but they were convinced that they counted for something because they belonged to "scientific circles." At a more popular level of the Christian community, however, an interclass saying like "God is the Father of all" became a widely held maxim used to reaffirm truths which had been thrust out of sight and evaded. The new expression was merely the virulent recrudescence of an old phrase in a new context. The traditional words of the text then came to be used polemically.

YAHWEH TAKES SIDES

The sturdy, realistic mentality of the ancient East did not allow any idealization of the poor. The poor person is one who looks to his own physical frame as his sole means of help. In this sense everyone is basically a poor and defenseless being, a feeble thing. Hence, for the moment, riches and power are gifts which accrue to him from without and which give him greater viability, being only in a certain sense necessary. "Life" includes a notion of *strength,* which thins out in the sick but has its complete and perfect manifestation in success, victory, and riches (Ps. 128). There is, therefore, a "positive" attitude to the world: riches are good, poverty calls for help.

But then, riches and poverty are the antithetical results of exploitation. The biblical statement is not simply a religious message. Yahweh is not a transcendent and neutral divinity but continually demands an account of what happens, and only having understood what has happened does he in fact respond to the question of the prostrate or the proudly successful. The prophet—that is, the man who announced the divine oracle to the people—based his discourse on very precise analyses of the situation, analyses which would appear still more precise to us if we knew the detailed historical circumstances under which each prophet lived. What stands out clearly, however, is the denunciation of social injustice and of the religious ideology in which it is cloaked. The prophet denounced the "sin" of the people, or rather of the leading circles, giving the true facts about precise social and political matters.

The criterion for recognizing "sin" (meaning in Hebrew "to miss out," "to go astray") is not the *commandment* but the *community relationship* which has been violated. The article of the law, if one may use the expression, has the function of highlighting the communion between members of the fellowship, protecting the weak. The primary reference is always to the communion disrupted by injustice, not to the abstract violation of a decree. And the protection of the economically feeble is the almost continual theme of the legislation.

In the ancient East the socially and economically feeble were considered as people with whom God had a special relationship. But this may be understood in two ways. The fact that Yahweh places himself on the side of the poor man (Ps. 146) also means that he intervenes to raise up the lowly and to punish those in high places. This is asserted in strong and manifesto-like terms in 1 Samuel 2:1–10, where it is said:

> The bow of the strong is broken
> and the weak are girded with strength.
> Those who had plenty sell themselves to have bread,
> but the hungry cease from their travail. . . .
>
> It is Yahweh who makes a man poor or rich,
> who brings down or raises up,
> who lifts up the weak from the dust
> and raises the poor from the dunghill.

The fact that Yahweh is on the side of the poor is always a genuine protest against those who trample right and justice underfoot. On the other hand, passages like this suggest the notion that God is particularly close to the poor, that the state of poverty constitutes a privileged situation of proximity to God. Affirmations to the effect that Yahweh is on the side of the poor have given rise, strangely enough, to interpretations such as "the poor man is closer to God." With this, poverty becomes sacrosanct (there will always be poor people), which is in stark contrast to the sense of social justice which runs through the great prophetic witnesses and is at the root of the legislation. Once the state of poverty is considered a privileged situation, the way lies open to *quietism*.

CHRISTIAN PRACTICE

There was nothing particularly new or original in early Christian practice concerning wealth and poverty. There was the experience of the greed of the rich together with the awareness of the rarity of just judges. On the other hand, Christians organized mutual assistance on a vast scale. Thus the texts frequently speak of the rich who sell all they have to give to the poor (Luke 19:18; Acts 2:45, 4:36; Mark 10:21; Luke 18:22; Matt. 19:21). Apart from this, there are exhortations to shun avarice, to give generously, and not to hoard riches (Luke 12:13-21, 33-34), or descriptions of the reversal of the lot of the rich and the poor in the other world (Luke 16:19-31, cf. the woes pronounced against the rich, Luke 6:24-26). The Jerusalem community helped a large number of poor people: Paul organized a collection for their benefit in the churches around the Aegean Sea.

The texts referred to belong for the most part to Luke. The author of the third Gospel and the Acts is particularly sensitive to the problem of riches. He shares this preoccupation with the author of the epistle of James. In the framework of the data to be collected from the New Testament, these are the two authors in whom the terms rich and poor recur with the greatest frequency.[1]

For James, the passages 1:9-11 and 5:1-6 are characteristic. The attitude of the rich is an example of sin in its worst form, while the poor man is the just man who is vindicated by God. The fact that the poor man does not resist increases still further the culpability and hence the punishment of the rich. Hope for relief from injustice looks to the future judgment (5:9).

Luke for his part takes up the theme in the style of the psalm found in 1 Samuel 2, quoted first in the Magnificat:

> [The Lord] intervenes with the might of his arm,
> he scatters the proud, confusing the thoughts of their mind;
> he deposes the mighty from their thrones
> and raises up the lowly;
> he fills the hungry with good things
> and sends away the rich empty-handed [1:51-53].

Luke then has Jesus born within the circle of the pious poor. Mary's Magnificat is in fact very like Jewish compositions of the period in question. God reveals that he is on the side of the lowly.

All these passages indicate that the Christian message would be distorted if it were taken as a neutral statement addressed to people regardless of their times and circumstances. It is obvious, on the other hand, that it would be anachronistic to look for a materialist analysis of history in these texts. The texts restrict themselves to hoping for a settlement of accounts at the future judgment. They exhort endurance under poverty and call for mutual aid.

At this point the following objection could be made: Jesus did not preach the gospel merely to the poor, but also to the rich. But it is too easy to say that the liberating message preached to the poor really *compels* the rich who wish to take it seriously to lose all, even if they are to benefit by it (Mark 10:21).

It is true that the welcome extended by Jesus to those who are kept furthest from God is not confined to the shepherds of Bethlehem. The welcome is even extended to the officials collecting taxes on behalf of the occupying power (Rome), who usually enrich themselves by dishonest means. A text of the period says that "for shepherds, extortioners, and tax-gatherers, repentance is difficult." The fact that Jesus accepted an invitation to dine with such persons (Matthew 9:9–13) is presented as something that caused scandal. But in the eyes of the evangelist it has the same liberating value as the gospel preached to "the least." Like the poor, the rich and dishonest extortioners bear witness to the way taken by Jesus, who made no demands on the former while he called on the latter to change their calling. The real point here is that he displayed his liberating authority in contrast to the enslaving authority of the Roman Empire. Jesus sees that under certain conditions men will be lost, whether they are shepherds or tax-collectors, and he contests such conditions. It is for him a question of freedom, of liberty. The New Testament texts proclaim this freedom by giving an analysis of the forces which are mutually opposed. Obviously, this analysis is not a materialistic one, nor could it be.

The problem for us, then, is this: Can we just replace the analysis provided by primitive Christianity with a modern scientific analysis of production relations? This may indeed be indispensable; but what are we to do with the text of the New Testament? There are three possibilities: (1) to pigeonhole it as completely outdated; (2) to maintain its validity, but only in a "spiritual" domain, kept well apart from the scientific; or (3) to consider that although it says nothing that interests us from the strictly scientific point of view it bears a dialectical relationship to materialism. In this last case, it will be quite evident that the "statement" of the New Testament cannot be properly understood by means of the type of historical investigation now prevalent (such as is made by summing up certain headings) but that more thorough research is necessary. The adventure begins here, because we do not know what we shall find, or whether we shall find it. But this is the only way in which we can throw more light on the origins of the interclass theory held by Christians. It arose out of the New Testament, but from an equivocation.

THUS GRACE REIGNS BY MEANS OF JUSTICE (ROM. 5:21)

The investigation begins with a text on which one never tires of meditating. If we replace the Greek terms of the original with more modern terms, the text reads more or less like this: "Look at your calling, brothers; there is a majority of powerless people among you—economically and socially feeble—without access to culture. But your call shows that God has placed himself on your side, that God has chosen you in order to make an end of the existing order and unmask the contradictions of the class that holds all power. So, no one has anything to boast of in the face of God. But through him you are in Jesus Christ, who has been made wisdom for you by God, and justice, sanctification, redemption (liberation), so that, as it is written, 'if anyone wishes to boast, let him boast of the Lord' '' (1 Cor. 1:26-31, quoting Jer. 9:23-24). This of course is a paraphrase, not a literal translation.

If we compare this text with those of 1 Samuel 2:1-10 and Luke 1:51-53, we can see that the structure is the same: the divine intervention is described by means of radical oppositions. But the formulation was created *ad hoc* by Paul, with the situation in Corinth before his eyes. The enthusiasm of the Corinthians is displayed in the community reunions. In the grip of enthusiasm, real life is forgotten and people feel that they are new beings. The Christian of Corinth, having attained the state of enthusiasm, feels that he is perfect, curses real life and the Jesus of history while exalting the Lord of glory. This attitude is held to be "wisdom" of a higher type and is in opposition to Paul's message, which speaks of Christ crucified. This message is "sheer folly" in the eyes of the Corinthians. When defending his theology, Paul takes up the term "sheer folly" and applies it to his preaching. Among other things, he points out that it is precisely because of this sheer folly of the way taken by God that the pagans believe and that they, the Corinthians, the economically and socially feeble, have been chosen. This means that the concrete reality of life is affirmed as being of relevance for the Christian message.

Paul's argument seems to be this: The election of the poorest strata demonstrates the "sheer folly" of God. The demonstration of the gospel is provided either by the pagan as he lines up under the banner of liberty represented by the name of Christ or by the fact that it is precisely the underprivileged classes that have been chosen. This choice is a fierce blow to power, riches, and culture. But the text also says that this is so that no one may have anything to boast of before God, which means that the poor have nothing and the rich have been reduced to nothing. The only value comes from God, because he had something to put into the balance: he made Jesus count. So if we, for our part, want to put forward something valid, we must also make the Lord our boast—the Jesus whom God has made justice, liberty and, if we may say so, culture. The argument is addressed to the poor, though the rich are not excluded.[2]

It is clearly stated that God "chose" the poor at Corinth, reducing the powerful to nothing. But what is the consequence of this "election"? There seem to be two answers: Either the lower classes at Corinth *ought* to make this real choice of God palpable in their history, and hence dismantle the system of oppression; or they must consider the divine choice as taking place at a supra-historical level, with no suggestion that the upheaval will come about in some historical period—that is, it becomes an other-worldly matter. In the latter case, another world which is the complete opposite of this world has to be invented. It must be a place where the justice of God will finally have the means of asserting itself. This conception prevailed during the Middle Ages.

Paul's theology, however, is never caught in an either-or position. He does not consign the realization of what he affirms to another world. The "justice of God" does not wait for another world to display itself. It has been displayed in Jesus Christ. It is impossible to read these verses outside their context, which is a polemical one, challenging notions of salvation which do not apply to the problem posed by the present world.

The Gospel is a scandal precisely because it does not evade action but proves itself in definite situations. Once the justice of God has become an accomplished fact in the person of Jesus crucified it is verified at once in practice. According to some, it is verified by the fact that the poor of Corinth assume a title of nobility as Christians. Taken this way, the text is denied all social relevance. Christ will simply be the sublimation of the Corinthians' frustrations. Christ will be enthusiasm. The text has to be understood differently. The "election" of the Corinthians, being pagan and poor people, is a key to the interpretation of reality. The "wisdom" of the Corinthians cannot but be the ability to assess all events in the light of the justice of God. There is a categorical refusal of "the way of power" in favor of "the way of the cross" which also leads to the rejection of the powerful as an "institution."

On the other hand, Paul opposed the idea that the Corinthians should regard God's decision to manifest himself as realizable through their own strength and in revolutionary action. The conditions at Corinth certainly called for the emancipation of women and of slaves, but Paul did not encourage this movement. Of course, the changes called for did not compare with the modern concept of "revolution"; nevertheless, it must be affirmed that there was in fact at Corinth a move or tendency towards "realization." This move was not based on contrasting the other world with the present world but was based on a much more subtle notion: the person who has been saved must not re-enact the schema from which he has been liberated.

In the text under consideration, we also find the formula "to be in Christ," which is characteristic of Paul. We may consider this as an alternative to "realization": the Corinthians owe it to God that they are in Christ (1 Cor. 1:30). The formula "to be in Christ" indicates a correlation. The Corinthians partake of reality to the extent that they relate to Jesus Christ in a complete way. What has happened to them has absolutely changed them. This relationship constitutes their being: they are correlatives of Christ. Paul uses the word "analogy," but if we find this too difficult we can always translate it into "consistency." Then the Pauline invitation to "live according to the analogy of faith" (Rom. 12:6) means that we should live a life consistent with the justice of God revealed in Christ and not a life conforming to "this world." The important thing for Paul is not realization but to "be always part of the event"—just as, according to Paul, the person of Jesus Christ does not signify a doctrinal system but the event of revelation. Our *action,* therefore, is determined by this event. There will be the danger that our desire to *act* may make us rely too much on our own conceptions of justice, but this should not paralyze all our initiatives. There can be human initiative which remains within the ambit of correlation to Christ. The aim of Paul's quest is really to define this correlation in *action*. The concept he uses for this precise purpose is that of *agape,* which describes a practice which "is not puffed up, does not seek its own interest, delights in the truth," etc. (1 Cor. 13:4-7). *Agape* is not an ethical concept. Only those who are free can love, and only those are free who have been chosen outside the patterns of worldly "wisdom." The saved are those who have been reduced to nakedness and stripped of all their pretensions. So their only possible course of action in this world is that of people who renounce all efforts to institutionalize themselves. If Paul contrasts "gift" and "exploitation"—that is, the justice of God, which is a gift, and the human wish to exploit one's own position—correlative and consistent action becomes that which unmasks exploitation. But this is not all; it is only one side of the question. If the behavior in question is to be described as *agape* one has to consider the concept of *liberty,* which defines clearly our being in Christ and *remaining* there.

Given the scope of this paper, we cannot afford to dwell on the dialectics of liberty and *agape.* But we have to point to a third important element of "being in Christ." Christians are called upon to put the event into practice on the basis of what is considered to be its scandalous element for the world. Therefore Paul insists on the following point: reality is henceforth an unstable place and a battlefield. Christians are experiencing the end of one world and the beginning of another. Real life means a life passed in friction and conflict. But this is not simply "realizable" through transformative action, important as it is. Here, the *word* is a crucial element. What is really characteristic of the Christian concept of dynamic reality is that the *word,* much more than action, corresponds to being, to reality. But the point is that the word should always be used in relation to action. And unless the practice goes with it, the relationship between the word and Jesus Christ can only be a false one.

We have noted that Christian life does not repeat the pattern from which it has been liberated. Hence the refusal of self-assertion and exploitation is a radical one. It would be wrong, however, to transpose this into ethical terms. Nothing more than the exhortation to humility and resignation could come of it. As far as we are concerned, the interclass approach in the writings of the New Testament is always rather fluid. Later the church was to develop along one definite line. It is important to know whether these developments can be traced back to the beginning and whether other developments may be substituted for them.

To sum up this section very briefly: The "justice of God" is implemented when power is stripped of its mystique and when it is unmasked as folly. This has been a notion which had been developing for a long time in Israel, and here Paul is drawing on his Jewish heritage. God gives up revealing himself in the garb of royalty, equipped with the symbols of power. The cross of Christ signifies a change in the concept of God. He manifests himself henceforth in a way which is rather "democratic" and proletarian, but without ceasing to be—or rather, being still more radically—the God who brings down the mighty from their thrones. The originality of the Christian contribution was that it tried to understand more deeply the significance of the cross. This was also done from the standpoint of the justice of God. The Jewish ideal, according to which God rewards the good (i.e., the poor) and punishes the wicked (i.e., the rich) could not be accepted by Christianity. And one would have to be rather naive to try at the present time to deduce the class struggle from the Jewish premise in question, as if this is what the class struggle means and as if it could thus be transformed into a sort of "holy war." Christianity sees the justice of God being implemented in a different way, since it justifies sinners and in fact sends away the just empty-handed. And how is such a procedure even thinkable? The procedure is thinkable if one considers that it is really the coming of this justice which establishes the boundaries of poverty and riches and that it is really the result of the manifestation of this justice that "many of the last become first and many of the first become last." The justice of God does not show itself subsequent to the good or bad actions of men, to reward or to punish, but is displayed in what happened on the cross and in the concrete repercussion of the cross on the people of Corinth or in the people gathered at Jesus' feet on the mountain of the Beatitudes, to name but two examples. This manifestation of God's justice brings about the separation between rich and poor, oppressed and tyrants, exploited and exploiters. And it still does so today, just as on that Friday at Jerusalem.

In saying this, it was not our intention to "spiritualize" the whole procedure again. The interclass conclusions which could be derived from this argument are known to all, but it cannot be abandoned, since this would mean abandoning an essential aspect of the Gospel message. Two discussions will ensue. One will be with interclass-oriented Christians, to see whether they find it normal that the churches should be religious clubs, so to speak, where people get together to comfort themselves with fine traditions while they forget all that is happening in the world. The other will be with the overdogmatic materialist, who has to be told that any fatalistic approach to class must be rejected. We recognize that what makes people fighters for justice is their actual situation in production relationships, but we do not wish this to be taken in a fatalistic sense. For it seems to us that a mighty force in history has been provided by those who acted from a sense of vocation. The commitment of many is founded on their situation with regard to the cross of Jesus.

The interclass tradition in Christianity—in spite of all that we have tried to say—was quickly established in the Pauline churches and as such was canonized. The epistle of James, with its "populism" of a slightly Jewish tinge, displays clear evidence of this. Paul, with his extremely fine sense of dialectics, was quickly abandoned. The fate of Paul was left to the word. When it passed into the phase of ethics and exhortation, all hope was given up. Masters and slaves are to be of one mind, in the light of their common divine paternity, obeying the same Lord and so on. The poor have one function, the rich another, and the church supplies the needs of the former and offers them to the latter as an opportunity of good works (1 Tim. 6:17). This was still acceptable to Calvin, who wrote in this connection, "when the rich have the wherewithal to do good and the poor thank God for having something to eat, they all glorify God" (Commentary on Deut. 16:11). *Agape* is transformed into a great charitable enterprise which tries to obviate the social calamities of the ancient world as it goes down to ruin. And the Emperor Julian, who would have liked to revive paganism, wrote angrily: "The Galilean atheists not only sustain their poor, they also sustain ours."

To come to more recent times, and to remain within the domain of Protestantism, it is well known that the interclass approach is interwoven into the history of Protestantism. The Gospel was reduced to individualistic ethics, which in practice really excluded the proletariat but in theory tried to impose on it the same profound bourgeois morality. And there was the political theory which on the face of it should have enabled people to come to agreement on the basis of equality by means of rational negotiations. There was no question of any sort of "charity" any more than there was a question of any heroic and exceptional "holiness." In practice, it did no more than sanction exploitation. This Protestantism wrongly seeks to survive the collapse of bourgeois society. With the early Barth, a new page has already been turned. What he rejects is ethics, and what he rediscovers is really the very special character of transcendence in the sense of Paul. But Barth too is critical with regard to the pride of revolutionaries while trying to develop a political theory in which the state corresponds to the justice of God. Perhaps the interclass illusion is an incurable illness of Protestantism?

1.	An interclass reading of the Bible is illegitimate.
1.1	Both we and the text are conditioned by society.
1.2	The justice of God is revealed in the gospel.
1.2.1	The justice of God is not automatically implemented in the course of history; it is not postponed till the end of history; it comes in the cross of Christ.
1.2.2	The justice of God is manifested in the "disclosure" of the pretensions of those who claim to be just and are not—that is, of those who claim to be on the side of reason and are hypocrites. It is likewise manifested in the fact that it takes the side of the persecuted.
1.2.3	A "positive" message which is not also "negative" has nothing to do with the gospel message.
1.2.3.1	Faced with such a positive/negative message, one cannot remain neutral. No one can stay with generalities in order to claim credit for himself on all issues (to be always right).
1.2.3.2	The message may not be spiritualized in such a way that only the interior life of humanity is in question. It is wrong to say that preaching considers the sins committed by the poor and the sins committed by the rich in the same light.

1.2.4   The hearing of the word of the gospel unmasks our efforts to exploit the situation. It makes us free.

1.3   It is meaningless to speak of the word of God apart from an event.

2.1   We are now in a position to work out scientifically the theory of exploitation and to trace poverty and riches to precise causes.

2.2   Once the causes have been made clear, it is impossible not to try to think out measures for changing the production relationships which result in exploitation. The change has to be undertaken as a human task. It should not be regarded as the implementation of metaphysical presuppositions.

2.2.1   It is impossible in fact, just as it would be wrong, to work in such a way that deeds and words were not precisely directed to this end or could be held aloof from the question; such procedures would nullify the Christian vocation.

2.3   All classist "fatalism" is contrary to the gospel.

2.4   The Christian vocation must be worked out in materialist practice. There is no such thing as a Christian practice which would be the implementation of Christian presuppositions. The Christian reaffirms the complementarity of a practice and a language which make the search for truth possible.

2.4.1   As evangelical Christians, when we speak of a language which makes the search for truth possible, we mean the language of the Bible.

2.4.2   Humanity needs a language that will not enslave it but set the truth free. The gospel language does not enslave.

2.4.2.1 Religion can have a bad influence on people or it can express a true experience of liberation. A state that tolerates religion only as "the opium of the people" shows a false conception of freedom.

3.   There can be four different types of biblical reading:

3.1   an interclass reading, the traditional one (see above);

3.2   a reading in which the scientific analysis of production relationships would be dressed up in a biblical apparatus of which it really has no need, an apparatus in which the texts would only be used in an evocative way, independently of the underlying historical problems in the light of which they should be understood. This way of quoting the Bible has no interest for us.

3.3   A third way of reading the Bible would be the pietistic and dogmatic way. That is, faith would be nourished on biblical truth in a rather literal way but would have an ethical orientation of immediate relevance. In a word, one would have to see how various circumstances would work out among people who have various beliefs. The main problem is that of "consistency."

3.4   In a fourth type of reading, the value of the texts would be assessed in relation to our practice and the understanding of our practice.

4.   The reading of the Bible cannot be used to deduce pointers for what may be opportune or tactically useful in political moves.

NOTES

1. Out of a total of 28 occurrences in the New Testament, the term *rich* appears 11 times in Luke and 5 times in James; the term *poor* occurs 10 times in Luke and 4 times in James out of a total of 34 times for the whole of the New Testament.

2. In this particular case, the argument is addressed to poor people whose enthusiasm makes them feel rich (1 Cor. 1:5 and 4:8). Paul makes the point that they must take their material poverty seriously. The aim is not to place the rich and the poor on an equal footing. The problem, therefore, is to understand how the Corinthians are to regard their material poverty.

5

DAVID LOCHHEAD

The Liberation of the Bible

People read the Bible from different points of view and see different mean-ings in its texts. Since the eighteenth century, we have come to realize that such a "partial" or "prejudicial" stance is a necessary aspect of our knowing anything. "Ideology" refers to the social, economic, cultural, and political dimensions of one's point of view. The Bible itself is not ideologically neu-tral, nor do all its parts form a harmonious ideological unity. The Bible does not prescribe an ideology for our time in any simple or direct way.

By insisting on full and honest analysis of the ideological assumptions of the Bible and of our own ideological assumptions, it is possible to increase our awareness of what we hold to be true (theory) and of what we do (praxis). By gaining more consciousness through the interaction of theory and praxis, we also make it possible to change our ideology. In Bible study, this process can both free the Bible *from our naive prejudgments about it and* free us *to alter our judgments about ourselves and our society.*

Reprinted from David Lochhead, *The Liberation of the Bible* (Student Christian Movement of Canada, 1977, and the World Student Christian Federation of North America, 1979), pp. 4–7, 18, 27–28, 40–52. Available from Service Center, 7820 Reading Rd., Cincinnati, Ohio 45237.

INTRODUCTION

If the point of this book could be put in one sentence, it is this: *You can't take anything out of context.* If that is true—well, what is the context? Who am I? What is the social and historical situation of the author? To whom is the book addressed? Why?

I suppose that the story of this book really begins in 1973 when, after a period of teaching, administering, and chaplaining in university situations, I took my first full-time position as the minister of a congregation.

During my years in the university, as a student, as a teacher, etc., I had suffered as one who attended church on Sunday mornings. My suffering was due to what I perceived in many of the sermons I heard as a simple lack of integrity in the way in which many preachers dealt with the Bible. I resolved, when I became a pastor, that my preaching should be biblical.

The discipline of producing a "biblical" sermon each week, together with the necessity which circumstances forced on me to come to terms with the charismatic movement, led me to reflect on my own praxis in relation to the Bible. The whole train of thought was triggered by a very simple remark by a charismatic friend. In the middle of a conversation he remarked that the Bible could be considered to be infallible *as long as it was interpreted in context.*

This is a rather commonplace remark, but for the first time it struck me how significant this qualification *in context* really is. This insight became an important tool for analyzing my own approach to the Bible as a preacher. I pursued the logic of this remark to the point at which the interpretation of the Bible became, for me, the crucial contemporary theological issue.

But that alone would not have produced a book. While being preoccupied with my own praxis as a preacher, I happened to receive a request from Alan Rimmer, then General Secretary of the Student Christian Movement of Canada, as well as a former classmate in theology, to attend a Board meeting of the SCM and to teach the Movement how to think theologically!

Well, I wasn't totally out of touch with the SCM. My university had hosted the National Council in the last few months of my university career. I knew something of where things were at. I also knew that it was not possible to construe theological reflection as it might have been construed in those days in the early '60s when Al Rimmer and I were theological students and co-conspirators in the local SCM.

In brief, the problem was this: In the late '50s and early '60s there was a great interest in existentialism. We approached theological questions through existential questions—personal identity, dialogue, estrangement as sin, God as ultimate concern—and all that. Of course, the existential questions were never solved. The later '60s took care of that!

Under the impact of the '60s, the existential questions gave way to political questions. The SCM, which had always had political concerns, gave these concerns first priority. Regionalism. Socialism. Economic Disparity. Land Use. That is what SCM national programs were about. How do you do theological reflection about that?

You don't start with existential questions! When the request came to me I could not see—and I still do not see—any basis for theological reflection on political questions apart from a dialogue with the Bible—the story of God's presence in the politics of Israel.

So it came to pass that on Thanksgiving weekend, 1975, I met with the Board of the Student Christian Movement of Canada to do Bible study. We did a study on "prosperity."

While I was preparing this presentation, Al undertook to send me an article by someone I had never heard of: an Italian pastor named Sergio Rostagno. As far as I could make out from a quick look at the mimeographed article which Al sent me, Rostagno was saying that an interpretation of the Bible which meant the same thing to people in different contexts (in this case, people of different social classes) was not possible. I noted my mental agreement and set the article to one side.

Well, the session with the SCM Board went well. I continued the theoretical development of my analysis, preparing a paper for the Canadian Theological Society, and was beginning to feel that I had spent enough time on hermeneutics. Just when I figured that I had done enough, the SCM called again. It seemed that this Sergio Rostagno had produced more than one paper. In fact, the World Student Christian Federation had bound a number of essays by Rostagno together under the title *Essays on the New Testament: A "Materialist" Approach*. It was supposed to be a study document for the affiliated movements, including the Canadian SCM.

The Rostagno essays are good, solid stuff. They are mainly thorough analyses of some central Pauline themes from a radical perspective. In the process, Rostagno makes important criticisms of the dominant liberal tradition in biblical criticism. The problem was that the essays are just too sophisticated for undergraduate use. They are written at a level which would be more suitable for use in a graduate seminar in theology. So—could anything be done?

Consequently this book is prepared with the needs of the Canadian SCM in mind. It assumes a readership of people who are involved in very concrete ways with the major issues of our time. It also assumes a readership of people who want to relate their involvement to a Christian commitment—even though they might not be sure what that means.

The title and shape of this work have been chosen for a variety of reasons. In the pastorate, I am particularly aware of the pressure of the religio-political right wing. I want to challenge as forcefully as I can the assumption that the Bible is a reactionary book.

The other major reason for the title and shape of the work comes from my persuasion that the only rigorous program which relates faith to the total context of life is that of "liberation" theology. Yet at this point I feel a certain embarrassment. This is not a work in liberation theology. At best, it is prolegomena to an indigenous Canadian liberation theology.

The reason for my embarrassment is simply this: I am white and male and North American. On every count I am numbered with the oppressor! At the same time, I am very aware of my own powerlessness. I believe that the basic insight of liberation theology is quite correct. God does identify himself with the oppressed. The struggle for liberation in the third world, in the women's movement, among racial minorities, in native groups—that is where the theological action is! Yet that is not where I am!

Where I am—and where the people are with whom I must deal day by day—is terribly ambiguous in a theological sense. I and my parishioners are people of good will. We are people who are concerned about, and are willing to sacrifice for, the oppressed of the world. We, too, are oppressed. We are powerless. We lack either the will or the determination even to influence the future of our immediate environment. We doubt that we could change things, even if we had the will and the determination. So we watch, immobilized, while our orchards are appropriated for the recreational use of people from the city. No option but immobility seems reasonable in our circumstances.

Yet coexisting with the consciousness of our powerlessness is the fact that we know we are being paid very well. The farmer who sells his orchards for recreational use can look forward to a reasonably comfortable and independent retirement. We all benefit from the fact that North America pays low prices for raw materials and receives high prices for manufactured goods. I benefit because I am unilingual in English rather than in French. I benefit from my sex and my color. I am oppressor and oppressed—and I don't seem to have much choice about either.

I do not believe that I am alone in this sense of ambiguity. It is precisely in the recognition of the ambiguity of our situation that any white, male, North American theology of liberation must begin. We do not need a theology for the oppressor. We have that in abundance. What we need is a theology for the oppressed who are simultaneously the oppressor. That is much more difficult. Prior to that, we need to understand ourselves better. We need an adequate analysis of the ambiguity of our situation. This task, as fundamental as it is, is not attempted in this book. It still awaits us.

For some, the theoretical openness that this work leaves to ideological pluralism will be offensive. I leave this option open for a number of reasons. First, I do not believe that the Bible is of one ideological piece. Only a falsification of history could, for example, represent the royal theology of the Old Testament as expressing identical ideological interests to the prophetic theologies—at least, during the period of the monarchy. Secondly, I believe that we North Americans have a lot of listening to do both to Scripture and to the world before our options can become sufficiently clear. Thirdly, I am convinced that the truth of a statement like "God identifies himself with the oppressed" is not at issue. What is at issue is the *praxis* which is associated with this kind of affirmation.

A few final remarks about my use of words: The word *"praxis"* is used frequently in liberation theology and in radical political circles. Its meaning is not always clear. During the writing of this book, it became apparent that, among the group which gathered to react to each chapter, the word meant different things to different people.

Words are like that. Particularly when a word is gaining currency, the boundaries of the word's meaning will not be at all clear. And while not subscribing to the linguistic antinomianism of Humpty Dumpty who tells Alice that words can mean whatever he chooses them to mean, when a word has a range of possible meanings it is important to indicate which of the possible meanings is used here.

By *praxis,* I mean the way that theory and practice fit together. I say certain things; I hold to certain opinions; I do certain things. How are these interrelated? How does what I think fit together with what I do? That interrelatedness, that "fitting together," is my *praxis.* That is how the word is used here. Other uses may be quite legitimate, but those other meanings are not intended in this work.

I use the words "prejudice," "perspective," "viewpoint," and "ideology" more or less synonymously. Furthermore, the terms "prejudice" and "ideology" are never meant in a disparaging sense. I argue that, in understanding reality, our understanding always reflects our perspective on reality. For every view of reality, there is always a "point of view." The term "prejudice" is used when it is important to emphasize that we come to reality with certain expectations of what we are going to find. Any perspective "prejudges" reality in certain ways. The term "ideology" is used to emphasize the social, cultural, economic, and political dimensions of one's "point of view."

The treatment of ideology in the first chapter may seem hopelessly idealistic. It could be read as if I believed that ideologies were caused by people deciding to have one ideal rather than another. No such thesis is intended. I am quite aware of those theories which would see ideologies as reflections of social relationships. I have no argument, in general, with such a thesis. My point in chapter one is simply to identify certain ideals as typifying (not causing) ideological commitments in order to see, in a simple model, what happens when the Bible is read from an ideological point of view.

In case any theologians should happen to pick up this work, I should add that I am aware of the many questions I have begged or over-simplified. I am not writing for theologians. In case any biblical scholar should be listening, I plead *nolo contendere.* I am not a biblical scholar. But neither are those who are my intended readers. We all have a desperate need to hear. This book is not about what to hear, but *how* to hear. It is a book for communities of people who are not content to leave the *doing* of theology to the experts.

THE MIRROR OF THE MIND

One of the dominant myths of modern Western culture is that the mind is something like a mirror of reality. The mind knows the world. What the mind "knows" is like an image of reality—a re-presentation. Ideally the mind itself neither adds to nor subtracts from the facts which it encounters in the world. Like a good mirror which represents what is placed before it without distortion, the mind should reproduce in the form of knowledge only what exists in the world independently of mind.

But just imagine if things were the opposite. Imagine that, in the encounter of the mind and the world, it was the *world* which resembled the mirror. Instead of having knowledge which represented an objective world, what we would "know"—what we would perceive in the world—would simply be a reflection of ourselves.

The contrast between these simple analogies—the mind as mirror vs. the world as mirror—illustrates a basic tension in our recent intellectual history. In the seventeenth and eighteenth centuries the idea of knowledge as an objective representation of reality was certainly dominant. Yet many of the major thinkers of the nineteenth and twentieth centuries have raised the possibility of an alternative: Perhaps what we know, however it may represent a world which exists quite independently of our minds, may also reflect something that our minds contribute as well. Perhaps, at least partly, what we see when we look at the world is our own reflection.

The question of how much we see our own reflection in what we "know" puts the problem of an ideological captivity of the Bible in a radically new perspective. Ideological readings of the Bible are not *simply* attempts to manipulate the texts to our own purposes. If it should be a condition of knowing that we must see the world from the perspective of our own prejudices, we have to read the Bible that way too. We need to consider the implications of the possibility that prejudice is a necessary condition of having any knowledge at all. . . .

It has not been the purpose of this chapter to endorse any particular view which has been briefly sketched here. It has been the intention, however, to endorse the major conclusion which has emerged: *The world is "known" only from the unique perspective of the knower. What is understood reflects not only the reality which is understood but the perspective from which it is understood.*

At the same time we must be clear that we are not endorsing a kind of reductionism, which might be suggested by some of the views we have discussed. Among Marxists, for example, it is sometimes suggested that economic factors are the only significant variables in understanding. Similarly, McLuhan often seems to hold that everything can be explained by media studies. We don't wish to move in this direction. What we want to stress is that every "knower" has a unique perspective on the "known." We each belong to some particular social class in a particular socio-economic system. Each of us has a unique set of parents and a unique upbringing. We speak a particular language with a particular grammatical structure. We are part of a particular culture in which particular media of communication are used. Each of these factors plays a role in defining the perspective from which we experience and understand our world. Each of these factors is reflected in what we see in the world.

It will be clear that if everything that we understand reflects our own unique perspective, this will also be true of how we understand the Bible. There is no reason to complain about this or deplore it. Without a perspective—without prejudices—we could not begin to understand anything. The important thing is to be aware that this is so. It is just not possible to talk about what the Bible says as if our exposition of the biblical view of things were quite independent of our own perspective on reality. To ignore this is to make the Bible captive to our prejudices. Our task is to read the Bible in such a way that it is liberated from our blindness to the relativity of our own point of view.

To put this point another way, we have to learn to read the Bible so that it is able to liberate us from the bonds of our own perspective. To a remarkable degree, our point of view is not something of our own making. We are not asked when we want to be born, what nationality and social class we will have, what language we will speak, what ideological framework will accompany our instruction in Sunday School, and so on. The temptation is to force the Bible to fit the perspective we have inherited. Yet a Bible which must "fit" a perspective is not one that is going to tell us anything new. It becomes an ideological weapon in our defense of our own version of the status quo.

In this study we will henceforth assume the relativity of knowledge. In making this assumption it is important to make a few qualifications. In particular it should be clear that while any given expression of truth is relative to the perspective of the beholder, it is quite another thing to hold that truth itself is relative. The latter position is a metaphysical theory which we shall not discuss. Relativism can be used as an excuse for the abdication of any intellectual and moral seriousness. It can justify exploitation and irrationalism. This is not the conclusion we wish to draw here. Rather we wish to ask, given the fact that any understanding of the Bible reflects the relativity of the perspective from which it is read, how we can proceed in our search for valid theological insight which is relevant to the reality in which we live? . . .

THE POLITICS OF UNDERSTANDING

We have seen that our goal of the liberation of the Bible is closely related to our ability to see the text in its own contexts. To be more precise, a liberated and liberating reading of the Bible must, at the level of *explicatio,* fulfill two conditions. First, the method must be available to groups of ordinary people who wish to listen to the Bible as a part of their reflection on the reality in which they live and on their own relationship to that reality. Secondly, the group must be free and able to distinguish the perspective of the group from the perspective of the text.

Yet at this point the method as we have outlined it is in danger of falling into a contradiction in practice. The problem is this: The method requires that the participants be aware of the context of the text. This awareness involves a relatively sophisticated knowledge of biblical scholarship. "Where," groups ask, "can we find the information we need to establish the contexts of the passages we study? How do we discover the passages which are relevant to the reality we are addressing?"

The temptation is to call in an expert. The expert locates the relevant texts. The expert supplies the background material.

Here the contradiction is introduced. The expert has a point of view too! The expert has ideological commitments. The very selection of the passage has to be studied; the way that the background material is structured cannot help but reflect the perspective of the expert. From the beginning the expert dominates the course of the study. There may be no intention to manipulate on the part of the expert. The contradiction is built into the expert's role.

The contradiction poses the dilemma which plagues many attempts at Bible study. The choice seems simple. One can do away with the expert in a burst of anti-intellectual populist enthusiasm. We know the result. The group is then dominated by the more aggressive representatives of the unofficial ideology of the group: the most pious or the most militant. What is worse, in dispensing with the expert the group dispenses with the kind of information that the expert can provide. Such an approach must, therefore, take history less than seriously. Turning one's back on the historical reality of the world of the Bible means that the text is treated, in practice if not in theory, as a fairy tale, a once-upon-a-time kind of story. (Note that the socio-economic environment of Goldilocks is not very relevant to the story *Goldilocks and the Three Bears*. The date of Goldilocks' visit to the home of the bears is also irrelevant.) In theological terms, this denial of the relevance of history to the study of the Bible may be seen as a practical denial of the reality of the word of God.

The first approach, then, has the virtue of recognizing and rejecting the dominance of the expert. It fails to be liberating because, transforming history into fantasy, it is vulnerable to various kinds of ideological manipulation.

The alternative approach, of course, is to affirm the dominance of the expert. Thus the relevance of the special knowledge and skills which are possessed by the expert is affirmed. The price is that the group is submitted to the prejudices and the personal agenda of the expert. Such an approach cannot be called liberating.

Is there a way out? Let us look at the problem again. We have assumed that all understanding involves prejudice. If so, it follows that no attempt to understand a text can be free of the perspective of the interpreter. If an ideologically free reading of the Bible is what we mean by liberation, we might as well forget it. There can be no such thing.

Then what is the problem? If our understanding of the text is going to be "contaminated" by ideology anyway, why not "sin the more that grace may abound"?

What we need to clarify is that the problem of the liberation of the Bible is not ideology itself. The problem is the *dominance* of our ideology over the text. The struggle of *explicatio* is a struggle against the ways in which we allow our ideologies to *control* our reading of the text. Thus, in the use of experts, we are in danger of surrendering our reading of the text to the control of the expert's point of view. If we dispense with the expert, we apparently surrender control of our reading to prejudices we share, largely unconsciously, with our peers.

The aim of *explicatio* must be to approach the world of the text as consciously and as critically as we can of our own prejudices. The truth or falsity of our prejudices is not at issue here. What is at issue is that our prejudices should not dominate the text. On the contrary, we should be in a position to allow the text to expose and illumine the prejudices we bring to it. Our experience in entering the world of the text should be a form of consciousness raising.

But how? The information we need to enter the world of the text has to come from somewhere. We need the expertise of the specialist. Yet our very need seems to place us under the domination of the expert. We still have the dilemma. It is a dilemma which has plagued the churches since the rise of modern historical and critical Bible scholarship. In churches where this dependence on the expert has been rejected, the Bible is a living and powerful force in the lives of the people. In churches which have accepted the historical-critical method, and thereby the dominance of the expert in biblical studies, the people are alienated from a book which, they assume, is too difficult and too remote to understand.

It would be possible to examine this apparent alienation of people from the Bible in "liberal" churches from a number of perspectives. The dynamics are complex and take varied and subtle forms. At base, however, the study of the Bible has tended to become a problem of marketing biblical knowledge. The scholar produces knowledge about the Bible. The preacher is the distributor of the scholar's product. The layperson is the consumer. Given this underlying structure to our attitude to the Bible, it is not surprising that so many attempts to deal with the problem of biblical illiteracy have the appearance of a search for a new and better package for the product. No wonder people are alienated!

Without wishing to labor the analogy, it should be clear that if we wish to speak of the liberation of the Bible, the kind of marketing of biblical knowledge which moves from producer through distributor to consumer needs to be challenged. But how?

Let us recall what is involved in *explicatio*. There are two basic questions here. The first involves getting as complete a picture as we can of the world of the text. Here, it must be granted, some source of information is necessary. We can't all carry around the knowledge of archaeology, history, and textual studies that we require for any text we might wish to study. Yet we must recognize that what we need is not information about what the Bible *means,* but about the *context* within which the text has its basic meaning. There is a difference and, at this point, a very important one.

The "meaning" of a text must be understood in context. However, the meaning of a text is not identical to the context. One could know all there is to know about the context of a text and still miss the point. One can know relatively little about the context of a text and still make a pretty good guess about its basic intention. Ultimately, the intuition of what a text means in context is not a matter of expertise. It is a matter of creative insight.

What we look to the specialist for is not an exposition of a given text. Rather we need the background information which will help us to listen to the text in its own context. This distinction does not entirely remove the threat of the domination of a reading by the expert's viewpoint. If this distinction is ignored, however, the domination is virtually inevitable.

We might state this conclusion in another way by saying that the role of the specialist in biblical reflection is that of a resource rather than of an "expert." The problem of the group which is engaged in biblical reflection is that of finding resources. How do you go about it?

It means work. Unless a group includes a number of members with a relatively sophisticated knowledge of the history and culture of the ancient Middle East, it will be necessary to research the background of the text before the group deals with it. The questions which should be answered are these:

1. When was the text written?
2. Who was the author of the text?
3. What important historical events and developments were taking place at the time of the text?
4. What forms of social organization are reflected in the text?
5. To whom is the text addressed?

The answers to these questions will be found most easily in general introductions to the Bible and in commentaries. Groups should be careful to do their research with more than one resource. Every resource has its own set of prejudices. Watch for them!

We have stressed the necessity of reading any text in relationship to its social and cultural context. Depending on the specific dating of the events recorded in the Bible, the story from Abraham through Paul spans about two thousand years. It will be clear that, given this period of time, we are not dealing with a single sociocultural context. It may be helpful to distinguish the principal epochs in the biblical account from this point of view. Anyone wishing to engage in serious study of the Bible should have a general familiarity with each of these periods.

In the Old Testament, the first two periods we can distinguish are a nomadic period, which would include the experience of slavery in Egypt, and the period of the settlement of Canaan. In these periods, society is organized along tribal lines. We have only isolated passages in the Old Testament which can be reasonably assigned to these times. The nomadic and settlement periods can be dated from about 1750 B.C. to 1020 B.C.

The settlement era is followed by the monarchy. The period of the monarchy may be dated from 1020 B.C. to the fall of Jerusalem and the exile in Babylon (586 B.C.). It produced most of the major writings in the Old Testament. The greatest part of the Pentateuch, most of the historical writings contained in the deuteronomic history, certain prophets—Amos, Hosea, First Isaiah (chapters 1-39), Jeremiah—belong to this period.

The next era is relatively brief—the exile. The exile in Babylon can be dated from 598 B.C. to 539 B.C., a period of about sixty years. During this time the Jewish elite were settled in Babylon while the "people of the land" remained in Palestine under Babylonian rulers. The most important works of these years were Ezekiel and Second Isaiah (chapters 40-55).

The final epoch of Old Testament times we may describe as a colonial period. In 539 B.C. the Babylonian Empire was overthrown by the Persians. The Jews were permitted to return to Palestine under Persian supervision. From this point on, Palestine is ruled as a province of one of a series of empires culminating in New Testament times in Roman domination. During this era the Jewish people enjoyed more or less autonomy in the practice of their religion. Major works of this era include the Chronicle's history, including Ezra and Nehemiah, much of the so-called "Wisdom" literature (Ecclesiastes, Job), the books of Ruth and Jonah, which can be seen as reactions to the exclusiveness of Ezra-Nehemiah, and the book of Daniel, a revolutionary tract from the time of the Maccabean revolt (c. 166 B.C.). Many of these works are preoccupied with the problem of the survival of Israel in a colonial situation.

In the New Testament, three distinct sociocultural situations must be distinguished. Many texts in the Gospels are related to the Galilean ministry of Jesus. This is a rural, hinterland world populated by fishermen, tax-collectors, and other outcasts, and Pharisees who represent the religious establishment. Other texts in the Gospels and some in the book of Acts are set in Jerusalem. This is an urban and much more cosmopolitan context. The *dramatis personae* are quite different. A few of the Galileans remain on the scene, but the supporting characters are now Romans, some Hellenistic Jews (i.e., Greek-speaking) and the religious establishments of the Temple and the Sanhedrin. The third period takes us out into the Greco-Roman world where both Christians and Jews are distinct minorities in cosmopolitan centers such as Ephesus, Corinth, and Rome.

Virtually all of the New Testament comes from the third period. Nothing in the New Testament was written during the life time of Jesus. Nothing in the New Testament can be demonstrated to be a product of the Jerusalem church although a Judean origin is sometimes argued for some of the books.

Given this rough analysis of the different periods of the biblical record, let us see what it implies for the task of *explicatio*. We will start with a simple case.

Perhaps a passage from one of Paul's letters would present the fewest complications. Here it is easy to obtain the answers to the questions which are relevant to the determination of the context. If we wish to discover the context of, say, Paul's letter to the Galatians, we simply consult some introductions to the New Testament and some commentaries on Galatians. We will discover that the work was indeed written by Paul (But who was Paul? Dig deeper here. Paul's background as a Pharisee is very relevant.), that it was written probably quite early (maybe before 50 A.D.), and that its exact recipients are unknown (Galatia covers a big area). Even more importantly we will discover something of the controversy to which Galatians is addressed and we will be directed to portions of the book of Acts which bear upon the same problem. Having done our homework, we can then proceed to read the text in this context.

The situation is more complicated if we select a passage, say, from the Gospel of Luke. The passage we select will have an apparent context in the life of Jesus. It is written in the form that we have it, however, sometime later. The context of the author is that of a member of a Christian minority in the Roman world (the third period, above).

The interpretation of such a passage will involve at least two contexts. Most obvious is the context in the life of Jesus. However, the stories in the Gospels are not simply eyewitness accounts. They are stories which were preserved and told and retold in the primitive church. The accounts which were preserved were those which were important and relevant to the experience of the early Christian community. The actual form which the stories took was determined by the situation of their retelling. The stories are thus "about" Jesus but they reflect also the situation of the narrator.

In reflecting on a Gospel passage, then, we have to ask two questions concerning context. The first question concerns what the story meant for the early church. The second question asks what the significance of the story was in its original setting.

Initially, this may seem a formidable task. For practical reflection on the Bible, however, it is not as difficult as it first appears. One must simply keep in mind that texts such as these have two levels of meaning. Otherwise the process of discovering the context is the same.

In fact, much of the Bible has this feature of multiple contexts. The passage from 1 Samuel which we studied in the previous chapter is a case in point. There we discovered at least three possible contexts: the context of the deuteronomic editor of the exilic period, the context of the basic formulation of the sources in the period of the united monarchy, and the situation of the actual establishment of the monarchy in Israel. This passage is not atypical of much of the historical material in the Bible. Except for isolated passages, virtually all of the narrative portions of the Old and New Testaments have passed through a number of hands between the event recounted and its final form in the Bible.

The fact that a text may have multiple levels of meaning may be a little frightening at first. To some extent we have all been conditioned to expect a relatively straightforward meaning and a simple application of any given biblical text. How can we use texts which are so ambiguous?

Multiple levels of meaning are actually no threat to the "utility" of the Bible as a source for theological reflection. We must remember that, even for a text which is simple and straightforward, there is no direct route from *explicatio* to *applicatio*. For any text, however simple, the decision of how the text applies to contemporary reality is a *decision* of the interpreter. It is not imposed by the text. If a text has multiple levels of meaning, the need for an interpretive decision may be more obvious. That is all to the good. The simple text whose application seems self-evident and automatic is deceptive. The so-called "ambiguous" text need not be ambiguous in the praxis which follows reflection upon it.

We have looked at the problem of the domination of the expert in coming to understand the Bible. We have suggested ways in which a group can cope with this threat by transforming "experts" into "resources." However, this is only one aspect of the politics of understanding.

Understanding is always political in this sense: What we "know," what we understand, always takes place in a social context. The social context is constituted by a complex system of social relationships. Among other things, these relationships are power relationships. They are relationships between the dominating and the dominated. This fact of the sociology of understanding is put very simply in Marx's remark that the dominant ideas of any society are the ideas of the dominant classes of that society. Put more generally, we can say that understanding never occurs in a political vacuum. Dominance and submission in the realm of ideas is still dominance and submission.

There can be no escape from this kind of politics of understanding. In terms of our analysis of the method of biblical reflection, relations of dominance and submission arise at every stage. *Who selects the text? Why is this text chosen? What interests are reflected in the resources which the group is using? In whose interest is it to read a text the way we do? Why do we analyze our contemporary reality the way we do? Why do we apply the text in one way rather than another?* In relation to all our questions we need to ask, *Whose interest is being served?*

If we find this notion disturbing, it is very likely our liberal conditioning at work. In the understanding of the feudal church (an understanding which survived in the Roman Catholic church at least until Vatican II and which still appears to be alive and well in the Curia) there was no question about the right of the hierarchy to dominate the church's theory and practice of faith.

In many right-wing groups there is similarly no question about the right of the leader who is "blessed by God" to dominate the thinking of the group. On the left, radicals understand quite well—particularly in the relation of class interest to ideology—the connections between understanding and power.

The problem is not to eliminate relationships of power from the study of the Bible. That would be an illusory task. Neither is the problem to legitimate those relationships. That would be oppressive. The problem is to be aware of the politics of biblical reflection. Only when we are aware of the power relationships which we bring into the process of reflection can we begin to think and act freely in relation to them.

The power relationships which are relevant to biblical reflection exist on two levels. First, there are the external power relationships; the relationships which order society as a whole. Since we live our lives in the context of these relationships, we necessarily bring to the task of biblical reflection a type of thinking which is molded by the world we live in. We then have to ask, in relation to any specific text, the question of class interest. Who stands to benefit if we read the text one way rather than another? Secondly, we have to deal with the internal relationships within the study group. Who is dominating the discussion? How is he doing it? Why? On both levels, a liberated reading of the Bible must be accompanied by a healthy exercise of suspicion.

DOING THEOLOGY

When we speak of the "liberation" of the Bible we mean two things. First of all, we mean the liberation of the Bible in quite a public sense. We observed that in the media there has been a tendency for the Bible to be presented as a reactionary document. The question we face, then, is how we can effectively challenge this view of what the Bible is. At the same time, most of us who have been raised in the so-called "main-line" denominations face another kind of captivity. The Bible as we have been exposed to it in Sunday School and in sermons is a very liberal document, setting forth the brotherhood of man under the fatherhood of God. So here the challenge of the liberation of the Bible is a challenge to something that is very much part of ourselves. How can we get the kind of critical distance from our own assumptions so that this kind of ideological captivity can be questioned?

This brings us to the second meaning of the term "liberation." In liberating the Bible from its various captivities we find that we have to engage in a process of personal liberation as well. The mechanisms which allow the Bible to be placed in ideological captivity are built into the very nature of understanding. We have found that self-criticism and consciousness-raising are absolutely necessary in any attempt to engage in a liberated reading of the Bible.

To help ourselves along the way we have formulated a "method" for Bible reflection. The "method" consists of four steps in two movements. The first movement takes us into the world of the text. It consists of (1) determining the context of the text and (2) reading the text in the light of its context. We have called this movement *"explicatio."* The second movement, which we have called *"applicatio,"* brings the text into relation with our contemporary reality. *Applicatio* consists of two steps: (1) reflection on the similarities and differences between the world of the text and our world and (2) a decision on how the text might be relevant to our reality in the light of this reflection.

Now it must be confessed that the "method" is really not a method at all. The "method" is simply a formalization of what happens of necessity in any theological reflection on the Bible. To read a biblical text, one must presuppose a context for it. If we do not know the context of a text, we must imagine one. We may very well imagine wrong. It is not possible to understand a text in abstraction from any context at all. Similarly to decide that a text applies to our world in a specific way is to assume that our world is sufficiently like the world of the text to make our application appropriate.

What the "method" does is simply to analyze the act of theological reflection and to identify the steps we perform. What is important is that we recognize what we are doing and to acknowledge the need to perform each step in a responsible way.

This formulation of the steps involved will be helpful to those who are new to biblical reflection. To this extent, it is appropriate to see the formalization as a method. As a method, however, it is meant to be put aside once its purpose has been achieved. Ultimately biblical reflection cannot be separated neatly into *explicatio* and *applicatio*. To enter the world of the text, in *explicatio,* is already to gain new perspective on one's own world. *Explicatio* involves *applicatio.*

There are two major weaknesses in the formalization when it is considered as a "method." The first weakness is that no method can program creative insight into the reading of the Bible. Yet without creativity it is difficult to see how any reading could be described as liberated and liberating.

In *explicatio,* we have already indicated the need for creative insight. It is one thing, for example, to know everything that there is to know about the world of Paul. It is quite another thing to see that world through Paul's eyes. The latter step is an act of creative imagination. Here method is no substitute for creativity.

The role of creativity in *applicatio* is just as decisive. Here creativity takes the form of seeing new possibilities in the text, the risk of departing from old and well-worn applications.

Recently, in a small seminar of Canadian pastors, the American theologian Paul Lehmann dealt with two passages of scripture in which both the possibilities and the risks of creative *applicatio* were brilliantly illustrated. The passages discussed by Dr. Lehmann were Genesis 13:1–13 and Matthew 25:31–46.

The first passage deals with Abraham and Lot dividing the land between them. Lot chooses the valley land toward Sodom while Abraham is left with the hill country to the west. Dr. Lehmann pointed out that Abraham and Lot were coming from the south, and, therefore, in turning to the east, Lot was turning to the *right*. To the right lies Sodom, which Dr. Lehmann interpreted as the symbol of organized dehumanization.

In his discussion of Matthew 25, Dr. Lehmann repeated the familiar fact that those who were chosen by the King—those at his right hand—are those who unknowingly have ministered to the poor and powerless. But then he appealed to the geometric fact that the right hand of God is the *left* hand of the world.

Bringing both of these studies together, Dr. Lehmann proceeded to comment on the "correspondence between theological and political designations of left and right," that the sheep don't know they are sheep and the goats are sure they are not goats, that the political move to the right is a move to what he called the "Brazilianization" of the world, to the point at which planning and power reach an equilibrium so that no effective challenge can be mounted. In short, to the right lies Sodom. To the left is where room is made in the world for the poor and powerless.

The dangers of this kind of *applicatio* are obvious. In the hands of a less capable thinker this kind of approach could easily degenerate into a kind of proof texting, providing a kind of blanket legitimization of any and every left-wing ideology. Lehmann avoided the traps by not pretending that he was engaged in *explicatio* and by confining the theological meaning of "left" to the movement to make room in the world for those whom Sodom would exclude. What emerges from Lehmann's analysis is a set of symbols which relate the biblical texts to the contemporary ideological realities. The analysis is undoubtedly debatable. What it does show is the kind of creative insight and risk which must be involved in *applicatio,* the kind of imaginativeness which cannot be programmed by a method.

The first weakness of the formalization, considered as "method," is that it does not create imaginative insight. The second weakness lies in apparently isolating *applicatio* as a discrete step in the "method." It seems that once you have done everything else, it is time to make up a moral to the story. When actually performed that way, the applications come out sounding pompous and cliché ridden. To consider the relevance of a text as a distinct step in the process of biblical reflection is to expect too little and too much. It is to expect too much of a formal process to hope to capture in words the impact of the text on our world. It is to expect too little of *applicatio* to confine it to a formal step in biblical reflection.

Applicatio is theological praxis. It is "doing theology." The term *praxis* designates the interrelationship of thought and action. *Applicatio* is the bridge between reflection and action.

What we have to notice is that biblical reflection is not something which is autonomous. It is possible, of course, to attempt a kind of autonomous Bible study. One could discuss the application as a kind of ideal, leaving it quite open and optional whether the discussion would actually affect the lives of the participants. Indeed, this is often done. We have to insist that this kind of reading of the text is not liberated because it is not liberative. By stopping the application at the level of ideas, the Bible is held in a kind of captivity which, if not ideological, is at least idealistic. It is only when *applicatio* is construed as praxis that we can speak in any genuine sense of the liberation of the Bible.

What this implies is that a liberated and liberating reflection on the Bible is possible only on the basis of a theological commitment. Biblical reflection involves a commitment to listen to Scripture and to act on the word we hear.

To this point we have avoided traditional theological language as much as possible. It is time we drew some connections between what we have been saying and some of the theologisms which we are used to hearing. By calling Scripture "the word of God," the church has expressed the confidence that in a faithful hearing of Scripture the will of God can, in fact, be encountered by human beings. The qualification "faithful" is important. It implies that not every hearing of the word of Scripture is a hearing of the word of God. The church has further made the qualification that only the Holy Spirit is the legitimate interpreter of Scripture—a warning that no automatic and mechanical application of Scripture is possible. *No method will ensure a liberated and liberative reading of the Bible.*

It is not the purpose of this study to elaborate on the traditional theological formulations. Yet the term "faith" needs particular attention. This word has had an unfortunate history in that it has been perennially interpreted as something which is contrasted with human *activity.* Thus, if we think of human life in terms of thought, emotions, and activity, faith tends to be understood as a kind of thinking or a kind of feeling. In doctrinaire churches, faith has tended to be understood as a kind of belief, as a matter of one's religious opinions. In revivalistic churches and sects, on the other hand, faith has come to be associated with the emotions, a matter of the heart. In neither case is faith interpreted directly as a matter of activity.

This assigning of faith to what we may call human passivity (as opposed to activity) is not something new. When the Pauline doctrine of salvation by faith alone gained some standing in the early church, it was opposed by the Epistle of James, for just this reason. The author of James assumes that faith is something other than activity. "Show me your faith apart from your works, and I by my works will show you my faith. You believe that God is one; you do well. Even the demons believe—and shudder"(James 2:18-19). Clearly faith is here equated with belief.

It is worth setting against James something that Paul says. In the epistle to the Romans, Paul had been concerned to spell out his objections to a doctrine of salvation by works of the law. Yet after stating and restating his conviction that salvation can only be by faith, Paul remarks: "If you confess with your lips that Jesus is Lord and believe in your heart that God raised him from the dead, you shall be saved" (Rom. 10:9). It might be easy to miss the significance of this remark. We must remember that in Paul's context the confession "Jesus is Lord" was not a kind of automatic doctrinal cliché. To confess with one's lips that Jesus is Lord was, to those in Paul's time, a political act of no little consequence. What Paul suggests, here and elsewhere, is that "faith" somehow includes activity with thought and feeling.

Instead of seeing faith as a matter of belief or of feeling, we are well advised to see faith as *praxis*. Faith, in relation to Scripture, is the commitment to listen to Scripture and to act on the word we hear. Faith is presupposed in any genuine *applicatio*.

The association of the words "faith" and "belief" is very strong in our culture. And, of course, they are connected. They are not, however, identical.

Let us characterize "belief" as belief of doctrines. (In philosophy of religion, a distinction is often made between "belief that" and "belief in." The latter is close to what we mean by "faith." We are considering belief as "belief that.") Belief expresses itself as the assent to certain propositions about God and man. "I believe that there is a God." "I believe that Jesus is the Son of God." "I believe that Jesus died to save mankind." "I believe that there is life after death." And so on.

It is important to understand the nature of doctrine which is the substance of belief. The classical creeds—particularly the Apostles' Creed and the Nicene Creed—can be seen as models of doctrinal statements. What are the creeds? And where do they come from?

Recall the basic principle with which we insisted the Bible be interpreted. Texts must be understood in context. The context of the creeds is the life of the early church. The creeds arose out of the *praxis* of the early church. As Christians moved between the poles of listening to the testimony of the Apostles and facing the challenges of the reality in which they lived, certain statements became important as expressing the difference between an authentic *praxis* and a false one. Behind each creedal statement lay practical issues which the church felt were matters of life and death for the community.

What happens, however, when these statements are formalized into creeds and passed on from generation to generation is that the creeds become statements without a context. It is assumed that in the creeds we have statements which can say essentially the same thing in any and every context.

In fact, the creeds have done rather well in presenting a distillation of belief to which Christians in various eras have been able to give their assent. The assumption that belief can be constant in changing circumstances is naive and fallacious, however. Only propositions of mathematics have this kind of constancy. Statements of substance are always embedded in history.

We need to make a distinction here between theology and doctrine. This distinction may have to be drawn at the price of making a bit of a caricature of the word "doctrine." If so, I apologize. The distinction is important even though some may wish to dispute the words with which the distinction is made.

Theology is the community's reflection on its *praxis*. Theology is the representation in terms of ideas which arises from the community's hearing of

Scripture and its acting on the word it hears. Theology is, therefore, part and parcel of the ongoing life of the community.

Doctrine is what happens when theology is presented in abstraction from the concrete life of the community in which it arises. Doctrine is saying that Jesus is "very man and very God" without reference to the very concrete temptations which the church of the fifth century faced to say that Jesus was *not quite* "very man" and *not quite* "very God," and without reference to the implications that such temptations held for the life of the Christian community.

This distinction is necessary to talk about the "theological commitment" which we have claimed to be necessary for a liberated and liberative reading of the Bible. The point which has to be made is that what we call a "theological commitment" is not necessarily a "doctrinal commitment."

Faith is not equivalent to belief. Theology is not equivalent to doctrine. A doctrinal commitment would be a commitment which placed *a priori* limitations on what could be heard from Scripture. It would determine in advance what Scripture would have to tell us. This kind of limitation is just a variant on what we have called the "ideological captivity" of the Bible.

What we mean by theological commitment can be put most simply in biblical terms: "He who has ears to hear, let him hear." There is no need to set doctrinal pre-conditions here. Obviously a person to whom all "God-talk" is simply nonsense will not have much desire to listen. The theological commitment is simply commitment to a *praxis* of hearing and acting. In the process of doing theology, the problems of doctrine will present themselves in their own place and in their own way. It would be improper, indeed self-defeating, to determine them in advance.

Theological commitment is commitment to *praxis*. We need to be warned. Biblical reflection is not something one does as a hobby, in one's spare time. Biblical reflection is not something which can be done as a kind of philosophical discussion, a kind of playing with ideas because ideas are interesting. Biblical reflection cannot be separated from the response we make to the reflection in the face of the concrete questions and concerns which life throws at us. In biblical reflection we are responsible to each other, not only for our ideas but for our *praxis* as a whole. One cannot liberate the Bible privately. That is an individualistic illusion characteristic of our liberal heritage. The liberation of the Bible can happen only when people come together in faith and hope and love to seek a unity of belief and action which is the essence of theological *praxis*.

The forms which this coming together may take can vary quite widely. It may happen in issue-oriented groups who wish to get a theological perspective of the questions with which they are already involved. It may happen in groups who gather simply to study the Bible and find what they are hearing directs them to grapple with specific personal, social, and political issues. It may even happen in the ongoing life of a local congregation in its recurring movement from world to word and back again. Yet it is only when this coming together happens that the Bible demonstrates its freedom to speak to the world in which people live.

Let us close where we started: the problem of ideology. We have seen that there is no simple correspondence between the ideological options of the contemporary world and those of the world of the Bible. Further, we have seen that although the Bible is not ideologically neutral, neither is it an ideological unity. The Bible does not prescribe an ideology for our time in any simple and direct way.

Yet we live in a world where crucial ideological issues are at stake. How are we to live in a world and to mold the future of a world in crisis—a world divided between rich and poor, oppressor and oppressed, powerful and powerless? And what does theological *praxis* have to do with it? How do we choose our options with theological responsibility?

These questions can be answered only in the *doing of theology*. An ideological choice which could be specified *a priori* would simply bind the Bible once again to ideological bondage. It is only in the commitment to hear and to do that the Bible can demonstrate its relevance to the world we inhabit.

6

JOSEPH L. HARDEGREE, JR.

Bible Study for Marxist Christians: The Book of Hosea

Marxist Christians committed to Bible study will need to formulate their own sociopolitical identity and to engage the biblical text with the realization that they may find no immediate point of contact with some biblical texts, negative contact with others, and constructive encounter with yet others. Openness to clarification and change in political and religious theory and practice will characterize the mind set of such Bible study.

Instead of "canned" summaries of the meaning of the Bible, groups need to pose their own questions, gather their own resources, and struggle together for a meaning that matters to them. How this process might be carried through is illustrated with preparatory materials and questions concerning the Book of Hosea.

Reprinted with minor revisions from *The Bible and Liberation: Political and Social Hermeneutics,* 1st ed., ed. N. K. Gottwald and A. C. Wire (Berkeley: Community for Religious Research and Education [Radical Religion], 1976), pp. 166–73.

PART I
GENERAL CONSIDERATIONS FOR BIBLE STUDY

The Necessity for Defining Who We Are

It is a mistake for us to assume that we can enter into the study of the Bible as if we were not particular people in a definite history. Nevertheless, that seems to be the assumption, usually unexamined, that people commonly make. The idea appears to be that we should, as much as possible, seek *tabula rasa* mentalities in order to be fully receptive to the Bible's "true message." Such an approach is deceptive.

We all bring our own agendas to the study of the Bible. These agendas affect everything from our approach to the Bible in the beginning to the "truth" we see in the end. As long as these agendas remain hidden from us, as long as we do not investigate our underlying assumptions, then our study is most likely to result in little more than a proof texting of our preconceptions.

But if we begin by thinking about who we are, what we believe in and live by, and especially what our political commitments and goals are, then Bible study can begin to take on dimensions of reality. On this basis it becomes possible to make a *comparative study* of what we believe and the beliefs expressed in various parts of the biblical material.

The study of the Bible becomes real in those moments of perception of the similarities and differences between ourselves and whatever segment of the Bible we happen to be studying. Through our collective meditations about these moments our own insights can be challenged, deepened, and, perhaps, changed.

Here I shall focus on the task of self-definition in the political sense. Coming as we do out of a religious milieu in which the personal and the psychological have been overemphasized, we should now begin to underline the social and political. We also live in an age when problems of revolutionary social change must be dealt with. I believe it would be a retreat from responsibility to seek escape into a personal, privatized religion when society's contradictions have grown so acute.

We begin, therefore, by declaring our politics and trying to sort out what that means. At least three things might be said by Marxists, for example, at the beginning:

1. Marxism is *the* critique of our present political-economic system and what is wrong with that system. We must push for clarity about what *is* wrong and how we, and everybody else, are affected by it.

2. Marxism presents an alternative to the present order: Socialism replacing capitalism. What kind of society do we expect this socialism to be?

3. Marxism is a revolutionary theory and practice for social transforma-

tion. How do we plan to get from where we are now to where we hope to be?

These suggestions are meant to be illustrative of how we might begin the process of self-definition. I acknowledge that such a process may well be more extensive than, and may not necessarily start from, the above.

What We Expect to Find in the Bible

Broadly speaking, there are three results we should expect from our Bible study. The first of these is *no result* at all. It is always the case that, at any given time, parts of the Bible are not relevant to the present situation. Sometimes, of course, a genuine relevance may be latently present if we but dig a little deeper. But the Bible records a very long time span and a multitude of sociopolitical situations and human possibilities. Many situations in the Bible are sufficiently different from our own that it is difficult or impossible to have a true encounter with them. At any given moment, some parts of the Bible have nothing to say to us.

The Christian contribution to North American society will, no doubt, take on a different form after a socialist revolution. What will need to be struggled against and what will need to be supported then will be different from what they are now. When that happens our spiritual map will be rearranged and so will the Bible. We and the Bible change with the dialectic of history. What speaks to us now may not speak to us then. What has nothing to say to us today may be the primary message for tomorrow.

A second result grows out of the fact that there are parts of the Bible we can only understand in a *negative* sense. If we take ourselves and our times seriously, we can only conclude that the writers of certain passages were in error. We may be wrong, certainly, in some of our judgments about them. But even with proper precaution we must be prepared to accept the reality of aspects of the Bible with which we disagree.

An example is the masculo-centric language and general male-chauvinist attitudes we find in the Bible. The Bible must not be forgiven at this point; it must be defeated. How this is to be done is not yet entirely clear. For the present we must be firm in our argument against such evils or limitations as they are found in the Bible, for example, refusing to use any such offending passages in liturgical expressions without rewording them into language that shows full appreciation for women as well as men.

Fortunately, a third result is possible or we would not be doing Bible study at all. There are sections that allow for a *genuine encounter.* Sometimes these lead to a deepening and, perhaps, a re-nuancing of what we already know and believe. At other times we may be led to change our opinions when confronted by a different perspective. We also will, on occasion, be challenged by ideas that appear to grow out of experiences similar to our own but which lead to different conclusions than we have previously drawn. The important thing is not to determine which view is correct, but to use the optional answer as creative ''space'' within which we may reconsider our own decisions and commitments. We must never become so tied to dogma (either religious or political) that our theory and practice are not open to change.

Bible Study as a Collective Effort

I have already said that the concept of Christianity as individualistic piety must be rejected. Our study, therefore, should be basically a social, not a private, endeavor, especially if our purpose is to strengthen group efforts toward political transformation. In any event, it is only by centering our study in the midst of our collective life, sharing and mutually supporting one another, that we shall discover the widest possible range of help available to us in Bible study.

It is very important that we constantly struggle against all ideologies that seek to divide us and require us to define ourselves in terms of competition and separation. The content of the Bible is not just about individuals, it is about the human condition, about societies, about history: both under judgment and with possibilities for redemption. Personal Bible study, as a main emphasis, is contradictory to all that Christianity (and socialism) stand for.

Two exceptions are immediately recognized. One is the necessity for private Bible study as *preparation for* group study and as *follow-up of* group study. The important thing is to remember which is primary and which is secondary. The other exception is "emergency" situations such as being in prison or other forms of isolation. One may or may not wish to engage in Bible study during those times, but Christians and others often derive benefit from the Bible under those circumstances. (Huey P. Newton and Nestor Paz are two recent examples.)

Formulating the Right Questions

Part of our preparation for Bible study is a relatively precise formulation of what it is we are looking for. This question divides into two parts: (1) What do we *look for?* and (2) What do we *look at* in order to find it? Unless we clarify these questions we tend to overlook many things that would be helpful to us.

Recently I was involved in an academic course on the Old Testament prophets. Our principal concern was to discover the "social location" of each prophet, assuming that this would be helpful to our understanding of the prophetic messages. At one class meeting a young black woman brought to our attention certain problems in the prophet Jeremiah dealing with black people (Ethiopians from the land of Cush). By doing so she opened up possibilities for understanding that I (and, I think, most of the class) had overlooked in a fairly careful reading of the same material. By formulating the question of racism, we discovered biblical material of real interest to us that we previously had missed. (Read the twelfth chapter of Numbers with an appreciation for the delicious irony in verse ten.)

During the same course we attempted to discover the social and political situation of each prophet. Part of this meant giving special attention to direct and indirect references to political and economic conditions. Another part involved reading background and reference materials which helped to "flesh out" what we found in the Bible. I discovered that my understanding and appreciation for the *theology* of each prophet grew in direct proportion to my increasing understanding of the "real world" within which the prophet worked and spoke. By *looking at* the society, we better saw what we were *looking for,* i.e., the prophet's message and program.

Background Materials

All serious Bible study must take advantage of the tools that have been developed for our use. What we need and how we use it requires careful consideration. It seems to me that there could be a great deal more conversation among Christians who wish to make the Bible a part of their lives and biblical scholars whose job it is to provide the help needed.

One thing we do *not* need very much of is what is called "exposition." We do not need to be told what the Bible means. It is our job to discover varying possibilities of meaning. At the most, an occasional sharing of meaning interpretations from other collective Bible study groups might be helpful as examples of what can be done. Most presentations of "meaning," however, tend to short-circuit a process we should be doing ourselves.

We also need scholars who are prepared to admit the ideological nature of doing scholarship and are willing to make their commitment toward a humane and just socialist revolution foundational for the work they are doing. In short, we need more Marxist biblical scholars who are willing to seek clarity about who they are, politically and socially, and who are also willing to seek new ways of working together to help create the proper materials we need.

It seems to me that there is a real gap in Bible study materials of the sort needed. On the one hand, when serious Bible scholars write books and articles, even when they are trying to write for general audiences, either they are way above the heads of ordinary people or they offer generalizations about "what the Bible means." On the other hand, a great deal of lay Bible study guide material is so much pap. It is an insult to the intelligence of serious Christians and has as much depth as floor wax. The helpful middle ground between scholars writing for one another (which is certainly legitimate) and "popular" trash would be a literature of "tools for better Bible analysis." Some of these tools would include the following:

1. Political-social-economic histories which help us to place each part of the Bible in its total context. Additionally, we need indications of where the evidence comes from in order that we may make some judgments about the use of evidence in the writing of these histories.

2. Literary histories (including form criticism, tradition history, and redaction history) of each part of the Bible, together with information about

both the original speakers and writers and the later editors, as far as can be determined, along with the evidence mentioned above.

3. A strong element of class analysis in both of the above.

4. Special studies of particular concerns within limited parts of the Bible (such as "eschatology" among the prophets) and general histories of particular aspects of the Bible such as those dealing with women, blacks, etc.

5. Explanatory notes about obscure references.

6. Extensive cross-references of biblical material both for similar and for contrary passages.

Obviously, much of this has already been done although usually in forms not readily accessible to lay people. Other parts of the task imply further discussions with biblical scholars about what we expect from them and what they expect from us. This discussion between scholars and lay readers is long overdue.

Theology and Ideology

The word "ideology" has already been used and needs some clarification in order for me to make my final point.

Popular usage of this word usually assumes a negative definition of "false consciousness." Ideology is understood to be the distorted understandings of reality which particular power groups in society have a vested interest in perpetuating. This definition is essentially correct and is a helpful concept to people striving for socialist revolution.

However, there is another tradition about ideology which also may be helpful to us in our Bible study. Mao Tse-tung has written:

> In class society everyone lives as a member of a particular class, and every kind of thinking, without exception, is stamped with the brand of a class.[1]

We stand for active ideological struggle.[2]

Mao is using "ideology" in a nonpejorative general sense to stand for the particular point-of-view toward reality each person has. It is not a question of whether or not one has an ideology. Everyone does. The question is: What is your ideology? Does it represent the interests of the ruling class, maintaining the status quo? Or is it, perhaps, the petty-bourgeois mentality, somewhere in the middle of the various social contradictions? Or does it represent the interests of the oppressed for whom the system must be transformed into socialism if their basic problems are to be solved?

It is this meaning of ideology that I am using when I suggest that particular attention must be paid in Bible study to theology as ideology. Every part of the Bible represents a point of view. Our central task must be to try to determine what that is. Sometimes it is expressed in the words or actions of God.

At other times it is revealed in the particular way a story is narrated or in the selection process used in writing a particular history.

Traditionally this has been called "theology." I am proposing that it be called ideology, or, at least, "theological ideology." The trouble with calling it theology only is that this lends itself to concepts of timeless truth over and above historical reality. We are not interested in the arrangement of the Platonic forms; we are interested in what is to be done. By understanding biblical theological ideology as timely perception rather than timeless truth we can engage in a real conversation with the Bible. For a little while, at least, this concept of ideology, used in a positive sense, may be helpful to this end of grasping theology as timely truth.

Transition

This concludes the discussion on method for the moment. The problem shifts from theory to practice. The following section uses the prophet Hosea as an example of how to gather and coordinate preparatory materials for Bible study.

We should keep in mind that theory and practice have a continuing dialectical relationship with one another. We need to sort out and evaluate on a regular basis what our preconceptions and methodologies are. It is only as we try these out in actual experience that we can gain a proper perspective for evaluating and changing our preconceptions and methodologies.

A document such as this should be considered a working paper. It should be revised on a regular basis to incorporate new and better ideas that arise out of the "practice" of the people.

Many of the sources suggested here were provided by Professor Norman Gottwald for his class on "The Social Location of Israelite Prophecy and the Continuing Prophetic Tradition" (at the Graduate Theological Union, Berkeley, California, Fall quarter, 1975). Admittedly, sitting in such a course facilitates the task of putting together Bible study proposals. Many Bible study groups will not have such easily available resources.

At the same time, this may serve as one example of a model of the kind and arrangement of materials we would ask biblical scholars to provide for us. Perhaps the emerging trend of "biblical sociology" will help solve some of these problems. Nevertheless, we should not be afraid to try to dig out our own resources when "professional" help is not readily available. "Self reliance" can work in all fields, even this one!

PART II
STUDY MATERIALS FOR THE PROPHET HOSEA

Introduction

The following is offered as an example of the kind of materials Marxist-Christians, and other socially committed Christians, need to engage in Bible study relevant to their political commitment. It presupposes that the majority will not have formal theological training.

The additional readings suggested are intended to be helpful but not absolutely necessary. Perhaps various members of the group might choose from among those suggested and report their readings to the others. The above does not apply to the biblical parallel readings. It is strongly recommended that these be read by all members of the group as necessary preparation for the study of Hosea.

Later Additions to Hosea

While debate is not entirely closed, most scholars agree that some or all of the references to Judah were added by later editors, including the following: 1:7; 1:11a; 4:15; 5:5b; 6:11a; 8:14b; and 10:11b, as probably also the reference to "David their king" in 2:5. The final verse (14:9) is widely recognized as a later "wisdom style" addition.

Biblical Parallels

1. *2 Kings 14:23-18:12.* This section is the basic historical source within the Bible for Israel (the northern kingdom) during the time of Hosea. It begins with the reign of Jeroboam II, during whose last days it is possible that Hosea began his public activity, and ends with the fall of Samaria, which occurred about the time Hosea's work was concluded.

2. *Amos.* Amos and Hosea should actually be studied together since they were both active in the northern kingdom at approximately the same time, with Amos preceding Hosea. Even though Amos prophesied somewhat earlier than Hosea, mainly during the stable and "prosperous" reign of Jeroboam II, he tells us much more than Hosea about the general economic and social distresses suffered by the under classes. The problems pressing down on the poor certainly did not get any better and probably got worse during Hosea's time.

3. *Numbers 25.* In Hosea 9:10 there is a reference to Baal-peor, which probably refers to the event narrated in Numbers 25. A second possible reference to this incident and/or to Baal worship in general is in Hosea 4:13-14. A suggestive interpretation of the Numbers story as a religious response to bubonic plague is provided by George E. Mendenhall *(The Tenth Generation).*[3]

4. *Jeremiah 2-4.* A century later, Jeremiah was influenced by the tradition of Hosea's prophecy. Jeremiah 2-6 is probably from the earliest period of the prophet's activity. Chapters 2-4:4 should be read *after* your study of Hosea to see how Jeremiah adopts and adapts some of the ideas of Hosea.

The Political History During Hosea's Time

1. Hosea and Amos were the only two classical[4] prophets to function in the northern kingdom of Israel instead of the southern kingdom of Judah. Amos

was said to be a native of Tekoa, in Judah, whereas Hosea was a native of Israel.

2. Hosea's public activity is usually dated either from toward the end or from shortly after the long and relatively stable reign of Jeroboam II (786–746) and continued to about the time of the fall of Samaria (721), which ended the existence of the kingdom of Israel.

3. After the death of Jeroboam II, the general political history of Israel is dominated by two developments: political intrigues and royal assassinations, and increasing military threat from and eventual take-over by the Assyrian Empire, notably under the leadership of Tiglath-pileser III (744–727).

When Jeroboam II died he was succeeded by his son Zechariah (746–745) who lasted only six months before he was murdered by Shallum. Zechariah was the last king of the Jehu dynasty, referred to in Hosea 1:4.

Shallum (745) lasted one month and was murdered by Menahem (745–738), who was the only king of Israel after Jeroboam II to die a natural death while still in power.

He was followed by his son, Pekahiah (738–737), who was murdered by an army officer, Pekah (737–732), who, in turn, was murdered by Hoshea (732–724). When Hoshea withheld tribute from Assyria he was deposed and imprisoned. During his imprisonment and the long siege of Samaria, leading to the city's fall in 721, Israel had no functioning king.

After a period of relative weakness the Assyrian Empire had once again grown large and powerful under the leadership of Tiglath-pileser III, who is sometimes referred to in the Bible as Pul. Beginning with Menahem, the kingdom of Israel was forced to pay a heavy tribute to Assyria. Pekah formed an alliance with Syria and tried to get Judah to join in a general revolt against Assyria. Judah refused, Pekah was defeated, and large parts of Israel were divided into three Assyrian provinces.

Hoshea was probably helped to power by Tiglath-pileser but when his patron died he made an alliance with Egypt in order to attempt another revolt. Shalmaneser V (726–722), Tiglath-pileser's son and successor, quickly forced Hoshea to capitulate, deported him, and began the three-year siege of Samaria. Shalmaneser's successor, Sargon II (721–705), finally defeated Samaria (721), deported the ruling class and brought a large number of settlers from other parts of the empire to colonize what had formerly been Israel. These colonists mixed with the Israelites who remained to form the so-called Samaritans.

4. An excellent integrated narrative of the whole period (with some differences in the dating) is in Norman K. Gottwald's book *All the Kingdoms of the Earth.*[5] Abundant material may be recovered piecemeal by reading the following articles, in order, in *The Interpreter's Dictionary of the Bible,*[6] Jeroboam (no. 2); Zechariah (no. 14); Shallum (no. 1); Menahem; Pekahiah; Pekah; Hoshea (no. 4); and Tiglath-pileser III.

Cult Practices

1. In addition to Hosea's animosity toward the royal politics of his time, he was strongly upset over the Canaanitic cult practices which had been integrated into Yahweh worship as well as having a very widespread life of their own among the people. Essentially it was a fertility cult which included ritual prostitution by both sexes and sometimes human sacrifices. Wine was often used to help induce ecstatic frenzies. (See the article on "Fertility Cults" in *The Interpreter's Dictionary of the Bible.*)

2. Roland de Vaux in *Ancient Israel,*[7] argues that Canaanite religious practices and those of Israel were never so dissimilar as one might assume. Nevertheless, Hosea expressed very strong judgments against such practices during the last years of Israel's existence. What was he getting at?

The Social Situation

Edward Neufeld describes the social process going on in monarchic Israel in this way:

> The following basic factors were mainly responsible for the growing economic tension and social cleavages. The geographical division of land ownership according to which the lowlands were inhabited by the wealthier groups of the population, while the stony highlands and the plateaus were held by the mass of poor peasants most of whom had to seek employment during the winter months; the transition from nomadic existence to a sedentary agricultural life, which, among others, produced, even in the days of Abimelech and Jephthah, a landless element; the growth of urbanization which undermined old ideas of kinship; and the transformation and, in particular, the expansion from a barter into a money economy which destroyed small landowners. The economic and social differentiation and cleavages were greatly speeded up by the domestic policy of the monarchy of centralizing life in cities. This changed the old system of the Hebrew organization causing detribalization, many hardships, unemployment and extreme poverty.[8]

Add to this a realization of the rapid deterioration of this oppressive system during the last two decades of Israel's existence and you begin to get a picture of what was happening to the people during Hosea's time.

A Class Analysis of Hosea

Who was Hosea? What were his class origins and inclinations? Who supported him and who opposed him? My purpose here is not to answer these questions but rather to give some background and some suggestions for how study groups may approach them.

1. The place to begin in background reading is with Max Weber.[9] Weber contends that the prophets were essentially "genteel intellectuals," outside of official circles, who were faithful to an older, more primitive, pre-monarchic religious tradition. He also calls them "demagogues" in their political activity, saying they were not "champions of democratic ideals" nor did they succeed with the peasantry. They were against the kingship altogether, although they were in the midst of so much political strife they could not help but be identified with one faction or another. Weber calls their politics "utopian" partly because they were dependent on a "nomadic ideal" and partly because they advocated total dependence on Yahweh rather than on human alliances and revolutions.

2. Peter Berger carries on the discussion begun by Weber[10] by arguing that the prophets were reforming radicals from within official cultic circles rather than alienated intellectuals on the periphery. James G. Williams[11] takes issue with Berger by insisting that it is difficult and perhaps impossible to determine the prophet's social location on the basis of extant writings and that, in any case, their attacks on the cult largely show that they were not cultic figures.

3. Further readings about Hosea include: Gerhard von Rad, *Old Testament Theology,*[12] Georg Fohrer, *Introduction to the Old Testament,*[13] and the article on "Hosea" in *The Interpreter's Dictionary of the Bible,* which is especially helpful for an historical overview of the varying interpretations of Hosea.

4. Some clues to the prophet's class connections within the book of Hosea itself include the following:

1:4–5	In forecasting the fall of the Jehu dynasty was Hosea involved in palace politics?
3:2	Note purchase price of a wife; does this indicate his economic standing?
5:1	Criticism of priests and kings who are "responsible for justice."
6:9	Priests are like robbers.
7:3	People accused as severely as kings.
12:7–8	Opposes dishonest accumulation of merchant wealth.

Hosea's Marriage(s)

1. There is disagreement whether Hosea was married to one woman twice or to two different women. The article on "Hosea" in *The Interpreter's Dictionary of the Bible* gives much information about the standard interpretations of Hosea's marriages.

2. R. E. Clements[14] argues that this story from Hosea's personal life must

be interpreted in light of the general message of Hosea and not the other way around. The prophet's message determined the symbolic actions.

3. Another way of looking at the relationship between Hosea's marriage(s) and his message is to note that he understands his personal situation as being grounded in a larger historical phenomenon. Each is related to the other. Does this suggest anything to us?

4. Hosea's wife (or wives) was probably involved in cult prostitution, a generally honored social activity among Canaanites, as also in some Israelite circles. Both for her and for Israel as a whole the term "harlotry" is frequently used and condemned. How helpful or destructive is Hosea on the situation of women?

Eschatology and/or Retribalization

1. In a very good article on "Prophecy and Eschatology," T. C. Vriezen summarizes the development of eschatology in the writing prophets, showing the place of each in an overall development. In his section on Hosea, Vriezen argues:

a. The judgment of Yahweh "cannot be the end but through it salvation is obtained."
b. This judgment is an act of "God in his [sic] love."
c. "Ultimately God will grant restoration."
   This will include:
   (1) Peace among animals.
   (2) Destruction of implements of war.

Vriezen adds: The principal new elements (in Hosea) are the positiveness with which God's judgment is announced and the absoluteness of the necessity of conversion; it is only through the judgment and this conversion that the restoration can break through, and this can only come to pass by a miracle of God.[15]

2. Another valuable resource on eschatology in the prophets is Gerhard Von Rad.[16]

3. Norman K. Gottwald has become one of the chief proponents of the thesis that during the two and one-half centuries preceding the monarchy (1250–1000) Israel existed as an "egalitarian society" in a "liberated existence" of "re-tribalization" in Canaan—a form of social life by no means simply culturally derived from pastoral nomadism. At that time its social existence and its theological formulations were based upon a unique, relatively simple, and highly just social order. Gottwald puts it this way:

I propose a societal model for early Israel along the following lines: Early Israel was a slowly converging and constellating cluster of rebellious and dissenting Canaanite peoples distinguished by an anti-statist form of social organization with de-centralized leadership. This Israelite "devolution" or "winding down" from the city-state form of social organization took the shape of a "re-tribalization" movement among agriculturalists and pastoralists organized in economically self-sufficient extended families with egalitarian access to basic resources. Israel's religion, which had intellectual and cultic foundations in ancient Near Eastern-Canaanite religion, was idiosyncratic or mutational in a manner that its society was idiosyncratic and mutational, i.e., one integrated divine being existed for one integrating and egalitarianly structured people. Israel became that segment of Canaan which wrested sovereignty from another segment of Canaan in the interests of village-based tribally-oriented "low politics" over against city-state hierarchic "high politics."[17]

The question this raises concerning the prophets is whether or not the "utopia" (Weber) they were seeking was actually a call for a strengthening or renewal—perhaps after destruction of the state—of the re-tribalization process which had seriously lapsed under the monarchy. Is this what eschatology (in Hosea, at least) is all about? A similar approach is made by George E. Mendenhall in *The Tenth Generation,* and in an article, "The Monarchy."[18]

God Talk

According to José Miranda,[19] to "know God" in the Bible is to "know justice." He quotes Hosea 4:1b–2 as one of his first examples (p. 45). How well does this conception—that God's presence is justice happening in the world—hold up in the "God talk" of Hosea?

NOTES

1. Mao Tse-tung, *Selected Works,* 4 vols. (New York: China Books, 1961–1965), Vol. 1 (1924–1937), p. 296.
2. Ibid., 2:31.
3. George E. Mendenhall, *The Tenth Generation: The Origins of the Biblical Tradition* (Baltimore: Johns Hopkins University Press, 1973), ch. 4.
4. "Classical" refers to those prophets whose speeches and writings are collected in biblical books bearing their names. The "nonclassical" or "non-writing" prophets Elijah and Elisha had been active in the northern kingdom before Amos and Hosea.
5. Norman K. Gottwald, *All the Kingdoms of the Earth: Israelite Prophecy and International Relations in the Ancient Near East* (New York: Harper & Row, 1964), pp. 119–46.
6. George A. Buttrick, *The Interpreter's Dictionary of the Bible,* 4 vols. (Nashville: Abingdon, 1962).
7. Roland de Vaux, *Ancient Israel: Its Life and Institutions,* Vol. 1: *Social Institu-*

tions, Vol. 2. *Religious Institutions* (New York: McGraw-Hill, 1972), pp. 438–40.

8. Edward Neufeld, "The Emergence of a Royal-Urban Society in Ancient Israel," *Hebrew Union College Annual* 31 (1960): 31–53; this quotation, pp. 44–45.

9. Max Weber, *Ancient Judaism* (New York: Free Press, 1952), chaps. 11 and 12.

10. Peter Berger, "Charisma and Religious Innovation: The Social Location of Israelite Prophecy," *American Sociological Review* 28 (1963): 940–50.

11. James G. Williams, "The Social Location of Israelite Prophecy," *JAAR* 37 (1969): 153–65.

12. Gerhard von Rad, *Old Testament Theology,* 2 vols. (New York: Harper & Row, 1962, 1965), 2: 129–30, 138–46.

13. Georg Fohrer, *Introduction to the Old Testament,* 10th ed., trans. David Green (Nashville: Abingdon, 1968), pp. 418–25.

14. R. E. Clements, *Prophecy and Tradition* (Atlanta: John Knox, 1975), pp. 29ff.

15. T. C. Vriezen, "Prophecy and Eschatology," *VTSup* 1 (1953): 199–229; esp., p. 207.

16. Von Rad, *Old Testament Theology,* 2:99–125.

17. Norman K. Gottwald, "Domain Assumption and Societal Models in the Study of Pre-Monarchic Israel," *VTSup,* Edinburgh Congress volume (1975): 93–94.

18. Mendenhall, *Tenth Generation,* ch. 1 and 6; idem, "The Monarchy," *Int* 29 (1975): 155–70.

19. José Miranda, *Marx and the Bible: A Critique of the Philosophy of Oppression* (Maryknoll, N.Y.: Orbis Books, 1974).

7

GEORGE V. PIXLEY

Biblical Embodiments of God's Kingdom: A Study Guide for the Rebel Church

The kingdom of God is always presented in the Bible as God's rule in relation to some particular "historical project," or sociohistoric embodiment, of which six such projects or embodiments are described:

1. God's kingdom in the religious cult of the temple

2. God's kingdom in the early intertribal peasant revolution against Canaanite city-states

3. God's kingdom in the monarchy

4. God's kingdom in the priestly or hierocratic society

5. God's kingdom in Jesus' attack on the temple economy and its tie to the Roman slave society

6. God's kingdom in the congregations of Christians spread over the Greco-Roman world

Some of these forms of God's kingdom were oppressive, or at least ambig-

---

Reprinted from George V. Pixley, *God's Kingdom. A Guide for Biblical Study* (with Foreword by Harvey G. Cox, pp. viii–xi) (Maryknoll, N.Y.: Orbis Books, 1981), pp. 1–9, 101–105.

uous, in their original settings, while others were highly liberative, especially the kingdom of God in tribal Israel and in the strategy of Jesus.

Working class people in Latin America today are critically assessing the Bible, so often used against them, to determine the adequacy of Christian faith and its sources as a contribution to effective liberation from sociopolitical oppression. The various ideological roots and uses of the Bible must be brought to light. Analyses and strategies for liberation, which are not provided by the Bible, must grow from our own experience. Theological production will become the work of Christians engaged in social struggle and in struggle with the biblical text.

FOREWORD
BY HARVEY G. COX

"My kingdom is not of this world," said Jesus to Pilate at his trial. And what a twisted trail of confused misinterpretations and questionable applications have followed in the path of this single text. If Jesus did not intend his kingdom to come in this world, then why did he so boldly confront the rulers of this world in Jerusalem when he might have remained safely secluded in Galilee? Why did he invade the temple, the political and economic power center of his time and place, causing such a stir that the remaining events of Holy Week—his arrest, trial, condemnation, and execution—became inevitable? Why does the last book of the New Testament confidently foretell that it is the kingdoms of *this* world that "shall become the kingdoms of our God and his Christ"? Above all, why does Jesus instruct his disciples to pray for the coming of God's kingdom "on earth as it is in heaven"?

Throughout Christian history the argument over just how earthly the kingdom of God is supposed to be has been fought along quite predictable lines. Those who are rich or content or powerful or comfortable here and now prefer a kingdom to come that will not alter our earthly reality very soon or very much. They like it the way it is now. They have devised theologies of inward, figurative, or post-historical kingdoms, or kingdoms that begin only after death. No wonder. The powerful would prefer their "casting down" that Mary sings of in the Magnificat to happen in some other world, not this one. The rich, reading of the woes that Jesus promises them in Luke's Gospel, have an equally understandable preference that such woes be inward and psychological, something a skilled therapist can help them cope with. No outward or worldly woes, please.

The disinherited, on the other hand, have frequently insisted on a much more commonsensical and straightforward reading of what Jesus was saying and doing. When he speaks of emptying the prisons, they refuse to reduce this to "spiritual prisons," since the cell blocks they and their friends and loved ones languish in are made of stone and steel. When he talks about cancelling debts, they think first of all not of infractions of social decorum but of their unpaid bills and the hot breath of their creditors. When he speaks of filling the hungry, they think not of communion wafers, but of rice and beans and bread: "Thy kingdom . . . on earth."

Who has been right and who wrong in this age-old hermeneutical class struggle? Not surprisingly, since most scholars and theologians for most of history have worked for the privileged and not for the poor, the weight of scribal evidence seems to be on the side of the wealthy and well-situated. Books and articles and monographs have piled up over the centuries to document and demonstrate the transcendental or interior character of the kingdom Jesus said was at hand. The theological ideologues of the ruling elites have poured contempt on the "crude," and "literalistic," or—still worse—the "utopian" wrong-headedness of the poor's demand that the promised milk and honey should be something hungry people can actually eat and drink.

The elite version of what the kingdom means has held sway, with several important exceptions, for centuries of Christian theological history. But recently it has come in for a serious challenge. This book by George Pixley is at once eloquent evidence and an erudite expression of that challenge. Pixley has not only looked at the issue through the eyes of the poor (an angle of vision made possible by his life of work in Latin America) but has utilized the most refined tools of critical scholarship to lay out his case. No thoughtful reader can ever again dismiss the interpretation he advances as simplistic or unlettered. To my mind, in fact, he clinches the case: from now on those who take the traditional elite view of what the "kingdom of God" means in the Bible will have the burden of proof.

Perhaps in describing what Pixley has done one should use the word "inquiry" rather than "case." He is interested in something far more important and more profound than simply winning an argument. To his credit he does not want merely to prove his scholarly case against someone else's, the all-too-familiar contest in academic one-upmanship. Rather, what Pixley wants to do is to ask this question: "Is the kingdom of God preached by Jesus good news for the poor today?" His historical exploration of what Jesus and the movement around him meant by the kingdom of God is thus not just the leisurely pursuit of an antiquarian. It is a real question, urgently asked by millions of real people today. It is not by any means a rhetorical question, and, for Pixley, the answer is far from obvious. The book leaves the reader not with the comfortable feeling that a question has been decisively answered; rather it leaves one with the troubled feeling that a far more important question has been unavoidably asked.

"Not of this world?" What did Jesus mean? That in God's kingdom no one would "lord it over" others as he had said earlier? That God and not some worldly intermediary—Temple or Emperor—would rule in human hearts and communities? Whatever Jesus meant, Pixley believes that the question of whether the message of that reign is good news for the poor today must be answered on the plane of present historical and political engagement and not in the realm of past historical research, even research as skilled and as winsomely presented as his.

I have an advantage over the reader who is just picking up this splendid new contribution to the growing body of excellent biblical scholarship that is strengthening the liberation theology movement. Since Pixley has served as rector of the Baptist Seminary of Mexico where I have taught off and on during the past half decade, I discussed many of the ideas in this book while it was in the making. Even then I could see that Pixley, who is not only an accomplished biblical scholar but also a Christian with a burning commitment to the Latin American liberation struggle, was on to something important. Since receiving the galleys from the publisher several months back I have had a chance to share its ideas with students in my classes and seminars at Harvard. I can assure anyone who foresees using the book in such a setting that it goes over remarkably well. Inundated by scholarly books with little political relevance or with political ones that often lack scholarly depth, students find this volume a welcome surprise. It also helps students to see that even though, understandably, the leading voices in Latin American liberation theology are those of our Roman Catholic colleagues, still Protestants are beginning to play a vital role too. For all these and many more reasons it is a special joy for me to introduce this fine book—by one who is both *amigo* and *compañero*—to an English-speaking audience. My hope is that it will enable all its readers to take a bit more seriously what it is we are really asking for when we pray, "Thy kingdom come, on earth. . . . "

INTRODUCTION

The author was asked to write a word study of the biblical phrase "kingdom of God," and the present study is in response to that request. The genre of the biblical word study is well established and known to pastors and laypersons in the many Bible dictionaries in wide use among our churches. Studies of certain significant biblical words such as "love" (*agape*), "peace" (*shalom*), and "spirit" (*pneuma*) have played a role in Christian belief even at the parish level. No one can doubt the value of this kind of semantic investigation for the renewal of some of the key expressions in our Christian language, which had become stale through much use and abuse.

Nevertheless, we have learned in Latin America to be suspicious of the kind of idealism that seeks "true" concepts in their purity. Often behind the beauty and desirability of the concept in the abstract lies the intention to legitimate structures that in concrete history produce misery and oppression. No better example of this fatal disease of the mind can be found than the way in which "freedom" has been used to justify misery. In the name of freedom labor unions have been broken up (because they are said to distort the "free" play of the market by introducing "artificial" levels of wages). In the name of "scientific freedom" universities have refused to serve the needs of people, preferring to devote their research facilities to the novel and complicated machinery that interests the transnational corporations. In the name of professional freedom doctors struck against the Popular Unity government in Chile seeking the right to serve whom they chose (concealing the fact that they chose to serve those who could pay best). In the name of the freedom of the marketplace price controls have been resisted always and everywhere by merchants large and small. In principle, of course, nobody can be against the freedom of human persons. However, freedom or any other concept or value never encounters us in the abstract but rather in terms of some particular historical project. And in terms of that project it may contribute to the struggle for life and salvation, or it may serve merely to justify and conceal the destruction of life.

For this reason, our study of the biblical phrase "kingdom of God" begins with the suspicion that if it were investigated in its purity as "the biblical concept of the kingdom of God" it would be easily usable for purposes not favorable to the lives of God's people. We shall confirm in our study of the Bible that there is no "biblical concept" of the kingdom of God. That God, some God, however conceived, rules the world is a very widespread idea, and certainly not limited to the Bible. Within the Bible this idea is central. However, the idea has no existence in its purity as an abstraction. It must always find expression in some particular historical project, a project that may well exclude other projects that also claim to embody the kingdom of God. We would, then, give a fundamentally false impression if we did a study of the kingdom of God in the Bible in abstraction from the particular historical embodiments that that idea found. For a Christian people that wishes to follow Jesus in a particular historical circumstance, the historical embodiments of the idea are necessary for our guidance. We do not want to follow beautiful dreams that may exist only in our heads, but to find guidance for the way to a better world where we can live more fully as sons and daughters of our God.

We shall not study the phrase "kingdom of God," then, in order to identify a supposedly pure concept. We are not interested in concepts except as they serve to guide us toward salvation—real, concrete, historical salvation. What we seek with this study of the kingdom of God in the Bible is to know both how such a fundamental notion guided the people of Israel toward a free and just society and how it was used to submit the people of Israel to tyranny under Solomon. We shall see how God's kingdom was a call by Jesus to struggle for a better life for Galilean peasants, and how it became an unhistorical ideal for the unclassed peoples of the cities of Asia Minor and Greece. In other words, we shall see how the idea of God's kingdom was used in the Bible both for good (salvation) and for ill (oppression). We do so in full awareness of the historical struggles in which Christians in Latin America are engaged, and of the need to put our faith in the service of the historical redemption of our Latin American peoples.

In undertaking the study of the phrase "kingdom of God" we are not just looking at one among many biblical ideas. This is a foundational idea: The announcement of the imminence of the arrival of God's kingdom was the main content of Jesus' preaching. Everything Jesus said and did can be subsumed under his urgent conviction that the kingdom of God was at hand. Many studies have been devoted to clarifying exactly what he meant. But in general not enough attention has been given to the fact that Yahweh's kingdom is the seminal idea of the Old Testament, so that Jesus was not preaching something new, but announcing a hope with a long history in Israel. If it is true that we cannot understand the kingdom of God in abstraction from its concrete historical embodiments, it is also true that we cannot understand the first-century hopes pinned on it without understanding its particular history in Israel.

Palestine in the century that we now call the first of the Christian Era was one of the major centers of revolt against the empire that the Romans had built on slave labor. The inspiration for this rebellion came from the holy writings of the Jews. Yahweh's kingdom, proclaimed by the prophets, was the utopia that inspired peasant masses in their resistance to Roman domination. As one would expect in such a situation, several groups attempted to interpret the oppressed situation of the people, and each proposed its own strategy for overcoming that situation. Zealots, Essenes, Pharisees, and "Christians" all tried to channel the people's rebellion with the use of biblical categories. Only the Sadducees understood the tradition as a support for political accommodation with the authorities then in power.

Amidst these political currents appeared John, a desert prophet of Yahweh's kingdom. He was aware of the incipient movement that had gathered around the Galilean Jesus, and from jail he challenged him with the fundamental question: "Are you the one who is to come or shall we wait for another?" Jesus' answer provides a good entry to our subject:

> Go and tell John what you hear and see: the blind receive their sight and the lame walk, lepers are cleansed and the deaf hear, and the dead are raised up, and the poor have the good news preached to them [Matt. 11:4–5].

Good news for the poor! The Galilean Messiah interpreted his powerful works on the bodies of Palestinian poor men and women as the beginning of God's kingdom, which the prophets announced as salvation for the poor and vengeance on their oppressors (Ps. 146; Isa. 11:9; 61:1–3). Nevertheless, the solitary prophet was executed in his imprisonment, and shortly afterward the Galilean Messiah was also executed.

Jesus' death did not finish his movement. Out of that movement came the Christian church, which is still a factor in our history. However, we do not know whether this continuation was good or bad news for the poor to whom Jesus had announced a coming kingdom of justice and peace. Forty years later Mark wrote a "gospel" in the midst of the chaos of the Judeo-Roman

War (A.D. 66–70).¹ Recalling words of Jesus, he announced the near solution to all the people's aspirations: "Truly, I say to you, there are some standing here who will not taste death before they see the kingdom of God come with power" (Mark 9:1).

Yet in less than three hundred years the church born in a Palestine on fire with rebellion was embracing the Roman Empire under the leadership of the "Christian Emperor" Constantine. History would provide new expressions of this marriage between the hope of God's kingdom and the class societies of the world. When the Spanish Empire reached America in the sixteenth century, it was accompanied by a supporting Christian church. In the nineteenth and twentieth centuries, when United States imperialism penetrated into Latin America, it was accompanied by Protestant missions.

This tragic history cannot be brushed aside. It must be understood. Was it a betrayal of a potentially liberating rebel movement, or was the movement of Jesus the Messiah from its beginning a false announcement of freedom for the oppressed? Today in Latin America we are witnessing the birth of a rebel church that identifies with the struggles of oppressed people against their exploiters. It is essential for this struggle that we examine anew the sources of Christian faith. The Bible has often been used against the lives of ordinary working people. If this is not to happen again we must know our sources and their potential for good and for ill.

According to the Gospels, the people of Jerusalem initially received Jesus as the Messiah they had been awaiting. Surrounded by a multitude of jubilant well-wishers, Jesus and his following of Galileans entered the Temple to face the priestly hierarchy that was "doing business" there. In the short span of a week's time, the people of Jerusalem changed positions. When given a choice, they preferred the Zealot Barabbas to the Messiah Jesus of Nazareth.

We must seriously ask ourselves whether this crowd understood correctly its interests. Later history showed the limitations of the Zealot option. The multitudes followed the leadership of the Zealots into the war of 66–70 and saw Titus lead his legions into the city of Jerusalem and destroy its Temple. The Zealots, then, were not the answer. But would the crowd have done any better by choosing to follow Jesus? Would they have achieved freedom from Roman domination? Could the tragedy have been avoided that the Christian church has meant for the working peoples of the world? This matter is not of purely academic interest. The rebellious church that emerges from the Latin American people tries to join forces with the working people of the cities and the countryside against their oppressors—and also against a church that is allied to the oppressors. This strategy is valid only if it is possible to recover in the Bible a political and religious current that will give the lie to the church of the powerful and genuinely offer good news for ordinary working people. This is what is at stake in a study of the biblical history of the idea of God's kingdom.

But study alone will not be sufficient to answer so momentous a historical question. It is the hope of the author of this small book that it will motivate

Christian groups to study the Scriptures that inspired those defeated rebellions against the Roman Empire in search of guidance for the different struggles of our time. This is a new kind of Bible study. It is not an exercise of Christian devotion. Nor is it an objective, scientific, intellectual exercise. The Bible study we need must question our faith in the light of the strategic requirements of the struggle for life and freedom. The theme of God's kingdom is exciting because of its importance in the beginnings of the church and because many believe it is relevant to the struggle that we are today carrying on for a just social order. But we do not know that it is genuinely relevant. The author as a professional of biblical studies does not know. Collectively, we Latin American Christians do not know. Only the working people in their struggle for life will prove or disprove that the kingdom of God is good news for the poor. It is this vital concern that moves Christian people to investigate again God's kingdom in the Bible.

This study is divided for convenience into six parts. Each unit could be called an adventure of God's kingdom. That is, we want to study this idea historically, in its various embodiments. Only thus can we determine the advisability of striving for a new embodiment in our generation. The six chapters of our study are the following:

1. The celebration of Yahweh's kingdom in the cult as revealed in the Psalms and by the prophets. This is probably the least important incorporation of Yahweh's kingdom. But it is also the most religious one, and that closest to the beliefs of neighboring peoples. God was celebrated as king in the royal cult of Jerusalem, and the texts of this cult, the Psalms, had a lasting influence on the Jewish and Christian religions.

2. Having looked at the religious meaning of Yahweh's kingdom in monarchic times, we shall next study the role of that kingdom as the revolutionary project of the peasants of the Canaanite hills in the formation of the nation Israel. This is the first and normative incarnation of God's kingdom. All the later history of the idea must measure itself against this original historical expression.

3. The revolutionary project of Israel was after some two centuries domesticated into a class society not unlike those from which Israel had escaped in Egypt and Canaan. In this third chapter we shall document the use of God's kingdom as the official ideology of the Davidic state in the tenth to the sixth centuries before Christ.

4. When the Davidic monarchy was destroyed it was succeeded by a class society in which a priestly caste dominated the working people of the land. This hierocratic society also had a use for the idea of God's kingdom.

5. With the Zealots and with Jesus, God's kingdom again became the political project of justice and freedom for the working people of Palestine, and especially of Galilee. In the new context of a slave society, the attempt was made to again incarnate God's kingdom as a hope for the poor. After the period studied in the second chapter, this is second in importance in the biblical history of God's kingdom.

6. Finally, we shall see how God's kingdom was preached by the Christian successors of Jesus who had left the territory of Galilee where his historical vision had taken shape. Under the leadership of the missionary Paul, the kingdom became a spiritual kingdom, a shift of basic consequence for the church through the centuries.

We shall end by suggesting some tasks for today's Christian communities. This book is of necessity provisional and unfinished. It needs to be completed through the analyses and strategies of the people that still considers itself Christian even if it is not sure that this is good news. Even more, it needs to be completed by the struggle for life and justice for the working people of the world, a struggle that alone will show whether God's kingdom is a hopeful promise or a dangerous illusion.

To send forth a little book like this one, addressed to groups of churches, assumes that Christian people are capable of a critical study of their Scriptures. If this turns out not to be the case, we as Christians shall have little to offer a people that needs to criticize all its social foundations—economic, political, and cultural—since all have been converted into instruments of its oppression. . . .

WHAT IS TO BE DONE?

In abstract and general terms, God's kingdom means in the Bible a society of justice, equality, and abundance. In concrete terms, it directs different historical projects under different circumstances. At two seminal moments the kingdom meant liberation, a struggle against class systems that systematically exploited the working people of Israel.

First of all, in Canaan, to accept Yahweh as the king of Israel meant to repudiate the kings who were exploiting the productive villages and along with the kings to reject the religious superstructure that gave them legitimacy. For the rebellious peasants of Israel, God had revealed himself in Egypt as a liberator, and they found it impossible to worship Yahweh and also accept the kings who were exploiting and enslaving them. Inspired by this Yahweh, Canaanite peasants rose up and formed tribal alliances to face their exploiters. However, this project was subverted from within when David of Judah, in the name of Yahweh, founded a dynasty stronger and more powerful than those rejected by the tribes of Israel. In this new order, Yahweh's kingdom became the ideological support for the exploitation of working people.

In the first century of the Christian Era, under the impact of Roman oppression, God's kingdom once again became the inspiration for rebellion and the promise of liberation. Still, none of the strategies to make the kingdom a reality was successful. Jesus and his movement did not achieve the mass support needed to set in motion their historical project before it was cut off by Jesus' crucifixion. The Zealots had their moment of glory when they consolidated the rebel forces in an armed struggle, but they were defeated by the superior military power of Rome. And the Pharisees and their rabbinical successors have continued to wait for the kingdom for centuries. From the messianic Jesus movement there arose a universal, spiritual, and individualistic religion that offers inner salvation to oppressed men and women within various class systems.

These are the materials concerning God's kingdom with which we have to work. What real possibilities do they offer the poor in our day?

In the first place, this biblical investigation has placed tools in our hands for the necessary task of unmasking religion that conceals and justifies domination. We have learned how Yahweh's kingdom could be used as an ideological support for an oppressive regime in Israel. We have learned how, in the analysis made by the Jesus movement, the temple of Yahweh and its religion had become the principal enemies of the liberating kingdom of Yahweh. Then we saw how this rebellious message was deflected toward a religion that was individualistic, spiritualizing, and ahistorical. It was in this form that it was presented to the urban, uprooted working people of the empire. And this was done in the name of Jesus the Messiah and of the kingdom he proclaimed.

All of this should put us on guard against a preaching of a gospel that may not be good news. We will not find protection against this problem in biblical language or right doctrine. Even within the Bible, God's kingdom was exploited for quite different purposes. It is necessary to look critically at what is being proclaimed in our day as good news for the poor. We should learn to ask, ''What are its real consequences in history?'' The answer to this question can hardly be given in general terms. It must be formulated by each Christian group in its place, in the light of its historical juncture.

Even so, the general statement can safely be made that Protestant churches in Latin America have been the allies of imperialism. In order to penetrate traditional societies, monopoly capital has needed to break the bonds of solidarity and to create individuals who lead their lives as personal projects. For this it has found Protestantism useful, and we have often not seen how we were being used. Comparable judgments could be made of Catholic Christianity. Therefore, an important continuation of this study of the kingdom of God in the Bible will be the analysis within each group of the shape that the kingdom takes in *its* preaching and *its* practice.

In the second place, our biblical investigation shows the need for conjunctural analysis and the formulation of strategies of liberation based on it. Such strategies cannot be formulated in abstraction from an understanding of the mechanisms of oppression. Jesus and the Zealots formulated different strategies of liberation because they understood the conjuncture of first-century Palestine differently. We cannot know whether Jesus' strategy had more possibility of success than that of the Zealots. That is not what is important. Neither the one nor the other can be applied to our dependent capitalism. We must make an analysis of our situation in order to formulate relevant strategies of liberation. In doing so, we can count on a significant liberating tradition within our sacred texts. But the Bible will do neither our analyzing nor our strategizing. This is the task of Christian groups in their particular places.

The first task, that of unmasking the ideological uses of the "gospel," is a necessary preparation for the second task. These tasks must be carried out together with people committed to liberation who are not necessarily believers. In its original biblical expression, God's kingdom was for the poor and not for believers.

We take for granted that analysis and strategy will be part of a political practice of struggle for liberation. There remains a third task peculiar to the community of faith. This is the task of theological production. We need to articulate theoretically the nature and work of the God who freed Israel from the Egyptian Pharaoh and from the Canaanite kings. This involves criticism of a theology done for a dominating church. Over against the self-sufficient creator God of a church that felt itself mistress of society and at peace with the natural world, we must affirm a God who is historical and who actively strives to arouse the oppressed and to destroy their oppressors. Classical philosophy and theology must be examined for its class content. This is a somewhat technical task for which we shall need persons well equipped biblically and philosophically. But, to be valid, the task must be carried out in close contact with working people who are struggling for their liberation.

Only experience will tell if the biblical kingdom of God can be truly good news for the poor, the exploited workers of Latin America. There seem to be some positive elements here, but only their incarnation in effective strategies of liberation will confirm that this is not a matter of illusions, of stones when the people ask for bread. The liberation of the people of Latin America is imposed on us today, and for those who believe in God's kingdom we have a divine ally in our struggle. History must say whether our faith is well placed. "The proof of the pudding is in the eating."

NOTE

1. The tradition of the Fathers of the Church and the majority opinion among modern interpreters is that Mark wrote his Gospel in Rome. Irenaeus, bishop of Lyons, informs us (*Adv. haer.* III, 1.2) that this happened after the death of Peter (A.D. 64), and in this the chaotic situation of Jerusalem described in Mark 13 offers confirmation. Most commentators think that the Gospel was written during the war (66–70) but before its final outcome. Some, among them Wellhausen, Brandon, and Belo, consider that Mark 13 already presupposes a knowledge of the destruction of the temple and that therefore the correct date of composition is a little after 70. With Werner Georg Kümmel we can conclude cautiously: "Since there are no decisive arguments for a year before or after 70, we must be content to conclude that Mark was written around 70" (*Introduction to the New Testament* [Nashville: Abingdon, 1966], p. 71).

8

CARLOS MESTERS

The Use of the Bible in Christian Communities of the Common People

The typical grass-roots Bible study setting among Brazilian Catholics is a community of people meeting around the Bible who introduce the concrete reality of their own situation into the discussion. Using language studded with the pungent speech of the people themselves, the author notes obstacles they face and how they surmount them: inability to read, slavish literalism, differing conceptions of time, dependence on the learned expert, lack of tact in pastors and teachers, erudite language, and fundamentalist dogmatism.

As the ordinary Christian Bible readers gain in confidence to claim the Bible as their own, dislocations or shifts in interpretation take place: from an upper class toward a lower class perspective, from biblical text to real life, from a text enclosed in itself to a text with meaning for us, from an abstract individualistic understanding to a community sense, from neutrality to taking sides in society, and from overly spiritualized concepts to the concrete meanings and demands of faith in a present lived situation.

Reprinted from Sergio Torres and John Eagleson, eds., *The Challenge of Basic Christian Communities,* Papers from the International Ecumenical Congress of Theology, February 20–March 2, 1980, São Paulo, Brazil (Maryknoll, N.Y.: Orbis Books, 1981), pp. 197–210.

119

PRELIMINARY OBSERVATIONS

Limitations of This Report

The information I am going to pass along to you is limited for several reasons. First of all, I am going to talk to you only about Brazil because I am not that familiar with the rest of Latin America. Second, I am going to talk only about the Catholic church in Brazil because I know relatively little about other Christian churches. I am just now beginning to make an acquaintance with them. Third, my report is limited by the fact that there is this "opening-up" process now going on in Brazil. That may well force me to rethink a lot of the things I am going to say about the past twelve years or so in Brazil. Finally, my report is limited by my own eyesight. Even though I wear glasses and have good intentions, I find it hard to grasp certain sides of reality—the political side in particular. That may be due to the fact that when I got my education the social sciences and their findings were not a part of the picture.

The Importance of the Bible in Grassroots Christian Communities

The Bible is very important in the life and growth of grassroots communities. But its importance must be put in the right place. It's something like the motor of an automobile. Generally the motor is under the hood, out of sight. It is not the steering wheel. The history of the use of the Bible in grassroots communities is a bit like the history of car motors. Way back when the first cars came out, the motor was huge. It was quite obvious and made a lot of noise. It also wasted a lot of gasoline and left little room for passengers. Today the motors are getting smaller and smaller. They are more powerful, but they are also quieter and better hidden. There's a lot more leg room and luggage room in the car. Much the same is true about the Bible and its function in the life of Christian communities. The Bible is supposed to start things off, to get them going; but it is not the steering wheel. You have to use it correctly. You can't expect it to do what it is not meant to do.

My Relative Optimism

Perhaps what I am going to say to you may seem a trifle optimistic. If so, it is something like the optimism of a farmer watching the grain surface above ground. A storm may come later and wipe out the whole crop. But there is room for optimism, and it's good to be optimistic.

INTRODUCING THE ISSUE: THREE BASIC SITUATIONS

First Situation

In Brazil there are many groups meeting to focus on the Bible. In this case the motivating occasion for the group is some pious exercise or special event:

a feast day, a novena, a brotherhood week, or what have you. The people meet on the parish level. There is no real community context involved. The word of God is the only thing that brings them together. They want to reflect on God's word and put it into practice.

Second Situation

In Brazil some groups are meeting within a broader context. They are meeting on the level of the community and its life. I once went to give a course to the people in such a community. In the evening the people got together to organize the course and establish basic guidelines. In such groups you generally get questions such as these: "How do you explain the Apocalypse? What does the serpent stand for? What about the fight between David and Goliath?"

The questions, you see, are limited to the Bible as such. No hint of their own concerns, no hint of real-life problems, no hint of reality, no hint of problems dealing with economic, social, and political life. Even though they are meeting as a community, the real-life problems of the people are not brought up.

Third Situation

To introduce the third situation, I am going to tell you a typical story about my experience in this area. I was invited to give a course in Ceará, in northeast Brazil. The group was made up of about ninety farmers from the backlands and the riverbanks. Most of them couldn't read. In the evening we met to get things organized. They asked me about a dozen basic questions, but these are the ones I remember:

1. What about these community activities we are engaged in? Are they just the priest's idea? Are they communism? Or do they come from the word of God?

2. What about our fight for land? (Most of them had no land. But they had plenty of problems and fights on their hands.) What about our labor struggles and our attempts to learn something about politics? What does the word of God have to say about all that?

3. What about the gospel message? Does it have to do just with prayer, or is it something more than that?

4. The other day, in a place where there was a big fight going on between the landlord and his tenants, this priest came, said Mass, and explained the gospel in a way that made the landlord right. Then the local priest of the parish read the same gospel and explained it in a way that made the tenant farmers right. So who really is right?

5. The landlord gives catechism lessons that teach subservience and bondage. In our community we have a catechetics of liberation, and the landlord persecutes us for it. So how do we settle the matter and figure it all out? We want to know whether the Bible is on our side or not!

Here we have three basic situations. In the first situation the group involved comes together solely for the sake of discussing the Bible; the Bible is the only thing that unites them and they stick to it. In the second situation the people focus on the Bible, too, but they come together as a community. In the third situation we have a community of people meeting around the Bible who inject concrete reality and their own situation into the discussion. Their struggle as a people enters the picture. So we can formulate the following basic picture:

Community
the con-text

Hearing the word
of God today

the Bible   *Reality*
text   the pre-text

We find three elements in the common people's interpretation of the Bible: the Bible itself, the community, and reality (i.e., the real-life situation of the people and the surrounding world). With these three elements they seek to hear what the word of God is saying. And for them the word of God is not just the Bible. The word of God is within reality and it can be discovered there with the help of the Bible. When one of the three elements is missing, however, interpretation of the Bible makes no progress and enters into crisis. The Bible loses its function.

When the three elements are present and enter the process of interpretation, then you get the situation that I encountered when I gave a course in Ceará. People asked me to tell them the stories of Abraham, Moses, Jeremiah, and Jesus. That is what I did. But in their group discussions and full meetings, the Bible disappeared. They hardly ever talked about the Bible. Instead they talked about real life and their concrete struggles. So at the nightly review the local priest asked them what they had learned that day. They quickly got to talking about real life. No one said anything about the Bible. Ye gods, I thought to myself, where did I go wrong? This is supposed to be a course on the Bible and all they talk about is real life. Should I feel upset and frustrated, or should I be satisfied? Well, I decided to take it easy and feel satisfied because the Bible had achieved its purpose. Like salt, it had disppeared into the pot and spiced the whole meal.

It's like what happens when you take a sponge and dip it in a little bowl of water. The water is soaked up and disappears inside the sponge. At the end of the nightly review the people were asked what they had learned from the biblical explanations. They squeezed the sponge a bit and let a few drops of water out. I could see that the sponge was filled with water. At the final ceremony for the week, which lasted four hours, they squeezed the sponge completely and everything inside came out. I realized that when the three elements are integrated—Bible, community, real-life situation—then the word of God becomes a reinforcement, a stimulus for hope and courage. Bit by bit it helps people to overcome their fears.

Conclusions

1. When the community takes shape on the basis of the real-life problems of the people, then the discovery of the Bible is an enormous reinforcement.

2. When the community takes shape only around the reading of the Bible, then it faces a crisis as soon as it must move on to social and political issues.

3. When the group closes itself up in the letter of the biblical text and does not bring in the life of the community or the reality of the people's struggles, then it has no future and will eventually die.

4. These three factors or situations characterize the use of the Bible by the common people and reveal the complexity involved. The three situations can be successive stages in a single ongoing process, or they can be antagonistic situations that obstruct and exclude each other. It all depends on how the process is conducted.

5. It doesn't matter much where you start. You can start with the Bible, or with the given community, or with the real-life situation of the people and their problems. The important thing is to do all you can to include all three factors.

SOME OBSTACLES AND HOW THE PEOPLE ARE SURMOUNTING THEM

It is not always easy to integrate all three factors in the interpretation of the Bible. There are many obstacles along the way that the people are trying to surmount in various ways.

Many Don't Know How to Read

Many people don't know how to read, and the Bible is a book! Sometimes no one in the group knows how to read. They are inventing ways to get around this problem. They are using song and story, pictures and little plays. They are thus making up their own version of the "Bible of the poor." Thanks to songs, for example, many people who have never read the Bible know almost every story in it.

Slavish Literalism

Another obstacle is slavery to the letter or fundamentalism. This usually occurs when the Bible is read in dissociation from a real-life community and concrete situation. The circle closes and the letter becomes a source of further oppression rather than of liberation.

The Bible is ambiguous. It can be a force for liberation or a force for oppression. If it is treated like a finished monument that cannot be touched, that must be taken literally as it is, then it will be an oppressive force.

Three things can help to overcome this obstacle. The first is the good sense of the people. In one community composed of blacks and other farmers the people were reading the Old Testament text that forbade the eating of pork. The people raised the question: "What is God telling us today through this text?" Their conclusion was: "Through this text God today is ordering us to eat the flesh of pork." How did they arrive at such a contrary conclusion? They explained: "God is concerned first and foremost with life and health. In those times eating the flesh of pork was very dangerous to people's health. It was prohibited in God's name because people's lives had to be protected. Today we know how to take care of pork meat, and the only thing we have to feed our children are the piglets in our yards. So in this text God is bidding us to eat the flesh of pork."

A second thing of great importance in breaking through enslavement to the letter is the ongoing action of a local church that takes sides with the poor. The ongoing movement of the church in this direction is helping to ensure that questions focused exclusively on the letter of the biblical text gradually give way to others. Literalist questions are falling from the tree like dry leaves to make room for new buds. The larger complex of a local church that sides with the poor and joins their fight for justice is very important in correctly channelling the people's interpretation of the Bible.

The third thing has to do with various devices of a fairly simple kind. For example, we can show people that many of the things we talk about in words cannot be taken literally. Symbolism is an integral part of human language. In many instances the first step towards liberation comes for people when they realize that they need not always take the biblical text literally. They discover that "the letter kills, the Spirit gives life." This realization unlocks the lid and lets new creativity out.

The Conception of Time

Another problem or obstacle is the people's conception of time. Often folks will ask questions like these: "Did Abraham come before or after Jesus Christ? Did David live before or after Cabral discovered America? Was it Jesus Christ who created the world?" Such questions may seem to indicate a great deal of confusion to us, but I think not. Apart from a certain amount of ignorance about the content of the Bible, I don't think it is a matter of confusion at all. Instead it is an expression of their circular conception of time. In such a conception you don't know exactly what comes at the beginning and what comes at the end. A simple explanation will not suffice to change this view of time, because it is a cultural problem rather than a problem of mere ignorance. In their minds the people simply don't have a peg on which to hang a concept of linear time.

How do we help them to overcome this obstacle? How do we unroll the carpet of time in their consciousness? Perhaps the best way we can help is to help them discover their own ongoing journey in their lives today. We can help them to recover the memory of their own history, of struggles lost and forgotten. We can help them to begin to recount their own history. In Goiás a group of farmworkers was asked: "How did the Bible come about?" An old farmer gave this reply: "I know. It was something like this. Suppose fifty years from now someone asks how our community arose. The people will reply: In the beginning there was nothing here. . . ." Thanks to his own concrete journey in life, the old farmworker perceived that the Bible had arisen from narrative accounts, from stories people told to others about their history. He realized that the Bible was the collective memory that gave a people its identity.

Dependence on Informational Knowledge and the Learned Expert

You often hear people say something like this: "I don't know anything. You or Father should do the talking. You're the ones who know things. We folks don't know anything." In the past we members of the clergy expropriated the Bible and got a monopoly on its interpretation. We took the Bible out of the hands of the common people, locked it with a key, and then threw the key away. But the people have found the key and are beginning again to interpret the Bible. And they are using the only tool they have at hand: their own lives, experiences, and struggles.

Biblical exegetes, using their heads and their studies, can come fairly close to Abraham; but their feet are a long way from Abraham. The common people are very close to Abraham with their feet. They are living the same sort of situation. Their life-process is of the same nature and they can identify with him. When they read his history in the Bible, it becomes a mirror for them. They look in that mirror, see their own faces, and say: "We are Abraham!" In a real sense they are reading their own history, and this becomes a source of much inspiration and encouragement. One time a farmworker said this to me: "Now I get it. We are Abraham, and if he got there then we will too!" From the history of Abraham he and his people are drawing the motives for their courage today.

Now here is where the danger comes in. Some teacher or learned expert may come along. It might be a pastoral minister, a catechist, or an exegete. This expert may arrive with his or her more learned and sophisticated approach and once again expropriate the gains won by the people. Once again they grow silent and dependent in the presence of the teacher or expert. Our method is logical. It involves a reasoning process, a careful line of argument. We say it is scientific. When the people get together to interpret the Bible, they do not proceed by logical reasoning but by the association of ideas. One person says one thing; somebody else says another thing. We tend to think this approach has little value, but actually it is just as scientific as our approach! What approach do psychoanalysts use when they settle their patients into a chair or couch? They use the free association of ideas. And this method is actually better than our "logical" method. Our method is one for teaching information; the other is one for helping people to discover things themselves.

Lack of Tact on the Part of Pastoral Agents

Another obstacle that crops up at times is the lack of tact on the part of pastoral workers among the people. They are in a hurry and have no patience. They ride roughshod over some of the natural resistance that people have to our interpretations of the Bible. One time a nun went to give a course on the Old Testament. Halfway through she had to close down the course because no one was showing up. The people said: "Sister is destroying the Bible!" A certain priest offered an explanation of the Exodus. Many people never came back. "He is putting an end to miracles," they complained.

Meddling with the faith of the people is very serious business. You must have deep respect and a delicate touch. You must try to feel as they would and intuit their possible reaction to what you are going to say. The people should be allowed to grow from the soil of their own faith and their own character. They should not be dragged along by our aggressive questions.

Erudite Language

Another obstacle is erudite language, abstruse words. We talk a difficult idiom, and the language of translations is difficult. Today, thank God, various efforts are being made to translate the Bible into more popular terms. Nothing could be more desirable. People now feel that they are getting the point at least. The first and most basic requirement is that people talk in such a way that their listeners can understand them. It sounds simple enough, but often it is very hard to do.

Another important point is that we must not lose the poetry of the Bible. We must not reduce it to concepts. The Bible is full of poetry, and poetry is more than a matter of words. It is the whole way of seeing and grasping life.

From Confrontation to Practical Ecumenism

Another problem crops up on the grassroots level with "fundamentalist" groups. They head for people's homes with the Bible in their hands and make it clear that they have the only right answer. This leads to a defensive reaction and sectarian apologetics. It is hard to foster any ecumenism around the Bible in such an atmosphere.

In some areas, however, practical biblical ecumenism is growing from other starting points. Roman Catholics and Protestants are meeting each other and working together in labor unions, in fights for land ownership, and in other real-life struggles. Gradually other sectarian issues are taking a back seat to practical ecumenism.

CHARACTERISTICS OF THE PEOPLE'S INTERPRETATION OF THE BIBLE

In a sense we can say that the tabernacle of the church is to be found where the people come together around the word of God. That could be called the church's "holy of holies." Remember that no one was allowed to enter the holy of holies except the high priest, and he was allowed in only once a year! In this holy of holies no one is master—except God and the people. It is there that the Holy Spirit is at work; and where the Spirit is at work, there is freedom. The deepest and ultimate roots of the freedom sought by all are to be found there, in those small community groups where the people meet around the word of God. One song in Ceará has this line: "It is the tabernacle of the people. Don't anyone touch it!" Certain characteristics are surfacing in this tabernacle, and I should like to point them out here.

The things I am going to mention now are not fully developed and widespread. They are more like the first traces of dawn in the night sky. We are dipping our finger into the batter to savor how the cake will taste when it is baked and ready. The following characteristics are just beginning to surface here and there in the ongoing journey of various communities. I think they are very important.

The Scope of the Biblical Message

In the eyes of the common people the word of God, the gospel message, is much broader than just the text itself. The gospel message is a bit of everything: Bible, community, reality. For the common people the word of God is not just in the Bible; it is also in the community and in their real-life situation. The function of the Bible, read in a community context, is to help them to discover where God is calling them in the hubbub of real life. It is as if the word of God were hidden within history, within their struggles. When they discover it, it is big news. It's like a light flicking on in their brains. When one leper in Acre made this discovery, he exclaimed: "I have been raised from the dead!" He used the idea of resurrection to express the discovery he had made.

Theologians say that reality is a *locus theologicus*. The common people say: "God speaks, mixed into things." A tinker defined the church this way: "The church is us exchanging ideas with each other to discover the idea of the Holy Spirit in the people." If it hadn't come from Antonio Pascal, I would have said it came from St. Augustine. But it came from Antonio Pascal. It is us exchanging ideas with each other to discover the idea of the Holy Spirit in the people. Not in the church, in the people!

So you see, when they read the Bible, basically they are not trying to interpret the Bible; they are trying to interpret life with the help of the Bible. They are altering the whole business. They are shifting the axis of interpretation.

The Unity of Creation and Salvation

The common people are recovering the unity or oneness of creation and salvation, which is certainly true in the Bible itself. The Bible doesn't begin with Abraham. It begins with creation. Abraham is not called to form some separated group apart. Abraham is called to recover for all peoples the blessing lost by the sin of Adam. This is the oneness between life and faith, between transforming (political) activity and evangelization, that the people are concretely achieving in their praxis.

The Reappropriation of the Bible

The Bible was taken out of the people's hands. Now they are taking it back. They are expropriating the expropriators: "It is our book! It was written for us!" It had always been "Father's book," it seemed. Now it is the people's book again.

That gives them a new way of seeing, new eyes. They feel at home with the Bible and they begin to link it with their lives. So we get something very interesting. They are mixing life in with the Bible, and the Bible in with life. One helps them to interpret the other. And often the Bible is what starts them developing a more critical awareness of reality. They say, for example: "*We* are Abraham! *We* are in Egypt! *We* are in bondage! *We* are David!" With the biblical data they begin to reflect on their real-life situation. The process gradually prompts them to seek a more objective knowledge of reality and to look for a more suitable tool of analysis elsewhere. But it is often the word of God that starts them moving.

The rediscovery of the Bible as "our book" gives rise to a sense of commitment and a militancy that can overcome the world. Once they discover that God is with them in their struggles, no one can really stop them or deter them. One farmworker from Goiás concluded a letter this way: "When the time comes for me to bear my witness, I will do so without any fear of dying." That is the kind of strength that is surfacing. A sort of resurrection is taking place, as I suggested earlier.

We who have always had the Bible in hand find it difficult to imagine and comprehend the sense of novelty, the gratitude, the joy, and the commitment that goes with their reading of the Bible. But that is why these people generally read the Bible in the context of some liturgical celebration. Their reading is a prayer exercise. Rarely will you find a group that reads the Bible simply for better understanding. Almost always their reading is associated with reflection on God present here and now, and hence with prayer. They live in a spirit of gratefulness for God's gift.

History as a Mirror

Another characteristic which I hinted at already is the fact that the Bible is not just history for the people; it is also a mirror. Once upon a time we used to talk about the Bible as "letter" and "symbol." Today we might do well to talk about it as "history" and "mirror." The common people are using it as a mirror to comprehend their own lives as a people.

We who study a great deal have a lot more trouble trying to grasp the point of images and symbols. If we want to get a handle on symbolic language, we have to go through a whole process of "demythologizing." We have to go through a long process of study to get the point of the symbol. To us images are opaque glasses; we can't see through them at all. To see at all, we have to punch out the glass and smash it. To the common people in Brazil, an image or symbol is a pair of glasses with a little dust or frost on it. They just wipe them a bit and everything is as clear as day.

I don't think we pay enough attention to this educational item. We are awfully "Europeanized" in our training. Take the question of the historicity of a text. I think you have to approach it very differently, or worry about it differently, when you are dealing with ordinary people. Very often pastoral workers are talking about the Bible and they ask questions like these: "Did that really happen? Did Jesus walk on top of the water? Were there only five loaves and two fishes?" They think that this is the most important problem that the people have with the text in front of them. I don't think so. Once, in Goiás, we read the passage in the New Testament (Acts 17:19) where an angel of the Lord came and freed the apostles from jail. The pastoral worker asked his people: "Who was the angel?" One of the women present gave this answer: "Oh, I know. When Bishop Dom Pedro Casaldáliga was attacked in his house and the police surrounded it with machine guns, no one could get in or out and no one knew what was going on exactly. So this little girl sneaked in without being seen, got a little message from Pedro, ran to the airport, and hitched a ride to Goiana where the bishops were meeting. They got the message, set up a big fuss, and Dom Pedro was set free. So that little girl was the angel of the Lord. And it's really the same sort of thing."

The people don't always take things literally. They are far smarter than you would think. Our question simply will have to take more account of the way that ordinary people understand history. They are far more capable of understanding symbols than we assume.

DISLOCATIONS

When there are only five people in a room, then each one can be pretty much at ease. When fifty more people enter the room, then the original five find themselves a bit crowded and some moving around has to take place. Well, the common people have entered the precincts of biblical interpretation and they are causing much shifting and dislocation.

A Shift in Standpoint

First of all, the Bible itself has shifted its place and moved to the side of the poor. One could almost say that it has changed its class status. This is important. The place where the people read the Bible is a different place. We read the Bible something like the wealthy car owner who looks out over the top of his car and sees a nice chrome finish. The common people read the Bible something like the mechanic under the car who looks up and sees a very different view of the same car.

The common people are discovering things in the Bible that other readers don't find. At one session we were reading the following text: "I have heard the cries of my people." A woman who worked in a factory offered this commentary: "The Bible does not say that God has heard the praying of the people. It says that God has heard the cries of his people. I don't mean that people shouldn't pray. I mean that people should imitate God. Very often we work to get people to go to church and pray first; and only then will we pay heed to their cries." You just won't find that sort of interpretation in books.

The Bible has changed its place, and the place where the common people read the Bible is different. It is the place where one can appreciate the real import of Jesus' remark: "I thank thee, Father . . . that thou hast hidden these things from the wise and understanding and revealed them to babes; yea, Father, for such was thy gracious will" (Matt. 11:25–26). If you take sides with the poor, you will discern things in the Bible that an exegete does not see. All of us have a slight blind spot that prevents us from seeing certain things.

From Biblical Text to Real Life

Another shift mentioned earlier has to do with the fact that the word of God has moved in a certain sense from the Bible to real life. It is in the Bible but it is also in real life—especially in real life. So we come to the following conclusion: the Bible is not the one and only history of salvation; it is a kind of "model experience." Every single people has *its own* history of salvation.

Clement of Alexandria said: "God saved the Jews in a Jewish way, the barbarians in a barbarian way." We could go on to say: "God saves Brazilians in a Brazilian way, blacks in a black way, Indians in an Indian way, Nicaraguans in a Nicaraguan way, and so on." Each people has its own unique history. Within that history it must discover the presence of God the Liberator who journeys by its side. The scope of this particular dislocation is most important.

From Meaning in Itself to Meaning for Us

Another dislocation is to be found in the fact that emphasis is not placed on the text's meaning in itself but rather on the meaning the text has for the people reading it. At the start people tend to draw any and every sort of meaning, however well or ill founded, from the text. Only gradually, as they proceed on their course in life, do they begin to develop an interest in the historical import and intrinsic meaning of the text. It is at this point that they can benefit greatly from a study of the material conditions of the people in biblical times: i.e., their religious, political, and socio-economic situation. But they do so in order to give a better grounding to the text's meaning "for us." In this framework scientific exegesis can reclaim its proper role and function, placing itself in the service of the biblical text's meaning "for us."

From Abstract Understanding to a Community Sense

The common people are doing something else very important. They are reintroducing faith, community, and historical reality into the process of interpretation. When we studied the Bible back in the seminary in the old days, we didn't have to live as a real community or really know much about reality. We didn't even have to have faith. All we needed was enough brains to understand Greek and Hebrew and to follow the professor's line of reasoning.

Now the common people are helping us to realize that without faith, community, and reality we cannot possibly discover the meaning that God has put in that ancient tome for us today. Thus the common people are recovering something very important: the *sensus ecclesiae* ("sense of the church"). The community is the resonance chamber; the text is a violin string. When the people pluck the string (the biblical text), it resonates in the community and out comes the music. And that music sets the people dancing and singing. The community of faith is like a big pot in which Bible and community are cooked just right until they become one tasty dish.

From Neutrality to Taking Sides

The common people are also eliminating the alleged "neutrality" of scholarly exegesis. No such neutrality is possible. Technology is not neutral, and neither is exegesis.

Clearing up Overly Spiritualized Concepts

The common people are giving us a clearer picture of concepts that have been excessively spiritualized. Let me give just one example. Some time ago Pope Paul VI delivered an address in which he warned priests not to become overly preoccupied with material things. He urged them to show greater concern for spiritual things. One farmworker in Goiás had this comment: "Yes, the pope is quite right. Many priests concern themselves only with material things, such as building a church or decorating it. They forget spiritual things, such as food for the people!"

This is what the people are doing with such notions as grace, salvation, sin, and so forth. They are dusting them off and showing us that these notions have to do with solid, concrete realities of life.

Putting the Bible in Its Proper Place

Finally, the common people are putting the Bible in its proper place, the place where God intended it to be. They are putting it in second place. Life takes first place! In so doing, the people are showing us the enormous importance of the Bible and, at the same time, its relative value—relative to life.

PROBLEMS, CHALLENGES, REQUIREMENTS

There are many problems, difficulties, and failings associated with the interpretation of the Bible by the common people. But every good tree has a strong, solid limb that can be pruned when the time comes. The point is that its roots are okay. The common people are reading and interpreting the Bible as a new book that speaks to them here and now. And this basic view of the Bible is the view that the Church Fathers of the past had when they interpreted the Bible.

Here I simply want to enumerate a few further points that need greater attention.

1. There is the danger of subjectivistic interpretation. This can be combated in two ways: by more objective grounding in the literal sense of the Bible and by reading the Bible in community.

2. It is possible to read the Bible solely to find in it a confirmation of one's own ideas. In this case the biblical text loses its critical function. Community-based reading and interpretation help to overcome this tendentious use of the Bible. In addition, people must have a little humility and a little signal-light in their brains that calls them up short when they are tempted to absolutize their own ideas.

3. People may lack a critical sense in reading and interpreting the biblical text. They may be tempted to take the ancient text and apply it mechanically to today, without paying any serious attention to the difference in historical context.

4. The above three points underline the proper and necessary function of scientific exegesis. Exegesis is being called upon to concern itself, not with the questions it raises, but with the questions that the common people are raising. In many cases the exegete is like the person who had studied salt and knew all its chemical properties but didn't know how to cook with it. The common people don't know the properties of salt well, but they do know how to season a meal.

5. We need biblical interpretation that will reveal the material living condi-

tions of the people in the Bible. We need a materialistic reading and interpretation of the Bible, but not a narrow and confined reading. It must be broad and full.

6. We urgently need to give impetus to ecumenism on the grassroots level. It is a hard and challenging task, but a beginning has been made here and there.

7. The Bible is a book derived from a rural environment. Today we live in an urban environment. Re-reading the Bible today here in São Paulo, in this urban reality, presents no easy task of interpretation.

8. There is the matter of revolutionary effectiveness and gratitude for the Father's gift. This is another matter that needs further exploration.

9. Criticism can be derived from the word of God to foster transforming action.

9

KUNO FÜSSEL

The Materialist Reading of the Bible: Report on an Alternative Approach to Biblical Texts

Three influential studies on the materialist reading of the Bible have been written since 1974 by Fernando Belo, Michel Clévenot, and Georges Casalis. They have as their aim to clarify how the biblical texts relate to their socio-historic settings as ideological productions. A combination of Marxist historical material analysis and of literary structuralism is employed to illuminate the literature as a product of the social formation which has its own unique character as a written system of symbolic codes.

The author briefly develops a materialist theory of literature and sets forth the steps typically involved in doing a materialist reading of a biblical text, including the distinctive mixture of sequential codes and cultural codes that are embodied in the structure of the writing. This type of biblical study is finding a widespread audience principally among lay groups in France,

Reprinted from Willy Schottroff and Wolfgang Stegemann, eds., *Der Gott der kleinen Leute: Sozialgeschichtliche Bibelauslegungen,* Vol. 1, *Altes Testament,* Vol. 2, *Neues Testament* (Munich: Kaiser; Gelnhausen: Burckhardthaus, 1979), Eng., *The God of the Lowly: Socio-historical Interpretations* (Maryknoll, N.Y.: Orbis Books, forthcoming).

Spain, and Italy, and among university-based groups in Germany, Austria, Switzerland, and the Netherlands. Leftist Christians, dedicated to changing their own sociohistoric circumstances, are aided by a materialist reading to grasp the connection between the biblical symbols they are nurtured on and the social practice of the biblical symbolizers.

CLASSICS OF THE MATERIALIST READING OF THE BIBLE

The year 1974 saw the appearance of Fernando Belo's *Lecture matérialiste de l'évangile de Marc.*[1] With this book, Belo, a Portuguese who was at that time living in French exile as a foreign worker and a laicized priest, set in motion a search for alternative readings of the Bible that has continued down to the present. His approach is not only fascinating but is marked by a certain inexorability; both qualities result from his ability to bring almost the entire arsenal of Parisian theoretical production in the linguistic and social sciences to bear on a single basic question: What is the connection between political and radical Christian practice? Or, to spell this question out in greater detail: How do economic, political, and ideological class struggles influence the production and reception of biblical texts? What material presuppositions, interests, and needs lead to which concepts, ideas, and theories? What are the laws regulating not only the exchange of goods but also the circulation of signs in those systems of a social formation that mediate meaning?

In the first part of his book Belo admittedly requires the reader to climb a whole mountain of methodological problems; the effort needed has certainly deterred many a reader from continuing with the book or has forced them to approach it in a different way. But as early as the second part of the book the reader's perseverance receives its first reward when Belo comes to the conclusion that the Old Testament is shaped by two main opposed lines of thought. These are the expression not only of distinctive religious and theological traditions but, at a deeper level, of contrary socioeconomic interests and power relationships. A system based on gift (a system that is Yahwist and concerned with equality and self-rule in the framework of tribal society) stands over against a system based on purity vs. pollution (this system is priestly, centralizing, and bureaucratic with its focus in the exercise of sacral and royal power).

The struggle between these two approaches continues into the New Testament. At their point of intersection stands the cross of Jesus. Belo shows why this was inevitable, by means of a clear analysis of the function of the temple in Israelite religion. The proceedings against Jesus are really concerned with the role of the temple as the economic, political, and ideological focus of power. Jesus dies because he wishes to tear down this temple and build a new one distinct from the old temple and outside the holy city. This purpose distinguishes him from the Zealots, who die for and in the temple.

In Belo's view, the entire development of theology that follows on the death of Jesus (it begins in the Bible, although least of all in Mark, whose Gospel Belo analyzes and comments on, sequence by sequence) must be described as an attempt to blunt and adapt the radical messianic practice of Jesus. Perhaps Belo is here throwing out the infant (theology) with its idealist bath, but no one can dispute his claim that to follow Jesus without accepting his messianic practice is simply to play games with labels.

In 1976 Michel Clévenot published his *Approches matérialistes de la Bible*.[2] His study picks up the main points of Belo's book but puts the latter into a form better suited to group reading. Clévenot not only provides a simple methodological introduction to the interrelations of historical materialism, linguistics, and Scripture study, but also makes stimulating comments in explaining the Bible as a collection of literary texts and in interpreting the Gospel of Mark as the story of the subversive practice of Jesus. As for the main task, which is to ascertain and map the traces of the practice of Jesus at the level of the various societal instances, Clévenot seeks to accomplish this by reconstructing the class relationships current around A.D. 70 and by deciphering the codes used in Mark's literary production.

In 1977 Georges Casalis published his book *Les idées justes ne tombent pas du ciel* [Correct Ideas Don't Fall from the Skies],[3] which describes numerous and varied approaches to a materialist hermeneutic that is valid not only for a materialist reading of the Bible but also for a theologico-political reading of Christian revolutionary practice in general. This brilliantly written account of the journey of a militant French professor of theology from a politically sensitive Barthian theology to a clear option for the oppressed classes may be regarded as a first contribution to a European theology of liberation. Casalis energetically continues the struggle, begun by Belo, against bourgeois logocentrism in theology (that is, the exorcism of rational thinking as a supposedly impartial grasp of objective thought-forms).

He shows that human alienation is not to be overcome by an ever-new submission to ever-new scientific considerations but only by liberation from what divides us from God, our neighbor, and ourself. In Casalis's view, theological thinking is primarily a trailblazing engagement in revolutionary practice; it is a risking of one's existence, and this usually means initially that one becomes an outcast in one's own church. Such an approach to theology means the end of theology as conceptual representation; it is a farewell to spectator theologians. Another characteristic of this new kind of theologizing is a new manner of reading, which does not get entangled in abstract problems of understanding but uses book lore in order to experiment on behalf of life and thus to change one's own practice. The world's structure of meaning, its intelligibility, "does not fall from the skies" as a gift, but must be created.

WHO ENGAGES IN AN ALTERNATIVE READING OF THE BIBLE, AND WHY DO THEY DO IT?

No one who is familiar with the professional scene will deny that, if the publication of technical studies be taken as a criterion, exegesis and the auxiliary biblical sciences have made great progress in the last thirty years. A decisive factor in this progress has been the acceptance of the historical critical method by all scholars in these disciplines, almost without exception. It seems, however, that the undeniable multiplicity of exegetical results has not satisfied an equally great number of diverse interests and needs. In fact, there is reason for thinking that scholarly exegetical interest and the hermeneutic which guides it (rather than the formal method as such) have been directed unilaterally to the acquisition of authoritarian knowledge in the service of an elitist claim to dominance on the part of a few "reading experts" in the church. Exegesis has thus become, in large measure, a legitimating science, and authentic exegesis has turned into ideology.

When Belo, Casalis, Clévenot, and many others denounce this tendency as idealist, they are at least able to point out how surprisingly little of real history appears in the immediate work done on the biblical text by outstanding representatives of the historical critical method, such as Rudolf Bultmann. At the very time (1941) when Nazi Germany was attacking the Soviet Union and Jews were being murdered in the concentration camps, Bultmann, who was certainly not a fascist, published his book *Neues Testament und Mythologie* in which he accepts the modern spirit as the criterion for interpreting the Bible. Yet Bultmann does not allow the pitiless consequences of this spirit and of the technological mind to which it has given birth, as seen in war and the Holocaust, to exercise any influence on his exegetical principles.[4] It is clear that even in Bultmann "history" still means simply such residues of the past as can be established and that criticism is limited to the analysis of world views, forms, redactions, and traditions. Nothing is seen of history as the presently operative product of the class struggle, or of a revolutionary "critique of the status quo" as a valid interpretive horizon for contemporary reading and for the discernment of spirits that is needed today.

In view of this observation, which is representative of many that might be made, we can understand the severity with which Belo criticizes this elimination of social contradictions and conflicts from the existential hermeneutic of the demythologization program:

> Bourgeois exegetes, working on the basis of anthropocentric logocentrism, have sought with varying success to undo the closure of the MYTH codes that play in the New Testament texts. The name of Bultmann especially is connected with this attempt at demythologization. For a symptom of the fact that the attempt is being made on the basis of

bourgeois logocentrism I need point out only the appeal to "the modern consciousness," to scientific reason, and to advancing modernity that seems always to be the ultimate argument in texts aiming at demythologization. This effort at demythologization fails to understand the Scriptures and the narrative of power (the messianic narrative). This bourgeois form of the theological discourse ends up in *interiority* (even if it be called spiritual experience or a spiritual attitude).[5]

Ecclesiastical authorities and the dominant exegetes have reacted strongly to the charge of idealism. Catholic exegetes especially insist that in matters of scriptural exegesis they will allow no alien gods besides them, and therefore any approach to the Bible that differs from theirs or represents a critical reaction to theirs is labeled as unbridled or unscientific or as a temporary fad (assuming that they do not join the bishops and reach for a stronger weapon, disqualifying other approaches as un-ecclesial or even un-Christian).

It is evident, therefore, that attempts at a nonidealist approach to the Bible do not originate in the academic world of university theology, but rather in the commitment of the leftist Christians who opt for the oppressed in the class struggles of our time and join them in the fight for liberation.

Revolutionary practice thus becomes the starting point for a comprehensive hermeneutic that not only makes possible a new interpretation of political and ideological reality in society but also becomes the basis for a new understanding of faith.

If a church of the oppressed is to be built and if the folly of the cross is to be taken seriously in politics, then there is need not only of bidding farewell to bourgeois religion and the church of the established classes, but also of forming a new identity. A materialist reading owes its existence to this need, springing from an altered practice, for a Christian-socialist identity and for an appropriation of the tradition of faith and its sources that will make this identity secure.

Like every conversion, this new beginning has its problems. There is a need to avoid two dangers: that of an individualistic, spontaneous biblicism, and that of a completely functional approach to the Bible which looks upon it solely as a source of motivation for political action. A conscious and sustained materialist reading is therefore compelled, first of all, to be clear about its own limitations, the methods required, and the state of utilizable preliminary work. It is here that Belo and, following him, Clévenot and Casalis have made a valuable pioneering contribution.

Numerous groups throughout the world (at present there are about a hundred) have therefore adopted the program suggested by these men and have made it the basis for their common study of the Bible. In addition, the groups have moved beyond the now prototypical Gospel of Mark and have applied the method to other texts of Scripture: in the Old Testament to the Books of Samuel and Kings, to Genesis and Jeremiah; in the New Testament, to 1

Thessalonians and 1 Corinthians, to the Gospel of John and the Acts of the Apostles. The Acts of the Apostles especially has attracted increasing interest, and this for two reasons. First, it provides a document in which the entire range of problems created by the entry of the church into the place left by Jesus ("Jesus went and the church came") may be studied. Second, it makes possible a closer examination of living conditions among the early Christians and especially of their common possession and sharing of goods.

In the Romance-language (and especially in the French- and Spanish-speaking) countries a materialist reading is practiced chiefly by groups made up of members from left-oriented church associations (in which an ecumenical composition is taken for granted), the trade unions, and the Christians for Socialism movement. The important thing seems to be not the reading as such but rather the liberation and enlightenment it brings within the family, at work, and in the Party. In terms of trade or profession, the members of the groups are quite varied: technicians, workers, elementary school teachers, nurses, housewives, students, retirees. There are few academic people or professional theologians.

The composition of the groups is quite different, however, in the German-speaking countries (West Germany, East Germany, Austria, Switzerland). Here the universities and the student associations provide the milieu for the groups devoted to the materialist reading of the Bible; in terms of methodology these groups frequently take their lead from the school of the Dutchman F. Breukelmann (thus, for example, T. Veerkamp and J. van Zwieten). Pastors, teachers, theology students, and church workers largely determine the manner in which these groups go about their work. The situation is similar in the Netherlands, although here the phenomenon of the base-level communities and the general ecclesial climate of tolerance also provide a favorable atmosphere. In both of these language areas, however, it can be said that Christians for Socialism play an important role in coordinating and giving guidance. This is true also of Belgium, England, Norway, Canada, Peru, Colombia, and Mauritius.

The work of these groups derives the essentials of its structure from the leftist Catholic periodical *Lettre* which is published in Paris[6] and has M. Clévenot as one of its editors. Since the appearance of Belo's book, *Lettre* has promoted the common cause in trailbreaking articles and has provided a forum for supraregional and international discussion. The Supplement to No. 237 (1978) may be regarded as a first comprehensive survey of the subject of alternative readings. It contains reports of new groups, new exegetical findings, and new tools of analysis.

With this Supplement as a basis and preparation, a first international meeting took place in Paris on November 11–12, 1978. There were more than 100 participants from sixteen countries; among these were "of course" Belo, Clévenot, and Casalis, but it was the laity, and not the professional textual analysts who gave the event its stamp. The pentecostal power of Christian-socialist internationalism supplied the normative codes: the primacy of experience, the equal standing of all readers, unity in political commitment, the impulse to ongoing personal work.

The Bible is, of course, not the only book these groups use in their often discouraging struggle against the establishment in church and society. Perhaps it is not even the most important of the tools they use.

Christians who sum up in the term "socialism" their ideas and suggestions for the improvement of the present social order realize that they cannot derive their views directly from the Bible. On the other hand, it would be at the very least imprudent to take it for granted that militant Christians can in their political involvement dispense with the rich treasures of the Bible and the stimuli it affords. On the contrary, it is to be presupposed that the texts of the Bible have something in common with the hope that keeps us going in the political struggle, the hope, I mean, of a society without oppression and alienation. Consequently, the Bible is an indispensable aid to survival on the long journey through the wilderness of capitalism. Many of the groups mentioned know from experience that a reading of the Bible done in common not only brings new knowledge and helps eliminate old misapprehensions of the Bible as being a collection of pious statements for use on feastdays, but also affords an authentic joy. Texts of the Bible and the reading of them have contributed to the loosing of the tongues of many in the groups. As a result, conflicts in the groups have found their voice and a solution, whereas previously they had been unadmitted and had unconsciously hindered practical action.

From this it can be seen that a materialist reading of the Bible has three goals. 1. It aims at showing that the Bible does not simply contain scattered expressions of the lives of the oppressed but has the poor for its real subject. 2. It aims therefore at rescuing the Bible from those who have wrongfully appropriated it and put it in chains. 3. It aims at reading the Bible in such a way that in its light our political practice will receive a new clarification, while at the same time this practice and its clarification will help us find in the writings of the Old and New Testaments hitherto undiscovered paradigms of a subversive practice.

WHAT DOES THE TERM "MATERIALIST" MEAN IN THIS CONTEXT?

Since it is undoubtedly the case that the materialist reading of the Bible is carried on in groups that are at least socialist, if not Marxist, in their orientation, this kind of basic politico-practical direction must be made the starting point in interpreting the word "materialist."

The primary point of reference for a materialist reading is "revolutionizing practice"[7] as a concrete epistemological principle. In other words, the transformative practice determines in each instance the range of concepts and theories that are developed, and serves as criterion of truth for statements made with the help of these. This applies to a hermeneutic for interpretation of the Bible.

The materialism in question here is therefore practical and not metaphysical. It begins with the concept of production which, according to Marx, is determinative for the human species. "The act by which they [living human individuals] distinguish themselves from animals is not the fact that they think but the fact that they begin to produce their means of subsistence."[8] Under the heading of productive activities Marx includes art and therefore literature as particular forms. "Religion, family, state, law, morality, science, art, etc., are only particular modes of production, and fall under its general law."[9] At the same time, however, there are serious differences between the various productive activities just mentioned, between art and science, for example: "The whole as it appears in the mind as a conceptual totality [scientific investigation of social reality in its entirety] is a product of the thinking mind, which appropriates the world in the only way possible to it, a way that is distinct from the artistic, religious, or practical appropriation of the same world."[10] But in order to appraise correctly the place of writing, reading, and literature (the Bible belongs here), recourse must be had to a materialist theory of literature.[11]

In regard to such a theory careful heed must be paid to the guideline Marx sets down for any and every scientific materialism: "It is, in reality, much easier to discover by analysis the earthly core of the misty creations of religion, than, conversely, it is, to develop from the actual relations of life the corresponding established forms of these relations. The latter method is the only materialistic, and therefore the only scientific one."[12]

By way of a rough and condensed formula, then, the following can be said with regard to a materialist theory of literature: Applying Marx's maxim to the literary production of texts we may assert that literature is to be understood as a product of social practice and derives its character from the relations at work in each case.

Literary production is a *form of ideological production*. Like every other ideological production literary production is determined by the relation between basis and superstructure and by the class struggle. The production of texts is the privileged field of the conflict between the rival ideologies at work on a social formation. The basic structure of literary texts emerges from consideration of this primary contradiction. In itself, therefore, literature is always incomplete, incoherent, and open to new readings. What is called "the unity of a work of art" is simply a metaphor for the effort to resolve social conflicts in a symbolic way and achieve a fictive reconciliation by creating a secondary semiotic system (= literary language).

A materialist theory of literature identifies types of texts and genres of texts as variations within a general social determination of literary form, and analyzes the religious, political, juridical, etc., themes of a text in light of its function. This emphasis on the objective character of literature as a reflection of real life means the rejection of a conception that regards literature as resulting from the genial or even fully mysterious creative action of individuals.

Once literature is understood as a particular form of ideological *practice,* it follows that it is not to be classified as an achievement of consciousness and removed from reality, but that it is a material, that is, a practico-transformative, factor of social reality. Literary texts are not simply mental products of material life but rather themselves in their turn play a part in shaping this life. To produce and utilize literature is always at the same time to intervene and take sides in the struggle between the rival ideologies at work in a social formation, and it is therefore to make an active contribution to the shaping and differentiating of its contradictions.

A materialist reading (this applies not only to the Bible) must therefore strive to do justice, in dealing with a text, to the viewpoints of productivity and materiality. But productivity and materiality must themselves be seen from two points of view, lest we fall into the error of an esthetics of production, on the one hand, or an esthetics of reception, on the other.[13] Productivity and reception must be considered in relation to the labor of the author, who makes the text out of the given material of his own language, but also in relation to the reader (interpreter), who makes the text his own by his reading of it, implants it in his own speech, and so incorporates it into himself. As far as reading is concerned, this process means that the constitutive elements must be interrelated: (a) the given language; (b) the author who uses it, and the original addressees of the text; and (c) the present-day reader—while paying attention to the conditions in which the text was produced and those in which it now discloses itself, as these conditions are determined by the social situation of the author and that of the reader.

Clévenot therefore sets down the following minimal requirements for a materialist reading: It must lead the reader to the point at which (a) at least the basic syntactical structure of the text and the structure of its statements or actions is clear; (b) the manner in which the author says something to others with the means which his language provides likewise emerges; (c) the author-reader relation and the influence of each on the other is clarified; and (d) enough information about the social situation of author and reader is brought to bear on the analysis of the text.[14]

WHAT METHOD IS TO BE PREFERRED IN READING?

The categories and methods a person needs and the degree of differentiation he claims for them will depend (a) on the field of practical needs and requirements in which he is taking his stand, and (b) on the degree of theory-development which he regards as obligatory and considers to be fruitful and helpful to him in his options. Since the reading groups are made up of militants and not of university professionals, much less theoreticians of science, the first of these two criteria will be decisive for the choice of linguistic methods.

For such an initial understanding,[15] which has not surveyed, and does not intend to survey, the entire discussion that goes on among modern theoreticians of texts, texts are to be regarded, in a quite general way, as linguistic entities which were produced under certain social conditions. Materially speaking, texts are collections of signifiers (signs that convey meaning) which are connected with one another by precise relations. The totality of these relations reveals the structure of the text. For a structural analysis of a text[16] one particular relation is especially important: the opposition between two elements (good/evil, stay/go, Jerusalem/Samaria, etc.). The oppositions that occur in a text reveal the purpose of the text. This is also one of the most important formal bridges to historical materialism with its methodological emphasis on contradictions.

The ascertainment of the conditions of production and reception requires not only reliable information on the pertinent social formation and its general instances: economy, politics, and ideology (consultation of the pertinent technical literature is indispensable here), but also a clarification of the type of text. What is meant by "type of text"?

Most people (this is something drilled into them in school) read texts (a newspaper, a book, a letter) either because they want to know what the author (a friend, a teacher, a politician, etc.) intended to say to them or others, or because they want to find out what happened, what it was really like then or now, who was involved, who did what.

Given these two basic interests, it seems plausible to divide the texts we meet in reading the Bible into two main groups: discourses or speeches, on the one hand (e.g., the letters of Paul), and stories or accounts, on the other (e.g., the Gospel of Mark).

A discourse is a text that establishes a relation between an I and a You and then fashions this relation (developing it, intensifying it, weakening it). At the level of linguistic features discourses are recognizable by the present tense of the verbs, the role of pronouns and adverbs, and the structure of the statements.

A story or narrative, on the other hand, eliminates references to the author's role in the process of expression. Events seem to narrate themselves, so that we do not know clearly who is speaking to whom. Consequently, the third person and the past tense are linguistic signposts of narrative. The change produced by the text is the change that takes place between the actants or agents who make their appearance in the text.

The distinction between discourse and narrative is usually made at the beginning of joint work on the text.

According to Roland Barthes (whom many study groups follow on this point in their reading), the mode of production peculiar to a text, and the structure that emerges from the text, are to be determined by deciphering the sequential codes used, whereas the insertion of the text into a particular situation can be known by the indicial or cultural codes.[17]

Sequential codes may be subdivided into three types: the actantial code, the analytic code, and the strategic code.[18] The working of these codes can be further specified depending on whether they are used in a discourse or in a narrative:

1. The actantial code enables us to see who the actors or actants are and what they do (Jesus, the Pharisees, the disciples, and so on).

2. The analytic codes show us how the actants read and analyze the events (the Pharisees and Jesus pass divergent judgments on cures worked on the sabbath).

3. The strategic code permits us to evaluate the behavior of the actants in terms of the attitudes they adopt toward each other (e.g., the summoning of a sick person into the midst of the synagogue).

Once the overall plan of the text is known, the indicial or cultural codes tell us how the individual components of it are related (e.g., place names), in order that we may thus come to grasp the meaning of the whole. The most important thing here is the serial connections among the individual terms (e.g., whether they all have to do with health, sickness, healing, and so on, or whether they deal with landed property, money, selling, contracts, and so on).

The most important cultural codes are the following:

1. The geographical code: it tells us the regions whence the information comes or where the action takes place.
2. The topographical code: it indicates locales, at least in a narrative: a house, the street, the sea, the temple.
3. The chronological code: it specifies the temporal sequence.
4. The mythological code: it establishes connections with the store of myths that were current throughout the entire East.
5. The symbolic code: it makes reference to the system of values and norms found in the Bible.
6. The social code: it indicates relations to the economic and political instances of society and to practical life generally.

Most groups begin their work by first investigating the way in which one particular code works and then adding code after code until the entire fabric has been reconstituted.

WHY HAS THE MATERIALIST READING UNDERTAKEN TO LINK HISTORICAL MATERIALISM AND STRUCTURALISM?

A materialistic reading of literary texts may be described, from the viewpoint of methodology, as an effort to draw profit, for an intensive reading, from the sociohistorical analysis of the production and reception of texts, on the one hand, and from the determination of their specific literary form, on the other.

In the process, the social background for the analysis is derived from historical materialism as a theory of the formation and history of societies. This is followed by a consideration of the text on the basis of linguistic structuralism. Is this combination of approaches accidental or necessary?

At least on historical grounds the claim that the conjunction is accidental can be dismissed. Ever since the beginning, in the twenties, of Russian formalism,[19] which continues to exert an influence on French structuralism by way of R. Jacobson and T. Todorov, there has been a complementarity (often ignored) between the problems dealt with in the Marxist/materialist theory of literature and those in the formalist/structuralist theory:

1. The Marxists insist on the need of showing how literary texts depend even in their multiplicity of meanings on the sociohistorical context.

2. The formalists are interested primarily in the way in which a literary text manages to establish between sign and reality a relationship that is free from any utilitarian compulsion to represent reality. It is in this freedom that the autonomy of the work of art consists.

3. In concrete work on texts each party gladly avoids the approach taken by the other or, by way of diversion, criticizes the other for neglecting its own (the criticizing party's) side of the investigation. There are only a few theories of literature that try to deal with both aspects at the same time and in a balanced way; some of the exceptions are W. Benjamin and T. W. Adorno, along with E. Balibar and P. Macherey.[20] Belo is very close to the last-named, even though he takes Julia Kristeva as his explicit point of departure.[21]

The attempt to link historical materialism and structuralism in a dialectical way when working on a text is in keeping with an older aspiration, although one that is difficult to satisfy. In this context a dialectical approach implies the need of remaining aware that both the esthetic and the sociofunctional aspects of a text are socially determined but are not on that account reducible to one another by any means. Theory of ideology and structural analysis of texts can therefore usefully complement one another when the goal is to explain how a literary work such as the Bible not only permits different and even contrary types of reading (one which confirms the dominant understanding of reality; another which shatters it), but is itself already the product of rival types of reading and represents their fictive reconciliation.

It is still possible, however, to argue about whether the alliance of methods and the practice of reading that are exhibited in this book are meaningful and helpful and carry us forward. It may be asked whether an equally fruitful or perhaps even more productive combination of the historical critical method and the analysis of societal formation may not be possible. In my opinion, the likelihood of a positive answer to these questions has for the first time increased, now that L. Schottroff and W. Stegemann have published their book[22] which so brilliantly combines readableness, thorough information, and knowledge of the present state of scholarship with the concern for a concrete sociocritical reading.

NOTES

1. Fernando Belo, *Lecture matérialiste de l'évangile de Marc: Récit—Pratique— Idéologie* (Paris: Du Cerf, 1974; 2nd ed., 1975); Eng. *A Materialist Reading of the*

Gospel of Mark, trans. M. J. O'Connell (Maryknoll, N.Y.: Orbis Books, 1981). I also refer the reader here to the exegetical journal, *Texte und Kontexte,* which is published by the Alektor-Verlag (Stuttgart) and contains contributions from the area of alternative interpretations of the Bible.

2. Michel Clévenot, *Approches matérialistes de la Bible* (Paris, 1976); Eng. *Materialist Approaches to the Bible,* trans. William J. Nottingham (Maryknoll, N.Y.: Orbis Books, forthcoming). In an appendix to the German translation of Clévenot's book, *So kennen wir die Bibel nicht* (Munich, 1978), I have gone more fully into the theoretical background; I refer the reader to it for a more detailed discussion of the subject.

3. Georges Casalis, *Les idées justes ne tombent pas du ciel* (Paris, 1977), Eng. *Correct Ideas Don't Fall from the Skies: Elements for an "Inductive Theology,"* trans. Jeanne Marie Lyons (Maryknoll, N.Y.: Orbis Books, forthcoming).

4. Cf. also Casalis's critique in Chapter 4 of his book.

5. Belo, *A Materialist Reading of Mark,* p. 286.

6. *La Lettre* is published by *Temps Présent* (68, rue de Babylone, Paris 7).

7. Marx's third thesis on Feuerbach, in L. S. Feuer, ed., *Karl Marx and Friedrich Engels: Basic Writings on Politics and Philosophy* (Garden City, N.Y., 1959), p. 244.

8. Karl Marx and Friedrich Engels, *The German Ideology,* Part I, in ibid., p. 409.

9. Karl Marx, *The Economic and Philosophical Manuscripts of 1844,* ed. Dirk J. Struik, trans. Martin Milligan (New York: International Publications, 1964), p. 136.

10. Karl Marx, *Einleitung zur Kritik der politischen Ökonomie,* in *Marx-Engels Werke* 13: 632-33.

11. I have indicated elsewhere the sources on which Belo and Clévenot depend; cf. my essay, "Anknüpfungspunkte und methodisches Instrumentarium einer materialistischen Bibellektüre," in M. Clévenot, *So kennen wir die Bibel nicht,* pp. 145-70.

12. *Capital,* trans. S. Moore and E. Aveling, Volume 1, Part 4, Chapter 15, Section 1 (New York: International Publications, 1967 [1887]), p. 372, n. 3.

13. Cf. P. V. Zima, *Kritik der Literatursoziologie* (Frankfurt, 1978), pp. 72-112.

14. Cf. M. Clévenot, "Lectures matérialistes de la Bible," in *Introduction à la lecture matérialiste de la Bible* (Geneva, 1978).

15. There is here an understandable difference in level between the reflections and researches of Belo and that which individual groups can absorb of these.

16. There is a survey of the various methods in M. Titzmann, *Strukturale Textanalyse* (Munich, 1977).

17. Cf. especially Roland Barthes, *S/Z,* trans. Richard Miller (New York: Hill and Wang, 1976).

18. Cf. Füssel, art. cit. (n. 11, above), pp. 150-52.

19. Cf. J. Striedter, ed., *Texte der russischen Formalisten* 1 (Munich, 1968); V. Erlich, *Russischer Formalismus* (Munich, 1964); M. Bakhtin, *Marxismus und die Philosophie der Sprache. Grundprobleme der soziologischen Methode in der Wissenschaft von der Sprache* (Leningrad, 1929; Frankfurt, 1976).

20. Cf. E. Balibar and P. Macherey, "Thesen zum materialistischen Verfahren," *Alternative,* no. 98 (1974), 193-221.

21. Cf. Füssel, "Anknüpfungspunkte," pp. 152-54; see Note 11 above.

22. Cf. L. Schottroff and W. Stegemann, *Jesus von Nazareth—Hoffnung der Armen* (Stuttgart: Kohlhammer, 1978).

Part III

SOCIOLOGICAL READINGS
OF THE OLD TESTAMENT

10

FRANK S. FRICK and NORMAN K. GOTTWALD

The Social World of Ancient Israel

Possibilities for using the social sciences in Old Testament studies have been greatly enhanced by broad advances in cultural and social anthropology, sociological theory, and historical sociology. A review of the sociological study of ancient Israel in the period 1880–1960 shows promising starts never systematically followed through.

Since 1960 there have emerged much more methodologically astute studies of Israelite origins by means of sociological and anthropological understandings of nomadism and tribalism and of Israelite prophecy and apocalyptic by means of social data on shamanism, spirit-possession, and millennial sects. The two primary social scientific models used in Old Testament sociological studies have been the structural-functional and the historical material models, respectively indebted to the theories and methods of Max Weber and Karl Marx.

Reprinted, with minor revisions of the notes, from *The Bible and Liberation: Political and Social Hermeneutics*, 1st ed., ed. N. K. Gottwald and A. C. Wire (Berkeley: Community for Religious Research and Education [Radical Religion], 1976), pp. 110–19.

The aim of this article is: (1) to identify emerging (and re-emerging) types of sociological study of the Old Testament in relation to other forms of biblical study, and (2) to explore the potentialities and implications of sociological method for our understanding of biblical Israel.

TASKS FACING A SOCIOLOGY OF BIBLICAL ISRAEL

Among Old Testament scholars there is a reawakening of interest in the social dimensions of ancient Israel and the beginnings of a determined effort to use sociological methods to supplement the more familiar methods of literary, historical, and theological study of the Old Testament.

This interest is fueled in part by factors external to the discipline, such as the worldwide impact of social ferment and revolution on the life and thought of the churches, and the expansion and refinement of method in the social sciences.

There are distinctive factors internal to the discipline that condition the forms and styles of current sociological inquiry into ancient Israel. For one thing, the social dimensions of biblical Israel were initially explored by a number of late nineteenth- and early twentieth-century scholars such as W. Robertson Smith, Max Weber, Antonin Causse, and Johannes Pedersen. They operated on a grand scale and attempted comprehensive analyses. Part of our current task will be to reassess the strengths and weaknesses of their presuppositions, methods, and results. Furthermore, the recent upsurge of sociological interest in ancient Israel coincides with a growing recognition that traditional methods in biblical studies (such as literary criticism, form criticism, tradition history, rhetorical criticism, redaction criticism, history, history of religion, and biblical theology) have not been able to contribute a satisfactory unified account of the early Israelites as producers of literature, history, and religion. There is reason to believe that a sociological "axis," "grid," or "map" of the field may be able to relate the traditional forms of biblical study to one another in a movement toward a more coherent picture of early Israel as a total life system.

Old Testament scholars can look to some impressive examples in historical sociology. Progress in cultural and social anthropology and in sociological theory—particularly with respect to social organization and social evolution—has been put to productive use in the study of several historical societies, e.g., ancient Mesopotamia, pre-classical and classical Greece, early Islam, and ancient China.[1] These projects have offered structural frameworks for viewing the interrelations of material, cultural, and spiritual sectors of those societies. An historical society can be seen as a structured system that changes through time, and it can also be compared and contrasted with other societies in a controlled manner. Instead of discounting or trying to replace the customary humanities approaches to a society's history, literature, and religion/philosophy, a social structural analysis and synthesis tends to stimulate new research directions in all the disciplines needed for treating the great range of phenomena present in any society. New possibilities for the collaboration of historians and social scientists are rapidly opening up.[2]

Controlled sociological method in biblical study will help to overcome two damaging tendencies in Old Testament scholarship that confuse and weaken the uses that are made of sociocultural data and theories. One tendency has been to localize attention on sociocultural data that happen to be heavily represented in particular biblical texts without serious examination of "balancing," "supplementing," or "countering" data in other texts and especially from nontextual sources. This may lead, for example, to exaggerated fixations on "cult" or on "purity laws" in a research context that is isolated from enrichment and correction by other sources and methods. Another tendency has been to cite cross-cultural parallels on the basis of real or fancied linguistic, thematic, or functional similarities without careful attention to the location of the compared items in their total societies. Many intriguing cross-cultural parallels between Israel and Greece or between Israel and Arabic/ Islamic societies have been dubious and untestable because the data, lifted out of context, were compared in a nonsystemic and unhistorical way.

THE ERRATIC HISTORY OF THE SOCIOLOGY OF BIBLICAL ISRAEL

We will now consider what there is to learn from the early "giants" in social study of the Old Testament. How does their work stand up today? In what respects can we correct them and go beyond them? Only by getting in critical and creative touch with that earlier tradition of biblical sociological study will we be able to minimize errors and false leads and begin to move beyond the present ambivalent and polarized situation. While some scholars flounder in unverifiable cult theories and impressionistic "parallelomania," others react by "sticking to the text," without a method for uncovering the wider contexts and structures of Israelite life which alone can properly elucidate even the text in a full exegetical sense.

W. Robertson Smith and Julius Wellhausen. Already by the end of the nineteenth century the growing disciplines of anthropology and sociology were being applied to the Old Testament. An early work by John Fenton provided a sociological analysis to supplement literary criticism, although he scarcely touched on the relation between social organization and the development of religion.[3] W. Robertson Smith and Julius Wellhausen compared the societal forms, customs, and rites of the Israelites with the ethnography of the pre-Islamic Arab Bedouins.[4] They pointed out significant parallels, but their overall interpretation was based on the prevailing assumption of the day that historical societies in the ancient Far East had evolved out of pastoral nomadic societies. Their work was eclipsed by a wave of interest in comparing Israel with Mesopotamian societies and also by general uneasiness about connecting Israel in such a fundamental way with "primitive" and "pagan" Bedouins. Nevertheless, the work of Robertson Smith and Wellhausen had one lasting and ultimately disastrous influence on biblical studies: although their conclusions were contested and dismissed in many details, their basic assumption that early Israel was a pastoral nomadic society was accepted uncritically until well past the mid-point of this century. In fact, that assumption is still the unchallenged operating scheme of most biblical scholars who have not had occasion to study the matter closely with the aid of improved social scientific understandings of pastoral nomadism.

Max Weber. As part of his monumental project to investigate the connections between religion and economics, sociologist of religion Max Weber studied the social groups and forces that interacted with the religious ideas and practices of the ancient Israelites.[5] Considering that he worked at a time when biblical study was largely literary criticism, Weber was remarkably successful in anticipating the significance of the cult, the covenant, and the role of the Levites in early Israel. Weber also recognized that early Israel was no simple unity but a coalition of socio-economic groups. The pastoral nomadic model of Israel's beginnings inhibited Weber from a full development of his intuitions, as did also his inability to distinguish clearly between the premonarchic and monarchic phases of Israelite social and political organization. Oddly enough, Weber's epic undertaking has never received the systematic criticism it deserves. This was partly because he was an "intruder" into Old Testament study without "proper" biblical scholarly credentials. Also, the style and organization of his volume on ancient Judaism—assembled after his death—are dense and contorted, and the English translation is clumsy and at points inaccurate.

Social Gospel and "The Chicago School." In the United States, the Social Gospel movement drew heavily on biblical sources and produced a spate of biblical sociological primers or segments of broader social ethical and theological works that summed up the social dimensions of the religion of the Bible.[6] These were addressed mainly to the broad religious community or to theologically-oriented audiences such as seminarians and pastors. They seldom issued a challenge or charted a program of inquiry and research for biblical specialists. North American biblical scholars were strongly under the spell of forms of European biblical scholarship that gave them few leads on how to pick up the biblical sociological emphases of the Social Gospel as a valid project for serious scholarship. For a time in the 1920s and 1930s biblical scholars at the University of Chicago—where sociology had made its first penetration into the American academic setting—tried to combine a broadly social approach with comparative religion in order to reconstruct Israel and the early church as living communities.[7] Their achievements were more extensive in New Testament studies than in Old Testament studies. "The Chicago School" did not develop precise sociological methods but tended in the direction of comparative cultural studies that did not take the social structure of biblical communities per se as a high priority. Eventually the University of

Chicago approach was overwhelmed by the tidal wave of Neo-Orthodoxy and biblical theology that struck North American religious and biblical scholarly circles in the late 1930s and the 1940s.

Form Criticism. Meanwhile, form criticism, with its concern to identify typical forms of biblical speech in typical "life-settings," affirmed a broadly social concern but failed to employ sociological methods.[8] Disappointingly, form criticism's main dependence on the social sciences was at the point of folklore studies and some limited aspects of rite and custom in primitive societies. This was much too narrow a spectrum of social scientific methods to carry out an adequate reconstruction of the community setting of traditions and their symbolic functions. The horizons of the "life-setting" (*Sitz im Leben*) were increasingly narrowed. Formal worship or cult, as one aspect of the social system, crowded out the other aspects. The cult itself was more and more treated by form critics as a self-contained entity without regard to social organization, economics, politics, or communal symbolizing.

Martin Noth. Martin Noth, both a form critic and a follower of Albrecht Alt's territorial-historical method, advanced the notion that early Israel's socioreligious organization as a league of twelve tribes in a common form of worship was parallel to the Old Latin, Etruscan, and Greek sacral leagues of tribes and city-states, as at Delphi (called in Greek an *amphictyony*).[9] Although incisive and comprehensive, Noth's hypothesis did not pay careful attention to many differences among the Mediterranean amphictyonies, nor did he study them in relation to other types of Greek leagues and confederacies, some of which seem closer at points to Israel's social organization than the sacral leagues. Most seriously, Noth did not ask the decisive question of the relative locations of the Greek and Israelite leagues in their respective social systems.[10] In fact he was comparing the primary and most inclusive social structure of Israel with a relatively minor, second or third level form of social organization in Greece. It did not occur to Noth—nor has it occurred to most of his critics—that a wide range of tribal constructs and inter-tribal confederate forms are available to illuminate the specifics of early Israelite tribalism or "re-tribalization." As a result, biblical interpreters have thought themselves trapped with the cruel choice either of hanging on to Noth's problematic amphictyonic model or of assuming the even more problematic conclusion that Israel lacked any sort of inter-tribal social bonding.

Antonin Causse. Antonin Causse, much indebted to the sociologist of religion Émile Durkheim, wrote an impressively synthesized account of Israelite sociocultural evolution. His premise was that Israel began as an ethnic pastoral nomadic community that gradually lost its organic solidarity as it settled down and diversified economically as a result of the pressure and attraction of Canaanite civilization.[11] The original bond between society and religion was severed and collective identity and responsibility dissolved into private interests. The previous harmony of social life and religious thought and practice was ruptured beyond repair. Prophets arose to address the new confusions and divided loyalties from the critical perspective of the old solidarities. Causse opposed a merely romantic notion of Bedouin life and emphasized that Israelite peasants retained the old norms and practices of social solidarity. His analysis, however, did not explain how peasants managed to retain pastoral nomadic values and habits, other than by some sort of ethnic memory. Also, it is now widely recognized that Causse's simplistic trajectory from collectivism to individualism needs radical reformulation and nuancing.

Causse's sociocultural view of ancient Israel as a people in transit from cohesive ethnicity to individuated religiosity is probably the most lucid expression of what still remains the "preferred theory" of Israel's social history. The big watershed in Israel is presumed to have been the move from harmonious self-contained pastoral nomadic modes of existence to divisive atomizing agricultural, craft, and trading modes of existence. In its sociocultural movement Israel is viewed as proceeding from "lower" to "higher" cultural adaptations, from "simple" to "complex" social and economic organization, as it transplanted itself from the desert to the sown land and then to city life. Neo-Orthodox and biblical theological "return to the Bible" movements were not very receptive to the evolutionary social development of Israel articulated by Causse, but they did not criticize this social developmental theory on the grounds of social data. Instead, they either ignored or rebutted it on general theological grounds. No coherent counterversion of the social history of Israel has been seriously proposed until recent years.

It should be stressed that this socioreligious evolutionary conception is not to be faulted for perceiving the organically social nature of Israel's religion, nor is it to be doubted that Israel's social organization changed adaptively throughout biblical history. The problem of the model is its tenuous connection with the empirical data and its rootage in antiquated anthropological and sociological models that have long been outmoded. Adherents of this two-stage Israelite progression—from (1) pastoral nomadism as a homogeneous form of labor in organic socioreligious solidarity to (2) agriculture and handcraft/merchant urban life as a fragmentary division of labor marked by socioreligious anomie and individualism—often interpret the first stage along the lines of Noth's sacral inter-tribal league. In all these formulations it is striking how little attention has been paid to the accumulating corpus of anthropological and sociological studies of nomadic communities, of tribal societies pursuing various economic modes, of the parameters of social and cultural innovation, of the interaction of city and countryside, plus many other relevant types of studies.[12] Once these materials are admitted into the discussion, the constructs of Israelite society favored in biblical circles are razed to their foundations.

Johannes Pedersen. Mention should also be made of Johannes Pedersen's psychosocial study of biblical Israel, notable for its treatment of the mana-like Hebrew conceptions of "name," "soul," "holiness," etc. This has been a work of considerable impact on biblical scholars seeking a way to overcome the fragmentation and hyper-rationalism of literary criticism.[13] Pedersen applied to Israel the folk-soul and group consciousness approach that the Danish historian of religion V. P. Grønbech had applied to old Nordic culture. He tended to see the social system as a kind of mirror reflection of the people's psychology or mode of perceiving reality. Actually Pedersen mixed two very different approaches in his mammoth study. Alongside the better-known psychically empathetic probe of key Israelite words, practices, and institutions, he introduced somewhat briefer but suggestive sketches of the social history in which he tried to show how the religion changed in pace with the social forms. The two approaches were never satisfactorily integrated, and Pedersen lacked the social scientific tools to fully realize his efforts at a socioreligious developmental history.

Albrecht Alt and William F. Albright. Over the last half century the two dominant traditions in Old Testament scholarship have been the form-critical and the territorial-historical approaches associated with Albrecht Alt and the archaeological and linguistic approaches associated with William F. Albright.[14] Their respective sets of methodologies for relating biblical and extra-biblical literary and material remains have been highly productive and not so opposed as some of their adherents have claimed. While neither founder of these approaches was markedly informed by sociological method and theory, it is correct to note in both these influential scholars a component of sociological interest which continued undiminished throughout their work, possibly intensifying toward the culmination of their long careers. In his last years Albright was fascinated with the *'apiru* (a Canaanite social grouping in some way related to the Hebrews) as donkey caravaneers, and some of Alt's most trenchant studies on social conditions under the monarchy were written toward the close of his life.

THE AMBIGUOUS PRESENT AND FUTURE PROMISE OF A SOCIOLOGY OF BIBLICAL ISRAEL

Limited Advances. The work of certain students of Alt and Albright gives fuller expression to the implicit sociological impulse in their teachers. From the Alt stream of scholarship came Noth's model of early Israel as an amphictyony. Alt also stimulated M. B. Rowton to pursue a territorial-historical study of the *'apiru* and to begin an ambitious study of different types of nomadism in the ancient Near East.[15] From the Albright stream of scholarship have come George Mendenhall's proposal that the Israelite covenant was a religious analogue to the suzerain-vassal political treaty,[16] and his hypothesis that the Israelite conquest of Canaan was a peasant's revolt instead of a nomadic invasion or infiltration.[17] Sometimes as offshoots of the Alt or Albright methods and sometimes more independently inspired, numerous detailed studies have treated a range of Israelite sociopolitical texts, offices, practices, and institutions in relation to similar phenomena in ancient Near Eastern societies.[18] Attentive to the rich literary finds from Ugarit, Alalakh, and Amarna, initial efforts have been made at reconstructing the social and political institutions of Syria and Palestine in the Late Bronze Age (1500–1200 B.C.) and later.[19] Unfortunately, in the application of these results to biblical studies, as in the case of the *'apiru* = Hebrew equation, there is a continuing tendency to examine limited social items but to neglect their systemic contexts. Nevertheless, the sociological impulse to bring these detailed studies toward a productive synthesis asserts itself ever more insistently. The complex socioreligious mutation of inter-tribal Israel, initially probed by Mendenhall, is receiving intensive sociological attention in recent research.[20] Likewise, more sociologically informed treatments of Israelite monarchic institutions and of the prophetic office are beginning to appear, although the desired comprehensive and integrated social theory still requires development for the monarchic era.[21]

Continuing Handicaps. All in all, there has been regrettably little practical application and synthesis of the significant detailed social studies of biblical Israel in context. Lack of familiarity with progress in the prehistory of the ancient Near East, in anthropology, and in social evolution and social organizational theory, still permits biblical scholars to write about Israel's supposed pastoral nomadic origins as though nothing on the subject of pastoral nomadism had been learned in the last fifty years.[22] Likewise, with some happy recent exceptions, biblical scholars talk about the city in ancient Israel in blissful disregard of historical and sociological studies on urbanization processes and urban organization.[23] Even Noth's widely accepted amphictyonic hypothesis and Mendenhall's generally rejected or ignored revolt model of the Israelite takeover in Canaan have drawn astonishingly little evaluation informed by sociological observation and theory.

Major stumbling blocks to progress in the sociology of biblical Israel have been the lack of communication among scholars who are doing Israelite sociology and the great lag time between basic research and publication of results. Many of the most important contributions to an adequate sociology of Israel remain unassimilated to the mainstream of biblical studies—and often unknown to other biblical social researchers—because they are buried in unpublished academic dissertations.[24] When the existence of these contributions is known and even bandied about at times in the journal articles (as in the case of John T. Luke's 1965 University of Michigan Ph.D. dissertation on pastoralism and politics at Mari), it is clear that few scholars have read them and that they are often misstating conclusions at second or third hand. It is to be hoped that the development of a continuing working group within the Society of Biblical Literature on the Social World of Ancient Israel can take steps to make research more readily available so that the element of "mystery" and misinformation about biblical sociology can be reduced. At the same time, the basic results and issues in these studies can be spread and discussed in all circles, including the churches, where an accurate understanding of biblical society and religion is likely to be prized.

Sociocultural "Background" Data. One additional sector of Old Testament studies may be loosely called sociological. These are the materials about daily life, customs, institutions, and general culture of Israel collected in introductory handbooks and reference works, the so-called "realia."[25] The best of these is Roland de Vaux's *Ancient Israel: Its Life and Institutions* (1961). Even so, De Vaux's invaluable compilation of social data lacks a sustained social historical perspective and is meager on sociological theory. Some of these social and cultural data are gathered in archaeological reports, in studies of Israel's neighbors, and in dictionary and encyclopedia articles.[26] For the most part sociocultural data are still thought of as "preliminaries" or "background" to the primary business of literary, historical, and religious study of the Old Testament. It will be admitted that Israel had "social" institutions such as family, clan, and tribe. Yet large tracts of social reality tend to be omitted—notably economics, but also important aspects of politics. Systematic analyses and syntheses in cross-section (synchronics) and over time (diachronics) seldom occur, the data rather being presented as so many discrete "facts." Sometimes the materials are organized fragmentarily as commentary on biblical texts or topics. From these sociocultural handbooks, the average exegete or scholar—not to mention lay reader—derives little sense of how to go about putting all the social pieces together in some kind of method or interpretative framework.

Archaeology. Archaeology has been so deeply engrossed in historical problems related to the Bible, such as the conquest of Canaan, that it has had little to contribute on social history. Excavations have been largely confined to walled sites; only in recent years have rural settlements and installations (such as waterworks and terraces) been taken up as objects of archaeological study.[27] The so-called "new archaeology," having contributed brilliantly to cultural and social reconstructions of American Indian civilizations, is lately stimulating some biblical archaeologists to a similar broad ethnographic view of their work.[28] Methods aimed at recovering aspects of ancient material culture, such as pollen analysis and tree-ring counting, are slowly finding their way into biblical archaeology. Increasing cooperation between prehistoric and historic archaeologists is called for. Because of lack of communication and differences in training, biblical archaeologists have made only limited use of models employed regularly by prehistorians (e.g., ecological, demographic, and systemic models).[29]

It is clear, therefore, that a social scientific ferment is at work among some biblical archaeologists. Instead of almost exclusive preoccupation with destruction levels in thirteenth-to-eleventh-century Canaan in order to determine the identity of the destroyers and the date of their attack, the more subtle and complex project of recapturing the settlement patterns and characteristic means of subsistence of the first Israelites is enlisting the imagination and resources of a growing number of archaeologists. One of the challenging tasks before social researchers of biblical Israel is to formulate models and specific research questions and inventories of needed data that can be addressed to archaeologists. Archaeologists in their turn will doubtless have questions and valuable "leads" to pass on to social researchers. In this way the material cultural artifacts and the textual artifacts will be drawn into closer communication along a much broader front than when they are mined solely for answers to precise historical questions.

TWO STRATEGIES FOR A SOCIOLOGY OF BIBLICAL ISRAEL

To round out this largely historical review of sociologically-oriented study of ancient Israel, a word will be said about two types of social scientific constructs that may serve to guide social research into biblical Israel. They are intended as examples with which the writers are familiar, in no sense exhausting possibilities or precluding other approaches.

The Typological Strategy. One crucial social scientific approach is *the typological strategy for elucidating social formations and institutions.* The model is broadly that of Max Weber's "ideal type," although the typology in any given instance may be more or less abstract than Weber's usual level of treatment and more or less historically fleshed out than in Weber's style of exposition.[30] A social type is really a cluster of social phenomena in a developed form that is viewed as "characteristic" or "normal," marked by typical traits "abstracted" out of concrete cases. Given the positing of the type, departures from the "type norm" (norm here understood as "the usual" rather than as "the morally obligatory") and combinations and interpenetrations of types may be empirically (including historically) noted and clarified.

Representative of the typological strategy are two works of particular value for Old Testament studies: S. N. Eisenstadt, *The Political Systems of Empires,* and G. Sjoberg, *The Preindustrial City.*[31] Eisenstadt studied numerous examples of the "type" he called historical bureaucratic empire and characterized that sociopolitical formation in rich detail. Sjoberg did the same, in somewhat more digested and compressed form, with the "type" he called preindustrial city. In both cases the examples are drawn from many geographic areas and many historical periods. Each scholar attempted to specify the respects in which the cited historical examples exhibit the type traits and to indicate factors making for skewed or asymmetrical specimens of the type.

Sometimes the typological study is heavily weighted in historical description culminating in type proposals. This style of social typology is more amenable to the usual historical cast of mind of the biblical investigator. An instance is E. Wolf, *Peasant Wars of the Twentieth Century.*[32] Wolf unfolds the history and principal features of peasant wars in Mexico, Russia, China, Vietnam, Algeria, and Cuba. In a concise conclusion he sets forth a preliminary typology that both generalizes and discriminates on the basis of the six historical case studies.

It is fairly easy to see the limits and vulnerabilities of social type studies. They aim at a given moment in time (synchronics) in the life of a social formation and can degenerate into formalism unless constantly checked by empirical data and supplemented by questions about what went before and what came after the given moment under investigation (diachronics). Also, social typologists are often criticized because they are not experts in all the societies from which they draw examples. Granting these liabilities, typological studies carefully executed are of immense value in suggesting and testing appropriate research strategies and theory designs for particular societies. They have a provocative and directive "mapping" function. Like good maps, the further knowledge that they stimulate is vital in correcting and refining the earlier type models in order to enhance accuracy and utility.

Typological studies are especially valuable in alerting researchers in limited social sectors to classes of data and interconnections among the phenomena that can easily be missed by an overly narrow "close in" view of the subject. Eisenstadt, for example, is exceedingly instructive for anyone trying to grasp the anatomy of Egyptian imperial rule in Amarna Canaan (15th–14th centuries B.C.) or of Assyrian imperial rule in its western provinces during the divided monarchy in Israel. Similarly, Sjoberg is a mine of insight and detail for those who wish to make sense of the structure of Israelite cities and their relations with their hinterlands.[33] Of course "the social type" is a generalization abstracted from many cases and in relation to which all cases are merely approximations. The positing of social types is a method of learning and of clarifying and refining the structure and function of social parts and wholes. The social type is a hypothetical formation drawn from empirical data in the first place and then played back against the data and continually corrected by the data. It can both reveal and conceal. The social type can bring out characteristic patterning of social phenomena and sharpen observation; on the other hand, it tells us little about how phenomena originate and why and how they change. That takes another kind of strategy, to which we now turn.

The Historical Cultural Material Strategy. A second crucial social scientific approach is *the historical cultural material or techno-environmental/ techno-economic strategy.* The model is broadly that of Karl Marx's identification of the succession of social forms in history in tandem with means of production and relations of production—i.e., with the concrete modes by which people sustain themselves and collectively reproduce their physical, social, and cultural existence. The methodological set is to focus on the convergence of factors that bring about nodal social changes with the intent of specifying typical and temporal priorities among the change-promoting factors.

Representative of the historical cultural material strategy are Marvin Harris, *The Rise of Anthropological Theory,* and Gerhard and Jean Lenski, *Human Societies,* to which one could add the work of the French Marxist anthropologists Claude Meillassoux and Emmanuel Terray.[34] Harris, who has written the first comprehensive history of anthropology in English since Robert Lowie in the 1930s, contends and demonstrates that structural-functional, culture and personality, ethnolinguistic, and other static modes of theorizing, completely fail to account for social evolution. Only as we relate social formations to their roots in economy and environment can we begin to account for stasis and change from society to society over time. The Lenskis, adopting what they call an "ecological-evolutionary" method, demonstrate that, in spite of the irrational bias directed at one or another caricature of "economic determinism," the single most important factor in societal change is the interchange between the social organism and its environment. They describe the biological foundations and parameters of sociocultural adaptations in which the variable of technological exploitation of the environment sets the direction of social adjustment and innovation.

Applications of the historical cultural material strategy to ancient Israel have been practically nil. The articles by Jan Dus on Joshua as liberator and religious founder of Israel,[35] and by Henri Mottu on the clash between the prophets Jeremiah and Hananiah,[36] operate chiefly within an historical cultural material framework. Their analyses are concentrated, however, on sociopolitical and ideological considerations to such an extent that the related techno-economic material cultural conditions are less adequately treated. This disproportion of analysis has unfortunate consequences for Dus's examination of modes of production in Canaan and early Israel, since he does not rigorously assess the naive scholarly consensus about Israelite pastoral nomadic origins.

Some limited attention has been given to the coincidence of the emergence of Israel with the introduction of iron and the invention of slaked lime plaster for making water-tight cisterns.[37] These technological breakthroughs have not, however, been studied as a part of the total Israelite cultural and social complexes, for example, in relation to the agricultural modes of production and the typical settlement patterns. Mention may be made of Lawrence Stager's work on ancient irrigation agriculture in the Buqei'ah Valley as an example of an "eco-systematic" archaeological approach which gives attention to ancient ingenuity within a regional ecology.[38] Only of late have features of the water sources, the agricultural terraces, the settlement patterns, and the political security system been brought together in the initial stages of an historical cultural material hypothesis about the origins of Israelite free peasant agriculture vis-à-vis Canaanite hierarchically expropriated agriculture.[39]

To be sure, any particular historical cultural material hypothesis is no more sacrosanct than any particular typological scheme. The criteria of judgment are similar: has the hypothesis taken all relevant evidence into account? Does any alternative theory explain the data better, in whole or in part, and is it possible to combine elements of two or more hypotheses in a more satisfactory explanation than either hypothesis alone provides? Moreover, adequate historical cultural material strategies normally require the incorporation of typological strategies in varying synchronic/diachronic combinations. It should also be obvious that a serious pursuit of the historical cultural material approach to biblical Israel will place demands on archaeology, historical and cultural geography, hydrology, climatology, demography, and numerous other disciplines so far only randomly and sporadically drawn upon for the elucidation of ancient Israel. This brief survey of the history and promise of biblical Israelite sociological research has omitted reference to many sub-topics in the general field, such as sociolinguistics, social leadership roles, form and function in genealogies, and we could go on at great length in such an inventory. Enough has been said, we hope, to provide the general reader with orientation and to stimulate biblical researchers in the application of proposed methods and in the articulation of alternative or additional methods. By all counts the protean and multifaceted field of Israelite sociology seems to be offering new and rich possibilities for biblical science and for the social self-understanding of the religious communities that base themselves on the Old Testament as sacred literature.

NOTES

1. Robert Mc C. Adams, *The Evolution of Urban Society: Early Mesopotamia and Prehistoric Mexico* (Chicago: Aldine, 1966); Igor M. Diakonoff, ed., *Ancient Mesopotamia: Socio-Economic History* (Moscow: Nauka Publishing House, 1969); G. Thomson, *Studies in Ancient Greek Society: The Prehistoric Aegean* (Secaucus, N.J.: Citadel Press, 1966); Alvin W. Gouldner, *Enter Plato: Classical Greece and the Origins of Social Theory* (New York: Basic Books, 1966), Part I (published separately as *The Hellenic World: A Sociological Analysis* [New York: Harper & Row, 1969]); W. Montgomery Watt, *Islam and the Integration of Society* (Evanston, Ill.: Northwestern University Press, 1961); P. Wheatley, *The Pivot of the Four Quarters: A Preliminary Inquiry into the Origins and Character of the Ancient Chinese City* (Chicago: Aldine, 1971).

2. G. Leff, *History and Social Theory* (Birmingham, Ala.: University of Alabama Press, 1969, and New York: Doubleday, 1971).

3. John Fenton, *Early Hebrew Life: A Study in Sociology* (London: Trübner and Co., 1880).

4. W. Robertson Smith, *Lectures on the Religion of the Semites: The Fundamental Institutions*, 3rd ed. with intro. by S. A. Cook, 1927, reprinted with prolegomenon by James Muilenburg (New York: KTAV Publishing House, 1972), and *Kinship and Marriage in Early Arabia,* 2nd ed. 1903 (New York: Humanities, 1972); Julius Wellhausen, *Reste arabischen Heidentums,* 2nd ed. (1897).

5. Max Weber, *Ancient Judaism* (New York: Free Press, 1952 [1921]), and see Weber's systematic analysis of major analytic concepts applied to Israel in *The Sociology of Religion*, trans. Ephraim Fischoff (Boston: Beacon, 1964).

6. Graham Taylor, *Syllabus of Biblical Sociology* (Chicago: P. F. Pettibone, 1900); W. Rauschenbusch, *Christianity and the Social Crisis* (New York and London: Macmillan, 1907), Ch. 1; T. G. Soares, *The Social Institutions and Ideals of the Bible* (Nashville: Abingdon, 1915); C. C. McCown, *The Genesis of the Social Gospel: The Meaning of the Ideals of Jesus in the Light of Their Antecedents* (New York and London: Knopf, 1929).

7. Louis Wallis, *A Sociological Study of the Bible* (Chicago: University of Chi-

cago Press, 1912); idem, *God and the Social Process: A Study in Human History* (Chicago: University of Chicago Press, 1935) and *The Bible Is Human,* reprint of 1942 ed. (New York: AMS Press, 1972); W. C. Graham, *The Prophets and Israel's Culture* (Chicago: University of Chicago Press, 1934); W. C. Graham and Herbert May, *Culture and Conscience: An Archaeological Study of the New Religious Past in Ancient Palestine* (Chicago: University of Chicago Press, 1936). Among the New Testament scholars were Shailer Matthews, Shirley Jackson Case, and Harold R. Willoughby; for a brief summary and critique of their work, see L. E. Keck, *JAAR* 42 (1974): 435-52.

8. John Hayes, ed., *The Old Testament and Form Criticism* (San Antonio: Trinity University Press, 1973), particularly the chapter on the study of forms by Martin J. Buss.

9. Martin Noth, *Das System der zwoelf Staemme Israels* (Stuttgart: Kohlhammer, 1930) and, in its condensed form, *The History of Israel,* 2nd ed. (New York: Harper & Row, 1960), pp. 85-138.

10. Extensive analysis of Greek leagues and confederacies in Jacob A. Larsen, *Representative Government in Greek and Roman History* (Berkeley: University of California Press, 1955), and *Greek Federal States: Their Institutions and History* (New York: Oxford University Press, 1968). A structural-functional and historical comparative critique of Noth's amphictyonic model appears in N. K. Gottwald, *The Tribes of Yahweh: A Sociology of the Religion of Liberated Israel, 1250-1050 B.C.E.* (Maryknoll, N.Y.: Orbis Books, 1979), pp. 345-86. For a summary of evidence against Noth's theory, see A. J. Hauser, *JBL* 94 (1975): 190-200.

11. A. Causse, *Du groupe ethnique à la communauté religieuse* (1937) and, in less developed form, in his *Les prophetes contre la civilisation* (1913), and *Les "pauvres" d'Israël* (1922). Assessment of Causse's sources and contributions to the sociology of Israel has been made by S. T. Kimbrough, Jr. *Israelite Religion in Sociological Perspective: The Work of Antonin Causse* (Wiesbaden: Harrassowitz, 1978).

12. See, for instance, J. T. Luke, "Pastoralism and Politics in the Mari Period: A Re-Examination of the Character and Political Significance of the Major West Semitic Tribal Groups in the Middle Euphrates" (Ph.D. diss., University of Michigan, 1965); N. K. Gottwald, "Were the Early Israelites Pastoral Nomads?" *Rhetorical Criticism: Essays in Honor of James Muilenburg,* ed. Jared J. Jackson and Martin Kessler, Pittsburgh Theological Monograph Series, No. 1 (Pittsburgh: Pickwick Press, 1974), pp. 223-55; M. D. Sahlins, *Tribesmen* (New York: Prentice-Hall, 1968); Morton H. Fried, *The Evolution of Political Society: An Evolutionary View* (New York: Random House, 1968); J. Helm, ed., *Essays on the Problem of Tribe,* Proceedings of the 1967 Annual Spring Meeting of the American Ethnological Society (Seattle: University of Washington Press, 1968); Homer G. Barnett, *Innovation: The Basis of Cultural Change* (New York: McGraw-Hill, 1953); Robert Braidwood and Gordon R. Willey, eds., *Courses Toward Urban Life: Archaeological Consideration of Some Cultural Alternatives,* Viking Fund Publications in Anthropology Series, No. 32 (Chicago: Aldine, 1962); Robert Mc C. Adams and Hans Niseen, *The Uruk Countryside: The Natural Setting of Urban Societies* (Chicago: University of Chicago Press, 1973).

13. Johannes Pedersen, *Israel: Its Life and Culture,* 4 vols. (New York: Oxford University Press, I-II, 1926, III-IV, 1940).

14. Albrecht Alt, *Kleine Schriften,* 3 vols. 1953-1959; idem, *Essays on Old Testa-*

ment History and Religion, trans. R. A. Wilson (New York: Doubleday, Anchor, 1968). William F. Albright, *From the Stone Age to Christianity: Monotheism and the Historical Process*, 2nd ed. (Baltimore: Johns Hopkins University Press, 1957); idem, *History, Archaeology, and Christian Humanism* (New York: McGraw-Hill, and London: Adam and Charles Black, 1965); idem, *Yahweh and the Gods of Canaan: A Historical Analysis of Two Contrasting Faiths* (New York: Humanities Press, 1968).

15. M. B. Rowton, "The Topological Factor in the '*Ḫapiru* Problem," *Studies in Honor of Benno Landsberger* (1965), pp. 375–87; the first two parts of Rowton's ten-part series on pastoral nomadism in the ancient Near East appeared in *Or* 42 (1973): 247–58, and in *JNES* 32 (1973): 201–15.

16. G. E. Mendenhall, *Law and Covenant in Israel and the Ancient Near East*, 1955, reprinted in *BAR* 3 (1970): 3–53.

17. G. E. Mendenhall, "The Hebrew Conquest of Palestine," *BA* 25 (1962): 66–87. (Reprinted in *BAR* 3 [1970]: 100–120); *The Tenth Generation: The Origins of the Biblical Tradition* (Baltimore: Johns Hopkins University Press, 1973).

18. A representative, though far from exhaustive, sample of this technical literature up to 1960 is given in a topically arranged bibliography in Roland de Vaux, *Ancient Israel: Its Life and Institutions*, 2 vols. (New York: McGraw-Hill, 1961 [1958, 1960], pp. 519–52, which can be supplemented by the bibliographical footnotes in G. Buccellati, *Cities and Nations of Ancient Syria: An Essay on the Political Institutions with Reference to the Israelite Kingdom* (Rome: Institute of Near East Studies, University of Rome, 1967).

19. Moshe Greenberg, *The Ḫab/piru* (New Haven: American Oriental Society 39, 1955); G. Buccellati, *Cities and Nations of Ancient Syria*; two extremely valuable critical review articles are published in M. Liverani, ed., *La Siria nel Tardo Bronzo* (1969): H. Klengel, "Probleme einer politischen Geschichte des spaetbronzezeitlichen Syrien," pp. 15–30, and M. Heltzer, "Problems of the Social History of Syria in the Late Bronze Age," pp. 31–46.

20. M. L. Chaney, "ḤDL-II in 1 Sam. 2:5; Judg. 5:7; and Deut. 15:11," paper delivered at the annual meeting of the AAR-SBL on October 24, 1974; and "ḤDL-II and the 'Song of Deborah': Textual, Philosophical, and Sociological Studies in Judges 5, with Special Reference to the Occurrences of ḤDL in Biblical Hebrew" (Ph.D. diss., Harvard University, 1976); N. K. Gottwald, "Domain Assumptions and Societal Models in the Study of Pre-Monarchic Israel," Edinburgh Congress Volume of *VTSup* (1975): 89–100, and *The Tribes of Yahweh*.

21. On monarchic institutions, T. N. D. Mettinger, *Solomonic State Officials: A Study of the Civil Government of the Israelite Monarchy* (Lund: Gleerup, 1971); J. R. Rosenbloom, "Social Science Concepts of Modernization and Biblical History: The Development of the Israelite Monarchy," *JAAR* 40 (1972): 437–44; W. E. Claburn, "The Fiscal Basis of Josiah's Reform," *JBL* 92 (1973): 11–22. On the prophetic office: P. Berger, "Charisma and Innovation: The Social Location of Israelite Prophecy," *ASR* 28 (1963): 940–50, with rejoinder by J. G. Williams, "The Social Location of Israelite Prophecy," *JAAR* 37 (1969): 153–65; B. O. Long, "Prophetic Authority as Social Reality," in *Canon and Authority: Essays in Old Testament Religion and Theology*, ed. George W. Coats and Burke O. Long (Philadelphia: Fortress Press, 1977), pp. 3–20; Robert P. Carroll, *When Prophecy Failed: Cognitive Dissonance in the Prophetic Traditions of the Old Testament* (New York: Seabury, 1979); Robert W. Wilson, *Prophecy and Society in Ancient Israel* (Philadelphia: Fortress Press, 1980).

22. Exemplary of the continuing deficiency of biblical scholarly treatment of pastoral nomadism are Manfried Weippert, *The Settlement of the Israelite Tribes in Palestine,* trans. James Martin, Studies in Biblical Theology, 2nd ser., No. 21 (Naperville, Ill.: Allenson, 1971), pp. 102–26; and M. S. Seale, *The Desert Bible: Nomadic Tribal Culture and Old Testament Interpretation* (New York: St. Martin's, 1974).

23. Studies of the Israelite city informed by sociological method and theory: F. S. Frick, *The City in Ancient Israel,* SBLDS 36 (Missoula: Scholar's Press, 1977); and J. H. Halligan, "A Critique of the City in the Yahwist Corpus" (Ph.D. diss., University of Notre Dame, 1975).

24. An initial, in no sense complete, list of sociologically oriented or sociologically relevant dissertations yet to be published is here appended: S. H. Bess, "Systems of Land Tenure in Ancient Israel" (Ph.D. diss., Princeton University, 1968); A. E. Glock, "Warfare in Mari and Early Israel" (Ph.D. diss., University of Michigan, 1963); P. A. Riemann, "Desert and Return to Desert in the Pre-Exilic Prophets" (Ph.D. diss., Harvard University, 1963); J. T. Luke (see Note 12); S. Schwertner, " 'Das Verheissene Land': Bedeutung und Verstaendnis des Landes nach den fruehen Zeugnissen des Alten Testament" (inaugural diss., University of Heidelberg, 1966); W. E. Claburn, "Deuteronomy and Collective Behavior" (Ph.D. diss., Princeton University, 1968); W. J. Dumbrell, "The Midianites and Their Transjordanian Successors: Studies in the History, Social Structure, and Political Influence of Related Transjordanian Groupings" (Th.D. diss., Harvard University, 1970); F. S. Frick (see Note 23); A. E. Glock, "Warfare in Mari and Early Israel" (Ph.D. diss., University of Michigan, 1968); D. A. Patrick, "A Study of the Conceptual Models of the Covenant" (Th.D. diss., Graduate Theological Union, Berkeley, 1971); R. R. Wilson, "Genealogy and History in the Old Testament," (Ph.D. diss., Yale University, 1972 [published as *Genealogy and History in the Biblical World,* Yale Near Eastern Researches, No. 8, New Haven: Yale University Press, [1977]); J. H. Halligan (see Note 23); M. L. Chaney (see Note 23).

25. Roland de Vaux (see Note 18); Martin Noth, *The Old Testament World* (Philadelphia: Fortress Press, 1966 [1964]); B. Reicke and L. Rost, eds., *Biblisch-Historisches Handwoerterbuch,* 3 vols. (1962–1966), plus the older and still useful work of G. Dalman, *Arbeit und Sitte in Palaestina,* 7 vols. (1928–1942).

26. A. G. Barrois, *Manuel d'archéologie biblique,* 2 vols. (1939–1953); G. E. Wright, *Biblical Archaeology,* rev. ed. (Philadelphia: Westminster, 1963); C. F. Pfeiffer, ed., *The Biblical World: A Dictionary of Biblical Archaeology* (Grand Rapids, Mich.: Baker Books, 1966); D. J. Wiseman, ed., *People of Old Testament Times* (New York: Oxford University Press, 1973); Willy Corswant, *A Dictionary of Life in Bible Times* , completed and illus. by Eduard Urech, trans. Arthur Heathcote (New York: Oxford University Press, 1960 [1956]). Of all the biblical dictionaries and encyclopedias, probably the one that has most fully integrated the *realia* into the body of biblical studies is U. M. D. Cassuto, B. Mazar, et al., eds. *'Entsīqlōpedyāh Miqrā'ith* (Biblical Encyclopedia), 1955—, so far available only in modern Hebrew and lacking one or two volumes to reach completion.

27. Z. Ron, "Agricultural Terraces in the Judean Mountains," *IEJ* 16 (1966): 33–49, 111–22; B. Golomb and Y. Kedar, "Ancient Agriculture in the Galilee Mountains," *IEJ* 21 (1971): 136–140; C. H. J. de Geus, "The Importance of Archaeological Research into the Palestinian Agricultural Terraces, with an Excursus on the Hebrew word *gbi**," *PEQ* 107 (1975): 65–74; see also J. E. Spencer and G. A. Hale, "The Origin, Nature, and Distribution of Agricultural Terracing," *Pacific Viewpoint* 2 (1961): 1–40.

28. For example, A. E. Glock, director of the Concordia-ASOR excavation at Tell Ta'annek (Jordan), in a seminar for resident fellows of the Albright Institute for Archaeological Research in Jerusalem on May 3, 1974, presented a paper on "Archaeological Systematics," advancing an ethnographic model for Palestinian archaeology that would view archaeological remains as the deposit of regional systems including paleo-environment, material culture forms on the site, and reconstruction of the social dynamics. Glock's paper will be published in revised and expanded form. For similar perspectives in Mesopotamian archaeology, see R. Mc C. Adams, "Archaeological Research Strategies," *Science* 160 (1968): 1187–92.

29. C. B. Moore, ed., *Reconstructing Complex Societies* (1975), is a volume of colloquium papers attempting to develop interdisciplinary dialogue and collaboration (Cambridge, Mass.: American Schools of Oriental Research, 1974).

30. For a recent discussion of Weber's "ideal-type" analysis and its utility in historical research, see M. Hill, *A Sociology of Religion* (Grand Rapids, Mich.: Basic Books, 1973), pp. 147–151.

31. S. N. Eisenstadt, *The Political Systems of Empires* (New York: Free Press, 1963), paperback with new preface (New York: Free Press, 1968); Gideon Sjoberg, *The Preindustrial City: Past and Present* (New York: Free Press, 1960).

32. Eric Wolf, *Peasant Wars of the Twentieth Century* (New York: Harper & Row, 1969). M. L. Chaney, in lectures at the Graduate Theological Union, Berkeley, California, has sought to show the extent to which early Israel met the conditions and criteria of successful peasant revolutions as elucidated by Wolf's study.

33. Frick's study (see Note 23) utilizes Sjoberg's theoretical framework in order to attempt a functional description and analysis of urban structures in the Old Testament, including various physical, social, economic, and political structures.

34. Marvin Harris, *The Rise of Anthropological Theory: A History of Culture* (New York: T. Y. Crowell, 1968); Gerhard Lenski and Jean Lenski, *Human Societies*, 3rd ed. (New York: McGraw-Hill, 1978); C. Meillassoux, *L'Anthroplogie économique des Gouro de Côte d'Ivoire* (1964); Emmanuel Terray, "Historical Materialism and Segmentary Lineage-Based Societies," *Marxism and "Primitive" Societies: Two Studies,* trans. Mary Kloppen (New York: Monthly Review Press, 1972 [1969]), pp. 93–186.

35. Jan Dus, "Moses or Joshua? On the Problem of the Founder of the Israelite Religion," in *The Bible and Liberation*, 1st ed., 1976, pp. 26–41.

36. Henri Mottu, "Jeremiah vs. Hananiah: Ideology and Truth in the Old Testament," in *The Bible and Liberation*, 1st ed., 1976, pp. 58–67; see Article 14 in this volume.

37. Y. Aharoni, "The Settlement of Canaan," *The World History of the Jewish People*, Vol. 3, *Judges*, ed. Benjamin Mazar (New Brunswick, N.J.: Rutgers University Press, 1971), pp. 97–98.

38. See the prospectus on Stager's project in *ASOR Newsletter*, No. 2, September 1972; see also *IDBSup* (1976); pp. 11–13.

39. In particular, see de Geus (cited in Note 27) and Gottwald, *The Tribes of Yahweh*, pp. 650–63.

11

Theological Issues in *The Tribes of Yahweh* by N. K. Gottwald: Four Critical Reviews

While recognizing the substantive importance of the book's hypothesis of Israel's origin in a revolutionary peasant movement, these reviewers of The Tribes of Yahweh *call attention to the challenge of its radical methodological proposal for biblical hermeneutics and for theology.*

A. Myers, noting that Gottwald premises social determinants for early Israel in the manner that religious historians have studied such factors in the origins of denominations and confessions, specifies "the urgent need to better ascertain the shared interests of and precise domain between [sociology and religion/theology]."

W. Brueggemann observes in Tribes *"the tilt toward a radical theology" in which religion not only integrates and legitimizes but also evokes, criticizes, initiates, and energizes. He connects Gottwald's program of biblical analysis with J. Habermas's formulation of a critical rationality that uncovers the social presuppositions and implications of every exercise of instrumental rationality and of hermeneutical rationality.*

F. Woo calls Tribes *"unabashedly incarnational," which means that traditional concepts of revelation and incarnation, redemption and resurrection, will have to be rethought with a new historical earthiness. At the same time,*

Reprinted from book reviews by Allen Myers in *The Reformed Journal* 31 (March 1981): 20–23, by Walter Brueggemann in *Journal of the American Academy of Religion* 48 (1980): 441–51, by Franklin Woo in *China Notes* 18 (1980): 142–43, and by Lucien Legrand in *Indian Theological Studies* 18 (1981): 78–86.

the religion of ancient Israel gains pertinence to the situation of Third World peoples, such as the Chinese, where a great socioreligious peasant revolt (the Taiping Revolution, 1851–1864) evidenced close parallels to Israel's peasant revolt.

L. Legrand sees in India some limited corroboration of aspects of the Israelite tribal system as outlined in Tribes *but is dubious whether a thoroughgoing social revolutionary model can account for the Indian castes and tribal systems. In questioning the adequacy of sociological interpretations of religion, Legrand poses the apparent "irreducibility" of three entirely legitimate ways of reading biblical developments: "It is not a matter of explaining the Exodus partly through the sociology, partly through Moses or Joshua, and partly through the intervention of God. It is rather entirely a matter of sociology, a matter of personalities, and a matter of faith." He further poses the issue of the continuing significance and authority of texts that live on after the social movements that produced them have disappeared.*

Norman K. Gottwald, *The Tribes of Yahweh: A Sociology of the Religion of Liberated Israel, 1250–1050* **B.C.E. (Maryknoll, N.Y.: Orbis Books, 1979), xxv plus 916 pp., $19.95 paper.**

1. ALLEN MYERS IN *THE REFORMED JOURNAL*

Only on the rarest of occasions in any branch of scholarship does a work come forth with the potential to radically alter that field. Norman K. Gottwald's ambitious study of the social world of ancient Israel has been hailed as such a moment in biblical scholarship, akin to the publication of Julius Wellhausen's *Prolegomena* (1878) and William F. Albright's *From the Stone Age to Christianity* (1940). Gottwald's radical departure is his attempt to synthesize standard biblical scholarship, oriented toward historical and literary matters, with "socially informed" analysis and to attain thereby a "social hermeneutic of the Bible that will be both scientifically and religiously cogent."

Although an offshoot of the author's long-standard introduction to the Old Testament, *A Light to the Nations* (1959), and his study of Israelite prophecy, *All the Kingdoms of the Earth* (1964), *The Tribes of Yahweh* differs substantially in scope and format. It is neither a textbook nor a reference work in the usual sense, but rather comprises an extended and meticulously dialectical methodological argument which is best considered step by step.

Gottwald first proposes a synchronic social structure for the two-hundred-year formative period of Israel's history, a pristine time when that people's social identity can be considered its norm. The aim is to develop a theoretical model, a system of "real hypotheses" which can be tested, reformulated, or complexified with the prospect of "increased explanatory power." Using recognized methods of biblical science (literary criticism, history, tradition history, and history of religion), he assesses the various literary sources regarding the rise of Israel and the "cultic-ideological framework" which is their biblical setting. To this construct of data and theory he applies social scientific methods to delineate early Israel as a total social system of which its religion is an integral dimension. By analyzing the terminology used to designate Israel as a whole as well as its internal structure (primary, secondary, and tertiary subdivisions), Gottwald concludes that early Israel was an alliance of various coexistent social organizational systems, a truly "ecumenical" body—socially, juridically, and even theologically. Citing major structural functional dissimilarities within their respective social settings, Gottwald discounts any formal similarities between the Greek amphictyony and the Israelite confederation, a consciously contrived surrogate "anti-state" serving its people as a protective association of tribes.

Particular attention is devoted to the conquest, settlement, and revolt hypotheses of the formation of Israel within Canaan. The three patterns are not absolutely distinct, and Gottwald's revolt model is "nuanced" as a gradual withdrawal or "progression into the area of redoubt." His preference for this mode is based on the assumption that the way that the people of Israel came into being is inseparably tied to the nature of the system which emerged, along with the shared goals and bonding structures of that system. The resultant society was an alliance through various modes and degrees of affiliation by an eclectic assortment of underclass and outlaw elements of Canaanite society (feudalized peasants, 'apiru mercenaries and adventurers, transhumant pastoralists, tribally organized farmers and pastoral nomads, and probably also itinerant craftsmen and disaffected priests) who subordinated their intrinsic differences in a unified strike against the source of their common misery, the Canaanite ruling class (the *yōshᵉvīm*, "inhabitants," of the early poetry). By no means a direct carryover from pastoral-nomadic tribalism, this conscious "egalitarian retribalization" was a definite reaction against Canaanite statism; its societal segmentation and intergroup bonding were adaptively related to the fundamental aims of escaping imperialism and feudalism imposed from without and preventing feudal domination from within.

To account for this "mutant" formation, Gottwald extends his structural-functional model into an historical cultural-material model. He subjects the emerging cross-section of normative Israel ("an egalitarian, extended-family, segmentary tribal society with an agricultural-pastoral economic base") to rigorous diachronic-comparative analysis with roughly contemporary social systems and economic modes: Egyptian political hegemony, indigenous Canaanite feudalism, and the functional interlock between the two; the specific adaptation to feudalism by the 'apiru subelement; and proposed sociopolitical models for the Philistines, Ammon, Edom, and Moab. Thus he seeks social "morphemes" to isolate emergent Israelite society on a cross-cutting grid of complementarity and opposition, of continuity and discontinuity. The resultant "provisional hypothesis" (pp. 660–663) shows how all that was specifically Israelite—even "the 'highest' reaches of its Yahwistic faith"—was "the expression of a total interpenetration of material and socioreligious factors in one single system."

Israelite religion, then, is neither an isolated nor a self-generating entity but rather an integral factor of Israelite society, one which is a function of it yet has an impact on that society. Coincident with the "great leap forward" from Canaanite *'apiru*-ism to Israelite egalitarianism was the conscious adaptation of El-worship, by then the symbol system of the hated Canaanite political-cultic complex, to the cult of Yahweh, introduced by the Exodus Levites as the powerful god who had defeated Egypt on its home ground and who thus could defend in Canaan this enlarged and reorganized anti-feudal, anti-imperial coalition. "Mono-Yahwism," this common religious identity (though probably broad enough to permit a spectrum of collateral cults), was in dependent relationship to the rise and maintenance of sociopolitical egalitarianism. At the same time, it was a most significant organizational and symbolic force through which the community was established as a unique attempt at ethical living, and an "intentional" means of cementing and motivating that balance of unifying and decentralizing sociocultural patterns which guaranteed the very survival of the system. Its function was that of a "servo-mechanism," a "feedback loop" by which the system could adapt or "correct" itself.

Ideology, in the current anthropolitical interpretation, is neither a belief system that could be determined empirically by an objective observer nor a people's self-image of their beliefs, but rather the unconscious "lived" relation between a people and their world. Accordingly, Gottwald "demythologizes" the "distinctives" of Israelite religion in terms of their function and expression within the total system: Yahweh—"the historically concretized, primordial power to establish and sustain social equality"; Chosen People—"the distinctive self-consciousness of a society of equals . . . demarcated from a primarily centralized and stratified surrounding world"; covenant—"the bonding of [these] decentralized social groups in a larger society of equals committed to cooperation without authoritarian leadership"; eschatology—sustained commitment to that society "with the confidence and determination that this way of life can prevail against great environmental odds."

Gottwald's failure, intentional or not, to consider the Israelite experience of the Holy or perceptions of Yahweh apart from characteristics related to the "ancient Near Eastern high god paradigm" may be excused as irrelevant to the place of Israelite religion in the dynamics of the premonarchic social system. More sensitive, however, is what might seem the implication that Yahweh, as the focus of that religion, exists not as an independent reality but merely as a function of the social system. The interrelationship and interdependence of religion and social factors actually may be so complex as to immerse efforts to determine preeminence in a hopeless "chicken-or-egg" debate over religious phenomenology (but note elsewhere the prevalence of socioeconomic, political, and ethnic determinants over the purely "religious," as frequently in the origins of denominations and confessions). At root are obvious conflicts in the modes of understanding of sociology and religion (theology), pointing to the urgent need to better ascertain the shared interests of and precise divisions between the two.

In this regard, Gottwald assails much of biblical scholarship for being "uncritically idealist," marked by a distinct "failure of sociological nerve." Even those for whose influence he is most grateful—John Bright, George Mendenhall, Georg Fohrer—have produced mere "anti-theories" or "nontheories" because they have failed to synthesize or interpret fully the results of their efforts. This he attributes partly to an unconscious pattern determined by lack of familiarity with social scientific method as well as the difficulty of shifting from such established patterns of causation as the "evasive Weberian co-determinacy of religion and social relations." Also at work, however, may be the lingering "bugaboo of 'reductionism' " and the fear that to admit systematic social influences on religion "is to deny the creativity and importance of religion" or even to invalidate it. (But certainly the Israelite religion of Gottwald's model is neither passive nor moribund.)

A number of Gottwald's presuppositions contrast sharply with those of traditional Christian thought, raising questions about both objectivity and relevance. In particular, many will be concerned with the author's unabashedly Marxist stance. In his own defense Gottwald points to the considerable success of Western scholars with Marxian methodology, largely accepted though often disguised either for fear of social rejection or because the intellectual roots of the method were unrecognized. Despite an occasional predilection towards 1960s leftist jargon (by no means the obstacle presented by the book's rampant "socialsciencespeak"), the work is not uncritically biased. For example, Gottwald favors Eric R. Wolf's assessment of peasant initiative over the early Marxian assumption that only an industrial proletariat could effectively foment socialist revolution. More importantly, the author's use of "conflict sociology" to elucidate Israelite decentralization is tempered by his reliance on functionalism, a basically conservative "consolidating" sociology, to show the internal cohesiveness of early Israel.

Gottwald himself addresses the danger of "contaminating presuppositions," citing the "new literary criticisms" which seek only antiseptic technical control of data, the "high" view of Scripture which would eschew all critical issues, and even the purportedly neutral "idealist" theology. Nevertheless, in his quest to make biblical scholarship "scientifically testable" and to find "new paradigms" which ask "new questions" and break with "the old way of knowing," Gottwald dares to set aside the stricture that primary sources be permitted to speak for themselves without imposed interpretive bias. Analytical models, often "felt to grow more out of the interpreter's immediate needs or out of his unexamined milieu than out of the biblical evidence itself," become heuristic devices to overcome gaps in data and to test theoretical adequacy ("the ability to account for the data over the widest range in the most coherent manner"). Accordingly, Gottwald demonstrates that the danger is not so much method per se as bad execution of method or failure to recognize the limits of method—"socially-informed" analysis included. Moreover, if indeed "all truth is God's truth," even the most unorthodox views must be risked on occasion, for they may be just the catalyst needed to reveal analogous forces and circumstances in ancient times and places.

The provisional character of this treatise is underscored by the author's recognition that the issues addressed require an open-ended and corporate process. Carefully he points out imperatives for future consideration, noting that the book is an "initial mapping" put forth "with the deliberate intention of inviting criticism and refinement," particularly in view of his own "lack of specific training and experience in those disciplines and skills vital to assembling the data for analysis of the economic and cultural-material foundations of early Israel." The book is a progress report, "no more than the first tentative step" of a project which Gottwald hopes to extend to the entire history of Israel (work purportedly has begun on a subsequent volume on the monarchy).

Despite these disclaimers, Gottwald has assembled an impressive mass of sociological data by skillful (though occasionally adventuresome) philological, form critical, and tradition-critical treatment of the literary and historical sources. In addition, he offers insights from such cultural-material factors as topography, demographics, and technology (improved iron tools, waterproof cisterns, and rock terracing). An epilogue is included to accommodate pertinent scholarship subsequent to completion of the text in 1975. Here Gottwald reiterates his "paradigm shift" in adopting Noth's pentateuchal model yet without reliance on his amphictyonic model; notes the current impasse regarding models of Israelite settlement; and reviews the work of M. B. Rowton on nomadism, C. J. de Geus on the Israelite tribe, and macrosociological theory as propounded by Marvin Harris and Gerhard Lenski. The text is supported by extensive documentation (nearly one hundred pages of notes), schematical charts, and comprehensive indexing (perhaps the only effective way to cross-reference a dialectical argument of such proportions). One regrets, however, the lack of a bibliography.

Much of the value of *The Tribes of Yahweh* transcends the book's concern for the formal aspects of methodology, stemming rather from its grasp of the substance of early Israel—a daring social experiment by actual human beings within a network of lived relationships and shared meanings, a people

> *. . . laughing, singing*
> *loving their people*
> *and*
> *all people who put love*
> *before power*
> *then*
> *put love with power*
> *which is necessary*
> *to destroy power without love.*
> (from the book's dedication)

No incongruity exists in the publication of such a major undertaking of biblical scholarship by a firm primarily associated with liberation theology and Third World issues. Gottwald sees the theologian's task as more than gaining descriptive, technical control of data. Rather, it is to "do" theology within an appropriately "engaged process" (Gustavo Gutiérrez's "liberating praxis"). Although many might object, Gottwald's "science" is not concerned with proving or disproving the Bible. His hermeneutic concern goes beyond mere explanation to "understanding," by which Gottwald implies empathy, identification, and participation. He defines the unique religious perception of incipient Israel as "its discovery through social struggle that the concrete conditions of human existence are modifiable rather than immutable conditions." The power of that religion "was precisely its integration within and penetration of a total struggle situation." Accordingly, modern attempts to apply the symbols of Israelite religion fail abominably (they become what Tillich called "dead symbols") apart from comparable circumstances of social struggle ("mono-Yahwistic affirmations that were socially 'progressive' in their origins become socially 'reactionary' when simplistically reaffirmed today"). This does not mean that the modern Jew or Christian must seek out a comparable pre-industrial retribalization (a purely antiquarian endeavor, "no more than a romantic primitivizing form of idealism at best"). Rather, the Judeo-Christian "faith" comes alive when one strives to "enable" egalitarian social forms "in which the cul-de-sac of the nation-state constellation of class divisions with their rampant repression of human life in the service of racism, provincialism, and war will be overcome."

The book's manifold potential for expanding the horizons of biblical scholarship is apparent, but its effect will be felt most immediately in the need for those in the field to retool, to become familiar with new vocabulary and modes of thinking and to acquire new technical skills. Gottwald's unorthodox presuppositions and innovative methodology will ensure a broad range of reactions, but certainly for those seriously concerned with the sociopolitical factors, the religious underpinnings, or the total ecology of early Israel, this venture will provide abundant seed for thought and innovative and challenging possibilities for reconstruction and application.

2. WALTER BRUEGGEMANN IN
JOURNAL OF THE AMERICAN ACADEMY OF RELIGION

Gottwald has wrought a peculiarly impressive intellectual achievement. There are few among us who could so capably move among the disciplines of critical sociology and Near Eastern history as he does. Along with that, Gottwald's book is an act of great personal courage, for he has staked out a provocatively imaginative position that will be disputed and controversial for a long time, one bound to be misunderstood in some quarters, for known or unrecognized reasons.

I

It is not too much to say that Gottwald's is a one-idea book. And that one idea is a radical methodological proposal: a most important and neglected interface for Old Testament studies is with *critical sociology*, as distinct from more conventional interfaces with the humanities, explicitly history and literature. More specifically the methodological proposal is that religion must be treated as a function of a coherent socio-economic structure, a function which both reflects that structure and peculiarly impacts that structure. Positively this means that the "religion of Yahwism" cannot be understood at all apart from the sociopolitical community which articulated, transmitted, and practiced the religion of Yahwism. Negatively the argument permits a criticism of Old Testament scholarship as uncritically idealistic. By "idealism" Gottwald means either that the religion of Yahweh is treated as a thing unto itself with no necessary or integral relation to its social counterparts, or that the religious factor is the decisive and initiative-taking one in forming a social community. Either way, religion is treated as the distinctive element in isolation. And this, Gottwald argues, will not do, for it naively ignores the whole development of critical sociology from Marx, Durkheim, and Weber.

Nowhere does Gottwald explicitly appeal to Marx's programmatic statement, as might be expected from his earlier articles in *Radical Religion*. Nevertheless, Marx's statement may be taken as a premise of the book: "Thus the criticism of heaven is transformed into the criticism of earth, the criticism of religion into the criticism of law, and the criticism of theology into the criticism of politics."[1] Though lacking that particular statement, Gottwald is explicit in his general appeal to a Marxist sociology. To ignore any longer the gains of critical theory in terms of the function of religion is intellectually naive and academically irresponsible. This matter is especially urgent because it appears that alternative directions in Old Testament scholarship (specifically the "new literary criticism") run the risk of bracketing out all the sociologically critical questions. And the result is an uncritical, unwitting embrace of conventional systemic values of American academia.

Gottwald's methodological proposal brings him close to two programmatic books which greatly illuminate his intent. First, it is instructive that one of Gottwald's early citations (p.13, n. 6) is to Gouldner's *The Coming Crisis of Western Sociology*. Gouldner has argued that Western sociology, by which he means noncritical positivistic sociology, has been largely a "kept" sociology, confined to technical reason. It has adopted a methodology which screens out the hard questions and operates as a tool for conformity to the way things are. By analogy Gottwald suggests that the "idealism" of historical criticism is also not neutral but serves interests about which it is not always aware. I suspect that the impact of Gottwald's book is first of all to call attention to a methodological crisis that is deeper than even Childs or Wink has hinted. Gottwald offers a new set of questions which must be asked. And that inevitably implies a shifted task for scholarship.

Second, at several points Gottwald uses the word "paradigm." Gottwald's book is a prime example of the offer of a new paradigm as Thomas Kuhn describes the function of paradigm in *The Structure of Scientific Revolutions*.[2] That is, Gottwald's book should not be taken simply as another critical analysis, but as a reorganization of the data around quite new categories. What is offered is a bold critical proposal that must be lived with and not simply voted up or down on the basis of data. As Kuhn has seen, a new paradigm, if it is radically new, does not receive or expect ready acceptance, but becomes a field for conflict and battle.

In this book we have a programmatic hypothesis which holds the potential of being an important historical moment in the discipline. Unless I greatly misjudge, the book holds promise of being a point of reference parallel in significance, potential, and authority to Wellhausen's *Prolegomena* and Albright's *From the Stone Age to Christianity*. As is well known, Wellhausen established a new scholarly base for criticism, both literary and historical, with his massive and ingenious synthesis. He broke with a *naive precritical historicism*. In turn, Albright broke with the *evolutionism* of Wellhausen. In a parallel move, Gottwald proposes a break with *idealism* toward a religious functionalism that reflects a dialectic which is profoundly materialistic, and a materialism which is profoundly dialectical.[3]

II

Now of course Gottwald's book is not simply a methodological proposal. The dominant *methodological* proposal of the book is matched by a sustained *substantive* argument: Early Israel, of which religious Yahwism is an important element, is a revolutionary social movement, radically egalitarian in contrast to the hierarchical systems of domination out of which it emerged and against which it worked. Gottwald studies in detail the historical and literary issues and pays attention to the institutional, political life of Israel. He shows that for 200 years (from Joshua to the monarchy, 1250–1050) Israel is a serious, concrete social experiment that was a *novum* in the political world of the Near East. This *novum* utilized, and cannot be understood apart from, both the subversive political actions taken and the triggering of religious Yahwism. The political actions and religious triggering together permitted an alternative social system out of which biblical Yahwism has come.

Among the elements of Gottwald's argument, we can note several of the more important:

1. Tribalism, as distinct from nomadism, is an important feature of the hypothesis. Gottwald does an acute investigation of the nomenclature. First, "tribe" is a sociological unit and not a kinship unit. Second, denying any evolutionism, he argues that tribalism comes *after* and in reaction against statism. So he inverts the evolutionary scheme, now dominant, to speak of "retribalization."

2. Gottwald stays close to the German hypothesis of tribal confederation, but takes careful account of the criticism made against Noth's amphictyony. But he does end up with a transtribal organization not unlike that proposed by Noth. His use of Noth's work is a good example of how paradigms shift with both continuities and discontinuities from previous scholarship.

3. Gottwald also posits something much like von Rad's credo or cult hypothesis. That is, after analysis of the "historical" conflict in Joshua and Judges, he understands the main Pentateuchal themes as constructs of the cultic ideological community, i.e., as the theological creativity of the community in providing ideological undergirding for a subversive, egalitarian social system. Gottwald's procedure is to deal with Joshua–Judges as historical foundation (though of course he does not uncritically handle the literature as "history") with Pentateuch materials as part of the "superstructure." Thus we are permitted both the "criticism of heaven" (in the Pentateuch) and the "criticism of earth" (in Joshua and Judges). In his assessment of the Pentateuch, Gottwald moves away from historical questions, very much in the direction of von Rad's more or less liturgical approach. He is, of course, not unaware of or inattentive to the criticisms of von Rad's hypothesis. In his own argument, Gottwald regards the Pentateuch as an ideological construction of an alternative social reality. He does not deny the existence of earlier elements, historical and ideological, but the creative formation is by and in the service of the egalitarian community.

III

Before coming to the main issue, three comments are pertinent to Gottwald's use of and feedback upon Old Testament scholarship:

1. Gottwald has found a way (even if he is not interested in it) of giving substance and credibility to the now discredited "mighty deeds of God" construct. As is well known, Childs saw the problem: "Mighty deeds of God" is a way of speaking that seems to float in the air without historical basis. The approach of Wright and von Rad had not solved the problem of "actual" history and "sacred" history. The recital of sacred history appeared to have no rootage in historicality. Gottwald has found a way for those who will speak in terms of "mighty acts." But now it must be faced that the recital is

an ideological articulation of a radical social movement. Obviously the implications for doing Old Testament theology are acute. Gottwald comes down sharply on Old Testament scholarship which has been idealistic about these matters, as though Israel's was a religion without close linkage to sociopolitical matters. As examples, he applies his strictures to John Bright, Georg Fohrer, and, perhaps surprisingly, George Mendenhall.

2. Gottwald proposes two very subtle and, I am not sure, very convincing constructs. I cite these to note that they are advances beyond the synthesis of Noth and to say they are (in this judgment) precarious. The first of these is the twelve-tribe configuration, which Gottwald sees as a backward projection from monarchical administrative districts which both utilized and impeded genuine tribal patterns (p. 363). I doubt if this is persuasive, though it should be noted that no other hypothesis at this point carries more weight.

3. The other oversubtle construct is the hypothesis of an Elohist Israel that is a seedbed for Yahwism. That is, it is already a potentially revolutionary grouping which still lacks the triggering of religious Yahwism (chapter 43). Of course, the problem of Israel's religious antecedents is notorious. I regard this as not much better or worse than other hypotheses.

Neither his proposal about the twelve-tribe system nor his hypothesis on a pre-Yahwistic Elohistic Israel is crucial to his main argument. Not much that is enduring, in this judgment, will hang or fall on these proposals. Both matters will need to be kept under review. In the long run these will not be found any more compelling than some of Noth's work which is now doubtfully regarded.

IV

The crucial issue in the book is the relation between sociology and religion, or, to put it alternatively, the extent to which Yahweh is a "function" of an egalitarian movement and the extent to which Yahweh is a free agent to be understood in religious categories. It may be that finally theologians must learn what they can from such bold sociology, but then must part company and be theologians. But they must learn *much* and make that move away only at the *very last moment*. But from a sociological perspective, and probably from the point of view of Gottwald, any such move toward the independent reality of God is a move toward the very idealism he is trying to combat. Then the substantive question is whether such a theological move can be anything other than mere ideology, an ideology which costs more than it gains.

The question before us is evident if we contrast Mendenhall and Gottwald on this point. Mendenhall is consistent in urging that the initiative runs from religion to social reality: "It is very difficult, if not impossible, for modern Western man to conceive of a new cultural synthesis stemming from a new religious ideology, just as it is virtually impossible to convince the usual secular university professor that religion has occasionally in the past functioned to create new and larger communities, rather than merely to create and perpetuate socio-cultural divisiveness."[4] And that line is pursued in his *Tenth Generation* in his advocacy of Israel's religion and in his strictures against "politics."[5]

By contrast, Gottwald (already in his 1974 Congress paper) had gone far in arguing that the move is in the opposite direction, from social reality to religion. His third domain-assumptive proposal is: "It is assumed that the initially or ultimately prominent or distinctive features of a society or culture must be viewed in the total matrix of generative elements and not overweighted in advance as the all-powerful sources of inspiration or as the selective survival factors in the societal development. Thus, a critical generative role may well have been played by cultural elements which have been lost to view and must be recovered by careful research. In particular, ideational factors must be looked at not as disembodied prime movers but as the ideas of human beings in determinate technological and social settings in which the total mix of culture will tend to exhibit lawful or patterned configurations."[6] And that, of course, is the present argument as well. But Gottwald is acutely sensitive on this point. He will not have Yahwism be *simply* a projection. And so he says: "If it turns out that not only is mono-Yahwism dependably related to sociopolitical egalitarianism, but that likewise sociopolitical egalitarianism is dependably related to mono-Yahwism, we shall be able to speak of the two social-systemic entities as interdependently or reciprocally related as functions one of the other" (p. 618).

Especially in Chapter 50, Gottwald not only acknowledges his awareness of the issue, but is extremely sensitive in handling it. He concedes that functionalism has limits in dealing with the question of priority, because it is a tool geared to analyze *interrelations,* but not *priorities.* So Gottwald seeks to move beyond functionalism to a "historical cultural materialism." After some consideration of Durkheim and Weber, he finds Marx (pp. 631ff.) to provide the most coherent strategy for research. Because he insists that religion is best understood on materialist grounds, he concludes (p. 646) that Israelite social relations have priority over Yahwist religion. But at the same time Yahwistic religion has a crucial role to play, not simply as a legitimator, but as a "facilitator" of the egalitarian movement (p. 642). My judgment is that Gottwald has gone as far as he can go to face the problem squarely and to give religion its just due. But he will not and must not move beyond his sociological presuppositions, or he would vitiate his entire hypothesis. He is, in his own words, "unsurrendered to the end."

Clearly hermeneutical categories from Marx are shown to be not just tools of subversion, but responsible ways of discerning the text. Gottwald has made the point in showing that Marxist criticism is not just one more tool along with all the others which can be used without changing the others. Rather he shows how these categories place all our methods under criticism in terms of their ideological service unwittingly given.

While the book is about ancient Israel, it unavoidably raises issues about the sociology of our own scholarship. The book pushes toward "canon within canon," a question in which Gottwald has no explicit interest. The problem is this: If this model of religion is understandable only in relation to this egalitarian social system, is it usable as a normative or absolute paradigm? I.e., is it "movable" to other contexts to be used as a critical principle *against* other social systems? Or in other social systems must there only be the matching or appropriate religious symbolization? Perhaps that is where theologians must part company with sociologists. Liberation theologians have gone far in taking this model of religion to use it not only as a *legitimator* and *energizer* of egalitarian movements, but as a *critique* against domination systems. Perhaps in a functionalist approach, that is a "function of dissonance." But in such a use, what is labelled "function" takes on the color of "norm" or of "truth." But then theologians have as their work an articulation of what is normative, work very different from that of a sociologist. Gottwald, of course, fully recognizes this issue. Theologians may wish to have the religion of Yahwism without linkage to that particular intertribal movement. But Gottwald trenchantly observes that is what happened in monarchic Israel, so that "the Yahwistic ideology and traditions were increasingly seen as a self-contained body of beliefs and practices separable from any particular kind of social order" (p. 597). And the social result is a reactionary sociopolitical practice making *reactionary use* of *radical theological rhetoric*. That is a characterization of ancient monarchic Israel, but there are ample contemporary parallels.

V

How can this work be received and assessed by a guild for which these are new questions? It may be useful to locate the book more precisely, epistemologically, in the field. Gottwald's book makes more coherent sense for the field if set in the grid of rationality of Jürgen Habermas.[7] Habermas argues that there are three levels or dimensions of rationality. First, technical knowledge (Habermas calls it "strategic" or "instrumental") is analytical knowledge which seeks only to establish technical control of the data. I suggest it applies especially to historical studies which seek for origins. There is increasing indication in Old Testament studies that scholars grow impatient with those questions. Witness the harsh current judgments on conventional archaeological scholarship.

The second level of rationality for Habermas is hermeneutics. Hermeneutics (by which is meant attention to symbolism and meaning in the interest of "understanding") is commonly regarded as an advance beyond and liberation from historical-critical issues which pursue explanation. In Old Testament studies this second level is especially evident in the new literary criticism and in structuralism, which means to bracket out many of the old critical questions for the sake of meanings. For Habermas, as Pierce was a model proponent of technical, instrumental reason, so Dilthey is an example of such a hermeneutical enterprise.

But it is clear in Old Testament studies that "the new literary criticism" tends to work with "history-less" texts and on the whole is uncritical of itself as a method. That is, it is not reflective that such closed attention to structure is tilted in a conservative direction with no impetus for newness. Everything falls before an avoidance of the "genetic fallacy." This hermeneutic interest is a reentry to "old truths," by which is meant in general old mythic structures not embarrassed by the scandal of Israel's liberation movement. I suggest Gottwald's program is a practice of Habermas's third form of rationality, a critical perspective that moves behind the hermeneutical to "unmask" its social presuppositions and implications (Habermas cites Freud as a practitioner of this kind of rationality). Gottwald, like Habermas's program, sees that religious symbols reflect, legitimate, energize, and criticize social systems. Thus Gottwald proposes an important task without which our hermeneutical fascination may be accepted too easily without attention to social implications. What Gottwald has done appears not to be an option which some scholars may take up, but an essential ingredient in scholarship, which means to be rigorously critical. Thus we may locate Gottwald by correlation with Habermas's scheme:

instrumental reason (Pierce)......historical criticism
hermeneutical (Dilthey)............structuralism and new literary criticism
critical (Freud).....................Gottwald's sociological investigation

I suggest that this indicates that Gottwald's program is essential to our common work.

VI

Gottwald's final pages suggest a passion that tilts his work in sociology toward a radical theology. These points are worth noting:

1. On pages 684ff., in his consideration of Yahweh's masculinity, the author refers to God as "he" with quotation marks. Clearly Gottwald intends a contemporary critique of such usage.

2. Gottwald comments on the inherent conservatism of Durkheim's sociology of religion (p. 697). But he makes a point that there is another kind of sociology of religion, reflective of Marx, which does not simply personify the spirit of the community. He quotes Buber that this alternative sociology of religion "represents the power which transcends it, happens to it, which *changes* it, even historicizes it; a power which in a formative hour drives it on to do the unaccustomed and untraditional, in a feud-overcoming gathering together of all clans as a single tribe." On such a material cultural base, there is a sociology of religion which offers the dynamic toward new possibility. Gottwald appeals to categories quite alien to most sociologists of religion who are dominated by Durkheim.

3. Gottwald uses the telling phrase, the "impossible possibility" (p. 701):

"The power of the religious symbolism in early Israel was precisely its integration within and penetration of a total struggle situation, so that it articulated a willfulness informed by the situation, illuminating a route for those divided Canaanite underclasses to follow as, step by step, they realized 'the impossible possibility' of free communal life in hierarchic Canaan."

In using the phrase "impossible possibility" in this way, Gottwald has in the end done both things which are important. On the one hand, he has used language which links his perception to the most subversive theology of our time. Indeed, Gottwald is fully aware of the theological implications of his sociological analysis for the contemporary scene. But on the other hand and at the same time, Gottwald is clear that the "impossible possibility" is not a contextless theological slogan. It has substance only when used in relation to intentional social struggle. Such religious symbolism has legitimacy only as a form of *praxis* (p. 702). Gottwald has moved well beyond an *integrationist functionalism* to an *historical cultural materialism* that is fully dialectical. Thus the fully dependable function of religious Yahwism is not simply a descriptive counterpart to social reality, but a powerful set of symbols which evoke, initiate, and energize, as well as legitimate. In this way it appears that Gottwald has impressively narrowed the gap between sociology and theology.

It is the impression of this reviewer that Gottwald has not resolved the issues of social criticism and the reality of God. But he has indeed reshaped the context and the issues for our discussion. The book abounds in careful critical detail, comprehensive documentation, and a complete index of authors, personal and geographical names, Scripture passages, and topics. In every way it will be a long-standing teaching instrument. Gottwald's passion for contemporary issues is matched by his peculiar boldness in scholarly questions. And that rare combination is crucial "in the long struggle of human liberation" (p. 709) which finally concerns him. Gottwald has made unmistakably clear that liberated and liberating theology must give careful and sustained attention to methodology, so that it does not at the outset concede the main point in question, or in turn become itself a noncritical ideology. He has shown us how to proceed in that.

Clearly the issue of method is not a formal question of preferring or not preferring Marxist critical categories. It is a substantive question about the nature of early Yahwism as a symbol system, an ideological vision, and a social system. Method cannot be determined on formal grounds, but only in terms of the material before us. And that is not likely to look the same again after Gottwald.

NOTES

1. Karl Marx, "Critique of Hegel's Philosophy of Right." Cf. David McLellan, *The Thought of Karl Marx* (London: Macmillan, 1971), p. 22.
2. Thomas S. Kuhn, *The Structure of Scientific Revolutions* (Chicago: University of Chicago, Press, 1974).

3. That dialectic is quite self-conscious: "In short, the basic tenet for future research and theory is clear and commanding: only as the full *materiality* of ancient Israel is more securely grasped will we be able to make proper sense of its *spirituality*" (*Tribes of Yahweh*, p. xxv).

4. George Mendenhall, "Between Theology and Archaeology," *JSOT* 7 (1978): 31.

5. See esp. his *The Tenth Generation* (Baltimore: Johns Hopkins University Press, 1973), chapter 7 and 8. The point may be traced in his book by the polemical and enigmatic footnotes concerning Harvey Cox, pp. 3, 65, and 202.

6. Norman K. Gottwald, "Domain Assumptions and Societal Models in the Study of Pre-Monarchic Israel," *VTSup* 28 (1974): 93. The contrasting domain assumption which Gottwald rejects is this: "It is assumed that the most idiosyncratic, prominent or distinctive element of the new socio-political phase, especially as viewed in retrospect, must have been the nuclear factor which initiated other sorts of changes and constellated them into a new social system or culture. Since the religio-symbolic and cultic dimensions of Israelite society appear to be the most idiosyncratic elements, particularly as viewed from the perspective of later Judaism and Christianity, Yahwism is to be regarded as the isolate source and agent of change in the emergence of Israel" (ibid., p. 91). The issue with Mendenhall could hardly be more sharply put, though of course Mendenhall has no monopoly on the matter. I submit that this question is the crucial one Gottwald asks of Old Testament scholarship.

7. Jürgen Habermas, *Knowledge and Human Interests* (Boston: Beacon Press, 1968); see also Thomas McCarthy, *The Critical Theology of Jürgen Habermas* (Cambridge: MIT Press, 1979), Ch.2.

3. FRANKLIN J. WOO IN *CHINA NOTES*

Norman Gottwald's *The Tribes of Yahweh* is a book about the struggle of disenfranchised peasants in Old Testament times for an egalitarian society. For a huge volume of 916 pages, it covers only a thin slice of some 200 years of the history of premonarchic Israel. To see how this history relates to an interest in China and religion is the attempt of this introductory review.

Gottwald is unabashedly incarnational. He sees the religion of people as having to do with their real life. There is always that intimate interaction between life and religion, as banal as this may sound. Gottwald, who is himself trained in humanistic historical methods, chooses to use sociological methods with consistent rigor in unfolding the sociopolitical realities in Canaanite society. He follows his methodology all the way, not giving in to traditional faith assumptions which might lead to a facile relegating of religion to that which comes from out of the blue. For him religion is a social product, and he wants to know the social forces that go into the process of shaping religion. (Instead of the term "religion" Gottwald prefers "ideology" in order to set "a methodological distance between sociological inquiry into Israel's religion and the more familiar historical and theological approaches to Israel's religion," p. 65.)

Gottwald's rigorous application of sociological methodology and his own fidelity to its structural integrity have resulted in what Walter Brueggemann regards as a third turning point in modern Old Testament scholarship. This methodological breakthrough is seen by Brueggemann as comparable to that of Julius Wellhausen's analysis of the Pentateuch and William F. Albright's synthesis of archaeology and biblical history.

The author sees himself as differing from other Old Testament scholars in that he is attempting to complement what they overlook or treat only as "social factors" which are subsumed under what they regard to be universal religious norms. For example, unlike John Bright who has influenced generations of biblical teachers and preachers, Gottwald hesitates to see the uniqueness of Israel in its unique religion while in other areas Israel is seen as similar in every way to other Semitic societies. For Gottwald the tribes of Yahweh were disparate peoples with overlapping concerns. The one basic commonality which they shared was their fighting for a place for themselves within Canaanite society of which they were the underclasses and to which they were marginal.

Gottwald's hypothesis is that there was a coalescing ("retribalization") of marginal peoples within the city-states of Canaan. The underclasses of Canaanite society were held down in their subservient status by the power and authority of the rulers, undergirded by Baal ideology. This hypothesis poses a challenge to prevailing hypotheses which are so familiar to generations of Christians: that the Israelites were pastoral nomads, and that they invaded and conquered Canaan, the land of milk and honey. Building on the work of George E. Mendenhall, especially his peasant revolt thesis, Gottwald nevertheless holds with tenacity to his sociological methodology while staying clear of any one-sided religious idealism. Starting with the known history of Israel, as did Martin Noth, the author finds in Noth a false analogy of the tribes of Israel to the religious league (amphictyony) of ancient Greece. Instead, Gottwald sees a coalition of different marginal peoples who were fighting for a place for themselves under the Canaanite sun. Monotheistic Yahwehism was their religion. It was, however, shaped by the different traditions which they themselves brought to the coalition, and it was commensurate with the egalitarian goals for which they fought.

This is an exciting book. As mentioned, it is an apparent breakthrough in modern Old Testament studies. Furthermore, for people in China concerns, Gottwald's major work offers a possibility of drawing significant parallels from other cultures where similar disenfranchised peoples have also struggled for a place within their own societies. One immediately thinks of the Taiping Revolution (1851–64) which involved millions of land-starved peasants in an expanding population in the Ching period in China. Under a cruel land tenantry system ruled by ruthless feudal elites who were undergirded by a Confucian ideology, the poor peasantry was driven to despair, desperation, and revolt. The already impossible situation was exacerbated by the import of foreign opium and the outflow of Chinese silver. In their quest for an egalitarian society the Taiping's religion was commensurate with the "Heavenly Kingdom of Great Peace" for which they struggled for fourteen years and in which over 20 million lives are estimated to have been lost. Against the Confucian social order their egalitarianism was based on a simple ideology of the fatherhood of God and the brotherhood of man (Taiping egalitarianism included women) provided by Christianity with a Confucian social milieu.

Gottwald says that it is easy for scholars including himself to cite all kinds of parallels between Israel and other peoples, but "far fewer have been able to assimilate and assess the comparative phenomena within an adequate theoretical framework" (p. 22). Much remains, therefore, to be done in assessing the role of religion in the Taiping Revolution and how religion was itself shaped by the sociopolitical realities of that historical situation. Here Gottwald's work is most suggestive, as well as providing a rigorous program of examining the Old Testament, part of the written foundation of Christianity, for the material bases of life and religion.

Moreover, what Gottwald's rigorous scholarship in sociological criticism of the Old Testament does in effect is to challenge people who are comfortable (as in Plato's Cave) with their understanding of their world, universe, and cosmos. The author begins with people and their historical realities. He does not begin with religion and then look for the people to fit into that religion. He is more interested in the canonizing process of scriptures and its politics than in the finished Canon itself, seen as being authoritative for all times and all places. For people who really want to know, even though such knowledge may be disturbing, Gottwald's pursuit is exciting. For established religion, however, his investigation can be viewed as iconoclastic, threatening, and therefore dangerous. Such time-honored religious concepts as revelation and incarnation, not to mention redemption and resurrection, will have to be seen in new historical light.

Gottwald's work may find much resistance and opposition in the Western world. On the other hand it may find much resonance in China, where from 1949 to 1966 over 3,000 research papers and 100 general books have been published, 50 kinds of source material collected, and 70–80 conferences and symposia on the national level held—all on the Taiping Revolution (see Tan Chung, "Peasant Rebellions in China" in *China Report,* Delhi, Jan.–Feb. 1980). In China, where biblical religion of the Old and New Testaments has never enjoyed an adherence of more than one percent of the total population in any given time of China's 1,300 years of contact with Christianity in its several forms, the problem of rigorous re-examination and self-criticism of faith assumptions may not be as acute as in Western culture.

In China, which has just finished another phase of peasant revolt, where eight people out of every ten in Chinese society are still required to produce food for a quarter of humanity, life is very hard indeed. But life is, as it always has been, also very precious and very much loved. In hardships, suffering, and struggle people form relationships which have dimensions of the sacred. In revolutions they have sought justice, liberation, and human fulfillment for themselves. Even without reference to an incarnator, life is and has been incarnate. Without an ordainer life is ordained so that the poor do rise up. Without any creation myth, creation is here and now. Life is down-to-earth, and revelation comes, if at all, from the very ground of suffering, struggle, and hope.

What is religion in this setting? A possible answer is that it is *survival*. It is the human struggle for life itself—its meaning, purposes, and destiny even among tremendous and impossible odds. Religion so defined is seen as an integral part of life which is God-given. It is not a *plus* to be appended to life. Though Norman Gottwald did not say these things in his book, his honest investigation of a very important period of the history of premonarchic Israel stimulates new ideas. This is the excitement of the heuristic nature of rigorous scholarship which is always open-ended. Such excitement awaits readers who are not discouraged or intimidated by this 3.4 pound paperback.

4. LUCIEN LEGRAND IN *INDIAN THEOLOGICAL STUDIES*

The title is modest. When I took the book in hand, I thought it would be one more of those highly technical monographs, going elaborately into endless technicalities, finally to come out with such meager results as a few precisions concerning the division of the narrative into sources or the geography and distribution of the tribes in Israel. But when I started reading the book, I realized that it was indeed scholarship but the kind of scholarship which is explosive! The subtitle should have warned me: it contains two terms which evoke very sensitive issues: A *Sociology* of *Liberated* Israel. There was another pointer to the nature of this study: the fact that it was published by Orbis Books, the missionary publishing firm which has specialized in missiological issues of a highly committed type and particularly in liberation theology. Gottwald's book on the *Tribes of Yahweh* shows that kind of relevance. It is certainly a solid biblical study. But the study of the past leads to challenging and even radical conclusions. In short, it is an important book not only for the scholar, but for anyone who takes the Bible seriously.

Starting from the externals, the book is important in terms of mere bulk. 709 pages to expose the thesis; 90 pages of notes in small print; various indexes of authors, biblical references, foreign terms, geographical and personal names, subjects, and an epilogue: altogether, a total of almost 950 pages in big format and tight print. They do not make them that big any longer nowadays! In the midst of a sterilizing output of over-specialized monographs dealing with irrelevant technicalities, Gottwald's study represents a return to the ambitious attempts of the humanists of old to produce broad syntheses encompassing the whole of the human situation. Since the author takes pain in the first part to oppose the humanistic and the sociological approaches to the text, it seems to be insensitive and vexatious to situate him in the old humanistic tradition. Yet, with due allowance to the important differences, I still think that the boldness of his project, the vastness of his syntheses can compare with the treatises written in the days when people took time to read, think, and write and when thinkers were not afraid to look at the human totality in all its aspects. Credit for this publication goes also to the publishers: it must have taken courage to accept a manuscript going to almost a thousand pages of solid scholarship and to produce it at the very decent price of 20 dollars. To finish with the externals of the book, I should add that the printing is excellent, barring a few instances of misplaced lines really disturbing (p. 85 line 2; p. 685 line 2; p. 686 line 1; p. 687 lines 2ff [ed. note: all but the last corrected in 2nd printing, Aug. 1981]).

Secondly, the book is important on account of the method it follows. The author is a professional exegete of the Old Testament. But he made an extensive study of sociology also. Of late, the interdisciplinary approach has been more and more frequently applied to the study of the biblical texts. The first chapters of Genesis, St. Paul, and the Gospels have been studied in the light of Freudism; there is another wave of structuralist analyses of the biblical narratives. It is only recently that systematic attempts have been made to combine exegesis and sociology and that in the context of liberation theology. But the professional scripturist is inclined to consider most of those attempts as exegetical light-weights. With N. K. Gottwald, we have solid Old Testament scholarship brought into the field. It is strange that it had not been done so systematically, so far. The very subject matter of the Old Testament is fraught with such sociological issues as tribal organization, family system, immigration, structures of power and administration, inter-racial relationship, etc. Moreover, the method of Form Criticism is supposed to be sociological since, for the individualistic approach to the text through the character and tendencies of an author, it substitutes an explanation through the concrete setting in the social life of the community. Gottwald draws Form Criticism to its full logical consequences. What is really the society which produced the accounts of the Exodus? A "Sociology of Liberated Israel" is the answer to the questions put by the analysis of Form Criticism. This method of Gottwald may seem to be the Columbus' egg of Old Testament criticism. But it must be added immediately that it calls for an extraordinary control of two widely different techniques. The reader is left gaping at the virtuosity of the author in both fields and begins to understand why it took almost a thousand pages to expose the results of that type of inquiry at two levels.

This original method yielded important conclusions or, at least, hypotheses. The book studies at length the sociological notions of tribe, clan (*mispaḥah*), extended family (*beth-abh*). He shows that the presupposition that the Israelite tribes followed a pastoral and therefore nomadic or semi-nomadic style of life is not scientifically justified: there are nomads who are not shepherds and there is a tribal system which is not bound to nomadism. M. Noth's amphictyonic system is also examined and found wanting in its application to Israel. The Greek amphictyony was only one of the confederate connections between the city states; there were several amphictyonies co-existing with other organs of confederation such as the military league, the federal union, local alliances, etc. The Hebrew confederacy, on the contrary, was unique; it penetrated the whole pattern of Israel's life and customs and functioned in lieu of any other centralized political power (see clear comparative tables on pp. 378–81).

But the main contention of Gottwald is that the origin of Israel is not to be found in a campaign or immigration movement coming from outside but in a revolt within the Canaanite society itself. Most of the studies on the Exodus follow the "conquest model" or the "immigration model." The first model, inspired by the book of Joshua, supposes an invasion of tribes coming from outside, joining battle with the Canaanite kingdoms and conquering the land. The second model, taking its clue from Judges 1, envisages rather a more peaceful movement of progressive immigration of marginal tribes attracted from the desert by the lure of rich cultivated lands "flowing with milk and honey." Neither of these two models is satisfactory, says Gottwald. They go against the evidence of biblical and archaeological data. Moreover, it is just not true that desert tribes lust after the fleshpots of agricultural lands: sociology shows that, on the contrary, nomads are reluctant to take to settled agricultural life, even when they are encouraged to do so. So the author returns to Mendenhall's suggestion that the Hebrew movement was mostly an "inside story," a development that took place within Canaanite society, a revolt of an oppressed peasantry against a political setup in which "they were exploited participants" (p. xxii). This does not exclude the participation of migrating and invading tribes but basically all the various groups which finally constituted Israel, "'*apiru,* transhumant pastoralists, *Shosu,* and peasants," found in Israel the catalyzing element that provided cohesion to their social tension and struggle. "With the appearance of Israel, the Canaanite 'tribe' at last found an ideological base and an organized mode for successfully challenging the Canaanite 'state' " (p. 485).

A long chapter follows that considers the many texts dealing with the hostility between Israel and Canaan and comes to the conclusion that, according to these texts, the hostility is not ethnic but social. Well understood they do not refer to a fight between ethnic groups but between classes, a struggle against "kings," "rulers," "princes," "armies," in other words, against the oppressive structures of the Canaanite state. In this connection, Gottwald develops a suggestion of Cross and Freeman that the Hebrew word *yoshev,* usually translated as "inhabitant," means rather, in a number of cases, "ruler," "people in authority," in short "the powers that be" (pp. 515–34): the term could be the basic appellation of that class from which the "Israelites" wrenched their freedom.

Yahwism provided an ideology for that class struggle. Loyalty to Yahweh, the only God, gave a sense of identity to those proletarian revolutionaries and undergirded a value system that focussed on social egalitarianism. Therefore it can be said that Yahwism issued from Israelite society and that Israelite society issued from Yahwism. It follows that the uniqueness of Israel is not just a matter of religious faith alone. This is the common idealistic explanation which insists on the many elements shared in common by Israel and the surrounding people, but isolates the faith of Israel, its monotheism, sense of the plan of God in history as the specific factors: Israelite society and culture would merge in the landscape of Western Asia; its religion only would be unique. For Gottwald, this is sheer idealism. What is unique in Israel is the social movement it crystallized, the egalitarianism it produced: the uniqueness of Israelite religion derives from the uniqueness of its sociological experiences. The emergence of Israel is not an insignificant episode which happened in a remote corner of Western Asia and in which God, by an arbitrary decision, resolved to hide a great grace. It was a highly significant sociological event which had a remarkable impact on world history and a uniquely symptomatic value.

A final chapter of the book develops the mutual relationship between biblical theology and biblical sociology. The main features of Israelite religion can be "demythologized" in terms of the sociological venture lived by Israel. The lesson given by the history of early Israel is that Yahwism and biblical faith can be really significant only in the context of a struggle for freedom, by a radical involvement in the values embodied in the "sociology of liberated Israel."

This too-rapid a summary cannot do justice to an exposition rich in learned analyses, in solid demonstrations, perceptive remarks, and fecund hypotheses. It will be sufficient, I hope, to give an idea of the amplitude of the thesis that tries to integrate the data of literary analysis, ancient history, archaeology, sociology, philosophy of religion, and of society finally to conclude on a manifesto of committed theology.

So ample a synthesis will evidently not get the approval of all the specialists in all its details. Mendenhall's hypothesis concerning the emergence of Israel as the outcome of an internal struggle within Canaan has not convinced many so far. Will the much enlarged demonstration of Gottwald carry conviction? Will the Hebrew dictionaries in the future give "ruler, powers that be" as one of the recognized meanings of *yoshev*? Does the analysis of the tribal system with its clans and joint families bring final clarity to the complex linguistic data? Can the complexity of Hebrew terminology as regards the tribes and their divisions be reduced to the three-tier system proposed by the author? Tribalism, nomadism, and pastoralism do not necessarily coincide: this is certainly a valid point made by the author. The tribal system that we know in India and in South Eastern Asia shows it. But precisely this tribal system raises many more problems than can be solved by an analysis of society in terms of class. The tribal system we know in India and in Asia has definite ethnic components.

Ultimately the basic questions raised by Gottwald's thesis are those which the "humanists" continue to put to the "sociologists." Let us at least mention a few:

1. The thesis of Gottwald follows the Marxist model obviously and avowedly. Is it not also inspired and conditioned by this model? Is it true that the other models of the "conquest" and of the "immigration" were also conditioned by an implicit ideology and presuppositions? The success of the "conquest model" in exegesis may not be immune from unconscious colonialism; the conquest of Canaan by Israel has even sometimes been explicitly taken as a justification of the colonial wars. The immigration model evokes the *Drang nach Osten,* the conquest of the American West, and other treks more or less glorious, more or less infamous. Every generation dresses the biblical heroes in its own garments. But is this not true also of the "revolt model"? Once the Marxist analysis is fed into the inquiry, is it not necessary, at the end of the process, to get a class revolt against oppressors? Can the various forms of tension in India be reduced to class struggles? Has Marxism really accounted for the caste system and the tribal system as we know them?

2. What leaves the "humanist" perplexed as regards sociology and especially Marxist sociology is its total (totalitarian?) claim: it explains everything. But does it? and can it be an integral explanation? The sociologist is inclined to condemn any reservation that can be made as an example of idealism. So does Gottwald. We can agree with him that the nonsociologists and particularly the biblical scholars are often guilty of illogism when they accept sociological explanation up to a point but refuse to go further and try to divide the field into two. Any scientific discipline is all-inclusive and we cannot expect sociology not to be so. Even a religious movement can be explained entirely by its sociological background. But is it not also explained entirely by its human promotors, their vision and dynamism, and by the spirit (Spirit?) that moves them? It is not a matter of explaining the Exodus partly through sociology, partly through Moses or Joshua, and partly through the intervention of God. It is rather entirely a matter of sociology, a matter of personalities, and a matter of faith. By its all-inclusive claim, does not sociology, like any other type of human reflection, ultimately destroy the object of its study through decomposition? It has been said that biblical exegesis has been the victim of an "exegetical pollution" in which the Word of God is stifled through analyses and technicalities. Sociology also could smother the text by embracing it too tightly.

3. Still another question concerns the value and significance of the historical method. Granting that Gottwald has finally succeeded in reconstituting the events which took place in Palestine between 1250 and 1100 B.C. and accepting that this was a set of events of unique sociological importance for mankind, does the significance of the texts produced by that movement disappear with the end of that movement? Is it just to be the report of a very interesting and symptomatic but dead movement of the ancient past? Do not words continue to live a life of their own? Have not the texts, when genuine human language, has not poetry or prophecy a transtemporal value? How is it we can still read Shakespeare and be moved by him though we live outside the Elizabethan pattern of society? What is the principle of continuity of the

Judeo-Christian tradition? Can we simply say that the Exodus texts became irrelevant and could only be futile distortions once the period of early egalitarianism gave place to the new feudalism of Solomon and of the successive kings of Israel and Judah? Recent studies on language, on *Wirkungsgeschichte,* on the way a text works as it were of its own dynamism, open other aspects and raise other questions than those raised by Gottwald. In the present conflict between the synchronic and the diachronic lines of approach, a study like that of Gottwald leaves unanswered all the questions raised by the critics of too onesided a use of the historico-critical method.

But this does not mean that we can neglect the questions Gottwald's book has put to Old Testament exegesis, to theology, and to biblical faith itself. The uncommon length of this review shows the importance I find in this book, in the conclusions it reaches and the questions it puts. The questions I have formulated are not meant to be refutations. A book of this type cannot be and is not to be refuted. It must be listened to attentively. The questions it raises are only a tribute to its significance.

12

NORMAN K. GOTTWALD

The Theological Task after
The Tribes of Yahweh

Socially and theologically, early Israel was embedded in its ancient Near Eastern world, but its distinctive mix of social organization and faith stood out as a critical variation of the general environment. The sociological method of Tribes *contributes to a present theology that understands the "God-talk" of the Bible as symbolic representations of a totalizing and directive sort that are not to be confused with sense perceptions or cognitive concepts.*

Theological representations are developed through critical reflection on active faith in the social sites where believers struggle with the realities of daily life. Such representations provide an "onlook" or orientation toward social theories, analyses, and strategies. Theological representations cannot be dissolved by sociological criticism of the Bible or of present society, but must nonetheless continually reshape themselves in the light of fresh understandings of the social sites where they appear.

The theological task, once sensitized to sociological criticism, is to review and rework Jewish-Christian history as an interplay between faith, theologi-

An address delivered at Yale Divinity School on October 28, 1981.

cal representation, and social practice. The recovery of an organic theological curriculum of study entails the disciplined exercise of a theory-practice "loop" that links biblical tradition to the present through the mediation of Jewish-Christian history in all its religious, theological, and social aspects.

The title could be heard to strike a pretentious note, as though I were proposing that my sociological study of early Israel now made possible an entirely new theology. The intention rather is to indicate how I believe the theological task is affected or shaped by a thoroughgoing application of sociological criticism to biblical texts. Some readers of *Tribes* have thought either that I announced the end of theology or that, whatever my intentions, no theology would be possible on the basis of such deconstructed reading of the Bible.

By deliberation *Tribes* did not undertake a new theological construction in method or content. Instead, I stated that "I do not present a new theology so much as the *preconditions* for a new theological method which would employ the biblical records as ideological products and instruments of the social formation of Israel" (emphasis added).[1] How then does one begin to spell out the theological implications of the hypothesis of the social revolutionary origins of Israel and of the method and theory by which that hypothesis is reached?

THEOLOGY IN ANCIENT ISRAEL

An important premise of my argument in *Tribes* is to locate ancient Israel in its social matrix and to identify the social structural and developmental-conflictual features which have hitherto been described largely as "religious" or, more broadly, as "historical" or "cultural." In doing so I pose a total social formation which includes religion and culture, and which clearly has its own history (although many of the details are inaccessible), but which encompasses the whole constitution and experience of Israelites as determinate human beings who engaged in concrete activities to bring their society into being and to preserve and develop it. A village-based retribalizing movement broke away from city-state control, and in the course of that historical project to enable economic and political emancipation through self-defense and mutual aid, the movement created its own culture.[2] Central to that culture was the religion of Yahweh with a sharply etched symbol system and a centralizing cult practice. This religion was a key factor in achieving unity and perseverance in the historical project of economic and political emancipation.[3]

The socioreligious system of early Israel may be analyzed from as many angles as there were elements that composed it and as there are means for tracing the interactions among the combining and interacting elements. We may, for example, focus on the crops and agricultural technology that formed the base for the solidifying of the movement in the hill country, and go on to clarify the economic impact on residential patterns, forms of governance, and religious cults and symbols.[4] We can also focus on the peculiar "retribalized" social structure of the Israelite movement and its adaptive relationship to the economic, military, and cultural priorities of the movement.[5] Or we can just as legitimately begin with religious symbol and cult and trace how the specific material environment and the forms of social organization came to expression in the religion.[6] What we can no longer do in good conscience is to isolate the religious factors from the total social setting as though, once the historical and social "accidents" are noted as "background," we are free to move on to the self-contained religious essentials.[7] For theology, this is of utmost consequence, not only because of the socially embedded nature of the subject matter in biblical texts, but because of our position as socially situated and conditioned believers and theologians.

In the last section of *Tribes* I try to develop a profile or cross-section of the theological structure of earliest Israel both in its congruence with ancient Near Eastern theology and in its distinctiveness.[8]

It is my judgment that ancient Near Eastern and early Israelite religion participated in or shared a common structure in certain key respects:

1. The high god (either sharing power as one god among others, or as the highest for a given purpose or moment, or as the exclusive deity) is individuated, given personal attributes, and elevated as the comprehensive generative or engendering power behind all that is, or all that has momentary relevance.

2. The high god is active in the world of nature, history, social order, and often in a moral order as well.

3. The high god is conceived by natural and human analogies, which come to expression in titles, iconic symbols, and expressions of the feelings and expectations of worshipers. These analogies include natural elements, atmospheric and meteorological phenomena, topographical features, animals and plants, and familial and sociopolitical roles.

4. The high god is manifested or experienced as powerful, just, and merciful, and likewise effectual in enacting or assuring power, justice, and mercy in human affairs past, present, and future.

5. The high god is in bond with a people, organized in a particular sociopolitical, territorial, and cultural formation, and this relationship tends to be reciprocal—even contractual—in the sense that god and people know what to expect of one another. The god frequently imposes sanctions on the people.

6. The high god is interpreted by human representatives who occupy recognized social roles in accord with the kinds of social organization typical among the worshipers. The relation between god and people is interpreted according to "punishments" and "rewards" which are code-concepts for

concrete gains and losses in the natural, historical, and social domains. In times of social conflict and political turmoil, the interpreters of the same god may disagree in their readings of the will or message of the god.

Amid this common theological structure of the ancient Near East, Israel at its inception introduced new developments that marked it as exceptional:

1. The sole high god usurps the entire sacred domain, calling for the exclusive recognition of one deity in the life of the people. The hyperindividuation of Yahweh can be traced in the rhetorical modes of expression concerning divine qualities and doings, in the domains of life where the god is involved, and in the behavior prescribed or prohibited by the deity.

2. The sole high god is alone active in the world. Where ancient Near Eastern polytheism tended to diversify, fragment, and disperse human experience, Yahweh's singularity tends toward a more integrated and coherent assertion of the totality of meaning in human experience. Where certain realms, such as death or sexuality, are not immediately penetrable by this sole god, they are nonetheless denied to any other divine powers. Symbolic reflection on *the* activity of *the* one God is encouraged, although it falls short of some alleged single divine plan until apocalyptic times.

3. The sole high god is conceived by egalitarian sociopolitical analogies, by which I mean that the representations of Yahweh are chiefly those of a warrior-leader who brings the distinctive intertribal community into existence and defends it. Of course one cannot properly speak of equality between Yahweh and people, since Yahweh is the superior leader and also creator who benevolently rules human community. The terms chosen to characterize deity, however, show Yahweh to be establishing equality among people by creating Israel. The concretization of El as Yahweh (Yahweh is probably an epithet of El that means "the one who creates the armed hosts of heaven and of Israel")[9] defines the special sphere of divine societal reconstruction as an intertribal network of peoples. By contrast, analogies from nature and narrowly cultic analogies diminish.

4. The sole high god is coherently manifested or experienced as powerful, just, and merciful. The content of the revelation is formally very similar to the content of ancient Near Eastern religious revelation in general, but the faithfulness, reliability, and consistency of the deity in dealing with the people is greatly stressed—to the point that Israel gives much thought to how power, justice, and mercy are interconnected, believing them to be established in one divine ground and thus not at variance with one another. There is an emphatic expectation that all parts of human experience in community will mesh and interact intelligibly and supportively.

5. The sole high god is in bond with an egalitarian people, an intertribal formation. This people is Yahweh's special manifestation, which to misconstrue would be to misconstrue Yahweh. This people is not a land, region, or city; not a descent group formed by actual kinship; not an occupational group or privileged caste; not the protector of single needy persons separated from the whole community. Women share in this equality as members of

equal households, and women figure prominently in early Israelite traditions. Yet it seems a chiefly male-led society and the dominant analogies for Yahweh are male, although in many respects it seems as appropriate to refer to Yahweh as "she" as to call Yahweh "he."[10]

6. The sole high god is interpreted by egalitarian functionaries. Consistent with a people of equality is the interpretation of Yahweh by various leaders whose roles are circumscribed and contained within the whole tribal system such that monopolies on priestly or lay leadership are checked. No central government is operative and social stratification is intentionally de-structured. The priestly establishment is sharply contained.

This theological structure of premonarchic Israel can be "demythologized" according to its socioeconomic and communal-cultural referents, in contrast to the usual program of demythologizing into states of existential or mystical consciousness.

"Yahweh" is the historically concretized, primordial power to establish and sustain social equality in the face of counter-oppression from without and against provincial and nonegalitarian tendencies from within the society. "The Chosen People" is the distinctive self-consciousness of a society of equals created in the intertribal order and demarcated from a primarily centralized and stratified surrounding world. "Covenant" is the bonding of decentralized social groups in a larger society of equals committed to cooperation without authoritarian leadership and a way of symbolizing the locus of sovereignty in such a society of equals. "Eschatology," or hope for the future, is the sustained commitment of fellow tribesmen to a society of equals with the confidence and determination that this way of life can prevail against great environmental odds.[11]

Several of the most baffling aspects of Israel's religion are illuminated in terms of their critical social functions. Yahweh's exclusivity and abnormal jealousy correspond to the singularity and excessive passion of the Israelite social revolutionary movement. Yahweh's purposive neglect of the underworld and rejection of sexual commodity fetishism deny elite rulers the power to manipulate people's fear of death and hunger for sex as tools of oppression. The limited socioeconomic demands of the priesthood prevent a theocratic political monopoly over the people. The "popular" historiography of early Israel shows that the people, and not a few privileged heroes, make history. The salvation paradigms of early Israel (exodus, wilderness wandering, seizure of power in Canaan) are ways of showing that the decisive feature of historical events is social struggle.

THEOLOGY TODAY

On the basis of my reading of the theological structure of early Israel, in correlation with the people's material-social organizational-cultural structure, I offered in *Tribes* the following brief sketch of what theology is *not* and what it *is*:

In our attempt to position the socioreligious nexus of mono-Yahwism [the sole high god belief] and egalitarian Israelite society within the context of a larger contemporary understanding of religion, it is necessary to take our cue from the methodological insight that religion is the function of social relations rooted in cultural-material conditions of life. This entails a rejection of forms of theology that separate religion from theology and that abstract religious beliefs from the socially situated locus of the religious believers. The uniqueness of the Israelite religious perception lay in its discovery through social struggle that the concrete conditions of human existence are modifiable rather than immutable conditions. . . .

There is but one way in which those ancient religious symbols can be employed today in anything like their full range and power, and that is in a situation of social struggle where people are attempting a breakthrough toward a freer and fuller life based on equality and communal self-possession. Even then it is a risky business to "summon up" powerful symbolism out of a distant past unless the symbol users are very self-conscious of their choices and applications, and fully aware of how their social struggle is both like and unlike the social struggle of the architects of the symbols.[12]

In the light of the sociotheological understanding expressed in *Tribes,* I wish to expand briefly on three aspects of the theological task today: the nature and limits of theological representations, the social setting or site of theologizing, and the revitalization of the theological curriculum or encyclopedia.

THEOLOGICAL REPRESENTATIONS

Theological representations or symbols, such as the representations of God as an actor in or a shaper of human affairs, are a special kind of thinking which arises at the immediate level of faith but leads on to critical reflection, both because nontheological experience and knowledge press for an accounting from theology and because faith seeks clarity about itself.[13] Theological representations are general ideas that do not give sense data or cognition such as directly represent the world or directly guide our action within the world; they cannot be operationalized. Theological representations are formed out of tradition, and are strongly internalized psychosocially, but they do not replace practical knowledge of all kinds. They are not simply a knowledge alongside other bodies of knowledge but a way of looking at environment and human agency and at the meanings and values associated with various kinds of knowledge. Theological representations are thus totalizing and directive without being exhaustive or prescriptive. They orient and dispose us toward certain kinds of relational perceptions and values and they move us in practical directions, although they are by no means the sole source of totalizing and directive meanings and values.

There are many aspects to the proper comprehension of theological representations. There is the striking inner-biblical tendency to construct, deconstruct, and reconstruct representations of God and of the divine will for people. We also encounter the imperative of analogical or metaphorical limits to our theological representations. Every analogy drawn upon to assert a likeness to God is at the same time qualified by its unlikeness in that God is negatively qualified as one who escapes every analogy. We need especially to recognize how our understanding of theological representations follows on Kant's distinction of ideas such as soul, world, and God as belonging to a different grounding category than sense perceptions and theoretical or operational concepts. Moreover, we need to go on to show how ideas evolve cumulatively and relationally in history (our debt to Hegel), how they ground and function conflictually in a material social base (disclosed by Marx), and how they reverberate intrapsychically (discerned by Freud). The evident universals of the Kantian ideas are seen to be malleable within the strictures created by a developing psychic and social history.

Theological representations belong in a family with art and literature and with ideology conceived as a kind of prevailing "onlook" toward reality, a set of apparent a prioris or preunderstandings which have to be continually raised to consciousness and critically reflected upon. Thus, the theological representations call for incessant movement from first order statements of faith to second order coordination of these statements in themselves and in relation to other orders of experience and thought. Theological representations give an "onlook" toward praxis, as unreflected forms of behavior are self-corrected through intentional commitment and activity in daily life, gathering the behavior that appears to relate to the theological representations into some kind of coherence and relating it to other behaviors which may have their coherencies from other sources. While these theological representations do not operationalize into specific behavior they give an "onlook" toward concepts whose theories can be operationalized.

THE SOCIAL SITES OF THEOLOGICAL REPRESENTATION

Theological representations are the thoughts of people in a particular context. Faith and critical reflection on faith are activities in a given social site. The pertinent site, from which we start and to which we return, is our own social location whose specificity must be felt and analyzed as a determinate one with its own history, special pressures and possibilities, and its own movement toward a future which we consciously or unconsciously help to shape. Past theological representations, rising out of ancient Israel and mediated and enriched through Jewish-Christian history, are totalizing and directive toward our present social sites. Theological representations, far from being "free-floating" universals that give us solutions to problems in every time and place, are rather "engaged" images or models that orient us either to thinking or unthinking life in the here and now. This is because the social world, in which theological representations are formed and communicated, is a humanly constructed world structured by power relations and by power-determined distributions of goods, privileges, ideas, and meanings. The theological representations of biblical Israel are highly political in their scrutiny of social power and the ends for which it is used.

Every way of articulating and prioritizing the theological representations is conditioned by a material base in which people actually produce and reproduce their lives according to certain limits, some of which may be immutable but many of which are changeable. These theological representations express particular social interests which in one way or another are negotiated or imposed. The theological representations can serve to cover over these power realities by denying them or can assist in bringing them to light to justify them or to contest for their change. In the process the theological representations dispose us toward one or another set of theories and operations for dealing with power realities.

Theological representations, like art, literature, and ideology, sensitize and motivate us to deal with power relations in certain ways, but they are not themselves the precise tools for treating power relations, which must rather be theories and methods more exactly tailored to institutional and operational application. We may, for example, entertain a "functional" theory that explains inequality as a rough approximation to people's actual merits, or as the precondition of a social system working at all. Or, we may espouse a "conflict" theory that understands inequality as a forceful or duplicitous imposition of one set of interests on another set of interests without regard to merit.[14] We may accompany functional or conflict social theory with psychological theory that explains how people either necessarily crave mastery and subordination or have been culturally induced to internalize their powerlessness so that they more deeply fear the risk of change than they desire its potential benefits.[15] In our own social sites in capitalist United States, although functional theory is very strong, the impact of the theoretical and methodological currents flowing from Marx and Freud are deepening and widening, precisely because they offer us a leverage on problems that long seemed to be insoluble mysteries, and before which theological representations alone are helpless and even dangerously obfuscating.

Now it is evident that the wielders of theological representations can try to mark off areas of social and psychic life as tabooed ground and thereby resist new theories and methods for a priori reasons. Or they may so rush to embrace new theories and methods that they naively equate theological representations with those theories and methods (for example, the much-too-facile strategy of making Christianity and Marxism mean exactly the same thing), failing to observe the proper ground and limits of theological representations. Or theological representations can be recognized to have no special power to dispose over theory and method but rather a critical negative function of summoning and voicing the interests, meanings, and values that any theory or method will serve or disserve. Both the autonomy and conjuncture of theological representations and of theories and methods must be observed.

In *The Tribes of Yahweh*, I have carried through a radical socioeconomic and religiocultural deconstruction of early Israel without leaving any remainder to save traditional theology by means of the ever-convenient "god who fills the gaps." I have done so by turning theory and method upon the genesis of theological representations in ancient Israel. What I have not done, and could not possibly do by such a project, is to undo the theological representations, both because they are given there in the history and because they inhere in a living tradition today. Just as sense data, theory, and method do not replace art, literature, and ideology, so theological representations coexist with theory and method in the world of praxis. The viability of theological representations rooted in faith and opened to critical reflection is, however, tested by being called upon to give an account of how theological representations relate to their material base and social sites over the whole course of Israelite-Jewish-Christian history.

No mere pasting together of "history of theological ideas" with "history of religious institutions" can possibly accomplish this deconstruction of the history of theological representations in the context of Jewish-Christian praxis within the wider social world from biblical times to the present. The project of *Tribes*, restricted to premonarchic intertribal Israel, needs to be carried forward through all the phases of biblical history, as George V. Pixley has initially sketched in his recent *God's Kingdom* and as Fernando Belo has attempted for one Gospel in *A Materialist Reading of the Gospel of Mark*.[16] At the same time, the material and social base of theologizing throughout the whole of post-biblical Jewish and Christian history must be relentlessly pursued. Simultaneously, the theory and method by which we analyze and reconstruct the social sites of theologizing must be constantly evaluated, corrected, and enriched. It is clear that both Marxist and Freudian traditions are undergoing great ferment in themselves and in interaction with one another. The fertility of the theories and their applications is shown precisely in their capacity to reflect upon themselves and to improve their analytic and operational powers.[17] In this way, around the rubric of the interface between theological representations and social sites, all the disciplines of the theological encyclopedia can be gathered.

THE THEOLOGICAL CURRICULUM/ENCYCLOPEDIA

In a recent article, Edward Farley tackles the forbidding topic of fundamental reform in theological education as a theological task.[18] The theological task is understood by him not as the elevation of traditionally defined dogmatic theology over all the other branches of the curriculum. Rather, the theological task is to grasp the unity of knowledge and understanding requisite to the church and its ministry. I believe that Farley's desiderata for theological reform of the curriculum are met by the following formulation: it is the theological task of the church to grasp the theological representations in their social sites and praxis settings throughout Israelite-Jewish-Christian history and to focus all that critically re-worked content on a self-critical praxis of the church and its leadership here and now.

The Reformation, Farley notes, offered a kind of theological vision that grounded the branches of the theological encyclopedia in a unitary study of divinity in which there was a clear movement out of the biblical revelation and the confessions of the church through history and into the ministry of the church in word and sacrament. Modernity has undermined that unitary study of divinity. Science as the theoretical feeder of technological applications has penetrated the theological structure, sapped the primacy of biblical revelation and confessional authority, and reshaped the dismembered branches of the curriculum into professional specializations with their own independent self-justifications, now busily trying to recover the vision by separate enterprises of "bridging the gaps."

Farley believes that the bridgings, redivisions, and rearrangements of curriculum won't work without a new grasp of the theological task. No doubt he is right. But where does one grasp the nettle? A theological curriculum of theory-praxis as the axis of every discipline absolutely requires a substantial base in the church and a faculty fully committed to it. At the moment the main power in the churches and seminaries does not lie in the hands of those who want to revision theologizing, church mission, and the process of leadership education. In short, our current social site favors utter amnesia and mindlessness toward critical thought and action. Nonetheless, the failures of the churches are so colossal, the urgencies of social crisis so insistent, and the resources of a critical social theology so available that new opportunities for deep-going re-thinking and re-acting of Christian faith may be forced by our very desperation.

To bring theological representations into unabashed and total interface with material base and social site calls for the most unrelenting restructuring of consciousness. Theology really ceases to be higher knowledge, as it also ceases to be the arcane elaboration of a privileged faith that stands apart from worldly experience and meaning. A renewed theological encyclopedia of this sort could only come from Christians with a radical regard for their tradition and with radical trust and courage to commit themselves to the conflictual and open-ended task of restructuring themselves and their world.[19] Just such radical regard, trust, and courage impelled the first Israelites, and it is in part for this reason that they entice and disturb us, making it worth our while to study them so intensively and comprehensively that they might be rescued from the platitudes and dogmas that have nearly cut them off from us.[20]

NOTES

1. Norman K. Gottwald, *The Tribes of Yahweh: A Sociology of the Religion of Liberated Israel, 1250-1050 B.C.E.* (Maryknoll, N.Y.: Orbis Books, 1979), p. 668.

2. Ibid., pp. 210-33, 323-37, 464-85, 489-97, 584-87, 592-602, 611-18, 894-900, 903-13.

3. Ibid., pp. 63-71, 493-97, 592-607, 618-21, 642-49, 692-703, 901-03.

4. Ibid., pp. 650-63.

5. Ibid., pp. 293-341, 611-18.

6. Ibid., pp. 618-21, 660-63.

7. Ibid., pp. 592-607, presents critiques of the pronounced tendency of biblical interpreters to abstract Israel's religion from its society, as exemplified in the work of John Bright, George E. Mendenhall, and Georg Fohrer.

8. Ibid., pp. 670-91.

9. Frank M. Cross, *Canaanite Myth and Hebrew Epic* (Cambridge: Harvard University Press, 1973), pp. 65-71.

10. Gottwald, *Tribes*, pp. 685, 796-797, 913.

11. Ibid., p. 692.

12. Ibid., p. 701.

13. My discussion of theological representations is greatly indebted to Alfredo Fierro, *The Militant Gospel: A Critical Introduction to Political Theologies* (Maryknoll, N.Y.: Orbis Books, 1975), pp. 182-256, 305-62.

14. Michael H. Best and William E. Connolly, *The Politicized Economy* (Lexington, Mass.: D. C. Heath, 1976) offers trenchant analyses of the functional and conflictual explanations of economic inequality.

15. Michael Schneider, *Neurosis and Civilization: A Marxist/Freudian Synthesis* (New York: Seabury, 1975).

16. George V. Pixley, *God's Kingdom: A Guide for Biblical Study* (Maryknoll, N.Y.: Orbis Books, 1981); Fernando Belo, *A Materialist Reading of the Gospel of Mark* (Maryknoll, N.Y.: Orbis Books, 1981).

17. See, among others, Bruce Brown, *Marx, Freud, and the Critique of Everyday Life: Toward a Permanent Cultural Revolution* (New York: Monthly Review Press, 1973); Stanley Aronowitz, *The Crisis in Historical Materialism: Class, Politics and Culture in Marxist Theory* (New York: Praeger, 1981); Alan Gilbert, *Marx's Politics: Communists and Citizens* (New Brunswick, N.J.: Rutgers University Press, 1981).

18. Edward Farley, "The Reform of Theological Education as a Theological Task," *Theological Education* 18 (Spring 1981): 93-117.

19. See, for example, Frederick Herzog, *Justice Church: The New Function of the Church in North American Christianity* (Maryknoll, N.Y.: Orbis Books, 1980).

20. Gottwald, *Tribes*, pp. 700-709, 901-903.

13

ROBERT R. WILSON

Prophecy and Society in Ancient Israel

A review of the history of scholarship on the social dimensions of Israelite prophecy shows spotty or lopsided focus on the social functions of prophets (mostly as ethical or theological innovators), on the nature of prophetic behavior (chiefly ecstasy), and on the social location of prophecy (primarily in the cult). When cross-cultural data on prophets in the ancient Near East have been introduced to the discussion, it has generally been in an arbitrary way that overlooks the total settings of the compared forms of prophecy.

Anthropological data on the social matrix of intermediaries between the spirit world and the human world (seers, shamans, prophets) can be used to formulate and test hypotheses about the social processes involving Israelite prophets. We discover a continuum of prophetic types who range from central (or established) intermediaries to peripheral (or marginal) intermediaries. Relatively informal prophetic support groups may develop into highly organized millenarian movements.

This essay represents excerpts from Chapters 1 and 2 of Robert R. Wilson, *Prophecy and Society in Ancient Israel*, copyright © 1980 by Fortress Press, Philadelphia. Reprinted by permission of Fortress Press.

201

This abundantly documented anthropological material directs our attention to neglected aspects of the sociology of Israelite prophecy and suggests new lines of research and theory concerning the role of society in the processes by which people became prophets, how and where prophets performed their roles, how prophetic types and roles may have shifted over time, and how society reacted to their activities.

PROPHECY AND SOCIETY IN OLD TESTAMENT RESEARCH

An Introduction to the Problem

Ancient Israelite prophecy was a complex phenomenon which has been studied extensively by biblical scholars. Since the beginning of the critical study of the Bible in the nineteenth century, they have produced a number of comprehensive treatments of prophecy and have written a great many books and articles on its various aspects. In recent years in particular, researchers have been able to elucidate many of the obscure features of Israelite prophecy and have contributed greatly to our understanding of the prophets themselves. Their theological views have been examined and placed within the context of Israelite religion. The prophetic literature has been thoroughly analyzed, and the literary history of the prophetic corpus has been traced. Scholars have succeeded in delineating the characteristic patterns of the prophets' words and in some cases have been able to relate the various forms of prophetic speech to their original social settings.[1]

In the light of recent advances in prophetic research, it is all the more surprising that we still do not have a clear picture of the role that prophecy played in Israelite society. For purposes of study, the prophets have usually been isolated from their social matrix, and no comprehensive attempt has been made to examine the complex relationships that must have existed between the prophets and their society. We know little about the processes by which people became prophets, and the role that their society may have played in these processes remains to be studied. The nature of prophetic behavior is not precisely clear, and we do not know how society may have influenced that behavior. More important, we have only a vague understanding of the way in which prophecy actually functioned in Israelite society. We are uncertain about what the prophets did (or thought they were doing) for their society, and the society's reactions to their activities are often obscure. In short, most of the social dimensions of Israelite prophecy remain unclear, and for this reason the prophets themselves emerge from recent scholarly research as lifeless individuals.[2]

Yet, in spite of the fact that there is still no comprehensive study devoted exclusively to the problem of the relationship between prophecy and society in Israel, discussions of prophecy have frequently touched on various aspects of the problem. By collecting these scattered and sometimes oblique treatments, it is possible to reconstruct a schematic history of scholarship on the social dimensions of Israelite prophecy. This history reveals that the interaction between prophecy and society has been treated, at least peripherally, both by students of Israelite religious phenomena and by form critics concerned with the shape of biblical literature. These treatments, which are sometimes contradictory, have dealt in a limited way with three aspects of the overall problem: the social functions of prophecy, the nature of prophetic activity, and the social location of prophecy.

Prophecy and Society in the Study of Israelite Religion

From Ewald to Hölscher: The Social Functions of Prophecy. Early critical scholars tended to see the prophets as inspired individuals who were responsible for creating the purest form of Israelite monotheism. This view of prophecy gave rise to works that concentrated on the intellectual and theological aspects of prophecy, with the result that little attention was given to the prophet as a human figure intimately related to a social setting. These early works on prophecy seldom comment on the precise nature of prophetic speech and behavior or on the social location of the prophet. Yet, at the same time, even the most theologically oriented studies do imply something about the social *functions* of prophetic activity. Heinrich Ewald, for example, saw the prophets as crucial figures in the history of Israelite religion. They were the first people in whom the divine spark of true knowledge was brought to consciousness by the spirit of God. For this reason they served as models of the spiritual heights which all people might someday reach. In this way the prophets functioned as individuals who had been divinely chosen to reform all aspects of human society.[3] Ewald thus saw the prophets as agents of social change, although he nowhere describes them explicitly in these terms.

A similar view of the social function of prophecy is implied in the early work of Bernhard Duhm. Like Ewald, Duhm saw the major significance of the prophets in their theology, which raised the level of Israelite religion to new moral and ethical heights. The prophets broke sharply with the ancient Israelite religious traditions, particularly those of the patriarchal period, and were powerful forces in shaping a religion free of superstitious cultic and magical practices.[4] Duhm thus believed that the prophets functioned as agents of social change, although their main contributions were moral, ethical, and theological. On the question of the nature of prophetic activity, Duhm had little to say. He was aware of the existence of ecstatic prophecy in the ancient Mediterranean world, but he drew such a sharp distinction between "pagan" ecstatics and the Israelite prophets that he felt it unnecessary to use any type of comparative material in his study. He also recognized that the early writing prophets, particularly Amos and Isaiah, sometimes exhibited ecstatic behavior. However, he believed that such behavior was present only early in the prophets' careers and that it was quickly replaced by normal, rational speech and behavior.[5] Although Duhm treated the prophets in particular historical contexts, he believed that those contexts played little role in shaping prophetic theology, which transcended particular historical settings. He therefore did not deal with the question of the social location of prophecy in any specific way.

Duhm's general approach to the question of prophecy and society was subsequently followed by a number of historians of Israelite religion. Wellhausen, who was otherwise the most influential of Duhm's contemporaries, made few contributions to the study of prophecy. He held that early prophecy in Israel had little impact on Israelite religion or society. Only with the work of the writing prophets were the older religious patterns destroyed and replaced by prophetic "ethical monotheism." In contrast to their predecessors, the writing prophets worked both inside and outside of the religious establishment in order to change it.[6]

Similar views were held by W. Robertson Smith, who recognized the existence of ecstatic prophecy within the Israelite religous establishment but who argued that this phenomenon contrasted sharply with the rational behavior and ethical insights of the writing prophets.[7] However, Smith's approach moved beyond previous research at two important points. First, he made at least limited use of extra-biblical material to describe prophecy outside of Israel and to elucidate Israelite religious phenomena, although he ultimately denied that this material was relevant to the study of the writing prophets.[8] Second, he recognized the complex relationship which exists between religious phenomena and their social setting. He therefore paid a great deal of attention to the historical setting of the prophetic writings, and he noted the different social locations and functions of the various types of Israelite prophecy.[9]

The Legacy of Hölscher: The Nature of Prophetic Activity. Although Smith's work on the question of prophecy and society treated some areas not previously considered, he still basically accepted the views of Duhm and Wellhausen. A major alternative view did not appear until the influential work of Gustav Hölscher, who shifted the focus of the inquiry from the social function of prophecy to the nature of prophetic activity.[10] Hölscher argued that all prophets, including those in Israel, shared the same ecstatic and visionary experiences. To prove his case, he systematically considered various psychological and behavioral characteristics of ecstatics and then demonstrated the existence of these characteristics among the Israelite prophets. Although Hölscher followed earlier scholars in maintaining that Israel's prophets received divine moral insights from their experiences, he stressed the cultural and historical links between Israelite ecstatic prophecy and ecstatic prophecy among Israel's neighbors. In spite of the thoroughness with which Hölscher treated the nature of Israelite prophecy, he made few comments on the social location of prophetic activity. He recognized that some early Israelite prophets were associated with the cult, but he denied that the writing prophets had cultic connections.[11]

Hölscher's work marks a turning point in the study of prophecy and society not only because of his conclusions but also because of the method which he employed. He made extensive use of comparative material and thus established a pattern followed by a number of subsequent religiohistorical treatments. Throughout *Die Profeten* his normal approach is to draw extensively on contemporary psychological studies of the characteristics of ecstasy and then to document the existence of those characteristics in antiquity.[12] In order to do this he uses a great quantity of ancient Near Eastern and classical material and relies particularly heavily on Arabic sources.

Hölscher's concern with the nature of prophetic activity has been shared by a number of subsequent religiohistorical studies, all of which have focused on the ecstatic character of prophecy and have tried to come to grips with the basic problem posed by Hölscher's work: the relationship between the "irrational," ecstatic nature of prophecy and the coherent, theologically sophisticated, sometimes highly structured oracles of the Israelite writing prophets.[13] Treatments of this problem have followed three major lines of development, but to date no single solution has proven completely satisfactory.

First, some scholars have simply denied that the writing prophets and those nonwriting prophets whose words have been preserved were ecstatics. There are two major variations on this theme. Following the approach of scholars writing before the publication of Hölscher's work, some critics have admitted the existence of ecstasy early in the history of Israelite prophecy but have flatly denied the presence of ecstasy among the writing prophets.[14] In its extreme form, this approach is forced to overlook clear indications of ecstasy among the writing prophets, and most scholars following this line admit the occasional presence of "mild forms of ecstasy" in the writing prophets.[15] Taking a different tack, some scholars have argued that the "true prophets" in Israel were not ecstatics, while the "false prophets" described in the prophetic literature were ecstatics.[16] By assuming that all of the writing prophets were true prophets, this view is able to dissociate them from ecstasy. However, this approach underestimates the problems involved in differentiating true and false prophets in Israel, and it also overlooks the fact that there is no good biblical evidence to indicate that all of the so-called false prophets were ecstatics.

A second major line of development has taken an approach followed by Gunkel before the publication of Hölscher's work.[17] In contrast to Hölscher, who believed that the prophets delivered their oracles while in a state of ecstasy, Gunkel suggested that the prophets produced their oracles after their ecstatic experiences had ended. The oracles were thus the products of rational

Robert R. Wilson

minds and were attempts to communicate what had transpired during the prophets' ecstasy. A number of scholars have accepted some form of Gunkel's position and have argued that the prophets composed their oracles either immediately after their ecstatic experiences or at a later date.[18] Although this view has the advantage of accounting for the more-or-less rational nature of the prophetic literature, it is based on very little evidence. In addition, there are clear indications that some prophets did deliver oracles while in a state of ecstasy. Jeremiah's oracle in 4:19 ("My anguish, my anguish! I writhe in pain!") seems closely connected to ecstasy, and the fact that Jeremiah's speech could be described as that of a madman (Jer. 29:26) suggests that at least some of the prophet's utterances were given while in ecstasy. Ecstasy is also indicated by Jer. 23:9, where the prophet describes himself as shaking and like a drunken man because of the words of Yahweh.

The third approach to the problem of ecstasy has been taken by scholars who admit that even the writing prophets may have had mild and infrequent ecstatic experiences of some type. These scholars argue, however, that the *content* of the prophets' words must be distinguished from the ecstatic *means* by which those words were received.[19] This argument has the effect of shifting the focus of scholarly inquiry away from the problem of ecstasy, but by doing so it leaves unanswered the form-critical question of the relationship between ecstasy and the prophetic literature.

The Legacy of Mowinckel: The Social Location of Prophecy. Just as Hölscher's work brought the question of the nature of prophecy to the attention of biblical scholars, so also Sigmund Mowinckel forced them to struggle with the problem of the social location of prophecy. Although Mowinckel's interests were primarily form-critical, he recognized the importance of dealing with the social setting in which stereotypical speech forms were used.[20] Therefore, in the course of his investigation of the Psalms, he suggested that the so-called prophetic psalms were originally prophetic oracles delivered in the context of the cult. His suggestion was made on the basis of the form of the language of the Psalms rather than on any actual description of prophetic activity in the cult, but he went on to argue that prophetic guilds functioned in the Jerusalem cult alongside the priests. To be sure, scholars had previously noted the existence of cult prophecy in Israel, but such activity was usually thought to have been confined to an early period in Israelite religious development.[21] In contrast, Mowinckel's work raised the possibility that cultic prophecy was to be found throughout the history of Israel and that even the writing prophets had cultic functions. On this last point Mowinckel was a bit vague, but he did argue that Joel and Habakkuk were cultic prophets, and he later extended his argument to include Isaiah and Micah as well.[22]

Mowinckel's work touched off a debate on the social location of Israelite prophecy which has persisted to the present day and shows no sign of abating.[23] So much has been written on the question of prophecy and the cult that it is impossible even to begin to sketch here a history of research after Mowinckel. However, it will be helpful to mention briefly three works which illustrate the types of approaches that have been taken.

The thesis that prophets in Israel were located in the cult was developed in a thorough way by Aubrey R. Johnson.[24] His work is significant not only because he concluded that Israelite prophets played an important role in the cult but also because he supported that conclusion with an analysis which recognized the complexities of prophetic phenomena. He collected evidence of the various types of prophetic figures and tried to distinguish their characteristic behavior and social functions. Although he took no stand on the relationship of the writing prophets to the cult, he did argue that they must be seen against the background of other types of prophecy.[25] Almost all of Johnson's arguments are supported by appeal to the biblical text alone, and he rarely uses extra-biblical data. In contrast to Mowinckel, who started from an analysis of speech patterns, Johnson makes little use of form criticism.

Alfred Haldar approached the question from a very different angle.[26] Haldar's work opens with a detailed analysis of various types of cultic functionaries in Mesopotamia and pays particular attention to the *bārû* (the diviner, whom Haldar considers a "seer" or "oracle giver") and the *maḥḥû* (the ecstatic). Haldar then tries to make a direct connection between these Mesopotamian figures and Israelite priests and prophets. The function of the *bārû* was performed in Israel by the seers (*rō'eh, ḥōzeh*) while the *maḥḥû* had a counterpart in the prophet (*nābî'*). Both the seers and the prophets were members of organized groups related to the cult, although the prophet's office was not hereditary.

A very different approach to the problem of prophecy and cult has been taken by the sociologist Peter L. Berger.[27] Berger's work is interesting not because of its conclusions, which will be familiar to biblical scholars, but because it is one of the few attempts to date to use a cross-disciplinary approach. Berger's basic concern is to test Weber's views of charisma against the contemporary scholarly consensus on the nature of Israelite prophecy. Berger focuses on the question of the social location of prophecy in Israel and specifically considers the relation of the prophets to the cult. After surveying recent research on the question, he concludes that biblical scholars today see little distinction between the writing prophets and the earlier nābîs'. In addition, he believes that most scholars would admit that the prophets were located in the cult. Berger then draws the important conclusion that charismatic figures such as prophets need not be only on the periphery of society but may function within established institutions as well. In practical terms this would mean that cultic prophets in Israel need not have been totally bound by institutional pressures but would have been free to promote innovative changes in their institutions. Whatever one may think of Berger's conclusions, it is unfortunate that he commits a common error in his use of evidence outside his own discipline: he assumes a consensus in another scholarly field where in fact no consensus exists.[28]

Prophecy and Society in Form-Critical Study

Because there are several recent treatments of the history of form-critical research on the prophets, we need to make only a few observations about form-critical perspectives on the relationship between prophecy and society.[29] Interest in the social dimensions of prophetic activity first arose in form-critical circles in the work of Gunkel. As early as 1906 Gunkel had developed the concept that all literary genres had a setting in the life of the people who used them. However, his discussions of this concept are somewhat vague. He sometimes uses the phrase "setting in life" (*Sitz im Leben*) to refer to the original social settings of the literary genres themselves, but he also employs the phrase to refer to the social occasion on which the genres were subsequently used.[30] The setting of the activity of using a literary genre and the original setting of the actual language and structure of the genre *may* sometimes be the same. For example, the language and structure of the lament originated on occasions of mourning, and the lament was subsequently used on similar occasions. However, the original setting of the language of a genre *may not* be the same as the setting in which the genre is actually used. In the case of prophecy, the social matrix of prophetic language and the social location of prophetic activity may not be identical. A prophet who delivers oracles in the temple court may not employ speech forms that originated in the temple.

Since the time of Gunkel form critics have had a great deal to say about the literary genres of prophetic speech and about the original social matrix of the language of those genres, but little attention has been paid to the way in which the prophets actually used their traditional speech patterns in Israelite society. Form critics have generally overlooked the question of the social location of prophetic activity. A clear case in point is the work of Claus Westermann, whose *Basic Forms of Prophetic Speech* is the most recent comprehensive study of prophetic literary genres. After a thorough survey of the history of research on prophetic speech forms and an examination of the relevant biblical material, Westermann concludes that prophetic speech was shaped by the notion that the prophet was God's messenger, who delivered divine messages to the people. The basic form of prophetic speech was the announcement of judgment against the individual, but this form later underwent a number of structural changes and was transformed into an announcement of judgment against the whole nation. In the course of Westermann's analysis he provides a thorough discussion of the various prophetic speech forms, but nowhere does he deal with the actual social settings in which the forms were used. His picture of the prophet as Yahweh's messenger suggests that prophets had the general function of serving as a bridge between the human and divine worlds, but the messenger image says nothing about the actual social location of prophetic activity. The title which Westermann gives to the basic prophetic literary genre *implies* that the prophets delivered their oracles in a judicial setting, but he does not actually press this argument.[31]

When form critics have considered the social location of prophetic activity, there has been a tendency to use the original setting of prophetic language to reconstruct the occasion on which the prophets used the language. An example of this tendency can be found in recent work on the *rîb,* the prophetic lawsuit. This genre was first analyzed by Gunkel, who suggested that it must have originally had a judicial setting.[32] This is an adequate explanation for the origin of the *language* and *literary structure* of the genre, but Gunkel's suggestion does not shed much light on the social setting in which the genre functioned. There is no biblical evidence that prophets normally delivered oracles in the course of judicial proceedings. Nevertheless, the judicial background of the language of the genre has led some scholars to *assume* that the prophets operated in legal contexts. Because God is also involved in the covenant lawsuit, some scholars have suggested that the prophets used this genre in a cultic trial in which the people were indicted for breaking their covenant with Yahweh.[33] Still, it must be remembered that there are no biblical accounts of cultic trials for covenant breaking, and there is therefore no solid evidence that prophets actually participated in such trials. Their existence is based solely on a deduction from a literary genre.

The Implications of Prior Research

On the basis of the above history of the study of prophecy and society, it is possible to make two generalizations concerning the present state of the inquiry. First, it is clear that scholars have generally avoided dealing with *all* of the social dimensions of Israelite prophecy. The problem of the social role that the prophets played in Israel has rarely been treated at all in recent years. There are a number of discussions of the social location of prophecy, but they have been primarily concerned with the extent of prophetic involvement in the cult. Similarly, current treatments of the nature of prophetic activity have focused either on the behavior of the prophets (religiohistorical studies of ecstasy) or on the structure of prophetic speech (form-critical studies of prophetic literature), but seldom are these two features of prophecy considered together. In addition, form critics concerned with the stereotypical structure of prophetic language have often simply ignored the questions of social location and function. Clearly, these fragmented approaches to the problem of prophecy and society must be superseded if any real progress is to be made. All of the social dimensions of Israelite prophecy must be considered before any accurate picture of the prophets can be formulated.

Second, the fact that no single approach has thus far been able to characterize accurately the distinctive social features of Israelite prophecy has gradually led scholars to recognize the complexity of the interaction between Israelite prophets and their societies. This tendency is best seen in Johnson's work on the different types of Israelite prophets and in Berger's work on the relationship between charisma and social institutions. Treatments of the problem of prophecy and society must take this complexity into account. It seems increasingly likely that not all of the Israelite prophets were related to their societies in the same way. In addition, different relationships may have existed at various times in Israelite history, and this historical dimension must also be considered.

Prophecy and Society: A Cross-Disciplinary Approach

The Use of Anthropological Evidence. Although it is easy to locate the weaknesses in prior research on the problem of prophecy and society, one of the chief reasons for these weaknesses must be readily acknowledged. In fact, there is very little biblical evidence on which to base a study of the social aspects of Israelite prophecy. Old Testament narratives describing prophetic activity can provide some clues about how the prophets may have been related to their society, and by carefully examining the literary history of the narratives it is sometimes even possible to reconstruct the changes that took place in these relationships. However, the major sources for the study of prophecy, the prophetic writings themselves, furnish little data that can throw light on the social matrix of the prophets. Only a few of the prophetic books contain accounts of prophetic activity, and even where such accounts exist it is often difficult to relate them to the oracles preserved elsewhere in the prophets' writings.

Because of this relative lack of biblical evidence, it will be helpful to approach the problem from another direction. In recent years contemporary anthropologists and sociologists have produced a number of competent field studies of a wide range of prophetic phenomena. Unlike the biblical material, these anthropological studies provide comprehensive accounts of the ways in which prophets are related to their societies. This comparative evidence indicates the complexity of the social dimensions of prophecy and can therefore suggest to the interpreter more precise and potentially useful questions that might be asked of the biblical text. In this way the anthropological data can provide a detailed background against which the biblical evidence can be better understood. By acquiring a more sophisticated understanding of the role of prophecy in modern societies, the interpreter should be better equipped to consider the social dimensions of prophecy in Israel.

Methodological Problems. The use of comparative material to elucidate Israelite religion raises certain methodological difficulties which must be faced at the beginning of any cross-disciplinary study. The value of comparative material is obvious, for it can supplement the meager biblical data on the nature and functions of prophecy. Yet, the methodological errors which we have already seen in the work of earlier scholars must be avoided. On the one hand, the interpreter must be fair to the biblical material by not imposing on it irrelevant and constricting external data. On the other hand, the interpreter must be fair to the comparative material by treating it properly in its own context. In order to avoid methodological errors, the following guidelines must be observed when comparative material is used.[34]

1. Comparative material, particularly anthropological and sociological material, must be collected systematically by a trained scholar. Obviously the biblical scholar must rely on secondary literature for most comparative data, but an attempt should be made to be sure that the scholars whose work is used are reliable and that they have not themselves been overly selective or biased in their presentation of the data. In the case of anthropological material, this means that biblical scholars must rely on work done in the twentieth century.

2. Comparative material must be properly interpreted in its own context before any attempt is made to apply it to the biblical text. Ancient Near Eastern cultural phenomena must therefore be seen in the whole context of the societies that produced them and must not simply be extracted from their own cultural matrix. Sociological and anthropological data on a particular phenomenon must be seen in the context of the whole society which produced the phenomenon. Only by doing this is it possible to understand the social function of the phenomenon. This means that the most useful comparative material will come from studies dealing with the totality of a single society or with the social function of a phenomenon within several societies. Theoretical or abstract studies that provide little hard data are likely to be less useful.

3. When using sociological and anthropological material, the biblical scholar must survey a wide range of societies that contain the phenomenon being studied. By doing this it is possible to avoid using atypical material for comparative purposes.

4. The biblical interpreter must concentrate on the comparative data that has been collected and if possible must avoid the interpretive schemata into which sociologists, anthropologists, and Near Eastern scholars have placed the data. By doing this the biblical scholar can avoid biased presentations.

5. When applying comparative material to the biblical text, the biblical scholar must be sure that the comparative material is truly comparable to the biblical material being studied. By limiting the comparative material in this way, the interpreter can eliminate data that might distort the interpretation.

6. When applying comparative material to the biblical text, the interpreter must allow the biblical text itself to be the controlling factor in the exegetical process. The comparative material can thus be used only to form a hypothesis which must still be tested against the biblical text. The exegesis of the text itself will then support, disprove, or modify the hypothesis. If the exegesis of the text fails to provide enough evidence either to support or to deny the hypothesis, then the question must be allowed to remain open with respect to that particular text. The lack of exegetical evidence cannot cause either the acceptance or rejection of the hypothesis. Comparative data thus has a dual function. On the one hand, it can broaden the horizons of the biblical inter-

preter and suggest a wider range of hypotheses than the interpreter might be able to produce on the basis of the biblical text alone. On the other hand, comparative material may lend support to or cast doubt on hypotheses previously advanced.

The Complexity of the Biblical Traditions. Before anthropological material can be used to interpret the biblical evidence on prophecy and society, the complexity of Israel's own prophetic traditions must be taken into account. Even a cursory reading of the sources reveals that the biblical writers had divergent and sometimes conflicting views about prophecy. These views were presumably the product of a long period of development, and it is now difficult to determine how accurately they reflect historical reality. However, there is no reason to suspect that the various biblical conceptions of prophecy were simply created out of whole cloth. Rather, they must be taken as an indication that the groups bearing the biblical traditions actually knew of different types of prophecy. If so, then each type must have had its own peculiar characteristics and must have existed for a definite historical period, while still developing in reaction to changing social, political, and religious conditions.

To suggest that the various biblical conceptions of *prophecy* are relatively accurate reflections of the types of prophecy that actually existed in Israel is not to suggest that all of the biblical pictures of individual *prophets* are historically accurate. The biblical writers sometimes allowed their personal attitudes about prophecy to influence their portrayal of particular prophets, with the result that these individuals are said to have spoken and acted in ways that conform to the authors' understanding of appropriate prophetic behavior but that are at variance with the individuals' actual behavior. Furthermore, relatively late conceptions of prophecy have occasionally been retrojected into an earlier time. Therefore, in some cases the biblical texts are a more reliable guide to the general nature of Israelite prophecy in the time the texts were written than they are to the actual characteristics of the prophets being described.

Although the groups that bore the Israelite traditions undoubtedly had a number of different conceptions of prophecy, only one of them can now be seen clearly in the biblical texts. The prominence of this one view of prophecy is due to the simple fact that almost all of the biblical narratives dealing with prophetic activity come from what is essentially a single theological and literary tradition. Scholars have long noted that the Deuteronomic History, the Elohistic layer of the Pentateuch, and the writings of Hosea and Jeremiah share certain traditions and theological perspectives. These sources also view prophecy in a similar way, and this distinctive view now pervades most of the prophetic narratives. Because all of these sources are usually thought to reflect a northern Israelite perspective, we will refer to them as representatives of the Ephraimite tradition.[35]

The groups who bore the Ephraimite tradition are difficult to identify with any certainty, but as a working hypothesis we will accept the theory that they originated in connection with some of the northern Israelite shrines during the period of the judges. Some of the members of these groups may have been priests who officiated at the northern sanctuaries before David established a central shrine in Jerusalem. A few of the priests, represented by Abiathar, may have participated in David's Jerusalemite cult, while others remained outside of the royal establishment. Northern priestly influence in Jerusalem ended in the time of Solomon, and thereafter Ephraimite theological traditions were carried in different geographical areas by groups that retained an independent identity throughout the history of the monarchy. These groups expressed their views at various times in what we now know as the Elohistic layer of the Pentateuch and the Deuteronomic literature.[36]

Although the Ephraimite view of prophecy now dominates the biblical texts, there are also a few traces of other views. Some of these views are embedded in the Ephraimite literary corpus itself, but most of them are found in sources that can be linked with Jerusalemite or Judean authors. We will therefore assume that these views reflect Judahite traditions originating in the south but preserved after the rise of the monarchy at the royal court in Jerusalem. Unfortunately, because of the scarcity of information about Judean prophecy, it is unclear whether the sources reflect one coherent Judahite tradition or portions of several variant traditions.

The Scope of the Inquiry. In the study that follows we will first examine the anthropological evidence on various types of prophetic phenomena and will pay particular attention to the way in which modern prophets interact with their societies. Using the data drawn from this examination, we will then consider ancient Near Eastern evidence on prophecy. In this way we will be able to test the usefulness of the comparative data before attempting to apply it to the biblical material. Finally, in the light of our anthropological research, we will study the Old Testament evidence on prophecy and society. Our inquiry will focus on the Ephraimite prophetic traditions, for they provide the clearest evidence for the relationship between prophecy and society in Israel. However, we will also examine briefly the data on prophecy in Judah. The bulk of this data will come from prophetic narratives that have been preserved in the prophetic books themselves and in the work of the Chronicler. However, we will also use the little evidence that can be safely drawn from the oracles of Judean prophets.

The study of the biblical material can be approached in two ways. First, several crucial biblical texts can be examined in detail, and on the basis of this examination hypotheses can be formulated and then tested in later studies. Second, all of the biblical evidence on prophecy can be surveyed. The first approach has the advantage of being able to take into account the complexity of the biblical texts, but the concentration on only a few texts necessarily restricts the range of prophetic phenomena that can be considered. The second approach prevents a thorough examination of individual passages but has the advantage of permitting all of the evidence to be treated. Because previous studies of the problem of prophecy and society have failed to take into account all of the available material, we will follow the second approach, realizing that future detailed studies of specific passages may require the modification of our conclusions. Nevertheless, by at least surveying all of the biblical evidence we will be able to suggest the general outlines of a social history of Israelite prophecy. . . .

PROPHECY IN MODERN SOCIETIES

The Social Functions of Intermediation

In addition to the obvious religious function of serving as links between the human and supernatural worlds, intermediaries also have important social functions. Some of these functions are common to both peripheral and central intermediaries but other functions are not. For this reason, it is necessary to consider these two types of intermediaries separately. However, at the outset, it must be recognized that the distinction between the two types is not absolute. Some intermediaries can be seen either as peripheral or as central, depending on the point of reference used to make the classification. Thus, for example, an intermediary who functions within a peripheral possession cult is peripheral to the society as a whole, for he is a minority voice in the society and plays no role within the central cult. Yet, when seen from the perspective of the peripheral cult, the intermediary must be considered a central intermediary, for he plays an important part in maintaining that cult. Members of the larger society would certainly consider intermediaries in peripheral cults to be peripheral intermediaries, but members of a peripheral cult might, under certain conditions, see themselves and their intermediaries as central and the rest of the society as peripheral. To complicate the picture even further, central intermediaries may have once been members of peripheral social groups, with the result that these individuals must be considered peripheral with respect to personal background but central with respect to their present function. When dealing with the categorization of intermediaries, it is therefore important to know the person or group responsible for assigning the categories and the point of reference that was used in the process.

The Functions of Peripheral Intermediation. Peripheral intermediation has several interrelated social functions. First, by becoming intermediaries people on the periphery of society are sometimes able to improve their personal situations. While a society might not normally grant the requests of such powerless individuals, when they speak as intermediaries they speak with the voices of the spirits, who have more authority and whose demands carry more weight. In most cases societies recognize the authority of the spirits and are willing to agree to the demands that are made through the intermediaries.[37]

Thus, seen from a personal perspective, peripheral intermediation is a tool that powerless individuals can use to modify their status and obtain additional benefits from the society. Sometimes these benefits are quite tangible. For example, in societies where women have little political or religious power and are completely dominated by males, some women become possessed by spirits that demand more money or better food, clothing, and living conditions for their intermediaries. These requests are usually granted, so long as they are not too outrageous, and the result is an improvement in the intermediary's material status. Other social outcasts may use the same approach, and, if they are interested only in improving their lifestyle, they may cease to be intermediaries when they have amassed sufficient wealth and power.[38]

More often, however, individuals derive less tangible benefits by becoming peripheral intermediaries. Higher status usually accompanies the intermediary's position, and by occupying this position individuals can increase the amount of respect that they receive from the society. If the intermediary becomes a member of a peripheral possession cult, he finds himself in a supportive environment where he enjoys a great deal of power. His importance and authority within the cult help to compensate for his powerlessness in the society as a whole.[39]

A second important function of peripheral intermediation is to help bring about social change. In this case the interests of the spirits and their intermediaries turn away from personal aggrandizement and focus on the society as a whole. Through their intermediaries the spirits demand changes in the social order. Because the intermediaries speak not only as representatives of the spirits but also as representatives of support groups, the demand for social change takes a form that is acceptable to the peripheral group which the intermediary represents. Group members who are also intermediaries communicate with the spirits, clothe the supernatural message in stereotypical language that meets group expectations, and then deliver the message, which is supported by the authority of the spirits and the group. In practical terms this means that the demands of the spirits and the demands of the support group are the same. Therefore, both the interests of the spirits and the interests of the group are advanced when the intermediary delivers his message. From the perspective of the support group, the intermediary becomes the means by which group goals, desires, and programs are communicated to the larger society. Because of the supernatural authority that lies behind the intermediary's message, the society is usually willing to make some of the desired reforms, and thus the intermediary's support group at least partially achieves its goals.

The social reforms demanded by peripheral intermediaries usually fall into one of two categories. Sometimes the intermediaries seek to arrest social change by reaffirming traditional values. The intermediaries, along with their spirits and support groups, are a conservative voice in a society undergoing rapid social change. In these cases the possessing spirits are frequently old deities that were once part of the society's central cult but that have been displaced by newer gods. The old deities seek a rejection of recent innovations and demand a return to a place of preeminence in the cult. A return to older social and moral practices may also be involved in this process. If the intermediary's support group once had an important position in the old social order, a demand for the restoration of this position may be included.[40]

More often, however, peripheral intermediaries seek innovative changes in the society. Through the intermediaries the spirits and the support group advocate new patterns of action and behavior. New deities may also be urged on a society in this way, and peripheral spirits may seek to upgrade their status. The group itself may demand a larger role in the society's affairs. A plan for the restructuring of society will be advanced, and the group will seek to institute a new social order built around previously powerless individuals.[41]

A final function of peripheral intermediation is to help maintain social stability. By becoming peripheral intermediaries, repressed and powerless individuals can communicate their frustrations to the larger society. Because these communications are attributed to the spirits, the society tolerates the behavior of the intermediaries and makes an effort to alleviate their frustrations. This process works on two levels. On the personal level, individuals are provided with a socially acceptable means of venting their frustrations. Because the intermediary attributes his behavior to the action of the spirits, he avoids taking responsibility for his actions and is able to do and say things that would not be permitted under normal conditions. By tolerating this sort of psychological escape valve, the society prevents the intermediary from working out his frustrations in a way that might endanger the social order.[42] On the level of the support group, peripheral intermediation provides the mechanisms through which the group can relieve its discontent by realizing part of its program. The group voices its demands through its intermediaries, and the society takes those demands seriously because they come from the spirits. Social stability is achieved when a balance is struck between the demands of the group and the desire of the society to preserve its structure intact. Neither the group nor the society ever achieves precisely what it wants. The group will effect some of its desired changes but not all of them. The society will make some alterations in its structure but will make as few as possible. Peripheral intermediation thus provides a dynamic way of alleviating tensions between minority and majority groups. The process is a continuous one, for peripheral groups continue to press their demands, and the central society continues to meet those demands grudgingly. Yet, so long as both sides want to maintain the unity of the society, the process of give-and-take results in relative social stability and orderly social change.[43]

Peripheral Intermediation and Witchcraft Accusations. We have noted at several points in our discussion that peripheral intermediaries can exist only as long as they have the support of a group and are at least tolerated by the society as a whole. To insure this support and toleration, intermediaries express themselves in a way that is acceptable both to the group and to the society. An analogous situation exists with respect to peripheral groups that use intermediaries to advocate reforms in the larger society. The peripheral group must make reasonable demands, or else it runs the risk of alienating the society by its unacceptable behavior. We must now consider what happens when the demands of peripheral intermediaries and groups become too outrageous. A powerless minority sometimes feels that the society is not responsive enough to the group's demands and that the supernatural message of the intermediaries is not being taken seriously. These feelings usually lead to an increase in the group's frustrations and to an escalation of its demands. This escalation in turn antagonizes the society. Social tensions between the group and society increase, and as these tensions grow the society comes to regard the group as a threat to social stability. When the point of toleration is passed, the society will take steps to reduce social tensions and to restore the social order.

Societies have various ways of dealing with situations of rivalry and social friction, but the one which is most important for our discussion is the witchcraft accusation. Accusations of witchcraft are employed in cases where there are social tensions that cannot be handled by normal rational or legal means. Individuals or groups in conflict with each other may resort to witchcraft accusations in order to repress the party regarded as the source of the conflict. Such accusations are not to be made lightly, for in most societies witches are regarded as "inverts," beings that in every respect are the opposite of normal human beings. Witches are stereotypically pictured as night creatures, who fly or walk upside down. They break all social taboos and indulge in such heinous acts as incest, infanticide, and cannibalism.[44] The witch is a cancer in the social organism and must be excised in order to preserve the society. Most societies therefore require the death penalty for witchcraft, for only in this way can the witch's power finally be curbed. The judgment against the witch is frequently rendered by the spirits themselves, after the accused has been subjected to an ordeal designed to execute the guilty and spare the innocent.[45]

In the context of intermediation, societies use the threat of witchcraft accusations to control peripheral intermediaries and groups. When the society accuses a peripheral intermediary of witchcraft, the initial judgment which the society made on the intermediary is in effect reversed. Rather than attributing the intermediary's behavior to benign spirit contact, the society accuses him of involvement with demonic powers. The witchcraft accusation is a radical way of dealing with a troublesome intermediary, for it solves the problem by physically removing the offender, either by killing or banishing him. In the case of peripheral groups, accusations of witchcraft lead inevitably to rupture in the social structure. By killing or banishing the group's intermediary, the society rejects the group itself, forces it out of the society, and in the process stills the group's demands for social reform. Both peripheral intermediaries and their support groups usually seek to avoid provoking the society into making witchcraft accusations, for once this step is taken all hope of realizing the group's goals is lost. The *threat* of witchcraft accusations is therefore an effective deterrent against the excesses of peripheral individuals and groups.[46]

The witchcraft accusation, however, is a two-edged sword. It can be used by societies that want to repress difficult minority groups, but it can also be used in various ways by minority groups and individuals. Sometimes peripheral groups will indirectly use this weapon by deliberately increasing social tension so as to *force* the society to use witchcraft accusations. In this way the groups are able to shatter the social structure and place the blame for the destruction on the larger society. Peripheral intermediaries usually simply use the authority of their position to present their message to the society, but they may also hurl witchcraft accusations at vulnerable individuals in the central social structure. Political leaders, priests, and other intermediaries are likely targets for such accusations, for these figures are prominent exponents of the society's views. By using this technique, the peripheral intermediary not only claims supernatural support for his own views but demolishes his adversary's views by attributing them to demonic origins.[47]

Because witchcraft accusations always result in the fragmentation of a society, they appear only when social tensions have reached the point that social fission is inevitable. The appearance of witchcraft accusations in a society can therefore be used as an index of the society's stability. When a society is able to integrate its peripheral groups successfully, accusations of witchcraft are rare. But as social instability and tension between groups and individuals increase, the number of accusations also increases. Societies where witchcraft accusations are common are likely to be highly unstable and in danger of fragmenting as dissidents break away to form independent groups.[48]

Intermediaries, Simple Support Groups, and Millenarian Movements. Up to this point in our discussion of the functions of peripheral intermediation, we have focused our attention on the roles that intermediaries play in their support groups and in the larger society. In dealing with these peripheral support groups we have spoken in general terms, for our interest has been in the intermediaries themselves. However, at this point in the discussion it is necessary to examine these peripheral support groups more closely, for in fact they are of different types and have different characteristics. For the sake of analysis, we will designate one common type of group a "simple support group." This sort of group is best exemplified by the typical peripheral possession cult, which we have already described, although simple support groups need not have such a formal structure. The other common type of peripheral support group that we will consider is the millenarian group. Anthropological material on millenarian groups and movements is probably more relevant to the study of Israelite apocalyptic than to the study of Israelite prophecy.[49] Nevertheless, because some scholars have used data on millenarian movements to interpret biblical prophecy, it is important to examine the relationship between simple support groups and millenarian groups.[50]

Anthropologists are still debating the precise nature of millenarian movements, and there are even arguments about the name that should be given to these movements.[51] Clearly, they are complex social phenomena, and it is unlikely that any single interpretive schema can be made to fit all of them. However, at the risk of oversimplification, we may list several features that usually characterize millenarian movements and groups.

First, millenarian movements are made up of people who are on the periphery of society. They lack political and social power and have little social status. Furthermore, they *recognize* that they are on the periphery. They feel repressed and deprived of something which they might reasonably expect to possess. The feelings of deprivation that these people experience may come from a number of different sources. At a basic level, these peripheral individuals may lack food, clothing, useful work, or adequate housing. At a more abstract level, they may be politically powerless and socially ostracized. They may feel that they no longer have a voice in the way in which the society or the government is run. They may even believe that they can no longer control their own lives and destinies. On the other hand, they may simply have the vague feeling that the quality of their lives is poorer than it was in a real or imagined past.

The sort of deprivation involved in millenarian groups is rarely absolute but is usually measured in relation to something else. People may measure their present condition against the condition of others in the same culture or in neighboring cultures, or they may measure their present condition against their own past condition. This process can be carried to a rather high level of abstraction. People who feel deprived because the quality of social life has deteriorated frequently measure present conditions against past conditions which may never have existed. There is a tendency for the past to be idealized, and as a result every generation feels that things were better "in the old days." The fact that "the old days" were not really any better does not keep feelings of deprivation from existing.

Although it is normal for there to be some feelings of deprivation in every society, certain conditions tend to intensify those feelings and create larger numbers of dissatisfied and deprived individuals. Such conditions are present particularly in times of rapid social change. Wars, famines, climatic changes, national economic reversals, and the shock of sudden cross-cultural contact can all lead to unusually widespread and severe feelings of deprivation. Not only do such periods of social upheaval produce political and social inequities that lead to genuine cases of deprivation, but crises such as wars and clashes with other cultures provide opportunities for people to compare their own situation with that of outsiders. These comparisons may lead to feelings of relative deprivation and fuel social unrest. Times of social crisis frequently give rise to millenarian groups, for in such times feelings of deprivation are increased beyond tolerable levels.

Although members of millenarian groups are peripheral individuals, it is important to note that they normally remain physically within the larger society. They may sense a gap of some sort between themselves and the rest of the society, but this gap is usually more psychological than spatial. Participants in millenarian groups do not always separate themselves from the society as a whole, nor do they always cut their ties to other groups in which they participate. They may remain within the larger society and still feel that they are a minority within it.[52]

The second characteristic of millenarian movements is that their members form themselves into groups having relatively cohesive structures. Group members share common beliefs, perspectives, and goals and sometimes pay allegiance to a single leader. Members perceive themselves as a corporate body, which is capable of directing its actions in a unified way. This perspective is shared by people outside the group, who see it as an entity capable of focused political and social action. The group has a visible system of governance that coordinates group efforts and provides mechanisms for the group's maintenance.[53]

The third characteristic of millenarian groups is that they contain some sort of catalytic agent to articulate the feelings of group members and to formulate a plan to relieve their discontent. In some groups this role is played by an intermediary, who brings from the spirits the encouragement necessary to sustain the group. The spirits, speaking through the intermediary, may also supply a plan designed to improve the group's powerless situation. In this case the intermediary is a crucial figure in the group, for he is the means by which the group gains access to the spirits, who are directing the group's journey toward salvation. The intermediary relays practical suggestions from the spirits and helps to set up short-term goals toward which the group can work. The achievement of these short-term goals is important, for it gives the group a feeling of success and accomplishment, without which group members would despair of ever reaching their ultimate goals. The intermediary may also represent the group in contacts with the larger society and help to articulate group plans and demands.

However, the catalytic agent need not be an intermediary but may be a "charismatic" leader, who holds the group together by making its members recognize their common bonds and goals. Once the leader has begun the process of group formation and has sketched a program for the group to follow, his actual physical presence within the group is no longer necessary for its successful growth. History is full of examples of charismatic leaders who were martyred or who simply disappeared early in the process of group formation. In many cases these leaders became more effective catalysts after their departure than they were before. Still, it would be a mistake to think that the catalytic agent in a millenarian group must necessarily be a single intermediary or leader. In some cases there may be a succession of intermediaries and leaders, or the leadership role may be taken by a group.[54]

The fourth feature of millenarian groups is that they have some sort of program for meeting the difficulties experienced by group members. Such programs are usually both forward- and backward-looking. The primary concern of millenarian groups is with the future, for they look forward to the solution of their present difficulties. If group problems cannot be solved in the future in this world, then they will be solved in "the world to come." They will be solved in a world which lies beyond this world of time and space. However, if a millenarian program is to be successful, it must deal with the immediate future as well as with the distant future and must provide group members with immediate realistic goals. If this is not done, the group may lose faith in its comprehensive program and eventually dissolve. A striking feature of millenarian programs is that they frequently look to the past for a picture of the future. Either they seek to *preserve* remnants of the past in the face of present threats, or they seek to *revive* the conditions believed to have existed before the present time of deprivation.[55]

The final characteristic of millenarian groups is that they provide their members with some practical means of realizing group programs. These means may be either active or passive. If a millenarian group uses active means, it will outline specific, usually rational, steps which group members can take to move the group toward its goals. If the group adopts a passive stance, it will take no direct action at all but will simply wait for the achievement of its goals by supernatural means.[56]

This brief sketch of some of the characteristics of millenarian groups is sufficient to illustrate the similarities and differences between such groups and simple support groups. Both groups are similar in their overall composition and social location. They are both composed of peripheral individuals who lack political and social power. The groups themselves function at the margins of the society and are always a minority within it. Periods of stress and rapid social change encourage the development of both types of groups. Both types support the activities of intermediaries and allow them to function, and in turn both may use intermediaries to articulate group attitudes.

However, there are also marked differences between simple support groups and millenarian groups. First, millenarian groups are organized more rigidly than are simple support groups. Although intermediaries must have a support group of some sort, it need not be formally organized. Members of the group may have in common only their support of a particular intermediary and may share no particular attitudes or goals. The composition of the group tends to fluctuate, and members may not even perceive themselves as a group at all. Even when a formally organized peripheral cult group is involved, members of the group may share only their experience with the spirits and may have no long-range plans or goals. In contrast, millenarian groups are more cohesive and better organized. Members think of themselves as a group. They share common feelings and goals and may recognize the authority of a single leader. There are mechanisms to insure group survival and to prevent the group from disintegrating. There is a well-articulated statement of group aspirations, and the group has a plan for reaching its goals. Second, the role of the intermediary is slightly different in the two types of groups. When the intermediary's simple support group is not formally organized, he may do nothing for it at all. The group supports the intermediary but the intermediary has no definite role in the group. He fulfills the expectations of his support group in his behavior, but he is not expected to be a spokesman for the group. Even if the intermediary joins a peripheral cult composed of people who have had similar experiences with the spirits, he simply becomes a member of the group. In this context he may help to articulate group views, but this role could also be played by others in the group. In contrast, intermediaries may be the focal point of millenarian groups and act as the catalysts that are necessary to make such groups cohere and develop. The intermediary is a leader within the group and is expected to formulate and express group hopes and plans. Finally, because simple support groups do not have a strongly developed structure, they are unable to exist outside of the larger society. They do not have the organization that is necessary to permit them to exist independently. In contrast, millenarian groups are sometimes capable of withdrawing from the larger society and surviving as independent units. On occasion political separation is involved, although usually the group simply becomes a new religious entity. In either case the group is capable of supporting itself.

In summary, then, we may say that all millenarian groups are capable of supporting intermediaries, but not all simple support groups are millenarian. The millenarian group is more specialized, more cohesive, and better organized than the simple support group. Still, distinctions between the two types of groups are not always easily drawn, and it is necessary to see them as part of a continuum. If we were to place both types of groups and their intermediaries on a continuum moving from loose group organization to highly developed organization, the following picture would emerge.[57] At one end of the spectrum would be intermediaries who have no social support and whose behavior is regarded by the society as an indication of illness. In this case no support group exists at all, and the intermediary cannot survive. Further along the spectrum would be intermediaries who are supported by their societies or by simple support groups but who play no formalized role in these groups. Members of the simple support group lack a sense of group identity and have in common only their support of the intermediary. Still further along the continuum would be those intermediaries who are members of formally organized peripheral groups which also function as simple support groups. These may be cult groups composed of individuals who have had "calls" from the spirits, or the groups may be organized along other lines. As these groups develop more structure, they shade into fully developed millenarian groups. These groups are well organized, and their intermediaries play a crucial role in communicating group programs. Finally, at the end of the continuum would be the central cult groups that are integral to the functioning of a society. These groups are highly structured and involve well-developed rituals, beliefs, and programs. The intermediaries that are supported by such groups have official duties connected with the promulgation of group ideas and are under great pressure to conform to group expectations. This pressure does not rob the intermediaries of all of their freedom to act as messengers of the spirits, but it does impose restrictions that are not shared by peripheral intermediaries.

Intermediaries and groups may originate at any point along this continuum. For example, an individual may receive from the spirits a message that articulates the feelings and hopes of his neighbors, and the result may be the formation of a millenarian group led by the individual. Similarly, an intermediary might bring supernatural messages that result only in the formation of a simple support group lacking a rigid structure. On the other hand, groups and individuals may move from point to point on the continuum. A simple support group may become more highly organized and become a full-fledged millenarian group capable of directed action and independent existence. A millenarian group might also be formed when a dissident segment of a central cult breaks away and is able to sustain itself as a peripheral group. It would even be possible for a group to travel the whole length of the continuum, developing from a simple support group into a millenarian group and finally into a central cult group. Such a development is not common, but it does occasionally occur.

The Functions of Central Intermediation. Central intermediaries occupy an established position within the social structure. They are sometimes part of a society's central cult, or they may simply be part of its political bureaucracy. In either case, they are the official links between their societies and the spirit world. Societies depend on their central intermediaries to provide access to the spirits whenever necessary and to relay important messages from the supernatural realm. When the spirits indicate their displeasure by sending sickness, social discord, or natural disaster, central intermediaries are expected to diagnose the problem and devise a remedy that will placate the spirits. In some societies central intermediaries are even responsible for preventing spirit-caused problems from occurring in the first place. Shamans, for example, are expected to protect their societies from malevolent spirits that might cause disease or natural catastrophes.[58]

Central intermediaries may also play important political roles. In times of war a society may depend on its intermediaries to supply supernatural guidance for the army. When a ruler dies or is deposed, intermediaries may play a crucial role in regulating the succession by communicating the leadership preferences of the spirits. If the intermediaries are attached to a royal court or to a royal cult, they may serve as political advisers to the ruler and will certainly supply spiritual support for royal decisions and policies.[59]

Central intermediaries, then, are primarily responsible for maintaining their societies and for promoting community welfare. The intermediaries therefore have not only the specific duties that we have already mentioned but also the general task of insuring social stability. This task is accomplished first of all by providing supernatural legitimation for the existing social order and by supplying divine sanctions for traditional religious, political, and social views. Because the social and political establishment constitutes the support group for central intermediaries, they are under strong pressure to conform to traditional behavioral expectations and to avoid doing and saying things that might lead to social instability. This means that central intermediaries are usually more conservative than their peripheral colleagues. Central intermediaries safeguard social stability by avoiding unnecessary innovation. They are cautious about accepting new ideas and usually resist outside influences. Still, central intermediaries are by no means totally opposed to social change. They are simply interested in regulating the speed at which changes take place. Central intermediaries foster gradual and orderly change in order to retain social tradition and to preserve social stability. They are therefore fully capable of criticizing their societies but are likely to do so under the guise of retaining or restoring traditional beliefs and attitudes. New practices and ideas are anchored firmly in the past. In this way innovations are integrated into the tradition and their disruptive potential is minimized.[60]

The second way in which central intermediaries preserve social stability is by easing social tension. They represent the supernatural world when speaking to the people, but they also represent the people when communicating with the spirits. This identification with the people allows the intermediaries to serve as representatives of public opinion. By virtue of the nature of their office, they are in a position to assess their society's moods and to observe developing attitudes and opinions. Diviners and mediums are particularly well-situated in this respect, for they are the specialists to whom people come for help in decision making. As long as the society is divided on a particular issue, the intermediaries will rarely express a definite opinion, for to do so would lead to social discord. However, when they sense that a consensus has developed, they will reinforce it by lending it supernatural support. In this way divisive issues are resolved, and group solidarity is restored.[61]

In a similar way, shamans, diviners, and mediums may provide the opportunity for people to air their disagreements and resolve them. This frequently happens in societies such as the Lugbara, where there is a well-developed ancestor cult. The ancestors are thought to retain an interest in their descendants and to become disturbed when social discord develops among them. When social conflicts develop, the ancestors may be invoked by one of the participants and asked to intervene. The ancestors respond by sending an illness to one of the involved parties, who must then be taken to an intermediary for diagnosis. As part of the diagnostic process, the patient confesses the nature of the social conflict, and the ancestor, through the intermediary, proposes a conciliatory remedy. In this way interpersonal disagreements are brought to light and publicly arbitrated. A version of this process also occurs in some shamanic performances, where the shaman seeks the cause of a disaster or illness by inviting confessions of wrongdoing from those present. People respond by confessing their sins against the society, and by the end of the session social problems have been aired and solved.[62]

Peripheral and Central Intermediaries. Both peripheral and central intermediaries can exist in the same society at the same time. Furthermore, the lines between the two are not always firmly drawn. Given individuals may move from one category to the other if their support group changes, and as this movement takes place, the characteristics and functions of the intermediaries will also change. As we have already noted, both types of intermediaries are part of a continuum, and individuals may move along that continuum in either direction. Thus, if a central intermediary violates the norms that his society has established, he may be forced out of his position and onto the periphery, where he may find a new support group and be able to function as a peripheral intermediary. As his status and social functions change, he will give up the formal, traditional behavior typical of central intermediaries and take on the freer, more spontaneous behavior of peripheral intermediaries. Conversely, a peripheral intermediary may be able to enlarge his support group to the point that it becomes a majority in the society. The intermediary then becomes a central intermediary. When this shift takes place, he takes on the appropriate functions and adopts the appropriate behavior patterns. His behavior becomes more rigidly controlled, and he takes a new interest in maintaining the society that supports him.[63]

Conclusions

The anthropological material we have surveyed suggests that the relationship between Israelite prophets and their societies may be much more complex than previous studies have realized. For this reason, biblical scholars can no longer confine their investigations only to the three aspects of the problem that have usually been treated, but the social dimensions of a whole range of prophetic activity must be considered. On the basis of the comparative evidence, we may expect Israelite society to have been involved in every phase of prophetic activity, from the prophet's "call" to the delivery of his message. To derive maximum benefit from this evidence, we must not oversimplify or schematize it but must apply it in all of its complexity to the biblical material. Still, at this point it will be helpful to indicate the major implications of the anthropological data for the three areas that scholars have traditionally considered when commenting on prophecy and society in Israel.

The Nature of Prophetic Activity. The anthropological material suggests that any study of prophetic behavior in Israel must take into account the role of social groups in creating prophets and in shaping their behavior. Although intermediaries may receive their messages directly from the spirits, those messages are expressed in words and deeds that conform to group expectations about how intermediaries should talk and act. As a result, all of the intermediaries within a particular group tend to act and talk in the same way. An attempt must therefore be made to determine whether or not Israelite prophets also exhibited stereotypical behavior. This attempt must move beyond the traditional discussion of the role of "ecstasy" in prophetic behavior, for ecstasy is itself only one stereotypical behavior pattern. Other forms of prophetic speech and action must also be considered. If stereotypical behavioral patterns are discovered, then their origins must be traced and they must be related to prophetic support groups or to the society as a whole. Divergent behavior patterns will imply different social situations and support groups, and this social complexity must be taken into account in analyzing biblical prophecy.

The Social Location of Prophecy. The anthropological material suggests that there are two dimensions to the question of the social location of prophecy. First, intermediaries in every society are related to some sort of support group that allows them to continue to function. Seen from a social perspective, these groups and their intermediaries are located either on the periphery of society or within the central social structure. Second, intermediaries actually carry out their activities in various physical locations within the society. Sometimes the intermediary carries out his activities only within the support group, but other locations may also be involved. Studies of Israelite prophecy must deal with both of these aspects of social location. The support groups of the biblical prophets must be investigated, and an attempt must be made to discover where these groups lay in the social spectrum. In addition, the physical locations in which the prophets operated must also be explored. This exploration must consider locations other than the cult, and the full range of possible social and political settings must be considered.

The Social Functions of Prophecy. The anthropological material indicates that the functions of intermediaries vary depending on the type of intermediation involved. In general, peripheral intermediaries are usually involved in advancing the views of the spirits and of the intermediaries' own support groups. The aim is to improve the status of peripheral groups and individuals and to bring about changes in the social order. In contrast, central intermediaries are concerned with maintaining the established social order and with regulating the pace of social change. The investigation of the social functions of the Israelite prophets must also take this distinction into consideration. The different functions of peripheral and central prophets must be recognized, and the relation of each type of prophet to the whole society must be explored. The tensions that existed between prophet and society must be analyzed, and an attempt must be made to discover how those tensions were finally resolved. Only by considering all of these issues can insight be gained into the complex functions of prophecy in Israel.

NOTES

1. For a brief survey of critical scholarship on prophecy, see R. E. Clements, *One Hundred Years of Old Testament Interpretation* (Philadelphia: Westminster, 1976), pp. 51-75. An extensive bibliography of research since 1932 may be found in G. Fohrer, "Neuere Literatur zur alttestamentlichen Prophetie," *TRu* 19 (1951): 277-346; 20 (1952): 192-271, 295-361; idem, "Zehn Jahre Literatur zur alttestamentlichen Prophetie (1951-1960)," *TRu* 28 (1962): 1-75, 235-97, 301-74; idem, "Neuere Literatur zur alttestamentlichen Prophetie (1961-1970)," *TRu* 40 (1975): 193-209, 337-77; 41 (1976): 1-12.

2. There have been a few scholarly attempts to deal with the social dimensions of prophecy, and these will be discussed below. In addition, see A. Jepsen, *Nabi: Soziologische Studien zur alttestamentlichen Literatur und Religionsgeschichte* (Munich: C. H. Beck, 1934); H. Junker, *Prophet und Seher in Israel* (Trier: Paulinus, 1927); P. Kleinert, *Die Profeten Israels in sozialer Beziehung* (Leipzig: J. C. Hinrichs, 1905); A. Guillaume, *Prophecy and Divination among the Hebrews and Other Semites* (London: Hodder and Stoughton, 1938); and J. Lindblom, *Prophecy in Ancient Israel* (Philadelphia: Muhlenberg Press, 1962), pp. 47-219.

3. H. Ewald, *Die Propheten des Alten Bundes,* 2nd ed. (Göttingen: Vandenhoeck & Ruprecht, 1867), Vol. 1, pp. 1-40.

4. B. Duhm, *Die Theologie der Propheten* (Bonn: Adolf Marcus, 1875), pp. 1-34.

5. Ibid, pp. 4, 19-24, 29-34, 86-91. Duhm later revised his views considerably in the light of subsequent research. See his *Israels Propheten* (Tübingen: Mohr, 1916; 2nd ed. 1922), pp. 1-12, 61-88.

6. J. Wellhausen, *Prolegomena to the History of Ancient Israel* (London: Adam and Charles Black, 1885; repr., Gloucester, Mass.: Peter Smith), pp. 414-19, 467-77, 484-91; idem, *Israelitische und Jüdische Geschichte,* 7th ed. (Berlin: Georg Reimer, 1914), pp. 72-77, 91-92, 104-13, 122-32; idem, *Israelitische und Jüdische Geschichte,* 7th ed. (Berlin: Georg Reimer, 1914), pp. 72-77, 91-92, 104-13, 122-32; idem, *Grundrisse zum Alten Testament,* ed. R. Smend (Munich: Kaiser, 1965), pp. 87-97.

7. W. R. Smith, *The Old Testament in the Jewish Church* (London: Adam and Charles Black, 1895). pp. 278-308; cf. his *The Prophets of Israel,* 2nd ed. (London: Adam and Charles Black, 1895.)

8. See, for example, the Arabic and Greek material cited by Smith in *The Old Testament in the Jewish Church,* pp. 285-87, 292, 294, 297-98. For a discussion of Smith's general use of comparative material, see R. R. Wilson, *Genealogy and History in the Biblical World* (New Haven: Yale University Press, 1977), pp. 13-14; and T. O. Beidelman, *W. Robertson Smith and the Sociological Study of Religion* (Chicago: University of Chicago Press, 1974), pp. 27-28, 49-52.

9. Note, for example, Smith's reflections on the way in which a prophet's message

is related to his psychological state and social setting ("Prophecy and Personality: A Fragment," *Lectures and Essays of William Robertson Smith,* ed. J. S. Black and G. Chrystal [London: Adam and Charles Black, 1912], pp. 97–108). Cf. his treatment of Elijah (*Prophets of Israel,* pp. 78–89).

10. G. Hölscher, *Die Profeten* (Leipzig: J. C. Hinrichs, 1914), esp. pp. 1–358.

11. Ibid., pp. 143–47.

12. The exact sources of Hölscher's psychological data are not always clear, but he seems to have been influenced greatly by the work of Wilhelm Wundt. See Clements, *One Hundred Years of Old Testament Interpretation,* pp. 56–66.

13. For an overview of solutions to this problem, see H. H. Rowley, "The Nature of Old Testament Prophecy in the Light of Recent Study," *HTR* 38 (1945): 1–38 (= H. H. Rowley, *The Servant of the Lord,* 2nd ed. [Oxford: Blackwell, 1965], pp. 95–134); and O. Eissfeldt, "The Prophetic Liberature," *The Old Testament and Modern Study,* ed. H. H. Rowley (London: Oxford University Press, 1951), pp. 134–45.

14. I. P. Seierstad, *Die Offenbarungserlebnisse der Propheten Amos, Jesaja und Jeremia* (Oslo: Jacob Dybwad, 1946); A. H. Heschel, *The Prophets* (New York: Harper & Row, 1962).

15. J. P. Hyatt, *Prophetic Religion* (New York: Abingdon–Cokesbury, 1947), p. 17; cf. J. Skinner, *Prophecy and Religion* (Cambridge: Cambridge University Press, 1922), pp. 3–6; H. W. Robinson, "The Psychology and Metaphysic of 'Thus Saith Yahweh,' " *ZAW* 41 (1923): 5–8; A. Causse, "Quelques remarques sur la psychologie des prophètes," *RHPR* 2 (1922): 349–56.

16. H. T. Obbink, "The Forms of Prophetism," *HUCA* 14 (1939): 25–28; S. Mowinckel, " 'The Spirit' and the 'Word' in the Pre-Exilic Reforming Prophets," *JBL* 53 (1934): 199–227; Jepsen, *Nabi,* pp. 208–17.

17. H. Gunkel, "Die geheimen Erfahrungen der Propheten Israels," *Suchen der Zeit* 1 (1903): 112–53; cf. his later treatment in "Einleitungen," H. Schmidt, *Die Schriften des Alten Testaments,* 2/2: *Die grossen Propheten,* 2nd ed. (Göttingen: Vandenhoeck & Ruprecht, 1915), pp. xxv–xxviii (= "The Secret Experiences of the Prophets," *The Expositor,* 9th series, 1 [1924]: 427–32).

18. T. H. Robinson, *Prophecy and the Prophets in Ancient Israel,* 2nd ed. (London: Duckworth, 1953), pp. 50–51; idem, "The Ecstatic Element in Old Testament Prophecy," *The Expositor,* 8th series, no. 123, vol. 21 (1921): 217–38; J. Hempel, *Die althebraische Literatur* (Wildpark-Potsdam: Akademische Verlagsgesellschaft Athenaion, 1930), pp. 62–63; S. Mowinckel, "Ecstatic Experience and Rational Elaboration in Old Testament Prophecy," *AcOr* 13 (1935): 264–91; G. Widengren, *Literary and Psychological Aspects of the Hebrew Prophets* (Uppsala: Lundequist, 1948), pp. 98–120; Lindblom, *Prophecy in Ancient Israel,* pp. 47–65, 105–8, 122–37, 177–82, 197–202, 216–19.

19. Rowley, "The Nature of Old Testament Prophecy," pp. 128–31; cf. Mowinckel, "Ecstatic Experience," pp. 279–80.

20. As our next section will show, this has not always been the case among form critics. For a thorough discussion of Mowinckel's form-critical work, see J. H. Hayes, "The History of the Form-critical Study of Prophecy," *SBLSP* 1 (1973), pp. 76–79.

21. See, for example, Hölscher, *Die Profeten,* pp. 143–47.

22. Mowinckel's original suggestion was made in *Psalmenstudien III: Kultprophetie und prophetische Psalmen* (Oslo: Jacob Dybwad, 1923), pp. 1–29. Cf. his later

statement in *The Psalms in Israel's Worship* (Nashville: Abingdon, 1962), Vol. 2, pp. 53–73; and note his article "Psalms and Wisdom," where he claims that "the majority of prophets formed an official class of cult functionaries . . ." (*Wisdom in Israel and in the Ancient Near East* [H. H. Rowley *Festschrift*] [*VTSup* 3; ed. M. Noth and D. W. Thomas Leiden: Brill, 1960] p. 206). Mowinckel argued that Isaiah and Micah were cult prophets in his *Jesaja-Disiplene* (Oslo: H. Aschehoug, 1926).

23. For a thorough discussion of the main lines of the debate, see H. H. Rowley, "Ritual and the Hebrew Prophets," *JSS* 1 (1956): 338–60 (= H. H. Rowley, *From Moses to Qumran* [New York: Association Press, 1963], pp. 111–38); and L. Ramlot, "Prophétisme," *DBSup* 8 (1972): 1121–66, where exhaustive, up-to-date bibliographies may be found.

24. A. R. Johnson, *The Cultic Prophet in Ancient Israel* (Cardiff: University of Wales, 1944; 2nd ed., 1962).

25. Ibid. pp. 29–30; cf. his remark in the preface of the 2nd ed., p. v.

26. A. Haldar, *Associations of Cult Prophets among the Ancient Semites* (Uppsala: Almqvist & Wiksell, 1945).

27. P. L. Berger, "Charisma and Religious Innovation: The Social Location of Israelite Prophecy," *ASR* 28 (1963): 940–50.

28. Berger's work was rightly criticized on this point by J. G. Williams, "The Social Location of Israelite Prophecy," *JAAR* 37 (1969): 153–65. However, the force of Berger's conclusion is underestimated when Williams argues that prophets could not have been located in the cult and still have criticized the cult.

29. For recent accounts of the history of form-critical research on the prophets, see Hayes, "History of Form-critical Study," pp. 60–9; R. R. Wilson, "Form-critical Investigation of the Prophetic Literature: The Present Situation," SBLSP 1 (1973), pp. 100–21; W. E. March, "Prophecy," *Old Testament Form Criticism*, ed. J. H. Hayes (San Antonio: Trinity University Press, 1974), pp. 141–77; and G. M. Tucker, "Prophetic Speech," *Int* 32 (1978): 31–45.

30. H. Gunkel, "Fundamental Problems of Hebrew Literary History," *What Remains of the Old Testament* (London: George Allen and Unwin, 1928), 61–62. The German original of this article was published under the title, "Die Grundprobleme der israelitischen Literaturgeschichte" in *Deutsche Literaturzeitung* 27 (1906), cols. 1797–1800, 1861–1866 and reprinted in Gunkel's *Reden Und Aufsätze* (Göttingen: Vandenhoeck & Ruprecht, 1913), 29–38.

31. Claus Westermann, *Basic Forms of Prophetic Speech* (Philadelphia: Westminster, 1967). For a critique of Westermann's use of the messenger image and for a discussion of the adequacy of his form-critical analyses, see Wilson, "Form-critical Investigation of the Prophetic Literature," pp. 100–9, 114–20.

32. H. Gunkel, *Einleitung in die Psalmen,* 2nd ed. (Göttingen: Vandenhoeck & Ruprecht, 1966), pp. 364–65.

33. E. Würthwein, "Der Ursprung der prophetischen Gerichtsrede," *ZTK* 49 (1952): 7–8, 12–16. For a survey of recent work on the prophetic lawsuit, see R. North, "Angel-Prophet or Satan-Prophet?" *ZAW* 82 (1970): 31–67.

34. For a more thorough discussion of these guidelines, see Wilson, *Genealogy and History,* pp. 11–18.

35. The continuity of the Ephraimite prophetic traditions has been clearly demonstrated by J. Muilenburg, "The 'Office' of the Prophet in Ancient Israel," *The Bible in Modern Scholarship,* ed. J. P. Hyatt (Nashville: Abingdon, 1965), pp. 74–97;

idem, "The Intercession of the Covenant Mediator (Exodus 33: la, 12-17)," *Words and Meanings: Essays Presented to David Winton Thomas*, ed. P. R. Ackroyd and B. Lindars (Cambridge: At the University Press, 1968), pp. 159-81. For references to earlier discussions of these traditions and for a consideration of their origins, see E. W. Nicholson, *Deuteronomy and Tradition* (Philadelphia: Fortress Press, 1967), pp. 58-106. Although the northern origin of the Elohistic and Deuteronomic traditions has occasionally been challenged, these challenges have not been serious enough to warrant modifying the scholarly consensus. For a recent discussion reaffirming the Ephraimite origin of these traditions, see A. W. Jenks, *The Elohist and North Israelite Traditions* (Missoula: Scholars Press, 1977), pp. 2-18, 83-129.

36. This theory about the bearers of the Ephraimite traditions is based on F. M. Cross's reconstruction of Israel's early priesthood and to a lesser extent on his analysis of the Deuteronomic traditions (*Canaanite Myth and Hebrew Epic: Essays in the History of the Religion of Israel* [Cambridge: Harvard University Press, 1973] pp. 195-215, 274-89). Although we cannot accept all of Cross's reconstruction, he has convincingly argued that when David set up a central sanctuary in Jerusalem, he also installed two priestly houses: Levitical priests from the old northern sanctuary at Shiloh (represented by Abiathar) and Aaronid priests from the southern Judahite shrine at Hebron (represented by Zadok). When Abiathar was exiled to Anathoth, control of the Jerusalem cult was left in the hands of the Aaronids, while the Levitical priests remained outside of the central cult. The suggestion that these Levitical priests were also the bearers of the old Ephraimite traditions, including the Deuteronomic traditions, I owe to S. Dean McBride, who will develop his suggestion in greater detail in his forthcoming commentary on Deuteronomy in the Anchor Bible.

37. For examples of this process in operation, see Y. K. Bamunoba and F. B. Welbourn, "Emandwa Initiation in Ankole," *The Ugandan Journal* 29 (1965): 13, 16; I. M. Lewis, *Ecstatic Religion* (New York: Penguin, 1971), pp. 66-116; J. Beattie, "Group Aspects of the Nyoro Spirit Mediumship Cult," *The Rhodes-Livingston Journal* 30 (1961): 11-38; F. B. Welbourn, "Spirit Initiation in Ankole and a Christian Spirit Movement in Western Kenya," *Spirit Mediumship and Society in Africa*, ed. J. Beattie and J. Middleton (New York: Africana Publishing Corporation, 1969), pp. 290-303; J. Beattie, "Spirit Mediumship in Bunyoro," *Spirit Mediumship and Society in Africa*, pp. 159-70; H. B. Barclay, *Buurri al Lamaab* (Ithaca: Cornell University Press, 1964), pp. 196-205; M. Leiris, *La possession, et ses aspects théâtraux chez les Ethiopiens de Gondar* (Paris: Librarie Plon, 1958), pp. 13-38; S. D. Messing, "Group Therapy and Social Status in the Zar Cult of Ethiopia," *American Anthropologist*, new series, 60 (1958): 1120-26; E. H. Ashton, *Medicine, Magic, and Sorcery among the Southern Sotho* (Cape Town: University of Cape Town, 1943), pp. 3-4, 28-32; E. Colson, "Spirit Possession among the Tonga of Zambia," *Spirit Mediumship and Society in Africa*, pp. 71, 78-90; S. Fuchs, *Rebellious Prophets: A Study of Messianic Movements in Indian Religions* (Bombay: Asia Publishing House, 1965), pp. 1-17; M. Gelfand, *Shona Ritual* (Cape Town: Juta, 1959), pp. 10-13, 121-23; B. Stefaniszyn, *Social and Ritual Life of the Ambo of Northern Rhodesia* (London: Oxford University Press, 1964), pp. 138-47; E. H. Winter, *Beyond the Mountains of the Moon* (Urbana: University of Illinois Press, 1959), pp. 22-25; and J. Nicolas, "Les juments des dieux": Rites de possession et condition féminine en pays Hausa," *Etudes Nigerienne*, 21 (IFAN-CNRS, 1968).

38. There are numerous examples of this function of peripheral intermediation. A

representative sample may be found in Lewis, *Ecstatic Religion, pp.* 66–116; J. Hamer and I. Hamer, "Spirit Possession and Its Socio-Psychological Implications among the Sidamo of Southwest Ethiopia," *Ethnology* 5 (1966): 400–401; G. Obeyesekere, "The Idiom of Demonic Possession: A Case Study," *Social Science and Medicine* 4 (1970): 98–101; G. Harris, "Possession 'Hysteria' in a Kenya Tribe," *AA,* new series, 59 (1957): 1046–60; I. M. Lewis, "Spirit Possession in Northern Somaliland," *Spirit Mediumship and Society in Africa,* pp. 189–90, 198–213.

39. On this aspect of an intermediary's membership in peripheral cults, see R. Firth, "Problem and Assumption in an Anthropological Study of Religion," *JRAI* 89 (1959): 144–45; R. Horton, "Types of Spirit Possession in Kalabari Religion," *Spirit Mediumship and Society in Africa,* pp. 28–47; S. S. Walker, *Ceremonial Spirit Possession in Africa and Afro-America* (Leiden: Brill, 1972), pp. 7–9, 85–91; P. Fry, *Spirits of Protest* (Cambridge: Cambridge University Press, 1976), pp. 36–38; H. Kuper, *An African Aristocracy* (London: Oxford University Press, 1947), pp. 165–69; J. G. Kennedy, "Nubian Zar Ceremonies as Psychotherapy" *Human Organization* 26 (1967): 189–90; S. J. Lee "Spirit Possession among the Zulu," *Spirit Mediumship and Society in Africa,* pp. 140–55; Messing, "Group Therapy and Social Status," pp. 1120–21; R. E. S. Tanner, "The Theory and Practice of Sukuma Spirit Mediumship," *Spirit Mediumship and Society in Africa,* pp. 284–86; A. Southall, "Spirit Possession and Mediumship among the Alur," ibid., pp. 232–45.

40. For examples of peripheral intermediaries reaffirming traditional social values, see Colson, "Spirit Possession among the Tonga," pp. 78–90; Beattie and Middleton, "Introduction," *Spirit Mediumship and Society in Africa,* xviii; R. G. Willis, "Kaswa: Oral Tradition of a Fipa Prophet," *Africa* 40 (1970): 248–56; Horton, "Types of Spirit Possession," pp. 25–28; G. Lienhardt, *Divinity and Experience: The Religion of the Dinka* (Oxford: Clarendon Press, 1961), pp. 73–83.

41. For further discussion, see Horton, "Types of Spirit Possession," pp. 31, 45–47; Beattie and Middleton, "Introduction," p. xxviii; Firth, "Problem and Assumption," p. 145; and M. Douglas, "Social Preconditions of Enthusiasm and Heterodoxy," *Forms of Symbolic Action: Proceedings of the 1969 Annual Spring Meeting of the American Ethnological Society,* ed. R. F. Spencer (Seattle: American Ethnological Society, 1969), pp. 70–73.

42. For detailed examples, see J. Belo, *Trance in Bali* (New York: Columbia University Press, 1960), pp. 124–35; D. Parkin, "Politics of Ritual Syncretism: Islam among the Non-Muslim Giriama of Kenya," *Africa* 40 (1970): 224–25; and A. Doutreloux, "Prophétisme et culture," *African Systems of Thought,* ed. M. Fortes and G. Dieterlan (London: Oxford University Press, 1965), pp. 224–39.

43. For further discussion, see Beattie, "Spirit Mediumship in Bunyoro," *Spirit Mediumship and Society in Africa,* pp. 167–70; Walker, *Ceremonial Spirit Possession,* pp. 97–99; Southall, "Spirit Possession," *Spirit Mediumship,* pp. 232–45; Colson, "Spirit Possession," ibid., pp. 89–90; M. J. Field, "Spirit Possession in Ghana," ibid., pp. 10–12, and Obeyesekere, "The Idiom of Demonic Possession," p. 104.

44. For a discussion of the stereotypical characteristics of witchcraft and the social functions of witchcraft accusations, see H. Debrunner, *Witchcraft in Ghana,* 2nd ed. (Accra: Presbyterian Book Depot, 1961), pp. 20–47; M. S. Field, *Search for Security* (Evanston: Northwestern University Press, 1960), p. 38; J. LaFontaine, "Witchcraft in Bugisu," *Witchcraft and Sorcery in East Africa,* ed. J. Middleton and E. H. Winter

(London: Routledge and Kegan Paul, 1963), p. 197, 202-14, 217; and M. G. Marwick, *Sorcery in Its Social Setting* (Manchester: Manchester University Press, 1965), p. 95.

45. In Africa various types of poison ordeals were traditionally employed for this purpose. For descriptions, see M. Douglas, *The Lele of Kasai* (London: Oxford University Press, 1963), pp. 241-44; and E. E. Evans-Pritchard, *Witchcraft, Oracles and Magic among the Azande* (Oxford: At the Clarendon Press, 1967), pp. 258-386.

46. For a discussion of the ways in which societies use witchcraft accusations to control obstreperous intermediaries, see Lewis, *Ecstatic Religion,* pp. 33, 117-26. For other examples of societies using witchcraft accusations to repress minorities, see M. Douglas, "Techniques of Sorcery Control in Central Africa," *Witchcraft and Sorcery in East Africa,* p. 126; T. O. Beidelman, "Witchcraft in Ukaguru," ibid., p. 87; J. Buxton, "Mandari Witchcraft," ibid., p. 107; and M. Gluckman, *Politics, Law and Ritual in Tribal Society* (Chicago: Aldine, 1965), pp. 216-26.

47. For examples of peripheral individuals using witchcraft accusations against superiors, see L. Mair, *Witchcraft* (New York: McGraw-Hill, 1969), pp. 204-21; Buxton, "Mandari Witchcraft," *Witchcraft and Sorcery in East Africa,* p. 108; Douglas, *The Lele,* 223; idem, "Techniques of Sorcery Control," 125; J. Middleton, "Witchcraft and Sorcery in Lugbara," *Witchcraft and Sorcery in East Africa,* p. 268; Middleton and Winter, "Introduction," ibid., pp. 13-14; and D. Tait, "Konkomba Sorcery," *JRAI* 84 (1954): 73-74.

48. Douglas, "Techniques of Sorcery Control," *Witchcraft and Sorcery in East Africa,* p. 124; M. G. Marwick, "The Social Context of Cewa Witch Beliefs," *Africa* 22 (1952): 232; J. C. Mitchell, *The Yao Village* (Manchester: Manchester University Press, 1956), pp. 125-65.

49. For an attempt to apply some of this material to Israelite apocalyptic, see R. R. Wilson, "This World—and the World to Come," *Encounter* 38 (1977): 117-124.

50. For an example of the use of millenarian material to interpret Israelite prophecy, see T. W. Overholt, "The Ghost Dance of 1890 and the Nature of the Prophetic Process," *Ethnohistory* 21 (1974): 37-63; and his "Jeremiah and the Nature of the Prophetic Process," *Scripture in History and Theology: Essays in Honor of J. Coert Rylaarsdam* (Pittsburgh: Pickwick Press, 1977), pp. 129-50.

51. Millenarian movements are sometimes referred to as prophetic movements, messianic movements, revitalization movements, deprivation cults, cargo cults, and crisis cults. For a discussion of the various designations that have been suggested, see W. La Barre, "Material for a History of Studies of Crisis Cults: A Bibliographic Essay," *Current Anthropology* 12 (1971): 3-44. General treatments of millenarian movements may be found in H. G. Barnett, *Indian Shakers: A Messianic Cult of the Pacific Northwest* (Carbondale: Southern Illinois University Press, 1957); I. C. Jarvie, *The Revolution in Anthropology* (Chicago: Henry Regnery, 1969); Kenelm Burridge, *New Heaven, New Earth: A Study of Millenarian Activities,* Pavilion Social Action Series (New York: Schocken Books, 1969); B. R. Wilson, *Magic and the Millennium* (New York: Harper & Row, 1973); W. La Barre, *The Ghost Dance* (New York: Dell, 1972); J. Mooney, *The Ghost Dance Religion and the Sioux Outbreak of 1890,* ed. A. F. C. Wallace (Chicago: University of Chicago Press, 1965); P. Lawrence, *Road Belong Cargo: A Study of the Cargo Movement in the Southern Madang District, New Guinea* (Manchester: Manchester University Press, 1964); P. Worsley, *The Trumpet Shall Sound,* 2nd ed. (New York: Schocken Books, 1968);

S. L. Thrupp, ed., *Millennial Dreams in Action* (The Hague: Mouton, 1962, and New York: Schocken Books, 1970); N. Cohn, *The Pursuit of the Millennium*, rev. ed. (New York: Oxford University Press, 1970); V. Lanternari, *The Religions of the Oppressed* (New York: Knopf, 1963); and W. Lofland, *Doomsday Cult* (Englewood Cliffs, N. J.: Prentice-Hall, 1966).

52. For a discussion of the role that relative deprivation and social crisis play in the millenarian movement, see D. F. Aberle, "A Note on Relative Deprivation Theory as Applied to Millenarian and Other Cult Movements," in *Millennial Dreams in Action,* pp. 209–14; Burridge, *New Heaven, New Earth,* pp. 9–10; B. Barber, "Acculturation and Messianic Movements," *ASR* 6 (1941); 664–68; Lanternari, *Religions of the Oppressed,* pp. 243–249; Fuchs, *Rebellious Prophets,* pp. xii, 2–3, 16–17; D. F. Aberle, "The Prophet Dance and Reactions to White Contact," *SJA* 15 (1959): 79–81; and A. J. F. Köbben, "Prophetic Movements as an Expression of Social Protest," *International Archives of Ethnography* 49 (1960): 117–64. For a critique of relative deprivation theory, see L. Spier, W. Suttles, and M. S. Herskovits, "Comments on Aberle's Thesis of Deprivation," *SJA* 15 (1959): 84–88.

53. On the importance of group structure and maintenance mechanisms, see A. F. C. Wallace, "Revitalization Movements," *AA* 58 (1956): 273–74; and Y. Talmon, "Pursuit of the Millennium: The Relation between Religious and Social Change," *Archives européennes de sociologie* 3 (1962): 134–35.

54. For a discussion of the various kinds of catalytic agents involved in the formation and maintenance of millenarian groups, see Wallace, "Revitalization Movements," pp. 270–73; Worsley, *The Trumpet Shall Sound,* pp. ix–xxxix; Fuchs, *Rebellious Prophets,* pp. 5–6; and J. Fabian, "Führer und Führung in den prophetisch-messianischen Bewegungen der (ehemaligen) Kolonialvölker," *Anthropos* 58 (1963): 773–809.

55. R. Linton, "Nativistic Movements," *AA* 45 (1943): 230–40; Talmon, "Pursuit of the Millennium," pp. 130–33; Fuchs, *Rebellious Prophets,* pp. ix–x, 11–15.

56. Wallace, "Revitalization Movements," pp. 273–78; B. Wilson, "Millennialism in Comparative Perspective," *Comparative Studies in Society and History* 6 (1963): 93–114; J. F. Zygmunt, "When Prophecies Fail: A Theoretical Perspective on the Comparative Evidence," *American Behavioral Scientist* 61 (1972): 245–68.

57. The following schema is a development of the one suggested by I. M. Lewis, "Spirit Possession and Deprivation Cults," *Man,* new series, 1 (1966): 322–29.

58. Netsilik shamans are supposed to insure a ready supply of game, control thunder and snowstorms, stop the cracking of ice, and ward off illness (A. Balikci, "Shamanistic Behavior among the Netsilik Eskimos," *SJA* 19 [1963]: 386–87).

59. For example, see M. Bouteiller, *Chamanisme et guérison magique* (Paris: Presses Universitaires de France, 1950), p. 31; G. K. Garbett, "Spirit Mediums as Mediators in Korekore Society," *Spirit Mediumship and Society in Africa,* p. 106; Southall, "Spirit Possession and Mediumship," ibid., pp. 246–52; and especially G. K. Garbett, "Religious Aspects of Political Succession among the Valley Korekore (N. Shona)," *The History of the Central African Peoples* (Lusaka, Northern Rhodesia: Rhodes-Livingston Institute, 1963), pp. 1–2, 5–17.

60. Lewis, *Ecstatic Religion,* pp. 127–77; Beattie and Middleton, "Introduction," *Spirit Mediumship,* pp. xvii–xxix; Garbett, "Spirit Mediums as Mediators," ibid., pp. 119–20; H. Horton, "Types of Spirit Possession in Kalibari Religion," ibid., pp. 22–24; S. F. Nadel, "A Study of Shamanism in the Nuba Mountains," *JRAI* 2 (1946):

30-31; E. Colson, *The Plateau Tonga of Northern Rhodesia* (Manchester: Manchester University Press), pp. 92-93; and Colson, "Spirit Possession," *Spirit Mediumship*, pp. 70-71, 73-78.

61. For examples of this ratification process, see Garbett, "Spirit Mediums as Mediators," *Spirit Mediumship*, pp. 119-25; G. K. Parr, "Divination and Its Social Contexts," *JRAI* 93 (1963): 197-200; W. Bascom, *Ifa Divination* (Bloomington: Indiana University Press, 1968), p. 70; Field, *Search for Security*, p. 76; and Firth, "Problem and Assumption," pp. 142-43.

62. J. Middleton, *Lugbara Religion* (London: Oxford University Press, 1960), pp. 79-148; J. H. M. Beattie, "The Ghost Cult in Bunyoro," *Ethnology* 3 (1964): 146-47; W. La Barre, "Confessions as Cathartic Therapy in American Indian Tribes," *Magic, Faith, and Healing,* ed. A. Kiev (New York: Free Press, 1964), pp. 36-49; Balikci, "Shamanistic Behavior," pp. 387-89, 394.

63. Colson, "Spirit Possession," *Spirit Mediumship*, p. 75; Walker, *Ceremonial Spirit Possession*, p. 91.

14

HENRI MOTTU

Jeremiah vs. Hananiah: Ideology and Truth in Old Testament Prophecy

The prophet enters a situation in which interpretation of events—and policies to change or influence the events—are being shaped. The prophet offers words and deeds (explicit cultural production) derived from a reading of the basic contradictions that the people face (implicit cultural formation). The prophecies compete with other words, deeds, and readings of the situation. The analyses and strategies of all the interpreters and persuaders are "ideology" insofar as they pretend to be universal and indisputable truth while being actually the point of view of a group or class. They become "truth" insofar as the conditioned character of the analyses and strategies can be overcome through changing the conditions by thoughtful action.

Hananiah and Jeremiah offer two different readings of the contradictions facing Judah in 594 B.C.E.

Reprinted from *The Bible and Liberation: Political and Social Hermeneutics,* 1st ed., ed. N. K. Gottwald and A. C. Wire (Berkeley: Community for Religious Research and Education [Radical Religion], 1976), pp. 58–67.

For Hananiah the primary contradiction is between the superpower Babylon and inferior Judah, while the secondary contradiction is between salvation prophecy that promises Judah early victory over Babylon (Hananiah's prophecy) and doom prophecy that promises a lengthy Judean defeat at the hands of Babylon (Jeremiah's prophecy). The two contradictions are smoothly aligned in Hananiah's mind, and there is no other contradiction to consider.

For Jeremiah, the undoubted political threat of Babylon to Judah is altogether overshadowed by the primary contradiction between the power- and wealth-seeking interests of the ruling class in Judah and the well-being and survival of the whole Judean people. The associated secondary contradiction lies between salvation prophecy (serving the ruling class) and doom prophecy (serving the common people). For Jeremiah the immediate resolution of the contradictions will be for Babylon to remove the oppressive Judean rulers from their positions over the Judean people, for the latter are not ultimately threatened by the Babylonians under whose "yoke" they will survive and be renewed.

ASSUMPTIONS

I begin these tentative "Marxian" reflections on Jeremiah 28 by explaining the two assumptions I make.

First, it seems to me that the problem the Old Testament and the New Testament faced long before us, the problem of pseudo- and authentic prophecy, could be reformulated today under the terms, analyzed by Marxist thought, of ideology and truth—or more precisely: *Logos* and *Praxis*. The question that I want to address to the text is this: What does it say to us as we face the problem par excellence that plagues our lives and thoughts: *how are we to differentiate an ideological from a true theoretical statement?* It seems to me that the old text of Jer. 28 was wrestling with this very question and that the text raised this question with the maximum consciousness available in its time. By this I do not mean that we now have to "translate" the message of the text in our own language ("actualization"); that could be paternalistic. Rather, I mean we have to find again, in our own terms, the very question that the text was dealing with. My assumption is that the text was precisely dealing with Logos and Praxis. I call this process of interpretation "trans-interpretation."

As a matter of fact the text sounds very "modern," for it has to do with the question of authority: who has the authority to tell me what is true and what is false? Who is in a position to differentiate for me the deceitful Logos from the true Praxis? The Old Testament has an answer: only the true prophet is in such a position. But what constitutes the true prophet? Jer. 23, 26, and 28 are in fact wrestling with the conditions of true and false prophecy and provide us a sort of critique of what constitutes true or false Logos, Word of God or Word of Man. These texts, reflecting on Jeremiah's own praxis, grapple with the possibility and the actuality of such a differentiation. The modern problem, I believe, is not that of theism or atheism, of transcendence or immanence, of whether there is a God or not. Rather, what plagues us, Christians and atheists alike, is what makes a true statement true and a false statement false, and who in the last resort has the authority to teach us anything about it. This problem implies questions of source of authority, control, institutionalization, and politics. The *"diakrisis ton pneumaton"* of the New Testament necessarily involves the problem of the church or of the party.

My second assumption is that one cannot be satisfied today as an interpreter (and every theologian and philosopher is a decipherer of signs nowadays) with mere allusions to this problem or with basic unconscious and unexplained assumptions—as, for instance, when we identify from the outset with Jeremiah against his opponents, for that is precisely the beginning of a subtle hermeneutical lie. When for instance Van der Woude finishes a study of false prophecy with the remark: "The type of Zion-theology conceived of by the pseudo-prophets as an ideology does not in fact differ from any other ideology: its dogmatism, its objectivism, in particular its false hope for the future,"[1] one cannot avoid asking: on what basis does Van der Woude know that the theology of pseudo-prophetism was in fact an "ideology"? He simply assumes this and as an exegete has other things to do than to reflect on the matter. Nevertheless he does say such things in passing. As interpreters of the texts, however, we cannot avoid the problem and we must *try to clarify the process by which a given statement becomes false or true within the text itself as well as in our modern pre-understanding.* The same process of clarification is required from us concerning a myriad of other concepts or notions thrown out by exegetes and theologians as judgments in passing and sometimes even as cheap happy endings. In brief, our task is to decipher the hidden meaning of such unexplained assumptions; in other words, to make a critique of the dominant theological interpretation itself. We said earlier: *trans*-interpretation; we now say: *pre*-interpretation. It means: we want to provide a critique of what is *beneath* all these so-called "religious" or "Christian" interpretations.

THE PROBLEM

The problem has to be faced in its frightening and banal radicality without any attempt to transcend it too quickly or easily. And I must say, whereas the Old Testament itself has been quite honest in this regard, subsequent interpretations can be seen as an ongoing attempt to minimize and to domesticate it. For instance, the Old Testament never uses the equivalent of "pseudo" or "false" prophet. *Pseudoprophétes* comes from the Greek translation of the Old Testament and was taken up by some New Testament texts, but there is no comparable Old Testament expression. Behind this significant silence we may have the belief that only God himself is in a position to declare a prophet true or false. It is revealing that Jeremiah's opponents used a similar term. Shemaiah can describe Jeremiah as "a madman who sets up as a prophet" (Jer. 29:26), and the party of Azariah and Johanan can reply to Jeremiah on another occasion: "You are lying; the Lord our God has not sent you . . . Baruch son of Neriah has incited you against us in order to put us in the power of the Chaldeans, so that they may kill us or deport us to Babylon" (Jer. 43:2–3). Here we encounter call of God against call of God, Word of God against Word of God, God against God. The abstract question as to whether there is a God—or as to what God, humanity, or the world is in reality—is here put in its sole concrete way: What makes the truth the truth and the lie the lie? Who is the true interpreter of the world in which we live? The problematic is not either God or Marx, either Lenin or Mao, either Barth or Bultmann, but rather: Where is the true God, the true Marx, the true Bultmann to be found and to be differentiated from the false? Where is the illusory Marx and where is the true one?

The French Marxist Louis Althusser develops the notion of "epistemological break" precisely to answer the question: How can it be that our thinking, our Logos, is at the same time false by definition, since it is necessarily caught in its "practico-social function" as reflex (thus falsified) but still is, on the other hand, capable in some way of participation in the truth?[2] In fact, Althusser's epistemological break serves to describe both the fact that our Logos is a mere ideological reflex of sociohistorical conditioning (our "lived relation" to the world) and the assumption that once the break has taken place, our discourse is then able to constitute itself as a theory of science. Among Christian exegetes, this process is presumably exhibited when they say: *Here* in Jeremiah, true prophecy! *There* in Hananiah, false prophecy! In their eyes Jeremiah is a so-called "canonical prophet," a dreadful designation that simply calls "scriptural" or "canonical" the text of the victors and rejects to abomination or forgetfulness the beaten text of the defeated.

When Jeremiah tries desperately to convince his people that "in very truth the Lord has sent me to you to say all this in your hearing" (26:15), he can only *assure* them that this is so. There is here no external legitimation, no public testimony; the legitimation comes solely from the truth itself, from internal legitimation and testimony. Only prophecy can decide about prophecy (see 1 Cor. 14:32). Only God can say which god is the true God; only the Spirit can judge other spirits. Yes, but like Pilate we are tempted to respond, "But *what* is truth?" (John 18:38).

Of course there are attempts in the Old Testament to give some formal as well as material criteria for differentiating true from false prophecy; but they are what Marxists call "rationalizations" or "reifications" of the problem, to the degree that they replace the reality of lived-through history with objectifications and autonomous entities nowhere accessible to our actual consciousness. The formal criteria refer to Baal, morality, dreams, visions, fulfillment of prophecy, orthodoxy (as in Deut. 18:20–22); in this sense, Jer. 26 is mainly working on the level of the means of revelation and its critique. The material criteria refer to doom prophecy versus salvation and peace prophecy; free prophecy versus cult prophecy, etc. But, as Quell[3] and many others have shown, neither the external nor the internal criteria help very much, since they are all judgments after the fact. They do not help in the midst of the act of differentiating true and false prophecy. As André Néher says, not without irony, "There have been occasional attempts in biblical history . . . to codify prophecy and to state a theory of false prophecy. But no one has ever been able to establish the code of true prophecy."[4] My assumption is that Jer. 28 is an eminent text, an eminent narrative, that contains a surplus of meaning concerning an underlying theory of false and true discourse capable of recovery with the help of Marxian tools. This is my wager.

IDEOLOGY

I begin with the comprehensive definition of ideology advanced by François Châtelet:

> . . . an ideology is a cultural formation (implicit) or a cultural production (explicit) that expresses the point of view of a social class or caste; such a point of view concerns man's relations with nature, imagination, the others, and himself. Ideology presents itself as having a *universal* validity; but in reality it not only expresses a *particular* point of view, but also it tends to *mask* its particularity by proposing compensations and imaginary or fleeting solutions. By "ideological function" of a cultural production—a moral doctrine for instance—one has to understand the intellectual action that brings such a production, an action by which this particular conception is being presented as a universal conception.[5]

In Hananiah's statements and symbolic act (Jer. 28:1–4, 10–11) we have thus to differentiate three aspects:

1. The implicit cultural formation (what stands or lurks behind or beneath his discourse and act);

2. The explicit cultural production (what he explicitly says and does);

3. The ideological function of both (what the effects of his discourse and act are).

The implicit cultural formation that lies behind Hananiah's words and act may be summarized as follows:

1. There is the assumption that God protects his people and saves them from the Babylonian imperialism at any price (Zion-election tradition). Israel is viewed as forever the chosen people of God. Israel's own cast of mind or

actions or economic/political structures (e.g. the royal court) cannot change this enduring salvation fact.

2. There is the assumption that God acts in a repetitive way at any time and in any situation in the same way that he always has acted (God's truthfulness or fidelity is a given, a "thing" at our disposal). As God in Isaiah's time forced the Assyrians under Sennacherib in 701 miraculously to withdraw from the siege of Jerusalem, so now—in the same manner—the Babylonians under Nebuchadnezzar will be compelled by Yahweh to retreat and to let the first deportees of 597 (Jehoiachin and the ruling group with him) come back to Jerusalem safely and intact. What has happened in 701 will happen again in 594–593. We have to trust God's fidelity (to "trust" is Hananiah's key word, see Jer. 28:15).

Now what do we gain by calling this an "implicit cultural formation"? It is tempting to say: everybody knows that already and we have no need of this complicated conceptual apparatus. Answer: we gain two things. First, we are able to specify Hananiah's "unconscious motives" and his "concealed motivations" as a formation that *we* reconstruct and that *we* define as a theology, without immediately stigmatizing it as an "ideology," since this would be a statement after the event. J. Philip Hyatt asserts that "Jeremiah brought these concealed motivations into the open,"[6] but in truth it was not Jeremiah but *we* who try to bring into the open Hananiah's implicit cultural formation (I prefer the term "implicit" rather than the term "unconscious"). Jeremiah cannot be seen as taking the risk of reconstruction for us and apart from us. Second, when we speak of an implicit cultural formation we presuppose that such a construction—located "behind" or "beneath" any discourse or action that we undertake to decipher—lies behind Jeremiah's own statements as well. "May it be so!" he says, following Hananiah's Word of God (28:6). Consequently, it is not the mere existence of an implicit cultural formation as such, or for that matter its particular content, that can decide about truth and falsehood, reality and illusion. It is only the *function* of any formation that has become embodied in a specific production, the actual *use* made of them, that can decide about truth and falsehood, reality and illusion (see below on "Praxis").

The explicit cultural production takes the following form in the words and act of Hananiah:

Hananiah takes up the *universality* of Israelite prophetic speech: "Thus says Yahweh of hosts, the God of Israel: I have broken the yoke of the king of Babylon . . ." (28:2). He explicitly takes up the Word of God as a universal Word, as *the* Word, whereas he in fact takes up *a* word, pronounced in a *particular* situation and responding to particular interests (cf. Isa. 9:4, "thou hast shattered the yoke that burdened them"). Such a process of making out of a particular statement a universal one, valid once and for all, is called by Jeremiah (23:30) a "stealing": the prophets "who steal my words from one another for their own use." And what Hananiah explicitly *does* is clear also: he acts symbolically, as is often the case in prophetism: he breaks the yoke and takes it off the neck of Jeremiah. Word against Word, symbolic act against symbolic act.

The ideological function of both cultural formation and cultural production may be analyzed in this way:

1. This discourse and this symbolic action have first the function of interjecting, so to speak, into the objective situation certain value-imbuing affirmations. These are value judgments or affirmations that deal with predications of worth. Hananiah's discourse functions in reality as a predication of value which leads the people to "trust" in Yahweh in terms of certain perceptions about good and evil, about friend and enemy, about what is near (and therefore of concern or value) and what is far (and therefore of little or no concern or value). The discourse functions in such a way that the people are led to see, to face, and to resist "the enemy"—namely, the Babylonian invader. Thus God is seen as the Friend, the Protector, the Near over against the "others" over there who intrude into our land, territory, and city. For Jeremiah, on the contrary, God is the Enemy: "am I a God only near at hand, and not far away?" (23:23). "Do I not fill heaven and earth?" (23:24) Nebuchadnezzar is bluntly designated by Jeremiah as "my [God's] servant" (27:6). God is beyond good and evil.

2. The ideological discourse functions secondly by leading the people to take into account only one aspect of the whole reality, one contradiction that is elevated to the status of principal contradiction, whereas it is only a secondary contradiction [see below on "Contradiction"]. Hananiah sees only the contradiction between the Babylonian Empire and Judah (more precisely: between Babylon and the ruling class of Judah, esp. of Jerusalem) without taking any account of the fact that this contradiction is *overdetermined* [7] by the internal conflict between the people of Judah and its ruling class and by the conflict between God and Israel's fall into nationalism. Jeremiah, by contrast, understands the whole and rightly sees the necessity of history proceeding on its course under these painful circumstances—inevitably the "bars of wood" will be changed into "bars of iron" (28:13).

REIFICATION

As a beginning point I take the definition of reification by Peter Berger and Stanley Pullberg:

> By reification we mean the moment in the process of alienation in which the characteristic of thing-hood becomes the standard of objective reality. That is, nothing can be conceived of as real that does not have the character of a thing. This can also be put in different words: reification is objectification in an alienated mode . . . Reification, on all levels of consciousness, converts the concrete into the abstract, then in turn concretizes the abstract. Also, reification converts quality into quantity.[8]

By means of the concept of reification, I shall attempt to reconstruct Hananiah's world—i.e., his subjective understanding of it or his "lived relation" to himself, to the people of Israel, to the world, and ultimately to God. The process of reification can be observed on four levels:

1. Process of Recurrence. To the degree that reification as a general phenomenon is "grounded in historically recurrent circumstances of human existence in society,"[9] one can say that Hananiah operates upon the belief that God's fidelity is simply a recurrent fact. "Recurrence" is a procedure of demonstration that consists in extending to all the terms of a series what is valid only for the first two terms. This is exactly what he does: he extends the events of 701 under Sennacherib to the events of 594/3 under Nebuchadnezzar without seeing those events in terms of the historical activity of Babylon and Judah. What is going on in Hananiah's mind is exactly "the autonomization of objectivity in unconnectedness with the human activity by which it has been produced."[10]

2. Process of Stealing. Reification occurs when certain people "steal" the praxis of others, which is the case when Hananiah "steals" (Isa. 9:4) from Isaiah and simply transfers a word said in a given situation into a quite different one. This process of "stealing" is a far-reaching one and covers many different situations, as illustrated by the German peasants who saw their praxis being "stolen" from their hands by the princes and by Luther,[11] or by the process in contemporary theology and church of "stealing" Marxian categories dislodged from their militant political context, or by the praxis and struggle of women today being "stolen" by males for their own advantages. So the text of Isaiah 9 becomes a "thing," even a commodity, at the disposal of anyone at any time. Jer. 23:30 speaks pointedly against this "reification" of the words of God.

3. Process of Fetishism. In his 1962 spring term lectures at Göttingen, Walther Zimmerli remarked that for Hananiah the "sacred" comes first and the people come only in second position. "Within two years I will bring back to this place all the vessels of the Lord's house . . ." (28:3), and the people come only after this: "I will also bring back to this place Jeconiah son of Jehoiakim, king of Judah, and all the exiles of Judah who went to Babylon" (28:4). "Reification in a capitalist society is a product of the fetishism of commodities, and it is spread through all social life by the institutions necessary to the market."[12] We can, I believe, transfer this to the situation of the text, even though the economy then was only a barter economy and not an industrial economy. Of principal importance are the vessels of the temple, and only secondarily the people of flesh and blood. The "world" of Hananiah is a world of commodities viewed as prior to people. The temple is the collective that concretizes the abstract, that incarnates dead vessels, frozen things. The fetishism of the temple is everywhere present among the "pseudo"-prophets (cf. Jer. 7:4 and Mic. 3:11). In addition, it is worthwhile to note that Hananiah is primarily concerned about the ruling class deported with the king.

4. Process of Reification in the Religious Realm. Marx has analyzed the process of reification (commodity, man as commodity, etc.) as a process paralleled by religious fetishism. It is clear that for Hananiah God is a product of what is seen as "given" in the representation. A fixed preconception stands opposed to what is actually present! God is a commodity or thing in the midst of other commodities and things, even in the most important and influential of them. So we meet a religious representation of reality concretized in the fetishism of the temple and the reification of the vessels, elevated above the people, combined in a thorough-going process of "thingification."

CONTRADICTION

We observed from the outset the decisive role played in the debate by the yoke as the medium for the two opposing symbolic acts: the wooden yoke that Jeremiah carries on his shoulders and the action of Hananiah in taking this yoke from the neck of his opponent, only to be replaced by Jeremiah with an iron yoke. We meet not only word against word but act against act, and this points up the fact that Judah lives under the pressure of history ("the yoke of Nebuchadnezzar," 28:11), under history's necessity. Thus the yoke in my view stands as a representation of the concept of necessity and, more precisely, for the basic contradiction that the people of Judah are living between the promise of their God and the actual inescapable reality posed by history. Judah is historically and theologically caught in the alternative: either to rebel against history's necessity and to restore Jerusalem and its temple or to let the events go their course. The latter alternative implies a radical new understanding of God's action in history and of the role of Jerusalem. Hananiah is a kind of Zealot who united religious restorative thinking and political resistance. In my jargon: the symbolic gesture of Hananiah taking the yoke from Jeremiah's neck is the religious symbol of Judah's lived contradiction between rebellion and necessity.

Now let us try to make use of Mao Tse-tung's famous model of principal or dominant contradiction and nonprincipal or secondary contradiction; as well as the principal aspect of the contradiction and secondary aspect of the contradiction.[13]

1. Hananiah, like Jeremiah and all of the Judeans, sees the dominant contradiction as embodied in the unequal power relationship between Babylon and the royal court in Judah. This is first of all what lies objectively behind the entire situation. As far as the secondary contradiction is concerned, Hananiah envisions it as the antagonism between pseudo-prophetism as embodied in doom prophecy à la Jeremiah and authentic prophetism as incarnated in the Zion-election tradition à la Isaiah. He sees the situation exclusively in these terms, and there is no *reflection* on his part about the "aspects" of the two contradictions. For him the contradiction is really "pure and simple."

2. Jeremiah, by contrast, rightly points out the complexity of this twofold contradiction. The two contradictions imply aspects that are not reducible to the contradictions between Babylon and Judah and between doom prophecy and salvation prophecy. Jeremiah rightly sees that what Hananiah views as the dominant contradiction is in fact only the dominant *aspect* of the contradiction and that the secondary contradiction between doom prophecy (pseudo-prophecy in Hananiah's eyes) and salvation prophecy (authentic prophecy in his eyes) is only the secondary *aspect* of it.

What then is the actual dominant contradiction in the situation? It is, I think according to Jeremiah, *the overdetermination of the conflict Babylon-Judah by another conflict,* a conflict altogether ignored by Hananiah— namely, by *the conflict between the subjective interests of the ruling class in Jerusalem and the objective interests of the people of Israel/Judah as a whole.* Note here the intriguing intervention on behalf of Jeremiah by "some elders of the land" (26:17) who probably represent the old North Israelite tradition of Amos and Micah (in fact, they quote Mic. 3:11-12). According to Jeremiah, the apparent principal contradiction of Babylon versus Judah is decisively overdetermined by the conflict between the people of the land and the people of Jerusalem who rule Judah. This internal conflict, because of its socioeconomic roots, is much more basic to the situation than the more easily observed interstate conflict between Babylon and Judah.

Consequently, as far as the secondary aspect of the contradiction is concerned, Jeremiah sees not only the religious aspect of the antagonism between pseudo- and authentic prophecy but also its concrete and practical social effects. Praxis against dogmatism. Hananiah's "world" remains a purely religious one. Jeremiah sees much better the socioeconomic aspects of this religious contradiction insofar as what is at stake in the last analysis is not the correct religion or doctrine but rather the *survival,* "the good" of people of flesh and blood (cf. Jer. 6:14, "They dress my people's wounds, but skin-deep only, with their saying 'All is well.' All well? Nothing is well!"). It is not only that sin brings forth doom, but also that at stake is the survival, the very life, of the people (cf. Jer. 27:12-13, 17, "serve the king of Babylon and his people and you shall save your lives"). For Jeremiah the secondary aspect of the contradiction is set into a social context in which the prophetic debate about truth and falsehood is merely a part. The secondary contradiction has an aspect that overdetermines it insofar as the question is not only a "theoretical" abstract one (truth/falsity) but a concrete one as well (survival). Thus, far better than his opponent, Jeremiah has seen the wholeness of the situation, a situation in which the religious secondary contradiction is never "pure and simple" but always overdetermined by the conflicts and power relationships among social groups with their respective interests (see the social components of Judah mentioned in Jer. 26).

What have we gained by this rather complicated analysis? I think we have gained two things:

1. First we have tried to recapture the complexity of the situation. We

believe that the so-called "contradictions" pointed out by the exegetes to date are to some degree helpful but ultimately invalid. For it is simply not true to see the contradiction between true and false prophecy in the mere opposition between doom prophecy and salvation prophecy (e.g., Osswald[14]). In that case, what about Jonah and Nineveh? The contradiction between cult prophecy and "outsider" prophecy is somehow romantic and does not help very much. In that case, what about the fact that Jeremiah comes from a priestly family? The contradiction between group prophecy and solitary or individual prophecy is wrong too. In that case, what of the fact that Jeremiah was not "alone" (cf. the martyrdom of Uriah, Jer. 26:20–23, to say nothing of Jeremiah's "school" and disciples, such as Baruch). Finally, the contradiction between North Israelite land prophecy and Zion-election-temple prophecy (e.g. von Rad[15]) is somewhat more helpful, although this is not decisive either, since after all Hananiah and Jeremiah alike come from Benjamin and, moreover, Jeremiah is saved by the elders of the land only at the last minute without himself being located in their tradition.

Against these somehow lazy and too easy "explanations," we have tried to differentiate dominant and secondary contradictions, viewed as mere external power relationships, from dominant and secondary *aspects* of these contradictions viewed as an *internal* overdetermination of the latter.

2. Secondly, I think we have shown that Marxism does not *reduce* the frightening question at stake to this or that *external* factor. On the contrary, the enigma remains intact while becoming analytically approachable and discernible in terms of the various forces at work and the various value predications which the disputants affirm. Naturally this judgment gives no blanket endorsement to all interpretations labeled "Marxist," since many of these have been crudely mechanistic or economist and quite as "undialectical" as the worst instances of biblical exegesis. We have emphasized here strands of Marxist analysis contributed by theoreticians such as Althusser and Antonio Gramsci.[16]

PRAXIS

Let us return to our main question: What is a true statement confronted with an illusory one? What differentiates Logos from Praxis? Since any kind of statement, whoever delivers it, is inescapably not only *dependent* on sociohistorical conditioning but also necessarily *situated* in a web of power relationships, how can such a true statement simply *be?* There is no "human condition" as such, but only situation. All thought is situated and participates in the strategy of desire, of sociality, and of will for power. Where is the "line of demarcation" (Althusser) separating the true and the false and how can we simply "draw" it?

This is the problem of modernity: epistemology (what is knowing? How can I know any object?) is met from the angle of illusion (Kant and the "transcendental illusion"). It is at this point that Marx and Freud come together,

Marx adding to Freud's analysis the power relationships and the relations of domination and dependence. As Ricouer observes,

> . . . in this respect, the fundamental contribution of Marx will not rest on his theory of class struggle, but on the discernment of the hidden relation which connects ideology to the phenomena of domination. This reading of ideology as symptomatic of the phenomenon of domination will be the durable contribution of Marxism beyond its political applications.[17]

Thus Hananiah not only lives in illusion (albeit a religious illusion) but also participates implicitly in the power relationships of his time. Without knowing it, he responds under the disguise of the prophetic Spirit to the wishful thinking of the royal court and of the temple fans. But still, how are we to draw the line of demarcation? How do we know that Jeremiah is right and who tells us that this is the case? From what source do we assume what we more or less consciously assume and identify with? There are, I think, three solutions that are available to us, and I will briefly discuss them: (1) History draws the line of demarcation with its sole necessity and certainty; (2) Philosophy of consciousness; the "true" and the "false" consciousness; (3) "Philosophy of the praxis" (Gramsci).

1. History as the Criterion. The sly "solution" of this line of interpretation rapidly proves itself to be a slovenly answer that no one can be satisfied with, but that has often been considered as the Marxist doctrine and as a secularization of the Christian predestination doctrine. This is in fact a dreadful escape, but a very cunning one that still lies in our minds as the way to read any text, including biblical texts. Even if success may prove the validity of our knowledge and practice, the difficulty is that such a realization always comes after the event. History, contrary to what Hegel has said, is not the ongoing self-recognition of the Spirit. History teaches us only one thing: that there are victors and victims, dominators and dominated, texts of victors that remain and texts of the defeated that have disappeared. In brief, such hermeneutics work under the delusive assumption of relations of domination and dependence.

It is sheer bad faith to give Jeremiah the pre-eminence over Hananiah simply because history has justified him *a posteriori*; here the sly moralism of many commentaries should be checked. This has often been the "moralistic theological" reading of Jer. 28: one saves Jeremiah from the ambiguity and opacity of history by using *a posteriori* the entire "Marxist" arsenal in order to disqualify Hananiah. The "reflex" theory is then fully applied to Hananiah but *never to Jeremiah himself,* as if it would have been possible to differentiate them in the midst of the original action—which was precisely impossible. The proof from history is the false infinite of the theologian.

2. Philosophy of Consciousness. This is the exegetical solution of Edmond Jacob: "Thus what we customarily call 'false prophecy' would only be the temptation to which any prophet is constantly exposed."[18] This line of interpretation would focus on the "temptation" of Jeremiah as a prophet torn apart who exhibits the rise of personal subjectivity (who am I?); the temptation; the bad faith; etc. We would then have a *tragic* situation. Accordingly, there is *no way* to draw our much-desired line of demarcation. We are in the dark of existence. Two duties, two spirits, two words equally valid and valuable in and of themselves; only existence can decide (decision!). But we thereby renounce any attempt to arrive at objectivity. The world is on the verge of disintegration within the choice of consciousness. Are we not back to idealism, whereby consciousness gives birth to the world?

3. "Philosophy of the Praxis." Against the assumption that every statement, whatever it may be and whoever announces it, is "ideological" and thus untrue, Marxism has always emphasized the breakthrough ("the working through") of the praxis. In Marxism the "epistemological break" only takes place under the auspices of the praxis (this is to be affirmed against Althusser). Praxis does not mean "to be where the action is," since it means in Marxism not only the practical response to a person's conditions of life (need, material conditions, work), but also "the comprehension of this practice" (Marx's Thesis 8 on Feuerbach). Ultimately praxis serves in Marxism the function of "authentic consciousness" in existentialism over against "false consciousness," insofar as praxis is the mediation necessary to solve the problem of human dependency on our conditioning and, at the same time, of human participation in the truth: "The coincidence of the changing of circumstances and of human activity can be conceived and rationally understood only as revolutionizing practice" (Marx's Thesis 3 on Feuerbach). Thus praxis in Marxism plays the role of paradox in existentialism. This is why Marxian tools are originally and fundamentally *open tools* of criticism, including self-criticism. *Praxis does not "solve" anything; it just poses the problem in its right terms and in its correct scope* and it does so in opposition to loose talk about history's automatic "judgment" and against a kind of existentialist irrationalism.

Jeremiah "works" the truth of his God, the hidden God. He is the man of the Praxis rather than of the Logos. Why? For four reasons:

1. There is in Jeremiah a tremendous *process of "working,"* of work that is not only external labor but of work turned upon interiority and then turning back to exteriority. Here we should refer to Hegel's analysis of the Slave/Master relation in *Phenomenology of Mind,* Chap. IV: the Master is idle, he encounters nature and raw material only through the mediation of the Slave who is in direct contact with the real world. Hence the Master cannot be ultimately "satisfied"; the Slave, on the contrary, "works through"—i.e., he forms and educates himself through his fighting for recognition and his struggle with nature and other people. Hegel has a tremendous definition of "work": work, he says, is "repressed Desire, an arrested passing phase" and therefore only work, not enjoyment, is able to "form-and-educate."[19] That is why only the Slave is really able to make history. Marx of course will take up

later these considerations of Hegel in his own concept of alienated labor.

One sees how readily we can apply such a scheme to the diametrically opposed attitudes of Hananiah and Jeremiah. Jeremiah is the Slave who confronts his God, disputes with him, works over the meaning of a God who remains fundamentally *hidden,* far away, and who therefore has to be searched. Nothing is taken for granted. *Tu es deus absconditus.* There is at work in Jeremiah a fight over meaning and against illusion, a process of purification (for him God's word is both hammer and fire, Jer. 23:29–30). Not in the givenness of culture and "tradition" is the intellectual locus of Jeremiah to be found, but in the process of formation-and-education, at once dramatic and prosaic. There is in his attitude something that we could call "critical reflection" which permeates his work and search. One recalls his "Amen. May it be so!" in response to Hananiah and his reflection following this sigh (28:6–9). This is not a "word," a powerful Logos said in the name of Yahweh; on the contrary, this is only a reflection, an objection addressed to Hananiah which says: this should give you pause for thought, this should be considered also! A human and even rational reservation is here subtly and ironically opposed to a so-called "Word of God."

2. Beyond this reflective capacity is the agony too, *the agonizing confrontation with the silence of God.* Previously we said that unlike Hananiah, for whom God is here and now given and revealed, for Jeremiah God is problematic, far away, not obviously given. Now we must even say that for him God is silent and absent. "And the prophet Jeremiah went his way" (28:11). It is interesting to note that Jeremiah always put himself on the side of the cheated and deceived, of his people's lostness and helplessness (e.g., 4:10). Praxis meant in our first point the critical "working through" of the truth, the reflection that takes *distance,* the difference; now praxis means also the deep *solidarity* of the prophet with his deceived people, with the lost and powerless.

3. We must also include here Jeremiah's concrete and theoretical fight against alienation and reification on every level. In addition to praxis as a critical reflection and as passion and agony, praxis means also *the concrete liberating struggle against alienation.* Note the critique of the idols, of Judah's infidelity and untruthfulness, of royal and ruling class deeds (e.g., 22:13–17, against Jehoiakim).

4. Finally, we must emphasize the openness of Jeremiah's praxis to newness and *innovation.* It is striking to notice Jeremiah's own attitude of openness toward new deeds that may be accomplished by God, new horizons opened by history. Zimmerli understands Jeremiah's going away and apparent escape and silence as a self-criticism (28:11): "The Word of God is not his own Word."[20] Of vss. 12–14, Zimmerli says: "To the prophet who has departed the scene obediently *to listen afresh,* the mission is given anew."[21] As far as the new horizons opened by history are concerned, I would say that Jeremiah is simply a far better interpreter of his time, and of the time to come, than Hananiah—a better interpreter of Babylonian imperialism and,

beyond that, of exile, purification, and possibility of renewal. (See the promise of a *new* covenant, Jer. 31:31-34.) "The Lord has not sent you" (28:15) can be translated: "You did not persevere in the discipline of listening," so that the discipline, cost of discipleship, means not only critical reflection but also discipline, hard work to *listen to new facts,* to the newly emergent.

To return to Châtelet's definition of ideology, one can say therefore that Jeremiah's *implicit cultural formation* (the hidden God as the Other/God coming under the auspices of history's inescapability and leading to the agony of Israel through exile, death, and loss of world toward the promise of new life) and his *explicit cultural production* (the transforming of the wooden yoke into "bars of iron," i.e., the relation of inexorable dependence on the Babylonian Empire) are just as much an "ideological" formation/production as Hananiah's own "ideological" formation/production. The only difference—which is decisive indeed—is *how* this formation/production is used and thus how it *functions* within the sociohistorical conditions. Our assumption, our wager, is that Jeremiah's "ideology" functions as a praxis—as a breakthrough permitting the maximum *actual* consciousness of Israel's people to be transformed into the maximum *potential* consciousness, and as a "working through" of what has been made of them by history.

Praxis as critical reflection, as agony, as denunciation of alienation, and as innovating process makes possible a breakthrough toward newness, toward fresh fields of possibility, toward project. This is of course not to imply that Jeremiah's statement would suddenly and miraculously appear as a non-ideological one (fairy's wand), but this is simply to say that praxis permits us to dispose of a relative criterion of differentiation and of a relative means of participating in the truth—despite, or better *because* of, our conditioning.

Against idealism, whereby consciousness itself seems to give birth to the world of things, the strength of Marxism has always consisted of its insistence that one succeeds in putting human thought *at a distance* from its conditioning—a conditioning that it never ceases to reflect—only to the degree that *human thought proves itself capable of transforming the world, of transforming the very conditioning that it reflects.* That is the deepest meaning of the philosophy of praxis, innovating praxis.

On the other hand, however, the great contribution of phenomenology is also that it reminds us that such a distance can only be achieved as thought proves itself capable of positing to itself, *of returning to itself the question of the foundation of what it affirms as true.* This is the phenomenological *epochè* or "suspension" of meaning (see again 28:6, "May it be so!"—suspension of judgment; Jeremiah simply does not know). Hegel asserted: "What is *familiar* is not *known,"* which is exactly the epistemological presupposition of Jeremiah's whole attitude. This must be said against forms of materialism and naturalism whereby consciousness is seen as automatically engendered by the things, by the world, and by conditioning itself.

Praxis and *Epochè:* these are the two modern names for Jeremiah's words and deeds. How now to reconcile Marxism and phenomenology, Marx and

Kierkegaard, I do not know. This is the problem of my generation. In any case, throughout this whole discussion we have dealt with the central problem that I see as the modern problem par excellence: *where* does illusion cease and *where* does truth begin? What are the conditions for the actualization of such a process? What is a *critique* of theological Logos today in the light of Kant and of the three masters of suspicion: Marx, Nietzche, and Freud?

We are brought to say that the stake of all importance, at the heart of ourselves, between the authentic and the inauthentic is the meaning that we give to the affirmation. What do we affirm? What is our source, our resource of affirmation?[22]

My wager, I repeat, is that this old text already knew and dealt before us and for us with this ultimate question. Logos *or* Praxis? *Nobody* can finally give us a sure answer to that—and this is good. Those who use Marxism to avoid this darkness with a lazy historicism or economism not only do not know Marxism but do not know themselves. What I have said only is that with praxis we may find the concept of our question, the origin of our agony; but we are still in search of a new source of affirmation.

NOTES

1. A. S. Van der Woude, "Micah in Dispute with the Pseudo-Prophets." *VT* 19 (1969): 260.

2. For the notion of "epistemological break" see Louis Althusser, *For Marx,* trans. B. R. Brewster (New York: Random House, Vintage Books, 1970), especially the introduction, pp. 21-39. For definitions of all the Marxist terms used in this article, see the glossary, pp. 249-57.

3. Gottfried Quell, *Wahre und falsche Propheten* (1952).

4. A. Néher, *L'Essence du prophétisme* (1955), p. 102.

5. Quoted by J. P. Siméon, "Pensée et idéologie," *Esprit* 1 (1972): 31.

6. J. P. Hyatt, *Commentary on Jeremiah, IB,* p. 1016.

7. "Overdetermined" is Althusser's term, drawn from Freud, emphasizing that a contradiction or aspect of a contradiction may be "subordinated to" or even "deprioritized by" another contradiction or aspect of a contradiction. In other words, a contradiction is never "pure and simple." See *For Marx,* pp. 87-128, "Contradiction and Overdetermination."

8. P. Berger and S. Pullberg, "Reification and the Sociological Critique of Consciousness," *New Left Review* 35 (1966): 61, 68.

9. Ibid., p. 76.

10. Ibid., p. 59.

11. Jean-Paul Sartre, *Search for a Method,* trans. Hazel E. Barnes (New York: Knopf, 1963, Random House Vintage, 1968), p. 68.

12. B. Brewster, in discussion with Berger and Pullberg in *New Left Review* 35, p. 74.

13. Mao Tse-tung, "On Contradiction," *Selected Works,* 4 Vols. (New York: China Books, 1967, repr. of 1937 ed.), Vol. 1, pp. 311-47.

14. E. Osswald, *Falsche Prophetie im Alten Testament* (1962).

15. Gerhard von Rad, "Die falschen Propheten," *ZAW* 10 (1933): 109-20.

16. Antonio Gramsci, *Selections from the Prison Notebooks,* trans. Quinton Hoare and Godfrey Smith (New York: International Publishers, 1973), and Guiseppe Fiori, *Antonio Gramsci: Life of a Revolutionary* (New York: Dutton, 1971), with bibliography.

17. Paul Ricoeur, "The Critique of Religion," *USQR* 28 (1973): 206-7.

18. Edmund Jacob, "Quelques remarques sur le faux prophètes," *ThZ* 13 (1957): 483.

19. A. Kojève, *Introduction to the Reading of Hegel,* ed. Allen Bloom, trans. James H. Nichols, Jr. (New York: Basic Books, 1969), p. 24.

20. W. Zimmerli, "Das Wort und die Träume," *Der Grundriss* (Schweiz. reform. Monatsschrift, 1939), p. 202.

21. Ibid.

22. Paul Ricoeur, "The Language of Faith," *USQR* 28 (1973): 224.

15

PHYLLIS A. BIRD

Images of Women
in the Old Testament

The status and role of women in ancient Israel, while generally subordinate to men, varied considerably at different periods and in different social circles as expressed in various literary genres. There are frequent expressions of informal powers exercised by women that were not recognized by law or custom.

According to Old Testament laws, women were legally and substantively dependent on men, although they possessed certain rights and responsibilities under particular laws. In the Proverbs, woman is either mother who instructs and nurtures, or wife who looks to her husband's interests, or adulteress who endangers man's status and life. In historical writings, we meet women predominantly as mothers and wives who are adjuncts of men, although they also appear as harlots, prophetesses, cult singers, mediums, wise women, professional mourners, midwives and nurses, and household servants of kings.

This essay was originally published in Rosemary Radford Ruether, ed., *Religion and Sexism: Images of Woman in the Jewish and Christian Traditions* (New York: Simon and Schuster, 1974), pp. 41-88. Copyright © 1974 by Rosemary Radford Ruether. Reprinted by permission of Simon & Schuster, a Division of Gulf & Western Corporation.

The economic, cultic, and legal restrictions on women appear as cultural givens, a kind of base line that is sometimes exceeded by women who in fact and/or in theory (by means of patriarchal compensation) act or are thought of as equals to men in one regard or another. The creation stories recognize a general equality of sexes which rises above the average of woman's actual place in ancient Israel.

For most of us the image of woman in the Old Testament is the image of Eve, augmented perhaps by a handful of Bible-storybook "heroines," or villainesses, as the case may be (Sarah, Deborah, Ruth, Esther, Jezebel, Delilah). Some may also perceive in the background the indistinct shapes of a host of unnamed mothers, who, silent and unacknowledged, bear all the endless genealogies of males. But it is the named women, by and large, the exceptional women, who supply the primary images for the usual portrait of the Old Testament woman. These few great women together with the first woman (curiously incompatible figures in most interpretations) fill the void that looms when we consider the image of woman in the Old Testament. For the Old Testament is a man's "book," where women appear for the most part simply as adjuncts of men, significant only in the context of men's activities.

This perception is fundamental, for it describes the terms of all Old Testament speech about women. The Old Testament is a collection of writings by males from a society dominated by males.[1] These writings portray a man's world. They speak of events and activities engaged in primarily or exclusively by males (war, cult, and government) and of a jealously singular God who is described and addressed in terms normally used for males.[2]

But women appear in these pages more frequently than memory commonly allows—and in more diverse roles and estimations.[3] In some texts the woman of ancient Israel is portrayed simply as a class of property. In others she is depicted as possessing a measure of freedom, initiative, power, and respect that contemporary American women might well envy. This essay attempts to examine that full range of Old Testament images of women, with attention to the contexts in which they were formed and formulated and the meaning given to them by the various "authors."

Only a reading of the Old Testament can give an adequate impression of the variety of viewpoints and expression represented in its words about women and also expose the common threads that run through them. Here we can do no more than sample that literature. The short selections offered below aim only to suggest the compass of the evidence upon which the following analysis is based.

Most blessed of women be Jael
   the wife of Heber the Kenite,
   of tent-dwelling women most blessed.
. . . . .
She put her hand to the tent peg
   and her right hand to the workmen's mallet;
she struck Sisera a blow,
   she crushed his head,
   she shattered and pierced his temple [Judg. 5:24, 26].[4]

I brought you up from the land of Egypt,
   and redeemed you from the house of bondage;
   and I sent before you Moses, Aaron, and Miriam [Mic. 6:4].

Now when the Queen of Sheba heard of the fame of Solomon concerning the name of the Lord, she came to test him with hard questions. She came to Jerusalem with a very great retinue, with camels bearing spices, and very much gold, and precious stones . . . [1 Kings 10:1-2].

So Bathsheba went to King Solomon, to speak to him on behalf of Adonijah. And the King rose to meet her, and bowed down to her; then he . . . had a seat brought . . . and she sat on his right [1 Kings 2:19].

Everyone who curses his father or his mother shall be put to death [Lev. 20:9].

The peasantry grew plump in Israel
   they grew plump on booty
When you arose, O Deborah,
   arose, a mother in Israel [Judg. 5:7].[5]

Out of the window she peered,
   the mother of Sisera gazed through the lattice:
"Why is his chariot so long in coming?
   Why tarry the hoofbeats of his chariots?"
Her wisest ladies make answer,
   nay, she gives answer to herself,
"Are they not finding and dividing the spoil?—
   A maiden [lit., womb] or two for every man . . ." [Judg. 5:28-30].

Now King David was old and advanced in years; and although they covered him with clothes, he could not get warm. Therefore his servants said to him, "Let a young maiden be sought for my lord the king . . . let her lie in your bosom, that my lord the king may be warm." So they sought for a beautiful maiden throughout all the territory of Israel, and found Abishag the Shunammite, and brought her to the king [1 Kings 1:1-4].

. . . the men of the city, base fellows, beset the house round about, beating on the door; and they said to the old man, the master of the house, "Bring out the man who came into your house, that we may know him." And the man, the master of the house, went out to them and said to them, "No, my brethren, do not act so wickedly . . . here are my virgin daughter and his concubine; let me bring them out now. Ravish them and do with them what seems good to you; but against this man do not do so vile a thing" [Judg. 19:22-24].

When you go forth to war against your enemies . . . and you take them captive, and see among the captives a beautiful woman, and you have desire for her and would take for yourself as wife, then you shall . . . [permit her to] bewail her father and mother a full month; after that you may go into her and be her husband, and she shall be your wife. Then, if you have no delight in her, you shall let her go where she will; but you shall not sell her for money, you shall not treat her as a slave, since you have humiliated her [Deut. 21:10-14].

When Rachel saw that she bore Jacob no children,
she envied her sister; and she said to Jacob,
"Give me children, or I shall die!"
Then God remembered Rachel and God hearkened to her and opened her womb. She conceived and bore a son, and said, "God has taken away my reproach" [Gen. 30:1-2, 22-23].

. . . If a woman conceives and bears a male child, then she shall be unclean seven days. . . . But if she bears a female child, then she shall be unclean two weeks [Lev. 12:2, 5].

A certain woman threw an upper millstone upon Abimelech's head and crushed his skull. Then he called hastily to the young man his armor-bearer, and said to him, "Draw your sword and kill me, lest they say of me, 'A woman killed him' " [Judg. 9:53-54].

My people—children are their oppressors,
and women rule over them.
O my people, your leaders mislead you,
and confuse the course of your paths [Isa. 3:12].

Now when Athaliah the mother of Ahaziah saw that her son was dead, she arose and destroyed all the royal family. . . . [and she] reigned over the land for seven years [2 Kings 11:1, 3].

The Lord has created a new thing on earth:
and a woman protects [lit., encompasses] a man [Jer. 31:22].

A good wife. . . .
She considers a field and buys it;
with the fruit of her hands she plants a vineyard.
She girds her loins with strength
and makes her arms strong.
She perceives that her merchandise is profitable [Prov. 31:10, 16–18].

Rejoice in the wife of your youth,
a lovely hind, a graceful doe.
Let her affection fill you at all times
with delight,
be infatuated always with her love [Prov. 5:10–19].

A continual dripping on a rainy day and a contentious woman are alike
[Prov. 27:15].

The daughters of Zion are haughty
and walk with outstretched necks,
glancing wantonly with their eyes,
Mincing along as they go,
tinkling with their feet [Isa. 3:16].

The lips of a loose woman drip honey,
and her speech is smoother than oil;
but in the end she is bitter as wormwood,
sharp as a two-edged sword [Prov. 5:3–4].

How fair and pleasant you are,
O loved one, delectable maiden!
You are stately as a palm tree,
and your breasts are like its clusters.
I say I will climb the palm tree
and lay hold of its branches.
Oh, may your breasts be like clusters of the vine
and the scent of your breath like apples,
and your kisses like the best wine . . .[S. of S. 7:6–9].

. . . I found him whom my soul loves.
I held him, and would not let him go
until I had brought him into my mother's house,
and into the chamber of her that conceived me [S. of S. 3:4].

The daughter of any priest, if she profanes herself by playing the harlot, profanes her father; she shall be burned with fire [Lev. 21:9].

I will not punish your daughters
  when they play the harlot,
nor your brides when they commit adultery;
for the men themselves go aside with harlots,
  and sacrifice with cult prostitutes [Hos. 4:14].

So God created man in his own image, in the image of God he created him; male and female he created them [Gen. 1:27].

The variety of images apparent even in this limited selection of tests suggests that no single statement can be formulated concerning *the* image of woman in the Old Testament. At the same time an attempt must be made to discover what unity and coherence may exist within this plurality of conceptions. This process cannot be short-circuited by simply focusing upon the image of woman presented in the creation narratives. While those accounts have been rightly recognized to contain statements of primary importance concerning the nature of man and woman, their place within the total Old Testament literature has been virtually ignored. The task of this essay—to present the *Old Testament's view*—requires that an effort be made to locate the creation accounts within the larger testimony of the Old Testament.

One consequence of such an effort must be the recognition that Eve—or the first woman—is nowhere referred to in the Hebrew Old Testament outside the accounts of origins found in Gen. 1–4.[6] Because of this limited context of reflection upon the original woman, these too familiar passages are treated last in this essay, after a picture of woman has been formed from references contained in the legal, didactic, historical, and prophetic writings.

The diversity in the Old Testament conceptions of women may be attributed in part to differences in the time of composition of the writings and in part to differences in socioreligious context. The texts span close to a millennium in their dates of composition (twelfth to third century B.C.), while particular themes, motifs, images, and languages may derive from even earlier periods and cultures. However, since the "prehistory" of these texts can be assessed only by speculation that moves beyond adequate controls and scholarly consensus, they must be judged in their present form as products of that society known to us as Israel and as reflecting primarily the beliefs and practices of the period of their composition.[7]

That millennium saw enormous changes in the social, economic, political, and religious life of Israel. The texts on which this study is based reflect social patterns and images of semi-nomadic tribal society and of settled peasant agriculturalists. They mirror the modest and homogeneous life of the village, but also the cosmopolitan and stratified society of the capital and major cities. They embody the religious and cultural heritage of Mesopotamia and of Canaan and presuppose the differing political organization of autonomous clans, tribal league, independent monarchies, and the exile communities and subject provinces of a series of foreign imperial states. With these political changes went changes in the economic and religious life. New forms of social and religious organization emerged, new offices, new roles, new classes, new ideas and definitions—of man, and woman, of God and of his people. Some of the differences in the Old Testament conceptions of women must be attributed to these changes.

They may also be related to the individual authors, to the nature of the literature in which they are found, and to the particular situations they address. Thus prescriptive statements must be distinguished from descriptive, and attention must be given to the fact that different literary genres (e.g., myths, proverbs, admonitions and instruction, hymns, law, history, tales, sermons, and prophetic discourse) follow rules of their own and reflect in different ways and different places the changing images of the society. Hence the references considered below have been roughly grouped by literary types.[8]

THE IMAGE OF WOMAN IN THE OLD TESTAMENT LAWS

Though the laws of the Old Testament give only a partial view of the norms of ancient Israel, they are nevertheless a primary source for reconstructing the ideals and practices of that society. They are preserved, for the most part, in several large "codes," or collections, ranging in date from premonarchic (before 1,000 B.C.) to postexilic (500–400 B.C.) times.[9] Each collection, however, in its own prehistory has taken up material of different ages, and each combines laws of different types, including both "secular" law (the "law of the [city] gate"—where deliberation of cases took place) and religious law (the law of the sanctuary or religious assembly). Despite this variety, however, none of the "codes" can be considered comprehensive. All are samplers of one kind or another. All presuppose the current existence of a system that they seek not to formulate but to preserve from dissolution and destruction. Thus the laws frequently deal with areas in which changes have occurred or threaten, while the common assumptions of the society are left unspoken and must often be inferred from the special cases treated in the collections.

In many respects Israelite law differs little from that of ancient Mesopotamia and Syria. It is testimony to Israel's participation in a common ancient Near Eastern social and cultural milieu. Salient features of this shared culture revealed in Israel's laws are patriarchy (together with patrilineal descent and patrilocal residence as the usual norm), a more or less extended family, polygyny, concubinage,[10] slavery (under certain conditions), and the thoroughgoing institutionalization of the double standard. Israel's laws differ most notably from other known law codes in their unusual severity in the field of sexual transgression and in the severity of the religious laws that prescribe and seek to preserve the exclusive and undefiled worship of Yahweh, the national deity. These two unique features are interrelated, and both had significant consequences for women in ancient Israel.[11]

The majority of the laws, especially those formulated in the direct-address style of the so-called apodictic law (the style used primarily for the statement of religious obligations), address the community *through its male members.*[12] Thus the key verbal form in the apodictic sentence is the second person *masculine* singular or plural. That this usage was not meant simply as an inclusive form of address for bisexual reference is indicated by such formulations as the following:

Thou shalt not covert thy neighbor's wife [Exod. 20:19].

You shall not afflict any widow or orphan. If you do . . . then your wives shall become widows and your children fatherless [Exod. 22:22–24 (Heb. 21–23)].

You shall be men consecrated to me [Exod. 22:31].

Similarly, the typical casuistic law (case law) begins with the formula "If a *man* does X. . . ." The term used for "man" in this formulation is not the generic term, *'ādām*, but the specifically and exclusively masculine term, *'îš*. Even if one argues that these laws were understood to apply by extension to the whole community, it must be noted that the masculine formulation was apparently found inadequate in some circumstances. Thus *'ādām* is substituted for *'îš*, or the terms "man" and "woman" (*'îš, 'iššāh*) are used side by side where it is important to indicate that the legislation is intended to be inclusive in its reference.[13]

The basic presupposition of all the laws, though modified to some extent in the later period, is a society in which full membership is limited to males, in which only a male is judged a responsible person. He is responsible not only for his own acts but for those of his dependents as well. These include wife, children, and even livestock, in the extended and fluid understanding of household/property that pertained in ancient Israel (Exod. 20:17, 21:28–29). The law addresses heads of families (the family is called appropriately a "father's house" in the Hebrew idiom), for it is the family, not the individual, that is the basic unit of society in old Israel.[14]

But this definition of society as an aggregate of male-dominated households was modified in Israel by a concept of the society as a religious community, a religious community composed in the first instance exclusively of males, or perhaps originally all adult males.[15] This is the understanding of the covenant congregation, or the "people" (*'am*), Israel, addressed by Moses on Sinai:

So Moses went down from the mountain to the people [*'am*]. . . . And he said to the people [*'am*], "Be ready by the third day; do not go near a woman" [Exod. 19:14–15].[16]

It also coincides with the understanding of the "people" (*'am*) as the warriors of the community, a usage illustrated in certain texts pertaining to the premonarchic period.[17]

> The Lord said to Gideon, "The people [*'am*] are too many for me to give the Midianites into their hand" [Judg. 7:2].

> Sisera called out all his chariots . . . and all the men [*'am*] who were with him . . . [Judg. 4:13].

In both cult and war the "true" nature of Israel manifested itself.[18]

The coincidence in Israel of these two male-oriented and male-dominated systems (the sociopolitical and the religious) created a double liability for women, enforcing upon them the status of dependents in the religious as well as the political and economic spheres. Discrimination against women was inherent in the socioreligious organization of Israel. It was a function of the system. And though this systemic discrimination need not be represented as a plot to subjugate women—and thereby liberate the male ego—the system did enforce and perpetuate the dependence of women and an image of the female as inferior to the male.

This is illustrated in the legal material by laws dealing with inheritance, divorce, sexual transgressions, religious vows, cultic observances, and ritual purity. One of the chief aims of Israelite law is to assure the integrity, stability, and economic viability of the family as the basic unit of society. In this legislation, however, the interests of the family are commonly identified with those of its male head. His rights and duties are described with respect to other men and their property. The laws focus mainly upon external threats to the man's authority, honor, and property, though they may occasionally serve to define and protect his rights in relation to members of his own household (slaves: Exod. 21:20–21; children: Deut. 21:18–22; wife: Num. 5:11–31). Only in rare cases, however, are the laws concerned with the rights of dependents (Exod. 21:26–27; Deut. 21:10–14, 15–17 and 22:13–21).[19]

The wife's primary contribution to the family was her sexuality, which was regarded as the exclusive property of her husband, both in respect to its pleasure and its fruit. Her duty was to "build up" his "house"—and his alone. This service was essential to the man in order for him to fulfill his primary role as pater-familias. It was as a consequence jealously guarded. Adultery involving a married woman was a crime of first magnitude in Israelite law (Lev. 20:10; Exod. 20:14), ranking with murder and major religious offenses as a transgression demanding the death penalty—for both offenders.[20] The issue was not simply one of extramarital sex (which was openly tolerated in certain circumstances). The issue was one of property and authority. Adultery was a violation of the fundamental and exclusive right of a man to the sexuality of his wife. It was an attack upon his authority in the family and consequently upon the solidarity and integrity of the family itself.[21] The adulterer robbed the husband of his essential honor, while the unfaithful wife defied his authority, offering to another man that which belonged only to him—and that which constituted her primary responsibility toward him.

The corollary of the unwritten law that a wife's sexuality belongs exclusively to her husband is the law that demands virginity of the bride.[22] The wife found guilty of fornication is, like the adulteress, sentenced to death. In this case, however, the crime is not simply against her husband but against her father as well.

Extramarital sex is treated quite differently when a husband's rights are not involved. The man who violates an unmarried girl must simply marry her, making the proper marriage gift (*mōhar*) to her father. The only penalty he suffers is that he may not divorce her (Deut. 22:28–29).[23] Prostitution seems to have been tolerated at all periods as a licit outlet for male sexual energies, though the prostitute was a social outcast, occupying at best a marginal place in society. Hebrew fathers were enjoined not to "profane" their daughters by giving them up to prostitution, and the prophets used the figure of harlotry to condemn Israel's "affairs" with other gods.[24]

Taken together, the various laws that treat of extramarital sex evidence a strong feeling in Israel that sexual intercourse should properly be confined to marriage,[25] of which it was the essence (Gen. 2:24) and the principal sign.[26] Thus the victim of rape, the slave girl, or the female captive taken for sexual pleasure, must become or must be treated as a wife (Exod. 21:7–11; Deut. 21:10–14). Polygyny was a concession to the man's desire for more than one sexual partner, with concubinage a modification or extension of this.[27] Perhaps prostitution was tolerated as a poor man's substitute. It must certainly have been strengthened by the increasing institution of monogamous marriage as the general norm.

The laws dealing with sexual transgressions represent a strong statement of support for the family. But they are all formulated from the male's point of view, the point of view of a man who jealously guards what is essential to the fulfillment of his role in the family. Thus a jealous husband who suspects his wife of infidelity, but has no proof of it, may require her to submit to an ordeal. If she is "proved" innocent by this procedure, the husband incurs no penalty for his false accusation (Num. 5:12–31).[28] Infidelity by the husband is not considered a crime.

Divorce was recognized in ancient Israel and regulated by law, at least in the later period of the monarchy. The extent of the practice and the circumstances in which it was sanctioned remain unclear; there is no doubt, however, that it was an exclusively male prerogative. Some scholars have interpreted the "indecency" (*'erwāh*) given as the ground for divorce in the law of Deut. 24:1–4 as a reference to sexual infidelity.[29] If so, it would represent a modification of the more severe law of adultery found in Lev. 20. Others have suggested barrenness.[30] The Israelite man must commonly have understood his conjugal rights to include the right to progeny, especially male progeny. A wife who did not produce children for her husband was not fulfilling her duty as a wife. In early Israel it was apparently customary for her to offer him a female slave to bear for her (Gen. 16:1–3 and 30:1–3); or the husband might simply take another wife (where economically feasible [1 Sam. 1:2])—or secure the services of a harlot (?) (Judg. 11:1–3). In the monogamous family of the later monarchy divorce must have been a more frequent alternative. All the Old Testament references to divorce are found in sources stemming from this period or later (Deut. 24:1–4; Jer. 3:8; Isa. 50:1; possibly Hos. 2:2).

The integrity of the family was also secured by inheritance laws that insured against the alienation of family property, that essential property which assured to each father's house its "place" in Israel. The basic inheritance laws are not contained in the Old Testament legal codes, but can be inferred from extralegal references and from a number of laws dealing with special cases in the transfer of family property (Num. 27:1–11 and 36:1–9; Jer. 32:6–8; Ruth 4:1–6). Two of these concern the inheritance of daughters. Since a daughter left her father's house at marriage to become a member of her husband's family, she normally received no inheritance. (Neither did the wife, since property was transmitted in the male line.) By special legislation, however, daughters were permitted to inherit where sons were lacking (Num. 27:1–11).[31] But they were only placeholders in the male line, which was thereby enabled to continue in their children.[32] The rare institution of the levirate (the marriage of a widow to the brother of her dead husband) may also have been designed to preserve the property of a man to his name—that is, for his male descendants.

In the patriarchal family system of Israel a woman had only a limited possibility of owning property, though responsibility for managing it may have been assumed with some frequency.[33] Normally, however, a woman was dependent for support upon her father before marriage and her husband after marriage. As a consequence, the plight of a widow without sons might be desperate. Her husband's property would pass to the nearest male relative, who was apparently under no obligation to maintain his kinsman's wife. She would be expected to return to her own family. The frequent impossibility of this solution, however, is suggested by the special plea for defense of the widow that occurs repeatedly in the ethical injunctions of the Old Testament (e.g., Isa. 1:17; Jer. 7:6 and 22:3; Zech. 7:10, Exod. 22:22).

The laws also illustrate, both explicitly and implicitly, disabilities of women in the religious sphere. As noted above, the oldest religious law was addressed only to men, while the sign of membership in the religious community was circumcision, the male initiation rite. Only males were required by the law of Deut. 16:16 to attend the three annual pilgrim feasts, the primary communal religious acts of later Israel.[34] Consonant with this bias was the assumption of the cultic law that only males might serve as priests (eventually restricted to the "sons of Aaron"). However, in keeping with the understanding of the family as the basic social unit, the priest's whole household shared in the holiness of his office and in the obligations imposed by it. Thus a priest's daughter who "defiled" herself by fornication incurred the sentence of death, since she had also defiled her father by her act (Lev. 21:9; see also 22:10–14).

Women also suffered religious disability that was only indirectly sex-determined. Israelite religion, following widespread ancient practice, excluded from cultic participation all persons in a state of impurity or uncleanness—that is, in a profane or unholy state. Various circumstances were understood to signal such a state, during which time (usually limited) it was considered unsafe to engage in cultic activity or have contact with the cult. Israel's laws recognized leprosy and certain other skin diseases, contact with a corpse, bodily emissions of all types (both regular and irregular, in members of both sexes), sexual intercourse and childbirth as among those factors that caused uncleanness (Lev. 12–15). The frequent and regular recurrence of this cultically proscribed state in women of childbearing age must have seriously affected their ability to function in the cult.

An explicitly discriminatory expression—or "extension"—of the idea of ritual uncleanness is found in the law determining the period of impurity occasioned by childbirth (Lev. 12:1–5). Seven days are prescribed for a mother who has borne a son, but fourteen for the mother of a female child. Another cultic law that gives explicit statement to the differential values placed upon males and females is the law of Lev. 27:2–8, which determines monetary equivalents for vows of persons to cultic service. According to this reckoning the vow of a male aged twenty to sixty years was valued at 50 shekels, while that of a woman in the same age bracket was worth only 30 shekels.[35] Thus it appears that a male of any age was more highly valued than a female.[36]

The reason for this differential valuation must have been in large part economic, though a psychological factor is also evident. As in most premodern, labor-intensive societies, a large family was prized, since it offered a superior labor supply and flexibility and sustaining power when faced with serious threats to its existence. The large family carried more weight in the community and assured honor to its head—and to his spouse.[37] Many descendants also assured the continuity of the father's house and name. But only males could perform this task, and only males remained as primary economic contributors. On both economic (labor value) and psychological grounds the significant size of the family was reckoned in terms of males.[38] Females were necessary as childbearers and child rearers, but they always had to be obtained from outside the family—and at a price. A man's own daughters left his house to build up another man's family. Thus an excess of female dependents was a luxury and/or a liability.

The picture sketched above is not a complete portrait of woman in ancient Israel; nevertheless it does present the essential features. Additions and qualifications are necessary at many points. Most stem from sources outside the legal material and are treated later, but a few, explicit or implicit in the laws themselves, must be noted here.

The ancient commmand to honor one's parents (Exod. 20:12; Deut. 5:16) recognizes the female as the equal of the male in her role as mother. It places the highest possible value upon this role, in which her essential function in the society was represented—the reproductive function.[39] The welfare of family and society and the status of the husband depended upon her performance of that task. Consequently she was rewarded for it by honor and protected in it by law and custom which "exempted" her (indirectly) from military service and "excused" her from certain religious and civic obligations.

Laws of this type, though positive (or compensatory) in their discrimination, may be classed together with those that discriminate negatively as laws in which the sociobiological role of the individual or his/her social value (= productivity) is a significant factor in the legal formulation. In a society in which roles and occupations are primarily sexually determined, sexual discrinimation is bound to be incorporated in the laws. At the same time, however, laws that do not regard the person, but only acts or states, may be "egalitarian" in their conception.[40] This is illustrated in the old laws of Exod. 21:26 and 21:28, which assess penalties on the basis of injury suffered, without regard to the sex of the injured person. Egalitarianism, or nondiscrimination, is characteristic of most of the laws concerning ritual impurity and is a consistent feature of the laws dealing with major ethical, moral, and cultic infractions. Thus illegitimate association with the supernatural incurred the same penalty whether the practitioner was male or female (Lev. 20:27; Deut. 17:2-7), and cult prostitutes of both sexes were equally proscribed (Deut. 23:17). Illicit types of sexual intercourse, with their equal and severe penalty (death) for both offenders, may also have been viewed as belonging to this category of offenses—that is, as practices of the surrounding peoples, abhorrent to Yahweh (Lev. 18:6-18; 20:10-21; Deut. 22:30).[41]

The only statements of equal "rights" in Old Testament law are indirect and qualified. They, too, pertain to the cultic sphere. The laws of Num. 6:2 ff. and 30:3-15 (both belonging to the latest of the law codes) indicate that women, as well as men, might undertake on their own initiative binding obligations of a religious nature. Num. 30:3-15 qualifies this, however, by upholding—while limiting—the right of a husband or father to annul a vow made by his wife or daughter (thereby allowing the interests of family to take precedence over the interests of the cult).[42]

The picture of woman obtained from the Old Testament laws can be summarized in the first instance as that of a legal nonperson; where she does become visible it is as a dependent, and usually an inferior, in a male-centered and male dominated society. The laws, by and large, do not address her; most do not even acknowledge her existence. She comes to view only in situations (a) where males are lacking in essential socioeconomic roles (the female heir); (b) where she requires special protection (the widow); (c) where sexual offenses involving women are treated; and (d) where sexually defined or sexually differentiated states, roles, and/or occupations are dealt with (the female slave or captive as wife, the woman as mother, and the sorceress). Where ranking occurs she is always inferior to the male. Only in her role as mother is she accorded status and honor equivalent to a man's. Nevertheless she is always subject to the authority of some male (father, husband, or brother), except when widowed or divorced—an existentially precarious type of independence in Israel.[43]

THE IMAGE OF WOMEN IN PROVERBS

References to women in the Book of Proverbs are limited and stereotyped. Three major types dominate: (1) the mother, (2) the wife, and (3) the "other/foreign" woman.

The woman is portrayed in Proverbs as a teacher, whose instruction a son is commended to heed. In this role she is typically ranked alongside the father (in the normal parallelism, father . . . mother [1:8, 6:20]), though in the instruction of 31:1-9 it is the mother alone who is mentioned as author of the advice. Elsewhere mother and father together represent the parents, who take delight in a wise son (10:1, 15:20, 23:24-5) and to whom honor is due (20:20; see also Exod. 20:12). In Proverbs, as in the laws, the mother is described in positive terms only. But here it is clear that the term "mother" does not refer primarily to her reproductive function but to her role in the nurture and education of the child. She is not merely the womb that bears a man but a source of wisdom essential to life.

The wife is depicted in a more varied and ambivalent light. The "good" wife, or "woman of quality," is described as the crown of her husband (literally, "master") and is contrasted with the wife "who brings shame," that is, who degrades rather than enhances her *husband's* reputation (12:4). She is also described as prudent (19:14) and gracious (11:16), with honor as her gain (11:16). Obtaining such a wife is deemed a gift from God (18:22, 19:14).

A detailed list of the activities and skills of the "wife of quality" is found in the acrostic poem of Prov. 31:10-31. Here we see a woman of the upper class, presumably from the time of the monarchy. She is manager of the household, directing the work of servants and seeing to it by industriousness and foresight that her family is well provided for in food and clothing. She engages in business transactions, apparently on her own initiative, buying land, setting out a vineyard with the profits reaped from her undertakings, and manufacturing clothing. She is generous and ready to help the poor and needy, possesses strength and dignity, is a wise and kind teacher. In consequence of her good character and her provision for her household, her husband is "known in the gates." He trusts her and profits by her. Recognizing his good fortune ("a good wife is far more precious than jewels" [vs. 10]), he praises her in company with his children. In this portrait the sexual attributes of the wife are not mentioned. She is characterized in wholly nonsexual terms as provisioner of home and husband, toward whom all her talents and energies appear to be directed. In this role "she does him good" (vs. 12).

A "bad" wife is also described in Proverbs, but not as a general type. She is identified primarily in terms of a single trait—contentiousness. The contentious woman is likened to a "continual dripping on a rainy day" (19:13, 27:15). It is better to live in a desert land or in the "attic" than to share a house with her (21:9, 19, 25:24). The bad wife is characterized as "one who causes shame" (12:4); she disgraces not only herself but her husband—which is the main point of the admonition.

In only one passage in Proverbs is the wife described as a sexual partner. The counsel to fidelity in 5:15-19 contrasts the "wife of your youth" with the "loose woman," advising the husband to "drink water from [his] own cistern" and not to let his streams flow for others (vss. 15-16; cf. Sir. 26:19-21). He should let her breasts delight him and be intoxicated always (and only) by her love. The ideal portrayed here is that of sexual pleasure identified with marriage; and it is monogamous marriage that is presumed.

This counsel to fidelity is paralleled by the admonition to beware the seductions of the "other/foreign" woman—the most common word concerning women found in the instruction literature (2:16, 5:3-6, 5:20, 6:24, 7:5, 22:14, 23:27-28; cf.31:3; Eccles. 7:26; "harlot": 7:10-23, 29:3). Characterized by the RSV translation as a "loose woman" or "adventuress,"[44] she is depicted as luring men to destruction (her house/path leads to death: 2:16, 5:3; cf. 7:22, 9:18, 22:14, 23:28) by her "smooth talk" (2:16, 5:3, 6:24, 7:5; cf. 7:21). She accosts her victim in the squares and marketplace and lies in wait at the street corners to entice him into her house (7:12, 9:14-15).

The loose woman in Proverbs personifies "folly" and is contrasted with the "wise woman," or "wisdom" personified (9:1-6, 13-18), while association with harlots and love of wisdom describe antithetical behavior (29:3). But wisdom is not simply the antithesis of the folly characterized by the loose woman; it is the antidote. Throughout these admonitions runs the idea that wisdom will protect a man from the disaster she portends.

As the counsel to fidelity shows, the condemnation of the "strange" woman and her ways is not a condemnation of erotic love but of its abuse—its employment as the tool of an unscrupulous woman, out of the man's control.[45] In Proverbs sex is subordinated to wisdom. It is not extolled, like wisdom, as a good in itself, but is praised and appreciated only when channeled and controlled within the confines of marriage. The control essential to its enjoyment (in this view) must be exercised by the man, to whom the words of advice are directed.[46]

Two references are made to an adulteress. In 6:26 she is compared with the harlot; while the latter takes a man's money ("may be hired for a loaf of bread"), the former may cost him his life. The thought, which is amplified in the following verses, is that adultery constitutes theft, and the wronged husband will avenge himself upon the adulterer. In 30:20 the adulteress is portrayed as an amoral woman who refuses to acknowledge her guilt: "She eats, wipes her mouth, and says, 'I have done no wrong.' "

The wisdom sayings and instruction literature of Proverbs give a somewhat different picture from that of the laws. A more homogeneous social milieu is assumed here: urban, monogamous, and relatively comfortable. It is a literature of the upper class predominantly; and it addresses men exclusively. A man's success depends upon heeding his parents' instruction and obtaining a good wife. His fortune is seen as determined in large measure by his relationships with women, relationships determined both by accident (providence) and choice. Practical and moral suasion are employed here to guide that choice. The evils he is warned to recognize and avoid apparently carry no legal penalties. Adultery is redressed only by a husband's jealousy, and prostitution, conceived as the primary threat to a man, appears to flourish unsanctioned. Woman are not chattel in Proverbs, nor are they simply sexual objects; they are persons of intelligence and will, who, from the male's point of view expressed here, either make or break a man. The man must learn to recognize the two types and abstain from harmful relationships. He does so by means of wisdom, wisdom gained first and foremost from his parents—of both sexes.

THE IMAGE OF WOMAN IN THE HISTORICAL WRITINGS

The historical writings amplify greatly the picture of woman obtained from the laws and proverbs. The descriptions they offer of the women of their day and of the legendary figures of times past add richness of color and detail to the outline already sketched, confirming in many instances the initial broad strokes, but demanding reassessment and the redrawing of some features. The composite portrait contained in these writings displays variety and ambiguity in the image and status of women not apparent in the laws.

Despite the quantity and diversity of the references and despite occasionally vivid and individualistic portrayals, the great majority of women referred to in the historical writings appear in reality more as types than as "real," historical individuals. Even where a woman (or a woman's name) has attained legendary stature, where force of character or peculiarity of vocation or position has procured a unique place for her, or where an author following his own sympathies or artistic aims has lingered over a particular female figure, the roles played by women in these writings are almost exclusively subordinate and/or supporting roles. Women are adjuncts to the men: they are the minor (occasionally major) characters necessary to a plot that revolves about males. They are the mothers and nurses and saviors of men;[47] temptresses, seducers and destroyers of men;[48] objects or recipients of miracles performed by and for men;[49] confessors of the power, wisdom, and divine designation of men.[50] They are necessary to the drama, and may even steal the spotlight occasionally; but the story is rarely about them.[51]

Only Deborah and Jezebel stand on their own feet—possibly also Miriam and Huldah. But far too little evidence survives about them to assess their actual position in Israelite society or their representativeness. The Queen of Sheba also appears as an independent figure, but, this legendary foreigner cannot be placed within the context of Israelite society; she is introduced only as an exotic rival of Solomon in wisdom and wealth, a figure who must have the status of an equal or near equal in order to test him and acknowledge his superiority (1 Kings 10:6-9).

The two most common images of woman in the historical writings are those of wife and mother, frequently combined when the woman is portrayed as a historical individual. Other types, such as the barren woman, the foreign woman, and the widow, represent subtypes or modifications of these two. Identification of women by occupation or profession other than wife-mother is found in a small though significant group of references.

The primary characteristics of the mother in the historical writings are compassion, solicitousness, and jealousy for her children; she also appears (indirectly) as a teacher or determiner of character and as a figure of authority and respect—usually in conjunction with the father (i.e., as co-parent). (See 1 Kings 19:20; 1 Sam. 22:3-4; Judg. 14:2-3, 16.) The special feeling of the mother for her child—and for a son in particular—is given frequent and varied expression: the mother of Sisera suppressing her premonition of disaster with self-assuring visions of the scenes of victory (Judg. 5:28-30); Rachel weeping inconsolably for her children (Jer. 31:15); Rizpah in mourning vigil over the bodies of her dead sons, moving both heavens and king to acts of sympathy (2 Sam. 21:8-14); the "true" mother in Solomon's famous test revealing herself by her willingness to give up her own child to another woman in order to save his life (1 Kings 3:16-27); the wealthy woman of Shunem cradling her dying child in her lap (2 Kings 4:18-20).[52] These adumbrations of the pietà show no distinctions of social status. Queen mother (Judg. 5), concubine (2 Sam. 21), and harlot (1 Kings 3) all exhibit in these representations a common maternal feeling, a special and enduring bond with the fruit of their womb that makes the loss of children a woman's greatest loss. In this bereavement all women are alike and all are equal.

Suffering also marks the other primary image of the mother, the image that predominates in the prophetic writings. It is the woman (Isa. 13:8, 21:3, 26:17; Jer. 4:31, 30:6, 48:41; Mic. 4:9-10; etc.) in childbirth who has fixed the poet's attention. Her pangs represent for him the greatest anguish known to man, and their vivid portrayal expresses the deep pain and turmoil of all persons in extremity. The male writer sees in them not only pain but helplessness and fear, so that he contrasts the woman in childbirth with the warrior, strong and courageous, and mocks the fearful army by calling them women (Nah. 3:13; see also Jer. 30:6).

Socioeconomic factors certainly played a role in Israelite attitudes toward children and toward motherhood. The loss, or threatened loss, of an only child, especially when the woman was a widow, might be an occasion for panic as well as pathos, for the mother's life and/or welfare might depend upon the life of the child (2 Sam. 14:2-17; 2 Kings 4:18-25). The barren woman shared with the woman made childless by bereavement the same precarious future. In addition, however, she suffered immediate social and psychological deprivation for her failure to achieve motherhood.

Barrenness was a shame and a reproach in Israel (Gen. 30:1-2, 22-23; 1 Sam. 1:3-7, 11); it was interpreted as divine punishment or at least a sign of divine displeasure (Gen. 16:2, 20:18, 30:26; 1 Sam. 1:5; 2 Sam. 6:20-23). It brought gloating derision from other women, especially from co-wives who had proved their fertility (1 Sam. 1:6; cf. Gen. 30:1, 8 and 16:4), and it threatened the woman's status as a wife (Gen. 30:1-2; 15-20). The barren woman was deprived of the honor attached to motherhood—the only position of honor generally available to women, representing the highest status a woman might normally achieve. Consequently the expression "a mother in Israel" could be used metaphorically to describe a woman or a city (grammatically feminine) of special veneration[53] (Judg. 5:7; 2 Sam. 20:19), and the reversal of a woman's fortunes might be depicted in the image of a barren woman giving birth to seven sons (1 Sam. 2:5). But motherhood brought more than honor, more than security and approval of husband and society. It brought authority. It offered the woman her only opportunity to exercise legitimate power over another person.[54] In the hierarchically organized patriarchal family, in which women of every age and status were subject to the authority of a male superior, this must have been a significant factor in a woman's desire for children. The only relationship in which dominance by the woman was sanctioned was the mother-child relationship.

The authority of the mother over her children is illustrated by relatively few examples, most of which pair the woman in this role with the father (there is no common term for "parents"). Her influence on the character of the child is indicated only indirectly in the historical writings.[55] Direct power and influence over the life of the child may be seen in a mother's dedication of a child to cultic service (1 Sam. 1:11), in her efforts to affect the choice of a son's wife (Gen. 27:46-28:2; cf. Judg. 14:3), and in attempts to have her own son (in a polygynous family) or a favorite son declared principal heir (Gen. 21:10; 1 Kings 1:15-20).

The interests of a mother in the fortunes of her son are especially apparent when he is a potential heir to the throne, since his ascension elevates her to the honored position of queen mother. This position appears to have been a recognized institution, at least in the Judaean monarchy in which the queen mother was referred to by the title "[great] lady" *(gᵉbī rāh)*, and her name was included in the regal formulas of each king.[56] The deference accorded the queen mother is illustrated in the account of Bathsheba's reception by her own son, King Solomon (1 Kings 2:19). The potential power inherent in the position is evidenced in Athaliah's successful seizure of the throne (and six-year reign) on the death of her son, King Ahaziah (2 Kings 11:1-3).

The primary category to which all these women belong is that of wife. It is the comprehensive category that describes the destiny of every female in Israel.[57] Yet the image of the wife is an elusive one. As wife alone she is all but invisible. Neither eulogized nor deprecated, she rarely appears unless thrust forward by some peculiarity of family, character, position, or deed or unless required to link two male figures (1 Kings 3:1, 4:11; 2 Kings 8:18; 1 Sam.

18:20–27; 2 Sam. 3:13 ff.) or two generations of males.⁵⁸ Wives figure most prominently in the patriarchial narratives, primarily because they are by their nature *family stories,* created and/or employed for the purpose of creating a history based upon a genealogical scheme. In these tales the wives are seen primarily, though not exclusively, as mothers, while daughters appear only as wives—accounting for external relations.⁵⁹ Wives also figure in the tales incorporated into the books of Judges, Samuel, and Kings and play significant parts in the court narrative of David, which also partakes of the story genre. But they are almost totally lacking in the "political" history of Joshua-Kings, except for an occasional word of warning about the danger of foreign wives—or of marriage with foreigners in general.

Hebrew has no special term for "wife," but uses the common word for "woman" *('iššāh)* in genitive "construct" with the name of the husband ("woman of NN")—a formula that can be applied to a concubine *(pilegeš)* as well as a full wife. There is also no specific term for "husband," though the relational term *ba'al* ("master") was frequently used in the corresponding genitival construction instead of the general word for man *('îš)* ("man/master of NN"). This usage is indicative of the nature of the husband-wife relationship in Israel. It suggests why the marriage relationship was appropriated as a metaphor for the covenant relationship of Yahweh to Israel, a relationship characterized by intimacy—and subordination.

The Hebrew wife has often been characterized as essentially a chattel. And in some respects this view is justified. Wives, children, slaves, and livestock described a man's major possessions (Exod. 20:17). Wives, or simply "women," are found in lists of booty commonly taken in war (Deut. 20:14; cf. Deut. 21:10–14; 1 Sam. 30:2, 5, 22; 1 Kings 20:3, 5, 7; 2 Kings 24:15), and wives are counted—along with concubines, silver, and gold—as an index of a man's wealth (1 Kings 10:14–11:8).⁶⁰ In these and other references in which mention of a wife serves simply to complete a reference to family, household, or possessions, she is usually anonymous and is not formally distinguished from other property.

Despite legal, economic, and social subordination, however, wives were not simply property. They could not be bought and sold, and it is doubtful that they could be divorced without substantial cause. Later law required a formal writ of divorce (Jer. 3:8; Isa. 50:1; see also Deut. 24:1–4).⁶¹ But the rights of concubine and wife were not fixed by contract (as in later Jewish practice) or by any surviving law. They were presumably customary and negotiated by agreements between the husband and the wife's family. A wife's rights and freedom within the marriage would depend in large measure upon the ability of her family to support and defend her demands. Thus the daughter of a rich and powerful man could expect better treatment as a wife. Her status as a wife would reflect the status of her family.

The wives depicted in the historical writings exhibit a wide variety of characteristics, yet a coherent picture is not difficult to obtain. The good (ideal) wife is well illustrated by Abigail, wife of Nabal (and later of David)

(1 Sam. 25:2-42), with supplementary traits drawn from other examples. She is intelligent, beautiful, discreet, and loyal to her husband (despite his stupidity and boorish character in the case of Nabal; see Jer. 2:2). Prudent, quick-witted, and resourceful, she is capable of independent action, but always acts on her husband's behalf. The good wife does not attempt to rule her husband, nor does she openly oppose him. She defers to him in speech and action, obeys his wish as his command, and puts his welfare first. She employs her sexual gifts for his pleasure alone and raises up children to his name.[62]

The Old Testament historical texts portray the woman as intelligent, strong-willed, and capable, and especially endowed with the gift of persuasion (see 2 Sam. 14:1-20, 20:16-22; 2 Kings 1:11-31). As a consequence, she was also potentially dangerous to the man, since, if she wished, she could use her sexual and intellectual gifts to undo him or to gain her own ends at his expense. Against this female power not even the strongest man could stand (Judg. 16:4-21). The danger presented by the woman to the man was greatest where the relationship was most intimate, namely, in marriage. And there the threat had a second root. For the wife was always to some degree a stranger in her husband's household, an outsider who maintained bonds of loyalty to her father's house and who might consequently be used by her kinsmen. This danger from the wife's external connections was magnified if she was a foreigner, a fact that is reflected in a demonstrated preference for ingroup marriage (Gen. 24:1-4, 26:34-35 and 27:46-28:5; Judg. 14:1-3)[63] and in numerous laws, preachments, and "case histories" that warn against the disastrous consequences of marriage with foreigners (Judg. 3:5-6; Ezra 9-10, esp. 9:1-2; Num. 31:15-16; see also 1 Kings 11:1-8).

The historical writings rarely portray the wife as a sexual partner or lover, though they assume (as ideal) a high correspondence between love and marriage.[64] In general they give too little information about the marriage relationship to permit substantial conclusions. Israelite marriage was essentially an arrangement between two families, usually initiated by the man or his parents (Judg. 14:12; Gen. 34:1-4, 8; Gen. 24). This male locus of the initiative is illustrated by the verbs and the actions that commonly describe the incorporation of the woman into the new household: she is "given," "taken," "sent for," "captured"—and even purchased, in the case of a slave wife. Some texts suggest, however, that the woman's role was not wholly passive or lacking in initiative (2 Sam. 11:2-5; 1 Sam. 18:20),[65] that she could refuse an "offer" (Gen. 24:5, 57-58) and make demands of her own (Judg. 1:15). Though a woman could not divorce her husband, the mistreated wife might simply return to her father's house (Judg. 19:2).[66]

Polygyny is a recurrent feature in the narratives of the premonarchic period, and efforts to assure equal rights to multiple wives (and/or their children) are evidenced both in the laws and the narratives (Gen. 30:15; Deut. 21:15; cf. Gen. 29:30-31).[67] By the eighth century B.C., however, and probably a good deal earlier, monogamous marriage was clearly the norm and the ideal.[68] It is presupposed by Hosea's use of the marriage analogy to speak of

Yahweh's exclusive and demanding relationship to Israel. This metaphor of Israel as the bride or wife of Yahweh, which is also employed by Jeremiah (2:2, 3:1, 4, 6–10) and Ezekiel (ch. 16), is always found in the context of an indictment of Israel's unfaithfulness. She is described in alternating images as harlot and adulteress, though the language of harlotry predominates.[69] The choice of the latter metaphor may be related to the conspicuous feature of cult prostitution in Canaanite religion,[70] but the fact that it becomes prominent only in the eighth century while dominating later theological language suggests that it should be correlated with the use of the bride/wife motif.

The harlot was the primary symbol of the double standard in Israel. She was in every period a figure of disrepute and shame (Gen. 34:31; Judg. 11:1; 1 Kings 22:38; Isa. 1:21; Jer. 3:3; Ezek. 16:30), at best merely ostracized, at worst (in circumstances involving infidelity and defilement) subjected to punishment of death (Gen. 38:24; see also Lev. 21:9). But the harlot was also tolerated in every period by men who incurred no legal penalties—or even censure—for the enjoyment of her services (Gen. 38:15 ff.).[71] Her status and image gained nothing, however, from this tolerance. The two best-known stories of harlots (Rahab, who saved the spies of Joshua [Josh. 2:1–21], and the two harlots who presented their case to Solomon for judgment [1 Kings 3:16–27]), often cited as evidence of their acceptance in Israelite society, also presuppose their low repute. In both accounts the harlot heroines are made to demonstrate in their words and actions faith, courage, and love that would scarcely be expected of the average upright citizen and thus is all the more astonishing and compelling as the response of a harlot—that member of society from whom one would least expect religious and moral sensitivity. They serve the storyteller's purpose in much the same way as does the poor widow—that member of society whose existence is most precarious and who is consequently a favorite for depicting great faith and generosity.

In addition to the primary roles of wife and mother, women appear in the historical writings in a number of other, more specialized roles, occupations, and professions. Except in the case of the harlot, these are normally not alternatives to the wife-mother role, but represent complementary or supplementary activities. Foremost among these is the prophetess, of whom the Old Testament canon knows three by name:[72] Deborah (Judg. 4:4–16), in the premonarchic period; Huldah (2 Kings 22:14–20), in the late monarchic period (seventh century B.C.); and Noadiah (Neh. 6:14), in the postexilic period (fifth century B.C.). Too little is known about any of them to speak confidently or in detail about women in this role. But some general statements are possible. None of the authors who introduce these figures into their writings gives special attention to the fact that these prophets are women—in contrast to Old Testament commentators, who repeatedly marvel at the fact.[73] Despite some compounding in the traditions relating to Deborah and consequent difficulty in interpreting her role(s), the descriptions of the words and activities of the three named prophetesses coincide closely with those of their male contemporaries in the same profession. There is no evidence to suggest that they were considered unusual in this role.

But if female prophets were accepted in Israel, they were also rare. No collections of their words have survived among the prophetic books of the Old Testament—at least none identified by a woman's name. Discrimination might be argued, discrimination that was broken through only in the periods of national crisis, when the three known prophetesses emerged. But Israel knew other crises when no women arose to prophesy. Most likely, female prophets were always few in number, and presumably not associated with guilds and disciples who might have collected and preserved their oracles. Their exercise of their calling must have been at best part-time, at least during child-rearing years, and may not even have begun until later in life.[74] For the Israelite woman such a profession could only have been a second vocation. Early marriage with its demand upon women of a primary vocation as wife and mother would have excluded the early cultivation of the gift of prophecy.[75] But its authenticity was not subject to doubt on the basis of sex. Prophecy was a charismatic gift, and as such, no respecter of persons. The person who had a message from God would be sought out, heeded, and accorded recognition if his/her message was understood to have validity. The message authenticated the messenger. The Old Testament accounts of female prophets are testimony to Israel's recognition that God could and did communicate with females as with males, entrusting to them messages of vital concern to the whole community.

Prophecy may be contrasted with cultic service as the only religious profession generally open to women throughout Israel's history. There are some suggestions that women did function in the cult of the earlier period: the portrayal of Miriam alongside the priestly figure of Aaron in Num. 12:1-2,[76] and reference to "serving women" in the tent of meeting (Exod. 38:8; cf. 1 Sam. 2:22). But any early openness to women in the cult seems to have been foreclosed by a strong reaction during the period of the monarchy to the religious practices of Canaan, especially to fertility rites that involved female cult personnel. Thus the women referred to in association with the cult of the monarchic period are all described as illicit practitioners of non-Israelite rites.[77] Reference to female (temple) singers is found in works of the postexilic period (Ezra 2:65; Neh. 7:67, 2 Chr. 25:5), though they are associated there with the pre-exilic (and exilic) cult. This service, performed both by males and females, was in any case clearly auxiliary to the main cultic office.

Women were also recognized as practitioners of occult arts ("mediums" and "sorceresses"), though they were banned in Israel together with their male counterparts (1 Sam. 28:7; Exod. 22:18; cf. Deut. 18:10; 2 Chr. 33:6).[78] The functioning of women in this capacity is analogous to that of the prophetess; the profession was in both cases based upon the exercise of a special "gift."[79] A related specialization of women, though less distinctly "professional," is illustrated by the "wise woman" (2 Sam. 14:2, 20:16). The women so designated seem to have been noted especially for astute counsel, persuasiveness, and tact.[80] Their reputations, built upon demonstrated skill or the efficacy of their words, might extend well beyond the boundaries of their own towns (2 Sam. 14:2). Thus wisdom was recognized as a gift that, like prophecy, was in no way restricted to men. It was honored and sought out whenever it manifested itself.

Other professional specializations of women (all part-time) were more closely related to the primary roles played by women in the society. These include professional mourners, or "keening women" (Jer. 9:17), midwives (Gen. 35:17, 38:28; Exod. 1:15–21), and nurses (Ruth 4:16; 2 Sam. 4:4; Gen. 24:59, 35:8; Exod. 2:7; 2 Kings 11:2; 2 Chr. 22:11). Female slaves or servants, particularly those of the king's household, were apparently trained in a variety of specialties, as "perfumers," bakers, and cooks (1 Sam. 8:13). In addition to these, female singers are mentioned as entertainers in 2 Sam. 19:35 and Eccles. 2:8.

The hundreds of references to women in the historical and prophetic books present many and varied images. Central to most, however, and underlying all are the images of wife and mother (or wife-mother), with the harlot as a kind of wife surrogate or anti-wife image. These two primary roles defined most women's lives, though in varying degrees and with varying meaning, depending on the size, structure, function, and status of the particular family. That is, for most women the sexually determined roles of wife and mother also described their *work,* since the division of labor was based almost exclusively on sex. In the limited roles open to her, however, the ancient Israelite woman contributed more substantially and more significantly to the welfare of family and society than the modern Western woman in the same role. She was not simply a consumer but a primary producer or manufacturer of much of the essential goods required by the household; in addition, she had charge of the basic education of the children. She apparently had considerable power, authority, and freedom of decision in this important realm that she managed,[81] and she could make significant decisions about her own life and that of her children (by religious vows, specifically)—though her husband (or father) was granted veto power in some cases.

While in certain limited circumstances a woman might be thought of only as a sexual object (Judg. 5:30; 1 Kings 1:2–4; see also Gen. 19:8; Judg. 19:24), nonsexual attributes predominate in most Old Testament references to women; in particular, intelligence, prudence, wisdom, tact, practical sense, and religious discernment recur in numerous characterizations of women, often replacing or preceding descriptions of physical appeal. The women of these texts are not depicted as silly or frivolous, except perhaps in the prophetic caricatures of the harlot or of the pampered ladies of the upper class (Isa. 3:16–4:1; Amos 4:1). Women may be portrayed as unscrupulous, but they are rarely, if ever, characterized as foolish.

Despite the family locus of most of the woman's activity, the knowledge and abilities of women were not confined to the family circle or limited to expression in strictly female activities. The possession of special gifts and powers beneficial to the larger community was recognized and acknowledged in women as well as men, with the result that some professional specialization was possible for a few women along with their primary occupation of wife and mother. Most of these involved the exercise or employment of special kinds of knowledge: practical wisdom (the "wise women" of Tekoa and Abel); ability in deciding legal disputes (Deborah as judge); power to receive divine communications (Deborah as prophetess, Miriam, Huldah, and possibly Noadiah); and ability to call up spirits from the dead (the medium of Endor).

Judged by economic criteria or in terms of interest in continuity of house and name, the woman of the Old Testament was deemed inferior to the man. In the realm of the cult her activity was restricted. And from the viewpoint of the law she was a minor and a dependent, whose rights were rarely acknowledged or protected. These several systems in which woman's roles and status have been described represent in large measure cultural givens which cannot be ignored. They mark the base line for any discussion of the image of Old Testament woman; but they do not describe all situations or all points of view.[82] In many situations the woman was in fact and/or in theory an equal, despite manifold and combined pressures to treat her as an inferior.[83] She was recognized as equal (or superior) in the possession and employment of certain kinds of knowledge and in religious sensibility and sensitivity. In love she might also be an equal,[84] and could exploit (Judg. 16:4–22) as well as suffer exploitation. She was in general charged with the same religious and moral obligations as men, and she was held responsible for her acts.[85] Man in the Old Testament recognizes woman as one essentially like him, as a partner in pleasure and labor, one whom he needs, and one who can spell him weal or woe. From his point of view—the only point of view of the Old Testament texts—the woman is a helper, whose work as wife and mother is essential and complementary to his own. In a sense she completes him— but as one with a life and character of her own. She is his opposite and equal.

THE IMAGE OF WOMAN IN THE ACCOUNTS OF CREATION

Against the multitude of Old Testament references to women, actual and ideal, contemporary and past, the Bible has set two accounts of the first woman. Each belongs to a larger creation "story," and each shares many common features with similar accounts from the ancient Near East. In the mythopoeic world that was Israel's cradle, accounts of origins did not simply explain what happened in the beginning; they were statements about the nature of things as they "are" (or as they should be). In the recitation or reenactment of the myth the original drama of creation was repeated and the present order maintained through re-creation. Thus the Babylonian account of the creation of the world was a central feature in the liturgy of the New Year celebration, serving to insure that the forces of order (the created, present order) would prevail for another year over the forces of chaos (associated especially with the spring floods), and the account of the creation of mankind was the text of an incantation, recited by a midwife to assure a good birth.[86] The primary concern of a myth is not with the past but with the present.

Israel's accounts of creation draw heavily upon the myths current at their times of composition. The same basic themes occur, the same developments —even the same language is used in some cases. But the meaning of the biblical accounts differs radically from that of their prototypes, because the context of their employment is different. The Genesis accounts are no longer myth, but history—or a prologue to history. Creation has become the first of a series of events that extend on down to the writer's own day. That intervening period is never wholly collapsed in the biblical view. Creation stands always and only at the beginning—remote, complete, unrepeatable, the first of God's works. The God who performed that work continues to labor and to act, but in new ways. History is the drama of the interaction of God and the world that he created, the world to which he gave a life and a will of its own. The creation stories tell of man's place in that created world of nature and of his-her essential character. This is spelled out in Gen. 3 by an account of the first acts taken by that autonomous creation.

While the two creation accounts of Genesis differ markedly in language, style, date, and traditions employed, their basic statements about woman are essentially the same: woman is along with man, the direct and intentional creation of God and the crown of his creation. Man and woman were made for each other. Together they constitute humankind, which is in its full and essential nature bisexual.

The well-known word of the Priestly writer (P) in Gen. 1:27 is eloquent and enigmatic in its terseness: "God created mankind *('ādām)* in his own image . . . male *(zākār)* and female *(neqēbāh)* he created them." Two essential statements, and that is all. No exposition is given, no consequences stated, only the prefatory statement in verse 26 proclaiming the intentionality of this creation. The first statement has as its primary point the assertion that the human animal is distinguished from all others in being modeled or patterned after God himself ("in his image" is an adverbial clause describing the process of fashioning). In contrast to the other creatures, man's primary bond is with God and not with the earth; man's purpose in creation is to rule the earth. The second major statement is an expansion and a specification of the first. It does not relate a subsequent act of creation but only a subsequent thought of the narrator; and it does not explicate the meaning of the image. It simply makes the essential point that the genus, *'ādām,* is bisexual in its created nature.[87] There is no androgynous original creation in P.

The older, Yahwistic (J) account of creation in Gen. 2–3 is of a wholly different genre—a narrative. Here the art of the storyteller is seen in a work of great beauty and pathos, a narrative of beguiling simplicity, filled with yearning, compassion, and dramatic tension—the "soul" version of creation, in contrast to the cool, cerebral account of the priestly writer. In J's account the creation of man *('ādām,* deliberately ambiguous here)[88] is the beginning and the end of the story, with all of God's other creative acts bracketed in between. Here God's primary creation remains incomplete until, by a process of trial and error which populates the earth with creatures, that one is finally found for whom the man has waited and longed, namely, woman. With the creation of woman, man is finally his true self, a sexual and social being *('îš)*. J's account is a drama of the realization of the divine intention in creation.

The man in this creation drama recognizes the woman as his equal, as a "helper fit for him" (2:18). She is emphatically not his servant. "Helper" *(ēzer)* carries no status connotations, while the Hebrew expression translated "fit for" means basically "opposite" or "corresponding to." The statement simply expresses the man's recognition (the story is told from his point of view exclusively) that he needs her and that she is essentially like him. She is the "thou" that confronts him and the other that completes him. The story represents her as derived but not inferior. The fact that she is formed directly from the man is meant to emphasize the essential identity of man and woman. Woman is not a separate order of creation like the animals, each of which was created, like *'ādām,* from the earth. The scientific and symmetrical language of P, with his concept of one genus *('ādām)* in two sexes ("male" and "female"), is not used here, but the same idea is expressed in dynamic and dramatic language. The essential oneness of the two distinct persons (identified by the sociosexual terms "man" and "woman") is proclaimed in the man's recognition of and emotional response to the fact: "This one at last is bone of my bones and flesh of my flesh"![89]

In J's work the drama of creation forms part of a larger story of origins. The Yahwist's word about man and woman in their essential nature is not finished with the simple statement of their existence or of the "original" state of their existence; it is spelled out, as the account of creation itself, in the language of events. The true nature or character of man and woman is revealed only as they begin to interact with each other and with their environment as feeling, rational, and responsible beings. In this action/interaction their latent capacity for judgment, for disobedience, and for self-interest is actualized, and the pain and frustration that the author knows as a mark of human existence becomes a part of the history of the first couple and of mankind.

The author of this well-known and often misinterpreted account shared the age-old notion that misery is a sign of sin or guilt. Mankind's suffering was therefore conceived as punishment. The crime that the Yahwist depicts is the crime of disobedience, a crime committed by both man and woman.[90] The order of their transgressing is unimportant for the question of their guilt; the consequences of their acts (knowledge, shame—and pain) are described only when *both* have eaten the forbidden fruit.[91] The manner and the explanation of the responses of the pair is also inconsequential for the question of their guilt and punishment. Each individually and knowingly disobeys the divine command. But the way in which the response of each is portrayed may be understood to indicate something of the author's—or the tradition's—view of the character of man and woman. The woman in this portrait responds to the object of temptation intellectually and reflectively, employing both prac-

tical and esthetic judgment. The man, on the other hand, passively and un-
questioningly accepts what the woman offers him.[92]

In their common act of disobedience the man and woman become fully
human, identifiable with men and women of the author's own day. Losing
their original innocence, they become knowledgeable, responsible, and subject to pain and the contradictions of life. The "punishment" described in the
poem of 3:14–19 simply represents the characteristic burdens and pain of
man and woman as traditionally perceived in Israelite society. Ample testimony is offered by other Old Testament texts that the pangs of childbirth
were viewed as the most common and acute pain suffered by women. They
were at the same time indicative of the woman's primary and essential work
in the society—procreation. By no means an inclusive definition of her work,
it was nevertheless that to which all other work and all other roles were subordinated. The man's pain is described analogously as related to his work—
gaining a living from the soil. The work of the pair is here simply described as
the work of survival, biological (the work of the female) and material (the
work of the male). But it is not simply the pain of toil that the author
describes, it is the pain of alienation in that toil. The ground, the source of the
man's life and work, has become his antagonist rather than his helper, and
the man, the source of the woman's life and work, has become her ruler
rather than her friend.[93]

The words of Gen. 3 are descriptive, not prescriptive. J's story of the first
couple is heavily etiological; it offers an explanation for the primary characteristics of the human situation as Israel knew it. And this minimal statement
shows substantial agreement with the fuller account gleaned from other Old
Testament writings. But it is not normative. Israel did not use this legend to
justify the existing order or to argue for woman's subordination. She did not
need to. She understood the states described—for both man and woman—as
givens. J's view was larger than the common one, however, and marked by a
profound sense of wrongness of this order: given, but not willed, the tragic
consequence of man's exercise of his-her God-given reason and will. This was
also not J's final word about the human situation. In its present setting the
story has lost much of its etiological significance, for it is no longer simply a
description of things as they are but is the first act in a world-historical drama
that the historian has created as the context for Israel's history. For J, the
central figure in that drama is Yahweh, God, who continues to will, to act,
and to create. Adam and Eve are the beginning of his works, not the end.
Yahweh goes on in a play of many acts to create a new people and to enter into
a new relationship with them.

It is with that same understanding of the dynamic character of history that
the prophets speak of God's continued action in their own day, an action
portrayed typically as judgment upon a people who had replaced theological
norms with sociological ones (security, status, wealth, etc.). Neither the
prophets nor the theologians, such as J and P, succeeded in wholly escaping
the culturally determined understanding of male and female roles that they

had inherited. And their greater egalitarianism should not be too sharply contrasted with the overtly discriminatory laws and practices recorded in other Old Testament literature, since there, too, male-dominated language and structures disguised to a considerable degree the actual power, freedom, and respect of women in the society—respect based largely, though not solely, upon complementarity of roles. But distinctions of all types lend themselves to exploitation and to the creation of differential ethical standards. The historians of the Old Testament look behind the present state of division and alienation to an original and intended equality and harmony in creation, while the prophets focus upon the existing state of inequality and exploitation, addressing it with a concept of justice manifested in judgment—justice understood as a new act that God will perform to purge his creation, an act of retribution and rectification. The proud will be abased (Isa. 4:17), and the "men of distinction" will head the exile train (Amos 6:4–7); but she who is now an outcast in men's eyes will not be punished for her sin (Hos. 4:14).

Some among the prophets saw beyond the present day, beyond the present order and the impending judgment. They looked to a new act of God in creation, to a new order with new possibilities for human existence, radical possibilities that would abolish the present alienation and exploitation based on distinctions of species, age, sex, and social status. These prophetic visions speak of the knowledge of God in every heart, requiring no class of teachers to expound it (Jer. 31:31–34); of God's spirit free to all, so that old and young, male and female, bound and free shall prophesy (Joel 2:28–29); of lion and lamb, wild beast and helpless child living together in harmony and without fear (Isa. 11:6–9); and the reversal of the prevailing sexual roles: "a woman protects a man" (Jer. 31:22).[94]

The statements concerning the first man and woman must be read together with the statements of God's interaction with the world of his creation, his promises and his demands, his sending of saviors and spokesmen (both male and female), his judgments, his forgiveness and his new creation. Israel's best statements about woman recognize her as an equal with man, and with him jointly responsible to God and to cohumanity. That Israel rarely lived up to this vision is all too apparent, but the vision should not be denied.

NOTES

1. The term "patriarchy" is appropriate to designate such a society, but it is avoided here because of the fact that widespread indiscriminate use of the term has led to the blurring of significant social and cultural distinctions among various "patriarchal" societies. Whatever the terms employed, however, the characterization of ancient Israel as a male-centered and male-dominated society is meant as a descriptive statement. The aim of this essay is not to decry or to advocate but simply to record the perceptions of women found in the Old Testament writings and to analyze them in terms of their sources and consequences in ancient Israelite society and religion. Spec-

ulation concerning origins is renounced, and *Nachgeschichte* (the subsequent history of the ideas) is left to students of more recent periods in the tradition.

2. Exceptions to this latter rule are invariably deemed noteworthy by commentators. The extent and the meaning of gynomorphic language applied to the Deity has still to be assessed. See Phyllis Trible, "Depatriarchalizing in Biblical Interpretation," *Journal of the American Academy of Religion* 41 (1973):31–34. Whether the Old Testament use of feminine metaphors for God (always "mother" images, never "wife") is the product of Israelite monotheism or is a more general characteristic of language about certain types of deities (e.g., creator gods or tutelary deities) also needs to be explored.

3. See E. Deen, *All the Women of the Bible* (New York: Harper, 1955).

4. All citations are from the Revised Standard Version of the Bible (RSV) unless otherwise noted.

5. The translation is that of Marvin Chaney in "Israel's Earliest Poetry" (Ph.D. diss., Harvard, June 1974), based on a new understanding of the Hebrew; used by permission of the author.

6. Two references occur in later writings contained in the Greek canon: Tob. 8:6 and Sir. 25:24; cf. 2 Cor. 11:3, Tim. 2:13, and numerous references in the Pseudepigrapha (see index to R. H. Charles, ed., *The Apocrypha and Pseudepigrapha of the Old Testament in English,* Vol. II [Oxford, 1913]). References to Adam are more frequent, but only Job 31:33, in the Hebrew Old Testament, refers to him apart from genealogies and the original creation stories.

7. Thus all speculation concerning an "original" matriarchy is rejected in this essay as inconsequential for the period and the society under consideration.

8. A chronological arrangement, while desirable, has not proved feasible, because of the frequent impossibility of determining dates for individual texts. Of the four groupings created for this study (laws, proverbs, "historical" texts, and accounts of origins) the third is, unfortunately, too omnibus. Based primarily upon references in the historical books, it incorporates some material from the prophetic writings, which have received no separate treatment because of limitations of time and space. The third section of the canon, apart from the book of Proverbs, has also suffered neglect for the same reasons, though occasional references from that corpus have found their way into the discussion at places. These omissions are acknowledged with regret.

9. M. Noth, *The Laws in the Pentateuch and Other Studies* (Philadelphia: Fortress Press, 1966), p. 8.

10. Polygyny and concubinage appear to have been more common in early Israel and are not mentioned in later texts, except in connection with the royal household.

11. Israel's view of the proper place of sex and the harsh penalties laid upon sexual offenders presumably reflect a deliberate antithesis to the practices of the surrounding peoples (specifically Canaanites), but they may also be rooted in Israel's peculiar understanding of herself as a "holy people." Sexual offenses are religious offenses in Israel. They are not private matters but matters of vital concern to the whole community. See Noth, *Laws,* p. 55.

12. The whole community was bound by the law, however, sometimes explicitly and sometimes implicitly. E.g., the absence of any mention of the wife in the sabbath law (Exod. 20:10; Deut. 5:14), though sons and daughters and male and female slaves are listed, suggests that the wife was treated as one person with the man ("you," second person masculine singular), who is addressed by the law. (Whatever the interpretation, she is clearly not an independent person in this formulation.) In the

postexilic community the inclusive reference is made explicit; the assembly *(qāhāl)* convened to hear the reading of the law is described as consisting of "both men and women and all who could hear with understanding" (Neh. 8:2–3). In this late period the concept of the religious assembly itself has apparently been broadened to include women.

13. Compare Lev. 13:9 *('ādām)* and Lev. 13:38 *('îš, 'iššāh)* with Lev. 13:40 *('îš)*. See also Num. 6:2 *('îš, 'iššah)*.

14. Compare the idea, familiar even in contemporary Western society, of the citizen as property owner and/or family head. On the family and the place of the family in ancient Israel see J. Pedersen, *Israel,* I-II (Copenhagen, 1926; Oxford, photo reprint, 1964), pp. 46–96. See also R. de Vaux, *Ancient Israel: Its Life and Institutions* (New York: McGraw-Hill, 1961), pp. 19–40, 53 ff. Israelite family life and institutions are illuminated by references to recent and contemporary Middle East families in R. Patai, *Sex and Family in the Bible and in the Middle East* (Garden City, N.Y.: Doubleday, 1959).

15. Circumcision as the sign of the covenant (Gen. 17; Lev. 12:3; cf. Exod. 12:48) makes this explicit. This practice is in other societies a "rite of passage," performed at puberty and signaling the initiate's entry into the tribe as a full, adult member with all attendant privileges and duties, including marriage. See Exod. 4:26 and Josh. 5:2–7.

16. I.e., the men are to keep themselves "holy." Sexual intercourse was considered defiling in Israel. See Lev. 15:18; 1 Sam. 21:4–5; 2 Sam. 11:11.

17. The *'am* is first and foremost a kinship group—in a patriarchal society, "the sons of NN." It may be used in an inclusive sense as a designation for the whole community, including women (Judg. 16:30), or it may be restricted to the men, the community at worship and at war (Pedersen, *Israel,* I-II, 54–56).

18. See the evolutionary interpretation given to this phenomenon by Herbert Richardson, *Nun, Witch, Playmate* (New York: Harper & Row, 1971), p. 14: "What happened in ancient Israel was that the male group displaced the tribe as the primary social institution. It displaced the tribal family into a secondary position so that the family existed within the male group rather than vice versa."

19. The laws of Num. 27:1–11 and 36:1–9 are not concerned with the daughter's rights but with the father's, while the prohibition of Lev. 19:29 is a cultic proscription, not a defense of a minor's rights.

20. See Lev. 18:20. M. Noth, *Leviticus* (Philadelphia: Westminster Press, 1965), p. 150, sees the reference to the woman in 20:10 as an addition to the older law, representing a later interpretation, namely, that the woman is to be viewed not only as the object but as a fellow subject in the proceedings for breach of marriage. The actual practice and presuppositions reflected in historical, prophetic, and proverb texts point to a milder punishment, at least in the periods represented by those texts. See Jer. 3:8 and Hos. 2:2–7.

21. Incestuous sexual relationships, which were judged with equal severity (Lev. 18:6–18 and 22:10–21), may have been understood in a similar way as threatening the complex relationships of rights and authority within the extended family, and thus the order and stability of the family. See Pedersen (*Israel,* I-II, 65), who stresses the psychological aspect of these offenses. For another explanation, see below.

22. Likewise unwritten, but implied in Deut. 22:13–21.

23. See Exod. 22:16–17 and 2 Sam. 13:11–16. Genesis 34:1–7; 25–27 expresses a more severe attitude toward rape. In no case, however, are the girl's interests regarded by the law.

24. See Note 69 below. There is considerable fluidity in the metaphorical use of the terms for adultery and prostitution to describe idolatrous worship and "idolatrous" political relationships (see Hos. 2:2; Jer. 3:8–9; Ezek. 16:30–35). Israel's relationships with other gods and nations are usually described as harlotry, thus emphasizing the brazen and habitual character of the act. This figure presumes that the "marriage" bond with Yahweh has long been broken or disregarded. The figure of the adulteress lays more stress upon the "marital" relationship and the exclusive nature of its claim.

25. The common ancient Near Eastern understanding of the sexual act as holy (or at least potentially so) was emphatically rejected by Israel, though the Canaanite terms *qᵉdēšîm* (m.) and *qᵉdēšôt* (f.) ("holy/consecrated ones") were used to refer to illicit cult prostitutes. Sex in Israel belonged to the order of the profane, not the holy. Its proper uses included both enjoyment and procreation. Emphasis upon the former accounts for such literature as the Song of Solomon and also explains Israel's concession (in the male interest) to prostitution. For the most part, however, extramarital sex was discouraged for practical, moral, and religious reasons.

26. Sexual union as the sign of marriage is suggested by the designation of the wife as her husband's "nakedness" (Lev. 18:7, 14, 16). See Pedersen, *Israel*, I–II, 65.

27. In some circumstances concubines were treated much as wives (Judg. 19:2–9), though they did not have the full rights of free persons. There is some indication that the king's concubines were inherited by his successor, at least in the early days of the monarchy (2 Sam. 16:21–22; see also 2 Sam. 3:7–8 and 1 Kings 2:13–22), but this practice (which may have extended to all the king's wives on occasion [2 Sam. 12:8]) was probably a special feature of the royal household. See Patai, *Sex and Family,* pp. 41–43.

28. See the later law of Deut. 22:13–21, however, where the husband who slanders his wife with a false accusation of unchastity incurs a double penalty—corporal punishment and a fine.

29. See Patai, *Sex and Family,* p. 120 (citing Hos. 2:4 ff.; Isa. 50:1; and Jer. 3:8, all prophetic similes) and Gerhard von Rad, *Deuteronomy* (Philadelphia: Westminster Press, 1966), p. 150.

30. Pedersen thought this to be the most common reason for divorce, but could refer only to Gen. 29:34 as evidence (*Israel*, I–II, 71). Patai (*Sex and Family,* p. 120) notes that divorce for barrenness is never mentioned, but argues that the emphasis on procreation and the insecurity of the childless woman indicated in the patriarchal stories make barrenness a most probable cause for dismissal. In this connection it should be noted that the several conspicuously barren wives of the Old Testament all bear eventually (e.g., Sarah, Samson's mother, Hannah, and the "great" woman of Shunem). Their barrenness is a literary device that retards the action of the story, heightens anticipation and suspense, and gives a miraculous character to the birth. In most cases the real interest of the story is in the child that is finally born. Attention is focused upon him through this device. His existence is made to depend upon a special act of God in opening his mother's womb.

31. This special provision for female inheritance was further modified in the interests of tribal solidarity and the preservation of tribal land by a specification that the inheriting daughter marry within her father's tribe (Num. 31:1–9). From this it is clear that the daughter's husband was regarded as the real heir.

32. The property would otherwise pass to the father's nearest male relative and thus be lost to his name.

33. Von Rad (*Deuteronomy*, p. 107) notes that the "updating" in Deut. 15:12-17 of the old law of the Hebrew slave (Exod. 21:1-11) presupposes that the woman has in the meantime become capable of owning landed property and is thus able to sell herself into slavery for debt just as a male. Cf. 2 Kings 8:3-6 (though in this case the property claimed by the widow might possibly belong to her minor son).

34. Women may have been excused from this obligation in view of their more highly deemed—and confining—services to home and children. But the fact that they were dispensable in the practice of the cult would support any notion of their inferiority in that realm. Note, however, that against the law of Deut. 16:16, the custom of a single annual visit to a local sanctuary is described in 1 Sam. 1:3-8 (from the period of the Judges), in which the man was regularly accompanied by his wife or wives. Only the man sacrificed, however (vs. 4).

35. Further gradations by age and sex make it clear that it was labor value that was reckoned by this table of equivalents.

36. See Neh. 5:1-5, in which the impoverished Jews complain that in order to pay their debts they are being forced to sell their sons and daughters into slavery—and that some of their *daughters* have *already* been enslaved. The relatively greater expendability of females may also have found expression in female infanticide by abandonment, a practice attested among contemporary peoples of the Middle East and suggested for the Old Testament period by the image of the female foundling in Ezek. 16 (Patai, *Sex and Family*, p. 136).

37. See the blessing of Gen. 24:60: "[May you] be the mother of thousands of ten thousands."

38. See, for example, Gen. 46:8-27, in which wives are explicitly omitted from the tally given in vs. 26, and only one daughter is included among the 70 persons counted! See also Neh. 7:6-37, in which the number of persons returning from the exile is counted by families of men only.

39. Cf. Gen. 3:20, in which Eve's name is interpreted to mean "mother of all living."

40. It must be noted, however, that inequality of opportunity may make equal responsibility discriminatory in effect.

41. For a different interpretation, see Note 21, above.

42. The widow and the divorcée are alone free to make binding vows, since they alone bear no immediate responsibility to a male whose interests might be hurt by the action (vs. 9).

43. The prostitute, as a pariah, existed for the most part outside the primary authority structures of the society.

44. The Hebrew word used in most of these passages means simply a "stranger" or "foreigner"; only in 7:10-22 and 29:3 is the professional term "harlot" *(zōnāh)* employed. Scholars dispute whether the woman in question was actually a foreigner or simply a woman whose mores made her a social outcast and therefore an "outsider" (see W. McKane, *Proverbs* [Philadelphia: Westminster, 1970], pp. 285, 287). Some see in the descriptions of her a reference to a devotee of a foreign cult and thus a cult prostitute (ibid., pp. 284, 287). For the discussion here it is sufficient simply to designate her as the "other" woman, contrasting her with the wife. The admonitions against association with her are not religious or ethical but "practical." "She'll be the death of you," they predict.

45. See B. Childs, *Biblical Theology in Crisis* (Philadelphia: Westminster, 1970), pp. 186-90.

46. Ibid. In striking contrast to Proverbs, the Song of Solomon extols erotic love for itself as the most prized of human possessions. Its power and beauty are expressed in a relationship of complete mutuality, controlled neither by the man nor by the woman, and therefore (necessarily) apart from the marriage relationship with its structure of male domination and female subordination. In the Song the lovers alternate in initiating acts of lovemaking. There the woman is portrayed as seeking out her beloved in the very same language used by Proverbs to describe the aggressive enticement of the harlot—but with no hint of condemnation. For further comparison of the parallel passages in Proverbs and Song of Solomon, see Childs, *Biblical Theology in Crisis*, pp. 190–96. See also Trible, "Depatriarchalizing in Biblical Interpretation," pp. 42–47.

47. E.g., Jehosheba (2 Kings 11:2), Rahab (Josh. 2:1–21), Moses' mother and sister and Pharaoh's daughter (Exod. 2:2–10).

48. E.g., Delilah, Jael, the woman of Thebez (Judg. 9:53), Jezebel.

49. E.g., the widow of Zarephath (1 Kings 17:8–24; See also 2 Kings 4:1–7), the "great" woman of Shunem (2 Kings 4:8–37), Sarah, Samson's mother (Judg. 13:2–3).

50. E.g., Rahab (Josh. 2:8–13), Abigail (1 Sam. 25:28–29), the Queen of Sheba.

51. The exceptions, Ruth and Esther, are both encountered in works of a distinct literary genre, the novella, in which they are the central figures.

52. See also Hannah in her yearly visits to the child she had vowed to the service of Yahweh (1 Sam. 2:19) and Moses' mother boldly trusting in the compassion of another woman to save the life of her own son (Exod. 2:1–10).

53. Or, perhaps, one who protects, saves, or succors. Cf. Isa. 22:21 and Job 29:16.

54. Indirect or "underhanded" means of exercising power are the devices commonly employed by women in patriarchal societies. See Pedersen, *Israel,* I–II, 69.

55. In a rare acknowledgment of a woman's effect upon the political and moral life of the nation, the Deuteronomic historian judges the sibling kings, Ahaziah and Joram, in terms of the (evil) example of both parents, Ahab and Jezebel (1 Kings 22:52; 2 Kings 3:2, 13; see also 2 Kings 9:22 ff.) The widespread practice of cursing a man by cursing his mother may also be an acknowledgment of the mother's influence on the child. Compare Saul's reproach of Jonathan in 2 Sam. 20:30, "you son of a perverse, rebellious [= possibly "runaway"] woman," with the English deprecations "s.o.b." and "bastard."

56. The name of the queen mother is omitted from the formulas of two southern kings, Ahaz (2 Kings 16:2) and Jehoram (2 Kings 8:16–18). Jehoram's *wife's* name is given, however, which is unique in these records (she was the daughter of the notorious northern king Ahab). Normally the king's wives were of no interest to the official chroniclers or to the Deuteronomic historian. Only David's wives are known, because of the roles they play in the extended biographical history of David's rise and reign.

57. Exceptions only confirm the rule. See Judg. 11:37–40.

58. Rachel and Leah, together with their servants Bilhah and Zilpah, are in the first instance simply mothers of the twelve "sons of Israel," and are only secondarily fleshed out with individual characteristics as wives of Jacob. See M. Noth, *Das System der zwoelf Staemme Israel* (Stuttgart: Kohlhammer, 1930), p. 7.

59. See Gen. 34 (Dinah and Shechem—though the relationship failed to result in marriage, according to this account).

60. Despite the moralistic interpretation given by the editor, the enumeration of Solomon's wives and concubines was certainly intended to suggest his great means as well as his great appetite.

61. Even concubines and female prisoners of war taken as wives had limited rights, by virtue of their sexual union with the master, that distinguished them from ordinary slaves—or other property.

62. A case of extreme loyalty in this respect is exemplified by Tamar, who in desperation to fulfill her duty to her dead husband lures her father-in-law to impregnate her (Gen. 38). See Pedersen, *Israel,* I–II, 79.

63. Even half-sibling marriage seems to have been tolerated in David's time (2 Sam. 13:13), though later law prohibits it (Lev. 18:9, 20:17). See Pedersen, *Israel,* I–II, 64–65.

64. Compare Judg. 16:1 ff. and 16:4 ff. A man "goes in to" or "lies with" a harlot, but he is expected to take the woman he "loves" as a wife. Where he does not, the relationship is clearly an abnormal one (2 Sam. 13:1 ff. and 15–16). The major exception to this rule is found in the Song of Solomon, where love is extolled without thought of marriage.

65. In this case Michal's obvious love for David is exploited by her father, Saul, who makes an exorbitant demand as the bride price.

66. But a father might also step into the marriage and give a neglected daughter to another man (Judg. 15:1–2; 2 Sam. 25:44).

67. See Patai, *Sex and Family,* p. 44.

68. The major exception is the royal family (2 Kings 24:15).

69. The harlot as a metaphor for Israel is found in Isaiah, Hosea, Micah, Jeremiah, Ezekiel, and Nahum. The verb *zānāh* ("to play the harlot") is used to speak of apostasy in Judg. 2:17, 8:27, 33; Exod. 34:15–16; Deut. 31:16; Lev. passim; Num. 15:39, 25:1; Hos. 1:2, 4:12 and 15, 9:1; Jer. 2 and 3 (4 times); Ezek. (15 times); Ps. 106:39; 1 Chr. 5:25.

70. Note, however, that our chief source of information is the highly biased accounts of Hebrew prophets and theologians, who frequently describe all non-Yahwistic worship as simply prostitution.

71. See Patai, *Sex and Family,* p. 147. Patai argues that attitudes toward harlotry became more lenient in the later period of the monarchy, by which time harlots were an accepted part of urban society (1 Kings 22:38; Isa. 23:16; Exod. 16:24–25; Jer. 3:2, 5:7; Prov. 2:16; 5:3, 8; 6:24–25; 7:5, 10, 11, 12; 9:14, 15; Sir. 9:3–9; 19:2;26:9). His argument that later Hebrew attitudes toward prostitution involved no essentially moral judgment is supported only by citations from Prov. and Sir., both of which represent a genre of literature characterized by practical rather than moral judgments.

72. The enigmatic unnamed prophetess *(hannᵉbîāh)* of Isa. 8:3 is excluded from this analysis since nothing is known about her prophetic activity and her identity and role are disputed.

73. "Why did a chief priest inquire of a woman? And who was she? The question has been asked since at least Kimchi's day" (J. A. Montgomery, *A Critical and Exegetical Commentary on the Book of Kings* [Edinburgh: T. & T. Clark, 1960], p. 525).

74. Deborah and Huldah are both referred to as married women; it is generally assumed that all women of marriageable age and condition were married.

75. This pattern may be contrasted with that of the prophet Jeremiah, who knew himself to have been called as a "youth" (Jer. 1:7) and whose vocation obliged him to

renounce normal family life (16:2). Other male prophets are known to have been married. But marriage was never considered a vocation for males, as it was for females, and would generally have interfered far less with their "choice" and exercise of a profession.

76. Her "punishment" (vss. 9–14), in which she is made cultically unclean and excluded from the holy camp, also suggests a cultic interpretation of her role. In Exod. 15:20 she is described as a prophetess, but the meaning of the term for this early period is disputed. See Mic. 6:4.

77. These included the *qᵉdēšāh* ("holy/consecrated" woman) (Deut. 23:18 [Heb.; Eng.: vs. 17]; Hos. 4:14; cf. Gen. 38:21, 22) and devotees of the Canaanite mother goddess, *Asherah* (2 Kings 23:7). In addition to cult personnel, women are also singled out as worshippers of foreign gods in Ezek. 8:14 (women weeping for Tammuz, a Sumerian god, whose death was annually lamented by women) and Jer. 7:18, 44:17–19 (women making offerings to the Queen of Heaven, a female deity of Assyro-Babylonian or Canaanite provenance). It is significant that the syncretistic rites with which Israelite women are explicitly connected are associated solely with female deities or with deities whose cult was predominantly female. See T. Jacobsen, *Toward the Image of Tammuz and Other Essays on Mesopotamian History and Culture* (Cambridge: Harvard University Press, 1970), pp. 29, 73–101. Compare also the practice of Elephantine Jews, whose cult included a female deity. See R. Patai, *The Hebrew Goddess* (New York: Ktav, 1967), and W. F. Albright, *Archaeology and the Religion of Israel*, 2d ed. (Baltimore: Johns Hopkins University Press, 1946).

78. The old law of Exod. 22:18 refers to "sorcery" alone of the magic arts, citing it along with bestiality and sacrifice to other gods (vss. 19–20) as practices demanding death. The clause concerning sorcery stands out from the rest by its feminine formulation ("you shall not permit a sorceress to live"). The practice was presumably considered a female specialty at that time. The later list of seven proscribed types of magic or divination in Deut. 18:10 is entirely masculine in its formulation (and probably inclusive in its intended reference). By this time, at least, sorcery and necromancy were clearly not regarded as exclusively female arts. See *Interpreter's Dictionary of the Bible (IDB)*, ed. G. A. Buttrick (New York and Nashville: Abingdon, 1962): I. Mendelsohn, "Magic, Magician," III, 223–25; "Familiar Spirit," II, 237–38; and "Divination," I, 856–58.

79. See Mendelsohn, "Magic," *IDB*, III, 224. The "gift" employed by the magicians consisted largely of special techniques, knowledge, or talismans that could be learned or acquired and passed on. As a consequence, sociological factors, including sexual distinctions, might be expected to play a larger role in the identification and classification of these manipulative artists than of the charismatics (prophets).

80. The adjective "wise" as applied to both men and women covers a wide variety of meaning and usages. While it frequently designates a class of counselors found in the court (see Judg. 5:29, where it describes the ladies who counsel the queen mother of Sisera), it may also be used of persons skilled in various arts and crafts (such as the keening women of Jer. 9:17 or the spinners of Exod. 35:25), and may be used in an even broader sense of one who is prudent, discerning, capable in solving problems and in counseling profitable action. See S. H. Blank, "Wisdom," *IDB*, IV, 852–61.

81. As a consequence, it is women who are the saviors of men when the threat is felt within the house or living quarters, the woman's province. See Exod. 1:15–2:10; Josh. 2:1–7, 15–16; 1 Sam. 19:11–17; 2 Sam. 17:17–20; 2 Kings 11:1–3. But the home can

also be a battlefield if the woman chooses (Judg. 4:18–21, 5:24–27; see also Judg. 16:4–22).

82. Notably absent from all these references to women is any conscious reflection upon woman's place and being in society, including any theological interpretation of her purpose and portion.

83. The actual status of women is exceedingly difficult to judge in a patriarchal and patrilineal society, where systematic bias in favor of the male characterizes language, laws, and most formal structures and relationships. The compensation that necessarily exists in such a system is rarely visible in formal documents and is hard to assess. Whether formalized or informal, it generally serves to re-enforce the system by making it bearable for those discriminated against. Thus the honoring of the mother is a necessary compensation, since the mother's role is an essential one to the maintenance of the society. Informal compensation is represented in the "underhanded" tactics used by women to get their way. But significant attempts were also made in Israel, against prevailing cultural norms, to recognize women as equals in the covenant community. Glimpses of this can be seen in some of the laws and especially in prophetic judgments (Hos. 4:14) and prophetic eschatology (Joel 2:28–29 and Jer. 31:32).

84. See especially the Song of Solomon. Phyllis Trible ("Depatriarchalizing in Biblical Interpretation," p. 47), sees in these poems an expression of Paradise regained, of the possibility of nonexploitative male-female relationship.

85. See, for example, the nondiscriminating laws and Isa. 3:16–4:1, 32:9–12; Amos 4:1–3; Jer. 44:20–30.

86. The text as it has been transmitted is complete with rubrics addressed to the midwife and the pregnant woman.

87. The P formulation implies an essential equality of the two sexes. But its implications were only partially perceived by the priestly writer, whose own culturally determined ideas concerning appropriate roles and activities of men and women generally fail to reflect this insight. Thus male genealogies and an exclusively male priesthood dominate the rest of his work.

88. '*ādām* in Gen. 2 is both the genus and the first individual, who appears as male and not androgynous, though the woman is formed from him. That he is conceived as a man in this naive version is clear from the statement concerning his loneliness (2:18); but he is not yet sexually aware. His true nature as a sexual being is manifest only as he is confronted by the woman. Thus he is at once truly male and truly man when joined by woman.

89. Gen. 2:23; see also vs. 24. In J's view the sexual act that unites man and woman is the sign of an intended and original union. The man and woman do not simply exist alongside one another as partners in work—though they are that; nor is their sexuality created primarily for procreation (as in P). They are created *for* each other, to complete each other. Their union in "one flesh" is a reunion. The fact that this is expressed by a man from his point of view should not obscure the basic intention and significance of the statement.

90. The crime is devoid of malicious intent, and is "softened" still further by the introduction of an instigator external to the man and woman. The serpent is the seducer, and he is made to bear the blame and punishment for the seduction. But the pair who succumbed to his tempting must pay the consequences of their common sin, the sin of disobeying the divine command.

91. The sequence of events in the narrative and the roles of the man and woman in it

derive, presumably, from a much older story, whose basic characters and meaning have been radically transformed in this Israelite appropriation of it. See J. S. Bailey, "Initiation and the Primal Woman in Gilgamesh and Genesis 2-3," *Journal of Biblical Literature* 89 (1970): 137-50.

92. In Trible's characterization ("Depatriarchalizing in Biblical Interpretation," p. 13) the man's one act is "belly-oriented," while the response of the woman is that of a theologian. I doubt that the minimal description given here of the man's response can support substantial inferences concerning the character of the man. According to Trible, "the man is passive, brutish, and inept," in contrast to the woman, who is "intelligent, sensitive, and ingenious" (ibid.) The man acts here in his normal role at mealtime: he accepts the food offered to him by his wife. No qualification is necessary of the general rule of male dominance in a patriarchal society. More important, however, is the fuller description of the woman's response. It, too, presents a picture that is consonant with the portrait of woman found in other Old Testament sources, where she is indeed "intelligent, sensitive, and ingenious."

93. The ambiguity in human existence and the interrelatedness of pleasure and pain are more clearly shown in the case of the woman, since her work is described in relational terms. That definition is given in the culture and the tradition with which the author had to work. The focus of this passage is upon the couple's work, not upon the male-female relationship. Consequently the asymmetry in the description of the man's and the woman's lot should not be overinterpreted. The man's desire for the woman is quite as prominent in this author's mind (2:23-24) as the woman's desire for the man (3:16).

94. Literally, "a woman encompasses a man." See W. L. Holladay, "Jer. 31:22b Reconsidered: 'The Woman Encompasses the Man,'" *Vetus Testamentum* 16 (1966): 236-39.

16

CAROL L.MEYERS

The Roots of Restriction: Women in Early Israel

During the Late Bronze Age, wars, famines, and plagues—especially the latter as attested in Exodus and Numbers—caused severe depopulation in Canaan. In that situation women of child-bearing age were at a premium. The new peasant movement of Israelites placed high priority on women as child bearers and as agricultural laborers alongside the men. At about the same time, when goddesses were excluded from the religious cult of Israel, women were excluded as cult servants, perhaps also affected by the urgent need for all able-bodied women to bear children.

Under the monarchy, after the original demographic crisis had passed, the former socioeconomically functional significance of women's restricted roles was perpetuated and hardened into fixed practice based on ideological subordination of women to men. This theologized endorsement of an older functional necessity was passed along to later Jews and Christians as normative tradition and behavior.

Reprinted from *The Biblical Archeologist* 41 (1978): 91–103.

Perhaps the most significant advances in biblical studies in recent years have come about through scholarly efforts to understand the emergence of earliest Israel in terms of its social dynamics. These studies of the origins of Israel, which benefit from anthropological analyses of group behavior and social change, have made it no longer possible to contemplate the beginnings of biblical tradition as theological history or as a kind of history of holiness. To do so, however pious the motives, becomes instead an ultimately irrelevant and perhaps irreverent exercise because it precludes full understanding. Rather, attempts at reconstructing any period in antiquity must involve a sensitivity to and consideration of the entire historicocultural spectrum which affects human development, individually or in groups.

In a sense, the archaeological investigation of the Near Eastern past has fostered and facilitated such a contextual approach to scriptural study by making available the nonbiblical materials essential for understanding the matrix of Israelite life. Ironically, however, the very archaeological revolution which brought about this new approach also became a serious stumbling block for reaping all its benefits. Archaeology, enamored of and elated by its intimate contact with objects of the past, felt itself in possession of the key to that past.

For a long time, the exclusive preoccupation with material relics and political history (with little or no attention given to the social dynamics of the people who left these relics) limited the analysis of the archaeological data. But now, aided by the insights of modern social science, archaeologists are in a better position to understand how ancient societies operated and what social and ideological changes occurred in the ancient world. Such investigation of the process of social change has been particularly important in the study of ancient Israel's early formation and development.[1]

If the emerging interest in reconstructing all dimensions of a crucial era in human history is to be expressed in thorough and balanced investigation, then it cannot do what so much of social history in the past has done, systematically omit or slight roughly half of humanity. In the natural and social history of any groupings of people, that slighted half—women—controls certain unique and critical functions within society. As the Harvard social historian David Herlihy puts it, women "carry the new generation to term, sustain children in early life, and usually introduce the young to the society and culture of which they will be a part. [In other words,] women begin the processes through which human cultures strive to achieve what their individual members cannot—indefinite life, immortality."[2]

Moreover, an examination of women's social position, while eminently cogent and important for historical studies of any period of our past, becomes extraordinarily pertinent and imperative in consideration of biblical society, especially in its formative and idealistic period. That specific period is the one in which the biblical community was formed, a community bound in covenant with God through the leadership of Moses and developing its characteristic and radical new way of looking at the world and living in that world in the few centuries after Moses and before the Davidic monarchy. Archaeologically, this formative period coincides with the closing decades of the Late Bronze Age and the beginning of centuries of the Iron Age in Palestine.

Concern for the evaluation of the social history of women during the early Israelite experience arises from the fact that this is precisely the period in which one of the major—if not *the* major—transitions occurred in the history of the position and role of women in the world. Some three thousand years of male dominance in Western civilization, and in particular in religious institutions, have clouded our vision of the prebiblical past and have led to the belief that the exclusion of females from regular leadership, at least in public and/ or religious life, has been the norm in human history. Further, it is difficult, psychologically and emotionally, to deal with the fact that the liberating principles of Mosaic Israel and the egalitarian society which it set about to establish turned out to be the very force which caused a dramatic turnabout in the history of women. Yet, as more and more material from the ancient world becomes available to us, the realities of the status of women in ancient societies, including their role in religious life, are becoming invisible behind the double veils of time and misapprehension. It is being discovered that the position and role of women in society were very different in some crucial areas than what they became subsequent to the beginnings of Israel.

For this reason, historical investigation of women in the formative period is crucial—otherwise, it is too easy to fall prey to the same process which has led to the gradual later misogynistic interpretations of early biblical tradition. It is needed to correct anachronistic interpretations as well as statements taken out of context and used dogmatically and authoritatively. Moreover, this investigation is necessary to identify long-ignored functional aspects within a particular setting of what appears in the finished scriptural product as God-given sanctions.

Perhaps this point should be illustrated before proceeding. The story of the Garden of Eden provides a parade example. The creation and early activity of male and female in the stories of the glorious garden of Genesis 2 and 3 present no evidence for any theory of subordination or inferiority of women.[3] If anything, the opposite is true. Read on its *own terms*, the story shows a primordial male who appears passive and submissive. This ancient tale must have been understood this way for centuries as part of Hebraic literature.

Yet somewhere and gradually along the line, complicated sociohistorical processes which cannot be traced here turned the edenic paradigm upside down. By the late biblical period, a rash of religious literature, produced by Jewish groups and nascent Christianity, took considerable pains to demonstrate that Eve was significant not as the source of life but rather as the source of death and evil;[4] and, therefore, women needed to be controlled and dominated by their male relatives.

Centuries of such distortions resulting from later interpretations of biblical traditions involving women can come to an end, it seems, only by going back to the very beginnings of Israelite life, where it all began, for it was then that there occurred a shift in sexual roles and meanings that was to have a profound and longlasting impact.

In order to appreciate this shift, it is important to consider the Near Eastern cultures from which Israel emerged. The Bronze Age religious ideology against which early Israel rebelled was the product of a millennia-old pattern. The pantheons of divine beings exalted in Near Eastern antiquity represented those forces in nature upon which humanity was dependent but which humanity could not bring under its control. Fertility was an underlying concern. Fertility cults in which mankind could create mechanisms for exerting control of or at least influence over the capricious natural world helped resolve humanity's helplessness and anxiety in the face of rainfall or lack of it, sunshine or lack of it, blight or lack of it. The great goddesses and great gods mated, producing a union of earth and sun/rain necessary for productivity. Cultic rehearsals of this union, while tantalizingly vague and distant in the face of our modern inquiries, seem to have taken place within the context of what is described by the suitably ill-defined phrase "fertility cult."

The particular Canaanite manifestations of such religious ideologies are generally described in terms of their relationship to the impoverished—in comparison to Egypt or Mesopotamia—resources of Syria-Palestine. Thus, the emphasis tends to focus on fertility of the soil. Yet, concerns with human fertility should not be excluded from the parameters of pagan religion. Particularly in the land bridge of Syria-Palestine, and in contrast to the relative stability and tendency toward over-population in the Nile and Tigris-Euphrates Valleys,[5] frequent outbreaks of violence added to the natural insecurity or continuity of human life. The repeated prophetic warning in the Bible about the triple threat of death through famine, pestilence, and the sword bears with it an urgent concern for the continued existence of any sociopolitical group. Warfare, famine, and disease were inseparable forces posing continuing threats to human existence. At certain times of upheaval, population losses far exceeded natural increment. Depopulation—i.e., decline in population—was a recurrent fact, archaeologically demonstrable.[6] Population growth, or the replenishing of the population, was a societal aim, expressed in Israel's national literature, in the face of considerable environmental odds at various points in ancient Palestinian history.[7]

The biological experiences of women in Bronze Age society were undoubtedly keyed to this fact. The fertility cults, however crucial for a concept of agrarian productivity, were no less crucial for notions of human reproduction. In this respect, the Near Eastern high-goddesses are featured in the role of the Great Mother who some believe was the supreme deity in the ancient world until the third millennium.[8] She was revered and worshipped as the creator of all life, as the female principle which was the source of life. The mystery of birth and of all creation and thus of human existence itself rested in the female power. From as early as the Old Stone Age onward (ca. 30,000 B.C.E.), material expressions of religious convictions by which mankind sought to establish links to that divine creative power have been found.[9] In the various places of Stone Age habitation, the naked female figurines with exaggerated sexual features are found, attesting to the cult of the Great Goddess. By the time of the great Bronze Age cultures of the Near East, the supreme Mother Goddesses were joined by or in some cases superseded by male deities. The societal changes connected with this transition have yet to be explored fully, since they are difficult to retrieve from the limited documents of antiquity.

Though it seems that a patriarchal system replaced the primary role of women in primitive agricultural-village economies, reflected in and by the Great Mother Goddess, the primacy of the female role nonetheless persisted in a limited way. The documents of Mesopotamian and Egyptian cities show women involved in a variety of public positions and occupations, exercising economic and legal rights, which varied from place to place and from time to time.[10]

Perhaps the most important arena within which women functioned was the temple precincts. Priestesses served the gods and goddesses. The elaborate temple organizations within the royal bureaucracy included female public servants. Some women functioned sexually in such occupations, as references to cultic sexuality attest. Others, it seems, refrained from sexuality and marriage by entering a sort of convent existence.[11] It is hard to reconstruct the social motivations for such a choice. Indeed, certain kinds of temple service for women may have represented an escape from the high risks and rigors of childbirth, and/or a way to provide economically for unmarried women. At least certain ancient mythographers saw a relationship between those cultic roles for women involving chastity and celibacy and the social necessity for population control by the limiting of child bearing.[12]

Whatever the social dynamics of the situation in the Late Bronze Age urban life may have been, certain facts about female roles emerge, dimly perhaps, but nonetheless apparent. The persistent strengths and appeals of Anat and Asherah (cf. Judg. 3:7; 1 Kings 15:13 = 2 Chr. 15:16; 1 Kings 18:19; Jer. 44:15ff.) in the Bible itself are evidence of the active participation of women in cultic, and therefore public life. Women served female deities and the female deities served women in return, affirming their ultimate creative worth.

All the above is in a sense introductory and thus is over-simplified and generalized as a preface to the problem posed at the outset, namely, investigating the social grounding for the transformation of women's position during early Israel to the limited and subordinate status that had become normative by late biblical times.

Early Israel, it has been shown, constituted a radical break with the city-state feudalism and nation-state imperialism of Late Bronze Age Palestine.[13] The description of the motivation for that break (and the implementation

through the Yahwistic covenant of a liberating replacement for city-state oppression) involves an understanding of the life of the peasantry.[14] The natural
resources of Palestine could no longer support an inflated urban bureaucracy
and thus Late Bronze Age peasant society was at the subsistence level. The
so-called Israelite "Conquest" represents a return of a full share of products
of the land to the people, a cessation of the continuous draining contributions
to urban bureaucracies.[15] The fact that nearly half of the Book of Joshua is
concerned with tribal allotments points to the early Israelite recovery of land
so that the people, according to their several tribes, would derive the benefit
therefrom.

Claims to land ownership, once the domination of the city-based power
structures had broken down, depended to a great extent on populating that
land (cf. Exod. 23: 23–30). In addition to establishing local tribal control over
certain territories formerly administered by oppressive city-states, the
Israelite federation was about to embark upon the settlement of previously
uninhabited territories, namely, the core of Palestine, the central hill country.

This territory was largely empty throughout the Bronze Age, except for
occasional, usually minor sites near springs and in valleys.[16] Generally poor
soil and scarce water supplies precluded significant habitation, particularly if
Bronze Age urban centers siphoned off a portion of the meager productivity.
If anything, the Late Bronze Age had even fewer settlements in the hill country proper than the preceding Middle Bronze Age centuries.

The ensuing Iron Age, in sharp contrast, brought an extensive settlement
of this region.[17] Technically, the storage of water in lined cisterns, the introduction of iron in the manufacture of farm tools, and the development of
methods of agricultural terracing resolved the environmental difficulties and
made this demographic shift possible. An enormous amount of human
energy was required, however, to clear land that had never before been tilled,
to build homes and villages where none had existed, and to cut back forests
and undergrowth that had covered the landscape since time immemorial.

This understanding of early Israel as an agrarian peasantry is dispelling the
romantic attachment to the notion of a biblical bias in favor of some sort of
Bedouin or semi-nomadic ideal. This understanding likewise affords an appreciation of a biblical undercurrent protesting—understandably so considering the ills and evils of Late Bronze Age Canaanite cities—against urban
life. The first city, for example, is built according to biblical tradition by the
first murderer (Gen. 4:17). The concluding exhortation of the Holiness Code
(Lev. 26:25–26) links city life—"if you gather within your cities"—with
famine, disease, and violence. The negative experience underlying such a bias
is clear. The orientation of the period of the judges rejected the urban centers.[18] In this process there arose social sanctions, ultimately translated into
law, which strengthened and favored land-based village life.

Against this background, what was life like for roughly half the population? How were women to do their share in espousing and furthering the

Yahwistic ideals of a free peasantry? Thus far, two major issues emerge in the attempt to answer these questions. Both of these had dramatic effects upon women and, while seemingly independent of each other, may prove ultimately to be interrelated.

The first issue concerns the biological need for productivity, the need to effect a population increase. Israel was obsessed both with having descendants to inherit its portion and with keeping its land-holdings within its kinship-based groups. In investigating this issue, anthropological and paleo-osteological studies which seek to describe fluctuations in ancient populations are extremely valuable.[19] Such studies inevitably lead to descriptions of mortality rates—or life expectancies—in the premodern world. In particular, the analysis of skeletal remains from various periods of Palestinian history provides information about life expectancies.[20] Excavations in Palestine have included—and in a sense began with—the investigation of tomb groups. Ironically, the skeletal remains of human beings from these tombs have so far received relatively slight attention; tomb studies have tended to focus on typologies of grave goods or of the tomb chambers themselves. However, although osteological studies have been carried out on relatively small numbers of the actual skeletal remains, the results present valid evidence for general demographic conditions and fluctuations in ancient Palestine, since the results of those studies correspond exceedingly well to the results of similar studies on all premodern populations.[21]

To begin with, the death rate was clearly highest among the preadult population. In one tomb group, 35 percent of the individuals died before the age of five, and nearly half of the individuals did not survive the age of eighteen.[22] For those who did survive to adulthood, another clear pattern existed: the mortality rate of females in the child-bearing years greatly exceeded that of the males.[23] In a population in which the life expectancy for men would be 40, women would have a life expectancy closer to 30. Consequently, it should not be surprising that the elders of any ancient tribal system were males, since a greater proportion of males would have survived into the chronological seniority which was at the basis of political seniority and leadership. It is no wonder that ancient biologists, Aristotle among them, proclaimed that the males of all species live longer than the females. It is a relatively modern phenomenon that the converse is true for humans. Women in antiquity were a class of humanity in short supply.

Paleo-pathologists have established that the cause of half, if not more, of all deaths, whatever the age of the individual at the time of death, was the presence of endemic parasitic disease, that is, infections which occur in a community more or less all the time without much alteration in their effects from year to year or even century to century.[24] The biblical term "pestilence" (*deber*) seems to be used in reference to such endemic disease. Very young children and old people, being the most susceptible to such infections, were the most likely to succumb. This fact is archaeologically evident in the high infant mortality rate as well as in the scarcity of people past forty. To put it bluntly, in normal times, families would have had to produce twice the number of children desired in order to achieve optimal family size.

The outbreak of epidemics, or the *abnormal* occurrence of acute infectious disease, reduced the usual low life expectancy even further. Epidemiological statistics, for historic periods in which records were kept, show the devastating effects of plague upon mortality rates. For example, in the plague-free early medieval years in Europe, life expectancy has been estimated as being between 35 and 40 years. For the generations during and immediately following the Black Death (1348–1349), which introduced an epoch of recurring plagues, the average life expectancy was as low as 17 or 18 years. It took nearly 100 years or more thereafter for life spans to creep back up to around 30.[25]

The Bible has a word that seems to describe such abnormal outbreaks of disease. This word, *maggephah,* normally translated "plague" (as opposed to "pestilence"), appears in several biblical accounts, chiefly in certain non-priestly narratives of Numbers, and also once in Exodus. Despite the layers of later explanations, these passages have preserved certain critical incidents of Israel's formative period and thus provide important information about public health and population density.

One such episode is Korah's rebellion in Numbers 16. The nature of the violent power struggle within the Israelite camp depicted here is peripheral to the present discussion. What does attract attention is the devastating plague associated with this rebellion in the mind of the biblical writer. The 250 leaders of the Korahites were consumed in a fire coming forth from the Lord. But God's wrath did not stop there; before Moses could carry out his efficacious atoning acts, 14,700 more deaths were recorded. There can be little doubt that this devastating plague, however that large and symbolic-sounding figure is to be interpreted, decimated the nascent community.

Num. 21:6 recounts another population loss. In this instance, the actual word *maggephah* is not used. Nonetheless, the description seems to reflect a plague situation: "Then the Lord sent fiery serpents among the people, so that many people of Israel died."

Another passage, Num. 11:1–3, while not mentioning plague or pestilence specifically, describes in similar language the effects of the wrath of God at a place called Taberah, which in itself means "Burning."[26] At this particular place God's anger—attributed to the complaining of the people—was kindled and the "fire of the Lord burned among them, and consumed some outlying parts of the camp." The destructive fever of plague, an outbreak of some kind of epidemic disease, seems to be the life situation, theologically interpreted, which gives rise to the association between divine anger and punitive, consuming heat/fire. The text does not give the number of casualties, but the losses in the Israelite camp must have been severe.

Num. 14:11 is another relevant text: except for Joshua (who brings back a good report), the spies who had gone into Canaan are said to have died from the plague.

Another incident, the unfortunate sequence of events at Beth Baal Peor, stems from the Mosaic period and is recounted in Numbers 25.[27] In some sort of orgiastic rite, various Israelite men participated in sacrifice to the Baal of Peor (Peor seems to be related to a Hittite word for "fire," which underlies that English word) and in relationships with the local unmarried Midianite girls. God's anger was kindled and turned upon Israel. No fewer than 24,000 people died in that epidemic which broke out among the people.

Exodus 32 provides one additional text dealing with death by plague. In the story of the Golden Calf, a plague caused the loss of an unspecified portion of the population (v. 35: "And the Lord sent a plague upon the people, because they made the calf which Aaron made").

Epidemic disease was clearly rampant. This clustering of biblical texts dealing with the age of Moses and using the word "plague" or *maggephah* reflects a public health crisis. Furthermore, nearly every extrabiblical source from the Late Bronze Age indicates the devastation wrought by epidemic infections. Perhaps the most famous of these is the Plague Prayer of Mursilis,[28] though disruption and devastation because of plague are recorded in other sources, such as the Amarna letters. A similar situation did not occur again in Palestine until 200–250 years later in the period of the Philistine wars, for which there is another clustering of biblical texts reflecting a plague situation.

The biblical passages cited above as well as the extrabiblical sources mentioned can be associated with what has been identified archaeologically as a massive disruption of the urbanized life of the petty kingdoms—or kinglets— in Palestine at the end of the Late Bronze Age. City after city suffered violent destruction. In many cases, if not all, the termination of Bronze Age culture in these cities is marked archaeologically by a thick layer of ashes, indicating a conflagration of major proportions.

These burnings of cities, it seems, are an aftermath of military conquest or overthrow rather than a part of it. If anything, military conflicts of guerrilla warfare took place outside the city walls, so well constructed were the fortifications of the Late Bronze cities. It is quite possible that the widespread burnings were not so much related to military actions as they were to a kind of primitive and desperate public health measure.[29] The fiery destruction of plagues needed to be fought with fire. Immediately following the recollection of the destructive plague of Baal Peor in Num. 31:21–23, the instructions to the Israelite warriors stipulate that "only the gold, the silver, the bronze, the iron, the tin, and the lead, everything that can stand the fire, you shall pass through the fire, and it shall be clean. Nevertheless, it shall also be purified with the water of impurity; and whatever cannot stand the fire you shall pass through the water." Thus, the unconscionable *herem,* or utter destruction of cities as presented in the book of Joshua, perhaps can be seen as a kind of plague control. It is difficult in the Western world today, with relatively little experience of such epidemics, to grasp the enormity of the plagues and the staggering death tolls which devastated the premodern world. Yet, the effort must be made to comprehend the drastic measures taken to stop epidemics in light of the ancient context.

Recognition of the existence of a period of widespread plague and death at the end of the Late Bronze Age is crucial, because that factor even more than famine and warfare (or at least in combination with those other two evils) created a life situation—or rather a death situation—of monumental proportions. The measures taken within the emergent Israelite community to deal with this situation are the ones that profoundly affected the lives of the female segment of the population.

Plague severely reduced the population of the peasantry at the time when sheer numbers counted most.[30] The normal difficulties in maintaining rural population in Palestine were compounded dramatically during this period. The biological creativity of females, a matter of vital concern even in normal times because of high infant mortality rates and the often fatal complications of childbearing, was most sorely needed in the aftermath of plagues. The devastation of plague had caused a demographic crisis. The repeated biblical exhortation, "Be fruitful and multiply" is singularly appropriate to this situation.

The strength and solidarity of the family were the basis for the vitality of the restored peasantry in early Israel and its ability to occupy the hill country of Palestine. At the most basic level, Israelite society urgently required a replenishment and even a surge in population to combat the effect of the famine, war, and disease at the end of the Late Bronze Age and to provide the human factor necessary for normal agricultural efforts. Moreover, this need for population increase was intensified as settlement of virgin areas proceeded. In addition to their specifically biological contribution, the full participation of women in the chores of a land-based economy was essential.[31] Further, since males were called away for occasional military duty in the absence of a standing army, the woman's role in managing all aspects of a household would increase.

From all perspectives, then, female creativity and labor were highly valued in early Israel. This female worth was not biological exploitation but rather part of the full cooperation of all elements in society in pursuing the goals of the Israelite people. Further, the early Iron Age experience of Israel was within the liberating matrix of the covenant with Yahweh, which emphasized ethical concerns and sought to maintain all human dignity. The precepts of the Decalogue and the Covenant Code are dedicated passionately against the exploitation of any groups of human beings or even animals. The Fifth Commandment (Exod. 20:12) bears this out. Both parents are to be honored, for on the two together depends the existence of Israel. The second part of this commandment is not a vague generality but rather an intrinsic complement of the familiar first half of that commandment ("Honor your father and your mother"). It expresses a hope for continued life and a restoration of public well-being: "That your days may be long in the land which the Lord your God gives you" (i.e., that life expectancies will stabilize above the low level characteristic of plague epochs).

The Bible generally reflects the fact that there were relatively fewer women of child-bearing age than men of the same age, a condition which Israel shared with the rest of the ancient world. Perhaps the existence of the *mohar*, translated variously as "bride price" or "marriage present," illustrates one way in which the community dealt with a shortage of marriageable women. The *mohar* may be compensation to the bride's family, since a daughter contributed through her work to a parent's household.[32] This bride-gift, a kind of reverse dowry, indicates that grooms had to compete for relatively few brides. Likewise, the financial burden of setting up a new household lay with the male, another indication of the socioeconomic dimensions of the shortage of brides. The dowry was rarely if ever bestowed in biblical times.[33] Fathers did not need to entice husbands. (Compare European history: it is perhaps not until the central Middle Ages that a combination of relative peace and a new urban economy brought about a relative increase in female population and led to the reversal of the terms of marriage. Girls became excess economic burdens and fathers gave dowries and paid for weddings to entice young men to take these girls off their hands.[34])

Beyond this, however, the intensified need for female participation in working out the Mosaic revolution in the early Israelite period can be seen in the Bible. Looking again at Numbers 31, an exception to the total purge of the Midianite population is to be noted. In addition to the metal objects which were exempt from utter destruction, so too were the "young girls who have not known man by lying with him" (Num. 31:18). These captives, however, were not immediately brought into the Israelite camp. Instead, they and their captors were kept outside the camp for seven days in a kind of quarantine period. (Note that the usual incubation period for the kinds of infectious diseases which could conceivably have existed in this situation is two or three to six days.[35]) Afterward, they thoroughly washed themselves and all their clothing before they entered the camp. This incident is hardly an expression of lascivious male behavior; rather, it reflects the desperate need for women of child-bearing age, a need so extreme that the utter destruction of the Midianite foes—and the prevention of death by plague—as required by the law of the *herem* could be waived in the interest of sparing the young women. The Israelites weighed the life-death balance, and the need for females of child-bearing age took precedence.

Such a source of female population, however, was not to be regularized. Instead, the extraordinary needs for female reproductive power in the tribal period precipitated strong sanctions against the expending of sexual energy in ways that either detracted from the primary reproductive channels or interfered with the strengths of nuclear family life or the transmission of family-based land ownership. The whole array of sexual customs and rules which exist in the Bible and which had the ultimate effect of relegating women to a narrowed and eventually subordinate position in later biblical times are in many cases radical changes from what had existed previously in the ancient world. These changes, which limited human sexual contacts and options, must be reconsidered in light of the demographic crisis of early Israel. Sanctions that eventually became expressed in biblical laws dealing with incest, rape, adultery, virginity, bestiality, exogamy, homosexuality, and prostitution require reexamination and reevaluation within the dynamics of the socio-economic situation and human crisis of the earliest days of Israel.[36] The dimension of purity and polemic in sexual sanctions is not to be ignored; but the role of the concern for repopulation and the need for human resources must also enter the picture.[37]

This is a vast project and one which is beyond the scope of this paper. However, progress can tentatively begin by looking at one expression of sexuality and the way the societal pressures of ancient Israel transformed it. Harlotry is a good example, since it leads directly to considering the second major issue which effected the turnabout in the status of women in ancient society.

Until the period of the judges, the existence of harlotry was an accepted, if not condoned fact.[38] Courtesans and prostitutes have existed at least since the dawn of recorded history without accompanying moral judgement or moral condemnation of harlotry *per se*. It was a legitimate though not necessarily desirable occupation for some women. In the Genesis story of Judah and Tamar, Tamar is not condemned for her temporary identification as a prostitute nor is Judah condemned for lying with her, except insofar as it signaled an evasion of his responsibilities toward his sons' widow (Gen. 38). Similarly, Rahab the harlot of Jericho is actually a heroine who helped the Israelite spies, in return for which they spared the destruction of her family (Josh. 2 and 6).

By the time that biblical legislation records attitudes toward harlotry, a considerable change had occurred. Lev. 19:29 is explicit: "Do not profane your daughter by making her a harlot, lest the land fall into harlotry and the land fall into wickedness." A father was responsible in the patriarchal system for his daughters. He was to limit their choice of occupation. Prostitution was not a possibility. The priorities and values of early Israelite existence had made family-centered life the chief, if not the only, course of action for a young woman.

There was another reason for closing out the option of harlotry in early Israel besides the need to have all available women of child-bearing years integrated into self-sufficient families. Harlotry was closely associated with the special use of sexual energy involved in ritual or cultic prostitution in the nature religions of the ruling urban elites. The efforts to secure productivity in the Israelite village and rural settings were to be separated from the rituals of the fertility cults. The sexual fetishism of Late Bronze Age society was "integrated into the hierarchic social order."[39] Because Israel rejected that order and also rejected the magical and mythological associations between the human reproductive process and the ritual enactment of such process, it of necessity prohibited the involvement of cult functionaries, male or female (Deut. 23:17), in such sexual activity.

In biblical law, the particular emphasis on the dissociation of the priests from harlotry can only be understood in this context. In Lev. 21:17, 14–15, priests are commanded to marry virgins. They are forbidden to marry any of four categories of women (widows, divorcées, "defiled" women, and harlots) whose sexual energies may already have been somewhat dissipated and whose fitness for child-bearing may have been reduced. Harlots in this law are not singled out as detestable or illegal members of society at large. However, in the same passage, the daughters of priests are condemned to burning by fire should they play the harlot (v. 9). This extraordinarily strong penalty for prostitution is aimed specifically at women who lived near or in the Israelite sanctuary area, the daughters of priests. It indicates the danger of pagan cultic expression that existed when men and women were together in cultic contexts, a danger that to some extent necessitated the removal of one of the two sexes from cultic services.

In the Bible, it is apparent which sex was barred from cultic leadership, but the reasons for such a limitation have not been properly explored. The priesthood of the Old Testament represents a radical break with the nature of priesthoods in the history of the ancient world; the priesthood of biblical religion is, from the outset, portrayed as a strictly and absolutely male profession.

The traditional answer to the query as to why the priesthood is male no doubt would have invoked the notion that the anthropomorphizing tendencies in the Bible made God out to be a male deity, some sort of macho warrior at one end or loving father at the other end. Male deities would naturally require a male priesthood. This response, however, does not account for the nonsexuality and nonhumanity of Yahweh's unity. Gender-oriented language for Yahweh is metaphoric. Furthermore, in addition to the all-too-familiar andromorphic images of Yahweh, there are a multitude of gynomorphic images, once one is open to reading them as such.[40]

Still, the establishment of an exclusively male priesthood was in a sense a natural development at the end of the second millennium. While a few millennia earlier a female priesthood in service of the Great Mother might have been the paradigm, the urban social systems of the Bronze Age were male dominated. Male deities outnumbered the goddesses. Thus, the kings, priest-kings, and priests were the dominant figures and provided the models for early Israel.

The priesthood before the monarchy was no doubt a decentralized and purposefully limited factor in Israelite life.[41] The egalitarian economy of the re-established peasantry of the period of the judges rejected the bureaucratic concentration of wealth that an elaborate priesthood requires. Circumscribed as it may have been, a priesthood nevertheless was established and thus siphoned off some portion of manpower as well as some economic surplus. The possibility of female service within any sort of cultic context could be eliminated purely on the basis of the felt priorities of early Israel in its allocation of human energies. Female energies were desperately needed in the family setting.

Partially as a rejection of the mythological and cultic sexuality of prebiblical religion and its integral connection with the urban power centers, and partly under pressures to concentrate female energies within the home and family, the Israelite priesthood emerged as a male occupation. In ancient Israel, thousands and thousands of years of female participation in this most crucial of all public institutions, an organized cultus, were terminated. One might speculate as to whether or not women might have entered priestly roles once the demographic crisis had been alleviated were it not for the continued attraction of the nature religions, particularly after the establishment of the monarchy and the return to urbanized life as the dominant mode in Israel. Thereafter, the social sanctions against such occupations as harlotry achieved the status of divine laws governing a priesthood distinct from that of pagan religion. From that situation, the moral judgment upon this kind of female sexual activity outside the family was only a step away.

Two major factors, then, appear to be primary causes of the profound change that occurred in the status and role of women during premonarchic Israel. The first was the drastic need to concentrate human energy, male and female, into family life and into intensive cultivation of the land, including considerable new territory. This meant a sex ethic, the primary societal function of which was to make childbirth and sexuality within the family crucial societal goals. Reversing the devastating depopulation of the Late Bronze Age was an enormous task. Likewise, setting about to re-emphasize an agricultural economy and even to settle new lands was a highly ambitious goal which called for the labor of women alongside men. The second factor was the rejection of pagan deities in favor of a covenant with a unified Yahweh. In cultic terms, this translated into a male priesthood. Neither of these two factors *within their contemporary settings* was particularly exploitive of male or female. On the contrary, strong female involvement in an agricultural economy and in the birth of new generations of Israelites who would literally inherit the land meant that women and men worked together to achieve the covenant ideals.

It is indeed an irony of history, then, that this very tight channeling of female (and male) energies into domestic affairs, which was a liberating event in its own time, became, ultimately, the *raison d'être* for continued and exclusive confinement of female energies to that sphere. A functional restriction to meet a demographic crisis of critical proportions became so deeply engrained that with the passing of the crisis the restrictions remained and ultimately became the basis for ideologies of female inferiority and subordination. Once the pattern of female nonparticipation in other spheres of life—the priesthood in particular—became established, society adhered to it in ways that became limiting and oppressive to women.

This was particularly true with the establishment of the monarchy and a gradual movement toward urbanization. Women became less important as participants in economic survival and therefore diminished in social importance. They were also the first to suffer when urban centers drained off the productivity of the land to support the monarchy and the military. Hard work under conditions of increased population and reduced nutrition meant even greater risks of death in childbirth. The introduction of slave wives under the phenomenal growth of the Davidic empire no doubt also contributed to the reduced importance of women. Thus, it was likely during the monarchy that the functional restriction of women in society became transformed gradually into an ideological restriction.

By this time opportunities for women to assume important roles outside the family, possibilities which had previously existed in ancient Near Eastern societies, especially in aristocratic settings, had been more or less systematically cut off in order to meet the needs of the emerging tribal groups. Yet, the exceptional leadership of women such as Miriam, Deborah, and the wise women of Tekoa and Abel are not so much "dynamic remnants"[42] of a time when women could hold natural positions of leadership within a community, positions which would have been based in inherited power structures (as queens or noblewomen); rather, their existence gives testimony to an epoch of liberation in which stratified hereditary leadership was abolished and anyone, women included, could rise to irregular positions of authority. They thus testify to the notion that God's spirit or wisdom could rest upon any individual, male or female, and grant that person a certain role in the community based on personal gifts rather than on social status. However, the patriarchal structuring of egalitarian tribal life with males as heads of families and of clans, with the elders of Israel becoming leaders, meant that women did not participate regularly in any sort of public political life, just as they did not perform priestly duties. The famous biblical women just enumerated occupy a kind of exceptional position, a nonrecurring charismatic participation. It is important to recognize that, however limited in proportion to males such leadership may have been, it was thoroughly accepted and acceptable. No notion of female inferiority intruded.

The reality for most women in the biblical world during the monarchy was one in which the vigorous equal-participation momentum of the formative period had been transformed gradually into a kind of masculine domination and female subordination. However, various biblical texts which depict a kind of harmonious ideal or balance between the sexes preserve the premonarchic situation.[43] The creation chapters of Genesis are one such text. Both the Priestly account in Genesis 1 ("So God created mankind in his image, . . . male and female he created them. And God blessed them and said to them, 'Be fruitful and multiply and fill the earth and subdue it' [i.e., till it together]"; Gen. 1:27–28) and the Yahwistic narrative in Genesis 2 affirm the existence of two sexes as the necessary and equal balance in human life.

In addition to the creation stories, the Song of Songs presents a beautiful picture of human love. The maiden and lad share in their desire and love for the other and in their expression of that love. Ideas of subordination or inferiority of one or the other are absent.

Also, the very anthropomorphism of Yahweh, when it is expressed in feminine terms, reaffirms and encourages the female in society. God, the warrior, is only half of the Exodus event. God, the provider of food and water, sustains the refugees from Egypt until they reach arable land. The redemptive acts of Yahweh, to be sure, are neither masculine nor feminine, but the working out of those actions involved the might that masculine imagery expresses and also the love and caring—and even the giving of birth—that feminine imagery conveys.

These latter, then, are the biblical ideals which can provide the balance in the endeavor to sort out the realities of life for women in ancient Israel amidst the social changes through which it passed. One can wonder to what extent these ideals were constantly at work within biblical society itself, even as the course of women's participation in society was being altered for millennia to come.

NOTES

1. The social history approach is exemplified by the work of such scholars as Mendenhall, Gottwald, and Campbell, especially for the period of concern in this paper, premonarchic Israel. Various works of theirs are cited in the following Notes, except for E. F. Campbell, Jr., "Moses and the Foundation of Israel," *Int* 29 (1975): 141–54. And Norman K. Gottwald's book has been published since this paper originally appeared: *The Tribes of Yahweh: A Sociology of the Religion of Liberated Israel, 1250–1050 B.C.E.* (Maryknoll, N.Y.: Orbis Books, 1979).

2. David Herlihy, "The Natural History of Medieval Women," *Natural History* 87 (1978): 56.

3. P. Trible, "Depatriarchalizing in Biblical Interpretation," *JAAR* 41 (1973): 35–42; J. Higgins, "The Myth of Eve: The Temptress," *JAAR* 44 (1976): 639–48.

4. B. P. Prusak, "Woman: Seductive Siren and Source of Sin," *Religion and Sexism*, ed. R. R. Ruether (New York: Simon and Schuster, 1974), pp. 89–116.

5. A. Kilmer, "The Mesopotamian Concept of Overpopulation and Its Solution as Represented in the Mythology," *Or* 41 (1972): 166–72.

6. J. L. Angel, "Ecology and Population in the Eastern Mediterranean," *World Archaeology* 4 (1972): 88–105.

7. T. Frymer-Kensky, "The Atrahasis Epic and Its Significance for Our Understanding of Genesis 1–9," *BA* 40 (1977): 150, 152.

8. E. Neumann, *The Great Mother,* Bolligen Series 47, 2nd ed., trans. R. Manheim (Princeton, N.J.: Princeton University Press, 1963).

9. E. O. James, *Myth and Ritual in the Ancient Near East* (New York: Praeger, 1958), pp. 113 ff.

10. B. F. Batto, *Studies on Women at Mari* (Baltimore: Johns Hopkins University Press, 1974); R. Harris, "Woman in the Ancient Near East," *IDBSup* (1976), pp. 960–63.

11. R. Harris, "The Nadītu Woman," *Studies Presented to A. Leo Oppenheim* (Chicago: University of Chicago Press, 1964), pp. 106–35.

12. Kilmer, "Mesopotamian Concept of Overpopulation," pp. 171–72; Frymer-Kensky, "Atrahasis Epic," pp. 149–50.

13. N. K. Gottwald, "Domain Assumptions and Societal Models in Pre-Monarchic

Israel," *VTSup* 28 (1975): 93–98; G. Mendenhall, *The Tenth Generation: The Origins of the Biblical Tradition* (Baltimore: Johns Hopkins University Press, 1973), pp. 194–97.

14. G. Mendenhall, "Social Organization of Early Israel," *Magnalia Dei: The Mighty Acts of God,* ed. F. M. Cross, W. E. Lemke, and P. D. Millar (Garden City, N.Y.: Doubleday, 1976), pp. 133–38; M. L. Chaney, "Ancient Palestinian Peasant Movements and the Formation of Premonarchic Israel," forthcoming in *Biblical Archeologist.*

15. G. Mendenhall, "The Hebrew Conquest of Canaan," *BA* 25 (1962): 66–87.

16. T. L. Thompson, *The Settlement of Palestine in the Bronze Age*, Beihefte zum Tübinger Atlas des Vordern Orients, Series B (Wiesbaden: Reichert, 1975), pp. 39–50.

17. Ibid., pp. 66–67.

18. A purely ideological understanding of this rejection is problematic, since it is related to some extent to the military-political and also the economic situation of post-Mosaic Israel. Further, the notion of tribal orientation is, at least for some scholars, actually a "retribalization" based on long-standing tribal patterns. Cf. Gottwald, "Domain Assumptions," pp. 93–95.

19. The difficulties inherent in the task of deducing population fluctuations in antiquity are not to be minimized, as Petersen makes clear; cf. W. Petersen, "A Demographer's View of Prehistoric Demography," *Current Anthropology* 16 (1975): 227–44. Nonetheless, the recurrent patterns visible in tomb studies and skeletal analyses for various parts of the premodern world do allow certain qualified judgments.

20. M. Giles, "The Human and Animal Remains," in O. Tuffnell, *Lachish III: The Iron Age* (London: Oxford University Press, 1953), Appendix A, pp. 405–12; "The Human and Animal Remains," in O. Tuffnell, *Lachish IV: The Bronze Age* (London: Oxford University Press, 1958), Appendix B, pp. 318–22; D. R. Hughes, "Report on Metrical and Non-metrical Aspects of E.B.-M.B. and Middle Bronze Age Human Remains from Jericho," in K. Kenyon, *Excavations at Jericho* (London: British School of Archaeology in Jerusalem, 1965), Vol. 2, Appendix H, "Human Bones," pp. 664–85; P. Smith et al., "Human Skeletal Remains," *Publications of the Meiron Excavation Project,* ed. E. Meyers, Vol. 3, Ch. 7. 2, forthcoming.

21. S. Genovés, "Estimation of Age and Mortality," *Science in Archaeology,* ed. S. Brothwell and E. Higgs (London: Thames and Hudson, 1969), pp. 440–52; M. S. Goldstein, "The Paleopathology of Human Skeletal Remains," ibid., pp. 480–89.

22. Smith et al., "Human Skeletal Remains."

23. Genovés, "Estimation," pp. 441–43; Goldstein, "Paleopathology," p. 486.

24. R. Hare, *Pomp and Pestilence: Infectious Disease, Its Origins and Conquest* (London: Victor Gollancz, 1954), pp. 32–66.

25. Herlihy, "Natural History of Medieval Women," p. 56.

26. Mendenhall, *The Tenth Generation,* p. 109 and Notes 17 and 18.

27. Ibid., pp. 105–21.

28. *ANET*, pp. 394–96.

29. Similar extreme and seeming cruel action in restricting homes or districts or even whole towns afflicted by the plague is well documented in European history. Instead of the healthy removing themselves from infected situations, the infected areas were isolated. Houses and sometimes entire towns were boarded up or walled in, along with all the inhabitants, sick or healthy. Nearly all of the latter then perished along with the former as a result of the disease itself or from suffocation or starvation. See Hare, *Pomp and Pestilence,* pp. 150–52.

30. Archaeological evidence bears out the literary evidence, both biblical and extra-biblical, for a massive disruption at the end of the Late Bronze Age; cf. G. Mendenhall, "Change and Decay in All Around I See: Conquest, Covenant, and *The Tenth Generation,*" *BA* 39 (1976): 152–57. Studies of death, longevity, reproductive capacity, ecology, and population density in the East Mediterranean have provided an estimated dramatic drop-off in people per square kilometer (km^2) from 30 in the Late Bronze Age, a high point for all of the Bronze Age, to 19 or probably less per km^2 in the Iron I period. In other words, the Iron Age begins with an overall reduction in population of over one-third, with some scholars positing as high as a four-fifths reduction. See J. L. Angel, "Ecology and Population in the Eastern Mediterranean," p. 93 and Table 28.

31. E. Friedl, *Women and Men: An Anthropological View* (New York: Holt, Rinehart and Winston, 1975), pp. 46–48.

32. O. J. Baab, "Marriage," *IDB* (1962) Vol. 3, pp. 283–84.

33. C. R. Taber, "Marriage," *IDBSup* (1976) Vol. 3, p. 575.

34. Herlihy, "Natural History of Medieval Women," p. 60.

35. T. C. Eickhoff, ed., *Communicable Diseases,* Vol. 3 of *Practice of Medicine* (Hagerstown, Md.: Harper & Row, 1977).

36. Friedl, *Women and Men,* pp. 86–98.

37. Anthropological analyses of the roles of women and men in various types of agrarian economies provide an untapped and potentially very fruitful resource for reconstructing the roles of various family members in early Israel. Particularly as archaeology provides more and more information about Iron I agricultural techniques and crop selection and also about cultural and/or commercial isolation, comparative studies will aid in the delineation of the family basis of Israelite society. It is indeed likely, as Friedl explains (p. 100), that "social structures and attitudes toward sex are together a consequence of strategies of control developed, sometimes unconsciously, by members of society as a means of regulating the ratio of land and food resources to the population."

38. O. J. Baab, "Prostitution," *IDB* (1962) Vol. 3, p. 932.

39. N. K. Gottwald, "Biblical Theology or Biblical Sociology?" *Radical Religion* 2 (1975): 53.

40. Trible, "Depatriarchalizing," pp. 31–35.

41. A. Cody, *A History of Old Testament Priesthood,* Analecta Biblica 35 (Rome: Pontifical Biblical Institute, 1969), pp. 1–61.

42. P. Trible, "Women in the Old Testament," *IDBSup* (1976), p. 965.

43. Trible, "Depatriarchalizing."

17

WALTER BRUEGGEMANN

Trajectories
in Old Testament Literature
and the Sociology of Ancient Israel

*By drawing lines of connection between the work of G. E. Mendenhall and
N. K. Gottwald on premonarchic Israel, F. M. Cross on the priesthoods
during the monarchy, and P. D. Hanson on exilic and postexilic apocalyptic,
Brueggemann "maps" two major lines of tradition-formation in the Old
Testament which show close linkages between theology and social organization. These are traceable as competing "trajectories" that run through all the
major Old Testament periods.*

*The "Mosaic liberation" trajectory emerges in an early Israelite peasant
revolt, in the Mushite priesthood of Shiloh and Nob, in the prophetic critiques, in the Deuteronomists before they later harden into dogmatists, and
in postexilic visionaries from the displaced Levitical priesthood and other
"have nots." The "royal consolidation" trajectory surfaces in the Davidic-
Solomonic state coup, in the Aaronid priesthood of Hebron and Jerusalem,*

Reprinted from *Journal of Biblical Literature* 98 (1979): 161–85.

in the institutions of monarchy, the Priestly writer, and in the postexilic Zadokite priesthood and other empowered "haves."

Various points of tension and conflict between the trajectories and their intermixture in particular Old Testament documents are explored. In the Old Testament, "the shape and character of human community are in question along with the God question," with very large implications for biblical interpreters and scholars in all religious disciplines, since "there is no disinterestedness in the text or in the interpreter."

It has long been recognized that there are two circles of tradition in Israel's literature concerning covenant, one derived from Moses and the other Davidic in its formulation.[1] The biblical tradition itself wishes to suggest that the two are continuous, so that the Davidic is a natural derivation from that of Moses and fully faithful to it. Undoubtedly, the circles around David urged this perception of the matter. Recent critical scholarship, however, has now made it reasonable to assume that these two articulations of covenant are not only distinct but also came from very different centers of power and very different processes of tradition building.[2]

Tension, and in some ways, conflict between the traditions can be sensed even when one is not attempting to be precise about the points of origin or settings for the two circles of tradition. Recent traditio-historical analyses confirm such a judgment.[3] Two additional observations need to be made in order to provide a better understanding of these circles of tradition. First, we may speak of trajectories running through the tradition. To my knowledge, the categories of Robinson and Koester[4] have not been applied to Old Testament studies. They urge that pieces of literature and tradition should not be studied in isolation nor in terms of mechanical dependence and relationship through a literary process, but that special attention should be paid to the continuities which flow between various pieces of literature. As a result of social value, use, and transmission, continuities both in terms of cultural context and in terms of theological perspective[5] become decisive for interpretation. Applied to the two covenantal traditions in the Old Testament, "trajectories" suggest that we might be able to trace continuities in the literature shaped and energized by the Mosaic and Davidic covenants. Specifically, as will be evident in what follows, the Mosaic tradition tends to be a movement of protest which is situated among the disinherited and which articulates its theological vision in terms of a God who decisively intrudes, even against seemingly impenetrable institutions and orderings. On the other hand, the Davidic tradition tends to be a movement of consolidation which is situated among the established and secure and which articulates its theological vision in terms of a God who faithfully abides and sustains on behalf of the present ordering.[6] As is clear from the work of Robinson and Koester, attention to trajectories is at best imprecise and does not permit a rigid schematization. It does, however, provide a way to see a coherent and persistent *Tendenz* in each stream.

Second, the presence and meaning of two alternative covenant traditions are richly illuminated by the recent attention to sociological factors. While we still do not have a comprehensive overview of this data, the recent work of George Mendenhall, Norman Gottwald, and Paul Hanson provide some beginnings. Such work makes clear that the literature that stands within the various trajectories is never sociologically disinterested nor singularly concerned with matters theological. Each text and each trajectory reflect important socioeconomic and political concerns.

The following discussion will consider the two covenant traditions in terms of literary trajectories and sociological considerations which may be related to them. Thus far, scholarly presentations have been concerned only with smaller historical periods and not with a comprehensive pattern for the whole. This paper suggests the provisional discernment of a comprehensive pattern which may significantly alter our understanding of the theological import of the texts and the literary-historical questions relating to them.

I

It will be useful to consider recent scholarly literature in terms of various periods of Israel's history which have been subjected to study. Our presentation will reflect a certain periodization of Israel's history; however, that periodization is used simply as a way of reporting various scholarly studies. None of the scholars mentioned has urged a pattern of periodization, so that it may be regarded simply as organization of convenience. For the present discussion, the stress is on the continuity of the trajectory rather than the periodization.

As early as 1962, Mendenhall proposed a fresh way of understanding the conquest and the premonarchial period of Israel (1250–1000 B.C.).[7] In contrast to the dominant views of conquest, either by invasion or infiltration, Mendenhall urged that Israel was formed by an intentional "bond between persons in an intolerable situation."[8] Oppressed people with an alternative vision of social order were able to "reject the religious, economic, and political obligations to the existing network of political organizations."[9] The "habiru" mounted a revolution against tyrannical Canaanite city-kings, rejecting the given social order. Bound to a nonhuman overlord by covenant and the solidarity of the newly formed community, they set about fashioning a deliberate alternative social ordering which became Israel. Thus Mendenhall has interpreted the "conquest" in the categories of oppressed people revolting for liberation versus tyrannical city-kings. In what follows, it will be suggested that these categories provide entry into the two dominant trajectories of Israelite literature.

Related to this hypothesis, several observations emerge from sociological considerations. First, the dominant view of early Israel as nomadic has been sharply placed in question. The sociological data, summarized by Mendenhall,[10] Gottwald, and Frick,[11] require a fresh sociological realism about Israel as an alternative to the city-state. What is different is not mobility or lack of a place but a social ordering which is characterized by political decentralization and social egalitarianism in contrast to urban centralization and social stratification with the power in the hands of an elite. In his preliminary paper, Gottwald contrasts the city and the countryside as available alternative models,[12] whereas Mendenhall presents Israel's egalitarian movement as a more radical step. Thus, Israel is not to be understood as a group of geographical outsiders but as sociopolitical outsiders who were only geographically present but not permitted to share in the shaping of their own destiny. Their marginality is not geographical in character, but rather social, economic, and political. Thus, instead of nomad, the suggested sociological identity is that of peasant, a term which means the politically-economically marginal element of society from whose produce the elite draw their life. Peasant is characterized as one whose labor yields produce enjoyed by others.[13]

Second, Mendenhall has urged a rethinking of the notion of "tribe" in characterizations of early Israel.[14] Tribe, he urges, is not to be understood as a natural ethnic grouping but as an intentional community deliberately committed to a different ideology and a different social organization.[15] Such a notion suggests that the central social unit in early Israel is not to be confused either with conventional notions of nomadism nor with anthropological ideas of kinship groups.

These groups are historical and not natural. In Israel they did not originate because of necessity or nature, but through historical decision-making. The tribe in Israel is to be contrasted with the state, a distinction that has received various presentations in the history of sociology. It is especially to be noted that the historical decision-making from whence comes such a tribe is an intentional action which is the first step away from historical marginality.

Third, such an understanding of the social unit provides a way by which greater stress may be placed on covenant as an ideology and form of social organization. The hypothesis of covenant (anticipated by Buber[16] and articulated especially by Baltzer[17] and Mendenhall[18]) of course provides a major conceptual category for understanding Israel. But that conceptualization has in scholarly discussion stayed largely in the sphere of theological interpretation. Indeed, Baltzer's excellent study is confined to literary and form-critical concerns. Only recently has the notion of covenant been handled sociologically to suggest that it provided ground for a "systematic, ethically and religiously based, conscious rejection of many cultural traits of the late Bronze

Age urban and imperial cultures.''[19] The covenant, then, is more politically radical and historically pertinent to early Israel than has often been recognized, for it permitted a political *novum* in history and a radical break with urban culture. Mendenhall has in schematic fashion contrasted the regnant social organization and the alternative made possible by covenant.[20]

While Mendenhall in 1954[21] did turn scholarship in a new direction, his major sociological intent has been neglected. Mendenhall's crucial presentation had two parts. The first dealt with the "treaty-form" and ancient Near Eastern parallels discovered in Hittite and Assyrian texts. The second was concerned with the innovative social vision and social organization derived from a covenant-treaty. Scholarship has largely embraced the former and has busily identified elements of the treaty form in many places, although some identifications are exceedingly doubtful.[22]

Until very recently, Mendenhall's major concern for social vision and social organization has not been recognized or pursued by scholars. It has been Mendenhall's own more recent work which has indicated that covenanted Israel embodied not only a theological novelty but also a social experiment as well.[23] The theological factor has required a quite new discernment of God as a faithful covenanter who engaged in the history of Israel and who was impacted by Israel's history, her acts and praises, but nonetheless a faithful covenanter who has independent purpose and authority not derived from his covenanted partner. Conversely, the theological self-understanding of Israel permitted a new people which had no other identity—linguistic, racial, ethnic, or territorial—except exclusive allegiance to its God. That much has been widely observed.[24]

What has not been sufficiently appreciated are the social implications of this theological novelty. Covenantal commitment to this God, unknown by name and without credential in the empire, carried with it a rejection of loyalty to the gods of the empire and a rejection of the ways of ordering that society.[25] Thus, the theological vision, either as impetus or as justification,[26] made possible a radical discontinuity in the social organization of Israel. Israel was no longer bound to the religion of the empire, which had now been effectively delegitimated, and Israel could no longer and need no longer rely upon the self-securing technology of the empire.

This way of interpreting the data presumes a close link between theological vision and sociological organization. A totalitarian, hierarchical social order has its counterpart and justification in the static religion of the empire in which the gods have no independent existence but are only an integral part of the social system.[27] Most obviously, the pharaoh, manager of the social process, is at the same time embodiment of the gods. There is an identity of social process and theological vision, an arrangement which assured changelessness and which denied any standing ground for theological criticism of social reality.[28]

When the "new" God of freedom and justice is accepted as covenant partner, the totalitarian, hierarchical social order is no longer necessary or viable. Thus the Israelite order from Moses until the time of David, 1250–1000 B.C., represents a sociological experiment to determine if a society is possible when not sanctioned and protected by the imperial gods. It is admittedly a precarious social experiment based on a precarious theological vision. That experimentation stands in sharp discontinuity with its political context as well as its theological milieu and is justified only by the bold theological novelty of Yahwism, a novelty focused on justice and freedom.[29]

So far as I am aware, Mendenhall at no point appeals to a Marxist criticism of society. Gottwald, however, does allow for it.[30] The discernment of the new situation is in keeping with the insight of Marx that the ultimate criticism is the criticism of heaven which then radically criticizes all earthly historical institutions.[31]

This insight, only recently reasserted by Mendenhall in a discussion of the covenant hypothesis, presents a quite shifted paradigm for biblical study, one that will need carefully to be studied, tested, and considered. In both the "peasant revolt" theory of "conquest" and the "covenant law" theme, Mendenhall has understood Israel in sharp discontinuity with its context. It may be argued that this is simply a "class conflict" reading of the text, or perhaps the emergence of an alternative consciousness.[32] In any case, it provides a way to hold together (a) a sense of religious radicalness which either is unexplained or appeals to "revelation" and (b) the awareness of urgency about social reality evident in the text. For the moment, setting aside literary critical judgments, such a view permits us to understand the militancy of Deuteronomy[33] as it urges an alternative understanding of reality and the high-risk venture Israel's faith is shown to be in the Book of Judges. Much more is now seen to be at stake in the pressure of syncretism, for it is not just a choosing among gods or a matter of loyalty to this especially jealous one, but the shape and character of human community are in question along with the God question. Human society, as ordered by Moses, is covenantal because the covenant God both sanctions and expects it. And Israel must resist every religion and every politics which would dismantle the covenant.

These discussions of peasants, tribe, and covenant prepare the way for Gottwald's major study of early Israel as a community of radical liberation. His book has not yet appeared, but we have hints[34] about his argument that conventional historical interpretations do not appropriate the sociopolitical radicalness of a movement which is profoundly religious in its commitment to the God of the exodus and dangerously political in its rejection of the status quo with its oppressive consciousness and practice.

We do not have (nor are we likely to have) a parallel consideration of the religion of the tyrannical city-kings of Canaan. Obviously, that lies outside the scope of Israel's normative faith and is treated by the Old Testament texts only in reaction and with contempt and hostility. The social organization of the period, however, provides a clue to the religious ideology that undoubtedly legitimated it. We may presume that this religion concerned a god of order who surely served to legitimate the way things already were. While one cannot be very precise, clearly the structure of liberation faith vis-à-vis a religion of legitimated order is already evident. That trajectory of a religion of God's freedom and a politics of justice will be important for the subsequent periods.

II

The second period we shall consider is that of united monarchy. Obviously, something decisive happened to Israel in this period. The tensions revealed in 1 Samuel reflect a battle for Israel as to whether it will be "like the other nations" (1 Sam. 8:5,20) or whether it shall be *'am qadôš,* a people holy to the Lord. While that issue has long been perceived, it is now possible to conclude that this was not only a battle over gods and theological identity but also a battle concerning social values and social organization. The innovations and inventiveness of David and Solomon (expressed, e.g., in temple, bureaucracy, harem, standing army, taxation system, utilization of wisdom) embody an imitation of urban imperial consciousness of Israel's more impressive neighbors and a radical rejection of the liberation consciousness of the Mosaic tradition. While the texts shaped under the aegis [note the word] of the monarchy in their present form stress continuity with and purpose fidelity to the tradition of Moses, the discontinuities can scarcely be overstated.

Mendenhall has described this as the "paganization of Israel."[35] It is clear from his work that the social innovation of Moses and its corresponding theological novelty of a God aligned with the marginal ones was abandoned in monarchic Israel. Social innovation and theological novelty sustained the community for 250 years, but only as a marginal, minority community preoccupied with survival. That now is given up when the community has the resources and breathing space not only to survive but also to dominate its context, as Solomon was able to do.[36] The radical experiment of Moses is given up and there is in Israel an embrace of the very imperial notions rejected from Egypt.[37] This imperial consciousness combines a religion of a static, guaranteed God together with a politics of injustice and social domination, precisely antithetical to the religion of the freedom of God and the politics of justice introduced by Moses and kept alive in the community of premonarchic Israel.

The change can be observed in a variety of ways. First, the organizational and institutional changes are well known: from traditional to bureaucratic leadership, from tribal ordering to governmental districts, from "holy war" ideology to hired mercenaries, and the introduction of a harem as an appropriate royal accouterment. Thus the presuppositions of public life were drastically altered, indicating an abandonment of the vision which powered the "peasant revolt."

Second, the discernment of God's relation to the community is reshaped. That change may be presented in terms of tent and house. The old tradition of "tent" asserts a claim of mobility and freedom for God. The "house" tradition is surely royal in its orientation and stresses the abiding presence of Yahweh to Israel. Thus the tension of the freedom of God and the accessibility of God to Israel is now tilted in a new direction.[38] The older Mosaic tradition stressed the freedom of God and the notion of presence was precarious. Now the notion of presence is primary and God's freedom is severely constricted, for the royal regime must depend on a patron and legitimator who is unreservedly committed to the shrine and its social arrangement.

Third, in the context of social transformation and theological revision, Frank M. Cross has offered a persuasive construction of the history of priesthood in Israel.[39] Clearly, the priestly narratives must be read with attention to the conflicts and political interests that seems always to have been at stake. It is clear that David was able to achieve a remarkable balance in having two priests, Abiathar and Zadok, and it is equally clear that Solomon brashly dissolved the balance with the enhancement of Zadok and the elimination of Abiathar (1 Kings 2:26–27).

By carefully piecing together the fragmentary evidence, Cross concludes that David held together the priestly rivalry to serve his dominant interest of political unification. According to Cross, one priestly interest, represented by Abiathar, is the Mushite house with old links to Shiloh and Nob; the other is the house of Aaron, represented by Zadok, with roots in Hebron and, ultimately, in Jerusalem.[40] Further, after the period of the united monarchy, Jeroboam I, in setting up his two shrines, balanced a Mushite shrine in Dan with the Aaronid Shrine of Bethel.[41] Thus, the narrative, as Alt has recognized, shows David holding together the imperial and covenantal constituencies. In terms of social vision and organization, it is plausible that David managed the process so that he did not finally force the issue which was so clearly and ruthlessly forced by Solomon.

The Davidic-Solomonic tradition with its roots in Abrahamic memory provides an important alternative theological trajectory.[42] We may identify two theological elements which are surely linked to this movement and which are important to the subsequent faith and literature of the Bible. First, it is generally agreed that the emergence of creation faith in Israel has its setting in Jerusalem and its context in the royal consciousness.[43] The shift of social vision is accompanied with a shifted theological method which embraces more of the imperial myths of the ancient Near East and breaks with the scandalous historical particularity of the Moses tradition. The result is a universal and comprehensive worldview which is more inclined toward social stability than toward social transformation and liberation. Thus, creation theology, like every theological effort, is politically interested and serves to legitimate the regime, which in turn sponsors and vouches for this theological perspective.

Second, clearly from this tradition comes messianism, the notion of God's promise being borne in history by an identifiable historical institution. Thus, the Davidic house now becomes not only historically important but theologically decisive for the future of Israel and all promises and futures are now under the dominance of this institution. It will be clear that in both ways, creation and messianism, the royal perspective is in tension with the Mosaic tradition. In the Mosaic tradition, narratives of concrete liberation are much preferred to comprehensive myths of world order. In the Mosaic world, precarious covenant premised on loyalty is in deep tension with the unconditional affirmation of an historical institution. In these major ways, the Davidic-Solomonic period witnesses the emergence of an alternative both in theology and politics which is in radical tension with Mosaic tradition and congenial to the non-Mosaic and pre-Mosaic royal traditions.[44]

For purposes of tracing literary-theological trajectories, it is important to recognize that the Mushite priesthood was heir to the liberation faith rooted in Moses and preserved among the northern tribes, likely at the shrines of the confederation. Conversely, the Zadokite rootage, from what can be reconstructed, belongs to a royal consciousness based in an urban context. The priestly conflict is not just an in-house power struggle of priestly interests, but it is again a battle for the life of Israel between a liberation faith and a religion of legitimated order. The issue of the earlier period (to use the construct of Mendenhall) between "peasants" and "city-kings" appears to apply here.

On the basis of such a reading of the evidence, the Hebron/Shiloh, Aaronid/Mushite, Aaron/Moses pattern and the vindication of the former in each case shows that the consciousness of the united monarchy was finally shaped decisively by a tradition rooted in very old pre-Israelite royal traditions. Specifically, it provided a shrine which legitimated order at the expense of justice, which presented the king as the principle of order and not as a child of the torah, and which placed stress on dynastic continuity at the expense of critical transcendence in history.

The tradition of the Canaanite city-kings to whom Mendenhall has applied the term "tyrannical" found its continuation in the royal theology focused on creation and messiah. The Mosaic tradition found its muted continuation in the priestly house of Abiathar, in occasional prophetic criticism, in the symbolic but revolutionary rejection of the Davidic house (2 Sam. 20:1; 1 Kings 12:16), in protests against the institution of monarchy (1 Sam. 8; 12), and its "sacred space" (1 Kings 8:27).

III

The two trajectories can be discerned in development throughout the period of the divided monarchies, 922–587 B.C. For this period there has not been the enormous scholarly activity of a sociological character as for the other periods. The tensions revealed here are also better understood when placed in the frame of the earliest confrontation of peasants/city-kings.

The political institutions of the northern and southern kingdoms are likely vehicles for these two traditions of religion and social vision. Thus the split of 1 Kings 12 represents a departure of the community of historical liberation from the ordering regime of David. It is important that the split did not happen over a theological dispute, nor was it simply a gradual growing apart, but it was triggered by a concrete issue of political oppression and social liberation. There is no doubt that the royal consciousness was committed to the maintenance of order at the cost of justice. This is not, of course, to claim that the northern kingdom did not practice similar oppression as under Ahab, but the northern kingdom appears to have been peculiarly open to and vulnerable to the transforming impact of the Moses tradition.

This entire phase of Israel's history is easily understood as a confrontation of kings and prophets, thus continuing the claims of the Davidic-Solomonic commitment to order and continuity and the Mosaic affirmation of freedom even at the cost of discontinuity. We may mention four occasions of the traditions in conflict, in which these trajectories are at work.

1. The confrontation of Elijah/Ahab (Jezebel) in 1 Kings 21 is nearly a pure paradigm of the issue. Elijah stands in the old tradition of "inheritance" *(naḥalah)* whereas the royal figures are committed to the right of royal confiscation which overrides older inheritance rights *(yaraš).*[45] The prophet appeals to the unfettered work of Yahweh which calls kings to accountability and dismantles kingdoms (vv. 17-19), whereas the king utilizes mechanizations of the torah for the sake of royal interest. Elijah believes that covenant curses follow violations of torah, even against the royal person, whereas Ahab believes the torah is only a tool of royal policy.

2. The confrontation between Amos and Amaziah (Amos 7:10-17) is of the same character. Amos speaks against any who violate torah[46] or who try to stop the free word of Yahweh, even if it touches the king. By contrast, Amaziah does not doubt the authority of torah but believes the royal reality has immunity. Thus the king's world has created a situation in which there is no transcendence outside royal management to which appeal can be made. It follows that there is no free God who can evoke or sanction radical social change, precisely the situation Pharaoh wished for in the Egypt of the thirteenth century.

3. The confrontation of Isaiah and Ahaz (Isa. 7:1-9:7) is somewhat different because Isaiah is not so unambiguously placed in the Mosaic trajectory,[47] though of course he does affirm a transcendence beyond royal perception in his use of the key words "glory" *(kabôd)* and "holy" *(qadôš)*. Thus it is not quite so clear that his position in the face of the king is so unambiguously critical. Nonetheless, he calls the king to radical faith (7:8) and urges the king to a wholly new perception of reality which calls the king out from his self-securing posture.

The resolution of the unit on the Syro-Ephraimite War (Isa. 9:2–7) demonstrates the delicate balance worked by the prophet. On the one hand, the future is indeed Davidic, with appeal to the royal promissory tradition rooted in 2 Sam. 7. The promise indicates enormous confidence in the royal tradition and royal institution, for it makes reference to Yahweh's unreserved commitment to this institution. Thus, the expectation of the prophet (if it is in fact his poetry) is very different from the radicalness of Amos. Amos, in extraordinary boldness (now placed after the Amaziah encounter), had finally said "end" *(qēṣ)*.[48] There had never been a pronouncement more radical than this. In a different way, Isaiah in his appeal to the Davidic promise concludes "no end" *('în qēṣ)* (v. 6).[49] (If, as some argue, Amos is committed to the Davidic reality, then his word is against the north and not in conflict with Isaiah; but that seems unlikely, even if Amos' words refer to the north.)

4. A final example we cite of the tension of traditions in this period is in the poem of Jer. 22:13–19, in which Jeremiah contrasts two kings, Jehoiakim and Josiah. Jehoiakim, so quickly dismissed by the Deuteronomist (2 Kings 24:1–7), is presented as an embodiment of royal self-serving, dominated by injustice and unrighteousness. The son practiced oppression and violence, the father cared for the poor and needy, i.e., he understood covenantal knowing. The poetry of Jeremiah (passing over the death of Josiah) presents him as "well," i.e., faithful in covenant, and Jehoiakim as destined to an ignoble death (which did not happen). The poem is not a report on what happened but a projection of what may be anticipated from the tradition.

Special note should be taken of Josiah, who occupied a crucial place in this period near its end and who also holds an enigmatic position between the traditions. On the one hand, he is clearly a Davidic figure. His credentials are unquestioned and his conduct of office shows he did not flinch from that role. But it is equally clear that unlike almost every other Davidide, he subordinated his Davidic role to the claims of torah. In terms of traditions which concern us, the Davidic claims are subordinated to Mosaic claims.[50]

The contrast of Jehoiakim *(lô'-ṣedeq, lô'-mišpaṭ)* and Josiah *(mišpaṭ, ṣedeq)* articulates well the trajectories of the older period. Jehoiakim is obviously a practitioner of the same oppressions as the city-kings and no doubt had a theology of order to legitimate it. Josiah, from a religion of torah, engages in political practice quite in keeping with the liberation movement of Moses.

It is possible that the trajectories in this period can be discerned in the variant expressions of the normative tradition designated J and E. There is little doubt that J is an attempt at unitive and comprehensive theologizing, concerned both to secure the place of the Davidic house in normative theology and to make cosmic claims in terms of linking Jerusalem's centrality and creation theology.[51] Conversely, the E tradition, to the extent it is a distinct and identifiable piece, is a separatist statement concerned for the purity of the community and aware of the threat of syncretism.[52] Clearly, purity is no concern of J and unitive issues are remote to E. Thus the old trajectory of marginal people with a primary concern for freedom and established people with a large concern for stability are reflected in the shape of the J and E traditions. The main issue, in terms of community identity (south and north), communal function and office (king and prophet) and tradition (J and E), stayed alive until the loss of Jerusalem.[53]

IV

The next period we may identify is that of the exile, for which the conventional dates are 587–537 B.C. Even if those dates are somewhat problematic, this period presents an identifiable crisis and a responding literature which permits disciplined consideration.

It is clear that with the crisis of 587, the faith trajectories we have presented are thrown into disarray. Particularly is this the case with the Mosaic-prophetic covenantal trajectory which seems now to have failed. From the perspective of the normative literature of the Old Testament, the pre-exilic period is dominated by the Mosaic trajectory, with the royal alternative subordinated (though undoubtedly flourishing in practice). With the exile, we may in broad outline speak of an inversion of the traditions so that the Mosaic theme is in crisis and is apparently less germane, while the promissory royal tradition now becomes the dominant theological mode for Israel.

In recent scholarly discussion the following are relevant to our theme:

1. The deuteronomic corpus, either shaped or revised in the exile, represents an insistence upon the Mosaic way of discerning reality and its insistence on radical obedience.[54] It is a call for radical obedience to torah, an embrace of Yahweh's will for justice with appropriate sanctions (positive and negative) for obedience. Thus, it continues the urgent call for purity (2 Kings 17:7–41) with its militant, uncompromising social vision.

Following Von Rad, it has been argued that Davidic themes of assurance are also present in the corpus.[55] These may perhaps be found in the conclusion of 2 Kings 25:27–30, or in the three texts now generally regarded as later additions (Deut. 4:29–31; 30:1–10; 1 Kings 8:46–53).[56] It is possible that these somewhat tone down the uncompromising rigor of the literature, but it is equally clear that they do not measurably affect the main theme of the piece, namely, Yahweh's will for a community of obedience and justice.

There can be no doubt that this primal liberation word of Moses has now hardened into an ideology. It serves as a critique of comfortable, culture-accommodating religion, whether toward Babylonian imperialism or Canaanite city-kings. Thus the call for repentance and disengagement from culture religion persists.

2. In sharp contention with that trajectory, two pieces of literature growing out of the promissory tradition are rooted in another view of reality.

First, Albrektson has argued that Lamentations is a response to the harshness of Deuteronomy.[57] In the poetry of Lamentations, appeal is made to the claims of Jerusalem. Thus, Lamentations casts itself much more willingly upon the graciousness and freedom of Yahweh, the abiding faithfulness of Yahweh which is unconditional and unreserved. That modest affirmation (3:22-24) cannot be derived from the abrasion and urgency of the Mosaic tradition but appeals to an alternative theological model more likely rooted in the confidence of the Jerusalem traditions and institutions. Thus both the assurance of 3:22-24 and the confidence of 3:31-33 appear to be echoes of the promise of *ḥesed* in 2 Sam. 7:11-16. The allusions to the royal psalms which Albrektson has noted strengthen the likelihood of such an appeal.

In a similar though more frontal way, the poem of Job may be understood as a protest against the crisp certitude of Deuteronomy. If indeed Deuteronomy can in moralistic simplicity reduce everything to discernible moral causes, Job counters with an awareness that life will not be so easily explained, that mystery moves in ambiguity and lack of clarity, and that God in his freedom has other concerns than exact response to human behavior.[58] Thus the God of Job is not inordinately preoccupied with "the human condition." There is no doubt that Job protests the moral singularity of his friends who speak out of a perspective not unlike that of Deuteronomy. The speech of Yahweh completely rejects those categories.

The rootage of the alternative perspective of the poet is not so easy to identify. We may note two attempts pertinent to our investigation. Samuel Terrien has located the poem of Job in the new year festival in the Babylonian exile as a para-cultic drama of one for whom history no longer holds any promise.[59] The innocent sufferer "has lost all, and for all practical purposes of historical realism, he has died, but will live again by faith."[60] Terrien sees that an appeal to the creation myths (older than Israel's historical memories) makes possible "a poetic discussion of the theology of grace." Indeed the poet presents himself as "theologian of pure grace, over against the fallacies of proto-Pelagianism."[61] Thus the basic themes of the religion of the city-state, a royal person, and a creation myth, surface here as resources for Israel when the historicizing morality of Deuteronomy has failed. Such a difference of trajectory is apparent, even if linkage of the poem of Job to an historical crisis cannot be sustained.

From a quite different perspective, Cross has reached conclusions similar to those of Terrien.[62] "Yahweh the Lord of history has failed to act. El or Baal, the transcendent creator spoke."[63] In Job, opines Cross, the ancient myths regained their meaning. Cross draws the radical conclusion that Job brought the ancient religion of Israel to an end and evoked the resurgence of the oldest pre-Israelite myths, precisely those myths to which the creation faith of Israel made appeal.

We should not neglect the sociological implication of the embrace of older myth at the expense of historical self-awareness in a time of crisis. Needful though that choice was in exile, such a decision is inherently socially conservative. There is not within the return to myth the nerve or energy to take the actions which would transform historical circumstance. Indeed, it was the rejection of those very myths which permitted the Israelite novum in history and religion.[64] Conversely, such a "theology of grace" contains within it the acceptance of things as they are, and there is here no call to repentance in terms of historical engagement. Thus, from one perspective Job reacts against the passionate stridency of Deuteronomy which knows too much and asks too much. On the other hand, it reduces historical nerve and asks an embrace of helplessness in the face of the terror of history and the hiddenness of God. Thus Miles, in a socially conservative position albeit faithful to Job, sees that "there was truth in what had been excluded, and in the book of Job that truth returns."[65] The poet is challenged to retain the old knowledge against the new; and the old knowledge is that God is not always victorious and "Job's comforting is a play about the return of the truth that God and natural reality are inextricably one."[66]

The trajectories are clear in the apparent tension between Job and Deuteronomy. Job does indeed represent the "old truth" that oppressive life must be accepted as ordained, surely a comfort in exile, while Deuteronomy bears the "new truth."[67] Exile brings these truths to sharp conflict, the one offering assurance of grace, the other the urgency of repentance. Exile may be read, then, either as a destiny to be embraced or as an historical situation to be transformed.

3. Second Isaiah, it is commonly agreed, is the poetic matrix in which the crisis of the trajectories receives a new articulation.[68] In an earlier essay,[69] Bernhard Anderson showed the extent to which Deutero-Isaiah utilized the exodus traditions to announce that his own time was a time like that of Moses, in which Israel as a newness in history had been willed by God. Thus Second Isaiah is a statement about historical redemption, making ready use of the Mosaic tradition.

More recently and with more precise focus on covenant, Anderson has concluded that it is the Abrahamic/Davidic covenant which dominates Second Isaiah.[70] Moreover, "the Mosaic covenant is appropriately absent from Second Isaiah's prophecy, for obedience to commandments is not regarded as a prerequisite for blessing and welfare."[71] "The ground for hope, therefore, is not a change on the side of man but, so to speak, on the side of God."[72]

Second Isaiah is the primary locus in Scripture where the trajectories do come together in a remarkably synthetic way. Both the history-transcending God of Job and the militant historicality of Deuteronomy come to positive expression. But on balance, Anderson has rightly discerned that the promises of God are the ultimate word of the poet. Thus Second Isaiah shows how it was necessary in the exile to make a major reorientation in traditions and move the normative faith of Israel from the one trajectory to the other.

In Second Isaiah, as in Job, creation themes reshape Israel's memory and hope according to the Jerusalem trajectory. It is the royal theme of Abraham/Noah/David which gives the poetry of Second Isaiah its energizing power.[73]

Anderson's stress makes it unmistakable that in exile the Abrahamic tradition has gained a new centrality which tilts the religion of Israel essentially toward promise. In that context, we should note the bold proposal of Van Seters that the Abraham materials were formulated in this period to meet the situation of dislocation.[74] That perhaps claims too much. We can observe that the theological inventiveness of the period shows a tendency to return to the royal-creation-promise tradition with its social conservatism, the very tradition which the "new truth" of Moses challenged.

4. Finally for this period, we should note the way in which Wolff[75] has juxtaposed the traditions of D and P in the exile. He begins with the two-sided covenant formula: "I will be your God and you shall be my people," and argues that P and D, reflecting their two trajectories, each stress one part of the formula. P gives emphasis to "I will be your God," and D stresses "You shall be my people." That is a fair summary of the issue in the exile. Obviously, both statements bear a truth and both are essential in exile. The alternative stress indicates not only a different theological reading of the promise and of the resources but also a very different sociological analysis of what is required and what is possible.

V

The final period we shall consider, the postexilic period, may be briefly mentioned by reference to the work of Paul Hanson.[76] Hanson has presented a major proposal, admittedly too schematic, for organizing the postexilic literature of the canon. He proposes that the beginning point for understanding this literature is the dialectic Deutero-Isaiah articulated between vision and reality.

In the period after Deutero-Isaiah, various groups in Israel each embraced a part of the dialectic and made that part its standing ground for faith and literature. Thus, Second Isaiah provides poetic and theological rationale for both the "pragmatists" and the "visionaries." For Hanson, the pragmatists are identified as the group in power, centering around the accommodating priesthood in Jerusalem. The visionaries are those groups now shut out of power and driven to hope in a new act of God which would invert historical reality and bring them to power. This latter group, pressed by its "world-weariness" to apocalyptic, may be identified with the circles of the Levites who were previously influential and now had become increasingly marginal.

Hanson's work utilizes the sociological paradigm of Karl Mannheim with its definition of ideology as a self-serving justification for the status quo and utopia as the passionate hoping for an alternative future. In presenting such a paradigm, Hanson limits his attention to rootage in Second Isaiah and does not go behind this literature for his purposes. But for our purposes, it is important to observe that Second Isaiah is not the first articulator nor the inventor of this dialectic. It lies deep and old in the tradition of Israel. Thus the "visionaries" and "pragmatists" of the postexilic period continue, in a way appropriate to their time and place, the same stances already discerned in the hopeful liberation movement of Moses and the accommodating, embracing creation-royal faith of the Davidic circles. The visionaries continue the hope and passion of the liberation tradition which believes that the present order is sharply called into question by God's promises. The pragmatists continue the confident affirmation of the present as the proper ordering willed by God, perhaps to be gradually changed but on the whole to be preserved. It is the substantive connections between the work of Gottwald and Mendenhall in the early period, Cross in the history of the priesthood, and especially Hanson in the later period, which permit us to speak of trajectories.

VI

We may then suggest a schematic way in which the trajectories can be understood. A trajectory, of course, is not a straitjacket into which every piece of data must be made to fit, but it lets us see the tendencies which continue to occur and to observe the influences which flow from one period to another. Over the five periods we have considered, generally following the periodization used by recent scholars in delimiting their work, the continuities may be outlined in the form of a chart.

Up to this point, scholars have focused on the tension in various periods. Mendenhall and Gottwald have concentrated on the early period, Cross on the monarchial period, and Hanson on postexilic developments. The point argued here is that continuities may be traced through the various periods in each of the strands, thus permitting us to term them "trajectories."[77]

Moreover, we may suggest, again in quite schematic fashion, common elements which appear continuously in each of the trajectories. Among them are:

A. *The Royal Trajectory*
(1) prefers to speak in myths of unity
(2) speaks a language of fertility (creation) and continuity (royal institutions)
(3) preferred mode of perception is that of universal comprehensiveness
(4) appears to be fostered by and valued among urban "haves"
(5) tends to be socially conserving with a primary valuing of stability
(6) focuses on the glory and holiness of God's person and institutions geared to that holiness

B. *The Liberation Trajectory*
(1) prefers to tell concrete stories of liberation
(2) speaks a language of war and discontinuity
(3) preferred mode of perception is that of historical specificity
(4) appears to be fostered by and valued among peasant "have nots"
(5) tends to be socially revolutionary with a primary valuing of transformation
(6) focuses on the justice and righteousness of God's will

	I. Mosaic Period (emergence of liberation)	II. The United Monarchy ("paganization")	III. Divided Monarchy (the clash of traditions)	IV. Exile (traditions in crisis)	V. Postexilic Period
A. imperial power and city-kings		Zadok: the Aaronite priesthood, royal theology and creation faith	royal history	P: "I will be your God"	Zadokite priesthood: pragmatists urban "haves" scribes comfortable syncretists Ezekiel 44
			in tension 1 Kings 21: Ahab/Elijah Amos 7:10–17: Amaziah/Amos Isa. 7:1–9–7: Ahaz/Isaiah Jer. 22:13–19: Jehoiakim/Josiah	II. Isa. "Look to the Rock from which you were hewn" (51:1) "Behold, I am doing a new thing" (43:18)	
B. revolt of peasants		Abiathar: the Mushite priesthood	prophetic alternatives	D: "You will be my people"	Levitical priesthood: visionaries peasant "have nots" apocalypticists waiting purists Isaiah 60–62

To the extent that this schematic presentation is correct, it means that these tendencies will be found at every period in the appropriate trajectory. A history of traditions approach must include a sociological analysis so that we are aware of the social function of each of the traditions, the authority assigned to it, the claims made for it and the power and social vision deriving from it.[78]

VII

It is perhaps premature to speak of the emergence of a new paradigm for scholarship, but there are hints in that direction.[79] It is clear that the older syntheses are now generally perceived as inadequate. This applies not only to the evolutionary scheme of Wellhausen but in a less incisive way also to the credo-tradition hypothesis of Von Rad.[80] Evidences of the emerging consensus around this provisional paradigm are as varied as Westermann's proposal of a contrast of blessing and salvation[81] and the suggestive title of Cross's statement, *Canaanite Myth and Hebrew Epic*. Westermann, in a programmatic way, has shown that blessing and salvation represent quite different theological worlds. He has not gone on to draw sociological conclusions nor to suggest that Old Testament interpretation may be largely organized this way. Cross has finely shown the dialectic of epic, which seeks to be concretely historical, and myth, which moves in the direction of syncretism. Cross means both to move beyond the historical emphasis of the American and German schools and the mythic inclination of the Scandinavians to show that the perspectives of the two are mutually corrective.

1. It can be argued that such a reading of Israel's faith and history is possible only by an appeal to a particular theory of history. And there is no doubt that a Marxist class reading of the Bible is not unrelated to this paradigm. Concerning the early period, Gottwald acknowledges this influence and makes a deliberate use of such a frame of reference.[82] Concerning the later period, Hanson is decisively guided by the conceptualization of Mannheim.[83]

Having acknowledged the influence (explicit or not) of this theory of society, several comments are in order:

(a) There has been some critical objection to the use of such a model for interpretation. Alan J. Hauser[84] has objected to the decisive role played by a Marxist model. More judiciously, Brian Kovacs[85] observed that by the use of Mannheim's model, Hanson has been led to and permitted certain conclusions which would have been very different given a different sociological model. Undoubtedly, much more testing remains to be done, and a clear consensus in this direction is far from established.

(b) It will, of course, be tempting to dismiss the entire approach by a rejection of Marxist presuppositions.[86] In response to such a criticism, Robert McAfee Brown has rightly said that the real issue is not if Marxist categories may be used but if the presentation and discernment is correct in terms of the data and if the categories serve responsible interpretation.[87] When that question is answered, the issue of Marxist presuppositions becomes largely irrelevant.

(c) Most importantly, it will need to be recognized again that there is no "presuppositionless" exegesis. It is not a matter of using Marxist categories or continuing "objective" interpretation. The paradigm suggested here requires that the critical guild become aware of its own categories and, indeed, of its own "embourgeoisement."[88] For example, Hauser seems quite unaware of his own presuppositions and seems to imagine that his own critical approach is socially disinterested. In this view, John McKenzie seems also to misunderstand and deliver a polemic against Marxist categories without discerning what the argument is about. There is no doubt that every paradigm, that of Wellhausen, Von Rad, or any other, including this one, contains presuppositions which govern interpretation. Thus, the present sociological discussion presses hermeneutical considerations even upon our more "objective" work in literature and history.[89]

2. The trajectories suggested here may illuminate the various alternatives in current theological discussion. Most broadly, the alternatives may be grouped in terms of process hermeneutics and liberation hermeneutics.[90] In terms of our previous discussion, process theologies may be generally placed in the trajectory of royal theology which is concerned with large comprehensive issues, which regards the concreteness of historical memory as a matter of little interest, and which is concerned with the continuities of the process. Current scholarly investigation within this trajectory: (a) is likely seeking meaningful interface with current cultural forms; (b) is most likely to be lodged in university contexts and their epistemological commitments and not primarily interested in the forming of the synagogue/church as an alternative and distinct community of faith; and (c) is likely to have an inherent bias toward social conservatism. Of course, persons engaged in this scholarship may indeed be found elsewhere, but the reference group is likely to be the same. It is equally clear that persons in this scholarly tradition may themselves be concerned for an ethical radicalness, but it is not likely to be rooted in this epistemological tradition.

We may cite one recent example, the judgment of Miles about the "old truth" that "God and the harshness of nature, though they may not be One, are not separable."[91] Such an affirmation clearly inclines to seeing God simply as part of the process and runs the ready danger of giving sanction to the way things are because they cannot in any case be changed. Of course, Miles does not even hint at such an extrapolation. The slide from nature which is not separable from God and cannot be changed to history understood the same way, however, is not a difficult one. Such an understanding of the trajectory does not, of course, imply a criticism of the persons who work in the trajectory, for they themselves may be passionate in other directions. The *Tendenz* itself inclines toward uninterrupted development. Moreover, that *Tendenz* has a remarkable capacity to coopt and contain the specific angularities of the other tradition, as, for example, Solomon containing the ark in the temple.

3. Conversely, the various liberation theologies in their epistemological abrasiveness likely may be located on the trajectory rooted in Moses. They are inclined to focus on the concreteness of historical memory and regard more sweeping, unitive statements as less important and compelling. Current scholarly work in this trajectory: (a) is likely not so directly concerned with contact with cultural forms and values but is addressed to a particular faith community living in uneasy tension with the dominant cultural forms and values; (b) is most likely to be lodged in a confessing community or a school of it. It is inclined to be concerned primarily with the faithful effectiveness of the confessing community and to believe that the dominant rationality will permit no ready point of contact without coopting. And, if the scholar is

lodged in a university context, it is still likely the case that the main referent is a confessing group; (c) is likely to have an intrinsic bias toward social, ethical radicalness. This does not mean, of course, that in every case the person involved is socially radical, for he/she may in fact be conservative. But the practice of this scholarship will predictably lead to the surfacing of such issues, even without the person intentionally doing so.

The pursuit of this paradigm of trajectories from early Israel until current scholarship, informed as it is by sociological considerations, is important in two ways, both affirming that there is no disinterestedness in the text or in the interpreter. Such a paradigm will permit texts to be understood more effectively in terms of their placement in Israel's faith and life and in the traditioning process. Such a paradigm will regularly force more attention to the interest and hermeneutical presuppositions of the interpreter and his/her community of reference. The pursuit of these trajectories may be a major service biblical study can offer to colleagues in other disciplines, for it may provide ground from which to do serious criticism. This discernment might lead one to expect a very different kind of scholarship, each faithful to a stream of tradition, depending on the context of the interpreter.

NOTES

1. On the extensive literature, see L. Rost, "Sinaibund und Davidsbund," *TLZ* 72 (1947): 129–34; and "Erwägungen zu Hosea 4:14f," *Festschrift Alfred Bertholet,* ed. W. Baumgartner, O. Eissfeldt, K. Elliger, and L. Rost (Tübingen: Mohr, 1950), pp. 459–60; M. Sekine, "Davidsbund und Sinaibund bei Jeremia," *VT* 9 (1959): 45–57; A. H. J. Gunneweg, "Sinaibund und Davidsbund," *VT* 10 (1960): 335–41; Murray Newman, *The People of the Covenant* (New York: Abingdon, 1962); David N. Freedman, "Divine Commitment and Human Obligation," *Int* 18 (1964): 419–31; Delbert Hillers, *Covenant: The History of a Biblical Idea* (Baltimore: Johns Hopkins University Press, 1969); Tomoo Ishida, *The Royal Dynasties in Ancient Israel,* BZAW 142 (Berlin: de Gruyter, 1977), pp. 99–117; Ronald Clements, *Abraham and David,* SBT 2/5 (London: SCM Press, 1967); and the general comments of Dennis McCarthy, *Old Testament Covenant* (Richmond: John Knox Press, 1972), especially Chapters 2 and 5.

2. Murray Newman, *People of the Covenant,* had already argued that the Abraham-David tradition is derived from the south and the Mosaic tradition from the north. The difference, of course, is more cultural and sociological than geographical. Bernhard W. Anderson, *Creation versus Chaos* (New York: Association Press, 1967) has shown the creative power of the Jerusalem establishment as expressed in the various creation and royal traditions.

3. Cf. the summary of Douglas Knight, *The Traditions of Israel,* SBLDS 9 (Missoula: Scholars Press, 1973).

4. James M. Robinson and Helmut Koester, *Trajectories through Early Christianity* (Philadelphia: Fortress Press, 1971).

5. On the issue of continuity and discontinuity, see especially the discussions of

Peter Ackroyd, *Continuity: A Contribution to the Study of the Old Testament Religious Traditions* (Oxford: Blackwell, 1962) and "Continuity and Discontinuity: Rehabilitation and Authentication," *Tradition and Theology in the Old Testament,* ed. Douglas Knight (Philadelphia: Fortress Press, 1977), pp. 215–34.

6. See the summary of Claus Westermann, "Creation and History in the Old Testament," *The Gospel and Human Destiny,* ed. V. Vajta (Minneapolis: Augsburg, 1971), pp. 11–38. Westermann has observed how the different traditions yield very different presentations of God. He has not pursued the sociological dimension of the argument, but it is clear that the theological *Tendenz* of a trajectory serves specific interests.

7. George Mendenhall, "The Hebrew Conquest of Palestine," *BA* 25 (1962): 66–87. His alternative hypothesis has been given a positive treatment by John Bright, *A History of Israel,* 2nd ed. (Philadelphia: Westminster, 1972), p. 133, n. 69, and John L. McKenzie, *The World of the Judges* (New York: Prentice-Hall, 1966), pp. 95–98.

8. Mendenhall, "The Hebrew Conquest," p. 87.

9. Ibid., p. 75.

10. George Mendenhall, "The Conflict between Value Systems and Social Control," *Unity and Diversity,* ed. Hans Goedicke and J. J. M. Roberts (Baltimore: Johns Hopkins University Press, 1975), pp. 169–80; "The Monarchy," *Int* 29 (1975): 155–70; "Samuel's Broken Rib: Deuteronomy 32," *No Famine in the Land,* ed. James W. Flanagan and Anita Weisbrod Robinson (Missoula: Scholars Press, 1975), pp. 63–74, and his synthesis in *The Tenth Generation* (Baltimore: Johns Hopkins University Press, 1973), especially Chapters 1, 7, and 8. These studies are derivative from his early work on covenant in 1954. Only now is he exploring the sociological aspects of that study.

11. Norman K. Gottwald, "Biblical Theology or Biblical Sociology?" *Radical Religion 2* (1975): 46–57; "Domain Assumptions and Societal Models in the Study of Pre-Monarchic Israel," *VTSup* 28 (1974): 89–100, and "Were the Early Israelites Pastoral Nomads?" *Rhetorical Criticism,* ed. Jared J. Jackson and Martin Kessler (Pittsburgh: Pickwick, 1974), pp. 223–255; Norman K. Gottwald and Frank S. Frick, "The Social World of Ancient Israel," *SBLSP* (1975), pp. 165–78; cf. Article 10 in this volume.

12. For our argument and its implications, it is important to note that both Gottwald and Mendenhall are engaged in the construction of alternative models. Obviously, increased data can still be adapted to the regnant models, but the importance of their work is precisely in the proposal of a new comprehensive model for interpretation.

13. Eric Wolf, *Peasants* (Englewood Cliffs, N.J.: Prentice-Hall, 1966) has provided a basic study of this social factor. Cf. John H. Halligan, "The Role of the Peasant in the Amarna Period," *SBLSP* (1976), pp. 155–70. Concerning what is perhaps a contemporary parallel to this crisis in Israel, Hugo Blanco (*Land or Death* [New York: Pathfinder, 1972], p. 110) asserts, "We must always keep in mind that the historic problem of the peasant around which all others revolve is the problem of *land.*"

14. *Tenth Generation,* Chapter 7, and more recently, "Social Organization in Early Israel," *Magnalia Dei: The Mighty Acts of God,* ed. Frank Cross, Werner Lemke, and P. D. Miller, Jr. (Garden City, N.Y.: Doubleday, 1976), pp. 132–51.

15. Mendenhall, *Tenth Generation,* pp. 19–31.

16. Martin Buber, *The Kingship of God,* 3rd ed. (New York: Harper & Row, 1966), especially Chapter 7. It is remarkable that Buber had seen this long before the work of Mendenhall and Baltzer.

17. Klaus Baltzer, *The Covenant Formulary* (Philadelphia: Fortress Press, 1971; first published in 1964).

18. George Mendenhall, *Law and Covenant in Israel and the Ancient Near East* (Pittsburgh: Biblical Colloquium, 1955).

19. Mendenhall, *Tenth Generation,* p. 12.

20. Mendenhall, "The Conflict between Value Systems and Social Control." In tabulating the contrasts between social theories based on "covenant" and "law," it is likely that he uses "law" in the same sense as does Paul in his radical critique of the theological function of the law.

21. Mendenhall, *Law and Covenant.*

22. See the summary of Dennis McCarthy, *Old Testament Covenant.*

23. The earlier scholarly consideration of Mendenhall's work focused on the radical theological break with the religion of the day. Only more recently has the social counterpart of that radical theology been more widely considered. The links between the theological and sociological are evident in *Tenth Generation.* See also Gottwald, "Biblical Theology or Biblical Sociology?" and especially M. Douglas Meeks, "God's Suffering Power and Liberation," *JRT* 11 (1977): 44–54.

24. A model articulation of that insight is offered by G. Ernest Wright, *The Old Testament against Its Environment,* SBT 2 (London: SCM Press, 1950).

25. Gottwald, "Biblical Theology or Biblical Sociology?" is especially attentive to the social use and function of religion, an insight surely Marxist in its awareness. His summary of the break in sociology asserted by Yahwism is this: "In brief the chief articles of Yahwistic faith may be socio-economically 'de-mythologized' as follows: 'Yahweh' is the historically centralized primordial power to establish and sustain social equality in the face of oppression from without and simultaneously provincialism and non-egalitarian tendencies from within the society. . . . Yahweh is unlike the other gods of the ancient Near East as Israel's egalitarian inter-tribal order is unlike the other ancient Near Eastern social systems. . . . The social-organization principle in Israel finds its counterpart in a symbolic ideological exclusionary principle in the image of the deity" (p. 52).

26. Acknowledgment must of course be made of Feuerbach's criticism that every religious statement is indeed a projection of social reality. Gottwald (ibid., p. 48) appears to move in this direction. "It seems that it is primarily from the historico-social struggle of a sovereign inter-tribal community that the major analogies for conceiving Yahweh are drawn." Mendenhall more readily appeals to the category of revelation and exercises a kind of theological positivism. Thus there is a difference between them on this point. Mendenhall (*Tenth Generation,* p. 16) alludes to the problem. "Do the people create a religion, or does the religion create a people? Historically, when we are dealing with the formative period of Moses and Judges, there can be no doubt that the latter is correct, for the historical, linguistic, and archaeological evidence is too powerful to deny. Religion furnished the foundation for a unity far beyond anything that had existed before, and the covenant appears to have been the only conceivable instrument through which the unity was brought about and expressed." In any case, their critical approaches disclose in fresh ways the fact that not only the dominant theology but the dominant scholarly methodology is not disinterested.

27. My colleague, M. Douglas Meeks ("God's Suffering Power and Liberation") has discerned how a notion of God who is passionless serves well a psychology and a sociology which is passionless. This observation appears to be especially important to liberation movements as they address the theological and sociological paradigms of dominance. Cf. Jane Marie Luecke, "The Dominance Syndrome," *Christian Century* 94 (1977): 405-7, for a summary of the matter.

28. Mendenhall has seen that to the extent that God is continuous with the social, economic system, outsiders have no court of transcendent appeal against the dominant ordering. That linkage of sociology and theology is especially evident in Egyptian religion, which on the one hand is committed to order and on the other hand regards Pharaoh as an embodiment of that ordering divinity. On both sociological and theological grounds, revolution is unthinkable. See Henri Frankfort, *Kingship and the Gods* (Chicago: University of Chicago Press, 1948). The subtitle is telling: "A Study of Ancient Near Eastern Religion as the Integration of Society and Nature." Such integration brings with it social conservatism.

29. The Mosaic tradition is premised on the affirmation of a God who has freedom from the regime. On the freedom of God in this tradition, see Walther Zimmerli, "Prophetic Proclamation and Reinterpretation," *Tradition and Theology in the Old Testament,* pp. 69-100. Zimmerli sees the tradition as being concerned with the fact that "Yahweh in his freedom can utter his word anew."

30. In addition to the various articles in *The Bible and Liberation* (Berkeley: Radical Religion, 1976) which make primary use of Marxist critical tools, see especially Gottwald, "Early Israel and 'the Asiatic Mode of Production,' " SBLSP (1976), pp. 145-54.

31. Marx's programmatic statement in his "Critique of Hegel's Philosophy of Right," is: "Thus the criticism of heaven is transformed into the criticism of earth, the criticism of religion into the criticism of law, and the criticism of theology into the criticism of politics." Cf. *The Marx-Engels Reader,* ed. R. C. Tucker (New York: W. W. Norton, 1972), p. 13. My criticism of Gottwald, from whom I have learned so much, is that he has not given sufficient attention to a critique of heaven.

32. In Israel, poetry may be understood as the rhetoric of the alternative community which refuses to abide by the prose of the empire. On the act of poetry as an assertion of liberation, see David N. Freedman, "Pottery, Poetry and Prophecy: An Essay on Biblical Poetry," *JBL* 96 (1977): 5-26, and less directly, "Divine Names and Titles in Early Hebrew Poetry," *Magnalia Dei: The Mighty Acts of God,* pp. 55-107. In the latter essay, the discernment of "militant," "revival," and "syncretism" in poetry (pp. 56-57) is worth noting because these aspects suggest the social use of the poems. On rhetoric as a tool for an alternative community, see Rubem Alves, *Tomorrow's Child* (New York: Harper & Row, 1972).

33. See Norbert Lohfink, "Culture Shock and Theology," *BTB* 7 (1977): 12-21, on culture crisis and the constructive function of Deuteronomy. For an alternative understanding of the social function of Deuteronomy, see Joseph Gutmann, *The Image and the Word* (Missoula: Scholars Press, 1977), pp. 5-25. Gutmann appeals especially to the hypothesis of W. E. Claburn, "The Fiscal Basis of Josiah's Reform," *JBL* 92 (1973): 11-22.

34. The book promised from Orbis is entitled, *The Tribes of Yahweh: A Sociology of the Religion of Liberated Israel, 1250-1050 B.C.E.* [published 1979].

35. Mendenhall, *Tenth Generation,* pp. 16, 182, 195-96; "The Monarchy," pp. 157-66; "Samuel's Broken Rib," p. 67.

36. It is evident that the critical perversion came not with David but with Solomon. See Frank M. Cross, *Canaanite Myth and Hebrew Epic: Essays in the History of the Religion of Israel* (Cambridge: Harvard University Press, 1973), pp. 237–41, and W. Brueggemann, *In Man We Trust* (Richmond, Va.: John Knox Press, 1972), pp. 64–77.

37. On the Solomonic fascination with Egypt, see T. N. D. Mettinger, *Solomonic State Officials* (Lund: Gleerup, 1971) and G. Ernest Wright, *Biblical Archaeology* (Philadelphia: Westminster, 1957), pp. 120–63.

38. On this tension, see W. Brueggemann, "Presence of God, Cultic," *IDBSup*, pp. 680–83.

39. Cross, *Canaanite Myth and Hebrew Epic*, pp. 195–215.

40. Cross's location of Zadok clearly is an advance beyond the position of H. H. Rowley (see Cross, p. 209). Nonetheless, Rowley ("Zadok and Nehustan," *JBL* 58 [1939]: 113–41; "Melchizedeq und Zadok [Gen. 14 and Ps. 110]," *Festschrift Alfred Bertholet* [Tübingen: Mohr, 1950], pp. 461–72) had already seen that Zadok represents a cultic tradition essentially alien to the Mosaic tradition.

41. Cross, *Canaanite Myth and Hebrew Epic*, p. 211.

42. Here we are concerned with the traditioning process and not with consideration of historically objective issues. But note must be taken of the radical position of John Van Seters, *Abraham in History and Tradition* (New Haven: Yale University Press, 1975) and T. L. Thompson, *The Historicity of the Patriarchal Narratives*, BZAW 133 (Berlin: de Gruyter, 1974).

43. See Anderson, *Creation versus Chaos*.

44. On Ezekiel's resolution of the role of the Messiah in the Mosaic tradition, see Jon D. Levenson, *Theology of the Program of Restoration of Ezekiel 40–48*, HSM 10 (Missoula: Scholars Press, 1976), Chapter 2. On the reassertion of the older pre-Mosaic traditions, see Cross, *Canaanite Myth and Hebrew Epic*, pp. 343–346.

45. Questions of literary history and unity in the narrative are difficult. See O. H. Steck, *Uberlieferung und Zeitgeschichte im der Elia-Erzählungen*, WMANT 26 (Neukirchen-Vluyn: Neukirchener, 1968), pp. 40–53, and G. Fohrer, *Elia*, ATANT 53 (Zurich: Zwingli, 1968), pp. 24–29.

46. On Amos and the torah, see R. Bach, "Gottesrecht und weltliches Recht in der Verkündigung des Propheten Amos," *Festscrift Gunther Dehn* (Neukirchen-Vluyn: Neukirchener, 1957), pp. 23–24.

47. That the Isaiah traditions will not fit any neat scheme is evidenced by the decision of Von Rad (*Old Testament Theology* [London: Oliver and Boyd, 1965], Vol. 2, pp. 147–75) to place him in the Jerusalem tradition. For a more refined judgment see O. H. Steck, "Theological Streams of Tradition," *Tradition and Theology in the Old Testament*, pp. 193–94.

48. Ronald Clements (*Prophecy and Covenant*, SBT 43 [London: SCM Press, 1965], pp. 39–43) has observed that the drastic announcement of an end represents a new radical announcement in Israel.

49. It may of course be too subtle to relate the "end" of Amos to the "no end" of Isaiah, for Isaiah clearly refers to Davidic Israel, while Amos presumably refers to the northern kingdom. See also Frank Crüsemann, "Kritik an Amos in Deuteronomistischen Geschichtswerk," *Probleme Biblischer Theologie*, ed. H. W. Wolff (Munich: Kaiser, 1971), pp. 57–63.

50. It is clear that the Davidic promises do not function in the poetry of Jeremiah. Indeed it is precisely his opponents who continue to rely on them. And in

Deuteronomy, surely closely related to Jeremiah, the balance between Mosaic and Davidic factors is in dispute, but there is little doubt that the Mosaic tradition is decisive. The situation is quite different in Ezekiel, as Levenson has shown.

51. See W. Brueggemann, "David and His Theologian, *CBQ* 30 (1968): 156-81; "From Dust to Kingship," *ZAW* 84 (1972): 1-18; and Walter Wifall, "Gen. 6:1-4, A Royal Davidic Myth? *BT* 5 (1975): 294-301; "The Breath of His Nostrils," *CBQ* 36 (1974): 237-40.

52. See H. W. Wolff, "The Elohistic Fragments in the Pentateuch," *The Vitality of Old Testament Traditions*, by W. Brueggemann and H. W. Wolff (Atlanta: John Knox Press, 1975), pp. 67-82, and Alan Jenks, *The Elohist and North Israelite Traditions*, SBLMS 22 (Missoula: Scholars Press, 1977).

53. See J. A. Soggin, "Ancient Israelite Poetry and Ancient 'Codes' of Law, and the Sources of 'J' and 'E' of the Pentateuch," *VTSup* 28 (1974): 193-95.

54. The most recent discussion is that of Werner E. Lemke, "The Way of Obedience: 1 Kings 13 and the Structure of the Deuteronomistic History," *Magnalia Dei: The Mighty Acts of God*, pp. 301-26, unambiguously placing Deuteronomy in the tradition of Moses and the prophetic demand for obedience. Lemke further develops the direction of Wolff's important essay.

55. Von Rad, *Old Testament Theology* (New York: Harper & Row, 1962), Vol. 1, pp. 334-47. See my derivative discussion, "The Kerygma of the Deuteronomistic Historian," *Int* 22 (1968): 387-402.

56. See H. W. Wolff, "The Kerygma of the Deuteronomistic Historical Work," *The Vitality of Old Testament Traditions*, p. 91-97.

57. B. Albrektson, *Studies in the Text and Theology of the Book of Lamentations* (Lund: Gleerup, 1963), pp. 214-39.

58. The fact that both Job and Deuteronomy have important connections with Jeremiah make it quite plausible that Job is grappling with the issues forced by the Deuteronomist. Cf. James A. Sanders, "Hermeneutics in True and False Prophecy," *Canon and Authority*, ed. George Coats and Burke Long (Philadelphia: Fortress Press, 1977), p. 28: ". . . Job was surely written in part to record a resounding No to such inversions of the Deuteronomic ethic of election." There is, to be sure, a counter opinion among scholars that it is not possible to link the poem of Job to any specific historical situation. See especially J. J. M. Roberts, "Job and the Israelite Religious Tradition," *ZAW* 89 (1977): 107-14. Even if that be granted, the religious tendency of the poem is surely in a direction other than that of Deuteronomy.

59. Samuel Terrien, "The Yahweh Speeches and Job's Responses," *Rev-Exp* 68 (1971): 497-509.

60. Ibid., p. 508.

61. Ibid., p. 498.

62. Cross, *Canaanite Myth and Hebrew Epic*, pp. 343-46.

63. Ibid., p. 344.

64. The break and the discontinuity caused by the emergence of Israel has been stressed by Mendenhall. Cf. *Tenth Generation*, pp. 1-19, and "Migration Theories vs. Culture Change as an Explanation for Early Israel," *SBLSP* (1976), pp. 135-43. The problem with a history of religions approach to these issues is that it is ideologically and methodologically committed to continuity as the primary agenda.

65. John A. Miles, Jr. "Gagging on Job, or the Comedy of Religious Exhaustion," *Semeia* 7 (1977): 110.

66. Ibid., pp. 110-13.

67. The "new truth" of the Mosaic revolution contrasts with the "old truth" of which Miles writes. When the old imperial gods are embraced, social stability is assured. Freedman ("Divine Names and Titles") identifies Judges 5 among the poems of "Militant Mosaic Yahwism." It is the coming of the new God, unknown in the empire, which causes a new social possibility.

68. Deutero-Isaiah has the capacity to utilize all the various traditions. See Von Rad, *Old Testament Theology,* Vol. 2, pp. 238-43.

69. Bernhard W. Anderson, "Exodus Typology in Second Isaiah," *Israel's Prophetic Heritage,* ed. Bernhard W. Anderson and Walter Harrelson (New York: Harper & Row, 1962), pp. 177-95.

70. Anderson, "Exodus and Covenant in Second Isaiah and Prophetic Tradition," *Magnalia Dei: The Mighty Acts of God,* pp. 339-60.

71. Ibid., p. 356.

72. Ibid., p. 355.

73. It is the faithfulness of God to which appeal must be made in exile. In the categories of Freedman, now Israel must speak of "divine commitment" and not of "human obligation." On the abiding *ḥesed* of Yahweh to his people, see Otto Eissfeldt, "The Promises of Grace to David in Isaiah 55:1-5," *Israel's Prophetic Heritage,* pp. 177-95. While the point of connection is unclear, the oracle of 55:3 is not unrelated to the anticipation of Lam. 3:22-24.

74. See Note 42. Aside from the specific critical judgments he makes, Van Seters has made a strong case that a situation of exile and a theology of promise are precisely appropriate to each other.

75. Hans Walter Wolff, *The Old Testament: A Guide to Its Writings* (Philadelphia: Fortress Press, 1973), pp. 32-44.

76. Paul Hanson, *The Dawn of Apocalyptic* (Philadelphia: Fortress Press, 1975).

77. Steck, "Theological Streams of Tradition," has pursued a parallel investigation utilizing the word "stream." However, Steck's presentation tends to identify so many diverse streams that the concept is diffused. Here I suggest that several of Steck's streams might be considered together as belonging to the same general context.

78. An important resource for further investigation is the book edited by Douglas Knight, *Tradition and Theology in the Old Testament.* Knight's own essay, "Revelation through Tradition," suggests the decisive way in which the traditioning community is engaged in the process of trajectory development.

79. It is of course presumptuous to speak of an emerging paradigm. The definitional statement of Thomas Kuhn, *The Structure of Scientific Revolutions* (Chicago: University of Chicago Press, 1970) has created a new awareness of the ways in which scholarship changes and/or advances. Gottwald ("Biblical Theology or Biblical Sociology?" pp. 52,55) both critiques the paradigm of "biblical theology," by which he means a quite identifiable approach, and hints at the alternative informed by sociology. From quite another scholarly perspective, John Dominic Crossan, *Raid on the Articulate* (New York: Harper & Row, 1976), p. xiv, suggests that he is raising the question of "a shift of the master paradigms of our research." He quotes Kuhn in referring to "a reconstruction that changes some of the field's most elementary theoretical generalizations as well as many of its paradigm methods and applications." Such reasoning is not far removed from the issue raised by Gottwald in "Domain Assumptions and Societal Models in the Study of Pre-Monarchic Israel." While both Crossan and Gottwald may speak of a shift of paradigms, the substance of their urging is in quite divergent directions.

80. It is likely that Gottwald's critique of the paradigm of "biblical theology" refers especially to the method and synthesis achieved by Von Rad. Brevard Childs, *Biblical Theology in Crisis* (Philadelphia: Westminster, 1970) has presented a formidable critique of that synthesis.

81. Claus Westermann has developed this dialectic in various writings, but his major presentation is in the Sprunt lectures soon to be published, in which he contrasts the saving and blessing of God. Most telling is his assertion that the God who blesses cannot fail or suffer. Such a conclusion has enormous sociological implications.

82. Most evident in his utilization of the "Asiatic Mode of Production."

83. Hanson, *Dawn of Apocalyptic,* pp. 213-20.

84. Alan J. Hauser, "Israel's Conquest of Palestine: A Peasants' Rebellion?" *JSOT* 7 (1978): 2-19.

85. Brian Kovacs, "Contributions of Sociology to the Study of the Development of Apocalyptic," paper read at the 1976 meeting of the Society of Biblical literature.

86. See, for example, the review by John L. McKenzie of the book by José Miranda *(Marx and the Bible: A Critique of the Philosophy of Oppression* [Maryknoll, N.Y.: Orbis Books, 1974]) *JBL* 94 (1975): 280-81.

87. Robert McAfee Brown, "A Preface and a Conclusion," *Theology in the Americas,* ed. Sergio Torres and John Eagleson (Maryknoll, N.Y.: Orbis Books, 1976), p. xvii: "But the important question is, 'Is the analysis true? Does it make sense of what it is describing? Do we understand the world better when we look at it in this way?' "

88. The term is from Helmut Gollwitzer, "Kingdom of God and Socialism in the Theology of Karl Barth," *Karl Barth and Radical Politics,* ed. George Hunsinger (Philadelphia: Westminster, 1976), p. 105.

89. For a persuasive critique of ideological objectivism, see Alvin Gouldner, *The Coming Crisis of Western Sociology* (New York: Basic Books, 1970).

90. On an attempt to engage the two perspectives, see Burton Cooper, "How Does God Act in America? An Invitation to a Dialogue between Process and Liberation Theologies," *USQR* 32 (1976): 25-35. See also Robert T. Osborn, "The Rise and Fall of the Bible in Recent American Theology," *Duke Divinity School Review* 41 (1976): 57-72.

91. Miles, "Gagging on Job," p. 110.

Part IV

SOCIOLOGICAL READINGS
OF THE NEW TESTAMENT

18

ROBIN SCROGGS

The Sociological Interpretation of the New Testament: The Present State of Research

Sociological interpretation of the New Testament has vigorously revived with the introduction of more sophisticated social scientific theories and methods. Impatience with fragmented knowledge produced by biblical scholarship has encouraged the attempt "to put body and soul together again" after long overemphasis on the inner spirituality and doctrinal views of early Christians.

Two types of sociological interpretations are evident: social history *that tries to identify the social composition of Christian groups, and* sociological analysis *that seeks to discover the larger underlying dynamics at work within the groups and in their relation to the wider society. Significant contributors to social history are M. Hengel, E. A. Judge, A. Malherbe, and R. Grant. Sociological analyses have proceeded in diverse theoretical frameworks:*

From *New Testament Studies* 26 (1980): 164–79; reworked from an address given at the 1978 meeting of the SNTS in Paris. Reprinted by permission University Press; copyright © 1980, Cambridge University Press.

(1) Troeltsch-like studies of unconscious social protest in the work of R. Scroggs and G. Snyder; (2) cognitive dissonance theory as applied by J. Gager; (3) role analysis as practiced by G. Theissen; (4) sociology of knowledge in the instance of W. Meeks; and (5) Marxist historical materialism in the writings of M. Machoveč, F. Belo, and M. Clévenot.

In all these approaches, important issues of the appropriateness of single or eclectic methodology, of the adequacy of social data, and of the nature of sociological explanation in relation to other types of explanation (the so-called problem of "reductionism") are prominent.

INTRODUCTORY REMARKS

It is fitting that the first major attention given by the SNTS to sociological concerns should occur in Paris, the home of Auguste Comte (often called the father of sociology) and his circle. Actually there seem to have been many fathers and many more offspring, such that the present genealogy of the discipline presents an almost bewildering profusion of perspectives, goals, models, and methodologies.[1] This is a productive situation and a sign of health, but it suggests right away that I cannot analyze in this paper a single or simple sociology of the New Testament. Those of us who are experimenting—and that cautious phrase must be taken literally—with sociological approaches have come from different backgrounds and perspectives, borrowing from sociology where it seems useful and tentatively trying out various methods and models. The exploration has really just begun.

Interest in the social reality of early Christianity, of course, is nothing new. Especially during the preceding one hundred years keen interest has often been expressed in such matters. This interest peaked during the first third of this century, best exemplified by scholars such as Deissmann, Lohmeyer, Cadoux, and especially representatives of the so-called Chicago School (e.g., Shirley Jackson Case and Shailer Matthews) who with great energy focused on early Christianity as a social reality and upon Jesus as a social reformer.[2]

Those were the days of liberal Christianity and the social gospel; it is hardly an accident that a socially oriented theology would cause social questions to be asked of the New Testament. By the 1930s, however, not even the Chicago School was being heard in the United States. Neo-orthodoxy, with its emphasis upon theology and the Word, displaced the social gospel. The kinds of questions the liberals had asked became unfashionable. Symbolic of this change are the fortunes of Frederick Grant's monograph, *The Economic Background of the Gospels*.[3] Published in 1926, toward the end of the era, it long remained, at least in the United States, the only major statement about the economics of first-century Palestine. In fact, the book had to be republished in unaltered form in 1973, forty-seven years later, because nothing comparable had appeared in the intervening years.[4]

Today the pendulum has swung again. Interest in social questions is again substantial in some quarters. Whether this is the result of a neo-liberalism, or social tensions such as the Vietnam war, student revolutions, and severe economic and political oppression in various parts of the world, or all of these, is not clear as yet. Nevertheless, Gerd Theissen speaks for many of us when he notes a rising *Unbehagen* [uneasiness] about a discipline which limits the acceptable methods to the historical and theological. No one doubts the supreme importance of these time-honored approaches. They do not, however, ask, let alone answer, all of the important questions, those concerning social dynamic, the relation between earthly goods and faith, and the interaction between social reality and theological assertions.

To some it has seemed that too often the discipline of the theology of the New Testament (the history of *ideas*) operates out of a methodological docetism, as if believers had minds and spirits unconnected with their individual and corporate bodies. Interest in the sociology of early Christianity is no attempt to limit reductionistically the reality of Christianity to social dynamic; rather it should be seen as an effort to guard against a reductionism from the other extreme, a limitation of the reality of Christianity to an inner-spiritual, or objective-cognitive system. In short, sociology of early Christianity wants to put body and soul together again.

PROBLEMS CONFRONTING SOCIOLOGICAL ANALYSIS

This is not to say that all is easy for the new approach. Among the serious problems which the sociologist of the New Testament must deal with, let me mention three.

The Problem of Methodology

The current state of tremendous variety in sociological theories and models presents the New Testament scholar with numerous possibilities and understandable confusion at the same time. Which are valid? Which are appropriate for the data to be interpreted? If we use more than one method, are these compatible or in tension? Theissen implies by his work, probably correctly, that an eclecticism and pluralism is appropriate.[5] If the methods have true heuristic value, they should ultimately prove complementary and contribute to one's confidence in conclusions drawn from them. I suggest only two warnings here. First, we need to understand fully how the method works and to be clear that it *can* be applied to the data at hand. Secondly, we need to know both the theoretical presuppositions and implications of the use of the method. Is it compatible with other (e.g., theological) presuppositions we may hold?

The Problem of the Data

Most sociologists, particularly those using computer methods to study contemporary societies, would probably be aghast when they learned how little in the way of data was available for the sociological analysis of the New Testament. Furthermore, what we do have is not directly sociologically accessible. That is, most texts are speaking about theological verities, not sociological conditions. The sociologist must read the text as if it were palimpsest. This means the researcher must work with the utmost caution and strictness, with adequate guard against overenthusiasm. There can probably never be any complete sociological analysis of early Christianity. And yet there may be times when a sociological model may actually assist in our ignorance. If our data evidences some parts of the gestalt of a known model, while being silent about others, we *may* cautiously be able to conclude that the absence of the missing parts is accidental and that the entire model was actually a reality in the early church.

The Problem of Reductionism

There is no doubt that one can use sociological methods from a reductionist standpoint, that is, to explain any societal phenomenon completely in terms of hidden, unconscious social dynamic. Thus one could understand religion out of Feuerbachian, Durkheimian, or Marxist closed systems. It is at this point that the New Testament scholar should be careful about the implications of the method he or she selects, to ask whether that method implicitly or explicitly excludes all dynamic except the immanent social. For example, it is clear that the Weberian emphasis upon the charismatic prophet allows for relatively more freedom and novelty than the societal emphasis of Durkheim. Nevertheless, it is to be doubted that any sociological method, except that of the strictly orthodox Marxist, is incapable of being used by a scholar who wants to leave room for the transcendent. Let me make three brief observations on this issue.

1. Social dynamics may create the situation but may not determine the response to the situation. Jesus rejected the Zealotic option, and Paul had to decide, according to Theissen, between the rich and the poor in Corinth. He points out that a distinction must be made between the social conditions and the theological intention of a Paul.[6] (This is a solution which respects the freedom of the leader [Weber].)

2. Even a more Durkheimian approach, it seems to me, can be fitted into a theological scheme, if one takes seriously the doctrine of creation, or finitude. Subjection to social dynamic is as much a part of our finitude as any other dimension of society's impingement on individual freedoms. For example, when the exegete seeks sources for Jesus' or Paul's ideas in Judaism or Hellenism, he or she is working out of that same presupposition of finitude.

3. It also needs to be emphasized that sociological models are not to be

awarded absolute objectivity as if they were natural laws. They are rather the time- and culture-bound creatures of humans. They are useful in so far as they have heuristic value, that is, in so far as they serve to illumine the *unique* phenomenon the researcher is studying.

REPORT ON RECENT SCHOLARSHIP

I will now turn to an all too sketchy report on recent scholarship. For purposes of clarity I want to make a somewhat artificial distinction between historical research into social phenomena and sociological analysis. Let me illustrate this distinction. The *historian* may ask the question, "What was the social level of early Christians?" and answer it by evaluating data which are theoretically available to the conscious perceptions of those early Christians and by putting them into causal and time-sequential structures. The *sociologist* then takes the historian's data and asks what underlying, usually *unconscious,* dynamic is at work, how that social level interacts with other levels, what conflicts usually emerge in such circumstances, and whether knowing that dynamic in turn helps us interpret certain interrelationships or even certain truth assertions in our data. Sociology thus depends upon data but works with them in ways that historiography does not. Sociology is comparative, since it will most often come to data with a model of dynamics taken from analyses of other groups and other data. It thus also tends to be synchronic rather than diachronic. I cheerfully admit that this definition of sociology is quite narrow and can easily be disputed. It will serve, I nevertheless trust, to sharpen the following analysis.

What follows is of necessity illustrative rather than comprehensive. Furthermore the emphasis will be not so much on *content* as on *methods* and *models.* I will concentrate on *how* the researcher works more than on *what* the resulting conclusions are. The full contributions to the discipline of the scholars discussed will rarely emerge—for this I ask for the sympathy of my colleagues. Hopefully what *will* come to expression are the varied possibilities of current research.

Recent Research into Social History of the Early Church[7]

The first name that comes to mind as one turns to research into social history is that of Martin Hengel. In a series of publications too well known and too numerous to name, Hengel has concerned himself with the concrete political and economic history in relation to the first centuries of the church and particularly with regard to Jesus and his followers.[8] He has, furthermore, offered us a useful model in the relevance of such social history for reflection in the church today.[9]

Recent years have seen the publication of a number of valuable studies by other scholars. A book with slowly growing influence was published in 1960 by E. A. Judge, titled *The Social Pattern of Christian Groups in the First*

Century.[10] Much useful information is contained in a series of essays under the title: *The Catacombs and the Coliseum: The Roman Empire as the Setting of Primitive Christianity* (1971).[11] Most recently two books relevant to the topic have appeared in the United States: *Social Aspects of Early Christianity* (1977) by Abraham Malherbe, and *Early Christianity and Society* (1977) by Robert Grant.[12] Mention should also be made of a study group under the auspices of the Society of Biblical Literature in the United States. Under the title "The Social Description of Early Christianity" (Wayne Meeks and Leander Keck, co-chairpersons), this group has been working for the last several years in a kind of sociological trench study of the city of Antioch, attempting to discover as much as possible about societal reality in that city, thus the better to understand the interaction of the Christian community with the larger social situations and dynamic.[13]

I can illustrate the work of these and other researchers only by one—albeit important—example, the question of the socioeconomic level of Christians. It is Deissmann who seems to get the credit for the view that early Christians were of the lower social classes—peasants, slaves, artisans.[14] In 1960 Judge mounted his, at that time somewhat lonely, protest.[15] True, he argued, the Christian community did not attract the true Roman nobility, but it did not draw to itself the other end of the spectrum either—peasants and farm slaves. Otherwise, Christians came from all strata in society.

It is interesting to note the data to which he appeals. (1) Middle- and upper-class people are mentioned in Acts and in the Pauline correspondence. (2) Barnabas, who donated the proceeds of a land sale to the Jerusalem church, is a representative of "the foreign community in an international resort," and it can be assumed that this class would be composed of "persons of means."[16] (3) The church enjoyed the "hospitality of wealthy and respectable patrons."[17] (4) The main passage of debate, 1 Corinthians 1:26–28, shows the opposite of what is commonly concluded, namely that there *were* Corinthian Christians who were from at least relatively privileged classes. Judge can then conclude: "Far from being a socially depressed group, then, if the Corinthians are at all typical, the Christians were dominated by a socially pretentious section of the population of big cities."[18]

Writing seventeen years later, Malherbe shows how the pendulum, at least in his judgment, has swung. Malherbe believes it even possible to speak of a "new consensus" emerging which places the social level noticeably higher than did Deissmann.[19] Theissen seems to be moving in the same direction when he speaks of a leading minority of upper-class Christians at Corinth, over against a lower-class majority.[20] Hengel, basing his judgment on Paul and the Pliny-Trajan correspondence, agrees: "Das heisst Glieder der christlichen Gemeinden fanden sich in *allen* Bevölkerungsschichten, vom Sklaven und Freigelassenen bis zur örtlichen Aristokratie, den Dekurionen, ja unter Umständen bis zum senatorischen Adel."[21]

Robert Grant's book, while moving far beyond the New Testament period, pictures a church which is essentially conservative, both politically and economically, reflecting the main concerns of the empire at large. While Grant does not exactly say it, he gives the impression that early Christians were as snobbish about their class status as anybody else in the contemporary world.[22] Supporting the political conservatism is the article, "Social Unrest and Primitive Christianity," by Clarence Lee in *The Catacombs and the Colosseum*. He finds no evidence to support the contention "that Christianity swept across the Roman world on the coattails of a social revolution."[23]

What is interesting about this "new consensus" is that it reaches a conclusion so different from Deissmann's, while working with precisely the same data—almost exclusively that found in the New Testament (I, of course, am speaking only to the conclusion for the New Testament period). This raises the question how the same data can produce such different conclusions. Tentatively the following can be observed. (1) The "new consensus" places relatively less emphasis upon the social implications of the Synoptic material. (2) It places relatively more emphasis upon the material in Acts *and its historical veracity*. (3) It seems, at least to this reviewer, to place almost exclusive weight upon *economic* factors to the exclusion of other sociocultural dynamics in determining social level.

The implications of the "new consensus" for the social interpretation of early Christianity are immense and thus its conclusions must be tested with great care. Such testing is out of place in this report; I do, however, raise the following questions. (1) Should not the Synoptic material (e.g., the strong protest against wealth) be given more weight, even if it does not reflect the same Hellenistic urban context of the Pauline letters? Surely the Synoptics speak for important segments of the first-century church and in their final form do not necessarily reflect only a rural setting. (2) Is the Acts material as historically trustworthy as the proponents assume? (3) Even if it is, and granted the evidence of the epistles, should the presence of a few (is it not a universal tendency to remember and name the upper rather than the lower?) wealthier members be allowed to change, in effect, the social location of the community as a whole? Is this not an elitist definition? (4) Should economic alienation be the only alienation considered? Do not all societies have categories of outcast individuals and groups who are not economically deprived?[24] (5) Finally (and here I am perhaps out of place) is there any relation between the "new consensus" and the change in our society from the more "revolutionary" period of the 1960s to the more "conventional" 1970s? Is there a need today to find a more "respectable" (i.e., middle-class) origin for the church? I am quite aware that the followers of Deissmann can be charged with a counter question: do they want to romanticize poverty?

Sociological Analyses of the Early Church

Here again I have space only for examples of recent sociological analyses and even so will do justice to no one example. I organize the discussion around the methods used rather than the total gestalt of the researcher.

Typologies. In an article published in 1975 I looked at some Synoptic material from the perspective of the religious sect.[25] I researched post-Troeltsch analysis of the sect by British and United States sociologists who now can base their conclusions on concrete studies of sects, both past and present. It was encouraging to see that there is basic agreement among these researchers as to what constitutes the dominant characteristics of the sect (Troeltsch's insights are mostly confirmed), although the sect is now interpreted over against the established social organization as a whole, rather than a sub-category named the "church." I summarized these arguments under seven heads. (1) The beginning point of the sect as protest (*N.B.,* not necessarily conscious). (2) The rejection of the assumptions of reality upon which the establishment bases its world and creation of a new world with different assumptions. (3) The egalitarian nature of the sect. (4) The vitality of love and mutual acceptance within the sect. (5) The voluntary character of the group. (6) The demand of total commitment to the new reality accepted by the sect. (7) And sometimes adventist, or millenarian expectations.

I argued that most of these characteristics were evidenced in the Synoptic material, which reflected the earliest Palestinian communities in their interaction with the larger social context. If so, this analysis gives us some new insight into the social dynamic—namely *unconscious social protest*—that helped bring the church into existence and that gave it the particular shape it took in those earliest years.[26]

Graydon Snyder, in an as yet unpublished manuscript, is working from quite a different typology.[27] Borrowing an anthropological model developed by researchers at the University of Chicago, Snyder sees early Christianity always in tension between dynamics he calls respectively the "trans-local tradition" and the "local tradition."[28] The trans-local tradition is the religion of the prophet, the universalist, the intellectual, the more-than-moralist (Weber). The local tradition, or social matrix, is the religion of the person rooted in land, community, family, moralism, or the one who uses religion to integrate people into the social matrix by the ceremonial marking of key-season and life-process days (Durkheim).

Any specific religious phenomenon, Snyder argues, will be a result of the tension between the two traditions in a given time and space. At times the trans-local tradition may dominate, at other times the local. Usually there will be some compromise, such that a phenomenon will rarely be a pure example of either tradition. Since writings are usually suspect as being primarily creations of the trans-local tradition, Snyder only begins in the post-New Testament period, when archaeological artifacts are available. In conversation, however, Snyder and I have concluded that it may be possible to use this typology as a grid to understand movement within trajectories in the New Testament itself. For example, it is possible that Paul himself represents a decisive victory of the trans-local tradition over the local, while the Pastorals reflect increasing assimilation by the local tradition of the Pauline thought world. At any rate, this typology should help us grasp more clearly some of the intramural conflicts within early Christianity.

Cognitive Dissonance. One major sociological study of early Christianity that has recently appeared in the United States is John Gager's *Kingdom and Community.*[29] In this many-faceted study the author uses varied models, unfortunately only one of which I can describe here. This is the theory of cognitive dissonance, a theory derived from sociological (or anthropological) theorists in the United States—although Gager will modify this theory in some respects.[30]

The theory asserts the following. When, in a community, religious or otherwise, a certain belief is held, specific enough for disconfirmation to be unavoidably clear, and given certain other conditions (named below), the likely result of any disconfirmation of the belief will not be the dissolution of the group but rather an intensification of its proselytizing. For example, if a community predicts the end of the world on a certain specific day, that belief can be disconfirmed, and such disconfirmation, while painful to the community, cannot be avoided by it.

In all, there are five conditions, according to the theory, which are necessary if proselytizing is to occur following disconfirmation. (1) The belief must be held with deep conviction. (2) There must be committed action on the part of the believers. (3) The belief must be specific enough that disconfirmation cannot be denied. (4) The believers must recognize the disconfirmatory evidence. (5) There must be communal support for the individual believer.

Gager claims that the community following Jesus fits all of the above conditions. The belief in question was that Jesus is the Messiah (although the author carefully hedges as to whether Jesus himself held this opinion). The death of Jesus is then the disconfirming event, for how could a messiah die? He writes:

> It would appear, then, that we are justified in maintaining that the death of Jesus created a sense of cognitive dissonance, in that it seemed to disconfirm the belief that Jesus was the Messiah. . . . Thus, according to the theory, we may understand the zeal with which Jesus' followers pursued their mission as part of an effort to reduce dissonance, not just in the early years but for a considerable time thereafter.[31]

To this Gager adds the disappointment of eschatological expectations. He claims that these expectations were also specific enough (the end was to come while the first generation of believers was still alive) for disconfirmation to occur. This then added to the missionary fervor of the first-century church.[32]

Gager is quick to say that he does not intend to explain the entire missionary endeavor by this one model, although he does not discuss what other dynamic might have contributed. This view of missionary dynamic may seem shocking and certainly clashes with the puristic, idealistic view so commonly held in theological circles. Ultimately both positions may have something to contribute to the complete picture of those very human early Christians making the missionary rounds. The question is whether both views can learn to live with each other.

Role Analysis. Surely the most prolific and provocative sociologist of the New Testament is Gerd Theissen. In an impressive series of articles and a book he has explored both the rural Palestinian setting of the *Urgemeinden* (original communities) and the urbanized church of the Hellenistic world.[33] In his writings there is a wealth of social data and luxuriant use of a number of sociological models, emerging out of a basic functionalist approach to social dynamic. Although it is a disservice to the productivity of Theissen, I can here choose only one example of his work, to illustrate the use of role analysis.[34] In role analysis one looks at the description of self-understanding of people who adopt or accept certain roles within the society, whether such roles are defined by social status, relationship of person to group, or kinds of activity expected of the role. How these roles *function* in the larger societal context is investigated.

By now most scholars are familiar with Theissen's analysis of the Palestinian Christian prophet as a "wandering charismatic." These were people who had given up all of their old life to proclaim the urgent gospel of the Kingdom of God. Homelessness, lack of family, lack of possessions, and lack of protection were characteristics of their new life. Jesus had commanded that they live this way and promised that they would be provided for by the people they served. To live as beggars was a sign of their trust in God.[35]

Paul, on the other hand, represents a different type—plays a different role, that of the community organizer.[36] The Hellenistic urban churches reflect a less radical, more middle-class society, in which the image of the wandering beggar would not be suitable, at least as Paul understood the situation. First Corinthians, however, reveals Paul on the defensive precisely because he would not accept payment from the Corinthians, i.e., would not put himself in the posture of a beggar. This passage has always puzzled exegetes. Why would not the Corinthians be happy not to have to pay their minister? Theissen believes he has solved the puzzle. The Corinthian situation has been created by the entrance into the church of wandering charismatics from Palestine who, living out the role of the faithful beggar, have seen Paul (and have tried to convince the Corinthians that Paul should be seen) as a faithless missionary. Paul, working independently of the community as an artisan, is not willing to follow the command of Jesus to give up all possessions. He is unwilling to put full trust in God's care.[37]

This ingenious analysis completely changes the picture we have traditionally held of Paul's opponents, and forces a radically different interpretation. The conflict is not between a good Paul and evil opponents, but between *conflicting roles*, between different understandings of the true missionary. Theissen's sociological analysis thus offers us a new perspective.

Sociology of Knowledge. For some of us, I suspect, the single most important approach within the field of sociology comes from the sociology of knowledge. It may also for others be the most threatening approach. This perspective teaches us that the world we live in, the world we think, or assume, has ontological foundations, is really *socially constructed* and is created, communicated, and sustained through language and symbol.[38] To denote this constructed world, whose relationship to the "really real" is by definition unknowable, many are using the phrases "social world" or "symbolic world."

What is potentially threatening is that language, *including theological language*, is never to be seen as independent of other social realities. *Thus theological language and the claims made therein can no longer be explained without taking into account socioeconomic-cultural factors as essential ingredients in the production of that language.* The difficult questions for the sociologists are, in concrete instances, *how* to move between language and social realities, and *which* social realities are to be related to *which* linguistic structures? These seem to me immensely important questions which are not yet adequately answered and thus the process does not currently have the proper methodological controls. I will, however, illustrate the immense possibilities in this approach by reporting an article which shows provocatively how one scholar believes it possible to bring language and social realities together—"The Man from Heaven in Johannine Sectarianism," by Wayne Meeks.[39]

Here Meeks wishes to understand the Johannine christology of the descending/ascending savior. He doubts that this christology was taken over from already existent gnostic myths and suspects, rather, that it represents John's own contribution to the march toward gnosticism. To understand the reason why the motif was created, Meeks raises the question, what *social function* this myth may have had in the community itself.

Why is it, Meeks questions, that the revelatory discourses are so opaque? With regard to chapter 3, for example, he writes: "Thus the dialogue with Nicodemus and its postscript connected with John the Baptist constitute a virtual *parody* of a revelation discourse. What is 'revealed' is that Jesus is incomprehensible. . . . Even for an interested inquirer (like Nicodemus) the dialogue is opaque."[40] The motif of descent/ascent in every instance in the Gospel "points to contrast, foreignness, division, judgment."[41]

But these are characteristics which apply to the entire Gospel. This writing sets itself against the world and in turn appears incomprehensible to that world. The book is simply a "closed system of metaphors."[42] Here lies, in Meeks' judgment, the clue to the function of the Johannine christology. As the community itself feels alien and over against the world, so the book and specifically the christology express this same alienation. If the church is not of this world, then neither can be its Lord. "One of the primary functions of the book, therefore, must have been to provide a reinforcement for the community's social identity. . . . It provided a symbolic universe which gave religious legitimacy, a theodicy, to the group's actual isolation from the larger society."[43]

Thus the christology cannot be interpreted apart from the social context of the community. Actually the movement between the two is dialectical. The christological claims of the Johannine Christians result in their becoming alienated "and that alienation is in turn 'explained' by a further development of the christological motifs."[44] This startling dialectic should not be taken to mean that the christological language is no longer to be taken seriously. There is no reason to doubt that theological insights can emerge out of the pain of alienation. To the extent that Meeks' judgments are compelling, however, they should lead us to a greater caution about generalizing or universalizing the christological claims in John. But in this caution are there not significant measures of realism and honesty?

MARXIST INTERPRETATIONS

Before concluding, it is only appropriate to point to recent Marxist interpretations of early Christianity, since they at many points relate to sociological approaches. Marxist theory certainly deals with social process and dynamic, while sociological theory can accept the unconscious nature of the process. Marx himself is perhaps the first to have understood the basic premise of the sociology of knowledge.[45]

Important advances in sophistication have on occasion been made since Kautsky's book of 1920.[46] *Not* in that category is the volume by Martin Robbe, *Der Ursprung des Christentums* (1967).[47] Working from a traditional Marxist-Leninist perspective, he develops a view of Christianity's emergence purely as social process, as a protest against the class society and its injustice. The importance of the figure of Jesus completely disappears (no Weberian perspective here!); Robbe is not even concerned whether Jesus existed or not. Nothing would have been different had he not.

In sharp contrast with Robbe, however, is Milan Machoveč, the author of *Jesus für Atheisten* (1972), translated into English as *A Marxist Looks at Jesus* (1976).[48] Leaning on the humanism of the younger Marx, Machoveč goes in exactly the opposite direction to Robbe; for the Czech communist, Jesus is a supremely important, seminal figure. Kautsky is roundly criticized as reductionistic; ideas again assume an intrinsic, determinative role, particularly those of monotheism and eschatology. Jesus made his mark upon society because he taught that the future depends upon human action. "In modern terminology we should say that Jesus turns a future which is essentially alien to us . . . into an experienced, a human future."[49] Even more, Jesus embodied that experience in his own life; without such embodiment he could only have failed. Finally, Jesus' eschatological thinking is "concerned with the transformation of the *whole* man . . . not just . . . oppression, need, slavery, etc."[50] Machoveč equates Marxism with true humanism, and humanism with the total person. Here shines clearly the attempt to put all dimensions of a person together, without minimizing any element. He honors Jesus because he reads Jesus as caring for the total selfhood of persons. For Machoveč, a Marxist should not be interested in Jesus despite the fact, but precisely because he is a Marxist.[51]

The most sensational and startling production of this genre has been written by the Portuguese Christian Marxist, Fernando Belo: his *Lecture matérialiste de l'évangile de Marc* (1974).[52] Unfortunately this book and its popularization by Michel Clévenot, *Approches matérialistes de la Bible* (1976)[53] seem virtually unknown to English- and German-speaking scholars. What little discussion I have uncovered about Belo's work has been almost entirely in French.[54]

Belo needs a hearing! His book is difficult, eclectic, startling, threatening, and perhaps even offensive to some. Yet he writes with a passion and clarity of vision that has as its aim to force a *"re*-reading" of the Gospel, a challenge to us "bourgeois scholars" to turn away from our consistently "idealist" reading (i.e., perspective) of the Gospel to a "materialist" reading.

When one struggles to get behind the author's erudite structuralist and Marxist symbolism and terminology, his "materialist reading" of the Gospel can, perhaps too simplistically, be reduced to a few points. The basic tradition in Mark is susceptible to a materialist reading, although a movement toward ideological (i.e., theological) interpretation is also apparent in some of the (later?) tradition.[55] Putting the latter aside, the former, if looked at correctly, reveals a Jesus as teacher and *actor* of a messianic *practice* (act is more important than teaching, narrative than discourse).

And what is this practice? It is a rejection of the dominant code of society; thus it reflects a struggle of class. It is a rejection of the definition of the self as spirit and a reassertion of the importance of body. In the *economic* sphere the messianic practice means giving to each according to need.[56] In the *inter-relational* sphere, it means the end of the lord/servant relationship and its replacement by a community where there are only "des frères, tous enfants, tous derniers, tous serviteurs."[57] In the *ideological* sphere, it requires a conversion from reading the Gospel according to the dominant code of establishment society to that of the "subversive" messianic practice, which Jesus embodies and to which Jesus calls the reader.[58]

Contrary to the Zealots, however, this practice is communist (i.e., egalitarian), nonrevolutionary, and international.[59] It is a practice which remains open to the future—it is a *way*. Hence the *resurrection of the body* is perhaps the single most important symbol for Belo.[60] For this points the reader toward the future, yet a future which is life in the body (i.e., anti-idealist). This future can be realized only by following the messianic practice of Jesus. That means that any idealist reading of the resurrection which separates it from messianic practice *in* this world is to be rejected. As Clévenot comments: "Ce n'est qu'au sein d'une pratique visant à *l'insurrection* des corps que peut se poser valablement la *question de leur résurrection*."[61]

From the perspective of critical ("bourgeois") scholarship, there is much that is perversely unscientific which can be dismissed all too easily. Yet there may also be much that is stubbornly right in its materialist reading that calls the idealistic (docetic?) reading into serious question. At the least Trocmé is correct in his conclusion about Belo: "Il y a place pour des études expérimentales dont les auteurs s'efforcent de relire les textes bibliques à la lumière des grands débats de notre temps."[62] Is not Belo a challenge to our scholarly world, asking whether New Testament exegesis has, in fact, anything to say about ecology, human oppression, economic slavery, mass malnutrition—or whether we can only be silent and leave *that* Gospel to others?

Even this all too brief march through recent scholarship reveals great differences and tensions among the various researchers, whether historians, sociologists, or Marxists. Do they have anything at all in common? Ultimately, it seems to me, they at least all share the aim to show how the New Testament message is related to the everyday life and societal needs and contexts of real human beings, how the texts cannot be separated from social dynamic without truncating the reality of both speaker and reader (including the reader today). In the final analysis, the issue is not whether these authors are correct, but whether they make us think about the texts in fresh ways, and in ways which are not out of tune with "the great disputes of our age."

NOTES

1. Since in these Notes I hope to present as full a bibliography of sociological work on the New Testament as is suitable, given space limitations, it has been necessary rigorously to exclude mention, except when necessary for the discussion, of non-New Testament studies, whether those secular studies which form the groundwork for work on the New Testament, or those which deal with contiguous areas such as early Judaism or the Greco-Roman world. For the latter, the interested reader should consult the bibliography in J. Smith, "Social Description of Early Christianity," *RelSRev* 1 (1975): 19–25.

2. E.g., Adolf Deissmann, *Licht vom Osten* (Tübingen, 1908); Eng., *Light from the Ancient East: The New Testament Illustrated by Recently Discovered Texts of the Graeco-Roman World,* trans. Lionel Strachen, rev. ed. (Grand Rapids, Mich.: Baker Books, 1965); E. Lohmeyer, *Soziale Fragen im Urchristentum* (Darmstadt, 1921); R. Schumacher, *Die soziale Lage der Christen im apostolischen Zeitalter* (Paderborn, 1924); C. J. Cadoux, *The Early Church and the World* (Edinburgh and Naperville, Ill.: Allenson, 1925); S. J. Case, *The Evolution of Early Christianity* (Chicago: University of Chicago Press, 1914); idem, *The Social Origins of Christianity* (Chicago: University of Chicago Press, 1923); idem, *The Social Triumph of the Early Church* (Chicago: University of Chicago Press, 1934; repr. facsimile ed. Freeport, N.Y.: Books for Libraries); Shailer Matthews, *The Social Teaching of Jesus* (New York, 1897); idem, *The Atonement and the Social Process* (New York, 1930).

Some have argued that form-criticism itself opened the way for a sociological interpretation, or at least for the asking of social questions, by concerning itself with the *Sitz im Leben* of the pericopes. Cf. D. Gewalt, "Neutestamentliche Exegese und Soziologie," *Evth* 31 (1971), 88f., and K. Berger, *Exegese des Neuen Testaments* (Heidelberg, 1977), p. 219.

3. Frederick Grant, *The Economic Background of the Gospels* (London, 1926, repr. New York: Russell and Russell, 1973).

4. In this statement I am referring explicitly to New Testament scholarship. With regard to the social history of early Judaism there has been and continues to be careful work. S. Baron, *A Social and Religious History of the Jews*, Vol. 1, *Ancient Times to the Beginning of the Christian Era*; Vol. 2, *The First Five Centuries* (1937; 2nd rev. and enlarg. ed., New York: Columbia University Press, 1952) has long been standard. More recent is the work of H. Kreissig, e.g., "Zur Rolle der religiösen Gruppen in den Volksbewegungen der Hasmonäerzeit," *Klio* 43 (1965):174-82; "Zur sozialen Zusammensetzung der frühchristlichen Gemeinden im ersten Jahrhundert u.Z.", *Eirene* 6 (1967): 91-100; "Die Landwirtschaftliche Situation in Palästina vor dem jüdischen Krieg," *Acta Antiqua* 17 (1969): 223-54; *Die sozialen Zusammenhänge jüdischen Krieges* (Berlin, 1970). See also E. Urbach, e.g., "The Laws Regarding Slavery as a Source for Social History of the Period of the Second Temple, the Mishnah and Talmud," *Papers of the Institute of Jewish Studies* (Jerusalem, 1964), Vol. 1, pp. 1-50. Now there is the massive *The Jewish People in the First Century: Historical Geography, Political History, Social, Cultural, and Religious Life and Institutions,* ed. S. Safrai and M. Stern (Philadelphia: Fortress Press, 1974).

5. E.g., Gerd Theissen, *Soziologie der Jesusbewegung* (Munich, 1977), pp. 9-13, Eng., *Sociology of Early Palestinian Christianity,* trans. John Bowman (Philadelphia: Fortress Press, 1978).

6. Gerd Theissen, "Soziale Integration und sakramentales Handeln: Eine Analyse von 1 Cor. xi:17-34," *NovT* 16 (1974): 200-202.

7. The reader must understand that I must limit myself to recent work only.

8. Among Martin Hengel's many contributions one can note the following: *War Jesus Revoluntionär?* (Stuttgart: Calwer, 1970), Eng., *Was Jesus a Revolutionist?* (Philadelphia: Fortress Press, 1971); *Gewalt und Gewaltlosigkeit: Zur "politischen Theologie" in neutestamentlicher Zeit* (Stuttgart, 1971), Eng., *Victory over Violence: Jesus and the Revolutionists,* trans. David E. Green (Philadelphia: Fortress Press, 1977); *Judentum und Hellenismus,* 2 vols. 2nd ed. (Tübingen, 1973), Eng., *Judaism and Hellenism: Studies in Their Encounter in Palestine during the Early Hellenistic Period,* trans. John Bowden (Philadelphia: Fortress Press, 1975); *Eigentum und Reichtum in der frühen Kirche* (Stuttgart: Calwer, 1973), Eng., *Property and Riches in the Early Church,* trans. John Bowden (Philadelphia: Fortress Press, 1975); *Christus und de Macht* (Stuttgart: Calwer, 1974), Eng., *Jesus and Power,* trans. Everett Kalin (Philadelphia: Fortress Press, 1975). Hengel has been particularly concerned with the problems of political force and the question of war violence. This topic has been much discussed in recent years; here I can mention only Oscar Cullmann, *Jesus and the Revolutionaries* (New York: Harper & Row, 1970), and George R. Edwards, *Jesus and the Politics of Violence* (New York: Harper & Row, 1972).

9. In *Gewalt und Gewaltlosigkeit* Hengel argues that only when the social *context* bears some analogies with the contemporary setting can the teaching of Jesus about violence be relevant for today's world. See my introduction to the English translation, *Victory over Violence,* pp. ix-xxiv.

10. E. A. Judge, *The Social Pattern of Christian Groups in the First Century: Some*

Prolegomena to the Study of the New Testament on Social Obligation (London: Tyndale Press, 1960).

11. S. Benko and J. O'Rourke, eds., *The Catacombs and the Colosseum: The Roman Empire as the Setting of Primitive Christianity* (Valley Forge, Pa.: Judson Press, 1971). Covering some of the same ground is the collection of essays by Hans von Campenhausen, *Tradition und Leben: Kräfte der Kirchengeschichte* (Tübingen, 1960).

12. Abraham Malherbe, *Social Aspects of Early Christianity* (Baton Rouge: Louisiana State University Press, 1977), and Robert Grant, *Early Christianity and Society* (New York: Harper & Row, 1977). Cf. also S. Bartchy, *Mallon chresai: First-Century Slavery and the Interpretation of 1 Corinthians 7:21* (Missoula: Scholars Press, 1973), and Richard Batey, *Jesus and the Poor* (New York: Harper & Row, 1972); Leander Keck, "The Poor among the Saints in the New Testament," *ZNW* 56 (1965): 100–137; idem, "The Poor among the Saints in Jewish Christianity and Qumran," *ZNW* 57 (1966): 54–78.

13. Many papers were produced by working members of the group on various social *realia* in Antioch, processing what information is known about Jews and Christians in the early centuries. Two papers that originated the discussion of the group have been published: L. Keck, "On the Ethos of Early Christianity," *JAAR* 42 (1974): 435–52, and J. Smith, "Social Description" (cf. Note 1 above). The recent volume by Wayne A. Meeks and Robert W. Wilken, *Jews and Christians in Antioch in the First Four Centuries of the Common Era* (Missoula: Scholars Press, 1978), lucidly summarizes many of the findings of the group, as well as including translations of some relevant texts (Libanius and Chrysostom). Cf. also the essays of several American scholars translated in *Zur Soziologie des Urchristentums,* ed. Wayne A. Meeks (Munich, 1979).

Two projects begun by the group are still underway. One is a bibliography, under the direction of Leander Keck, expected to be completed by 1979. Cf. L. Keck and J. Louis Martin, eds., *Studies in Luke-Acts* (Philadelphia: Fortress Press, 1980). The second is a prosopography for Antioch which is being completed by the Disciples Institut zur Erforschung des Urchristentums in Tübingen. According to F. Norris, director of the project at the Institut, completion is not expected before 1985.

14. Deissmann, *Light from the Ancient East.*

15. Judge, *Social Pattern.*

16. Ibid., p. 55

17. Ibid., p. 57.

18. Ibid., p. 60.

19. Malherbe, *Social Aspects,* p. 31. In addition to the authors cited here, Malherbe has supporters in Wilhelm Wuellner, *The Meaning of "Fishers of Men"* (Philadelphia: Westminster, 1967); idem, "The Sociological Implications of 1 Corinthians 1:26–28," *Studia Evangelica* 4 (1973): 666–72; and G. Buchanan, "Jesus and the Upper Class," *NovT* 7 (1964–1965).

20. Gerd Theissen, "Soziale Schichtung in der korinthischen Gemeinde," *ZNW* 65 (1974): 232–72.

21. Hengel, *Eigentum und Reichtum,* pp. 44–45: "This means that the members of the Christian communities were found in *all* social classes, from slaves and freed slaves to the local aristocracy, the members of municipal and colonial senates, and possibly even to the senatorial nobility."

22. Grant, *Early Christianity,* pp. 83–95.

23. Clarence Lee, "Social Unrest and Primitive Christianity," in *The Catacombs and the Colosseum,* p. 134.

24. Cf. R. Scroggs, "The Earliest Christian Communities as Sectarian Movement," in *Christianity, Judaism and Other Greco-Roman Cults,* ed. J. Neusner (Leiden: Brill, 1975), Vol. 2, p. 3. I am dependent here on Werner Stark, *The Sociology of Religion: A Study of Christendom,* 5 vols. Vol 2: *Sectarian Religion* (London, 1967; New York: Fordham University Press, 1967 and 1972), Vol. 2, pp. 6–29.

25. Scroggs, "Earliest Christian Communities."

26. My analysis concerned only the rural setting of Palestinian Christianity, and it cannot without alteration be applied to the urban churches of the Hellenistic mission. Howard C. Kee, in a recent work using sociological analysis believes that the Markan church in the late sixties is still non-urban: *Community of the New Age: Studies in Mark's Gospel* (Philadelphia: Westminster, 1977), pp. 104–5.

In the Paris meeting of the SNTS in 1978, however, Wayne Meeks addressed the question whether sectarian analysis would fit a Pauline church. He concludes that the evidence is ambiguous. His address, " 'Since then you would need to go out of the world': Group Boundaries in Pauline Christianity," has now appeared in *Critical History and Biblical Faith: New Testament Perspectives,* ed. J. T. Ryan (Villanova, Pa.: Catholic Theology Society, 1979), pp. 4–29.

At least some of the suggested essential characteristics of the sect are clearly present, however, in the Hellenistic churches, *at least in the earliest period.* Recent investigations have shown, for example, the basic egalitarianism that existed within the communities—the test case being the relation between male and female. For discussion and bibliography, cf. R. Scroggs, "Paul and the Eschatological Woman," *JAAR* 40 (1972): 283–303; and W. A. Meeks, "The Image of the Androgyne: Some Uses of a Symbol in Earliest Christianity," *HR* 13 (1974): 165–208. Before the New Testament period is over, however, this egalitarianism has disappeared, at least in those churches representing emerging "orthodoxy."

27. Graydon Snyder, professor of New Testament at Bethany Theological Seminary, Oak Brook, Illinois. Cf. his "Survey and 'New Thesis' on the Bones of Peter," *BA* 32 (1969): 3–5, and an unpublished paper he presented to the SNTS Seminar on Social Background and History of the Early Church, Tübingen, 1977: "The Great Tradition and Its Local Complement in Early Christianity."

28. Key here are Robert Redfield, *Peasant Society and Culture: An Anthropological Approach to Civilization* (Chicago: University of Chicago Press, 1965); Melford E. Spiro, *Buddhism and Society* (London, 1971, and New York: Harper & Row, 1972); and R. Thouless, *Conventionalization and Assimilation in Religious Movements* (Oxford: Oxford University Press, 1940).

29. John G. Gager, *Kingdom and Community: The Social World of Early Christianity* (Englewood Cliffs, N.J.: Prentice-Hall, 1975). This has stirred up quite an active response in the United States. Cf. three recent review articles, all appearing in *Zygon: Journal of Religion and Science* 13 (1978): D. Bartlett, "John G. Gager's *Kingdom and Community*: A Summary and Response," pp. 109–22; J. Smith, "Too Much Kingdom, Too Little Community," pp. 123–30; D. Tracy, "A Theological Response to *Kingdom and Community,* " pp. 131–35.

30. L. Festinger, H. Riecken, and S. Schachter, *When Prophecy Fails: A Sociological and Psychological Study of a Modern Group that Predicted the Destruction of the*

World (New York: Harper & Row, 1964). The "modern group" in question was an actual flying saucer cult in the U.S. The thesis, however, does not rest primarily on study of this group alone but involves analysis of many other millennial cults. The theory of cognitive dissonance has been used by at least two other scholars in related studies. Cf. U. Wernick, "Frustrated Beliefs and Early Christianity: A Psychological Enquiry into the Gospels of the New Testament," *Numen* 22 (1975): 96–130, and W. Zenner, "The Case of the Apostate Messiah: A Reconsideration of the 'Failure of Prophecy,' " *Archives de sciences sociales des religions* 21 (1966): 111–18, the latter dealing with the history of the Zabatean movement.

31. Gager, *Kingdom and Community,* p. 43.

32. Ibid., pp. 43–46.

33. Gerd Theissen, "Wanderradikalismus: Literatursoziologische Aspekte der Überliefungsform von Worten Jesu im Urchristentum," *ZTK* 70 (1973): 245–71; "Soteriologische Symbolik in den paulinischen Schriften," *KuD* 20 (1974): 282–304; "Soziale Integration und sakramentales Handeln: Eine Analyse von 1 Cor. xi, 17–34," *NovT* 16 (1974): 179–206; "Soziale Schichtung in der korinthischen Gemeinde: Ein Beitrag zur soziologie des hellenistischen Christentums," *ZNW* 65 (1974): 232–72; "Theoretische Probleme religions-soziologische Forschung und die Analyse des Urchristentums," *NZSTR* 16: (1974): 35–56; "Legitimation und Lebensunterhalt: Ein Beitrag zur Soziologie urchristlicher Missionäre," *NTS* 21 (1975): 192–221; "Die Starken und Schwachen in Korinth: Soziologische Analyse eines theologischen Streites," *EvTh* 35 (1975): 155–72; "Die soziologische Auswertung religiöser Uberlieferungen: Ihre methodologische Probleme am Beispiel des Urchristentums," *Kairos* 17 (1975): 284–99; "Die Tempelweissagung Jesu: Prophetie im Spannungsfeld von Stadt und Land," *ThZ* 32 (1976): 144–58; "Wir Haben Alles Verlassen (Mark: 10:28): Nachfolge und soziale Entwurzelung in der jüdische-palästinischen Gesellschaft des I. Jahrhunderts n. Chr.," *NovT* 10 (1977): 161–96; *Soziologie der Jesusbewegung: Ein Beitrag zur Entstehungsgeschichte des Urchristentums* (Munich, 1977).

34. Of this method Theissen says simply, "Die Rollanalyse untersucht typische Verhaltensmuster," *Jesusbewegung,* p. 10.

35. Ibid., pp. 14–21 see also "Wanderralikalismus," *ZTK* 70.

36. Theissen, "Legitimation und Lebensunterhalt," *NTS* 21, pp. 202–5.

37. Ibid., pp. 205–17. Two other authors who have recently wrestled with the problem of the bases of apostolic authority in the Hellenistic churches, both of these in dialogue with the Weberian analysis of charisma and legitimation, are J. H. Schütz, *Paul and the Anatomy of Apostolic Authority,* Society for New Testament Studies Monograph Series, No. 26 (Cambridge: Cambridge University Press, 1975), and Bengt Holmberg, *Paul and Power: The Structure of Authority in the Primitive Church as Reflected in the Pauline Epistles* (Lund, 1978, Philadelphia: Fortress Press, 1980).

38. A sociological work that has had great influence, perhaps especially in the United States, is P. Berger and T. Luckmann, *The Social Construction of Reality: A Treatise on the Sociology of Knowledge* (New York: Doubleday, 1966). These authors are themselves dependent on A. Schutz. Cf. my paper read at the Tübingen SNTS meeting in 1977: "A Theological Apology for Using Sociological Methodology"; W. A. Meeks, "The Social World of Early Christianity," *Bulletin of the Council on the Study of Religion* 6 (1975).

39. Wayne A. Meeks, "The Man from Heaven in Johannine Sectarianism," *JBL* 91 (1972): 44-72. For a critique of Meeks' view, cf. K. Berger, *Exegese*, pp. 230-31.

40. Meeks, "The Man from Heaven," p. 41.

41. Ibid., p. 67.

42. Ibid., p. 68.

43. Ibid., p. 70.

44. Ibid., p. 71.

45. Cf. his famous sentence, "It is not the consciousness of men that determines their being, but on the contrary, their social being determines their consciousness." This is from the Preface of *Zur Kritik der politischen Ökonomie*, and I take it from the translation of T. Bottomore, *Karl Marx: Selected Writings in Sociology and Social Philosophy* (New York: McGraw-Hill, 1964), p. 51.

46. Karl Kautsky, *Der Ursprung des Christentums* (Stuttgart, 1921); Eng. trans., *Foundations of Christianity: A Study of Christian Origins* (New York: International Publications, 1925). Interesting here also is B. Stasiewski, "Ursprung und Entfaltung des Christentums in sowjetischer Sicht," *Saeculum* 11 (1960): 157-79.

47. Martin Robbe, *Der Ursprung des Christentums* (Leipzig, 1967).

48. Milan Machoveč, *Jesus für Atheisten* (Stuttgart, 1972); Eng. trans., *A Marxist Looks at Jesus* (Philadelphia: Fortress Press, 1976).

49. Ibid., p. 88; references are to the English edition.

50. Ibid., p. 97.

51. Ibid., p. 31.

52. Fernando Belo, *Lecture matérialiste de l'évangile de Marc* (Paris: Du Cerf, 1974). By 1976 there was already a third edition. English ed., *A Materialist Reading of the Gospel of Mark,* trans. Matthew J. O'Connell (Maryknoll, N.Y.: Orbis Books, 1981).

53. Michel Clévenot, *Approches matérialistes de la Bible* (Paris: Du Cerf, 1976); Eng., *Materialist Approaches to the Bible,* trans. William J. Nottingham (Maryknoll, N.Y.: Orbis Books, forthcoming).

54. Although I am sure that this list is not complete, I have noted the following reviews: by Poulat, Herrieu-Leger, Hadot, and Ladriére in the *Archives de sciences sociales des religions* 40 (1975): 119-37; by E. Trocmé in *RHPR* 55 (1975): 293-94; by M. Bouttier in *Etudes théologiques et religieuses* 50 (1975):89-91; by Vanhoye in *Biblica* 58 (1977): 295-98. Cf. also the interesting comments of E. Trocmé in "Exégèse scientifique et idéologie: de l'ecole de Tubingue aux Historiens Français des origines chrétiennes," *NTS* 24 (1977/78): 461-62. P. Pokorny discusses Belo and other Marxists in "Die neue theologische Linke," *Communio Viatorum* 19 (1976): 225-32. From the same perspective, cf. S. Rostagno, "Is an Interclass Reading of the Bible Legitimate?" *Communio Victorium* 17 (1974): 1-14, see Article 4 in this volume; and the paper delivered at the Paris SNTS meeting in 1978 by K. Tagawa, "Possibilité de l'interprétation matérialiste: un essai de l'exégèse de Marc 6:7-12."

55. Belo, *A Materialist Reading,* pp. 233-340, references are to the English edition.

56. Ibid., pp. 244-45.

57. Ibid., p. 248: "There will be only brothers, with everyone a child, everyone last, everyone a servant."

58. Ibid., pp. 251-55.

59. Ibid., pp. 261-62.

60. Ibid., p. 288-95. Cf. also Pokorny in *Communio Viatorum* 19, p. 227.

61. Clévenot, *Approches matérialistes,* p. 152: "Is it not at the heart of a praxis aiming at the *insurrection* of bodies that it is possible to pose validly the *question of their resurrection?*"

62. Trocmé in *RHPR* 55, p. 294: "There is a place for experimental studies in which the authors strive for a re-reading of biblical texts in the light of the great disputes of our age." An equally provocative study is that of José Miranda, *Marx y la Biblia* (Salamanca: Sígueme, 1971), Eng., *Marx and the Bible: A Critique of the Philosophy of Oppression,* trans. John Eagleson (Maryknoll, N.Y.: Orbis Books, 1974).

19

JOHN PAIRMAN BROWN

Techniques of Imperial Control: The Background of the Gospel Event

To a greater degree than source critics and form critics of the Gospels have allowed, it is possible to visualize the Jesus movement among the rural poor of Galilee and in confrontation with priestly-Roman rule in Jerusalem. The Gospels are saturated with glimpses of how Rome ruled Palestine through the native Jewish elite, with the result that the imperial effects were felt everywhere, although more visibly in the capital than in the countryside.

Serious economic dislocation and deprivation, as well as social stigmatization of the poor, stand out starkly in the incidence of physical suffering, in the psychosomatic "demonic" diseases by which oppression was internalized, and in the persistence of resistance movements against Rome. The Roman imperial apparatus is apparent in a rich vocabulary in the Gospels that refers to banking, military, and bureaucratic structures. Jerusalem as a city under foreign military occupation is amply documented by innumerable de-

Reprinted from *The Bible and Liberation: Political and Social Hermeneutics,* 1st ed., ed. N. K. Gottwald and A. C. Wire (Berkeley: Community for Religious Research and Education [Radical Religion], 1976), pp. 73-83.

tails of the Passion narrative concerning Roman governance, trials, and criminal punishment.

We will have to grasp more concretely the history of oppression and alienation that Jesus and his followers faced if we want to understand his word about the kingdom.

What is the nature of the event which the Gospels partly record, partly themselves constitute? I am using "event" to describe a new historical emergent, like the American Revolution or the Methodist revival, which covers a period of years or decades, which has its preparation and its consequences. Such events require a substantial society of people in readiness for change and one or more striking individuals who both embody the needs of that society for change and illustrate the beginnings of the new thing in their own lives. A large part of the event is constituted by what purports to be the record of the event: the American Constitution, the Methodist hymnody. The Greek victory over Persia in 480 B.C. gave the Greeks unprecedented self-confidence and universalism of interests; the history of Herodotus not merely records the birth of that novelty but also constitutes one of its chief monuments. What event happens in the Gospels?

Harnack saw the meaning of the first Christian centuries as a Hellenization of Christian theology. If we go a step beneath that description to concrete social realities, we will say: the early church represents a shift from a movement of poor country people on the fringes of the Roman Empire to a movement of poor city people at the heart of the empire. If we go a step beneath that social framework to psychic states, we must say something like the following. Jesus and the Gospels embody an unprecedented level both of alienation and hope of poor people on the land. Paul in his letters translates those levels to the life of poor people in the imperial cities. The early church, remaining almost wholly in the cities, smoothes off both the peaks and the abysses to an oscillation that can be dealt with inside normal life rhythms.

I am writing from the conviction that the Gospel event, as I am describing it, is normative for my life. That means that the closer a contemporary event approaches the social and psychic realities of the Gospel event, the more it stands in the line of the Gospel. The Methodist revival, which spread from the British establishment and British slums to the American frontier, is a kind of shift backwards from the early church and Paul to Galilee. The closest parallels to the work of Jesus today are agrarian nonviolent organizing movements such as those of Danilo Dolci in Sicily and of Cesar Chavez in California. An historian who does not share my conviction about what is normative for his life, but who does share my analysis of what constitutes an event, should find exactly the same kind of help in Dolci or Chavez for understanding Jesus that I do.

The contemporary New Testament academic establishment finds it almost impossible to use the Gospels as evidence for a movement in Galilee and its culmination in Jerusalem. It uses them almost exclusively as evidence for the inner life of the urban churches which compiled and treasured the Gospels. I suppose this springs primarily from fear of dealing with the explosive concrete images in which the alienation and hope of the Gospels is expressed; the abstract concepts in which Paul expresses an equal alienation and hope are more easily dealt with in a library. But this is bad history. If we go to the ancient world asking for documents of the life of the rural poor from within their society, at an early period the near-contemporary books of Hesiod and Amos stand by themselves; under the Roman Empire the Gospels stand by themselves with more concreteness and fullness. The shipwreck of Acts has gone through much less literary transformation than the shipwreck of the Odyssey. The Passion narratives are unique witnesses to the gritty texture of imperial oppression from the point of view of the oppressed. If we rule these documents out of court, we are really passing a class judgment that the history of the poor cannot be written. By what right do those who can write classify all evidence about those who cannot write as "secondary sources"?

Sherwin-White, approaching the same question from the point of view of the practical working of Roman law, comes to the same conclusion, which the academic skeptics should ponder:

So, it is astonishing that while Graeco-Roman historians have been growing in confidence, the twentieth century study of the Gospel narratives, starting from no less promising material, has taken so gloomy a turn in the development of form-criticism that the more advanced exponents of it apparently maintain—so far as an amateur can understand the matter—that the historical Christ is unknowable and the history of his mission cannot be written. This seems very curious when one compares the case for the best-known contemporary of Christ, who like Christ is a well-documented figure—Tiberius Caesar. The story of his reign is known from four sources. . . . These disagree amongst themselves in the wildest possible fashion, both in major matters of political action or motive and in specific details of minor events. Everyone would admit that Tacitus is the best of all the sources, and yet no serious modern historian would accept at face value the majority of the statements of Tacitus about the motives of Tiberius. But this does not prevent the belief that the material of Tacitus can be used to write a history of Tiberius. The divergences between the synoptic gospels, or between them and the Fourth Gospel, are no worse than the contradictions in the Tiberius material.[1]

The Synoptic Gospels, where the scene shifts once and decisively from agrarian Galilee outside direct Roman control to urban Jerusalem under Roman control, prefigure the shift from Jesus to Paul and the early church. In this paper I attempt to sketch the social background of the Gospel event, which I hope will be in good proportion and uncontroversial. Like the Gospels I move from Galilee to Jerusalem, in each place giving some evidence how the psychic state of alienation, and the beginnings of hope, rest on the social reality. In a sequel I want to indicate how Jesus' life and message are a response to that psychic state and social reality, starting my analysis from the inexhaustible themes "Kingdom of God" and "son of man."

GALILEE

Palestine had been ruled from Alexandria by the Ptolemies during the years 323–200 B.C. In that brief period they imposed on Palestine the old Egyptian administrative system, which lasted until well into the Roman period.[2] Villages were grouped into administrative districts called "nomes" in Egypt and elsewhere "toparchies," "rules over a place." Probably there were five toparchies in Galilee.[3] Nobody seems to have noticed that the Gospel Greek records this usage: "He sent them to every city and place (*topos,* 'district') where he would come" (Luke 10:1); "whatever *topos* does not receive you" (Mark 6:11). Since the Ptolemaic regime was a military occupation, the governor of a toparchy was called a "commandant" *(strategos);* the term is well attested for the realm of the Nabatean king Aretas IV (9 B.C.–40 A.D., 2 Cor. 11:32).[4] The good slave of Luke 19:17–19 is given rule over ten or five cities, a Decapolis or Pentapolis; in real life Galilee he would have become commandant of a toparchy.

In the lifetime of Jesus and John the Baptist, Galilee was ruled directly by Herod Antipas, named by his father Herod the Great after his grandfather Antipater of Edom. In the New Testament he is called only by the dynastic title "Herod."[5] There was no Roman military occupation because Antipas toed the line. When Herod the Great died in 4 B.C., Antipas and his two brothers went to Rome and accepted slices of their father's kingdom: Archelaus became ethnarch of Judea until his deposition in A.D. 6, Philip "tetrarch" of Batanea in the northeast, and Antipas tetrarch of Galilee and of Peraea (the east bank of the Jordan). The original meaning of *tetrarches,* "ruler of a fourth part," had been lost, and it now marked its holder as ruling a Roman protectorate in a status inferior to that of a nominally independent king. But although he is called "tetrarch" by administrative texts he is called "king" (Greek *basileus,* Aramaic *malka)* by popular ones (Mark 6:22).[6] Everyone knew how the power of the brothers had been acquired: "A nobleman went into a far country to receive a kingship" (Luke 19:12). Antipas stayed in favor, through many shifts of Roman policy, until 39 A.D.; not for nothing that Jesus called him "jackal" (Luke 13:32). The emperor himself was glad to be called "king" in the Greek half of the empire, where the bad associations of *rex* at Rome were lacking. He had the reality of the old Persian and Hellenistic title "King of kings," although it seems not to have been applied to him.[7] It is applied to the Christ (Rev. 19:16) with some kind of glance at royal cults; a first-century rabbi called God "King of the king of kings."[8]

What more universal symbols of Roman hegemony could be found than the axe of the fasces, the sword, the wolf, the eagle? We have at least to allow for some imposition of Roman symbolism on John and Jesus when their poetry gives prominent place to the *axe* laid at the foot of the tree, the *sword* which will destroy all those who take the sword, the *wolves* among which the sheep are being sent out, the *eagles* (vultures?) which gather around the corpse. Yet there were no Roman soldiers or tax-collectors operating in Antipas' Galilee, although his army and taxation (as we shall see) were integrated into the Roman system. On the south, Judea, including Jerusalem, was after 6 A.D. ruled in contrast directly from Rome by a prefect attached to the proconsular legate of Syria. On the north, Galilee nowhere touched the Roman province of Syria since the territory of Tyre and Sidon, cities with local autonomy, came down to its northwest boundary (Mark 7:24, 31). Powerless as Antipas was, his Galilee was still a kind of privileged sanctuary for the pre-Zealot guerrillas, where the issues of collaboration, direct Roman taxation, and Roman affronts to the Law did not have to be daily faced. Suspended between the dependent kingship of Antipas and the distant kingship of Tiberius (14–37 A.D.), Jesus saw himself as a herald commissioned to announce the inbreaking kingship of God.

The villages of fertile Galilee were bigger than those in Egypt; Josephus claims 200 of them with over 15,000 population each (*B. J.* 3:43, *Life* 235), certainly an exaggeration. Mark (8:23–27) accurately calls Bethsaida in Philip's tetrarchy a "village," similar in status to the villages ruled by Philip's capital Caesarea (Panion), which was a true Hellenistic city with some autonomy and its own coinage. The Gospels often loosely call the big Galilean villages "cities," but Mark coins the precise term *komopoleis,* "villages the size of cities" (1:38). A village was administered by a "village scribe" (*komogrammateus,* Josephus, *A.J.* 16:203). In the Gospels this person is called the "judge"; a certain "city" had an unjust one (Luke 18:2), and Jesus refuses that office (Luke 12:14). The parable of the adversary (Luke 12:57–59 =Matt. 5:25–26) outlines village judicial procedure, un-Greek and un-Roman,[9] which could hardly have been invented or understood after Galilee became part of Judea in 44 A.D.[10]

The only true Greek city in Galilee was Tiberias, built by Antipas and named after Tiberius, issuing Antipas' coinage and (under Claudius) its own. It was built on a cemetery, perhaps intentionally to exclude Jews and attract pagans, some of whom were newly freed slaves (*A.J.* 18:36–38); it had Antipas' bank and archives (*Life* 37–39). Jesus evidently avoids it both as being pagan and the capital (cf. "the leaven of Herod," Mark 8:15); it appears in the Gospels only where "boats from Tiberias" arrive and provide a ride across the lake (John 6:23). The only other even half-way Greek city of Galilee—Sepphoris, four miles north of Nazareth—never issued autonomous coins before Trajan. Early in the Roman rule Gabinius had made it the capital *(synedrion)* of Galilee (*A.J.* 14:91). After Herod's death in 4 B.C. while the three sons were in Rome, the arsenal of Sepphoris was looted by Judas, son of the guerrilla leader Ezekias who had been executed by Herod the Great (*A.J.* 17:271-72; 14:159 = *B.J.* 1:204). The legate of Syria, P. Quinctilius Varus (later massacred with three legions in Germany), marched south with auxiliaries from Beirut and Aretas IV, retook and burned Sepphoris, and enslaved its people (*A.J.* 17:287-88). The scene lingers on in folk-memory: "The king was angry, and he sent his troops and destroyed those murderers and burned their city" (Matt. 22:7—the royal parables are a fund of suppressed political comment). Antipas quickly rebuilt it and made it his capital until the founding of Tiberias; the *tektones* (carpenters and masons) of Nazareth must often have commuted there. The Gospels only mention it in a confused reading;[11] probably like Tiberias it was largely pagan, for Josephus (*Life* 30) found it pre-Roman in 66 A.D., and its Jewish population attested by the Talmud may be of later date.[12]

Galilee at all periods was "the frontier" and its Israelite character problematical. When we first see it, it is "Galilee of the Gentiles" (Isa. 9:1), captured by the Assyrian in 733 B.C. (2 Kings 15:29). In 163 B.C., early in the Maccabean revolt, there was only a minority of Jews there, since they had to be evacuated to Judea (1 Mac. 5:23); but there are Jews taxed there in 152 B.C. (1 Mac. 10:30). Aristobulus (103–102 B.C.) forcibly Judaized part of it (*A.J.* 13:318-19). At least some of the Talmud's complaints about the laxness of Galilean Jews date from the first century.[13] Strabo says that Galilee, along with other parts of Palestine, contained Egyptians, Arabs, and Phoenicians (16.2.34). Perhaps each village was religiously and socially homogeneous as in present-day Lebanon, and the local administration had a religious character. Then the statement "Gentiles do this" could be verified daily in the next village.[14] Jesus states that Gentiles would come into the kingdom before its own sons (Luke 13:29), and he is shown as open to individual non-Jews but is not given a general mission to them; perhaps its presuppositions were lacking. The prohibition "Do not go into a Way of the Gentiles" (Matt. 10:5) is quite intelligible as the product of a Palestinian Jewish-Christian community.[15]

Mark (6:21) gives us the impression that the entire ruling elite of Antipas' realm, his "courtiers and rulers of a thousand and leading men of Galilee," could be gotten into one room, whether his birthday party happened at Tiberias as Mark suggests or at the fortress Machaerus in Peraea (Josephus, *A.J.* 18:119). His little militia aped Roman ways, for the executioner of Mark's narrative has a Latin title (*speculator,* Mark 6:27), which has also gone into Talmudic Aramaic.[16] The "centurion" of Capernaum is no Roman officer but an old-fashioned "ruler of a hundred." We would naturally take him to be a Jew, so that Matthew 8:10 may originally have meant "With no one *else* in Israel have I found such faith." John (4:46) calls him a "king's man"; he is one of Mark's "courtiers" (6:21) like the steward Chuza (Luke 8:3) and Antipas' boyhood comrade Manaen (Acts 13:1), perhaps the grandson of that Menahem the Essene (Josephus, *A.J.* 15:373) who predicted the accession of Herod the Great.[17] Probably the centurion's job is policing the toll-office of Capernaum (Mark 2:13, etc.); Jesus is surprised at his faith not because he is a pagan but because he is in so unsavory an occupation. John the Baptist found soldiers[18] beside the tax-collectors at the ford of the Jordan, evidently on the same assignment; his prophetic word to them, "Rob no one by violence or false accusation, and be content with your wages" (Luke 3:14), shows the general reputation of Antipas' force. Extortion was their forte; they were soundly beaten in battle by Aretas' irregulars (*A.J.* 18:114). The "leaders of a thousand" copy Roman military tribunes, who have the same name *(chiliarchos)* in Greek. But we hear of no unit in Antipas' force as big as a legion (6,000 men), so Josephus is wildly boasting when he claims to have personally raised 100,000 in Galilee (*B.J.* 2:576); it is total conscription when one "king" with ten thousand goes out against another with twenty (Luke 14:31).

Herod held his realm by favor of Augustus and Tiberius, and was removed by Caligula (*A.J.* 18:252). We can be sure that he paid the emperor tribute, but our sources give no figure. When first appointed (*A.J.* 17:317) he was allowed by Augustus to keep only 200 talents annually from the taxes of Galilee and Peraea; perhaps this was his private income, and the adminstrative budget, building program, and tribute were separate accounts.[19] Taxes in Judea and Syria generally were a heavy burden under Augustus,[20] and we can be sure that Antipas did not lag far behind, although a "chief tax-collector" (Luke 19:2) is attested only for Judea. From various sources we have evidence for a poll tax and for taxation of farm products, fishing rights, purchases and sales, and goods transported by road.[21] The tax-collectors of Galilee were subjects of Antipas who made a living, meager and despised, off the excess over what they had contracted to pay. John's word, "Collect no more than is appointed you" (Luke 3:13), would have reduced them to destitution. The orthodox called Jesus' followers "tax-collectors and sinners" (Mark 2:16, etc.) or "tax-collectors and harlots," and Jesus adopted it as a name for his own (Matt. 21:31). The Pharisees considered the testimony of a tax-collector as inadmissible evidence, and the stick with which he rummaged through Gentile bags as ritually unclean.[22] But they regarded nearly everybody else in Galilee as ritually unclean also, and the real complaint against the tax-collectors was the universal assumption, shared by John, that their occupation was dishonest.[23] Grant estimates the total tax at 25 to 40 percent of all income; presumably the bulk of it went to Rome, directly or indirectly. Was there any value received? Strabo (16.2.20), speaking of Philip's tetrarchy, says that the former robber bands had been broken up "through the good government coming from the Romans, and the security maintained by the Roman soldiers quartered in Syria." Syria had recently seen the invasion of Tigranes the

Armenian in 68 B.C., the Iturean occupation of the Palestinian coast in 63 B.C. and the invasion of Pacorus the Parthian in 40 B.C. But these were possible because Rome had destroyed the former regimes which policed the desert frontier: the Seleucids and the Maccabees.

In a Jewish village of Galilee, the local administration may have been more theocratic than in the realm as a whole. The local judge has jurisdiction over inheritance (Luke 12:14), a subject also regulated by the Mishnah; thus in Galilee a widow like Jesus' mother could go on living in her husband's house.[24] Also the synagogue had judicial authority. The synagogue at Nazareth is ready to execute the disrupting rabbi (Luke 4:29); the "synagogue ruler" is a person of weight (Mark 5:22); arguments and fights are brought before the synagogue council (Matt. 5:22); it has the power of corporal punishment for offenses at best vaguely indicated (Luke 12:11; Matt. 10:17; 23:24; cf. Luke 6:22). Thus the sabbath disputes run up against what was at once a religious and a civil jurisdiction. The "scribes of the Pharisees" (Mark 2:16) or those who "come down from Jerusalem" (Mark 3:22) help form local legal practice. In Galilee it was the lay Pharisees who had the real power, and two things are said of them: "they love the best seat in the synagogues, and salutations in the market" (Luke 11:43), for their power lay in both places. Their extortions of extra donations (Matt. 23:35=Luke 11:39; Mark 7:11) had a basis in both religion and law. When Jesus took them on, he was taking on both church and state, since there was a concordat between them. The charges leveled against him of blasphemy (Mark 2:7; 3:22) and what amounts to treason (Luke 13:31) could not be clearly separated; so Herod executed John on the charge of inciting revolution (*A.J.* 18:118). Through the hold which the Jerusalem-oriented lawyers exercised on village administration, the peasants were subjected to a second level of religious taxation for the benefit of the scattered Galilean priests and of the temple. A dozen-odd items in money or kind can be found, in which the tithes of produce dominate.[25] The parable of the Pharisee and publican is given special point when we realize that the two men are colleagues and competitors in shearing the very same sheep! And still Galilee was a Jewish enough state that we can probably assume that non-Jews were under even a heavier burden of unrecorded civil disabilities.

It seems plain that the Herods seriously dislocated the economy: this is perhaps the greatest cause of the widespread alienation.[26] The responsibility lies with Herod the Great, who at the same time turned a large part of Palestinian revenue over to Rome *and* perpetuated his name by a crash building program inside and outside Palestine. With so heavy a burden farmers came more and more to work the fields of an absentee landlord; the regime was killing off the goose that laid the golden egg. For Galilee was and is the best farming area of Palestine, a garden of Eden. The melting snows of Lebanon and Hermon create a water table tapped by the wells into which the blind, animals, or children (Luke 14:5 variant) may fall. The parable of the sower (Mark 4:3–8, see *B.J.* 3:42) emphasizes the variety of the soils and the excellence of the best with a yield of from 30 times to 400 times; it is accurate in the details of how sowing precedes plowing.[27] The Gospels are full of the annual miracle of the grain, exported to Tyre and Sidon (Acts 12:20). Josephus praises the variety of fish in the Sea of Galilee (*B.J.* 3:506–8), the walnuts and dates (3:517); its grapes were not gathered from thorns nor its figs from this-tles. The Talmud makes it clear that the olive was the chief crop; Josephus tells of the fortune which his rival John of Gischala (Gush Halab) made by an olive monopoly (*B.J.* 2:591–93). The good and bad trees of which John and Jesus speak are the olive. This was where the advent of the kingdom would be: "I will go before you to Galilee" (Mark 14:28).

The Gospels are obsessed with riches and poverty, wages and coins, the overriding questions of subsistence and survival. The text shows three social levels: the rich who benefit from taxation or at least escape it; the hardwork-ing poor kept on subsistence by taxation; and the destitute who have given up the unequal struggle. Jesus' initial manifesto states a simple contrast between rich and poor. The alternatives are laid out in the tale of the rich man's stew-ard, who if fired without resources has the choice of manual labor or beggary (Luke 16:1–8): "I cannot dig, to beg I am ashamed." But in spite of Jesus' exhortations that we should give to beggars (Luke 6:30), we meet no beggars until we get to Jericho (Mark 10:46): in Galilee the villages took care of their own, and outside Tiberias and Sepphoris there was nobody to beg from. The contrast of Dives in purple and fine linen with Lazarus at his gate (Luke 16:19–20) cannot be without base in social reality. Jesus, with a look at "king" Herod, says that "those who are clothed in fine garments live in kings' houses." Sherwin-White[28] remarks, "At Antioch or Ephesus one would not need to look so far"; but in Palestine there was no middle class.[29]

The village scenes of the Gospels show this subsistence life barely idealized. The house has one lamp (Mark 4:21), one bed (Luke 11:7, 17:34), one day's bread (Luke 11:5), one calf (Luke 15:23), one fig tree (Luke 13:7). Two sons may be the only hands available for the grape-picking (Matt. 21:28–30); with the addition of two men hired by the day they are a boat's crew (Mark 1:20). Even if the vineyard owner has a steward, he goes out himself to hire field hands in the market as needed (Matt. 20:1–16). The younger son might just as well cash in his lesser share of the inheritance and seek his fortune, leaving his brother with two or three hired men (Luke 15:11). How then could a man with five sons, like Mattathias the first Maccabee or Joseph (Mark 6:3) pro-vide for them all? There is no middle ground between these tiny landowners and the rich farmer who buys more fields and builds bigger barns (Luke 12:18); we are not actually shown the "rich neighbors" (Luke 14:12). The real rich are absentee, living in Tiberias or Jerusalem or some resort; they will let out the land to tenants (Mark 12:9), or manage it through a steward who must always be on the alert for his sudden arrival (Luke 12:35–48; Mark 13:33–37). Only such an estate is worth the thief's attention (Luke 12:39).

The landless day laborers could never rise out of that status, even if they had steady employment. A day's wage was a Roman denarius (Matt. 20:2).

To feed a big crowd would take 200 denarii, out of the question to raise (Mark 6:37): even so, 5,000 people (like all crowd estimates) must be high, a day's wage could hardly feed 25. A spell of bad luck would quickly get him on the downward path of debt. Typical moneylenders have debtors owing 50 or 100 or 500 denarii (Luke 7:41; Matt. 18:24) or 100 measures of oil or wheat (Luke 16:1-8). A hundred denarii (ten minas) could set you up as a moneylender in your own right (Luke 19:13). Obviously interest is being charged (Matt. 25:27=Luke 19:23) in contravention of the Law (the Mishna is silent on this point); in Nehemiah's time it was apparently at one percent per month or 12 percent per annum (Neh. 5:11) just as today. The scale of operations of the moneylender was beyond comprehension; in a parable, a court official could be thought to owe the king 10,000 talents, 50 years of Antipas' income (Matt. 18:24-28). And what if laborers could not find a job? They became the poor, maimed, lame, blind (Luke 14:21, 23; Matt. 15:30) who are always ready to come in from the roadside for a free meal. It was a narrow line between poverty and outlawry; when Jesus and his friends went through the fields plucking grain, they were availing themselves of provisions for the poor, but they were accused of lawbreaking (Mark 2:23). There were experiments at communal living: in Qumran, in the early church, in John's community (Luke 3:11).

The multiple levels of oppression which I have outlined had several consequences: direct physical suffering; psychosomatic diseases; and a resistance movement.

Direct Physical Suffering. Some at least of the maimed and lame were so as a result of the sack of Sepphoris; some of the mourning (Matt. 5:4) was for those lost there. The poverty and hunger which the Beatitudes presuppose, like poverty and hunger in the twentieth century, had the same cause: unequal distribution of wealth. Some of the blindness, as in the Middle East today, may have been glaucoma from an unsettled life and poor sanitation. None of the "leprosy" of Leviticus or the Gospels was true leprosy, or Hansen's disease (known but rare in the ancient world);[30] much of it no doubt was correlated with poor sanitation and malnutrition (I saw scurvy—Vitamin C deficiency—among American women dieting during a debilitating Beirut summer.) Some of the lameness may have been from poliomyelitis (although in Lebanon before the advent of sanitation it was rare in the villages, since infants almost universally acquired a mild case while they still retained uterine immunity). The itinerancy which Theissen[31] takes as a radical innovation of Jesus and the apostles was in fact the natural state of thousands of migratory workers and unemployed: far from setting them apart, it enabled them to melt into the landscape and move around freely under opposition, as Catholic Worker folks melt into Skid Row, farm worker union organizers melt into the fields, and beyond doubt the Zealots also into the Galilean countryside.

Psychosomatic Diseases, Psychosis, "Demons." The Gospel record is wholly exceptional in the degree to which the oppression generates concrete symbolic physical symptoms. That much of the disease was psychosomatic is proved by the fact that Jesus could heal it. If we look carefully at the sequence of Jesus' sayings in both Mark and the "Q-document," we will see that his announcement of the time of salvation, the Kingdom of God, *precedes* his healings, and that initially it is the suffering who seek him out and persuade him that he can heal either themselves or their family. Jesus does not initially come on as a healer; he points to the evidence of the healings only *after* they have happened. The diseased or their associates understood on some level of consciousness that their symptoms would respond not to an ordinary doctor but to the bearer of such a message as Jesus carried. It must have been a problem, as with faith-healers today, when Jesus came up against true physical ailments that would have been unresponsive to his word; the epileptic boy of Mark 9 is the record, apparently much worked over, of a borderline case.

We can distinguish two likely patterns at work. On the one hand the unemployed might develop a paralysis of the legs or arms which would at once justify and symbolize their social situation. But on the other hand some of the diseases represent a *partial cooptation, against resistance*, of the sufferer by the *oppressive forces*. The Pharisees said that most Galileans were unclean; some believed it and acquired skin diseases. The Pharisees said their testimony was inadmissible; they acquired speech impediments. The Pharisees "locked the kingdom of heaven against men" (Matt. 23:13), said they were unable to enter it; men became lame. (Jesus both heals the lame and says men *can* enter the kingdom.) The Pharisees said they were "guides to the blind" (Rom. 2:19, turned around by Jesus, Luke 6:39) who could not see the truth of God; people became blind. The Pharisees (no doubt) said the Galileans were deaf to the word (Isa. 6:10, probably turned against them by Jesus, Mark 4:12); the Galileans believed them.

The relation of the Pharisees and other legalists to the oppressive front was ambiguous. On the one hand they supported the village theocracy in Galilee, and through it the power of Antipas; he doubtless supported them, recognizing which side his bread was buttered on. But on the other hand their rigidity toward the Law could lead them in the direction of the Zealots (who like their prototype Phinehas were zealots for the Law) and thus ultimately into opposition to Rome and its puppets; or in the direction of the Essenes and the Covenanters of Qumran, who wrote or preserved the Scroll of the War of the Sons of Light against the Sons of Darkness and were at the last rally of resistance in 73 A.D. at Masada. The perception that the Pharisees should be a focus of resistance to external oppression only reinforced and legitimized their internal oppression.

But the Gospels also record some spectacular symbols of cooptation by unambiguous oppression. Taxation had been bleeding the country to death for decades; a woman is walking the streets who has been bleeding for twelve years, and has spent all she had on doctors to no effect (Mark 5:25–26). This instance perhaps can be disputed. Indisputable is the case of the Gerasene demoniac with a multiple personality, who is aware of his own uncleanness, has acquired superhuman strength, breaks any chains that are laid upon him, lives in the place of death, and bruises himself with stones toward his own death. His name is "Legion for we are many" (Mark 5:9): *legio* is a Latin loan-word which has gone equally into Greek and Talmudic Aramaic. Here is one, perhaps a survivor of Sepphoris, who by sheer froce has been taken over by the very essence of Roman militarism. But not without struggle; Antipas with his executioner and his captains of hundreds and thousands, is one who has been taken over without a struggle.

New Testament Greek ascribes these diseases to *daimonia*.[32] As a name for a prevalent thing, "demon" is as useful as "psychosis" and explains as little or as much. Jesus takes up the word and uses it. The legend of his temptations, which I hope to treat elsewhere, is an excellent analysis of the Palestinian situation. For Jesus, something is demonic to the degree that it stands directly over against God: God has his kingdom, and Satan has his (Luke 11:18-20). When men are behaving most demonically they are contrasted directly with God:[33] they have been coopted by the united front of oppression. His best-attested coinage is *Mammon*. It is a good Aramaic word meaning "money, security, capital." Jesus found it used with a good sense; Rabbi Jose, for example, said "Let the mammon of thy associate be as dear to thee as thine own."[34] In Jesus' mouth it signifies a master who, like God, is a jealous Lord (Luke 16:13). Such contrasts should make it clear that at Mark 12:17 "the things of Caesar" are being contrasted with the "things of God," not set in parallel with them in a coordinate realm as Luther tended to say. Political power is part of the demonic front. The "rulers and authorities" of Luke 12:11, whose names are identical with the "principalities and powers" of Paul, are alternatively translated "governors and kings" (Mark 13:9). Since the name Beel-zebul, "master of the house" (Matt. 10:25), is unattested before the Gospels, it may be Jesus' own coinage for the "chief magistrate" (Luke 11:15) of the demonic powers that face him. This Beel-zebul is the Usurper or Squatter par excellence, the prototype of all the forces that move into the houses of people's lives, swept and garnished, that turn a house of prayer into a den of thieves, that do not enter themselves but turn the key against others.[35]

The Resistance Movement. Ever since Alexander conquered the Near East there had been sporadic resistance movements, now studied in a stunning book by Eddy.[36] When Rome took over from the Hellenistic kingdoms, it inherited both their methods of imperial control and the resistance to them, of which the Jewish resistance was the most impressive. We badly need a translation of Hengel's big book on the Zealots.[37] It is most unfortunate that Brandon's fundamentally wrong-headed book[38] dominates the literature in English; besides his questionable extension of the name "Zealots" backwards to cover the whole movement,[39] he builds up a house of cards to argue Jesus' nonviolence out of existence.

That Galilee was one fountainhead of the Zealot movement seems clear from the history of Judas of Gamala (in Philip's tetrarchy, *A.J.* 18:4) who is also called "the Galilean" (*A.J.* 18:23). He may or may not be identical with the Judas son of Hezekias who took Sepphoris; but he is certainly the Judas of Acts 5:37 and the father and grandfather of Zealot leaders in the revolt of 70 A.D. It was at the deposition of Archelaus (6 A.D.), when the legate of Syria was sent to conduct a census in Judea in order to put it under Roman rule, that Judas of Galilee and his comrade Sadok the Pharisee "appealed to their people to make a bid for independence" on the ground that God was their only ruler.

The Gospels are our best evidence for the resistance in Galilee in the following decades. Seven of the first thirteen apostles—two Simons, two Judases, two Ma(tta)thiases and John—were named by their fathers after the Maccabees.[40] One Simon is said explicitly to be or have been a Zealot (Luke 6:15). John (6:15) preserves a precious testimony that after the great meal in the desert there was an attempt to make Jesus "king," which helps us interpret the much worked-over passage (Mark 8:33), where Jesus seems to forbid Peter to call him "Christ." The tendency of the Twelve is to take the violent course (Luke 9:54–55; 22:35–38; Matt. 26:52; John 18:36). What above all is the Sermon on the Mount about? To the extent that it is phrased in imperatives and negative commands it must be a polemic against views actually held by the audience rather than by somebody else; and the prohibition of violence is at the middle of it. Its passage through the hands of the church is chiefly marked by the mutual assimilation of its commands to the Passion narrative:

Sermon	*Passion*
". . . conscripts you one mile" (Matt. 5:41)	
	"And they conscripted Simon . . ." (Mark 15:21)
". . . if you kiss only your brethren" (5:46)	
	"Judas kissed Jesus" (14:45)
". . . give him your cloak" (5:40)	
	"They divided his garments" (15:24)
"if anyone hits your right cheek" (5:39)	
	"They hit him [on the cheeks," *Syriac*] (14:65)

But this leads us on to our next section.

JERUSALEM

Jeremias wrote a big and original book entitled *Jerusalem in the Time of Jesus* (Philadelphia: Fortress Press, 1969), which nowhere takes cognizance of the fact that this Jerusalem was a city under foreign military occupation! Against this book it is important to affirm that his Jerusalem was a Romanized city, that the New Testament is nearly as Roman a book as the *Aeneid*, and that the Passion narratives are its most Romanized parts. However it is also important to discern what image swims up in our inner eye when we hear the word "Rome." For English historians, from Gibbon to the *Cam-*

bridge Ancient History, that image was the British Empire. A recent collective work on the Roman background of the early church is very much in this tradition: "There can be no doubt that the economic conditions of Syria-Palestine improved greatly under Augustus' firm control."[41] Biblical students need to know that there is a revisionist history of the empire: Rostovtzeff[42] was a White Russian who saw the work of Diocletian as a Stalinization of the empire, and Syme[43] sees Augustus through the eyes of an Englishman looking towards the continent in 1939. But correctives continue to be needed on every level of scholarship and in every area of study.[44]

Sherwin-White has an excellent chapter on the trial of Jesus which shows that the Gospel accounts can be understood as actual accounts of Roman provincial administration. Rather than summarize, I will here illustrate the Romanization of Jerusalem from the standpoint of language and vocabulary. Where several languages coexist, a lingua franca emerges, especially in the noun-vocabulary. In an imperial situation, it is always the subject language that gives way: Vietnamese is full of Americanisms, but the Vietnam vets have not brought Indochinese words back to the States. Since Rome governed the Eastern half of the empire in Greek, building on the base of the successor kingdoms, the vocabulary of the imperial administration is partly Latin and partly fixed Greek equivalents.[45] The best witnesses to the lingua franca are the New Testament on one side and Talmud and Midrash on the other. I here pass by the common elements of vocabulary which witness to the previous Hellenization of Palestine in the general areas of Greek culture (Greek *synedrion,* "council," taken over as Hebrew *Sanhedrin*), luxury goods, and terms of the market. The elements of the lingua franca of Roman date overwhelmingly illustrate the techniques of imperial control.

In the New Testament as in the Talmud, the Roman weights, measures, and coins with their Latin names (*litra, mile, denarius,* etc.) dominate.

It was the Greeks that brought banking to Palestine, and their words have made their way into the New Testament and Talmud. But there was also a partial Hellenizing of Roman financial practice in the second century B.C., so that many of the same words come into the popular Latin of Plautus, some temporarily and some permanently. Such Greco-Hebraic-Latin words, whose role in imperial control needs no underlining, are: *trapezites,* "money-changer" (Matt. 25:27); *thesauros,* "treasure"; *emporion,* "market" (John 2:16); *gaza,* "royal treasury," a Persian word (Acts 8:27); *kollybos,* "small change" (cf. Mark 11:15); *daneistes,* "money-lender," Lat. *danista* (Luke 7:41).

Some samples of Hebrew and Aramaic infiltrated from the two languages (Greek and Latin) of the imperial bureaucracy will show the ambiguous feelings of the subject people to their lords. *Kosmokrator,* "world-ruler," has a politico-demonic sense at Ephesians 6:12; in an inscription it is applied to the Emperor Caracalla. The Talmud uses it to delimit imperial power: "A king may have for *patronus* the governor of one province (*eparchy*) and not of another; even if he is a *kosmokrator,* his power is limited by the edges of the land, he does not rule over the sea. But God is equally sovereign of sea and land."[46] The Midrash on Psalm 18:14, a dangerously subversive text, has Pharaoh bring up each of the resources of, remarkably, the Roman army, only to be decisively checked each time by God: "The Holy One took away the ensigns (*signus*) of the Egyptians. . . . Pharaoh tried again and brought up siege-engines (*ballistae*). . . . Pharaoh then sought to hearten his host with all kinds of bugles (*bucina*), horns (*shopars*), and trumpets (*salpinx*)."[47]

More often the Jews were trapped into taking their masters' view of the matter. God's action in creation and history is compared "to a country that rebelled against its king, whereupon the king sent a strong *legion* and marched them round it, so that the inhabitants might see it and fear him."[48] The Romans called Jewish revolutionaries *sicarii*, "assassins" (cf. Acts 21:38), and the Midrash uses the same word: the "chief of the *Siqarin*" in Jerusalem burned the storehouses "because so long as the precious stores were intact the people would not jeopardize their lives in battle."[49] A soldier's ration is *opsonion* (Greek loan-word, in Latin *obsonium*); it is used in Antipas' army (Luke 3:14) and in both good and bad senses by Paul. The Midrash compares God's gifts of commandments to men to "a king distributing *opsonion* to his *legiones* through his generals (*dux*), officers (*eparchs*), and noncoms (*stratiotae*)."[50]

Let us go through the Passion narrative in sequence and see how the text would have sounded to poor folk in Palestine.

The Poll Tax. "Is it lawful to pay the tax (*census*, Latin loan-word in Greek) to *Caesar*?". . . "Bring me a *denarius*" (Mark 12:14-15). *Census* is common in Greek of the East and has gone into Palestinian Syriac and perhaps Talmudic; the tax, its coin, and the recipient are all Latinisms in imperial Greek.

Rebels and Prison. "Have you come out as against a rebel (*leistes*) to take me?" (Mark 14:48); "Lord, I am ready to go with you to prison (*phylake*)" (Luke 22:33); "Barabbas was a *leistes*" (John 18:40) who had been "thrown into prison (*phylake*) because of sedition" (Luke 23:19). *Phylake* represents Latin *custodia* in one of its senses, and has also made its way into the vulgar Latin of Plautus. *Leistes* represents Latin *latro*: it is the pejorative "bandit," which Josephus uses to describe political rebels. Jesus himself is shown as using *leistes* in the bad sense of "a den of bandits." The Midrash attests to the presence of both words in popular Aramaic with the establishment sense:

It is like the case of a robber (*leistes*) who sat at a crossroads and over powered passers-by. Once a legate (?—Aram. corrupt) passed by to collect the taxes (Greek *demosia*) of that province. The robber arose, confronted him, and overpowered him, taking away all that he had. After a time the robber was captured and put in prison (Greek *phylake*).[51]

Prisons are maintained by a beneficent government to punish robbers and other criminals.

The Military Tribune and His Cohort. "So the cohort (*speira*) and its officer (*chiliarchos*, "ruler of a thousand"), and the servants of the Jews took Jesus" (John 18:12). The cohort also appears in the Synoptic narrative later at Matthew 27:27. In contrast to Antipas' "rulers of a thousand" this is a genuine Roman military tribune, commanding a cohort or tenth of a legion (600 men, expanded by the romantic Greeks to a thousand). The Greek terms are translations of the Latin standard since Polybius and were fully naturalized into Semitic. The Midrash gives Jehoshaphat a *speira*;[52] a Nabatean inscription of *klyrk* shows that the Nabatean army had a parallel structure to that of Antipas.[53] There are also many standard Greek equivalents of Latin terms which have gone into Semitic: *dogma*, "edict" of the emperor (Luke 2:1); *epitropos*, "procurator" (Luke 3:1 Western reading); *anthypatos*, "proconsul" (Acts 13:7).

The Blow. "And some began to hit (*kolaphizein*) him" (Mark 14:65). Vulgar Greek *kolaphos*, "box, cuff," went into the vulgar Latin of Plautus *colap(h)us*, and thence rose in the linguistic scale as French *coup*, Spanish *golpe*, etc. The Palestinian Syriac simply transliterates. The Old Syriac as we saw adds "on his cheeks"; it sees a fulfillment of the prophecy "I gave my back to the smiters, and my cheeks to those who pulled out the beard" (Isa. 50:6). Jesus speaks in the same tradition, "If anyone strikes you on the right cheek" (Matt. 5:39); all three texts describe a long-standing pattern of ritual humiliation.

The Tribunal. "While Pilate was sitting on his *bema* . . ." (Matt. 27:19). This term is standard Greek; it went over into Semitic where it was confused with another name of a pagan thing, *bama* for "altar" (probably the source of Greek *bomos* "altar").

The Accusation. "What accusation (*kategoria*) do you bring against this man?" (John 18:29). This is the standard Greek and Talmudic for *delatio* or *accusatio* (I should note that the Passion narrative was quite transparent to Jerome, who translates all the Greek terms by their correct Latin equivalents). *Kategor* (Rev. 12:10) in Greek and perhaps in Talmudic is also a name of Satan the *diabolos*—both Greek words mean "accuser." Satan's ambiguous legitimacy in Jewish mythology is similar to that of the Roman legal system, and it is appropriate that they should be associated! Did Satan originally acquire that status under Persian imperial control?

The Flogging. "And having scourged (*phragellosas*) Jesus, he delivered him to be crucified" (Mark 15:15). (The same verse contains a literal equivalent of Latin *satis facere*.) The cat-o'-nine-tails was such a characteristic Roman innovation that it was unknown elsewhere and carried its name, suitably distorted (Lat. *horribile flagellum*, Horace *Sat.* 1.3.119), wherever the eagles went. It strikes me as very seditious that John (2:15) should represent Jesus as driving the moneysellers from the temple with a *phragellion*. In the form *pargol* it runs through the Talmud. A beautiful parallel to the Passion narrative is a catechism of Jewish martyrs several times repeated in the Talmud:

"Why are you being led out to be decapitated?"
"Because I circumcised my son to be an Israelite."
"Why are you being led out to be burned?"
"Because I read the Torah."
"Why are you being led out to be *crucified*?"
"Because I ate the unleavened bread."
"Why are you getting a hundred *pargol*?"
"Because I performed the ceremony of the Lulab."[54]

This text, which somehow survived the self-censorship of the Talmud in matters relating to both Rome and the church, shows how similar the situations of Jesus, Jewish martyrs, and Christian martyrs were.

The Governor and the Praetorium. "Then the soldiers of the governor (*hegemon*) took Jesus into the *Praetorium*, and they gathered the whole cohort (*speira*) before him" (Matt. 27:27). Both terms go into the Talmud with an honorific sense: "A man received a governorship (*hegemonia*) from the king; before he reaches the seat of his authority, he goes as an ordinary citizen."[55]

The Mocking. "They clothed him in purple (*porphyra*) [Matt. 27:28 "a cloak (*chlamys*) of scarlet"] and put a crown of thorns on his head" (Mark 15:17). Although Semites invented purple, they took back its Greco-Latin name: "It is like a general (*dux*) to whom his *legiones* have thrown the *porphyra*."[56] Philo (*Contra Flaccum* 37) describes the public mocking in Alexandria of an idiot who is given a diadem, *chlamys*, and sceptre and is hailed in Aramaic as *Marin*, "Lord." Both tales are very ambiguous. For the Alexandrians, while seeming to mock King Herod Agrippa, by the very style of the parody affirm the legitimacy of the regal symbols; and the Evangelists obviously mean us to understand that the Roman soldiers, while intending to mock Jesus' supposed royal claim, in a deeper sense are affirming it.

Conscription. "And they conscripted (*angareuo*) a passer-by, Simon of Cyrene . . . to carry his cross" (Mark 15:21); "If anyone conscripts you one mile, go with him two" (Matt. 5:41). Conscription (*angareia*) was a Persian practice, and Herodotus (8:98) says they call their post-service *angareion*; the word is probably Aramaic or Akkadian, although the root is not certain. The Romans picked up the practice from the Hellenistic monarchies, together with the Greek name which went into Latin as into Semitic.[57]

Crucifixion. The royal inscriptions of the Assyrian and Persian kings constantly affirm how they have flayed or impaled their rivals, and Herodotus attests the same of the Persian kings. The punishment was known to Plato (*Gorgias* 473C) and to Polybius (1:86). In each of the languages it has a characteristic native name, probably in every case vulgar, derived from the instrument used, whether pole or cross. The Romans apparently first took it over from the Carthaginians (in whom Semitic and Hellenistic streams flowed together); with them it has come down in the social scale, and is used much more extensively, but now for slaves or those being treated as slaves.

I see no reason to doubt that Psalm 22, "they have pierced my hands and my feet" (vs. 16), was originally conceived as a lament of a crucified one, with some self-censorship in view of whatever the foreign power at the time may have been. Isaiah 53 is not quite so clear a case but is most easily understood as a development of the same theme: "his appearance is so marred" (52:14), "he was wounded for our transgressions" (53:5). Since the Romans stepped so accurately into the old imperial pattern, we can give a very objective sense to the idea of fulfillment of prophecy: the old pattern repeats itself, this is the expected fate of a prophet of justice under imperial rule. Thus it is not really very bad history when the evangelists quote the laments: "for my raiment they cast lots" (Ps. 22:18), "they gave me vinegar to drink" (Ps. 69:21), and so on. Also it is not so surprising that Jesus in the Sermon should use the examples of being struck on the cheek, being deprived of one's garments, and being conscripted so many miles; none should have known better than he what route he was setting out on.

The Sentries. "Take a guard (*custodia*, Latin loan-word in Greek)" (Matt. 27:65). Again in Semitic the police power is a parable of God's action: "It is like a settlement in the desert (*ereme*) which was kept in disorder by invading bands. What did the king do? He appointed a command(er) *(custodianus)* to protect it."[58]

To Summarize. The Galilean parts of the Gospels, much fuller than the Jerusalem part, give a very concrete and detailed picture of the society and economy. The texture of the language is not very Aramaic, and if it represents a popular Greek of Galilee it is not easily identifiable as such. In contrast, not merely does the Jerusalem part of the Gospel present an intelligible historical picture, but also the linguistic texture as lingua franca constantly agrees with Talmudic Hebrew and Aramaic in showing the effects of Roman rule. The poverty and psychic alienation in the North has its complement in the naked oppression and cultural-linguistic dislocation in the South. If we can affirm anything about Jesus' intentions, we can affirm that he knew some day he would go to Jerusalem and act. So if in speaking of the Kingdom of God he took into account in any way the historical situation around him and the psychic dislocations that it generated, we will have to grasp that history and that alienation if we want to understand his word about the kingdom.

NOTES

1. A. N. Sherwin-White, *Roman Society and Roman Law in the New Testament,* (Oxford: Oxford University Press, 1963), pp. 187–88.

2. A. H. M. Jones, *The Cities of the Eastern Roman Provinces,* 2nd ed. (Oxford: Oxford University Press, 1971), pp. 240, 272–74.

3. Michael Avi-Yonah, *The Holy Land from the Persian to the Arab Conquests* (Grand Rapids: Baker Books, 1966), p. 97; Prof. John H. Elliott has helped me to understand this administrative system.

4. The commandants of Nabatea figure in the flight of Antipas' wife to her father Aretas (Josephus, *A. J.* 18:112); *strategos* is a Greek loan-word in Aretas' Aramaic

inscriptions (G. A. Cooke, *A Textbook of North-Semitic Inscriptions* [Oxford: Oxford University Press, 1903], No. 96, p. 247).

5. A really good book on Antipas and his Galilee is now available, Harold W. Hoehner's *Herod Antipas,* NTSMS 17 (Cambridge: Cambridge University Press, 1972). Also the studies of John the Baptist are relevant: see Walter Wink, *John the Baptist in the Gospel Tradition,* NTSMS 7 (Cambridge: Cambridge University Press, 1968); the books by Goguel, Lohmeyer, Kraeling, and Scobie cited in Wink, *John the Baptist,* p. ix; and Eero Repo, *Der "Weg" als Selbstbezeichnung des Urchristentums,* Annales Academiae Scientiarum Fennicae, ser. B., tom. 132.2 (Helsinki, 1964).

6. Hoehner, *Herod Antipas,* pp. 149–151.

7. Adolf Deissmann, *Licht vom Osten,* 4th ed. (Tübingen, 1923), pp. 303, 310; Eng., *Light from the Ancient East* (Grand Rapids, Mich.: Baker Books, 1965).

8. Mishna *Aboth* III.1.

9. Sherwin-White, *Roman Society,* p. 133.

10. The Talmud appears to confirm the judge as Galilean when it says (Jerus. Talm. *Sotah* IX.10, iv.2.36, trans. Schwab) that Galilean courts had one judge while Judean ones had three. This may refer to the resettlement of Pharisees in Galilee in the second century of our era: A. Büchler, *Der Galiläische 'Am-Ha'areṣ des zweiten Jahrhunderts* (Vienna, 1906, repr. Hildesheim, 1968); J. Neusner, *The Rabbinic Tradition about the Pharisees before 70,* 3 vols. (Leiden: Brill, 1971), Vol. 3, p. 32.

11. Cambridge MS of John 11:54.

12. Jerus. Talm. *Pesahin* IV.2.

13. Johanan B. Zakkai: "Galilee, Galilee! Your hatred of the Law will class you in the end among the oppressors" (Jerus. Talm. *Sabbath* XVI end). Undated: the Galilean student did not learn from a single master; Galileans had a slovenly pronunciation of gutturals (Bab. Talm. *Erubin* 53a, trans. Soncino, p. 371); see A. Neubauer, *La géographie du Talmud* (Paris, 1868), pp. 177–240.

14. Luke 12:43;Matt. 6:32; Matt. 5:47; 6:7; 23:15.

15. Biblical atlases speak of the "Way of the Sea" (Isa. 9:1) and pre-Roman roads, but it appears all conjecture. After Galilee was incorporated into Judea, actual Roman milestones stood north, west, and south of Tiberias (Michael Avi-Yonah, *The Holy Land,* World Cultural Guide Series [New York: Holt, Rhinehart and Winston, 1972], pp. 181–87), and these would indeed be "ways of the Gentiles."

16. S. Krauss, *Griechische und lateinische Lehnwörter im Talmud, Midrasch und Targum,* 2 vols. (Berlin, 1899).

17. For Menahem the Essene, see also Mishna *Hagigah* II.2 and Bab. Talm. *Hag.* 16b. Zahn with great ingenuity said that the officer of Capernaum was Menahem, since the officer is the person of highest rank converted in the Gospels, and Manaen is the highest-ranking convert in Acts; Ernst Haenchen, *Acts of the Apostles: A Commentary,* repr. (Philadelphia: Westminster, 1971), p. 394.

18. W. R. Farmer makes the soldiers to whom John spoke actual Zealot units, "an organized resistance to Rome" (art. "John the Baptist," *Interpreter's Dictionary of the Bible* ii.190b). But this totally misreads the situation under Antipas, who held his tenure on condition of preventing any such organization.

19. Hoehner, *Herod Antipas,* pp. 75, 298–300.

20. Tacitus *Ann.* 2.42; Josephus *A.J.* 17:205, 18:90.

21. See the ground-breaking work of my late teacher Frederick C. Grant, *The Economic Background of the Gospels* (Oxford: Oxford University Press, 1926; repr. New York: Russell, 1973).

22. Mishna *Nedarim* III.4; *Kelim* XV.4.

23. Michel, art. "telones," *Theol. Wörterb. z. N.T.* VIII.88–106; John R. Donahue, "Tax Collectors and Sinners: An Attempt at Identification," *CBQ* 33 (1971): 39–61.

24. Mishna *Ketuboth* IV.12.

25. Grant, *Economic Background,* pp. 95–96.

26. J. Klausner, *Jesus of Nazareth: His Life, Times, and Teaching,* trans. H. Danby (New York: Macmillan, 1949), pp. 190–92.

27. Joachim Jeremias, *The Parables of Jesus* (New York: Scribner's, rev. ed., 1963).

28. Sherwin-White, *Roman Society,* p. 140.

29. M. Rostovtzeff, *Social and Economic History of the Roman Empire,* 2nd. ed., rev. by P. M. Frazer, 2 vols. (Oxford: Oxford University Press, 1957),Vol. 2, p. 664.

30. R. K. Harrison, art. "leprosy," *IDB,* pp. 111–13.

31. Gerd Theissen, "Wanderradikalismus . . . ," *Zeitschr. f. Theologie und Kirche* 70 (1973): 245–71.

32. The Aramaic original is unclear. Sometimes the Syriac translates it *daywah,* which is Old Persian *daiva,* "demon" (but originally "deity"!), a nice illustration of the influence of Zoroastrinianism on Semitic demonism.

33. God and men contrasted: Luke 16:15; Mark 8:33; 10:9; 11:30; Acts 5:29.

34. *Aboth* II.17.

35. See George B. Caird, *Principalities and Powers: A Study in Pauline Theology* (Oxford: Oxford University Press, 1956); H. Schlier, *Principalities and Powers in the New Testament* (New York: Herder and Herder, 1961).

36. Samuel K. Eddy, *The King is Dead: Studies in the Near Eastern Resistance to Hellenism, 334–31 B.C.* (Lincoln: University of Nebraska Press, 1961).

37. Martin Hengel, *Die Zeloten* (Leiden: Brill, 1961).

38. S. G. F. Brandon, *Jesus and the Zealots* (New York: Scribner's, 1968); Hengel is answering it; for now see M. Hengel, *Victory over Violence: Jesus and the Revolutionists,* trans. David E. Green (Philadelphia: Fortress Press, 1973).

39. Morton Smith, "Zealots and Sicarii . . . ," HTR 64 (1971): 1–19.

40. William R. Farmer, *Maccabees, Zealots, and Josephus* (New York: Columbia University Press, 1956, repr. Wesport, Conn.: Greenwood Press, 1974), p. 28. The Maccabees brought in new fixed naming patterns. Semitic often alternates two names between generations, so it is reassuring to find an Aramaic dedication from Capernaum showing a "Zebida son of Johanan" as alternate generation from a "John son of Zebedee": G. Dalman, *Aramäische Dialektproben* (Leipzig, 1927), p. 38.

41. Stephen Benko and John J. O'Rourke, eds., *The Catacombs and the Colosseum: The Roman Empire as the Setting of Primitive Christianity* (Valley Forge, Pa.: Judson, 1971), p. 230.

42. Rostovtzeff, *Social and Economic History of the Roman Empire.*

43. Ronald Syme, *The Roman Revolution* (Oxford: Oxford University Press, 2nd ed., 1960).

44. Recommended are: Nathaniel Lewis and Meyer Reinhold, *Roman Civilization: Selected Readings,* 2 vols. (New York: Columbia University Press, 1951–1955); Ramsey McMullen, *Enemies of the Roman Order: Treason, Unrest, and Alienation in the Empire* (Cambridge: Harvard University Press, 1966); little overlap with this paper.

45. D. Magie, *De Romanorum Juris Publici Sacrique Vocabulis Sollemnibus in Graecum Sermonem Conversis* (1905); L. Hahn, *Rom und Romanismus in griech.-*

röm. (Osten, 1906), with an excellent New Testament section; H. J. Mason, *Greek Terms for Roman Institutions: A Lexicon and Analysis,* American Studies in Papyrology, 13 (Toronto: Hakkert, 1973).

46. Caracalla: see Arndt-Gingrich *ad verb.* Jerusalem. Talm. *Berakoth* IX.I (tr. Schwabe I. 1. 152-53).

47. *Midrash on Psalms,* Judaica Series, No. 13, 2 vols., trans. William G. Braude (New Haven: Yale University Press, 1959), Vol. 1, p. 244.

48. *Bereshith Rabba, V. 6:* (Heb. and Eng.), (Brooklyn, N.Y.: Shalom Publications, n.d.), Vol. 5.

49. Midrash Rabba, 10 vols. (New York: Soncino Publications), in Vol. 7 on Ecclesiastes 12:1; art. "sikarios," *Theological Dictionary of the New Testament,* ed. Gerhard Kittel and Gerhard Friedrich (Grand Rapids: Eerdmans, 1971), Vol. 7, pp. 278-82.

50. Midrash on Song of Songs, I.2.5.

51. Midrash Rabba on Lev. 30:6 (p. 388 in Eng. trans.).

52. Midrash on Ps. 15:6 (Braude, Vol. 1, p. 193).

53. *Corp. Inscr. Sem.* II. 201.2.

54. Midrash Rabba on Lev. 32:1 (Freedman and Simon), Vol. 4, p. 408: *Mekilta* on Exod. 20:3-6, trans. Jacob Lauterbach, 3 vols. Library of Jewish Classics (Philadelphia: Jewish Publication Society of America, 1976), Vol. 2, p. 247.

55. Bereshith Rabba, L.2 (Eng. trans. Vol. 1, p. 435).

56. Exodus Rabba, XV.13 (Eng. trans. p. 176).

57. Talmudic testimonies to conscription (*angareia*): Strack-Billerbeck, I. 344-45.

58. Leviticus Rabba, XXXV.5 (Eng. trans., p. 449).

ADDITIONAL READING

Gerd Theissen, *Sociology of Early Palestinian Christianity,* tr. J. Bowden (Philadelphia: Fortress, 1978); Hans Kreissig, *Die soziale Zusammenhänge des judäischen Krieges, Klassen und Klassenkampf im Palästina des 1. Jahrhunderts v. u. Z.* (Schriften zur Geschichte und Kultur der Antike 1, Deutsche Akademie der Wissenschaften zu Berlin, Zentralinstitut für alte Geschichte und Archäologie; Berlin: Akademie-Verlag, 1970); Martin Hengel, *Crucifixion in the ancient world and folly of the message of the cross,* tr. J. Bowden with substantial additions by the author (Philadelphia: Fortress, 1977); Séan Freyne, *Galilee from Alexander the Great to Hadrian, 323 B.C.E. to 135 C.E.: A Study of Second Temple Judaism,* Univ. of Notre Dame, Center for the Study of Judaism and Christianity in Antiquity, 5 (Wilmington & Notre Dame: Michael Glazier & Univ. of Notre Dame, 1980). Of exceptional interest in many ways is Edward N. Luttwak, *The Grand Strategy of the Roman Empire from the First Century A.D. to the Third* (Baltimore & London: John Hopkins, 1976). Luttwak, a research professor at Georgetown University, is a military and strategic historian who writes in appreciation of the Roman Empire out of his identification with the American Empire: "We [Americans], like the Romans, face the prospect not of decisive conflict, but of permanent state of war, albeit limited. We, like the Romans, must actively protect an advanced society against a variety of threats rather than concentrate on destroying the forces of our enemies in battle. Above all, the nature of modern weapons requires that we avoid their use while striving to exploit their full diplomatic potential" (p. xii). Note especially his comparison (p. 81) of the dilemmas of the U.S. Department of Defense and the Roman Empire in policing geographically remote areas (in our case, Germany and South Korea): "It is for this reason that American troops must be stationed in the theater itself, with the resultant diseconomy of force, regardless of the obvious political functions that these deployments also serve." It throws a flood of light both on Roman imperialism and on U.S. imperialism for the one to be studied through the spectacles of the other.

20

GEORGE V. PIXLEY

God's Kingdom in First-Century Palestine: The Strategy of Jesus

Stimulated by the social readings of Gospel materials advanced by G. Theissen and F. Belo—who confine their analyses to the beliefs of early Christians about Jesus—the author attempts a coherent account of what Jesus understood himself to be doing. After a description of how the temple economy, headed by a Jewish elite, meshed with the empire-wide slave economy of Rome, he contends that Jesus set out to give a new embodiment to the Kingdom of God by overthrowing the priestly temple system and its ideology that masked the combined Roman/Jewish elite oppression of the great majority of Palestinian Jews.

The strategy of Jesus was to move about Galilee with a core band of followers in order to recruit people broadly to his understanding, in the course of which he awakened opposition from local religious establishments. Moving to Jerusalem, he disrupted the temple economy, but he was executed by an agreement between Jewish and Roman authorities when his popular sup-

Reprinted from George V. Pixley, *God's Kingdom: A Guide for Biblical Study* (Maryknoll, N.Y.: Orbis Books, 1981), pp. 64–87.

port crumbled. His abrupt death prevents us from knowing how he might have consolidated popular support had he been able to close down the temple, or what his strategy toward Rome would have been.

The organizational principles *of Jesus were equality among his supporters and the surrender of wealth and family. The allied enemies of Jesus and his movement were able to undermine their popular support because so many people in Palestine depended on the temple economy for a livelihood or had become psychically and culturally dependent upon it for national identity.*

The specifics of Jesus' historical project cannot be absolutized by us, the more so because it failed, although it is of significance that the central figure of Christianity led so concrete a religiopolitical project. For example, it is an error to treat the nonviolence of Jesus as a universal ethical norm. Jesus' nonviolence was strategic: he wished to neutralize Roman power while attacking the domestic Jewish religious and economic establishment and he wished to develop a disciplined and internally peaceful movement.

In our investigation of the kingdom of God within the Bible, this chapter is second in importance only to that on the origins of Israel (chapter 2). This is so because the historical project of God's kingdom of which the primitive Jesus movement was the bearer survived the debacle of the Jewish-Roman War to inspire the Christian religion that was to become the religion of Europe. Our entire study is based on the open question whether or not that Christian religion can be considered good news for the poor. By thus stressing the importance of the Jesus movement because of its seminal character for Christian religion we are recognizing an historical fact, not judging it. The judgment must be made if the poor are to achieve salvation, but a biblical scholar is not the one to make it. The decision whether the Christian faith offers hope for the poor must be made by the poor themselves. Nevertheless political decisions are not made without taking into account the realities of history, and Christianity is an historical reality to be dealt with, for good or for ill. And so, regardless of where we Latin American Christians come out in our political evaluation of the Christian message, the fact of the Jesus movement is a major historical reality with which we must deal.[1]

In this unit of our study what is most important, the Jesus movement in its origins, must remain largely hypothetical. About Jesus and his Galilean movement, about their strategy to bring about God's kingdom, we are informed only through the documents of a Christian church already uprooted from the Palestinian context in which it was born. That our investigation on this point is hypothetical does not mean that it is not serious or that it does not merit scientific respect. It will merit this respect to the extent that it does justice to the sources and succeeds in explaining the facts for which we have

trustworthy documents. A good hypothesis will then be confirmed or disconfirmed by the research it inspires on the documents.

It is not very difficult to establish the main outlines of the historical situation of Palestine in the first century of the Christian era. The various Jewish
movements inspired by the expectation of God's kingdom were so many attempts to answer the challenges of that situation. Any hypothesis about the
Jesus movement must rest on our knowledge of that situation, and then take
seriously the subsequent Christian texts that come mostly from outside of
Palestine. If it does so, it will not be just another projection of our desires like
that profusion of biographies of Jesus that liberal idealism has produced for
two centuries.[2]

We have divided our study of the first century into two parts. In this first
part we shall deal with Palestinian movements guided by the prophetic promises of the coming kingdom. Among these we shall emphasize the Jesus movement, because it is so seminal to our identity as Christians.[3] In a second part
we shall focus on the Christian communities scattered over the Greco-Roman
world outside of Palestine.

PALESTINE UNDER THE ROMAN EMPIRE

According to historical materialism, the introduction of private property
launched humankind on the irreversible path of making history. The irreversible character of the history thus launched has to do with the destruction of
the "natural" productive community, the peasant village. Once the village
structure was broken up, there was no turning back. Empirically, civilization
began with the introduction of a tributary mode of production in places like
Egypt, Mesopotamia, Mexico, and China. But in these societies the state was
superimposed on the village, and village structures persisted. It was the survival of the village that made possible the Israelite anti-statist revolution,
which was a more "primitive" society than the Canaanite society it replaced.
The breakup of village structures only occurred through the introduction of
private property, especially over land. Private property was first made possible by the introduction of slave labor. And the Roman Empire was the
greatest historical experiment in building a society on slave labor.[4]

The original accumulation of wealth in the city of Rome was achieved by
means of its commercial enterprises. To protect its commercial interests
Rome built a powerful army made up of the sons of the free peasants under its
sphere of influence. Slaves were introduced to work the lands, which passed
from the hands of villagers into those of wealthy nobles. Rome soon discovered that the cheapest way to acquire slaves was through war. Because slaves
did not reproduce themselves in captivity at a sufficient rate to maintain the
level of production desired, Rome was pushed to even greater militarism and
expansionism. By the first century of the Christian era it had achieved its
maximum extension.

In the course of its expansion, the Roman legions also conquered Palestine. It was Pompey who led the legions into Palestine in 63 B.C. Palestine was incorporated into the province of Syria, which was governed by a Roman proconsul. To a Hasmonean (the Jewish dynasty descended from the Maccabees) was entrusted the high priesthood, without administrative authority. The levying of tribute remained in the hands of the Syrian proconsul.

The mere presence of Roman authorities in Palestine did not overnight transform the character of Palestinian society. As we have seen, that society was organized according to an Asiatic mode of production. In the place of a royal court, the power of tribute over the productive villages rested in the hands of the temple personnel. Much remains to be done to understand how the tributary Palestinian society was meshed into the slave-based Roman Empire. It is clear, nevertheless, that slave production did not become the norm in Palestine. Cities were built on the Greco-Roman model, but they seem to have been enclaves within a society where traditional village life continued, and where the temple continued to play the role of the dominant class, it being in turn dominated by Roman military authorities. The interplay between these two types of class societies was basic for any strategy of popular liberation, and helps account for the various strategies we shall be examining. Not only is it difficult for us in the twentieth century to understand the interaction of these two class systems and their relative importance, those who struggled for liberation in the first century also differed in their interpretations of the reality of oppression they were experiencing. We shall return to this.

A further complicating factor was the rise of a local king, Herod the Idumean. Herod, whom Jews suspected of being a Jew only by convenience, was able through gaining the confidence of the Roman authorities to be recognized by the Senate in 40 B.C. as king with a good measure of autonomy. The Kingdom of Judea was separated from Syria and came to depend directly on Caesar. In exchange for his autonomy Herod gave military protection to this flank of the empire. During his reign (40–4 B.C.) Herod extracted an astonishing amount of wealth from the people of Palestine, as shown by the impressive buildings erected in Jerusalem and in the new city of Caesarea. His was a reign of terror and force, very effective principally through his good relations with Rome. He also understood Palestinian society, and became the principal sponsor of the temple. His extensive works of construction on the temple gave him a certain veneer of legitimacy in the eyes of the Jews.

This superimposition of a slave empire on the back of a tributary society worked very well during Herod's time, at the cost of considerable sacrifice by the working population. But ten years after Herod's death, A.D. 6, Judea was made a Roman province with its own proconsul who resided in Caesarea. Galilee meanwhile remained a semi-autonomous tetrarchy under the rule of a son of Herod (Herod Antipas). It was a highly unstable situation.

For the next century Palestine was one of the constant trouble spots of the empire. To understand this we must remember again that this tributary system centered in the temple. For six centuries the priestly class had been the ruling class. The religious ideology, with its symbolic center in the temple, was the principal justification for and concealment of class domination in Palestine since the reform of Josiah. During most of this time Palestine was under foreign domination. The extraction of surplus labor was carried out peacefully as long as the imperial authorities recognized the special characteristics of this society and allowed the temple its dominant role in the control and exploitation of the villagers. Difficulties arose only when the foreign rulers tried to alter this system by imposing cities in the Hellenistic style, with slavery and private property, and displaced Jerusalem and the temple from the center.

All social classes would see an attack on the temple as a threat, and its displacement from its privileged place would bring all classes together in opposition. This is what occurred when Antiochus Epiphanes tried to impose a Hellenistic social system on Palestine in the early second century B.C. Led by Judas Maccabeus and his successors, the Jews united in rebellion against the defiler of their temple. The situation in the first century of the Christian era was a similar one. Roman toleration for Palestinian ways was never secure, and latent opposition would break into open rebellion when a Roman emperor or procurator overstepped the bounds established by long custom.

The Maccabean revolt in the second century B.C. had led to the establishment of a semi-autonomous kingdom in Jerusalem with a dynasty that combined royal and priestly functions with the awkward but necessary support of the Seleucid kings. This foreign support, plus the fact that the Hasmoneans were high priests without belonging to the Zadokite family, took away legitimacy from the regime and began a process of secularization that continued into the century that concerns us.

There were several strategies for coping with the threat to the social fabric both from without and from within. The Essenes were a sect with deep concern for the purity of the temple, which they believed was defiled by an unworthy priesthood. In the hope that the future held a purification of the same and a restoration of legitimate worship, in the meantime they withdrew from national life and from any participation in the temple. They lived in separate communities, studied the Scriptures, and prepared themselves for the coming of God's kingdom.

The Sadducees were the party that supported the official arrangement of things and accepted the need for accommodating to the foreign authorities. They had their base in Jerusalem in the priestly aristocracy. Except for the most extreme situations, they always favored looking for a negotiated settlement with the ruling Romans.

The Pharisees focused on the need for fulfilling the law of Moses as the most important requirement of national life. They had their base among the villages, and were strong in Galilee. They were the direct religious leaders and teachers in the synagogues of the villages where the people gathered to learn their duties. They expressed the sentiments of the majority. Theirs was a central role in the struggles with the Romans. In ordinary circumstances they favored a policy of peace with the rulers and awaiting God's action on Israel's behalf. But each time that an emperor or a proconsul threatened to contaminate the temple or to prevent the exercise of obedience to the law they threw their influence against him and joined movements of rebellion.

Under Herod there was a situation of social calm, in spite of the intensity of the exploitation. He seems to have understood the system. He kept the temple in opulent style. It was with the incorporation of Judea as a province under a Roman procurator that the problems began that agitated Palestine until the destruction of Jerusalem A.D. 70.

A new "sect" arose, that of the Zealots. This movement was begun by Judas "the Galilean," who, at the time of the census of Cirenius, which occurred at the same time as the establishment of the province (A.D. 6), took up arms rather than pay tribute to the Romans.[5] The theological basis for their refusal to pay tribute was that by this action they would be recognizing a human ruler alongside God (Josephus, *B.J.* II. 118,433). If God was to be king, there could be no human king alongside him, not even a Jewish one. They revived the tradition of armed struggle against foreign domination that came from the Maccabees. But they were different in that they rejected monarchy. Theirs was a classic biblical position, reminiscent of that of Gideon. The difference was that they acknowledged the place of privilege of the temple, and therefore of the hierocratic class society.

The guerrilla movement that they carried on in the Galilean hills had its moments of importance. When the Emperor Caligula ordered that his statue be mounted in the temple (A.D. 40) the people joined them in readiness for armed rebellion. Caligula was assassinated before carrying out his intentions, and calm was restored to Palestine. The Zealots were again to play a dominant role when the entire people united in a war to restore the autonomy of the temple A.D. 66. Menachem, a descendent of Judas, was the chief of operations in Jerusalem in that year (Josephus, *B. J.* II. 433ff. and VII. 320ff.).

THE JESUS MOVEMENT AND THE KINGDOM OF GOD

With this background we are prepared to ask about the good news that Jesus and his followers had to offer to the villagers of Galilee. Luke summarizes Jesus' mission by having him quote from the book of Isaiah in his first public appearance in Galilee:

> The Spirit of the Lord is upon me,
> because he has anointed me to preach good news to the poor.
> He has sent me to proclaim release to the captives
> and recovery of sight to the blind,
> to set at liberty those who are oppressed,
> to proclaim the acceptable year of the Lord [Luke 4:18-19].

With this quotation Luke summarizes for his readers, most of whom presumably were not residents of Palestine, what was meant by preaching the kingdom of God. Mark does the same thing with a summary of Jesus' preaching of the gospel of God: "The time is fulfilled, and the kingdom of God is at hand; repent, and believe in the gospel" (Mark 1:15).

We are not interested here in Jesus' "messianic consciousness" or in his private understandings. Many generations of research in these themes have led to contradictory results. Our interest is focused instead on the historical project borne by Jesus and his Galilean movement, as it is told in the Gospel narratives (from which we try to strip the overlay of theological justification for Jesus' death; see Fernando Belo, *A Materialist Reading of the Gospel of Mark* [Maryknoll, N.Y.: Orbis Books, 1981]). The ways to discover the historical project are to look in the narrative for: (1) the strategy of the movement, (2) the organizational principles for the group of followers, and (3) the enemies of the movement.

Before looking at these three points, let us state our hypothesis in brief fashion: The Jesus movement saw the principal obstacle to the realization of God's kingdom in Palestine to be the temple and the class structure that it supported. In the terms of our analysis, their focus was on the Asiatic social organization rather than on the contradiction between the Palestinian (Asiatic) society and the Roman (slave) one. The latter became for the movement a secondary contradiction. Because the class domination of the priests rested principally on a deep-seated ideology, the strategy of the Jesus movement was one of ideological attack. Our Gospels give ample evidence that Jesus was executed by a broad coalition of groups that for different reasons were threatened by this historical project. This is our hypothesis.

As we look at the Gospels to flesh out this hypothesis a bit we must remember that the fact that the Jesus group preached the coming of God's kingdom hardly distinguished them from several other groups in first-century Palestine. This was a time of turmoil, and the prophetic preaching of a kingdom of justice and peace fired Jewish imagination. Essenes, Pharisees, and Zealots all expected the imminent dawning of the kingdom. Only the Sadducees with their concern for the temple ritual were cool to these expectations. Though there were differences of emphasis as to the content of the coming kingdom, the main differences were in the analysis of the Palestinian social structure and the consequent adoption of strategies of faith. Here Jesus and his followers had something different to offer Galilean peasants.

First, left us briefly look at Jesus' strategy. In keeping with well-established conclusions of New Testament scholarship, we favor the account of the Synoptic Gospels in looking for this strategy. Jesus moved about Galilee, drawing from that society a small band of followers who left their occupations to go about with him. The favorite example for the Gospel writers is that of Simon and Andrew, who left their fishing to become "fishers of men" (Mark 1:16–20). Jesus and his band were in constant movement, and their whereabouts were often not known to outsiders. For this movement they relied on the small fishing boats of some of the followers, in order to get away from the multitudes that pursued them seeking Jesus' reputed healing powers (Mark 4:35; 3:7, 13).

It is evident that the multitudes were important in their strategy both as the beneficiaries of the coming kingdom, as illustrated in his concern to feed and heal them, and as a recruiting ground for followers. But a distance was maintained by the constant movement of Jesus' band and by his teaching in parables: "To you has been given the secret of the kingdom of God, but for those outside everything is in parables" (Mark 4:11).

On the occasions in which the group went into one town or another they often ran into opposition from local representatives of the religious establishment, the "scribes and Pharisees" of the Gospels. Among many examples we can mention the healing of a paralytic at a house in Capernaum and the reaction it produced (Mark 2:1–12), and the incident over a man with a withered hand in a synagogue of an unnamed town (Mark 3:1–6).

Because of their analysis of the struggle as primarily one to be won on the ideological battleground, the movement needed the broadest possible contact with the people. This was surely the main reason for the constant movement they display. This also explains their occasional breaking up into teams of two to cover a larger territory (Mark 6:7–13; Luke 10:1–12). The preference for the hills, the wilderness, and the seashore are probably to be explained by the need for security, in case of pursuit, and also to avoid provoking local teachers of religion.

The second stage in the strategy of the Jesus movement is clearly marked in the Synoptic Gospels by the departure from Galilee in order to go to Jerusalem: "He went on his way through towns and villages, teaching, and journeying toward Jerusalem" (Luke 13:22); "on the way to Jerusalem he was passing along between Samaria and Galilee" (Luke 17:11); "and taking the twelve, he said to them, 'Behold, we are going up to Jerusalem, and everything that is written of the Son of man by the prophets will be accomplished' " (Luke 18:31); "as they heard these things, he proceeded to tell a parable, because he was near to Jerusalem, and because they supposed that the kingdom of God was to appear immediately" (Luke 19:11); "and when he had said this, he went on ahead, going to Jerusalem" (Luke 19:28); "and when he drew near and saw the city he wept over it" (Luke 19:41).

There is an intensity of purpose in the repetition of the direction of the group toward Jerusalem. Jerusalem, as we have seen, was the symbolic center of the "Asiatic" class system that prevailed in Palestine. The second stage in the movement's challenge to that system was to confront it at its most powerful point. The objective was not just the city but precisely the temple:

> And he entered the temple and began to drive out those who sold, saying, "It is written, 'My house shall be a house of prayer'; but you have made it a den of robbers" [Luke 19:45].

Several interpretations can be made of the attack on the temple business. Considering that the Roman soldiers could see all goings on in the temple from the Antonia fortress that overlooked it, it is unlikely that Jesus and his followers expected to take the temple. More likely, the intention was to dramatize their criticism of the temple before the multitude of pilgrims who were in the city for the festival of Passover. By attacking the banking and commercial aspects of the temple they were not attacking a minor sideshow. This was fundamental to the class system. It was by means of the trade and the taxes collected in the temple that the priests extracted the surplus labor of the peasants. Several of the teaching incidents put by the Gospel writers in the context of the temple in that week have to do with money (Caesar's coin, the widow's mite, Judas Iscariot's bargain with the priests). The economic base of the temple's domination was challenged by Jesus and his movement.

In the Gospel narrative, Jesus' movements during his stay in Jerusalem are very suggestive for understanding his strategy. During the day he went openly into the temple and sought contact with the multitudes that gathered there. This teaching was dramatized by the attack on the merchants. By this time, and as a result in part of his attack, Jesus' life was in danger: "And the chief priests and the scribes were seeking how to arrest him in stealth, and kill him, for they said, 'Not during the feast, lest there be a tumult of the people' " (Mark 14:1-2). Jesus was safe among the multitude, because he and his followers had achieved a measure of support. At night Jesus would withdraw, apparently to Bethany to the house of Simon the leper (Mark 14:3). This strategy of nightly withdrawal was broken when one of the members of the movement offered for a price to take his enemies where he could be found away from the crowd.

According to the theological reading overlaid on the narrative, Jesus went to Jerusalem to die. For that reason it is not obvious in the Gospels that his strategy was precisely designed to avoid falling into the hands of his enemies. But the narrative is clear enough. The priests had no need of a traitor except to find the hiding places where Jesus went when the crowds had dispersed. This contradiction within the Gospels enables us to separate the narrative from what overlies it and uncover the strategy.

The strategy of the Jesus movement was interrupted during the second stage by Jesus' execution. What the intended third stage was can only be a matter of conjecture. It must have involved some means of consolidating the popular support they expected to gain by their confrontation with the temple personnel in Jerusalem. A further step, also untouched in the Gospel narratives, would have faced the (for Jesus, secondary) contradiction with the Roman presence in Palestine. God's kingdom with its strong egalitarianism would have required dealing with this oppressive force sooner or later.

Meanwhile, during the phase of gathering support in Galilee and during the trip to Jerusalem, Jesus and his followers were embodying in their communal living the egalitarian principles of God's kingdom:

> You are not to be called rabbi, for you have one teacher, and you are all brethren. And call no man your father on earth, for you have one father who is in heaven. Neither be called masters, for you have one master,

the Christ. He who is greatest among you shall be your servant, whoever exalts himself will be humbled, and whoever humbles himself will be exalted [Matt. 23:8–12].

In the coming kingdom of God that Jesus was announcing, the poor would be exalted and the rich cast down (Luke 6:20–26). In the story of a rich man who asked to enter the kingdom, Jesus was quite harsh in insisting that he sell his goods, give them to the poor, and enter the movement as simply one of the brothers (Mark 10:17–22). In reflecting on his rejection, the text puts in Jesus' mouth that hard saying: "How hard it will be for those who have riches to enter the kingdom of God! . . . It is easier for a camel to go through the eye of a needle than for a rich man to enter the kingdom of God" (Mark 10:23–25).

Just as the demand for equality excluded the wealthy who were not ready to abandon their riches, it also excluded those who clung to the positions afforded them by their families. The need to break family ties to join the movement is dramatized by the story of Jesus' own distant attitude toward his mother (Mark 3:31–35). The same point is made in a more general manner in sayings (Mark 10:28–31; Luke 14:25–27) in which the willingness to abandon family position is made a condition for membership in the movement. The stress on equality within the movement is in keeping with our hypothesis that Jesus' affirmation of God's kingdom was a denial of the class structure that required privileges for the priests.

This brings us to an examination of the enemies of Jesus and his movement. Jesus' principal enemies were the Pharisees in Galilee and the priests in Jerusalem—in other words, the principal beneficiaries of the class system and the teachers of the religious ideology that supported it. Concerning the Pharisees the Gospels have many harsh words, though it is impossible to sort out what goes back to the Galilean days and what represents the anti-Jewish polemic of the church outside of Palestine:

Woe to you, scribes and Pharisees, hypocrites! For you tithe mint and dill and cummin, and have neglected the weightier matters of the law, justice and mercy and faith [Matt. 23:23].

Woe to you, scribes and Pharisees, hypocrites! For you are like whitewashed tombs, which outwardly appear beautiful, but within they are full of dead men's bones and all uncleanness. So you also outwardly appear righteous to men, but within you are full of hypocrisy and iniquity [Matt. 23:27–28].

The narrative also reflects many cases of confrontation with the Pharisees over Jesus' rather casual attitude toward the law. These are set in the period of the Galilean wanderings of Jesus' group.

The temple was the object of Jesus' attacks during his last week in Jerusalem. There is first of all the account of the attack on the banking operations of the temple. But there is preserved also a prophecy that the temple would be destroyed, and the accounts of the trial of Jesus record as one of the accusations that he announced the temple's destruction:

> And as he came out of the temple, one of his disciples said to him, "Look, Teacher, what wonderful stones and what wonderful buildings!" And Jesus said to him, "Do you see these great buildings? There will not be left here one stone upon another, that will not be thrown down" [Mark 13:1-2].

This hostility to the temple is a conspicuous theme of the Gospels, and fits with Jesus' analysis of the class situation of Palestine as that of domination by the priests.

Another of Jesus' enemies was the Roman authority, made personal in the procurator Pontius Pilate. The Gospels agree that Jesus was executed as a messianic claimant. This is quite understandable. During that century and the following there were many "messiahs" who were taken to fulfill Isaiah's promises that God would raise a descendant of David to sit on his throne. These were regularly the occasion for disturbances, and the Romans would have viewed any movement of this sort as a threat. The most important case was that of Simon Bar Cocheba, which set off a major rebellion A.D. 132. The title on Jesus' cross read, "the king of the Jews," a clear indication of why the Romans had him crucified. Mark informs us that during that Passover week there had been an armed uprising with some casualties (Mark 15:7). Besides Jesus, Pilate crucified two *lestai*, a word which can refer either to common highway robbers or to armed insurrectionists. In this case, in the wake of the Jerusalem uprising, probably the latter is correct. To the Roman authorities Jesus appeared, like the Zealots, as a rebel.

The Gospels, however, make a clear distinction between Jesus and the Zealots. They report that the crowds at Jerusalem also saw a difference. Pilate is said to have offered them a choice between the Zealot Barabbas and Jesus, at which they chose the release of Barabbas. This was the same multitude for fear of which the priests did not capture Jesus in broad daylight. Of course, the multitude was manipulated by the priests and Pharisees. It is not hard to understand the desire of these two groups to do away with Jesus. Nor is it hard to understand the fears of the Roman authorities. But Jesus and his movement sought to speak for the masses who were oppressed both by the Romans and by the priests (with the assistance of the Pharisees). It is, then, a problem that the crowd should have allowed itself to be swayed by the enemies of Jesus.

The choice of the multitude between Jesus and Barabbas dramatizes the difference between two social analyses and two strategies of liberation, that of the Jesus movement and that of the Zealots. The crowd of the Gospels chose the Zealot option when forced to a choice between the two. It must remain an open question whether they were right, in terms of the historical possibilities of Jesus' strategy. But it is not difficult to understand their choice.

First of all, a large proportion of the population of Jerusalem depended on the temple for their livelihood.[6] This included a large crew of artisans and builders, for there was permanent building activity going on during this whole period. It included a large population that lived from servicing the pilgrims who came to the city (innkeepers, merchants in food and sacrificial animals, etc.). And it included the bankers and moneychangers who were the immediate object of Jesus' attack. This part of the multitude had a vested interest in the temple, and would reject Jesus' strategy in favor of one which aimed rather at the Romans.

Secondly, for many of even the poorest elements of the population, the Roman domination would have seemed more visible and opprobrious than that of the priests. This would have included many people among the pilgrims. Perhaps they sympathized with what the Jesus movement represented but, offered a choice, preferred the strategy of direct confrontation with Rome.

The result is well known. Led by the priests, the principal enemies of Jesus and his followers, the multitudes supported the charges of sedition before the Roman authorities, who executed Jesus. With the death of Jesus the movement entered into a new and difficult phase of re-evaluation that is mostly lost to us.

Before discussing the Zealot strategy for the Kingdom of God, a word should be said about the principal alternative hypothesis about the nature of Jesus and his movement. This historical reading stresses the sayings of Jesus on making peace, finding his option to be that of reconciliation and nonviolence. Jesus advised his followers to learn to love their enemies (Matt. 5:43–45). They were to seek forgiveness from those whom they had offended (Matt. 5:21–26). They were to suffer evil rather than retaliate (Matt. 5:38–42). According to the reading of the Gospels that makes this a way of nonviolence that Jesus taught as universally valid, Jesus did not intend to have enemies. Their enmity was due to their hostilities, and Jesus' only response was to avoid provocation.

This reading of the Gospels is attractive to a sector of the modern church. However, it does not seem to apply to what the Gospel narrative tells us of Jesus. We would understand, rather, that here the Jesus movement was trying to distinguish its tactics from those of the Zealots. The Zealots saw the Roman presence as the principal cause of the oppression of the Palestinian population. And the only way to rid the country of a military domination was by military means. Jesus and his movement, however, did not see Rome as the principal enemy. In their priorities, it was first necessary to do away with the temple domination. For this, they had to avoid provoking military conflicts. Our hypothesis does not hold Jesus to have categorically rejected military tactics. It does hold that he did not espouse them for ridding the country of priestly oppression.

The other context for the saying on forgiveness is that of the internal demands of the movement. This is clearly the context of the sayings on forgiveness and reconciliation in Matthew 18, including the injunction to forgive seventy times seven (Matt. 18:21–22). It seems that the demands of internal peace within the movement and the need to avoid provoking military intervention by the Romans can explain these texts that form the basis of the alternative hypothesis about Jesus.

OTHER PALESTINIAN STRATEGIES FOR THE KINGDOM OF GOD

The destruction of the Jerusalem temple in the year 70 was the culmination of many of the events that had been taking place in Palestine during the early years of the Jesus movement. With this Roman victory over the holiest symbol of believers in Palestine, the messianic strategies of all Palestinian groups collapsed, with the partial exception of that of the Pharisees.

Jesus and his followers had tried to unite the people against the temple because they believed that *it* rather than the Romans was the primary source of Israel's oppression. For six centuries all the empires of the Near East had used the temple and its priests as instruments to dominate working people. In Jesus' view the temple was, as Jeremiah had put it at the beginnings of this system, a den of thieves and not the house of prayer for the nations, which was its original purpose (Jer. 7:11; Mark 11:17).

In one sense the destruction of the temple was a vindication of the Jesus movement. But only in a very minor sense. For its destruction to be part of the coming of God's kingdom, the working masses had to understand that the priests were their enemies and organize an alternative society. With Jesus' execution the real possibility of achieving this popular support for an alternative along the lines advanced by the Jesus movement disappeared. To survive, the Jesus movement soon abandoned the field and moved out of Palestine. Its strategy had failed well before the war broke out in A.D. 66.

The Sadducees followed a strategy of preserving within a Roman-dominated province a space for keeping up the liturgical life of the temple. They were the principal beneficiaries of the system and they owed their positions of hegemony to the imperial authorities. It was in their interest, then, to find ways of accommodating the Jewish tradition to the needs of the empire, widening as much as possible the temple's scope of action. Their political maneuvers responded to this strategy. They were always looking for alliances with those Roman leaders who were rising in the constant power struggles in Rome. As Roman impatience increased in the face of continual Jewish rebellion, the space for maneuvering was constantly narrowing. With the destruction of the temple, the Sadducee strategy was finished. History had proved their way to be a false one.

The Zealots also held the temple as the center of their vision of God's kingdom. Their strategy was, nevertheless, diametrically opposed to that of the Sadducees. They saw the physical presence of Roman troops in Palestine as a profanation of God's land and a blasphemous denial of Yahweh's sovereignty. So the first order of business for believers was the expulsion of the Roman presence. They were surely not unaware of Roman military superiority, but they were also convinced that God would struggle to restore his kingdom, as he had done in the days of Deborah and Gideon. With this conviction, they rushed into a truly suicidal struggle. They had their great opportunity in the year 66, when the Roman proconsul Gesius Florus withdrew from the temple treasury the sum of seventeen talents. This sacking, following as it did a long series of frictions between Jews and Romans, solidified the people behind the hard line the Zealots had been urging for sixty years. A considerable army was raised in Galilee to liberate that territory. Another force took the temple grounds and expelled the soldiers from the Antonia fortress that controlled the city. The high priest, who had appealed for moderation, was assassinated. There followed a series of victories that filled the people with euphoria. But, in the year 70, after long, hard battles, the Roman general Titus took the city and put an end to the brief existence of Jerusalem as a free city. This meant the failure also of the Zealot strategy.

The Essenes apparently joined in the broad coalition that faced the Romans in this war. They had long been waiting for the final war against the heathen. Their principal community near the Dead Sea was destroyed in the mopping-up operations by the Roman forces, and we hear no more from them.

Among the organized groups of Palestinian Judaism, only the Pharisees came through the war without a total collapse. Like the Zealots, Essenes and Sadducees, they too believed in the temple. But the centers for their ongoing activities were the town synagogues. Here the faithful gathered every week to read the Scriptures, to hear interpretations of them, and to pray for their own redemption. Here the people learned how to live a pious life of obedience to the law of Moses. These village people would make the pilgrimage to Jerusalem to offer their sacrifices in the temple only on special occasions. The rest of the year they made the synagogue and its teaching the center of their religious life. This was also the territory where the Pharisees held the hegemony. When the temple was destroyed, the synagogues became the only centers of Jewish life. The Pharisees emerged from the ruins as the most prestigious group.

In order to rightly place the gospel polemic against the Pharisees, it is important to realize that they were the principal rivals of the church in the later period. Much of the bitterness expressed in the Gospels against the Pharisees must come from this context rather than from the original Jesus movement. This is not to deny that Jesus and his followers also attacked the Pharisees. These pious teachers of religion were not rich. They were not directly exploiting the Galilean people. But they were the transmitters in Galilee of the temple ideology that Jesus and his movement were attacking. For this reason the Jesus strategy collided with the Pharisees before it even became a factor for the priests in Jerusalem. This initial opposition between the Pharisees and the

Jesus movement was deepened when Paul and other Christian missionaries began using the synagogues as recruiting grounds for the church in its missionary expansion. The synagogue survived the war as a viable institution and became the social base for rabbinic Judaism, which is the direct descendant of the Pharisaic movement.

About the Palestinian Jesus movement after Jesus' death our information is inadequate. Some things are known from the book of Acts of the Apostles, and others can be deduced from the Gospels, especially the sayings common to Matthew and Luke. From Acts we know of the establishment in the urban context of Jerusalem of a community that institutionalized the egalitarian practice of the itinerant group that followed Jesus. They practiced a communism of consumption, sharing the goods that they had acquired by private means (Acts 2:44–45; 4:32–35). Their leaders were James, the brother of Jesus, and Peter, one of the twelve chosen by Jesus as his closest circle. They lived in the expectation of the return of the Lord in glory (Acts 3:17–21; 1:9–11). The Gospel of Mark bears witness to the belief that this return would take place in Galilee (Mark 14:28; 16:7). At that time the Lord would restore the kingdom to Israel (Acts 1:6). Surprisingly, the Jerusalem Jesus community maintained a life of prayer in and around the temple (Acts 2:46; 3:1; 21:17–26), although they were regarded with suspicion if not hostility by other worshipers there.

One sector within this community maintained the original hostility to the temple. Not surprisingly, it was against this sector that the earliest persecution of "Christians" by the priestly class was directed. Acts, chapters 6 and 7, tells of how Stephen was selected as a target by the priests (6:8–7:1), how he defended himself by appealing to the biblical tradition of attacks on the temple (7:2–53), and how he was eventually killed by stoning (7:54–60). The Jerusalem community of Christians seems to have been destroyed during the war—that is, whatever remained after the persecutions had led many to flee for their safety. At any rate, they do not appear to have played a significant role in the historic events that led up to the war.

Recently, Gerd Theissen has made a good case for the existence of a continued Jesus movement in Galilee.[7] Its leaders were itinerant radicals of the sort who had followed Jesus, and there were sympathizers who assisted them in the villages. But they had no historical importance either.

Much remains to be learned about the Palestinian sequel to Jesus and his movement. It seems likely that the current interest in a sociological approach to the works of antiquity and in an archaeology of the material base of daily life will increase our knowledge in the next generation. What we have said here is no more than suggestive. Our New Testament shows very little interest in the Palestinian Jesus movement, and directs our attention instead to the founding of the church outside of Palestine. This is the judgment of posterity on a movement we should like to know better. This judgment is historically correct at least insofar as it is a fact that the Jewish-Roman war wiped out any possibility of success the movement may have had in becoming the bearer of good news for the peasantry of Galilee. Although it is impossible to overturn such a decisive historical judgment, our interest remains because the Latin American popular movement of our day knows that it must learn even from historical failures if it is one day to succeed in establishing a just society.

NOTES

1. In speaking of the Jesus movement rather than of the person of Jesus himself, we are stressing the fact that it is the social fact, of which the person is to be sure a part, that has historical importance. It is a bourgeois admiration for heroic personalities that focused much on New Testament research on the person of Jesus. It is a virtue of the recent work of Gerd Theissen to have pointed again to the importance of the movement. See his *Sociology of Early Palestinian Christianity* (Philadelphia: Fortress Press, 1978; German original of 1977). His hypothesis about the nature of the Jesus movement is very different from ours, but the virtue of his work is that he asks the right questions. This is a major advance over most previous New Testament scholarship.

2. The "search for the historical Jesus" has occupied many a liberal scholar dissatisfied with the Christ preached in the Christian churches. In his famous 1906 book, *Von Reimarus zu Wrede*, Albert Schweitzer showed the very high proportion of the projection of our desires that was present in the investigations of the great scholars of the nineteenth century (see the English translation, *The Quest of the Historical Jesus* [London: A. and C. Black, 1910]). In spite of this unmasking, the search has not ended, and it is unlikely to end while there are liberal Christians in need of a great personality for inspiration.

3. In our study, we are going to rely especially on the work of the Portuguese scholar Fernando Belo, *Lecture matérialiste de l'évangile de Marc* (Paris: Cerf, 1974), available in Spanish from Editorial Verbo Divino of Estella, Navarra, in a 1975 edition and now also available in English from Orbis Books. An important aspect of Belo's method is his examination of the narrative of the Gospel as a form with a history, and his focus on that narrative, in distinction from a search for the person Jesus or for the words themselves of Jesus. Much form criticism has focused on isolated pericopes and taken the structure to be a product of the final redaction. Belo shows that the sayings lose their significance when taken out of the narrative. The narrative has suffered that fate of all transmitted material, but it has its integrity, which makes possible a tentative history of the narrative. It is this basic narrative that interests us.

4. A classic and still useful description of the slave mode of production is that of the German Marxist Karl Kautsky, *Foundations of Christianity*, trans. Henry F. Mins (New York: S. A. Russell, 1953; German original, 1910). Kautsky's understanding of Christianity has basic flaws, though it is still suggestive. The best portion of his work is his analysis of the productive base of the Roman Empire.

5. On the Zealots, see S. G. F. Brandon, *Jesus and the Zealots* (New York: Scribner's, 1967), and the works of Martin Hengel, especially *Die Zeloten* (Leiden: Brill, 1961).

6. For documentation on the place of the temple in the economic life of Jerusalem, see Joachim Jeremias, *Jerusalem in the Time of Jesus* (Philadelphia: Fortress Press, 1969; German original, 1923).

7. Theissen, *Sociology of Early Palestinian Christianity*.

21

ELISABETH SCHÜSSLER FIORENZA

"You Are Not to Be Called Father": Early Christian History in a Feminist Perspective

The current discussion of the position of women in the early church, reaching far beyond a narrow "woman's issue," goes to the heart of an exegetical-historical problem that exposes the contemporary societal and ecclesial interests governing all interpretive models of early Christianity. Already in later New Testament times, male-centered interpretation and editing of earlier traditions both played down and covered over the important roles of women at key points in Christian beginnings, either because their roles were seen as unimportant or as threatening.

Patristic interpretation managed to present itself as the historically prior "orthodox" view, while whatever the church fathers did not like, such as equality of women in church leadership, was branded as "heresy" which mutilated the ancient faith. In fact, supporters of the ecclesial leadership of women could point to early support from traditions which the church fathers defamed as late heresy.

Reprinted from *Cross Currents* 29/3 (1979): 301–23.

The patriarchalizing and institutionalizing process in the early church is not a mere fait accompli but an early move in a continuing "power play" that requires a critical sociological and theological analysis to recover biblical and theological ground for woman's full place in today's church. The sexual equality of the Jesus movement and of the first Christian missioners must be reaffirmed by an egalitarian interpretive model that fully recognizes the conflict between equality and hierarchy within the early church—a battle that has been re-opened in our time.

For many Christians the reconstruction of early Christian history is not a problem. The impression remains widespread that Acts accurately reports what actually happened. Exegetes and historians of early Christianity, however, know all too well that this is not the case. But although most exegetes would agree that Jesus did not leave a blue-print for the organization of the church, their image of the actual development of early church history varies considerably. Questions regarding the historical importance of the Twelve, the relationship between charism and office, the juxtaposition of Paulinism and early Catholicism, the issue of apostolic succession and heresy, and the practical-ecclesial implications of early Christian history are answered in different ways.[1] Moreover, exegetes today more readily acknowledge that a value-free interpretation of early Christian texts and an objectivist reconstruction of early Christian history is a scholarly fiction that fails to account for its own presuppositions and scientific models.

The question whether women had a leading position in the development of the early Church intensifies all these interpretative problems and at the same time formulates the debated issues in a new perspective.[2] Nevertheless, most scholars have been hesitant to perceive this problem as an exegetical-historical problem, but understand it as a "woman's issue."[3] Seen as a "woman's issue," the question belongs to conferences and papers about and for women, and is given no place on the program of an exegetical-scientific symposium or in a scholarly *Festschrift*. In this way most scholars continue to perceive this question only as a topical or thematic issue, not as an issue of heuristic value for the interpretation of early Christian texts and history.

One usually justifies this attitude by pointing out that such a topic is ideologically suspect and does not proceed from an historical scientific interest since the topic is inspired by the women's movement, and therefore determined by ecclesial-societal modern interests. Such an argument, however, overlooks the fact that all scholarship on early Christian history is determined by contemporary questions and interests. Insofar as the Bible is not just a document of ancient history, but is Holy Scripture which claims authority and validity in the contemporary church, biblical-historical inquiries are always determined by ecclesial and societal interests and questions.

This dependency of historical-critical research on contemporary Christianity and society has, in my opinion, been correctly pointed out by J. Blank: "The interest in legitimization but also in the critique and reform of contemporary Christianity in all its forms and expressions is probably an essential, and even the most fundamental motive for the study of the history of early Christianity."[4] The objection that the search for the role of women in the early Christian movement is greatly determined by societal and ecclesial political interests, and is therefore unscientific, applies to any reconstruction of early Christian history inspired by the quest for the identity and continuity of contemporary Christianity with the early church. An androcentric reconstruction of early Christian history, therefore, is not value-free and objective but, consciously or not, legitimizes the present hierarchical-male structures of the contemporary church.

All historical reconstruction is a selective, contemporary analysis of the past in the present; it is not limited to the extant sources but is also conditioned by the societal perspectives of the present. The understanding of the past is never just antiquarian but always related to the contemporary situation of the historiographer. The hermeneutic discussion has shown that historians, like other scholars, can never totally free themselves from their existential presuppositions, experiences, ideologies, and commitments.[5] The personal presuppositions and societal position of the historian and interpreter determine the selection and definition of what was important in the past, and what needs to be studied today. Although the hermeneutical discussion and the sociology of knowledge have driven home the insight that historiography is determined by the experiences and interests of those who write history, this scientific consensus seems to disappear when scientific historiography and theology are denounced as "male." The problem is not only that most scholars are men but that our very understanding of reality is androcentric.

It is not enough, however, to expose the existential presuppositions of male exegetes and scholars: we must analyze the interpretative models from which they reconstruct the history of early Christianity. While descriptive historical studies analyze the available information and texts of early Christianity and presuppose a certain understanding of early Christian history, a constructive historiography makes this understanding explicit by developing heuristic and interpretative models[6] which enable us to reconstruct a total view of early Christian development. Such interpretative models place diverse information into a coherent interpretative whole which enables us to see the intellectual contexts and practical patterns of action in a certain perspective. An interpretative model should, therefore, not only be judged by whether it adequately lists various traditions and information, but must also be scrutinized as to whether it provides a comprehensive vision of early Christian history, making its emancipatory life-praxis and theology available to the contemporary church and society.

ANDROCENTRIC INTERPRETATION AND REDACTION

The thematic approach to "women in the Bible" overlooks the fact that references to women are already filtered through androcentric interpretation and redaction. If study of this topic is to help us in the scientific reconstruction of early Christian history, we must understand and make explicit the androcentric perspective of scientific-historical models as well as of early Christian tradition and redaction.

The systemic androcentrism of Western culture is evident in the fact that nobody questions the fact that men have been historical subjects and agents in the church. The historical role of women and not that of men is problematic because maleness is the norm, while femaleness constitutes a deviation from this norm. Whenever we speak of "man" as the scientific and historical subject we mean the male.[7] For the Western understanding and linguistic expression of reality, male existence is the standard of human existence. "Humanity is male and man defines women not in herself but relative to him. She is not regarded as autonomous being. He is the subject, the absolute; she is the other."[8] Therefore our societal and scientific structures define women as derivative and secondary to men. This androcentric definition of being human not only has determined the scholarly perception of men but also of women. In such an androcentric worldview woman must remain an historically marginal being. Therefore the androcentric scholarly paradigm has to thematize the role of women as a societal, historical, philosophical, and theological problem but cannot question its own androcentric scholarly horizon.[9]

Since the scientific reconstructions of early Christianity share in the androcentric paradigm of Western culture, they cannot integrate texts which speak positively about early Christian women into their overall interpretational framework. Because they generally presuppose that only men, and not women, developed missionary initiatives and central leadership in early Christianity,[10] texts that do not fit such an androcentric model are quickly interpreted in terms of an androcentric perspective. This happens in various ways. For example, most modern interpreters assume that Rom. 16:7 speaks about two leading men who had already become Christians before Paul and had great authority as apostles. However, there is no reason to understand Junia as a shortened form of the male name Junianus since Junia was a well-known female name. Even patristic exegesis understood it predominantly as the name of a woman.[11] Andronicus and Junia were an influential missionary team who were acknowledged as apostles.

Another example of androcentric intepretation is often found with reference to Rom. 16:1–3. In this passage Phoebe is called the *diakonos* and *prostatis* of the church at Cenchraea, the seaport of Corinth. Exegetes attempt to downplay the importance of both titles here because they are used with reference to a woman. Whenever Paul calls himself, Apollos, Timothy, or Tychicos *diakonos,* scholars translate the term as deacon, but because the expression refers here to a woman exegetes translate it as "servant, helper, or deaconess.'' While Kürzinger, for instance, translates the title in Phil. 1:1 as deacon, in the case of Phoebe he explains that "she works in the service of the community," and in a footnote he characterizes Phoebe as "one of the first pastoral assistants."[12] H. Lietzmann also understands the office of Phoebe in analogy to the later institute of the deaconesses which, in comparison to that of the deacons, had only a very limited function in the church. He characterizes Phoebe as an "apparently well-to-do and charitable lady, who because of her feminine virtues worked in the service of the poor and the sick and assisted in the baptism of women."[13] Origen had already labelled Phoebe as an assistant and servant of Paul. He concluded that women who do good works can be appointed as deaconesses.[14]

However, the text does not permit such a feminine stereotyping of Phoebe. As we can see from 1 Cor. 3:5–9, Paul uses *diakonos* parallel to *synergos* and characterizes with these titles Apollos and himself as missionaries with equal standing who have contributed to the upbuilding of the community in different ways.[15] Since Phoebe is named *diakonos* of the church at Cenchreae, she receives this title because her service and office were influential in the community. That Phoebe could claim great authority within the early Christian missionary endeavor is underlined by the second title *prostatis/patrona*. In a similar way 1 Thess. 5:12 and Rom. 12:8 characterize leading persons as *prohistamenoi*. Therefore, when Paul calls Phoebe a *patrona,* he characterizes her in analogy to those persons who had influential positions as representative protectors and leaders in the Hellenistic-religious associations.[16] G. Heinrici points out that in antiquity religious and private associations received legal protection and derived social-political influence from the patronage of eminent and rich members.[17] Nevertheless, E. A. Judge insists on interpreting the patronage of women in the early Church in an androcentric fashion:

> The status of women who patronized St. Paul would particularly repay attention. They are clearly persons of some independence and eminence in their own circles, used to entertaining and running their salons, if that is what Paul's meetings were, as they saw best.[18]

This misinterpretation reduces the influential role of women in the early Christian movement to that of housewives permitted to serve coffee after Paul's lectures!

Since exegetes of the New Testament take it for granted that the leadership of the early Christian communities was in the hands of men, they assume that those women mentioned in the Pauline letters were the helpmates and assistants of the apostles, especially of Paul. Such an androcentric interpretative model leaves no room for the alternative assumption that women were missionaries, apostles, or heads of communities independent of Paul and equal to him.[19] Since Paul's position was often precarious and in no way accepted by all the members of the communities, it is even possible that the women's influence was more established than that of Paul's. Texts such as Rom. 16:1-3 or 16:7 suggest that leading women in the early Christian missionary movement did not owe their position to Paul. It is more likely that Paul had no other choice but to cooperate with these women and to acknowledge their authority within the communities.

We must ask, therefore, whether it is appropriate to limit all leadership titles in the New Testament which are grammatically masculine to males alone. Predictably enough, androcentric exegesis interprets grammatically masculine terms in a twofold way, namely as generic and as masculine.[20] Grammatically masculine terms like saints, the elect, brothers, sons, which serve to characterize the members of the communities, are usually understood to refer to both men and women. Exegetes do not go so far as to understand Christian community in analogy to the Mithras-cult and to limit church membership or the New Testament admonitions and injunctions to men.[21] However, every time the New Testament uses grammatically masculine titles such as prophet, teacher, deacon, missionary, co-worker, apostle, or bishop, which refer to leadership functions within the Christian community, exegetes assume that the reference is exclusively to men. They have no interpretative heuristic model that could do justice to the position and influence of women like Phoebe, Prisca,[22] or Junia or could adequately integrate them into its conception of early Christian leadership. Such an androcentric perspective is easily misused to legitimize the patriarchal practice of the contemporary church.[23]

One could reject such an analysis and maintain that the androcentric interpretation of early Christianity is conditioned and justified by our sources because they speak about women and their role in the early church only rarely and mostly in a polemic argument. The historical marginality of women is not created simply by contemporary exegesis, but by the fact that women were marginal in the fellowship of Jesus and in the early Christian male church from the very beginnings. Jesus was a man, the apostles were men, the early Christian prophets, teachers, and missionaries were men. All New Testament writings claim to be written by male authors and the theology of the first centuries is called the "theology of the Fathers." Women do not seem to be of any significance in the early church nor are they allowed any leadership or teaching functions. The Christian marginality of women has its roots in the patriarchal beginnings of the church and in the androcentrism of Christian revelation.

Such a theological conclusion presupposes, however, that the New Testament writings are objective factual reports of early Christian history and development. The rarity of women's mention in the sources adequately reflects the actual history of their activity in the early Church. Such a presupposition, however, neglects the methodic insights of form, source, and redaction criticism which have pointed out that the early Christian writings are not at all objectivistic factual transcripts but pastorally engaged writings. The early Christian authors have selected, redacted, and reformulated their traditional sources and materials with reference to their theological intentions and practical objectives. None of the early Christian writings and traditions is free from any of these tendencies. All early Christian writings, even the Gospels and Acts, intend to speak to actual problems and situations of the early church and to illuminate them theologically. We therefore can assume that this methodic insight applies equally to the traditions and sources about women in early Christianity. Since the early Christian communities and authors live in a predominantly patriarchal world and participate in its mentality, it is likely that the scarcity of information about women is conditioned by the androcentric traditioning and redaction of the early Christian authors. This applies especially to the Gospels and Acts since these were written toward the end of the first century. Many of the traditions and information about the activity of women in early Christianity are probably irretrievable because the androcentric selection or redaction process saw these as either unimportant or as threatening.[24]

The contradictions in the sources indicate such an androcentric process of redaction, which qualifies information that could not be omitted. It is true that women were disciples of Jesus and witnesses of the resurrection, but none of them was a member of the twelve. Jesus healed women and spoke with them but no Gospel tells us a story about the call of a woman to discipleship. The images of the parables draw on the world and experience of women but the God-language of Jesus is totally masculine. The Gospels tell us that women discovered the empty tomb but the true resurrection witnesses seem to have been men.

Acts tells us about women, especially rich women who supported the early Christian missionary endeavor with their homes and wealth. However, the historical elaboration of Luke gives the impression that the leadership of the early Christian mission was totally in the hands of men. We find short references to widows and prophetesses, but Luke does not tell us any stories about their activity or function. Thus Luke's conception of history is harmonizing and does not acknowledge a "women's problem" in the early church.

Such a problem emerges, however, when one reads the Pauline letters. The meaning of the Pauline texts which speak directly about women is still unclear, although numerous attempts at interpretation have been made.[25] Exegetes are divided on the question of whether the influence of Paul was negative or positive with respect to the role of women in early Christianity. Paul presupposes in 1 Cor. 11:2–16 that women speak as prophets in the community worship but demands that in doing so they adapt to the prevailing custom. It is not clear, however, what the actual issue of discussion is between Paul and the Corinthians or how the individual arguments of Paul are to be evaluated and understood. The negative result of the injuction in 1 Cor. 14:33–36 is clear-cut, but exegetes are divided as to whether the famous "*mulier taceat in ecclesia*" (a woman is to keep quiet in church) is a later interpolation, since it seems to contradict 1 Cor. 11.

In Gal. 3:28 Paul proclaims that all distinctions between Jews and Greeks, free and slave, male and female are obliterated, but he does not repeat in 1 Cor. 12:13 that maleness and femaleness no longer have any significance in the body of Christ. Therefore no exegetical consensus is achieved on whether Gal. 3:28, like 1 Cor. 12:13, applies to the Christian community, or to the eschatological future, or refers to the spiritual equality of all souls. The Pauline lists of greetings mention women as leading missionaries and respected heads of churches, but it is not univocal on how much they owe their leadership position to Pauline approval and support. It is true that Paul values women as co-workers and expresses his gratitude to them, but he probably had no other choice than to do so because women like Junia or Prisca already occupied leadership functions before him and were on his level in the early Christian missionary movement.

That the sources are unclear and divided about women's role in early Christianity is also evident when one compares the information supplied by different New Testament writings. The Pauline letters indicate that women have been apostles, missionaries, patrons, co-workers, prophets, and leaders of communities. Luke, on the other hand, mentions women prophets and the conversion of rich women but does not tell us any instance of a woman missionary or leader of a church. He seems to know of such functions of women, as his references to Prisca or Lydia indicate, but this knowledge does not influence his portrayal of early Christian history. Whereas all the Gospels know that Mary Magdalene was the first resurrection witness, the pre-Pauline tradition of 1 Cor. 15:3-5 does not mention a single woman among the resurrection witnesses. The Fourth Gospel and its tradition ascribe to a woman a leading role in the mission of Samaria, while Acts knows only of Phillip as the first missionary of this area. While Mark knows of the discipleship of women (*akolouthein*), Luke stresses that the women who followed Jesus supported him and his male disciples with their possessions.

Reference to the Lukan works,[26] the major source of our knowledge of early Christian history, demonstrates how much the androcentric interests of the New Testament authors determined their reception and depiction of early Christian life, history, and tradition. Since Luke is usually regarded as the most sympathetic to women of all New Testament writers,[27] such a hypothesis may sound strange. However, such an androcentric tendency becomes evident when one analyzes the Lukan Easter narratives. The discussions of Paul with his opponents indicate that the leadership function of the apostle was of eminent importance for the developing Christian church. However, according to Paul, the apostolate is not limited to the twelve but includes all those who had received an appearance of the resurrected Lord and whom the resurrected Lord had commissioned to work as Christian missionaries (1 Cor. 9:4). Luke not only limits the apostolate to the twelve but also modifies the criteria mentioned by Paul;[28] only those males who had accompanied Jesus in his ministry from Galilee to Jerusalem and had become witnesses of his death and resurrection (Acts 1:21f) were eligible to replace Judas as apostle. In terms of these criteria, Paul cannot be called apostle because he did not know the earthly Jesus, but some women would qualify. According to Mark,[29] women were witnesses of the public ministry of Jesus in Galilee and Jerusalem. They were the only ones who were eyewitnesses of his execution since the male disciples had fled, and women were the first to receive the resurrection news (Mark 15:40f, 47; 16: 1–8). Whereas Mark does not tell us of an appearance of the resurrected Lord to anyone, Matthew and John report that Mary Magdalene, and not the male disciples, was the first to see the risen Lord.

Luke does not know of any appearance of the risen Jesus to women. His androcentric redaction attempts in a subtle way to disqualify the women as resurrection witnesses. He emphasizes that the twelve who heard about the empty tomb from the women did not believe them but judged their words as gossip (24:11). When the men checked out the message of the women, it proved to be true (24:24), but this did not provoke a faith response from the male disciples. Not until the appearance of the risen Lord before Simon (24:34) did the men believe in the resurrection of Jesus. However, this appearance before Peter is not narrated but proclaimed in a confessional formula. This formula corresponds to the tradition quoted by Paul in 1 Cor. 15:3–5, which mentions Cephas and the eleven, but not Mary Magdalene and the women, as witnesses of the resurrection. That Luke is interested in excluding women from apostleship is also supported by his condition that only one of the male disciples is eligible to succeed Judas (Acts 1:21).

This Lukan stress on Peter as the primary Easter witness must be situated within the early Christian discussion of whether he or Mary Magdalene is the first resurrection witness. This discussion understands Peter to be in competition with Mary Magdalene insofar as he complains constantly that Christ has given so many revelations to a woman. The Gospel of Thomas reflects this competition between Peter and Mary Magdalene.[30] The gnostic writing *Pistis Sophia* and the apocryphal Gospel of Mary further develop this motif. In the Gospel of Mary,[31] it is asked, how can Peter be against Mary Magdalene because she is a woman if Christ has made her worthy of his revelations? The Apostolic Church Order evidences that this discussion presupposes an actual ecclesial situation. While the Gospel of Mary argues for the authority of Mary Magdalene on the ground that Christ loved her more than all the other disciples, the Apostolic Church Order argues for the exclusion of women from the priesthood by letting Mary Magdalene herself reason that the weak, namely the women, must be saved by the strong, namely the men.[32] This dispute about the resurrection witness of Mary Magdalene shows, however, that Mary, like Peter, had apostolic authority in some Christian communities even into the third and fourth centuries. It also makes clear that the androcentric interpretation of the egalitarian primitive Christian traditions serves a patriarchal ecclesial praxis.

PATRISTIC INTERPRETATION AND CODIFICATION

The necessity of such an androcentric interpretation of early Christian traditions provokes the question whether the early Christian traditions and sources canonized by the Fathers manufacture the historical marginality of women in the church. In other words, was early Christian life and community totally and from its very beginnings patriarchally defined or was the patriarchal marginality of women in the early Christian sources a by-product of the "patristic" selection and canonization process? Is it possible to unearth an emancipatory tradition in the beginnings of Christianity or is the question of the liberating impulses of Christian faith historically illegitimate and theologically inappropriate? This question becomes all the more pressing since scholars of antiquity point out that the "feminist question" was much debated and the legal position of women was quite good in the Greco-Roman world. In order to address this question one has to challenge the patristic interpretative model that understands early Christian history and community as the antagonistic struggle between orthodoxy and heresy.[33]

The classic understanding of heresy presupposes the temporal priority of orthodoxy. According to Origen all heretics were at first orthodox but then erred from the true faith.[34] According to this model of interpretation heresy is not only a free defection but also an intended mutilation of the true faith. The orthodox understanding of history knows that Jesus founded the church and gave his revelation to the apostles, who proclaimed his teaching to the whole world. By its witness the orthodox church preserves the continuity of revelation in Jesus Christ and establishes the personal continuity with Jesus and the first apostles by maintaining the apostolic succession.

Since this understanding of the Christian beginnings is shared by all groups of the early church, they all attempt to demonstrate that their own group and teaching is in apostolic continuity with Jesus and the first disciples. Montanism, gnostic groups of various persuasions, and the patristic church claim apostolic tradition and revelation in order to substantiate (and to legitimate) their own authenticity. Both parties, the opponents as well as the advocates of the ecclesial leadership of women, claim apostolic tradition and succession for such a leadership.[35] The advocates point to Mary Magdalene, Salome, or Martha as apostolic disciples. They stress the apostolic succession of prophetesses in the Old and New Testaments and call attention to the women of apostolic times mentioned in Rom. 16. They legitimate their egalitarian structures of community with reference to Gal. 3:28. Others preserve the Acts of Thecla as a canonical book.

The patriarchal opposition, on the other hand, appeals to the example of Jesus, who did not commission women to preach or admit them to the last supper.[36] They quote texts like Gen. 2-3, 1 Cor. 14, the deutero-Pauline household codes, and especially 1 Tim. 2:9-15. Whereas egalitarian groups trace their apostolic authority to Mary Magdalene and emphasize that women as well as men have received the revelations of the resurrected Christ, patristic authors pit the authority of Peter against that of Mary Magdalene. While groups that acknowledge the leadership of women search the Old Testament Scriptures and the Christian writings for passages that mention women, patristic authors attempt to explain away or play down the role of women whenever they are mentioned. Origen, for instance, concedes that women have been prophets, but stresses that they did not speak publicly and especially not in the worship assembly of the church.[37] Chrysostom confirms that in apostolic times women traveled as missionaries preaching the gospel, but, he explains, they could do this only because in the beginnings of the church the "angelic condition" permitted it.[38] Whereas the Montanists legitimate the prophetic activity of women with reference to the Scriptures, the extant Church Orders justify the institution of deaconesses,[39] which granted women only very limited and subordinate ecclesial functions in relation to the prophetesses of the Old Testament and the primitive church.[40] While women who preached and baptized claimed the example of the apostle Thecla, Tertullian attempts to denounce the Acts of Thecla as a fraud.[41] This example indicates that the process of the canonization of the early Christian documents was affected by the polemics and struggle concerning the leadership of women in the church. The canon reflects a patriarchal selection process and has functioned to bar women from ecclesial leadership.

The acid polemics of the Fathers against the ecclesial leadership of women indicate that the question of women's ecclesial office was still debated in the second and third centuries. It also demonstrates that the progressive patriarchalization of church office did not happen without opposition, but had to overcome an early Christian theology and praxis that acknowledged the leadership claim of women.[42] We owe to these polemics the few surviving bits of historical, though prejudiced, information about women's leadership in various groups of the early Church. Unfortunately, early Christian historiography does not understand them as the outcome of bitter polemics but as historically adequate and theologically appropriate information.

The polemics of the patriarchal authors against women's ecclesial leadership and office ultimately resulted in the equation of women's leadership in the church with heresy. This progressive equation of women and heresy had as a consequence the theological defamation of Christian women. For example, the author of the Apocalypse prophesies against an early Christian prophetess whom he abuses with the name Jezebel.[43] This prophet apparently was the head of an early Christian prophetic school which had great influence and authority in the community of Thyatira. Since the author of the Apocalypse stresses that despite his warnings and denunciations the prophetess still was active within the community, her authority seems to have at least equaled that of John whom, in turn, she might have perceived as a false prophet. Her influence must have been lasting, since Thyatira, in the middle of the second century, became a center of the Montanist movement, where prophetesses had significant leadership and influence.

The attacks of Tertullian evidence how prominent women's leadership still was toward the end of the second century. Tertullian is outraged about the insolence of those women who dared "to teach, to participate in theological disputes, to exorcise, to promise healings, and to baptize." He argues that it is not permitted for women "to speak in the Church, to teach, to baptize, to sacrifice, to fulfill any other male function, or to claim any form of priestly functions."[44] He substantiates this exclusion of women from all ecclesial leadership roles with a theology that evidences a deep misogynist contempt and fear of women. He accuses woman not only of the temptation of man but also of that of the angels. According to him woman is the "devil's gateway" and the root of all sin. Finally, Jerome not only attributes to women the origin of sin but of all heresy.

With the help of the prostitute Helena, Simon Magus founded his sect. Crowds of women accompanied Nicholas of Antiochia, the seducer, to all impurity. Marcion sent a woman before him in order to prepare the minds of men so that they might run into his nets. Apelles had his Philumena; an associate in the false teachings. Montanus, the mouthpiece of an impure spirit, used two wealthy women of noble origin, Prisca and Maximilla, in order to first bribe many communities and then to corrupt them. . . . Arious' intent to lead the world astray started by misguiding the sister of the emperor. The resources of Lucilla supported Donatus to corrupt so many wretched in Africa with his staining rebaptism. In Spain the blind woman Agape led a man like Elipidius to his grave. He was succeeded by Priscillian who was an enthusiastic defender of Zarathustra and a *Magus* before he became a bishop, and a woman by the name of Gall supported him in his endeavors and left behind a stepsister in order to continue a second heresy of lesser form.[45]

PATRIARCHALIZATION AND INSTITUTIONALIZATION

This process of ecclesial patriarchalization, which climaxed in the identification of women's leadership with heresy, was also operative in the selection and formulation of the canonical New Testament writings. This becomes explicit in the later writings of the New Testament, which in turn serve to reenforce and to legitimize the patriarchalizing tendencies in the patristic church.

Since the genuine Pauline letters know of leadership roles of women in the primitive church and since exegetes debate the meaning and authenticity of 1 Cor. 11:2-16[46] and 1 Cor. 14:33-36,[47] scholars discuss whether or not this process of patriarchalization was initiated, or at least supported, by Paul. However, there is no question that the early Christian tendencies of patriarchalization claimed Paul for their cause and determined the history, theology, and praxis of the church in his name. Such an interpretation of Pauline theology is continued by modern historical-critical exegesis. Scholars presuppose the interpretative model of orthodoxy and heresy when they label the opponents of Paul as "gnostic" or "gnosticizing." The Christian women in the community of Corinth, who apparently occupied an equal position in the leadership and worship of the community, are, therefore, qualified as "heretic," whereas the theological admonitions and arguments of Paul are understood as "orthodox."[48]

The theological-historic claim of Gal. 3:28[49] is disqualified in a similar way when it is classified as a "gnostic" baptismal formula and denounced as enthusiastic spiritualization and illusion. Although the validity of this model for an historiography of early Christianity has been questioned, its patriarchal implications are not yet exposed. Even though exegetes disagree on Paul's own stance toward women, they acknowledge explicit tendencies of patriarchalization in the Deutero-Pauline and post-Pauline literature. The so-called household codes[50] of the Deutero-Pauline literature accept and legitimate the patriarchal family order. Ephesians especially gives a theological justification of the patriarchal relationship between husband and wife or slave and master, insofar as the author legitimizes it with reference to the hierarchically defined relationship between Christ and the Church.[51] First Peter, which belongs to the area of Pauline influence, identifies the missionary vocation of women with their subordination to their husbands, whom they can win over to Christianity without many words. The author admonishes women to imitate the example of obedience given by the women of the Old Testament. Sara becomes a prime example for the Christian woman because she acknowledged Abraham as her "lord." The husbands, in turn, are admonished to treat their wives with understanding since they are the "weaker sex." The expression "weaker vessel" implies the corporal, spiritual, intellectual, and social inferiority of woman. Peter concedes that women are also "heirs of the life," but theologically legitimates their secondary position. Indeed, the text not only justifies the submission of women, but also demands the submission of all Christians to the patriarchal political-societal order (2:13). Slaves are most especially enjoined to submit to the patriarchal domination; this is done with reference to the sufferings of Christ. The authors of 1 Peter, as well as Ephesians, do not shy away from developing a Christian theology that supports the patriarchal-hierarchical claims of the Greco-Roman state and society.[52]

1 Tim. 2:10-15 does not speak about the subordination of women to the patriarchal family order; but like 1 Cor. 14:33-36, it explicitly demands the silence and subordination of women in the Christian community. The goal here, a patriarchalization of the eccelesial leadership functions, is evident in the injunction of the author that women should learn in total submission and the categorical prohibition of women teaching and having authority over men. This patriarchal injunction is theologically substantiated by the argument that man was created first and that woman sinned first.[53] This negative theological understanding of woman's functions is used to legitimize the exclusion of women from leadership and office in the church. Woman's vocation is not the call to discipleship or the missionary; it is her patriarchally defined role as wife and mother that accomplishes her salvation.

This demand of the Pastorals for the subordination of women is formulated in the context of a progressive patriarchalization of the church and its leadership functions. The Pastorals require that the structures and leadership of the Christian community should be patterned after the patriarchal family structure. This is seen in the criteria for the election of male leaders: they should be married to one woman and have demonstrated their patriarchal leadership qualities in their own household; they should know how to rule their children and to administer and order their household authoritatively.[54] In such a patriarchal church order, by definition, there is no room for women's leadership.

It is clear, however, that such a leadership structure developed in conflict with a more egalitarian church order which it worked to replace because it needed an ideological legitimization for the exclusion of women. Thus it becomes obvious that the misogynist expressions of patristic theology are not only rooted in a faulty anthropology of woman but are also provoked by ecclesiastical-patriarchal interests to theologically legitimate the exclusion of women from ecclesial leadership and office. Such an exegetical-historical delineation of the patriarchalization of the church does not prove the historical necessity and unavoidability of such a development; it does not call for theological justification but for a critical-theological analysis.[55]

Contemporary exegetes and theologians usually understand the process of ecclesial patriarchalization as the necessary development from charism to office, from Paulinism to early Catholicism, from a millenarian radical ethos to a privileged Christian establishment, from the radical Jesus movement within Judaism to an integrative love-patriarchalism[56] within the Hellenistic urban communities, from the egalitarian charismatic structures of the beginning to the hierarchical order of the Constantinian church. Unlike the orthodoxy-heresy model, this interpretative framework does not justify the patriarchalization process of the early church on theological grounds, but argues with it in terms of sociological and political factors.

It implicitly maintains that, from a sociological-political point of view, the gradual patriarchalization of the early Christian movement was unavoidable. If the Christian communities were to grow, develop, and historically survive, they had to adapt and take over patriarchal institutional structures of their society. The institutionalization of the charismatic-egalitarian early Christian movement could not but lead to the patriarchalization of the ecclesial leadership functions—that is, to the exclusion of women from church office or to the reduction of their ecclesial functions to subordinate, feminine, marginal positions. The more the early Christian movement adapted to the prevailing societal institutions, thus becoming a genuine part of its patriarchal Greco-Roman society, the more Christian women had to be excluded from church leadership and office. They were reduced to powerless fringe-groups or had to conform to the feminine stereotypes of the patriarchal culture. For example, the patristic office of widow and deaconess had to limit itself to the service of women, and finally disappeared from history. Moreover, these leadership functions could no longer be exercised by all women but only by those who had overcome their femaleness by remaining virgins.

This interpretative model of the early Christian development seems to describe accurately the consequences and casualties of the gradual patriarchalization of the Christian church. However, it does not reflect on its own theological androcentric presuppositions, insofar as it overlooks that the history of early Christianity is written from the perspective of the historical winners.[57] Christian history and theology reflect those segments of the church which have undergone this patriarchalization process and theologically legitimated it with the formulation of the canon. Insofar as the sociological-political model presents the elimination of women from ecclesial office and their marginalization in a patriarchal church as an historical necessity, it justifies the patriarchal institutionalization process as the only possible and historically viable form of institutional church structure. It overlooks, however, that the institutional structures of the patriarchal household and state were not the sole institutional options available to and realized by early Christians; collegial private associations, philosophical schools, guilds, and some of the mystery cults accepted women and slaves as equal members and initiates. These groups, like the early Christians, however, were always politically suspect because their egalitarian ethos challenged the patriarchal structures of their society. Since women such as Phoebe or Nympha were founders and leaders of house churches, the missionary house churches seem to have been patterned after such egalitarian private organizations and not after the patriarchal household.

The theological implications of the patriarchal sociological model for the reconstruction of early Christian history are obvious. Women can occupy only subordinate positions in the contemporary church since they could only do so in the early church. The patriarchal character of church office is given with the institutionalization of the church. Women who claim to be called to church office and leadership violate the essence of ecclesial tradition and institution. Therefore, the androcentric sociological model for the reconstruction of early Christian history prepares the grounds for the theological claim that patriarchal church structures are divinely revealed, and thus cannot be changed.

Both the androcentric theological model and the sociological models for the reconstruction of early Christian life and community presuppose that the process of the patriarchalization of the church was historically unavoidable. They claim that the early Christian theology and praxis, which acknowledged women as equal Christians and disciples, was either "heretical" or "charismatic," and hence theologically and historically nonviable. Neither model can conceive of a Christian church in which women were equal. Therefore, it is not enough to re-interpret the biblical texts that speak about women in early Christianity. What is necessary is to challenge the traditional interpretative models for the reconstruction of early Christianity and search for a new model which can integrate both egalitarian and "heretical" traditions into its own perspective. Since such an interpretative model presupposes and is based on the equality of *all* Christians, it could be called feminist. Insofar as such a perspective attempts to comprehend the equality of all Christians within the early Christian church, it has to employ sociological analysis.

AN EGALITARIAN INTERPRETATIVE MODEL:
THE EARLY CHRISTIAN MOVEMENT AS A CONFLICT MOVEMENT

Such an egalitarian interpretative model is based on the insight that Christianity has not been patriarchally determined from its very inception, and has not been an integrated segment of the patriarchal Jewish or Greco-Roman society. If one asks which historical, as yet unrealized, emancipatory impulses in early Christianity, despite the patriarchalizing tendencies of tradition and church, are still accessible today, it is evident that the Jesus movement and the early Christian missionary movement have been "countercultural." These countercultural, egalitarian impulses have to become the defining elements of the interpretative model for the reconstruction of early Christian history.

Despite apparent patriarchal tendencies in the transmission and redaction of the Jesus traditions, the New Testament sources do not attribute to Jesus a single negative statement about women. This is remarkable because the Gospels were written at a time when the patriarchalization process of the Christian community was well underway. The stories about the healing of women especially indicate that tradition and redaction did not attempt to apologetically interpret Jesus' words and actions in a patriarchal way. Even New Testament texts which insist on the patriarchal submission of Christian women do not legitimize this injunction with reference to a word or action of Jesus but with reference to the Law and especially to Gen. 2–3.

The Jesus traditions are in no way patriarchally defined. The opposite is true.[58] They reflect that Jesus was criticized because he took women seriously, and that women were disciples and primary witnesses. Since discipleship and the community of the disciples dissolved and replaced traditional family bonds (Mark 3:35), the women disciples are no longer defined by the patriarchal order of marriage and family. It is not natural motherhood but Jesus' discipleship which is decisive. The commitment and fidelity of the women disciples is especially underlined in the Markan gospel. Women persevered with Jesus in his sufferings and execution. The women disciples were the primary witnesses of the empty tomb and the resurrection. The three women pericopes in Mark maintain that the women disciples were the primary witnesses for the three basic data of the kerygma: death, burial, and resurrection. These three women pericopes seem in narrative form to parallel the expression "Christ died . . . was buried . . . was raised" of 1 Cor. 15:3–5.[59] This tradition of the gospels concerning the women, especially Mary Magdalene, as primary witnesses and guarantors of the Christian gospel does justice to the critical criteria which historical-critical scholarship has defined for determining authentic Jesus traditions.[60] This tradition is found in two different areas, the Synoptic and the Johannine tradition. It cannot be derived from contemporary Judaism because women were not considered valid witnesses. It also does not owe its formulation to early Christian ecclesial interests, since later documents, as we have seen, attempt to play down the importance of the women disciples. Moreover, patristic and later church traditions speak of Mary Magdalene as "apostle to the apostles," although they attempt to diminish her importance, and in later ecclesial consciousness she becomes the "prostitute" and "sinner." Even modern interpreters attempt to explain away the significance of the women as primary witnesses and guarantors of Christian resurrection faith when they stress that, in distinction to Peter, the witness of Mary Magdalene was "unofficial."[61]

These traditions about the role of women in the discipleship of Jesus correspond to the character of the Jesus movement that has been worked out by the sociological interpretation of religion.[62] As a renewal movement the Jesus movement stands in conflict with its Jewish society and is "heretical" with respect to the Jewish religious community. The earliest Jesus traditions expect a reversal of all social conditions through the eschatological intervention of God; this is initially realized in the ministry of Jesus. Therefore, the Jesus movement can accept all those who, according to contemporary societal standards, are marginal people and who are, according to the Torah, "unclean"—the poor, the exploited, the public sinners, the publicans, the maimed and sick, and last but not least, the women. In distinction to other Jewish renewal movements, such as the Qumran community, the Jesus movement was not exclusive but inclusive; it made possible the solidarity of those who could not be accepted by other Jewish renewal groups because of religious laws and ideologies.[63]

Women could become disciples of Jesus, therefore, although they were socially marginal, religiously inferior, and cultically unclean persons. The seven-fold transmission[64] of the Synoptic traditions, which states that the first and the leaders should be last and slaves, shows that Jesus radically questioned social and religious hierarchical and patriarchal relationships. The fatherhood of God radically prohibits any ecclesial patriarchal self-understanding. The lordship of Christ categorically rules out any relationship of dominance within the Christian community (Matt. 23:7-12). According to the gospel tradition Jesus radically rejected all relationships of dependence and domination.[65] This demand for inclusiveness and domination-free structures in the Jesus movement provides the theological basis for the acknowledgment of women as full disciples.

This ethos of the Jesus movement also finds expression in the early Christian missionary movement. All social distinctions of race, religion, class, and sex are abolished.[66] All Christians are equal members of the community. Gal. 3:28 is a pre-Pauline baptismal formula which Paul quotes in order to prove that in the Christian community all religious-social distinctions between Jews and Gentiles have lost their validity. This pre-Pauline baptismal confession clearly proclaims values that are in total opposition to those of the Greco-Roman culture of the time. The Christian missionary communities, like the

Jesus movement, could not tolerate the religious-social structures of inequality that characterized the dominant Greco-Roman society. The new self-understanding of the Christians did away with all religious, class, social, and patriarchal relationships of dominance, and therefore made it possible not only for Gentiles and slaves but also for women to assume leadership functions within the urban missionary movement. In this movement women were not marginal figures but exercised leadership as missionaries, founders of Christian communities, apostles, prophets, and leaders of churches.

Contemporary exegetes, therefore, do not do justice to the text when they label this pre-Pauline baptismal formula as "gnostic."[67] As the Christian Jews remained racially Jews, so women remain sexually female although their patriarchally defined gender roles and dependency are annulled in the Christian community. Moreover, Gal. 3:28 does not claim, as later gnostic and patristic texts do, that "maleness" is the full expression of being human and Christian, and that women, therefore, have to become "male" in Christ. In addition, Gal. 3:28 must not be misunderstood as purely spiritual or eschatological, since the text does not maintain Christian equality of Jews and Gentiles regarding their souls or with respect to the eschatological future. Finally, Gal. 3:28 should not be misinterpreted as purely charismatic but as applying to the structures and organization of the Christian community. Egalitarian structures were not unthinkable at the time. Such communal, organizational forms, which eliminated the societal differences between slaves and free as well as between male and female are found in the religious and secular associations of the time, although they were always suspected as capable of sedition if they did not conform to the social, patriarchal dominant order.[68] Like other cultic associations, especially Judaism and the cult of Isis, the Christians had to face the accusation that they upset the traditional patriarchal order of the household, and therefore, the order of the Roman state and society, by admitting women and slaves to equal membership. Therefore, the thesis of G. Theissen that the radicalism of the countercultural Jesus movement was assimilated by the earliest urban Hellenistic missionary communities into a "family style love patriarchalism," in which the societal distinctions survived although in a softer mitigated form, cannot be substantiated. The household code traditions of the Pauline school do not demonstrate such a love patriarchalism for the initial stages of the early Christian missionary movement in the Hellenistic urban centers.[69] They are better understood as an apologetic development of cultural adaption that was necessary because the early Christian missionary movement, like the Jesus movement in Palestine, was a countercultural conflict-movement that undermined the patriarchal structures of the Greco-Roman *politeia*. Only an egalitarian model for the reconstruction of early Christian history can do justice to both the egalitarian traditions of woman's leadership in the church as well as to the gradual process of adaptation and theological justification of the dominant patriarchal Greco-Roman culture and society.

In conclusion, I have attempted a critical analysis of the theological and sociological androcentric models which are presupposed in a historical and theological reconstruction of early Christian history and theology. I have proposed instead an egalitarian model, which can do justice to all the New Testament traditions and does not have to eliminate or to downplay the traditions of women's discipleship and leadership in the Jesus movement and the early Christian missionary movement. Like any historical interpretation, an egalitarian reconstruction and interpretation of early Christian history is not only analytical but also constructive. It is not only motivated by interest in the past but also attempts to set free the emancipatory and egalitarian impulses and traditions for the present, and especially for the future.[70] It seeks to engender an emancipatory praxis of church and theology that would set free the egalitarian impulses of the Jesus movement in Palestine and of the early Christian missionary movement not only for women and the Christian community but also for Western society and culture.

NOTES

1. A. Meyer, *Die moderne Forschung über die Geschichte des Urchristentums* (Leipzig and Tübingen: Mohr, 1898); D. Lührmann, "Erwägungen zur Geschichtedes Urchristentums," *EvTh* 32 (1972): 452–67; R. Schnackenburg, "Das Urchristentum," in J. Maier and J. Schreiner, *Literatur und Religion des Frühjudentums* (Würzburg: Echter, 1973), pp. 284–309; J. Blank, "Probleme einer Geschichte des Urchristentums," *Una Sancta* 30 (1975): 261–86; S. Schulz, *Die Mitte der Schrift: Der Frühkatholizismus im Neuen Testament* (Stuttgart: Kohlhammer, 1976); F. Hahn, "Das Problem des Frühkatholizismus," *EvTh* 38 (1978): 340–57; H. Paulsen, "Zur Wissenschaft vom Urchristentum und der alten Kirche—ein methodischer Versuch," *ZNW* 68 (1978): 200–230.

2. Since this article presupposes the studies about the history of early Christianity as well as the literature on women in antiquity and in early Christianity, it is impossible to quote the literature pertaining to the topic. Adequate discussion of divergent hypotheses and opinions must be reserved for a more extensive book-length treatment.

3. This is evident in the fact that the studies on women in the New Testament or women in early Christianity have not influenced the scholarly reconstruction of the Christian beginnings.

4. Blank, "Probleme," p. 262.

5. This is illustrated by the work of G. Heinz, *Das Problem der Kirchenentstehung in der deutschen protestantischen Theologie des 20 Jahrhunderts* (Mainz: Mathias-Grünewald, 1974). Heinz highlights the theological presuppositions underlying the different reconstructions of early Christian beginnings. For the sociology of the biblical exegete cf. also R. L. Rohrbaugh, *The Biblical Interpreter* (Philadelphia: Fortress Press, 1978).

6. For the concept of "model," cf. T. S. Kuhn, *The Structure of Scientific Revolutions* (Chicago: University of Chicago Press, 1970); I. G. Barbour, *Myths, Models, and Paradigms* (New York: Harper & Row, 1974); J. Blank, "Zum Problem ethischer Normen im Neuen Testament," *Concilium* 7 (1967): 356–62, uses "model" in a somewhat different way.

7. Cf. Vera Slupik, "Frau und Wissenschaft," in *Frauen in der Universität, Journal No.* 6 (Munich: Frauenoffensive, 1977), pp. 8–20; I. Kassner and S. Lorenz, *Trauer muss Aspasia tragen* (Munich: Frauenoffensive, 1976); J. Janssen-Jurreit, *Sexismus/Über die Abtreibung der Frauenfrage* (Munich: Carl Hanser, 1976), pp. 11–93; H. Smith, "Feminism and the Methodology of Women's History," in B. A. Carroll, *Liberating Women's History: Theoretical and Critical Essays* (Urbana: University of Illinois Press, 1975), pp. 368–84.

8. Simone de Beauvoir, *The Second Sex* (New York: Knopf, 1953), p. 10; E. Janeway, *Man's World, Woman's Place* (New York: Dell, 1971) characterizes this as "social mythology."

9. Cf. my articles, "Für eine befreite und befreiende Theologie," *Concilium* 14 (1978): 287–94; and "Feminist Theology as a Critical Theology of Liberation," *ThSt* 36 (1975): 605–26; V. Saiving, "Androcentrism in Religious Studies," *JR* 56 (1976): 177–97; B. W. Harrison, "The New Consciousness of Women: A Socio-Political Resource," *Cross Currents* 24 (1975): 445–62.

10. Cf. my article on "Die Rolle der Frau in der urchristlichen Bewegung," *Concilium* 12 (1976): 3–9. For the relative emancipation of women in Hellenism, cf. G. Delling, *Paulus Stellung zu Frau und Ehe* (Stuttgart: Kohlhammer, 1931), pp. 2–56; C. Schneider, *Kulturgeschichte des Hellenismus* (Munich: Beck, 1967), Vol. 1, pp. 78–117; L. Swidler, "Greco-Roman Feminism and the Reception of the Gospel," in *Traditio-Krisis-Renovatio aus theologischer Sicht*, ed. Jaspert and Mohr (Marburgh: Elwert, 1976), pp. 39–52; W. A. Meeks, "The Image of the Androgyne," *History of Religions* 13 (1974): 167–80.

11. This is the reason why M. J. Lagrange, *Saint Paul, Epitre aux Romains* (Paris 1916), p. 366, decided in favor of a woman's name although this textual reading was abandoned by Protestant exegetes.

12. *Das Neue Testament* (Aschaffendorf: Pattloch, 1956), p. 214.

13. H. Lietzmann, *Geschichte der alten Kirche* (Berlin: De Gruyter, 1961), Vol. 1, p. 149.

14. *Commenteria in Epistolam ad Romanos 10:26* (PG 14, 1281B), 10:39 (PG 14, 1289A).

15. Cf. E. E. Ellis, "Paul and His Co-Workers,"*NTS* 17 (1970/71): 439; M. A. Getty, "God's Fellow Worker and Apostleship," in *Women Priests,* ed. A. and L. Swidler (New York: Paulist Press, 1977), pp. 176–82.

16. This is stressed by Ramsey MacMullen, *Roman Social Relations, 50 B. C. to A. D. 284* (New Haven: Yale University Press, 1974), pp. 74–76, 124.

17. G. Heinrici, "Die Christengemeinde Korinths und die religiösen Genossenschaften der Griechen," *ZwTh* 19 (1976): 465–526.

18. E. A. Judge, "St. Paul and Classical Society," *JBAC* 15 (1972): 28.

19. Cf. my article, "Word, Spirit and Power: Women in Early Christian Communities," *Women of Spirit: Female Leadership in the Jewish and Christian Traditions,* ed. Rosemary Ruether and E. McLaughlin (New York: Simon and Schuster, 1979), pp. 29–70.

20. For this distinction, cf. C. Miller and K. Swift, eds., *Words and Women: New Language in New Times* (New York: Doubleday, Anchor, 1977), especially pp. 64–74.

21. Small sectarian groups separate themselves from the world and distinguish between their members as insiders and the outsiders who are conceived as "the others." Not women but the non-Christians are the "others" in early Christianity. There is no evidence that church membership was restricted to males only, although the address

of the Christians is usually masculine. Cf. my article "The Study of Women in Early Christianity: Some Methodological Considerations," in *Critical History and Biblical Faith: New Testament Perspectives,* ed. J. T. Ryan (Villanova: Catholic Theology Society, 1979), pp. 30-58, and the contribution by W. A. Meeks, "'Since Then You Would Need To Go Out of The World': Group Boundaries in Pauline Christianity," in the same volume, pp. 4-29.

22. Among the outstanding figures of early Christianity only Prisca is mentioned among the leaders in the Pauline churches by Hans Conzelmann, *Geschichte des Urchristentums* (Göttingen: Vandenhoeck and Ruprecht, 1971), in Appendix I; Eng. *History of Primitive Christianity,* trans. John E. Steely (Nashville and New York: Abingdon, 1973).

23. This was already recognized and deplored by Elizabeth Cady Stanton, *The Woman's Bible,* new ed. (New York: Arno Press, 1974) in the last century. It is regrettable that the recent Vatican declaration against the ordination of women confirms this experience. For the international theological discussion of this document, cf. L. Swidler, "Roma Locuta, Causa Finita?" in *Women Priests,* pp. 3-18.

24. Many studies on women in the Bible do not perceive this process because they are often motivated by an apologetic defense of the biblical writers.

25. Cf. my article "Women in the Pre-Pauline and Pauline Churches," *USQR* 33 (1978): 153-66.

26. Cf. my plenary address "Women's Discipleship and Leadership in the Lukan Writings," at the CBA annual meeting in San Francisco in 1978.

27. Cf. e.g., C. F. Parvey, "The Theology and Leadership of Women in the New Testament," *Religion and Sexism,* ed. R. R. Ruether (New York: Simon and Schuster, 1974), pp. 137-46.

28. Cf. my articles "The Twelve" and "The Apostleship of Women in Early Christianity," in *Women Priests,* pp. 114-22 and 135-40 for the literature.

29. Since the Gospel of Mark portrays women positively, P. Achtemeier (*Mark* [Philadelphia: Fortress Press, 1975], p. 11) considers the possibility that the Gospel was authored by a woman. Although the tradition ascribes all New Testament writings to male authors, historical-critical scholarship has shown that we do not know the authors of most New Testament writings.

30. Logion 114, *PL* 99, 18-26. Cf. Edgar Hennecke, ed., *New Testament Apocrypha,* 2 vols. (Philadelphia: Westminster, 1963, 1966), Vol. 1, p. 522.

31. Ibid., p. 343.

32. Cf. J. P. Arendzen, "An Entire Syriac Text of the Apostolic Church Order," *JThSt* 111 (1902): 71.

33. Cf. A. Hilgenfeld, *Die Ketzergeschichte des Urchristentums,* new ed. (Darmstadt: Wiss. Buchgesellschaft, 1963); W. Bauer, *Orthodoxy and Heresy in Earliest Christianity* (Philadelphia: Fortress Press, 1971); H. D. Betz, "Orthodoxy and Heresy in Primitive Christianity," *Int* 19 (1965): 299-311; J. Pelikan. *The Emergence of the Catholic Tradition* (Chicago: University of Chicago Press; 1971).

34. Origen, *Commentary to the Song of Songs* 3.2.2; similarly also I Clem. 42; Tertullian, *De Praescriptione* 20; Eusebius, *Ecclesiastical History* 4.22.2-3; cf. also John G. Gager, *Kingdom and Community: The Social World of Early Christianity* (Englewood, N.J.: Prentice-Hall, 1975), pp. 76-92.

35. For extensive references cf. my article, "Word, Spirit, and Power."

36. Cf. *Didascalia* 15 and *The Apostolic Church Order* III, 6.9; J. Kevin Coyle, "The Fathers on Women's Ordination," *Eglise et Theologie* 9 (1978): 51-101; C.

Osiek, "The Ministry and Ordination of Women According to the Early Church Fathers," in C. Stuhlmüller, ed., *Women and Priesthood* (Collegeville, Minn.: The Liturgical Press, 1978), pp. 59-68.

37. Origen, *Commentarium in I ᵃᵐ/Epistulam ad Corinthios 14: 34-35.* Cf. C. Jenkins, "Origen on 1 Corinthians, IV," *JThSt* 10 (1908/09): 41 f.

38. E. A. Clark, "Sexual Politics in the Writings of John Chrysostom," *AThR* 59 (1977): 3-20, 15f; D. F. Winslow, "Priesthood and Sexuality in the Post-Nicene Fathers," *St. Luke's Journal of Theology* 18 (1975): 214-27.

39. Cf. especially A. Kalsbach, *Die altkirchliche Einrichtung der Diakonissen bis zu ihrem Erlöschen* (Freiburg: Herder, 1926), and R. Gryson, *The Ministry of Women in the Early Church* (Collegeville, Minn.: Liturgical Press, 1976).

40. *The Apostolic Church Order* III, 6.1-29.

41. Tertullian, *De Baptismo* 17. For the *Acts of Thecla* cf. C. Schlau, *Die Akten des Paulus und der Thekla* (Leipzig: Hinrichs, 1877); W. M. Ramsay, *The Church in the Roman Empire before A. D. 170,* repr. of 1904 ed. (Kennebunkport, Maine: Longwood Press, 1977, and New York: Baker Books, 1979), pp. 375-428; and the very interesting dissertation of R. Kramer, *Ecstatics and Ascetics: Studies in the Function of Religious Activities of Women* (Ann Arbor: University Microfilms, 1976), pp. 142-49.

42. Cf. also F. Heiler, *Die Frau in den Religionen der Menschheit* (Berlin: De Gruyter, 1977), p. 114. He surmises, however, that in the heretical communities women in office were not disciplined enough.

43. The accusation of sexual licentiousness is a stereotypical accusation leveled by pagans against Christians and by Christians against each other. Cf. K. Thraede, "Frau," in *RAC* 8 (Stuttgart, 1973): 254-66; L. Zscharnack, *Der Dienst der Frau in den ersten Jahrhunderten der christlichen Kirche* (Göttingen: Vandenhoeck and Ruprecht, 1902), pp. 78ff.

44. *De Praescriptione* 41.5 and *De Baptismo* 17.4. Cf. also J. K. Coyle, "The Fathers on Women's Ordination," pp. 67ff.

45. Jerome 1.48.

46. Cf. W. Munro, "Patriarchy and Charismatic Community in Paul," in *Women and Religion, Proceedings of the American Academy of Religion, 1972-1973,* rev. ed., ed. Judith Plaskow and Joan A. Romero (Missoula: Scholars Press, 1974), pp. 189-98; W. O. Walker, "1 Cor. 11:2-6 and Paul's View Regarding Women," *JBL* 94 (1975): 94-110; J. Murphy-O'Conner, "The Non-Pauline Character of 1 Cor. 11:2-16," *JBL* 95 (1976): 615-21.

47. For the literature and discussion of this text cf. G. Fitzer, *Das Weib schweige in der Gemeinde* (Munich: Kaiser, 1963) and my article "Women in the Pre-Pauline and Pauline Churches."

48. Paul's reaction is often understood as inspired by his Jewish past. For the danger of anti-Judaism in such an exegetical feminist explanation cf. J. Plaskow, "Christian Feminism and Anti-Judaism," *Cross Currents* 28 (1978): 306-9.

49. Cf. W. Schmithals, *Die Gnosis in Korinth* (Göttingen: Vandenhoeck and Ruprecht, 1956), p. 227 n.1; W. A. Meeks, "The Image of the Androgyne," pp. 180ff; R. Scroggs, "Paul and the Eschatological Woman Revisited," *JAAR* 42 (1974): 536.

50. Cf. J. E. Crouch, *The Origin and Intention of the Colossian Haustafel* (Göttingen: Vandenhoeck and Ruprecht, 1972); W. Leslie, *The Concept of Women in the Pauline Corpus* (Ann Arbor: University Microfilms, 1976), pp. 188-237.

51. Cf. J. P. Sampley, *And the Two Shall Become One Flesh* (Cambridge: Cam-

bridge University Press, 1971), and my article "Marriage and Discipleship," *The Bible Today* (April 1979): 2027-34.

52. Cf. the excellent analysis of D. Balch, *"Let Wives Be Submissive. . .": The Origin and Apologetic Function of the Household Duty Code (Haustafel) in 1 Peter* (Ann Arbor: University Microfilms, 1974).

53. Cf. S. Roth Liebermann, *The Eve Motif in Ancient Near Eastern and Classical Greek Sources* (Ann Arbor: University Microfilms, 1975).

54. Cf. A. Sand, "Anfänge einer Koordinierung verschiedener Gemeinde-ordnungen nach den Pastoralbriefen," in *Kirche im Werden,* ed. J. Hainz (Paderborn: Schöningh, 1976), pp. 215-37, 220.

55. For a positive interpretation of this development, cf., for example, W. Schrage, "Zur Ethik der Neutestamentlichen Haustafeln," *NTS* 21 (1974): 1-22.

56. For this expression cf. E. Troltsch, *Die Soziallehren der christlichen Kirchen und Gruppen* (Tübingen: Mohr, 1923), Vol. 1, pp. 67f, and especially G. Theissen, *Sociology of Early Palestinian Christianity* (Philadelphia: Fortress Press, 1978), and his various articles. However, in my opinion, Theissen too quickly ascribes the love-patriarchalism to the early Christian missionary movement in the Greco-Roman urban centers.

57. Cf. G. Gutiérrez, "Where Hunger Is, God Is Not," *The Witness* (April 1977), p. 6: "Human history has been written by a white hand, a male hand, from the dominating social class.The perspective of the defeated in history is different. Attempts have been made to wipe from their minds the memory of their struggles. This is to deprive them of a source of energy, of an historical will to rebellion."

58. Cf. Also Evelyn and Frank Stagg, *Woman in the World of Jesus* (Philadelphia: Westminster, 1978), p. 102.

59. Cf. M. Hengel, "Maria Magdalena und die Frauen als Zeugen," *Abraham unser Vater,* ed. O. Betz and M. Hengel (Leiden: Brill, 1962), p. 246.

60. For a short discussion of these criteria cf. N. Perrin, *What Is Redaction Criticism?* (Philadelphia: Fortress Press, 1971).

61. Cf., e.g., R. E. Brown, "Roles of Women in the Fourth Gospel," *ThSt* 36 (1975): 692, n. 12.

62. Cf. in addition to the work of G. Theissen, J. Gager, R. Kraemer, and W. A. Meeks also the article by R. Scroggs, "The Earliest Christian Communities as Sectarian Movement," in *Christianity, Judaism and Other Greco-Roman Cults* (Leiden: Brill, 1975), Vol. 2, pp. 1-23; J. A. Wilde, "The Social World of Mark's Gospel," SBLSP (Missoula: Scholars Press, 1978), Vol. 2, pp. 47-70.

63. Cf. M. Völkl, "Freund der Zöllner und Sünder," *ZNW* 69 (1978): 1-10; L. Schottroff, "Das Magnifikat und die ältesten Traditionen über Jesus von Nazareth," *EvTh* 38 (1978): 298-312, and especially her excellent book, L. Schottroff and W. Stegemann, *Jesus von Nazareth: Hoffnung der Armen* (Stuttgart: Kohlhammer, 1978).

64. Mark 9:35; 10:41-45;Matt. 18:4; 20:25-28; 23:11; Luke 9:48; 22:24-27. According to Billerbeck, *Kommentar,* Vol. 4, p. 722, women had the same social standing as slaves did.

65. Cf. P. Hoffmann and V. Eid, *Jesus von Nazareth und seine christliche Moral* (Freiburg: Herder, 1975), pp. 199ff.

66. Cf., e. g., H. D. Betz, "Spirit, Freedom, and Law: Paul's Message to the Galatian Churches," *Svenk Exegetisk Arsbok* 39 (1974): 145-60.

67. It is often claimed that the text is "gnostic" because it does away with the

creational differences between women and men. However, such a judgment, in my opinion, does not sufficiently distinguish between biological sex and social gender roles. For such a distinction and its cross-cultural documentation, cf. Anne Oakley, *Sex, Gender, and Society* (New York: Harper & Row, 1973).

68. Cf. the documentation and elaboration of this point by D. Balch, *"Let Wives Be Submissive. . . ,"* pp. 115-33.

69. The interrelation between the organizational forms of private or religious associations and the house-churches needs to be clarified. Cf. A. J. Malherbe, *Social Aspects of Early Christianity* (Baton Rouge: Louisiana State University Press, 1977), p. 92.

70. Cf. H. M. Baumgartner, *Kontinuität und Geschichte: Zur Kritik and Metakritik der historischen Vernuft* (Frankfurt: Suhrkamp, 1972), p. 218.

22

LUISE SCHOTTROFF

Women as Followers of Jesus in New Testament Times: An Exercise in Social-Historical Exegesis of the Bible

*Mary of Magdala was one of the women present with Jesus from the begin-
ning of his public work, doubtless a single woman among the indigent beg-
gar-wanderers, and not at all wealthy as Luke pictures the women accompanying Jesus. She was one of the disciples who proclaimed the imminence of
the kingdom and who lived together as "the family of God." She was among
the women who took the politically dangerous step of announcing the resurrection of Jesus, and became thereby, like Peter, a symbol of conquered fear.
Mary exhibits the full partnership which the male and female followers of
Jesus practiced. This equality of the sexes was born of a shared poverty and
of the hope for the impending kingdom of God, for "the Jesus movement in
Palestine was a self-help community of poor Jews."*

Prisca, and her husband Aquila, were fellow missioners with Paul, who as

---

An address delivered at Union Theological Seminary, New York City, February 16, 1981.

tentmakers were manual laborers who worked hard for meager wages, and were in this respect typical of the Pauline congregations. She is representative of a considerable number of women named or alluded to in the epistles and Acts as fully active in congregational affairs by organizing, speaking, prophesying, discussing, and praying in the public assemblies.

Paul's attempt to restrict this lively ecclesial practice of women by encouraging signs of submission on the part of women toward men probably was his concession to pressure from a Roman public opinion that was suspicious of excessive public activities by women. From this concession of Paul, which he probably thought rather minor, there was a direct line to later New Testament texts that returned women to a passive position as silent churchgoers while channeling them into the role of nurturers of men and children.

ON FOLLOWING JESUS IN PALESTINE BEFORE A.D. 70

I begin with an example: Mary of Magdala was just as important for the emergence of the Jesus movement in Palestine as Peter—we just know much less about her. Less in the first instance because the Christian sources of the first century are only too ready to keep silent about the women in the Jesus movement. For example, Mark's Gospel reports only in connection with the Passion story that women were present right from the beginning of the Jesus movement in Galilee (Mark 15:40-41). Up to that point, Mark wrote only about the men who followed Jesus. A further reason why we know so little about Mary Magdalene is the theological and exegetical tradition. According to church tradition, we incorrectly associate her with "the woman who was a sinner," the prostitute whose many sins Jesus forgave in Luke 7:36-50. According to the exegetical tradition of historical criticism, we would at most say that she was an "important woman."[1]

Unusually, Mary of Magdala is written throughout with an indication of her origin *(hē Magdalēnē)* probably at first because one had to distinguish her from the other women called *Maria* (or *Mariam* = Heb. *miryam*). She was not however distinguished by the normal addition of the name of a male relative (for example *Maria hē Iakōbou,* Mark 16:1). If she had still been living in the setting of a Jewish family this would hardly have been explicable. She comes from Magdala by the Sea of Gennesaret, but her name shows that at the time of the Jesus movement she had given up or lost her homeplace and no longer lived in Magdala. For she could hardly have been called *hē Magdalēnē* by the people of Magdala. Other Jews within and outside the Galilean Jesus movement would have called her that.

So she was a single Jewish woman probably without settled abode, at any rate at the time of the Jesus movement. She wandered around Galilee with the group attached to Jesus and also took part in the journey to Jerusalem (Mark 15:40–41).[2] That a woman should lead an unsettled life could mean that, like a wandering Cynic preacher, she had left home, family, and property. There is, as far as I know, only one reference in the classical sources to a female wandering Cynic philosopher: to Hipparchia, a beautiful young woman from a rich family, who journeyed as a Cynic philosopher in beggar's clothing, together with Krates, through Greece (Diog. L. VI, 96f). Luke imagined just this situation when thinking of the lifestyle of Jesus and his disciples: they leave their families, their wives, and all their property (see Luke 18:29; cf. 14:26).

However, for the women who follow Jesus this idea does not seem appropriate to Luke (8:1–3). Certainly Luke reports that women accompany Jesus and his disciples on the journey to the towns and villages of Galilee, but he imagines that, also on this journey, they have possessions with which they support Jesus and the twelve financially. The disciples take no money with them, not even a beggar's bag (Luke 9:3; cf. 10:4). They are poor beggar-prophets. The wealthy women walk with them on this journey. (Are we to imagine that they carry large money-bags behind the disciples?) Luke illustrates here from his own context the traditional reports of the wanderings of Jesus and his disciples, among whom were also women. He does this for the men with the *idea* of the ascetic wandering philosophers, for the women with the *idea* of ladies from a well-to-do house who support religious groups with their own possessions. Such women are known, for example, as pillars of the Jewish congregations in Rome, or indeed, as we know from Luke's Acts of the Apostles, as pillars of Christian congregations in Philippi and in Thessalonica (Acts 16:14–15; 17:4, 12).

Luke did not notice the incongruence in his description of the Jesus movement in Galilee. For him it was important that right from the beginning in Galilee women were there too. For that reason he already mentions them very differently from Mark in the description of Jesus' way through Galilee. The women, among whom Mary Magdalene is mentioned first (24:10), have in this way, according to his categories, the quality of witnesses to all of Jesus' work (Acts 1:21f), but not the status of apostles because, in Luke's opinion, twelve *men* were called (Luke 6:3; cf. Acts 1:21–22). Luke is interested from within the situation of his congregations to give emphasis to the women who followed Jesus. However he had no information about the historical reality of the women in Galilee at that time other than from Mark (15:40–41, 47; 16:1).

We return to the old pre-Marcan tradition which lies behind Mark 15:40—16:8. Mary of Magdala, like the other women who followed Jesus, shared his poor and vagrant life. We must not, like Luke, picture her life from the point of view of a relatively wealthy city-dweller far away from Palestine. We must work it out on one hand with help from the New Testament sources about the situation of the Palestinian Jesus movement, on the other hand from the extra-Christian historical sources from Josephus to archaeology. Mary Magdalene shared the life of the *ptōchoi,* "the poor," who formed the Jesus movement in Palestine.³ She belonged to the apparently very broad class of the poor among the Jewish population at that time. These people were not poor because they had given up property on account of the kingdom of God. They were poor because the Herodian family and indirectly the Roman Caesars took more from the population than was bearable, and because the increasing cultivation in large estates stifled the small farmers economically without offering enough jobs for day-laborers.⁴

Without lapsing into historical speculation we can, despite the scanty sources about Mary Magdalene, deduce much about her from the situation of the Jesus movement and of the Jewish population. Like many other people she lived at subsistence level: she could not be sure whether she would have to go hungry tomorrow, if today she was able to buy some bread. She could try, like the men, to find casual work as day-laborers. Women have (not only) in Palestine done the hardest work in agriculture, in building, and certainly also in the fish-trade by Lake Gennesaret.⁵ The often unemployed, unsettled, and single woman probably had, however, some education, in that she also followed the reading and interpretation of the Torah in the synagogue on the Sabbath. Perhaps she could even read and write.

She was familiar at any rate with the Torah to the extent that she could herself use its language when speaking; because, and here I return to the specific evidence relating to Mary Magdalene, she did not only wander with Jesus, but from the beginning she herself proclaimed the prophetic message of the coming of the kingdom of God. In Mark 15:41 it says that the women had already served Jesus in Galilee *(diēkonoun autō)*. That cannot mean the *diakonia* of serving meals, because then the singular would not be intelligible: Jesus was not *alone* when journeying. Aside from that, it is hardly possible in the overall situation of poor homeless people to imagine a *diakonia* in the sense of a housewife's activity. The *diakonia Christou* is much more a proclamation that Jesus is the Messiah and that the kingdom of God is imminent (in the sense of the usage in 2 Cor. 11:23; 6:4f).

The fact that Mary of Magdala and other women actively joined in the prophetic proclamation of the Jesus movement is shown also in their role after Jesus' death. We recognize from the largely pre-Marcan story of the so-called "empty tomb" that the execution of Jesus as a political trouble-maker caused his followers to disappear. Perhaps it was similar to the way Mark describes it: they ran away terrified. It would have been at any rate extremely dangerous to be recognized as a member of this movement. The Jewish authorities were very quick, as is clear from Josephus, to flog potential troublemakers and to hand them over to the Roman procurator (see Josephus, *B. J.* 6.300f). Going to the grave on Easter Day, if we can imagine it from Mark 16:1–8, was a risky act of solidarity with a person who had been executed for political reasons. We ought not to understand Mark 16:1–8 as an historical account about Easter morning, but as a kerygmatic story about the beginning of the proclamation of the risen Jesus. In any case this text remains a document of courageous solidarity.

It is not in my opinion the intention of Mark 16:1–8 to show that the tomb was empty or that the empty tomb did not become known for such a long time because the women said nothing (as in W. Bousset or R. Bultmann). Mark 16:1-8 relates a vocational epiphany: the calling of Mary Magdalene and some other women to proclaim the resurrection of Jesus. Or put another way: from Mark 16:1-8 we can deduce the historical fact that it was only through the courage and activity of Mary Magdalene and some other women that the Jesus movement carried on after Jesus' death. Even Mark, who in the final verse situates the women in the group of the disciples who were overcome by fear, tells this whole story against the clear background that *this* frightened Peter and *this* shaking Mary Magdalene then became the carriers of the message. For the Marcan congregation, characterized by fear, Mary Magdalene—like Peter and other men and women who followed Jesus—is a symbol of conquered fear.

I should like at this point to make some remarks about method. I have already said so much about Mary Magdalene, about whom the sources apparently relate very little, that from shortage of space I must forego discussion of other possible aspects. If one asks about the real situation of the people who lie behind the New Testament tradition, one can say an astonishing amount about them. It is just for that reason that I chose initially one person to make the method clear. The New Testament tradition is not restricted, then, to the history of thoughts and religious ideas, but rather the thoughts become part of the history of the followers of Jesus, their suffering, their praxis, their experiences together, their hope.

The women who followed Jesus before and after his death played a full part in the proclamation of the prophetic message of Jesus. There are no traces in the old part of the Synoptic tradition of a discussion about the special role of women. There is no pleading for their subordination to men as in Paul and in later Christian texts, but also no expression of their equality with men "in Christ" as in Paul (Gal. 3:28). The story of Mary and Martha certainly reflects problems with the role of women, but is however part of Luke's own awareness. We see this awareness elsewhere in Luke. Luke 10:38-42 cannot be used to reconstruct the history of the Jesus movement in Palestine.

In the Jesus movement the women were clearly and without question partners of the men. I see the causes for this on two levels. First, the economic, social, and political situation, which is well summed-up in the Greek word *ptōchos,* led to increasing breakdown of the family and of the organized roles of women among the Jewish population. The men leave to look for work. The women have to work with small children in the fields from sunrise until sunset, or go with them to swell the crowds of beggars and sick in the villages. What was seen in the apocalyptic tradition as a terrible sign of the end of the world was now happening: "a man is set against his father and the daughter against her mother and the bride against her mother-in-law" (Matt. 10:35).

The break-up of families, which is mentioned in the Gospels, was also related to the fact that the message of Jesus could lead to division among families. We should, however, not see this division in isolation from the family break-up caused by economic relations. A woman like Mary Magdalene and her Jewish sisters, who have to struggle to survive, is a partner in need for the men in the same situation. The socially defined role of women is superfluous for her as much as for the female and male slaves who work on the large Roman estates described by the Roman writer on agriculture, Columella.

In my opinion it is not historically accurate if, as constantly happens, we describe the freedom of Jesus in contact with women in sharp contrast to the dark picture of Jewish rabbis, who despise women and do not talk with them in public. The background in which the Jesus movement should be seen is *not* the patriarchal opinion of Jewish rabbis. It is much more the living-situation of the whole Jewish people at this time. The background is hunger, family break-down, exploitation of all, including women and children. In this background the Jesus movement shone out.

With that I come to the second reason for the equality between men and women in the Jesus movement: that is the *hope for the impending kingdom of God* and the collective life which resulted from that hope. They did not try to recreate the lost world of the patriarchal family, they founded a new family: the *familia dei*. They found the often accelerated break-up of existing families necessary (see for example Matt. 10:37). They did not try to define the special role of women, rather they understood the community of men and women as "one flesh" (Mark 10:8), as an indestructible community which they described in the enticing colors of a utopia: "from the beginning of creation God made them male and female. This is why a man must leave father and mother, and the two become one body. They are no longer two, therefore, but one body" (Mark 10:6f). Here speaks not a Jesus who anticipates church divorce laws, but a Jesus who shows us how wonderful it is to understand ourselves as God's creation. He shows that living with this understanding—as with living in the kingdom of God—turns sick beggars into people in a sense they could only dream about. This blissful experience of liberation, which speaks to us from many passages in the Synoptic Gospels, did not exist only in the *heads* of those involved. Above all in the healing miracles we can see that in the *familia dei* sick beggars become healthy people. We should not understand this as a metaphysical miracle to prove Jesus' divine qualities, but rather as a consequence, which we too can imagine, of the solidarity and love which was practiced in this movement of the poor.

Phrasing this as a fairly uninvolved historical report: the Jesus movement in Palestine was a self-help community of poor Jews. They tried in all ways to help each other, shared the little food that they had, and cared for each other's health. Those involved understood themselves as heirs of the religious tradition of Israel and their movement as the beginning of a bringing together of the entire people, as a restoration of the creation. Regarded politically, the execution of Jesus, and of many of his followers after his death, was from the point of view of the Romans thoroughly opportune. This movement could have become, at least in the long term, dangerous for Roman rule.

WOMEN IN THE PAULINE CONGREGATIONS

I begin again with an example.

Prisca, a Jewess with a Roman name, together with her husband Aquila, also a Jew with a Roman name, played just as important a role as Paul in the spreading of the gospel of the Messiah Jesus in the Roman Empire. Already in the old handwritten versions of the Acts of the Apostles there are changes in the text, which attempt to reduce the importance of Prisca, for example the Cantabrigiensis in Acts 18:2 (Paul *prosēlthen autō,* "went to see him [Aquila]," instead of *autois,* "went to see them [Aquila and Prisca]"), or in Acts 18:26 where in the same handwriting the word order is turned around: "Aquila and Prisca." The remarkable naming of the wife first, which is also to be found in Paul (Rom. 16:3), is, at least by such people as those who made such changes, understood as an expression of disproportionate importance for a woman.

We may infer that the married couple were full partners in the work for the gospel, if not that Prisca took on further tasks herself. It is anyway not a form of politeness when Paul and Luke name Prisca first. The work of this couple together ought not in any way to induce immediate associations for us ("Prisca probably wore the trousers in this marriage" or "Aquila preached while Prisca cooked"). Suitable associations would be much more Jesus' speech about the togetherness of man and woman in Mark 10:2-9: a married couple is trying here in extremely difficult circumstances to live in complete partnership. And Prisca and Aquila were not the only married couple; Philologus and Julia, whom Paul mentions in Rom. 16:15, perhaps Andronicus and Junia too (Rom. 16:7) can be regarded as couples who worked together for the gospel. Their partnership was not an expression of socially-determined roles, but of a lifestyle according to the essence of the message; they tried to live as "one flesh." Prisca has however only found recent appreciation from Adolf von Harnack, who even wanted to assign to her the composition of the Letter to the Hebrews.[6]

Prisca and Aquila earned their living like Paul as *skēnopoioi* (Acts 18:3). This profession is not mentioned outside the New Testament. It is according to the letters of Paul a craft (1 Cor. 4:12) which if necessary can be done at night (1 Thess. 2:9). It is work which allows frequent change of residence, perhaps even requires it, for Prisca and Aquila like Paul frequently moved from one town to another. I relate *skēnopoios,* "tentmaker," to the production of tents out of leather or wool; it is thus either the work of sewing leather or of weaving material from wool. The *lanarius,* "worker in wool," who also made tents, earned according to Diocletian's wage-scales (A.D. 301) even less than an agricultural day-laborer. The greatest demand for tents must have been from the Roman army. It is certainly plausible that the production of army tents played a role in Rome, Corinth, Ephesus, and Tarsus.

But even if the substance of the occupation *skēnopoios* must remain hypothetical, the indications from Paul are enough to see that Aquila and

Prisca are not "husband and wife employers,"[7] but manual laborers who work hard with raw material and who do not earn much. The wives of such manual laborers worked with them because the earnings of the husband were not sufficient. It is beyond doubt in this social situation that Paul worked with Aquila and Prisca together in Corinth (Acts 18:3); it is quite imaginable that the Western biblical tradition of the early church and of the Middle Ages had an interest in representing Aquila and Prisca as a well-off couple in whose business Paul was for a time employed, but who themselves did not have to work (see the history of the text, Acts 18:3: *ērgazeto,* "he worked"/ *ērgazonto,* "they worked"). According to the Greek-speaking upper classes of the Roman Empire, Prisca, like Aquila and Paul, is a *penēs,* a person who lives from manual work. The *penētes* are not as poor as the *ptōchoi*—the destitute—but they have to lead a hard life full of risk.

Altogether, the social situation of Prisca, Aquila, and Paul is, in my opinion, representative of the Pauline congregations in general. There are certain social differences within the congregations (probably 1 Cor. 11:21 is indicative of this). There are also regional differences: the congregations around Corinth are better off than those in Macedonia (2 Cor. 8:1–5 in the context of 8:6–7). But the Corinthian congregation is also not rich; it argues that it does not want to become hard-pressed through the collections for the *ptōchoi* in Jerusalem.

I cannot deal fully with the sources about Prisca, but should still like to say something about her political and Christian life. She was driven from Rome by the edict of Claudius against the Jews (A.D. 49—see Acts 18:2), but she also had experience later of the firm measures of Roman authorities. Paul says in Rom. 16:3 that Prisca and Aquila had risked their necks to save his life. Risk to the life of Paul and others like him came about in confrontation with the Roman authorities (see above all 2 Cor. 11:23; 1 Cor. 15:32; Rom. 8:35). Even if we do not know the particular circumstances, the assertions of Paul in Rom. 16:3 show pointedly just what a dangerous life these congregations of Christians led, what an important role mutual solidarity played, and that the women were just as much endangered as the men in conflicts with the authorities.

Prisca's work for the spreading of the gospel that Jesus is the Messiah probably began in Rome; she went to the synagogue on the sabbath in Rome as in Corinth (Acts 18:4). Whether she was able to read from the Torah and attest that Jesus is the Messiah we do not know. But in the gatherings of the Christian assemblies in private houses the women did speak in public, pray, and prophesy (1 Cor. 11:5), and also took part in discussions such as those with Apollos in Ephesus, who only knew the baptism of John (Acts 18:26). The active role of women in public within the Pauline congregations can be deduced from their relevance for all congregations, shown especially in the greetings-list in Rom. 16:3–16. In that list one-third of the persons mentioned by name are women (nine out of twenty-six), and women like men are distinguished by their work for the congregations, without any ranking between women and men being apparent.

This clear praxis of the Pauline congregations is already opposed in Paul by a contrary theory. In 1 Cor. 11:2–16 Paul shows, with a rather overdeveloped display of theological arguments, that the woman should publicly express her submission to the man by covering her head when praying and prophesying.

I do not want to go into detail about this text, but of fundamental importance is the question how one could arrive at such a theory within the setting of a contrary praxis. The question is moreover of fundamental importance because from this opinion of Paul there is a direct line to those Christian texts which have had such a disastrous effect for women: texts which demand that the women should keep quiet in the congregation or declare that she becomes blessed through bearing children, etc.

Why did this development take place? I can only state my hypothesis here, without really being able to substantiate it. The Roman state had an obvious interest in fighting against freedoms which women claimed publicly. It had a tremendous interest in the constant repetition of the picture of the ideal woman: she is only the wife of the man *(univira),* she practices the *lanificium—* spins wool, works at home, and obeys her husband. If a woman speaks in public, says Valerius Maximus, that shows that the state is shaken by anarchy. Paul, and other Christians with him and after him, have clearly given in to this pressure from outside. Why did they do that? How often has it been that women have been the oppressed among the oppressed? It does not reduce Paul in my eyes that he was a human-being like all others, that at a certain point he gave in to the pressure, which he probably did not find very important. It is *one* thing to make it clear why Paul behaved as he did in his historical situation. It is *another* how we deal with these expressions of opinion.

I should like to conclude by summarizing the methodological considerations concerning a social-historical exegesis. To do biblical exegesis means to see the connection between the realities of the lives of the people and the message of Christ they carried. I can, for example, only understand the message of the cross of Jesus when I grasp that those who preached that message were threatened by crucifixion, and that the symbol of the oppression of the Roman state became for them a sign of life. It is of critical importance theologically that the carriers of the gospel were the *ptōchoi* and the *penētes.*

The "reality of their lives" means their social reality in the widest sense: not only the spiritual and religious history, but also the political and social history. Or put in another way: Josephus is the most important New Testament commentator. It will not do that in New Testament studies the historical background remains a side-affair, and the social circumstances equally so.

To clarify further, biblical exegesis means that the social and political situation of the exegete is also part of the exegesis. As an exegete, it is necessary for me to consider my situation and to understand my exegesis in its own context. The phrase that man and woman should be one flesh can have quite a different sense depending on the context in which it is employed. It can also be a phrase which serves people's oppression.

Social-historical exegesis is an expression of *positive experience of the biblical tradition,* the experience that this tradition is capable of interpreting and changing my situation. From it we can understand that God is on the side of those who are made victims by the masters of this world.

NOTES

1. R. Pesch, *Das Markusevangelium II* (Freiburg, 1977), p. 505; M. Hengel, "Maria Magdalena und die Frauen als Zeugen," in *Abraham unser Vater, Festschrift O. Michel* (Leiden: Brill, 1963) pp. 243–56.

2. If Mark 15:40f has to be seen as the result of Mark's redaction-work, we can nevertheless draw the same conclusions from her name (Magdalene) and from her presence at the crucifixion of Jesus (Mark 15:47, 16:1).

3. Luise Schottroff and Walter Stegemann, *Jesus von Nazareth: Hoffnung der Armen* (Stuttgart: Kohlhammer 1978).

4. See esp. S. Applebaum, "Economic Life in Palestine," in *The Jewish People in the First Century II* (Assen/Amsterdam, 1976), pp. 632–700.

5. L. Schottroff, "Frauen in der Nachfolge Jesu in neutestamentlicher Zeit," in W. Schottroff and W. Stegemann, ed., *Traditionen der Befreiung,* (Munich, 1980), Vol. 2, pp. 91–133.

6. Adolf Von Harnack, *ZNW* 1 (1900): 16 ff.

7. K. Thraede, in G. Scharffenorth and K. Thraede, "Freunde in Christus werden . . ." (Gelnhausen, 1977), p. 97.

23

JOHN G. GAGER

Social Description and Sociological Explanation in the Study of Early Christianity: A Review Essay

A review of the social histories of early Christianity by R. Grant and A. Malherbe, and of the sociology of early Palestinian Christianity by G. Theissen, points up a number of key issues: the distinction between social description and sociological explanation, implicit and explicit use of sociological models, difficulty of establishing links between the religion and theology of early Christians and their social practice, confusion over how widely the categories "social/sociological" should extend, and the sociological import of a mixture of socially advantaged leaders and largely lower class followers in the early church. The reviewer gives his own views on the extent to which early Christian legitimation of empire (Grant's "Christian monarchism") was full endorsement of the state, and he also argues that rigid Roman class structure excluded people of high accomplishment and status from formal recognition and power until well into the third century.

Reprinted with permission, from *Religious Studies Review* 5 (July 1979): 174–80, published by the Council on the Study of Religion, Wilfred Laurier University, Waterloo, Ontario, Canada.

Robert M. Grant, *Early Christianity and Society: Seven Studies* (San Francisco: Harper & Row, 1977), x+21 pp., $10.00.

Abraham J. Malherbe, *Social Aspects of Early Christianity* (Baton Rouge and London: Louisiana State University Press, 1977), xii+98 pp., $7.95.

Gerd Theissen, *Sociology of Early Palestinian Christianity*. Translated by John Bowden (Philadelphia: Fortress Press, 1977), vii+131 pp., $4.50 paper.

There can be no denying that the simple passage of time contributes in significant, if imprecise ways to the open-ended character of all historical disciplines. Since the standpoint—call it the *Zeitgeist*—of all historians is subject to constant change, the historical subject itself, shaped as it is by the experience of historians, renews and transforms itself ceaselessly. In this sense, the intentions and actions of historians themselves are very much a part of the data. Herein lies the energy which constantly propels the resolution of all historical issues beyond the grasp of eager historians. For historians of early Christianity, then, the relevant data are never limited to the relatively constant mass of literary, epigraphic, or archaeological evidence.

For reasons that will not concern us here, the recent historiography of early Christianity has come increasingly to incorporate the pursuit of social history. But the term "social history" hardly conveys a full sense of the various species to be found under this general rubric. Indeed, the variety of species has given rise to occasional confusion about their proper definition. Terminological difficulties of this nature are bound to arise during the renaissance of any academic discipline and can be expected to recede as it moves toward maturity. One such instance involves the terms "social" and "sociological." Without seeking an elaborate justification, I would suggest that the term "social" should normally function to designate society or the social order. As such, it points to a particular aspect of our collective experience. But it does not indicate how we intend to approach or interpret whatever it is that we discover in the realm of the social. The term "sociological," however, clearly points us in the direction of a specific academic discipline—sociology—and thus introduces the full range of explanatory theories and hypotheses that characterize this discipline. To oversimplify, any sociological approach to early Christianity will be concerned with *explanations* of social facts, whereas a social history need not concern itself with anything more than a *description* of the relevant social data. The two approaches are certainly not antithetical; indeed, any sociological analysis must build upon the foundation of social historians. But neither are they identical. Each of these tasks is necessary *and* distinctive. It is a matter of good fortune that proponents and practitioners of these approaches have not been loathe to recognize this methodological pluralism and have resisted the urge to claim exclusive rights for any single direction. Parenthetically, I take this attitude of largesse as a measure of the maturity and self-confidence of the field as a whole.

As recently as five years ago, scarcely anyone would have ventured to predict a revival of interest in the social history of early Christianity. As things stand now, however, the case for the legitimacy and viability of the enterprise is clearly established and accepted. While it is still too early to determine whether this burst of energy will be sustained, it has already altered the shape of the field for all future members.

I

The three volumes under review in this essay illustrate nicely the major subdivisions within the broad framework of social and sociological studies of early Christianity. Abraham J. Malherbe's *Social Aspects of Early Christianity* concentrates, as the title suggests, on issues strictly within the early Christian movement as reflected in the writings of the New Testament: first, the social and educational level of its adherents, and, second, the organization of the early communities as house churches. Similarly, Robert M. Grant's *Early Christianity and Society* deals with social aspects and concerns of the Christian movement, though it is considerably broader in scope. Chronologically, it reaches to the end of the fourth century; and topically it covers the issues of population, politics, taxation, occupations, private property, almsgiving, and the financial base of Christian communities. Like Malherbe, Grant treats these topics by placing them squarely within the larger framework of Roman or Greco-Roman society. The third volume, Gerd Theissen's *Sociology of Early Palestinian Christianity,* shares Malherbe's focus on the earliest phase of Christian history, as reflected in the canonical Gospels and Paul's letters, and like Grant he stresses the importance of the immediate social and religious context, in this case Palestinian Judaism of the first century of the Christian era. What distinguishes Theissen from both Grant and Malherbe, however, is not the choice of topics or period, but rather his thoroughgoing sociological method. Though he never discusses particular theories in the text, and only rarely in the notes, and though he steadfastly—one supposes also self-consciously—refuses to identify himself with any particular school of sociology, he nonetheless presupposes and utilizes sociological theory throughout.[1]

II

Theissen's sociological perspective will create both excitement and frustration in many readers. His treatment of theory and method is limited to a scant two pages in the opening chapter. Sophisticated readers, schooled in the vagaries of recent sociological debate, will search in vain for clues to the sources of Theissen's own schooling and orientation. Worse still, the uninitiated or suspicious reader who harbors doubts about the viability of sociological treatments of any ancient religion, let alone early Christianity, will find it difficult to track down the theoretical literature that underlies Theissen's work at every point. Those who take the trouble to look into this literature will find it to be highly eclectic (see especially Theissen's theoretical essay).[2] Basically, Theissen's orientation is functional analysis, and within that tradition his mentors on this side of the Atlantic are Talcott Parsons and J. M. Yinger. Of the four chief functions of religion—domestication or socialization (described as integrating and restrictive; associated with Durkheim), compensation (described as antagonistic and conflict-producing; associated with Karl Marx), personalization (described as integrating and creative; illustrated by the work of Berger and Luckmann), and innovation (described as antagonistic, conflict-producing, and creative; associated with Weber's work on Protestantism and more recent studies of millenarian movements)—Theissen asserts that early Christianity falls into the category of innovation. Overall, he balances this functional analysis (Part Three) with a discussion of various external factors—economic, ecological, political, and cultural—which shaped the behavior of early Christians (Part Two) and a treatment of roles or "typical patterns of behavior" (Part One).

In calling attention to the theoretical infrastructure of Theissen's work, my intention is not so much to steer the discussion in a purely methodological direction, for such discussions tend to be pointless and endless, but to make two separate observations. First, and contrary to the impression created by the total absence of reference to sociological literature in the main body of the book, virtually every page relies on sociological assumptions of varying kinds and with clear pedigrees. This observation is not intended in any way as a criticism—indeed one of the attractive features of the book is its freedom from potentially distracting material—but to warn that it is not as methodologically simple and innocent as it might initially appear. Second, methodologically sophisticated readers may be surprised to discover the heavy reliance on older figures like Parsons and Yinger and the virtual silence on more recent developments. In particular, Theissen has totally passed over the extensive literature in English (Worsley, Burridge, Talmon, and Wallace among others) on chiliastic and millenarian movements in other parts of the globe. Once again, however, I make the observation not so much to criticize as to call attention to the particular configuration of Theissen's background and assumptions.

In the final analysis, with cooking as well as reviewing, the proof of the pudding lies in the eating. The ultimate test of any interpretation lies in its ability to bring new insights, to explain in broader terms and to reveal connections between apparently unrelated matters. And on these grounds, Theissen's efforts must be crowned with laurel. Among his numerous successes, the most striking is surely his work on the wandering charismatics in earliest Palestinian Christianity. By arguing that such figures constituted a basic type from the very beginning, he is able to demonstrate the existence of a "structural homologue" (p. 26)[3] in the Gospels between (a) images of Jesus,

(b) ideas of discipleship, (c) ethical injunctions, and (d) the life-style of these wandering charismatics. Each of these items reflects and reinforces the shape of the other. Furthermore, the life-style of these figures is in turn directly tied to socio-economic conditions of Palestine in the first century, conditions which are readily visible in other movements of the same period. As Theissen puts it, "the ethical radicalism of the synoptic tradition is connected with this pattern of wandering" (p. 15). Finally, he contends that it is no coincidence that we are able to uncover in the early tradition a convergence between small conventicles regarding themselves as "suffering outsiders" and a sharply dualistic and eschatological view of history.[4]

Two further aspects of the book deserve mention at this point. In the first place, he has made a significant advance over earlier discussions of the relationship between Palestinian Christianity and the broad religious and social setting of Jewish Palestine in the first century. No longer is it a matter of detecting "influences" of the Essenes or the Pharisees on the Christian movement. Instead we are urged to see these movements as differing responses—differing in part with respect to their "functions"—to a common set of circumstances. In accordance with this view, Theissen regularly draws parallels between other renewal movements, including the Essenes, the politically and religiously motivated groups of "robbers" cited by Josephus, the Zealots, and the Pharisees. At considerable length, he indicates some of their common traits: *economically,* these renewal groups drew heavily on the "many socially rootless people in Palestine" (p. 36), though he points out, as have other recent students of revolution, that the "social context of renewal movements within Judaism of the first century was not so much the lowest classes of all as a marginal middle class" (p. 46); *ecologically,* these movements reflected deep tensions between city and countryside, tensions which coincided in turn with a division between positive and negative attitudes toward Roman power and Hellenistic culture. In short, Christianity emerged as one among many social and religious experiments spawned by "a deep-seated crisis in Palestinian Jewish society" (p. 97).

In the final pages of this immensely stimulating study, Theissen turns his attention to the transition of Christianity from its Palestinian to its Hellenistic setting. His basic argument is that while the radical Christian experiment (wandering charismatics, eschatological expectations, hopes centered on the coming Son of Man) failed in its original Palestinian and Jewish setting, it survived in a profoundly transformed condition in the greater Greco-Roman world. Here the analysis is less successful. My own interest, however, is not to criticize but to suggest that the beginnings of a more adequate explanation of this transformation are already present in his earlier discussion of the wandering charismatics. In a chapter entitled "The Role of Sympathizers in the Local Communities," Theissen points to the existence of a second level and type of piety in the earliest gospel traditions—less radical, more community-oriented, and patriarchally structured. These scattered local communities functioned as support points for the wandering charismatics. But what Theissen apparently fails to recognize, or at least to emphasize, is that the less radical and more structured character of these communities provided the organizational bridge which made it possible for the movement as a whole to survive its traumatic transformation in the latter part of the first century. Also at this point, Theissen's discussion needs to be complemented and corrected by Malherbe's chapter on "House Churches and Their Problems." Malherbe mentions the importance of local communities in providing support to wandering figures like Paul, but unlike Theissen he does not overplay the differences between Palestine and the "Diaspora," nor does he reduce the local community in the early years to a peripheral and secondary status. Indeed, it can easily be maintained that the struggle between wandering and sedentary forms of leadership is just as visible during the early years in Palestine as in the later years of the "Diaspora."

The highest praise I can bestow on Theissen is to say that he has begun to do for primitive Christianity what E. R. Dodds[5] has done for Hellenistic Christianity. But a word of caution is necessary at this point. In his own words, Theissen's treatment of the Jesus-movement in Palestine is "based on a sociological theory of conflict" (pp. 114). But in turning to its expansion into the Roman world, where "it was given a positive welcome" (ibid.), he advocates "a sociological theory of integration [as] a more appropriate perspective" (p. 114f.). While I do not wish to deny the very real differences between the Palestinian and the extra-Palestinian stages of the Christian movement, I must note that Dodds' assessment of the Roman world and of Christianity's place in it is markedly different from Theissen's. And it draws heavily on the sociology and psychology of conflict.

III

Grant's volume makes no pretense whatsoever at sociological analysis. Like all of his work, it is lively, thorough, and intelligent. No one can fail to emerge better informed from a reading of his seven studies. Few readers will fail to be intrigued by his selection of topics and, in one or two cases, by his treatment of them. In the Preface, he hints at his principle of selection. "This book is intended for people whose interest in the life and thought of early Christianity is not strictly academic. In having to deal with the modern world, such readers have necessarily become interested in facts and figures, population trends, attitudes toward government, taxes and deductions, pros and cons of different occupations, property and charitable gifts, and buildings and capital funds" (p. vii). And so the chapters follow exactly this enumeration of modern interests. But we can hardly leave this list of topics without one or two observations.

In the first place, Grant clearly does not mean that the interest of his intended readers is "not strictly academic." What he means is that their interest is not strictly theological, exegetical, or ecclesiastical. In other words, he has focused much-needed attention on matters other than theology, liturgy, and ecclesiastical history—and he has done so in an academic manner. What he has not done is to explain how these "practical" problems connect with the "nonpractical" issues of theology, dogma, liturgy, and the like. And as a result he leaves us with the frustrating and surely incorrect impression that Christian social history and early Christian theology proceeded along two parallel but unrelated tracks. If we wish to avoid this serious misimpression, we have no choice but to enter the broad and dangerous realm of sociology.

In the second place, Grant's choice of topics reflects in many ways his own and his readers' social location as well-to-do, moderate, middle-class Americans. My quarrel is not with the social location as such. My point is rather that it may lead us, as scholars and readers, to overlook those places where the concerns of the past differ from our own. When we fail to correct for our biases, we inevitably miss voices other than our own.

Let me illustrate. In the section on early Christian views of work and occupations, it is surprising to find nothing about the largest single employer— then and now—the army. From Tertullian we know that the issue of military service was deeply controverted in certain circles. We also know that from the time of Constantine onward, the army was essentially a Christian institution. What happened in the third century to account for such a change? Surely, any explanation must take account of social factors. To take another example, in discussing the social status of early Christians, it would have been useful if Grant had treated such items as Christian views of pagan education, the educational level of the majority of Christians, and the emergence of distinctively Christian views on education. In treating alms, tithing, and endowments, more attention might have been directed to the eventual recipients of these benefices, i.e., those Christian and pagan poor cited by the emperor Julian. And finally, in discussing the extent to which "Christians shared the ideals of the dominant group in their society and did not innovate" (p. ix) Grant passes over completely the institutions of Christian asceticism and monasticism.

On matters of substance, the chapter entitled "Christian Devotion to the Monarchy" must be singled out for consideration, and in particular for its failure to deal with the problem of perspective. The central claim of the chapter is that with the exceptions of the Book of Revelation, Hippolytus, and Tertullian—Grant notes that the latter two eventually became sectarians— early Christianity was loyal to the emperor and to imperial institutions. Indeed, he characterizes the dominant view as "second-century Christian monarchism" (p. 25). Now a statement of this kind raises numerous questions:

1. Normally one speaks of loyalty to monarchy in a setting of diverse and conflicting political alternatives, as in reference to the loyalists among the early English settlers in America. Such was clearly not the case in second- or third-century imperial Rome. As a matter of practical experience, few people had ever known any political system other than a monarchy. Even the philosophical literature on political theory offered no real alternatives. Political

dissent in this literature is limited to the avowal that the monarchy occasionally fell into the wrong hands. Almost never do we find direct assaults on the idea of monarchy as such. Thus at a time when monarchy was the only practical or theoretical model available, it is not surprising or informative to learn that most Christian writers were devoted to the monarchy.

2. Nonetheless it remains true that numerous authors urged their fellow Christians to honor the emperor. This effort alone presupposes at least the possibility of disloyalty. But putting aside Hippolytus and Tertullian, Grant is correct in his conclusion that we will look in vain for a Christian literature of dissent. There are several possible explanations of this fact, among them the instinct for survival. But theological reasons must also have weighed heavily. For any denial of loyalty to the emperor brings us perilously close to a denial of divine creation and providence. One way around this difficulty was to uphold the view, as many Christian and pagan authors did, that while the empire itself was a providential institution, one could distinguish between good and bad emperors. Beyond this, if we look at other than literary sources, Christian political dissent can be found with ease. Without arguing the case at present, I would simply point to the Christian martyrs or again to the ascetics as figures who expressed their political dissent through the symbolic medium of the human body. To ignore such "dissenters" is to overlook a silent, though powerful minority in the early centuries of Christian development.

3. Finally, whatever one says about loyalty to the monarchy from the Christian perspective, the most serious objection arises from the fact that no influential pagan was ever convinced of Christian loyalty. From the very beginning, Christians proclaimed their political innocence—but never successfully. The problem was one of perspective. For their part, Christians failed to understand, or at least to accept, the idea that loyalty to the monarchy was not simply, as we would put it, a "political" matter. In pagan eyes, loyalty to Christianity, which entailed at the very least a denial of the preeminent role of the gods, was by itself sufficient proof of political disloyalty. And to confirm their doubts, they had only to look in the direction of the Christian martyrs. In so doing, I would argue that these pagan critics understood the latent political features of these figures better than did Christians themselves. In short, even if we could accept the idea of "Christian monarchism" as accurately reflecting the views of most Christians, we would still have to conclude that it never even approached the pagan understanding of "devotion to the monarchy."

IV

Like Grant, Malherbe is concerned with the social aspects of early Christianity. Unlike Grant, he focuses more narrowly and intensively on topics within the New Testament: "Social Level and Literary Culture" (Chapter 2) and "House Churches and Their Problems" (Chapter 3). In the "Prolegomena" (Chapter 1), he states the case for a social approach largely in terms of the social function of New Testament literary forms. "The sources that concern us are, primarily, the New Testament. . . . We must begin with these writings, and we must read them with a sensitivity to their social dimensions before we hasten to draw larger patterns" (p. 17). It is worth mentioning that while the author speaks here and elsewhere of the New Testament, it is really the letters of Paul that give the book its sense of continuity.

While placing himself in the tradition of earlier social historians such as Shailer Matthews, Ernst Troeltsch, and Adolf Deissmann, Malherbe is not hesitant to criticize their tendency to stress the total community (as witnessed by their concern for communal structure and leadership) and thereby to neglect or minimize the role of leaders like Paul. In fact, his stance on this particular issue is by no means inconsequential, for the importance of Christian leaders figures prominently in his argument that the social level and literary culture of early Christians are higher than has been traditionally assumed. "When Paul says that not many of the Corinthian Christians were from the upper social strata, he assumes that some, at least, were. Although they may only have been a minority, *they were a dominating minority*" (p. 72; emphasis added). I do not wish to deny that it is sometimes possible to eat one's cake and have it too, but in this instance we need to distinguish properly between the issues of political leadership and social constituency. There is no question—nor have many thought to assert otherwise—that the documents of early Christianity in general and of Paul in particular reflect a degree of literary skill on the part of their authors. But the methodological issue at stake here—and it is one that of necessity involves theories of social institutions—concerns the relative weight to be assigned to followers and leaders in any definition and description of the social world of early Christianity. Given this reservation, however, Malherbe has performed an important service in calling attention to certain distinctive features of early Christian literature. Whether Paul's literary style presupposes a second- or third-level schooling in rhetoric, he was neither unskilled nor untutored as a writer. Beyond this, and of greater social significance, is the strong influence of Septuagint mannerisms throughout the New Testament. For as A. D. Nock observes,[6] these usages "are the product of an enclosed world living its own life, a ghetto culturally and linguistically." Malherbe makes use of this observation to argue that the very language of the New Testament reveals "the mind-set of a minority group" (p. 38).

The issues raised by the phrase "the mind-set of a minority group" would seem to cry out for analysis in terms of contemporary work in sociology and anthropology. Although Malherbe has not chosen this path—indeed he seems rather dubious about its value—he has pursued the equally important task of looking closely at early Christian house churches as social institutions. Several aspects of these house churches bear directly on themes in early Christian literature: the emphasis on hospitality as an expression of *agape* (e.g., Rom. 13:8–13) suggests that talk about love in some communities was directly related to the mobility of apostles and other Christian travellers; the setting of the house church in an urban setting had the effect of heightening the minority group mind-set as well as creating a social context which offered a sense of "security and . . . belonging not provided by larger political and social structures" (p. 69); and the presence of members from different layers of Roman society leads Malherbe, following Theissen, to consider the possibility of a direct correlation between different social strata and the theological disputes which had splintered the community in Corinth. Although Malherbe pronounces himself unconvinced by Theissen's arguments, he does contend that a view of the early communities "as comprising a cross-section of most of Roman society" (p. 87) places earlier discussions (Georg Heinrici and Edwin Hatch) concerning relationships between Christian communities and pagan religious associations in a different light. In particular, he proposes that further attention be given to connections between house churches and *collegia* or guild halls.

As a concluding note, I should like to call attention to an instance of terminological ambiguity which may in turn conceal a deeper conceptual difficulty. As noted at the outset of this essay, there are important and obvious differences between social and sociological approaches to the study of religious traditions. Malherbe's approach is resolutely social and as such requires no further apology. Unfortunately, however, he persistently describes his approach as sociological, despite the presence of what I take to be a pronounced aversion to sociological analysis in the proper sense, i.e., the use of methods and models drawn from the field of sociology. The deeper uncertainty reveals itself in a warning against developing "excessive enthusiasm" for social interpretations (p. 11). This warning is followed by the remark that "the communities themselves came into existence in response to *preaching*, and social factors no doubt contributed to that response. But it was to the *preaching* that appeal was made in the documents that sought to direct the life and thought of the communities" (p. 11; emphasis added). Even within the arena of social, as distinct from sociological analysis, this attempt to circumscribe the influence of social factors rests on an underlying conceptual difficulty. Once one undertakes a social analysis of early Christianity, there is no need or justification for setting arbitrary limits to what can and cannot come under scrutiny. In particular, preaching would appear to be a natural candidate, for preaching is preeminently a "social fact"—it is both traditional and communal in nature (cf. 1 Cor. 15); it takes place in public and interactive settings; and it is coercive in its impact, that is, it constrains, elicits, and changes behavior. In brief, once we embark on the course of social or sociological analysis, there is no need to protect or preserve anything from our inquiry. For the goal of such analysis is not to reduce any phenomenon, whether preaching or the New Testament canon itself, to "purely social" factors, but to assess the significance of social factors in all forms of public behavior.

V

Recent social histories of early Christianity have returned repeatedly to the matter of social status. One common feature of these studies is a trend in the direction of upgrading the social location of many early believers. Malherbe speaks of "the emerging consensus on the social status of early Christians . . . as comprising a cross section of most of Roman society" (pp. 86f.). In large part, the proponents of this new view see themselves as correcting earlier presentations of early Christianity as exclusively proletarian, a movement of slaves, laborers, and outcasts of various sorts. While it may be seriously doubted that such a view ever existed apart from a few romantics and early Marxists, this renewed interest in the issue of social location will undoubtedly contribute to a better understanding of these persistently controversial matters.

At the outset it is important to observe that one factor has remained constant, even granted the new consensus. Earlier social historians were led to posit the proletarian constituency of early Christianity *in large part* to explain the "revolutionary" character of the new religion. In other words, this social surmise—perhaps it was more of a premise—was based on an underlying theoretical postulate that revolutions arise from the downtrodden mass of the lowest social classes. More recent work by historians, sociologists, and anthropologists has shown that the social sources of revolution lie higher up in the social order. Thus it could be argued that one impetus for upgrading the social status of early Christians stems from a continuing need to explain the revolutionary character of the religion while taking account of newer theoretical work on the social roots of revolutionary movements:

> One often comes across the rather naive idea that economic pressure leads to changes of attitude and protest predominantly among the lowest class. In reality, people are activated above all when their situation threatens to deteriorate. . . . This is why in many protest movements we find members of the upper classes—often in leading roles [Theissen, p. 39].

Theissen's salient remark points to a distinction that has often been neglected. If leaders constitute approximately 10 percent of the total membership in a particular community, it remains true that 90 percent are not leaders and that 90 percent of our information concerns this small, though important minority. Thus we must not draw hasty generalizations about the majority of believers from what we can conclude about their leaders. As Theissen observes, "most of the members of Christian communities came from the lower classes" (p. 116). Very much in line with this necessary and obvious distinction is Paul's much discussed and often overinterpreted comment in 1 Cor. 1:26 that "not many" of the Corinthians were wise, powerful, or of noble birth. At most we may infer from his words that a minority of the Corinthians thought of themselves as wise, powerful, or of noble birth. On the other hand, few have ever propounded any other reading of this text. While this minimalist interpretation does not mean, as Grant and others have properly cautioned, that Christianity was "a proletarian mass movement," neither does it mean, as Grant states in the same context, that "the triumph of Christianity . . . took place from the top down" (Grant, p. 11).

One further distinction is essential to any responsible analysis of social location in the later stages of pagan Rome—the distinction between social class and social status. Unlike most modern and Western societies, Rome defined its hierarchical class structure in clear and unmistakable legal terms. Senators and knights constituted the upper echelons (*honestiores*), even though they represented a small percentage of the total population. Below them fell the large mass of free citizens (*humiliores*) and still deeper came slaves and freedmen. Though the specific terms and regulations might vary from place to place, this system of classes or orders prevailed throughout the Roman Empire. Only with the social and economic crisis of the third century does the picture change materially as large numbers of newcomers are elevated, literally promoted, to the upper classes as replacements for the increasingly decimated old aristocracies. In unprecedented fashion, social status was converted into social class.[7]

With this brief sketch in mind, we must immediately add that such matters as wealth, education, and life-style could be and normally were quite independent of social class. These attributes regularly conferred social *status*; but until the third century they never qualified individuals for membership in a social *class*. Many freedmen enjoyed great wealth and education. But unless and until they were officially promoted to the ranks of the *honestiores*, their reward was status rather than class. As M. I. Finley remarks of the hero in Petronius' *Satyricon*, "Trimalchio . . . was no parvenu, it has been cogently said, for he never arrived."[8]

The distinction between class and status is important initially because it eliminates the pseudo-problem of having to account for the presence of relatively wealthy or cultured individuals in early Christian communities. To admit that some Christians were educated and wealthy does not alter the fact that these individuals, whatever their *status*, represented the lower levels of the Greco-Roman system of social *classes*. Furthermore, I would contend that it is precisely this distinction between class and status that makes it possible to explain why some persons of relatively high social status, but few of high social class, were attracted to Christianity in the first two centuries. At this point let me recall Theissen's comments quoted above about participation of members of the upper classes in protest movements (Theissen, p. 39) and draw attention to the pertinent observations of K. O. L. Burridge: "Where two groups or categories of persons share the same values or assumptions, but only one of these groups or categories has access to the rewards or benefits implied in the shared values, then the *guru* or prophet is generated, new assumptions enter the arena, a new group or category of persons may come into being."[9] With these words in mind we may give an altogether different reading of E. A. Judge's correct, though misleading statement that "far from being a socially depressed group . . . the Christians were dominated by a socially pretentious section of the population of the big cities."[10] They were drawn, one might say, to a religion with revolutionary implications precisely because of their frustrated social aspirations. For as a group they equalled and often exceeded the wealth and education of the *honestiores* but, like Trimalchio, found themselves denied access to the rewards reserved exclusively for those whose names were inscribed on the lists of the highest orders.

As a final comment, I cannot resist citing a line from Judge's study: "Modern Christians, uneasy about the respectability of a faith that is supposed to have revolutionary implications, like to cultivate the idea that it first flourished among the depressed sections of society."[11] Conversely, modern interpreters who advocate a social upgrading of the early Christians should be on guard lest their own respectability find its way into the machinery of their social analysis.

NOTES

1. For an excellent survey of Theissen's extensive list of publications, see John H. Schütz, "Steps toward a Sociology of Primitive Christianity: A Critique of the Work of Gerd Theissen." Schutz presented his review to the working group on the "Social World of Early Christianity" at the annual meeting of the AAR/SBL in December 1977.

2. Gerd Theissen, "Theoretische Probleme religionssoziologischer Forschung und die Analyse des Urchristentums," *NZSTR* 16 (1974): 35–56.

3. See also Mary Douglas, *Natural Symbols: Explorations in Cosmology* (New York: Random House, Vintage, 1973), pp. 98–100, esp. p. 98: "There are pressures to create consonance between the perception of social and physiological levels of experience."

4. Again, see Douglas, *Natural Symbols*, pp. 144–45, for a discussion of the relationship between dualistic cosmologies and "small bounded communities."

5. E. R. Dodds, *Pagan and Christian in an Age of Anxiety: Some Aspects of Religious Experience from Marcus Aurelius to Constantine* (Cambridge: Cambridge University Press, 1965).

6. A. D. Nock, "The Vocabulary of the New Testament," *JBL* 52 (1933): 35.

7. Peter Brown, *The World of Late Antiquity from Marcus Aurelius to Muhammad, 150–750* (London: Thames and Hudson, and New York: Harcourt, Brace, 1971), pp. 60–68.

8. M. I. Finley, *The Ancient Economy* (Berkeley: University of California Press, 1973), p. 51.

9. Kenelm Burridge, *New Heaven, New Earth: A Study of Millenarian Activities* (New York: Schocken Books, 1969), p. 95.

10. E. A. Judge, *The Social Patterns of Christian Groups in the First Century* (London: Tyndale Press, 1960), p. 60.

11. Ibid., p. 51.

24

ROBERT H. SMITH

Were the Early Christians Middle-Class? A Sociological Analysis of the New Testament

The stock picture of early Christians is that they were economically poor and socially deprived. Recent sociological studies of wandering charismatic Christian preachers and healers who lived on voluntary gifts (G. Theissen), of the rurally-oriented Marcan community (H. C. Kee), and of deprivation as a large factor in early Christian conversions (J. Gager) have underscored this customary view of the early Christians as overwhelmingly lower class.

On the other hand, the community of Matthew appears to be reasonably affluent, moderately educated, and much disturbed by excessive charismatic behavior. First Corinthians attests to a number of Christians with adequate and even ample means, as do also the reports of Acts. Jesus and the disciples were largely "free workmen, craftsmen, small businessmen, and independent farmers." Many early Christians could be justly called "middle class."

Reprinted from *Currents in Theology and Mission* 7 (1980): 260–76.

Our current stake in the social composition of early Christians needs to be more closely examined. Do we present Christians seek escape in a notion of bygone simplicity and "holy poverty"? Do we work off guilt about our own affluence and ineffectuality by idealizing the selfless early Christians? If there were many socioeconomic patterns and class levels among the first Christians, is any of them normative for us? Do we take a cheap and easy comfort in finding that many early Christians may have been economically comfortable like ourselves? Are we reassured or threatened by what we learn about the standards of living and economic practices of the first Christians? What is the relationship between psychological or sociological conditions and receptivity to the Christian gospel?

For a very long time Sunday sermons, Hollywood movies, and scholarly books have been unwitting collaborators. They have worked together to fix in the popular mind a graphic portrait of the social standing of Jesus, his first circle of disciples, the earliest Christian congregations, and the whole Christian church up to the time of Constantine in the early fourth century.

First of all, I want to display that popular picture so you can see for yourself whether it does not tally with what you have heard repeatedly in churches and seen time and again in theaters. One stream in contemporary sociological study of the New Testament supports that picture.

Then I will introduce contrary voices and allow a different picture to emerge. A swelling chorus today is declaring on the basis of biblical and later evidence that the pre-Constantinian church was very largely what we today call middle-class, not landless peasants or urban slaves, as in the first picture, and not noble aristocrats either. Matthew will serve as a test case within the New Testament era.

And finally it will be useful to raise some questions about relevance: why have so many of us found agreeable that popular picture of the earliest Christians as slaves and persecuted minority? What use should we make of our present-day deductions regarding the economic and social status of Jesus and his earliest followers? Must we today adopt their stance toward the larger society (whether they were revolutionaries or mystics or comfortably in the middle)?

THE STOCK PICTURE

"Like Jesus himself, the first Christians belonged to the lowest classes of society and were mostly rural peasants, poor urban laborers, or slaves; they shared generously with one another what little they had in the way of this world's goods, and a basic feature of their life was the daily or weekly communal meal; each was brother or sister to the other, and they recognized no hard and fast distinctions of higher or lower, of male or female, of slave or free among them; leaders and doers arose spontaneously to meet specific needs but there was no fixed or regular structure, no complicated internal politics, no division into clergy and lay, officer and mere member; all were spirit-filled charismatics enjoying divine guidance not through tradition and rule and office but immediately in vision, dream, and prophecy; they were all alike determined pacifists and rarely claimed public attention except in time of civil persecution, when, unjustly accused, they were dragged off to serve the public's craving for spectacle. Only later—long after the period represented by our New Testament documents, and perhaps not until Constantine, who became the first Christian emperor in A.D. 325—were the early charismatic fires banked and only then did the church gradually settle down and carve out a niche for itself in the world and become increasingly stratified, tradition-oriented, law-ruled, and bookish, comfortable, and even secular. And only then did Christianity begin to penetrate the middle and upper classes."

So goes the stereotype. It is safe to omit references to films like *Barabbas, The Robe, Ben Hur,* and all the others that have contributed to the picture. We turn to look at other sources and supports of the picture. It has been expanded and refined by a series of recent scholarly essays working with theoretical tools of modern sociology, and it has been nourished by attention to passages in the Gospels, in the early chapters of the Book of Acts, and by words of Paul in 1 Cor. 1:26–30. First a look at just a few sociological studies.[1]

Mark's Community and Cynic-Stoic Preachers

While Matthew will serve below as our chief focus and test case, it will be useful to begin with a description recently drawn of Mark's community, because it seems to fit the popular picture sketched above, and because Matthew, in using Mark, altered many details and so revealed his biases.

Howard Clark Kee thinks that while Mark may have been written in Rome (an old idea about the Gospel), it was more likely a product of "Eastern Mediterranean rural or village culture."[2] Even more specifically he thinks the Marcan community had its base in rural and small-town southern Syria, someplace in the boondocks outside Antioch and Damascus but not so far south as Palestine. Nevertheless Kee is more interested in the cultural than in the physical geography. He notes in Mark a "clear antipathy toward the city," an attitude that is in fact "anti-city."[3] In editorial sections of the Gospel (in the links between the traditional paragraphs of material, in the settings which Mark has himself supplied) Jesus is pictured as avoiding the cities. He characteristically teaches and acts "on a hill," "by the sea," "in the desert," "on the green grass." Down to the very end Jesus lives outside Jerusalem, entering the city daily to teach but retiring each evening. He announces the destruction of that city and is himself killed there.

In the ancient world Kee sees close parallels to the style of Jesus and the first Christians in the Essenes of Qumran (producers of the Dead Sea Scrolls) and in the Cynic-Stoic charismatic preacher-philosophers.

The Essenes stood in the Jewish-Hasidic-apocalyptic tradition: anti-city, anti-temple, anti-world, pious, devout and prayerful, looking for the resolution of cosmic conflict by divine intervention and for the early vindication of the faithful elect. Cynic-Stoic philosophers wandered from village to village and gained adherents by preaching, healing, and exorcisms and supported themselves by begging and depending on local hospitality.

The members of Mark's community did not retreat into the desert like Essenes but felt sent upon a worldwide mission like that of the Cynic-Stoic wandering teachers. They went out preaching and practicing exorcism (3:14; 6:12–13.) as Jesus had (1:39), and so exercised a prophetic-charismatic ministry. Members underwent a social and economic transformation as they abandoned their families and erstwhile means of livelihood, just as the first disciples had (1:20; 6:7–13; cf. Diogenes Laertius 6:13, 33). The community was marked by new forms of security and solidarity compensating for the call to abandon wealth and break family ties (10:28–31.). The Marcan community was also peculiarly open to women—even Gentile women—and children (1:31; 10:30; 15:41; 7:24–30; 9:33–37; 10:13, 16). The community was not a politically active entity but adopted a posture of deliberate pacifism (12:13–16; 10:42–45).

Kee's work is scholarly rather than popular and operates at a high level of sophistication with a variety of data. He examines every possible hint of Mark's social and cultural situation. In the end he sees Mark meshing rather neatly with Acts and 1 Corinthians and fitting comfortably into the popular picture. Of course he sharpens the focus, calls parallels to the witness stand, and works with a carefully articulated perspective.

Early Christianity as Millenarian Movement

In a celebrated work John Gager has offered a theoretical framework within which to ponder the origins and growth of the first Christian communities.[4] His ruminations seem to confirm the popular portrait and are close to Kee's hypothesis regarding Mark.

Gager's basic paradigm is neither the ancient Hasidic or Essene community nor the Cynic-Stoic troupe. It is the millenarian movement. (Kee regards the Essene and Cynic-Stoic movements as quite similar to millenarianism).

Millenarian movements attract the disinherited, and Gager proceeds to describe various facets of disinherited existence in first-century Palestine. (1) Political alienation was the pervasive Palestinian atmosphere under Roman occupation. (2) The Roman colonizers and occupiers practiced systematic taxation and rigid control of money, and a crisis of finance always generates a crisis of human dignity. (3) Religiously considered, the converts to the new movement seem not to have included any Pharisees other than Paul, any priests other than some of the poor and powerless men of the lower orders, or any Essenes. Thus the first converts did not represent the religious establishment but came from the ranks of the "impure outsiders" (the people of the land or *am ha-aretz*).

Deprivation is the best description of the situation of the earliest Christian community, according to Gager. The deprived who entered the church stood in the tradition of apocalyptic Judaism, politically unorganized but also uncontrolled by those in power and so perceived as a threat, not necessarily from the lowest social and economic classes but embracing an ideal glorifying poverty.

Gager believes that a prophet serves as catalyst in the generation of a millenarian movement out of a mass of deprived persons. He is sometimes not the direct cause of the movement but rather the symbolic focus of the concerns and aspirations of the community.

Being deprived outsiders had as its correlate an "intense preoccupation with the unity" of the congregation (p. 33) and Christians went through a "stage of anti-structure" in which they abolished all status and distinctions in their midst.

A caution is in order: Gager's analysis is more finely tuned than the preceding summary can indicate. He speaks of "relative deprivation" (p. 27), a sensing of a gap between actuality and expectation, of rising aspiration, frustrated by circumstance. He does not mean that every early Christian was dirt-poor, illiterate, and spit on by all comers. Yet he thinks deprivation is the best description of the situation (inner and outer) of those first drawn to the Christian movement.

Wandering Charismatics

A third example of sociological analysis may be cited even more briefly than the preceding two. Gerd Theissen[5] focuses on biblical texts which speak approvingly of the most radical forms of behavior: leaving father and mother and children, relinquishing house and home and job, releasing the grip on possessions, turning the back on all claims to defense and protection (see, for example, Mark 1:16-20; 10:28-30; Matt. 5:38-41; 6:25-32; 8:20-22; 10:10; 19:10-11). He seeks a home for all these texts. He asks questions such as "Who preserved these texts? Who lived by them?"

He believes that Christians in the years A.D. 30-70 fell into two major groups: (1) The decisive figures in early Christianity were wandering charismatics: traveling apostles, prophets, and disciples characterized by homelessness, lack of family, and the relinquishing of all wealth, possessions, and security. Not only were Peter and Paul travelers (1 Cor. 9:5), but at Antioch of Syria, for example, there were Christian leaders from all over the Roman world: Barnabas of Cyprus, Lucius from Cyrene, Menaen brought up with Herod Antipas at Rome or Jerusalem. (2) The wandering charismatics were supported morally and materially by sympathizers settled in local communities. The sympathizers were more moderate, making compromises with the world and not renouncing it totally as the radical, wandering charismatics had done (see Luke 8:2–3; 10:38–42; etc.).

The wandering apostles had an analogy in the itinerant Cynic philosophers, and the division of the complex movement into more radical and more temperate segments has an analogy in the Essene movement. While Cynics and Essenes are the basic analogies identified by Theissen, he finds parallels to some early Christian attitudes toward wealth and the wealthy landowners, toward the city, toward the temple with its cult and priesthood, toward Gentiles and the Romans in particular, not only among Cynics and Essenes but also among resistance fighters, prophetic movements (Jewish and Samaritan), and other groups.

These scholarly sociological studies of the early Christians seem largely to support the popular caricature, as they portray a movement inhabiting the cultural backwaters, led by charismatically endowed exorcists, healers, and teachers who had radically renounced the things of this world.

In significant ways these recent studies stand in a succession with older works of people like Karl Kautsky, Adolf Deissmann, and Ernst von Dobschütz. Kautsky analyzed Christian origins from the perspective of Marxist social and historical theories. For him the earliest Christians were proletarian—uneducated, disinherited, alienated—eagerly practicing the communism which they believed Jesus had taught. Later, as the gospel penetrated upward into monied and ruling classes, the revolutionary fervor died and the movement was co-opted by the very classes against which it had originally been directed.

Deissmann found the closest analogies to the language of the New Testament in the colloquial papyri recovered from the rubbish heaps of Egypt at the end of the last century. To Deissmann the language was an index of low social standing. Primitive Christianity was a movement of the weary and the heavy-laden, people lacking both power and position, the poor, the base, the foolish. And yet Deissmann insisted on adding to the preceding description the qualifying phrase "on the whole." Von Dobschütz attempted a description not merely of the dogmatic and ethical teaching of the earliest Christians but of their ethos, their actual behavior, style, attitudes, and patterns of life.

The work of Kee, Gager, Theissen, and others is an effort at renewing sociological analysis of New Testament texts by taking advantage of developments in the field of sociology after the time of these pioneers working in Germany and following upon the labors of the Chicago School, especially Shirley Jackson Case and Shailer Matthews.[6]

MATTHEW: A TEST CASE

Recent study of Matthew sees the first Gospel as revealing at least one influential early Christian author who does not fit the stock picture. Matthew and his community do *not* seem to fit the popular picture of unlearned evangelist and unwashed people. These results should make us hesitate to accept the popular portrait and should make us wonder about the adequacy (or at least the sole sufficiency) of the millenarian, the Essenic, or the Cynic-Stoic models.

Matthew's Community: Not Rural

Matthew has altered the setting of the ministry of Jesus offered in Mark, and in fact Matthew's Gospel has "an undeniable urban character." Throughout the first Gospel Jesus' activity is city-oriented. Capernaum is designated as "his own city" (8:1). From there he makes forays into the surrounding countryside, but he continually returns home to the city. His disciples traveled from city to city (10:11–15,23; 23:34). Matthew was most likely writing for an urban community, "for people who, like Jesus, have their home in the city." They were not rustics.[7]

Matthew's Community: Not Poor

Furthermore the audience seems to have consisted of "affluent Christian Jews who probably belonged to upper-class society." Genealogies were especially safeguarded as the historical records of the urban elite. They served to record a family's pedigree and defended its prestige. Matthew's audience apparently included many landholders, merchants, businessmen, and entrepreneurs. They were people who would appreciate the words on debtors and courts in 5:25–26, be startled by the suggestions regarding generosity (so unbusinesslike!) in 5:39–42 and the casual attitude toward sound financial planning in 6:19, be captivated by the dealer in pearls (13:45–46) and confounded by the logic of the landowner in 20:1–16, and would need the warning about the fate of those who have this world's goods but fail to share their resources with "the least of these my brethren" (25:31–46). Matthew has a more extensive vocabulary of coinage and wealth than Mark or Luke.[8] If Matthew's community contained a sizable group of relatively affluent merchants and businessmen, then it does not fit the popular portrait of early Christians.

Matthew's Community: Not Unschooled

The Gospel according to Matthew is a literary piece, sophisticated in construction and in theological argument, exhibiting a far greater mastery of the Greek language than his predecessor Mark.[9] Matthew had apparently enjoyed some considerable schooling, a privilege of the upper class. Most modern commentators on Matthew see the author mirrored not in the tax collector Matthew-Levi of 9:9, but in the scribe of 8:19 and 13:52. The scribe initiated into the kingdom, and that means taught by Jesus the messianic interpreter of the Torah, brings forth teachings old and new, both traditional and startlingly fresh. He does it like a man who pays out coins of various ages and reigns—all of them genuine, none of them counterfeit—so he is not afraid of the account he must render on the day of reckoning (13:52; 12:35-37).

It was Ernst von Dobschütz (1928) who suggested that the Gospel according to Matthew was written as a manual of discipline and catechism for Christian behavior by a rabbi trained in the Jewish school of Johanan ben Zakkai and subsequently converted to Christianity. Philip Carrington (1940) spoke of a Matthean school, whose teachers parallel the elders and teachers of ancient Judaism. G. D. Kilpatrick (1946) pictured Matthew's community at prayer, using pieces of the gospel tradition for liturgical reading and homiletical exposition in the midst of the worshiping community.

Krister Stendahl in reviewing the work of predecessors lauds the increasingly insistent accent on the actual life situation of the community and exploits the suggestion that the material in Matthew's Gospel has the character of a manual or handbook intended particularly for the leaders of the church.[10] He compares the Gospel of Matthew with the Qumran *Manual of Discipline (Rules of the Community,* 1QS) and the early Christian *Didache.*

Stendahl sees strong evidence of scholarly activity behind the production of the Gospel in its systematic teaching and its neat and symmetrical arrangement of material into clusters of threes, fives, sevens, and tens, in its developed casuistry (as opposed to the repetition of broad ethical principles), in its application of tradition to fresh situations in church life, in its reflection upon the duties and position of the church leaders and, above all, in its ingenious interpretation of the Old Testament in a method reminiscent of that practiced at Qumran. Jesus forbade his disciples to be called rabbi, father, or teacher (23:8-10), a caution with relevance only if something very similar to a rabbinic school existed in the church. Stendahl, opposing the notion that the Christian leaders were wandering missionary preachers, says it was the social pattern of the rabbi and his disciples which made the deepest imprint on the life of the early church as we see it in Matthew's Gospel.

Matthew's Community: Anticharismatic as Much as Charismatic

It is generally agreed that Matthew's Gospel comes from a Jewish-Christian community with a strong antipathy toward certain elements in the synagogue. No one needs to be reminded that Matthew includes sharp rebukes of his fellow Jews who refused to confess Jesus as "the Christ, the Son of the living God" (16:16). Chapter 23 is a notorious denunciation of scribes and Pharisees who teach Moses without Christ.

Less frequently observed are the attacks of Jesus upon certain charismatics.[11] Toward the end of the Sermon on the Mount, Matthew records Jesus' warning to the community about "false prophets in sheep's clothing" (7:15-20). These enemies of the community are Christians (sheep), not Jewish or pagan outsiders. They confess Jesus in language sufficiently orthodox:

"Lord, Lord" (7:21-22). That is also the cry of both sheep and goats in the parable of the last judgment (25:37,44), and throughout the Gospel it is the specifically Christian way of addressing Jesus. This correctly formulated way of hailing Jesus is probably not just liturgical convention or brief creed, but inspired utterance (see 1 Cor. 12:3). Nevertheless in spite of their inspired and orthodox confession, those Christian prophets are exposed as false by the fact that they are not bearing good fruit (7:15-20). They are "evildoers" or, more literally, "workers of lawlessness" (7:23).

Lawlessness *(anomia)* is a Matthean word and a Matthean worry. It describes the scribes and Pharisees once (23:28) but is used of Christians three times (7:23; 13:41; 24:12). Looking ahead to the days of the church and the end of history, Jesus says that many people will give up their faith and begin to betray and hate one another (24:10). Here hatred and faith are unexpected opposites; for Matthew both have a deeply ethical and equally religious content. Betrayal and hate are fertile ground for false prophets and their deceptions (24:11). And again it is rather surprising that deception is spelled out, not in doctrinal or speculative, but in ethical terms. Deception means there will be a spread of lawlessness. Lawlessness is the way Matthew describes the cooling love, the easy morality, the stance both in behavior and in teaching of those who come under the influence of the false prophets with their deceptions (24:12). He warns that at "the end of the age" (13:40; 28:20) the angels will gather up the doers of lawlessness and cast them into the fire (13:36-43).

Their exclusion from the kingdom comes as a surprise to them (25:1-13, 14-30,41-46; 22:11-14). But why are they startled? How could they possibly have expected to get in? On what basis? Apparently on the basis of their charismatic endowment. That is, they esteemed their spiritual gifts and powers as infallible evidence of God's indwelling and therefore of God's favor and acceptance of them as the children or people of God. They had no doubt that they were spiritual people, God's people, because the gifts of the Spirit were clearly displayed among them: tongues and spiritual utterance, exorcisms, prophecy, and the power to do miracles (7:15-23). The possession of the Spirit and the manifestation of the gifts of the Spirit had become their boast and the ground of their confidence.

Matthew, like Paul, is basically positive about the Spirit and about spiritual endowments. The very fact that Matthew speaks not simply of prophets and charismatics but also of "false" prophets shows that he assumed that there are "true" prophets and so "true" charismatics. He describes Christian discipleship in terms of charismatic deeds and charismatic speech in Jesus' mission discourse (10:5-20). Jesus was himself conceived by the Spirit (1:18,20) and endowed with the Spirit at his baptism (3:16; 4:1); and he performed charismatic deeds of healing, exorcism, and raisings of the dead (11:2-6). Matthew apparently uses "prophet" alongside "little ones," "righteous person," and "disciple" as synonyms, all equivalent to "Christian" (10:41-42). If "prophet" is a synonym for "Christian," then Matthew has a very high view indeed of the charismatic endowments in the congregations. If "prophet" designates only some especially gifted Christians, then Matthew still thought of all Christians as possessing the Spirit or as being alive in the Spirit (see Rom. 8:9). And of course Matthew's estimate of the Old Testament prophets is incomparably high.

Nevertheless, Matthew time and again betrays his uneasiness with certain charismatics. His formulation of the Beatitudes (which may be designed especially for church leaders) appears to include anticharismatic cautions. "Blessed are the poor *in spirit*" (5:3, italicized words not in the parallel, Luke 6:20) seems aimed at those who boast of their spiritual riches, just as "Blessed are the meek" (completely absent from Luke's list) may have in view those who are puffed up and arrogant because of their endowments (cf. Matt. 11:29; 21:5; 1 Cor. 4:6,18,19; 5:2; 8:1; 13:4).

Jesus' words on prayers uttered secretly behind closed doors and spoken simply without babbling or prating sound very much like Paul's instructions regarding tongues in 1 Cor. 14. Even the "much speaking" of Matt. 6:7 is reminiscent of Paul's words in 1 Cor. 14:19. Matthew omits the generous saying of Mark 9:38–41 (cf. Luke 9:49–50) concerning exorcisms performed by a charismatic leader who does not follow Jesus. It is simply unthinkable to Matthew that a true prophet or true charismatic is not simultaneously discipled to Jesus.

According to Matt. 25:31–46 it is not notorious public sinners who are excluded from the kingdom, nor is it the charismatically endowed who enter. It is doers of deeds of loving kindness, people who have exhibited love toward the deprived and disinherited. They are called sheep and righteous, and they enter the kingdom.

Finally, it is seldom noted that Matthew is silent about Pentecost. He neither has Jesus promise the Spirit nor does he describe the coming of the Spirit. And yet there is nothing incomplete about the portrait Matthew has drawn, and it is not necessary to fill in any gaps with paragraphs taken from the other Gospels or from Acts.

Jesus promises, "Where two or three are gathered in my name, there am I in the midst of them" (18:20). "Lo, I will be with you always" (28:20). His name, after all, is Emmanuel, which means "God with us" (1:23). The presence of God is experienced and known in the crucified and resurrected Jesus and not apart from him.

A church full (too full from Matthew's perspective) of boastful charismatics, prophets, visionaries, healers, and other claimants to spiritual endowment prompted him to say loud and clear that Jesus is himself still present. He did not say that in a merely anticharismatic fit, nor does he seem concerned for the authority of some ruling caste or for structure and orderliness in general against their threatened breakdown and dissolution. He is concerned for love, for discipleship, for the higher righteousness, for service in the world of human need, exactly as Paul (1 Cor. 13) and John (John 13–16; 1 John) were in their own ways, in the face of people who located the heart of their religion in pyrotechnic displays of spiritual virtuosity.

At the conclusion to his Gospel, Matthew declares that the same Jesus is present who had taught the Sermon on the Mount. For Matthew the resurrection means the conferring of unbounded authority upon Jesus of Nazareth, whose story the Gospel has rehearsed. He and he only is the Lord of the church. Matthew's Gospel holds before the church the picture of him who alone is norm of all churchly activity and teaching. With his words and deeds Jesus is the standard against which all fresh charismatic (or noncharismatic) activity is to be evaluated—not extinguished but distinguished.

The production of the Gospel met the need for controls over some forms of charismatic activity and for guidance for Christian leaders. The historical Jesus of Nazareth, who had exercised a charismatic ministry not only by healing and exorcising, but especially by rebuking lovelessness and by forgiving, by offering his life as a ransom, and by uttering the Sermon on the Mount, was the exalted one present in the community at prayer, study, and worship.

Back to the basic question: Are the earliest Christians aptly described as the disinherited and the disadvantaged, as those who felt political alienation acutely, as people shamed and gutted by Rome's control of their money, as a steamy hothouse of otherworldly virtues walled off from the predator-filled jungle of the world, as outsiders, as a family minimizing status and structure, as following the urgings of charismatic rather than of traditional or rational-legal leadership? The correct answer appears to be both "yes" and "no." There has been diversity in thought and style in the church from the beginning. But the "no" has usually been disregarded. The foregoing sketch of Matthew and his community constitutes one "no" vote.

Matthew emerges as urban, well-to-do, educated, and, in a certain sense, anticharismatic. An influential voice in the church from the beginning, he was not a wandering radical, but a settled critic both of traveling charismatics and of the stuffy emerging establishment, insofar as it swerved from the path of discipleship to Jesus. What may be even more surprising is that Matthew is not all alone in the New Testament, and there are contemporary voices declaring that many and perhaps most Christians in the period before Constantine were members of the middle class.

FIRST CORINTHIANS AND THE BOOK OF ACTS

1 Cor. 1:26–28 has probably been more influential than any other single text in shaping popular belief and scholarly opinion regarding the social origins of the earliest Christians. It has operated as a proof text for the low, proletarian origins of church members, and passages such as Acts 4:13, Mark 6:3, and John 7:15 have functioned as backup. The RSV translates the passage as follows:

For consider your call, brethren; not many of you were wise according to worldly standards, not many were powerful, not many were of noble birth; but God chose what is foolish in the world to shame the wise [1 Cor. 1:26–27].

The passage and its context have been subjected to rigorous analysis by Wilhelm Wuellner,[12] who concludes that the passage is written in the lively diatribe style of oral delivery. Paul tosses out lines to which his readers will respond with their automatic answers, and then Paul, assuming their response, proceeds with his own argument. The passage (including audience response) might be paraphrased as follows:

Paul: "Look, brethren! At the time you were called, isn't it true that many of you were wise according to human standards? Were not many of you powerful and of noble birth?"

Answer: "Yes, many of us were certainly well-endowed, but what about it?"

Paul: "Well, you seem to have forgotten that God has chosen what is foolish in the world to shame the wise, . . . so that no human being might boast in the presence of God." (And that's the basic problem of the Corinthians—their ingratitude, their boasting, their taking their stand on what they regard as their own strength, instead of standing on the grace of God alone.)

The congregation at Corinth may have recruited its members not only from the very poor, but also—and perhaps largely—from the well-to-do bourgeois circles and even from the upper classes.[13] Even if the suggested paraphrase is wrong, and the tradition is correct that only a minority was rich, powerful, and noble, that minority was dominant in the congregation.

The portrait of the Jerusalem congregation in the opening chapters of Acts has worked like magic, casting a spell over readers' eyes as they moved beyond those first chapters. Luke reports that the people of the first generation for a short time conducted an unsuccessful experiment in voluntary sharing. At least it was unsuccessful in the long run, unable to be sustained, as the Jerusalemites soon impoverished themselves, having depleted their capital resources by repeated liquidations, and they became dependent upon the generosity of Antioch, Asia Minor, and Greece.

In later chapters Luke pictures more well-to-do Christians and offers no hint of any effort to revive or copy the form of sharing attempted at Jerusalem. Perhaps the expectation of the imminent end of the world had nourished the voluntary poverty and selfless sharing, but that expectation dimmed and the church turned increasingly to the task of worldwide missionary endeavor. Luke's work as a whole documents the church's rapid adjustment to the ongoing history of the world together with its efforts not to be completely secularized.

In view of the recent widespread infatuation with portraits of Jesus and his first disciples as freedom-fighters (revolutionaries, liberationists, or radical reformers) or as wandering, homeless, world-renouncing charismatics, the number of publications picturing Jesus and his disciples as belonging to the ancient middle class is impressive.

Years ago George Adam Smith offered a quick and rather romantic portrait of Jesus' disciples:

In the ranks of those who pursued this free and hardy industry (fishing) Christ looked for His disciples. Not wealthy, they were independent with no servile tempers, and no private or trade wrongs disadjusting their consciences. This was one reason why our Lord chose him . . . Christ went to a trade with no private wrongs and called men not from their dreams but from work they were content to do from day to day till something higher should touch them. And so it has come to pass that not the jargon of the fanatics and brigands in the highlands of Galilee, but the speech of the fishermen of her lake and the instruments of their simple craft have become the language and symbolism of the world's religion.[14]

He wrote those words almost as an aside in his description of Galilee. The research of others has, however, confirmed the basic truth of his portrait of the independence and hardiness of the disciples and of Jesus.[15] Jesus was himself a skilled worker from the middle class, a kind of mason, carpenter, cartwright, and joiner all rolled up into one.[16] The Galilean fishermen called by Jesus were independent owners of family businesses. Zebedee was an entrepreneur who employed day-laborers.

It is a mistake to think that the recruits of earliest Christianity came primarily from the lowest ranks of society, from the unemployed or underemployed. Christianity was not a religion of slaves. The majority of its adherents in the whole period up to Constantine were members of the middle class of antiquity. They were primarily free workmen, craftsmen, small businessmen, and independent farmers; and as time passed more and more members of the upper classes entered the church, although it was not until after the conversion of the emperor that the aristocracy converted in any numbers, which is easy enough to understand in a hierarchically organized society.

Eusebius reports that the grandchildren of Jude, the brother of Jesus, were brought before the Roman emperor Domitian for questioning. They declared that they each owned property worth about 4,500 silver denarii. They farmed their land, supporting themselves and paying their taxes (*Ecclesiastical History* III 20.1–4).

Apocalyptic circles were critical of riches and may have promoted radical sharing, but the majority of Christians exhibited a positive evaluation of work, industry, business, and possessions and also very quickly established a comprehensive system of care for the poor.

At the beginning of the second century Pliny noted that Christians in Asia Minor were members of every class and were primarily city dwellers, disturbing Pliny in part because they were beginning to penetrate the countryside. In defense of the Christian movement an apologist of the second or early third century wrote, "We do not originate from the lowest levels of society," and, "If we refuse your purple robes of public office, it does not follow that our ranks are composed of the very dregs of the rabble" (Minucius Felix, *Octavius* 31:6; 8:4).

One of the larger conclusions at which Robert Grant arrives in his recent work on *Early Christianity and Society* is that the Christian movement as a whole in all the years up to Constantine was not "a proletarian mass movement," but a "relatively small cluster of more or less intense groups, largely middle class in origin."[17]

Retrospective Comments

The sociological approach is limited (as are the historical and literary approaches) but is so useful (ditto for the others) that it dare not be rejected or ignored. The Gospels are not simply biographies of Jesus but are the religious charters of the earliest Christian communities. With the emergence of the Christian movement, there arose a new world constructed and maintained by a new faith. The New Testament writings reveal the minds and hearts of their authors and of the communities which received them. They give voice to their profoundest convictions, their fundamental orientation, their perspective on existence, the basic generative forces invigorating them.

Diversity in thought and style was a fact from the beginning. All kinds of people became disciples of Jesus and still do. The church needed (and needs) prodding, but it has always had leaders and communities committed to crossing boundaries, whether they are geographical or cultural and social. Matthew's was itself a comprehensively mixed community, including many well-educated and well-heeled persons, because that community was inclusive rather than exclusive and practiced ecumenicity up and down the social and cultural ladder. At least Matthew had such a vision of inclusion and ecumenicity,[18] and his Gospel was received and preserved by his community.

Concluding Questions

All kinds of questions arise in my mind, and I offer some of them here in the hope that they might stimulate further questions and even some answers.

Why have preachers and congregations found the traditional picture of Christian origins so appealing? Is it part of a nearly universal yearning for a bygone simplicity, a lost paradise, an Eden in which the complexities of modern society disappear? Does the popular portrait of Christian beginnings function like a Grandma Moses painting, provoking and feeding a deep nostalgia for a simpler, brighter time? Do we desire to escape the demands of our culture and time? Is our yearning a sign that we should like to be out from under the burden of having to think and decide—and err? And is the dream of an old simplicity and a radical directness then ultimately a cry for absolution, for forgiveness, for purification?

Do preachers use the popular picture of radically obedient and self-sacrificing early Christians as a club or a whip with which to disturb their uneasily comfortable congregations? And are they misreading the texts and abusing their already battered congregations?

What if some of the very earliest Christians were slaves and some were free, some poor and some affluent? What if some sold all they had and laid it at the apostles' feet while others retained their inherited or earned wealth and donated from it as they were moved? Do any of the several ancient patterns lay an obligation upon us to conform? If there were many different ancient forms, even inside the covers of the canonical New Testament, are we then not freed to view those forms and patterns not as laws but as possibilities, stimuli, and encouragements from ancient fathers and mothers to experiment today with numerous patterns and forms appropriate to our own time and place?

What analogies really do best describe Jesus and his first disciples: revolutionaries or resistance fighters (liberationists), social reformers, healers (like M.D.s and psychological counselors), mystics, millennialists, charismatics? What is appropriate not only in our personal and individual lives, but in our larger social setting? Did the earliest Christians have a more global view (at least a larger, imperial or Mediterranean view) than most of us?

How much of our reading of the Bible and of early church history and how much of our analysis of the attitudes, organization, and style of ancient Christians is shaped by our own present social status and social prejudices? If we ourselves are middle class and not radical renouncers or the poor, do we enjoy hearing that many ancient Christians were also middle class? And do we feel uneasy and threatened by descriptions of the early Christians as ragged and uncouth? Or do we envy them their ability to throw off the encumbrances of civilization and the trappings of middle-class ease? How much of our study is controlled by our social-political-cultural biases?

Some of the sociological studies cited above seem to imply that deprivation was a necessary condition, a kind of prerequisite for becoming Christian. That view would seem to make deprivation in some sense the cause (necessary and sufficient basis) of the rise of the Christian movement. What is the relationship between psychological or sociological conditions and receptivity to the Christian gospel? What do inner and outer circumstances have to do with God's election?

When Jesus said that it is easier for a camel to go through the eye of a needle than for a rich man to enter the kingdom, did he not mean that rebirth as children of God is an impossible possibility for all of us? That it is ever a gift of God and never a natural or an easy passage?

NOTES

1. Only a few works out of a vast and growing literature can be mentioned here. Excellent introductions to various sociological approaches together with bibliographies can be found in (1) Leander E. Keck, "On the Ethos of Early Christians, *JAAR* 42 (1974): 435–52, (2) Jonathan Z. Smith, "The Social Description of Early Christian-

ity," *RelSRev* 1 (1975): 19–25, (3) Abraham J. Malherbe, *Social Aspects of Early Christianity* (Baton Rouge: Louisiana State University Press, 1977), (4) J. H. Schütz, "Ethos of Early Christianity," *IDBSup,* and (5) Howard Clark Kee, *Christian Origins in Sociological Perspective* (Philadelphia: Westminster, 1980).

2. Howard Clark Kee, *Community of the New Age* (Philadelphia: Westminster, 1977), p. 102. Very useful is James A. Wilde, "The Social World of Mark's Gospel: A Word about Method," in *SBL 1978 Seminar Papers,* ed. Paul J. Achtemeier (Missoula: Scholars Press, 1978), Vol. 2, pp. 47–70. Wilde employs a typology of religious responses to the world developed by Oxford sociologist Bryan Wilson and finds that Mark ranks high on the scale of thaumaturgy, conversionism, and revolutionism, while he ranks low on the scales of utopianism, reformism, introversionism, and manipulationism. Wilde is of course operating at a higher level of abstraction than Kee and raises important questions of method. There is no one reigning sociology, and interpreters of the New Testament employing sociological approaches use different typologies and vocabularies. On the work of Bryan Wilson see Donald E. Miller, "Sectarianism and Secularization," *RelSRev* 5 (1979): 61–74.

3. Kee, *Community of the New Age,* p. 104.

4. John G. Gager, *Kingdom and Community: The Social World of Early Christianity* (Englewood Cliffs, N.J.: Prentice-Hall, 1975). John Gager in a review of books by Theissen (cf. Note 5), Malherbe (Note 1), and Grant (Note 17) discusses social and sociological study of early Christianity, *RelSRev* 5 (1979): 174–80; see Article 23 in this volume.

5. Gerd Theissen, *Sociology of Early Palestinian Christianity* (Philadelphia: Fortress Press, 1978) and "Itinerant Radicalism: The Tradition of Jesus' Sayings from the Perspective of the Sociology of Literature," in *The Bible and Liberation: Political and Social Hermeneutics,* 1st ed., ed. N. K. Gottwald and A. C. Wire (Berkeley: The Community for Religious Research and Education, 1976), pp. 84–93.

6. Karl Kautsky, *The Foundations of Christianity* (New York: Russell & Russell, 1953; German edition, 1908); Adolf Deissmann, *Paul: A Study in Social and Religious History* (New York: Harper, 1957; first published in 1912) and especially *Light from the Ancient East* (New York: Harper, 1927; first German edition in 1908; rev. ed. Grand Rapids: Baker Books, 1965). Deissmann's review of Kautsky is published on pages 465–67 of *Light from the Ancient East.* Ernst von Dobschütz, *Christian Life in the Primitive Church* (New York: G. P. Putnam's Sons, 1904; German edition, 1902). Keck and Malherbe (Note 1) review the works mentioned in this paragraph among many others.

7. On this and some of the other material in the following paragraphs on Matthew see G. D. Kilpatrick, *The Origins of the Gospel According to St. Matthew* (Oxford: At the Clarendon Press, 1946) and Herman C. Waetjen, *The Origin and Destiny of Humanness* (Corte Madera, Cal.: Omega Books, 1976).

8. Many further details on money in Kilpatrick and Waetjen and in Jack D. Kingsbury, "The Verb *Akolouthein* ('to follow') as an Index of Matthew's View of His Community," *JBL* 97 (1978): 56–73.

9. According to James Hope Moulton, *A Grammar of New Testament Greek* (Edinburgh: T. & T. Clark, 1919), Matthew, as he deals with his predecessor Mark, was not only "an artist in his genius for compression" but he also frequently substitutes "literary flexions for popular" (p. 169), and yet all in all his is a "correct if rather colourless Greek which avoids the vulgar forms without displaying a mastery of the literary syntax" (p. 29). In the opinion of C. F. D. Moule, Matthew was "an educated

person commanding sound Greek with a considerable vocabulary (*The Birth of the New Testament* [New York: Harper & Row, 1962], p. 219). See also F. Blass and A. Debrunner, *A Greek Grammar of the New Testament,* trans. and rev. R. W. Funk (Chicago: University of Chicago Press, 1961), par. 485, 492.

10. Krister Stendahl, *The School of St. Matthew* (Uppsala: Gleerup, 1954).

11. Gunther Bornkamm, "The Risen Lord and the Earthly Jesus," in *The Future of Our Religious Past,* ed. James M. Robinson (London: SCM Press, 1971), pp. 203-29; Eduard Schweizer, "Observance of the Law and Charismatic Activity in Matthew," *NTS* 16 (1970): 213-30; J. Massingberd Ford, *Baptism of the Spirit* (Techny, Ill.: Divine Word, 1971); James P. Martin, "The Church in Matthew," *Int* 29 (1975): 41-56.

12. Wilhelm Wuellner, "The Sociological Implications of 1 Corinthians 1:26-28 Reconsidered," *Studia Evangelica* 6 (1973): 666-72.

13. Malherbe (Note 1) and E. A. Judge, *The Social Pattern of Christian Groups in the First Century* (London: Tyndale Press, 1960) arrive at the same conclusions as Wuellner concerning the social mix in the congregation at Corinth.

14. George Adam Smith, *The Historical Geography of the Holy Land* (New York: Harper & Row, 1966: reprint of the 25th edition published in 1931), p. 300.

15. Wilhelm Wuellner, *The Meaning of "Fishers of Men"* (Philadelphia: Westminster, 1967).

16. Martin Hengel, *Property and Riches in the Early Church* (Philadelphia: Fortress Press, 1974).

17. Robert M. Grant, *Early Christianity and Society* (New York: Harper & Row, 1977), p. 11.

18. Edgar M. Krentz, "The Egalitarian Church of Matthew," *CurTM* 4 (1977): 333-41, and Gunther Bornkamm, "The Authority to 'Bind' and 'Loose' in the Church in Matthew's Gospel," in *Jesus and Man's Hope* (Pittsburgh: Pittsburgh Theological Seminary, 1970), Vol. 1, pp. 37-50.

Part V

THE BIBLE
IN POLITICAL THEOLOGY
AND MARXIST THOUGHT

25

ARTHUR F. McGOVERN

The Bible in Latin American Liberation Theology

Four related biblical themes recur in liberation theology as the foundational expressions of an integral process of salvation involving all realms of life: God as liberator, notably in the Exodus; God's command to "do justice"; Jesus as proclaimer and doer of the Kingdom of God; and the political dimension of Jesus' conflicts with authorities.

Liberation theology is frequently charged with reducing faith to politics, one-sidedly stressing politics and human activity in the Bible, and using theology to justify pre-established political positions. These charges are shown to derive largely from misunderstandings of critics who display their own reactionary position or from revolutionary groups who employ the rhetoric of liberation theology in a simplistic way. The central claims of liberation theology, which understand liberation as a broad process inclusive of but not exhausted by politics, are consistent both with the Bible and with the role of critical faith in the present oppressive situation in Latin America.

Reprinted from Arthur F. McGovern, *Marxism: An American Christian Perspective* (Maryknoll, N.Y.: Orbis Books, 1980), pp. 188-97.

461

The critique of development policies and the critique of ideological elements in church doctrine supportive only of reformism led liberation theologians to a new awareness. Authentic liberation, Gutiérrez claimed, could come to Latin America only through a liberation from domination exercised by the great capitalist countries and their domestic allies who control the national power structure. Such a liberation would require creating an entirely new kind of society. It would mean being open to socialism; it would mean learning from Marxism about structural causes and from Paulo Freire about conscientization.[1] It would also require the active participation of the oppressed. "It is the poor who must be protagonists of their own liberation."[2]

This new awareness led to the discovery of new dimensions in scripture about God's liberating power, and to new convictions about the role of the church. Liberation, Assmann noted, means more than just freedom or improvement. It implies a judgment on, a condemnation of, the present state of affairs. It is a word of confrontation and conflict. It expresses a new historical awareness among Latin American peoples, and awareness that they are not just insufficiently developed but dominated and oppressed peoples.[3] But with this new consciousness of oppression came also a new way of experiencing God and understanding Christian faith.

What in the Bible and Christian faith speaks to hopes of liberation from conditions of oppression and bondage?[4] Four related biblical themes recur most often in liberation theology as a response to this question: God as liberator, with the Exodus as a special prototype; God's command to "do justice," reflected in the denunciations of the prophets; Jesus, liberation, and the kingdom of God; Jesus and the confrontations in his life which gave a "political dimension" to his actions. These four themes will serve as a basis for discussing new biblical dimensions in liberation theology.

GOD AS LIBERATOR: EXODUS

Through the influence of Greek philosophy on Christianity, God came to be thought of as eternal, unchangeable, and outside of human history. Theology consequently said little about God's role in history apart from the one moment of the Incarnation. Recent biblical scholarship, however, has placed great stress on God's part in history, noting that God revealed himself only gradually over a period of time and by entering into human history. Thus the expression "the God of Abraham, Isaac, and Jacob" communicates this sense of God gradually revealing more of himself to successive generations in the course of Israel's history. He reveals himself by acting in history to bring salvation.

God initiates human history by his gift of creation. He saves humanity from destruction by floods when he appears to Noah; he promises to make Abraham the father of a new nation; through Joseph he acts to spare the descendants of Abraham from starvation; through Moses he liberates the

Israelites from slavery in Egypt and leads them to the promised land. Thus, as Gutiérrez observes, "biblical faith is, above all, faith in a God who reveals himself through historical events, a God who saves in history."[5] The salvation which God brings, moreover, is not just the salvation of the soul in a life hereafter. As these historical events manifested, God acted to affect the lives of persons on earth, to free them from hunger and misery, to liberate them from Egyptian oppression, to bring them to a promised land.

The Exodus, especially, provides liberation theology with a striking paradigm of God's liberating power. The Exodus out of Egypt molded the consciousness of the people of Israel and revealed God's power to them.[6] It showed that God's actions take place *in* history and *as* history, and it showed the political character of this history, for it embraced the total life of the people.[7] The Exodus liberated the Israelites physically from the bondage of Egypt.[8] The Exodus speaks to the present situation of Latin America for it reveals that God works in history and not outside it, and God works to liberate the oppressed in the fullest political sense of the word.[9]

GOD'S DEMAND: "DOING JUSTICE"

God identifies with the poor and oppressed. To be a Christian one must share in this love. Love of God and love of neighbor, especially love of the poor, cannot be separated.[10] The central mystery of our faith is that God shared our humanity, so that every person must be seen as the living temple of God. The parable of the last judgment in Matthew 25 summarizes the very essence of the gospel message. Christ is to be found in the hungry, the thirsty, the naked. "Whatever you did for the least of my brethren you did unto me."

God's identification with the poor, however, is not just a question of charity but of justice. The prophets make this point clear: to know the Lord is to do justice. Míguez Bonino cites Jeremiah 22:16, in which Josiah is praised for doing justice: "He judged the cause of the poor and the needy; then it was well. Is not this to know me? says the Lord." Hosea 4:1–2 makes the same point by equating lack of knowledge of God with failure to do justice.[11]

José Miranda's *Marx and the Bible* provides a detailed study of this identification of knowledge of God and doing justice. Miranda argues first of all that Western translations of the Bible, since the sixth century A.D., robbed biblical texts of their force. What the Hebrew text intended to connote as "justice" the translations rendered as "almsgiving." Thus deeds we have come to consider works of charity or supererogation were in the original Bible texts called works of justice.[12]

Miranda's central theme is that one cannot claim to know Yahweh except by doing justice. To know Yahweh is to achieve justice for the poor. Miranda insists, moreover, that the Bible does not just mean that justice is one sign or manifestation of knowledge of God. It is *the* way. Citing another biblical scholar, H. J. Kraus, he concludes: "Amos, Hosea, Isaiah, and Micah know only one decisive theme: justice and right."[13] In the view of the Bible, Yahweh is the God who breaks into human history to liberate the oppressed. "I, Yahweh, have called you to serve the cause of justice . . . to free captives from prison and those who live in darkness from the dungeon" (Isa. 42:5–7). Or again in Exodus 6:3, God says, "Say this to the sons of Israel, 'I am Yahweh *and therefore* I will free you of the burdens which the Egyptians lay on you. I will release you from slavery to them,' "[14] Liberation flows from his very nature.

Miranda believes not only that injustice is denounced by Yahweh but that his justice is "fiercely punitive against the oppressors," that it is for their injustice that Yahweh defeats nations for Israel.[15] But it is likewise Israel's own injustices that are the direct cause of its rejection by Yahweh. Thus we read in Micah 3:9–12: "Now listen to this, you leaders of Jacob, rulers of Israel, you who loathe justice and pervert all that is right; . . . because of this, since the fault is yours, Zion will be ploughed like a field."[16]

In short, justice is decisive for God. One cannot claim to know, love, or worship God except through doing justice.

JESUS AND LIBERATION: THE KINGDOM OF GOD

Jesus proclaimed the coming kingdom of God. He preached primarily not about himself or even about God but about the kingdom. Jon Sobrino writes: "The most certain historical datum about Jesus' life is that the concept which dominated his preaching, the reality which gave meaningfulness to all his activity, was 'the kingdom of God.' "[17]

To understand the import of the term "kingdom of God," says Sobrino, we must understand what it meant to the people of Israel. They had suffered the destruction of the northern and southern kingdoms, the Babylonian captivity, and had failed to achieve national self-determination after these. But the prophets held out to them the promise of liberation, of a Messiah who would fulfill their hopes. This salvation was viewed as something radically new. Thus Yahweh announced: "Lo, I am about to create new heavens and a new earth; the things of the past shall not be remembered or come to mind. Instead there shall always be rejoicing and happiness in what I create" (Isa. 65:17). Jesus shared that prophetic vision and understood his task of proclaiming the kingdom in that context.[18]

The kingdom comes as a grace, it is due to God's initiative. But it is a salvation and liberation expressed in deeds. Jesus equates "proclaiming God" with "realizing God's reign in practice." His deeds, his healings, his driving out of demons, his raising to life, are signs of the coming kingdom. They also show that kingdom means transformation of a *bad* situation, of an oppressive situation. The kingdom must overcome sin, not merely personal sin but sin in its social and collective dimensions, in groups that oppress and the structures they represent.[19]

It is not enough, however, to know what the kingdom of God meant in

Jesus' time. It must be grasped in the light of present experience. Today in Latin America, Leonardo Boff asserts, the kingdom expresses a people's utopian longing for liberation from everything that alienates them: pain, hunger, injustice, death.[20] But it also conveys the absolute lordship of God who will carry out this liberation. Jesus proclaims that the kingdom will no longer be utopian but the real fulfillment of happiness for all people. This kingdom of God is not only spiritual but also a total revolution of the structures of the old world; it is *this* world transformed and made new. The cross symbolizes the suffering that unjust structures can impose on the world. The resurrection is an experience of liberation not only for Jesus but in every instance where elements of oppression are overcome and new life breaks through. If the church is to be the bearer of the kingdom, then demands of liberation are not only political demands but demands of the faith.[21] On this last point Gutiérrez writes: "To place oneself in the perspective of the kingdom means to participate in the struggle for the liberation of those oppressed by others. That is what many Christians who have committed themselves to the Latin American revolutionary process have begun to experience."[22]

JESUS AND CONFLICT: THE POLITICAL DIMENSION

Many Christians, Gutiérrez observes, take for granted that Jesus was not interested in political life, that his mission was purely religious. To look for the characteristics of a contemporary political militant, he continues, would be to misrepresent his life and witness. He rejected the narrow nationalism of the Zealots and their belief that they could realize the kingdom through their own efforts alone. He opposed all political-religious messianism which did not respect the depth of the religious realm and the autonomy of political action. He attacked instead the very foundation of injustice and exploitation, the disintegration of community. In doing so his actions took on a very definite political significance. He confronted the major power groups of his society. He called Herod a "fox"; he denounced the hypocrisy and legalism of the Pharisees; his teachings threatened the privileged position of the Sadducees; and he died at the hands of political authorities.[23]

Several other liberation theologians argue for the political dimension of Jesus' life by focusing on his confrontations and conflicts with authorities. Ignacio Ellacuría contends that Jesus lived in a highly politicized atmosphere in which all he did necessarily carried political implications.[24] His criticisms interfered with the whole socio-political power structure. In criticizing the Scribes and Pharisees he was attacking their monopoly over the faith and consequently he undermined the power base of the priestly class. He also threatened the power balance between the Jewish nation and the Romans. His condemnation of wealth carried the same political implications. Míguez Bonino adds that the universality of Jesus' love cannot be interpreted as a compromise with or acceptance of evil, and that he was *rightly* accused of taking the side of the oppressed against the constituted religious and political authorities.[25]

Sobrino emphasizes the targets of Jesus' denunciations. If Jesus does not speak in contemporary terms of unjust structures or institutions, his denunciations are almost always *collective*. They are aimed at the Pharisees because they pay no attention to justice, at the legal experts because they impose intolerable burdens on the people, at the rich because they refuse to share their wealth with the poor, and at the rulers of the world because they govern despotically. The anathemas are also directed against abuse of power, be it religious, intellectual, economic, or political.[26]

In a powerful chapter on the death of Jesus, Sobrino argues that the crucifixion can be explained only as the historical consequence of Jesus' life and preaching of the kingdom. Jesus proclaimed a God of liberation, a God concerned about human life and dignity, a God whose love is so deeply affected by all that is negative that *he suffers* from the death of his Son and from human suffering. But this God whom Jesus proclaimed conflicted with the God of religion, the God of external rituals and temple worship, the God in whose name privileged classes subdue others. Jesus was charged with blasphemy for proclaiming such a God, but he suffered the punishment imposed on political agitators (crucifixion) rather than the punishment dealt out to religious blasphemers (stoning) because his denunciations challenged every claim to power which does not embody God's love and truth.[27]

Jesus seems clearly to have renounced the use of violence in his own defense or as a means of confronting injustice. He drove moneychangers out of the temple. He did not, however, use or condone violence against persons. But given the violence of oppressive conditions in Latin America would not revolutionary violence be justifiable? Liberation theologians do not deal with this issue as often as one might expect. Gutiérrez, in *A Theology of Liberation*, speaks often of oppressive institutional violence in Latin America and of the necessity of class struggle to oppose it. But he does not discuss to any extent a recourse to revolutionary violence. Some liberation theologians have affirmed non-violence as an essential Christian stance on liberation. Leonardo Boff affirms that the power of God, to which Jesus bore witness, is love. "Such love rules out all violence and oppression, even for the sake of having love itself prevail." The apparent efficacy of violence does not manage to break the spiralling process of violence.[28] Segundo Galilea argues that liberation from violence, both from institutional violence and from subversive violence, is one of the most important tasks confronting Christianity. He holds that liberation theology and Christianity "tell us that violence cannot be overcome with purely human means or with other forms of violence."[29]

Juan Luis Segundo, on the other hand, believes that Jesus' message of non-violence is not a matter of faith but an ideological stance taken in a particular historical context. The Israelites felt that God commanded them to exterminate their enemies; Jesus insisted on love and nonresistance to evil;

each ideology had its own historical function to carry out. What theology must do is decide what ideology is needed in the light of the present situation of socio-political oppression in Latin America. Since it would be unrealistic to look centuries back to biblical situations for an answer, the best approach would be to ask: "What would the Christ of the Gospels say if he were confronting our problems today?"[30]

SOME COMMENTS ABOUT BIBLICAL PERSPECTIVES

Critics of liberation theology charge that it oversimplifies the biblical message of the faith and tends to reduce it to politics with a definite ideological thrust.[31] Their criticisms might be grouped and considered under three charges: that liberation theology reduces faith to politics, that it interprets political dimensions of the gospel one-sidedly, overemphasizing human efforts, and that it uses scripture to justify its own political positions.

Liberation theology is criticized for reducing faith to politics. Liberation theologians *do stress* the political dimensions and political implications of scripture because they see Latin America's most urgent problems as bound up with politics. But stress cannot be equated with denial of all other aspects. A theologian who writes on prayer is not accused of ignoring marriage. More qualifying statements within liberation theology might have averted some of the criticism. Segundo, for example, makes a claim for liberation theology which could be used as an objection to the response that it only stresses the political. He writes: "Liberation is meant to designate and cover theology as a whole" and it is "the only authentic and privileged standpoint for arriving at a full and complete understanding of God's revelation in Jesus Christ."[32] The fact that he moves on to discuss the political problem of socialism versus capitalism as a test of theology might add to the impression that liberation theology deals only with politics. But Segundo does not say that *politics* is the privileged standpoint or covers theology as a whole; he says that *liberation* is. Liberation has a much fuller meaning than political action. Certainly other liberation theologians in the same volume of *Frontiers of Theology in Latin America* quite clearly take liberation in a broad sense and say explicitly that politics is only one dimension of the faith.[33]

The second objection raised against liberation theology is that when it treats the political dimension of the Bible it gives a one-sided and oversimplified interpretation, and it overstresses human activity in achieving liberation. Some liberation theologians have presented one-sided interpretations of biblical passages. Miranda's *Marx and the Bible* falls into this. His major thesis that justice is the prevailing theme of scripture has been supported by other scripture scholars.[34] His book, moreover, contains a powerfully moving call to justice. But Miranda also makes strong, sweeping statements that do present only one dimension of the biblical message. He claims, for example, that the justice proclaimed by Isaiah is "fiercely punitive against oppressors," without mentioning numerous passages that extol God's great mercy.[35] He claims that not even the anarchist Bakunin made assertions more subversive of the law than St. Paul, overlooking Paul's admonitions that slaves obey their masters and wives their husbands.[36] Phillip Berryman, in an otherwise very positive presentation of liberation theology, comments on the extreme form of Miranda's arguments.[37] And as the title of the book would suggest, Miranda often does impose a Marxist framework on the Bible.

Biblical passages have many dimensions and hence lend themselves to different interpretations. The sources most often cited by liberation theologians could be used to show that liberation does *not* come through struggle and oppression. If the Exodus account serves as a paradigm of liberation, it is not an example of overthrowing oppressors. The Jews fled Egypt; they did not overcome their oppressors and establish a new social order in Egypt. Yahweh told them that it was not because of their efforts, but because of him, that they were liberated. They struggled and fought wars to gain possession of the promised land, but not against oppressors over land they could claim was due to them in justice. Yahweh told them: "It is not for any goodness of yours that Yahweh gives you this rich land to possess, for you are a headstrong people" (Deut. 9:6). Similarly, when the prophets denounced injustice they did not call for collective political action but for conversion of the powerful and wealthy. They insisted moreover that only God could provide true justice (Isa. 1:24ff.; Exod. 3:7-9). Neither did Jesus organize the masses to overthrow unjust structures.

These examples, however, do not negate the central claims made by liberation theology that God acts in history to bring human, physical liberation and that he defends the poor and denounces injustice. The examples only serve to illustrate Segundo's argument about the distinction between faith and ideology. These central claims of liberation theology pertain to faith; how they were acted upon in biblical times was conditioned by cultural ideologies. If exact imitation of what the prophets did or what Jesus did is made a matter of faith, then few of the institutional ministries of the Church could be justified. Jesus never started a school or built a parish church; nor did he instruct his apostles to do so. The essential thing is to discover and act upon the spirit and intention that underly God's revelations and Jesus' actions. Dorothee Soelle articulates this well:

> Social awareness of transformation cannot and need not be justified biblically. . . . It is not a matter of compiling in a biblicistic sense materials pertaining to the political activity of Jesus and using them to establish whether or not he was a revolutionary. The main thing is not to describe his concrete behavior and to imitate it, but rather to discern the intention or tendency of that behavior and to realize anew his goals in our world.[38]

Leonardo Boff's essay on "Christ's Liberation via Oppression" complements what has already been said about the meaning, spirit, and tendency of

Jesus' words and behavior. Jesus preached good news to the poor and was born and lived among them; he denounced injustice; he put human good above legalism when he healed on the Sabbath; he died for values he refused to compromise. Yet at the same time he forgave and he maintained a deep love for every person and respect for each person's liberty.[39] To combine the strength to oppose and overcome injustice with a love that is forgiving is, I believe, to live with the spirit of Jesus. Combining these, moreover, could be the distinctive contribution of Christianity to human liberation.

The third criticism raised against liberation theology is that it uses theology to justify political positions already taken. A criticism often heard about liberation theology is that it identifies God's will and Marxist socialism: it identifies the poor with the proletariat, prophetic denunciation with Marxist critiques of capitalism, God's liberation with socialist revolution, and the kingdom of God with a new socialist society. But if liberation theology made no effort to correlate the poor of the Bible with the poor in Latin America, and injustice denounced in the Bible with contemporary injustices, it would lose all meaning. The very purpose of liberation theology is to relate the word of God and historical praxis.[40] The issue is whether liberation theology determines in advance what it will find in praxis by adopting only Marxist categories. If the summaries we have given on biblical perspectives accurately reflect liberation theology as a whole, the identification of biblical and Marxist categories is *not* characteristic. Opponents of liberation theology, Galilea observes, often fail to distinguish between liberation theology as such and political documents published by revolutionary Christian groups. Some forms of liberation theology, he acknowledges, do tend to be "ideologized" and to rely on Marxist categories, but this current is limited and not representative of liberation theology as a whole.[41] To his remarks could be added those of other liberation theologians who criticize the "absolutizing" of any one ideological position.[42]

Quite often it is the opponents of liberation theology who read into theological statements a Marxist-Leninist identification. Bishop Alfonso López Trujillo's *Liberation or Revolution?* exemplifies this tendency. The book cover, not inappropriately in light of its tone, presents the title in dripping paint to suggest bloodshed. Where liberation theologians speak of the political dimension of Jesus' mission, López Trujillo treats them as militant proponents of violent revolution. "Is Christ a Zealot who seeks radical change by means of violence. . . . Does He impatiently seek the 'Kingdom,' and does He want to speed his mission by means of violence?"[43] In short, where facile identifications of liberation and Marxism are made, they are most often the product of opponents, or of militant political groups using liberation theology, not from within liberation theology itself.

A way of reading liberation theology more sympathetically, while at the same time testing the basic faithfulness of liberation theology to scripture, would be to list points that they hold and ask: "which of these should be *denied*?" Could any of the following be judged contrary to faith or scripture?

God reveals himself in history.

God desires the full human freedom of his people, at every level of their life.

God reveals a very special concern for the poor and is angered by injustice done against them.

Jesus sought to bring God's liberating power and justice to all.

Jesus identified in a very special way with the marginal people of society, the outcasts, the poor.

Jesus denounced those who placed burdens upon the poor and who placed legalism (law and order) over human need.

Jesus sought to "break the power of evil and sin" in the world.

Jesus' actions were seen as a threat to those in positions of power.

A similar set of statements could be drawn up to reflect the role of faith in the present as expressed in liberation theology. Which of these should be denied?

The issue of poverty and oppression is the gravest problem facing the great masses of people in Latin America.

Without denying the value of other ministries, primary importance should be attached to the work of helping the poor.

The poor of Latin America are the landless peasants, the marginal people in the barrios of the city, the underpaid, underemployed, or unemployed workers.

In Latin America capitalism has failed to serve the common good, and developmental policies have not succeeded in bettering the situation.

These failures suggest the need for a more profound analysis of causes, using the best tools available from the social sciences.

The church should be willing to evaluate its own social teachings to see if they are adequate to the present situation.

Some church teachings may reflect cultural attitudes or "ideologies."

To work directly with the poor is certainly consistent with the spirit of Jesus and the mission of the church. It might prove more effective for social change than educational work with upper and middle classes, a work which seems to have had very limited success in changing conditions in Latin America.

Working with the poor and striving with them for liberation can lead to a very enriching and new understanding of the faith.

In its concern for the poor and for ending injustice the church should be willing to take stands, even if this involves conflict with some of its own members, for example regarding land reform.

It may be argued that this list of statements, and other efforts made to strike a balance, are out of harmony with liberation theology which concerns itself with praxis and the process of liberation, not with theological propositions. But an important political issue is involved, namely, whether liberation theology wants to build support for its positions within the institutional church.

NOTES

1. Gustavo Gutiérrez, *A Theology of Liberation: History, Politics and Salvation*, trans. and ed. Caridad Inda and John Eagleson (Maryknoll, N.Y.: Orbis Books, 1973), pp. 88–92.

2. Ibid., p. 113.

3. Hugo Assmann, *Theology for a Nomad Church*, trans. Paul Burns (Maryknoll, N.Y.: Orbis Books, 1976), pp. 49–51.

4. See Jon Sobrino, S.J., *Christianity at the Crossroads*, trans. John Drury (Maryknoll, N.Y.: Orbis Books, 1978), p. 35. See also Leonardo Boff, "Christ's Liberation via Oppression," in *Frontiers of Theology in Latin America*, ed. Rosino Gibellini, trans. John Drury (Maryknoll, N.Y.: Orbis Books, 1979), pp. 100–131.

5. Gutiérrez, *Theology of Liberation*, p. 154.

6. See Assmann, *Theology for a Nomad Church*, p. 66 and Rubem Alves, *A Theology of Human Hope* (Washington, D.C.: Corpus Books, 1969), p. 89.

7. See José Míguez Bonino, *Revolutionary Theology Comes of Age* (London: SPCK, 1975); and U.S. edition, *Doing Theology in a Revolutionary Situation* (Philadelphia: Fortress, 1975), pp. 134–35.

8. Alfredo Fierro, *The Militant Gospel: A Critical Introduction to Political Theologies*, trans. John Drury (Maryknoll, N.Y.: Orbis Books, 1977), pp. 140–45.

9. Assmann, *Theology for a Nomad Church*, p. 35.

10. See Sobrino, *Christology at the Crossroads*, pp. 169–73, 204–5.

11. José Míguez Bonino, *Christians and Marxists: The Mutual Challenge to Revolution* (Grand Rapids, Mich.: Eerdmans, 1976), pp. 31–33.

12. José Miranda, *Marx and the Bible: A Critique of the Philosophy of Oppression*, trans. John Eagleson (Maryknoll, N.Y.: Orbis Books, 1974), pp. 14–15.

13. Ibid., p. 46.

14. Ibid., pp. 78–79.

15. Ibid., pp. 83 and 121.

16. Ibid., p. 165. In Scripture see also Amos 4:1–3 and Hosea 10:13.

17. Sobrino, *Christology at the Crossroads*, p. 41.

18. Ibid., pp. 42–44.

19. Ibid., pp. 50–55.

20. Leonardo Boff, "Salvation in Jesus Christ and the Process of Liberation," in *The Mystical and Political Dimension of the Christian Faith,* Concilium 96, ed. Claude Geffré and Gustavo Gutiérrez (New York: Herder/Seabury, 1974), pp. 81–88.

21. Ibid., p. 88. Opponents of liberation theology have accused it of identifying the kingdom as something human activity alone can achieve. Boff clearly does not, p. 89.

22. Gutiérrez, *A Theology of Liberation,* p. 203. Also, on the distinction noted above between the kingdom and human efforts, pp. 227, 231.

23. Ibid., pp. 225–32.

24. Ignacio Ellacuría, *Freedom Made Flesh*, trans. John Drury (Maryknoll, N.Y.: Orbis Books, 1976), pp. 31–45.

25. Míguez Bonino, *Revolutionary Theology Comes of Age*. pp. 121–124.

26. Sobrino, *Christology at the Crossroads*, p. 53.

27. Ibid., pp. 204–9. On God Suffering, pp. 224–26.

28. Leonardo Boff, "Christ's Liberation via Oppression," in *Frontiers of Theology in Latin America*, p. 120.

29. Segundo Galilea in ibid., "Liberation Theology and New Tasks Facing Christians," p. 175.

30. Juan Luis Segundo, *The Liberation of Theology*, trans. John Drury (Maryknoll, N.Y.: Orbis Books, 1976), pp. 116–17. See also Míquez Bonino, *Christians and Marxists*, p. 124, who comments only briefly on the question of violence by saying that if socialist revolution involves violence a Christian should be concerned with keeping it at a minimum.

31. See the criticism of the International Theological Commission "Human Development and Christian Salvation," in *Origins* 7 (November 3, 1977). As an advisory group to the pope, the Commission's criticism of "some forms" of liberation theology constituted the most formal critique. The criticisms focused chiefly on biblical interpretations which were found oversimplified. The Commission itself was criticized for not including a liberation theologian in its deliberations. Clark H. Pinnock, "Liberation Theology: The Gains, the Gaps," in *Christianity Today* 20 (January 16, 1976), is critical of liberation theology.

32. Juan Luis Segundo, "Capitalism versus Socialism: Crux Theologica," in *Frontiers of Theology*, p. 241.

33. Gutiérrez, "Liberation Praxis and Christian Faith," in *Frontiers*, insists that Christian liberation is not restricted to political liberation, but stresses its universal transcendence (p. 128). Also in *Frontiers*, Boff, pp. 107–8; Raul Vidales, "Methodological Issues in Liberation Theology," pp. 35–36, and Galilea, "Liberation and New Tasks," pp. 169–70.

34. See, for example, John R. Donahue, S.J., "Biblical Perspectives on Justice," in *The Faith That Does Justice*, ed. John C. Haughey, S.J. (New York: Paulist Press, 1977), p. 68.

35. Miranda, *Marx and the Bible*, p. 83.

36. Ibid., p. 187.

37. Phillip Berryman, "Latin American Liberation Theology," in *Theology in the Americas*, ed. Sergio Torres and John Eagleson (Maryknoll, N.Y.: Orbis Books, 1976), pp. 71–73.

38. Dorothee Soelle, *Political Theology*, trans. John Shelley (Philadelphia: Fortress, 1974), p. 64.

39. Boff, in *Frontiers*, pp. 100–31.

40. See Vidales, in *Frontiers*, p. 41.

41. Galilea in ibid., pp. 169–70.

42. In *Frontiers*, see Gutiérrez, p. 22–23; Vidales, p. 47; José Comblin, "What Sort of Service Might Theology Render?" p. 76; Enrique D. Dussel, "Historical and Philosophical Presuppositions for Latin American Theology," p. 212; Juan Carlos Scannone, "Theology, Popular Culture, and Discernment," pp. 218, 221.

43. Alfonso López Trujillo, *Liberation or Revolution?* (Huntington, Ind.: Our Sunday Visitor, 1977), pp. 16–17.

26

ALFREDO FIERRO

Exodus Event and Interpretation in Political Theologies

The function of the Exodus theme in the political theologies of J. Molt-mann, H. Cox, and J. Cardonnel is described. The objections of F. Biot that the Exodus was not seen as a revolutionary activity by the biblical writers and that biblical narratives do not constitute moral norms are carefully evaluated.

The author concludes that the precise prominence the biblical writers gave to the subversive political significance of the Exodus is not determinative since the attested event carries that significance by the way it is related. More-over, political theologies do not claim a direct moral norm for the Exodus any more than they do for the cross. Exodus and cross are "exemplary memories." Exodus is a liberative memory about the possibility of insurrection which takes away the religiously induced fear of revolution, certifying that insurrection is a stance or line of action that may be entirely appropriate for the believer in particular circumstances.

Reprinted from Alfredo Fierro, *The Militant Gospel: A Critical Introduction to Political Theologies* (Maryknoll, N.Y.: Orbis Books, 1977), pp. 140–51.

EXODUS THEOLOGY

Included in current political theology is an Exodus theology. The image of the church as an "Exodus community," which was made popular by Moltmann, has social and political connotations: "Christendom must dare to undertake the Exodus, viewing its societal roles as a new Babylonian captivity." A Christendom on Exodus means a group "that is not capable of being assimilated or conquered," that is ever ready to "flee the social roles that have been set for it by society."[1] Most importantly of all, it means that Christendom, as the bearer of the gospel hope, "enters into a polemical and liberative relationship not just with the religions and ideologies of human beings but even more so with everyday life." The hope of a Christendom on Exodus entails "practical resistance" and "creative refashioning" that calls into question the existing order and serves what is to come in the future.[2]

In Moltmann's thinking the Exodus is nothing but a theological category or a theological representation. Of course it contains an implicit reference to the historical fact of the Hebrews' liberation from Egypt, but the weight of his ecclesiology bears down more on the present moment than on the past historical model. His theology is a theology of hope more than it is an Exodus theology. In it the Exodus is simply one among many images serving to outline the community's attitude of hope.

Some other theologians have put more stress on the Hebrew Exodus as an event that really happened in past history. They forcefully underline its historical reality, its value as a model for Christian praxis, and its importance for the possibility of talking about God in terms of a liberation theology. Thus they formulate an Exodus theology in the strict sense of that term. The departure from Egypt is much more than a mere image designed to enrich theological representations; it becomes the primeval and fundamental happening of the history of divine revelation itself. The Exodus comes to constitute the prototype of divine revelation, the privileged moment in which God once manifested himself and now continues to do the same. At the same time the Exodus of history did not just signify a withdrawal from socially assigned roles. It was a liberative revolution in the strict sense, a socially subversive act comparable to slave rebellions or other struggles of oppressed peoples against imperialism. The significance of that act for the theologian lies in the fact that it was carried out under the inspiration of faith and interpreted as the portentous result of a divine revelation; even more importantly, it brought into existence a nation of people, the Israelites, who thereby began to serve as the bearer of God's promises.

The connection between the Exodus and the original divine revelation is clearly brought out by Harvey Cox. He sees it as the focal point of the theology of desacralization. It simultaneously symbolizes and realizes man's liberation from a sacral political order so that he may involve himself in history and social change. Picking up a traditional theme of biblical exegesis that underlines the fact that the God of the Bible reveals himself in the events of history rather than in physical or cosmic phenomena as other cosmic or nature deities do, Cox goes on to point out that the first and foremost event in which God spoke decisively to the Hebrews was a liberation event that brought them out of Egypt. He thinks it is of the utmost significance that the event in question brought about a major social change, that it was what we today would call a mass act of civil disobedience. Thus the Exodus, seen as an "act of insurrection," can support a theology of revolution. In his early work Cox prefers to talk about a "theology of rapid social change" rather than about a theology of revolution.[3] In Christian praxis the import of the Exodus is to encourage the abandonment of older immobilist attitudes. Once Christians are courageous enough to move out of the paralyzing structures of the present, God himself will furnish them with new ones. They do not need a detailed plan of the promised land before leaving Egypt.[4]

Latin American theology also stresses the fact that liberation from Egypt was a political act, noting the link between it and creation in the Hebrew experience; those two events are almost completely identified in the mind of the Israelites.[5] To be created by God is equivalent to being free. Indeed the very possibility of appreciating life and the world as creation depends on the concrete experience of liberation. People begin to see their own history as an Exodus before they begin to see the universe as the creative work of God. Divine revelation, including the fact that the world is God's creation, begins with the freedom inaugurated in the Exodus. As Jean Cardonnel says:

> Sacred history, the conscious history of a people, does not begin in Genesis but in Exodus. The concrete experience of liberation is the only way to discover the fact of creation. It is only the deeply lived experience of oppression that prompts man to work toward his radical liberation, in which process he can come to discover that the world is a creation.[6]

It is in the work of Cardonnel that Exodus theology finds its fullest elaboration and its most passionate tones. As he sees it, God makes himself known precisely by making the cause of the oppressed his own and intervening on the side of their liberation. Here the Exodus theme links with another theme of major importance in current political theology: the need to opt for the poor and oppressed because the gospel message is a proclamation of liberation addressed primarily to them. God's revelation is the announcement of his identification with the subjugated:

> It is first and foremost in making the cause of the oppressed his own that God does his work and manifests the fact that he is God. He reveals himself as the one who rouses and creates a people who had not existed

as such before. Whereas other deities simply endorse the victories of
their people, the specific character of the one and only God is the fact
that he intervenes in the very midst of abandonment and dereliction.
His divine revelation begins with the liberation of the most oppressed
and tortured people, who thereby move prophetically from oppression
to liberation.[7]

That is what specifically identifies the God of the Bible and distinguishes
him from the deity of metaphysics. In the outlook of Cardonnel an Exodus
theology is what clarifies Christian theology and gives it its essential and
distinctive character. Either theology is an Exodus theology or it is not Christian at all:

> The revealed God to whom I offer my faith is infinitely different from
> the deity of deism. He is not a "supreme being" whose loveless benevo-
> lence derives from his arbitrary power. Rather, he it is who intervenes in
> the history of human beings. The originality of revelation lies in the fact
> that God makes himself known by quickening the spirit of a people
> threatened with total defeat. That is the real meaning of Israel's des-
> tiny, which anticipates the passover of all peoples from a fatalistic order
> to an order of freedom. There is some undeniable affinity between God
> and weakness. The eternal one is revealed in the despised and oppressed
> in order to confound the powerful.[8]

So the Exodus is the first event of revelation and salvation. For the first
time human beings realize that they have been saved by God through their
concrete experience of liberation from oppression and the attainment of a
new freedom. The Exodus experience was a liberation experience,[9] and it
constitutes the archetypal event in the historical self-awareness of the Christian faith. Its profile gives form to the other historical commitments of the
believer. When theology tries to understand itself through its recollection of
the Exodus, it is proceeding as revolutionary theory does when it recalls the
historical precedents set for it by the French or Russian or Chinese revolutions. The memory evoked in this process is then incorporated into the praxis
of the present and its prospective hopes for the immediate future. It becomes
an image and a standard accompanying one's revolutionary understanding
of the time. In the case of theology, the Exodus is a symbol of throwing off
the yoke, breaking away from established institutions, and evincing the ability of a people to fashion or refashion a life for themselves. They throw off
the suffocating convenience of their age-old situation, lured on by the entice-
ments of a new promised land. The Exodus symbolizes a theological grasp of
history as the possibility for change and discontinuity, as malleable material
in human hands, as a line of action based on the awareness that one has been
liberated by God.

At this point one thing should be noted, however: Before it was an image or symbol that might be used like any other theological representation, the Exodus was an historical fact. When one talks about "conversion" or "charity" or "salvation," as we shall do in the next chapter, one is utilizing theological categories that are not empirical realities in any immediate or direct sense. There should be some material, tangible facts underlying these terms and giving them substantive reality, but the terms themselves are primarily theological categories; they are keys for representation and interpretation, not facts or happenings. The Exodus, by contrast, is a *matter of fact,* not a key for representation and interpretation. It must be considered in terms of its historical reality before one attempts to speculate on its symbolic import.

The same point holds true for the other historical paradigms cited here: prophetism as the historical stance of certain individual human beings and Jesus' clash with the public authorities of his day. The conclusions we arrived at concerning the Exodus apply equally to the other historical paradigms.

INTERPRETATION AND EVENT

Biot has made some sound and useful criticisms of Exodus theology. But if we stress the point that the Exodus must be viewed as a real event before being used as a theological category, we can narrow the scope of his objections. There is a twofold thrust to his objections. First of all, he wisely warns us against the precritical ingenuousness of some versions of Exodus theology. Biot reminds us that we must not make the mistake of extrapolating the biblical account of the Exodus in attempting to interpret its political import here and now: "It can be legitimate to view the Exodus happening as the prototype for present-day revolutionary activity, if we make sure to point out that no biblical author interpreted it thus." The legitimacy of such an interpretation is greatly diminished by Biot, however, as he makes it a matter of individual taste or preference: "As a matter of personal taste, someone may come to view the Exodus story as a confirmation of his own revolutionary commitment; but he must recognize that this interpretation itself is not biblical."

In addition to this criticism of an exegetical nature, Biot has another of a theological cast. Even if the Bible itself were to offer the aforementioned interpretation of the Exodus, "that in itself would not hallow or canonize revolution." His line of reasoning is based on an indisputable premise: "The historical events narrated in the Bible cannot constitute moral norms." Thus the fact of the Exodus does not point of necessity toward a theology of revolution.[10]

These criticisms are healthy warnings against oversimplistic versions of Exodus theology or a theology of revolution. But they also embody serious misunderstandings, an analysis of which will help us to see more clearly what the true import of the Exodus is as an historical model for political theology.

Insofar as Biot's first criticism is concerned, it is up to exegetes to decide the question. The interpretation of the Exodus event as an act of resistance, insurrection, and liberation is highly suggestive, but is that the biblical interpretation? It may well be that theologians of the Exodus have been too hasty in assuming a "yes" answer to that question. But Biot himself seems to to be rather hasty in assuming a "no" answer without spelling out his exegetical reasoning on the matter. There is every reason, of course, to try to find out exactly what the Bible thinks about the Exodus as a possible archetype for civil insurrection motivated by Christian hope in a new earth. But even here it is worth pointing out that the critical issue is not so much the Bible's interpretation of the Exodus happening as *the happening itself* which is related by the Bible. The important issue is not whether a political interpretation of the Exodus has a solid basis in the Bible; it is whether the happening itself is biblical. In short, it is a question of historical fact, not a question of hermeneutics.

If we consider the Exodus as an historical reality, then it is more or less beside the point whether the Bible does or does nor interpret it along the same lines as current political theology. The fact that the biblical authors might not have taken account of the subversive political significance of the flight from Egypt is not a crushing blow. The crucial point is that from the way they relate the event this subversive political significance seems to be clear and obvious. It flows from the very nature of the event itself, whether those who reported the event in the Bible were aware of it or not. The Exodus from Egypt was a political act, clearly bearing the stamp of resistance and rebellion. And if an action of that sort lies at the very origin of biblical tradition, then on that score there is justification for an Exodus theology and its prolongations in a theology of liberation. Political theology relates to the event of the Exodus itself, with the escape from Egypt as history, not (or not only) with the understanding and interpretation of that event by the biblical writers.

There is a real core of truth in Biot's second objection. Biblical facts and events do not give rise to moral norms; in fact they are not always exemplars either. This is obvious enough when the Bible itself condemns them as sinful. But even those deeds it regards positively or applauds loudly do not necessarily possess exemplary value by virtue of that simple fact. It would be naive to try to construct a theological or moral teaching on the story of Judith, for example. To that extent Biot's objection is very much to the point. But here again we find that it, too, has limitations and cannot be pushed further.

It is misleading to talk in generic terms about "the historical events narrated by the Bible," as Biot does, placing them alongside each other indiscriminately and then adding that they do not canonize anything. The Judith event is not on the same plane as the Exodus event; hence the former cannot have the same exemplary value as the latter. If we are talking about the most fundamental events of what is called salvation history, we cannot rightly say that they do not contain any import as models. Like the cross, the Exodus does have archetypal significance. Of course it would be a very different matter if one were to claim that they give rise to moral norms. Neither the cross nor the Exodus can be said to establish any moral norm.

The cross, for example, does specify a general moral attitude, but not a concrete norm. There is a theology and also an ethics of the cross, but there are no precepts arising directly out of it. In like manner there is a morality and a theology of the Exodus, though one cannot derive codifiable norms from it. The Exodus has exemplary and paradigmatic value, though it has no normative value in a case-book sense. This conclusion follows from the very nature of the sequence of events that faith accepts as salvation history. If salvation history, viewed as an overall process and in terms of its cardinal happenings, does not have any value for the Christian as exemplar and prototype, what possible import could it possess?

Let us grant, then, that the Exodus does not give rise to any moral norm prescribing and sanctioning revolution or any other social change. No obligation to revolution, and indeed no obligation whatsoever, follows from the fact of the Exodus. There is no moral precept to engage in revolution, or liberating insurrection. Moreover, one is making a gratuitous assertion if one claims that political theology tries to defend the existence of such a norm flowing from some event narrated in the Bible. But that does not mean that the Exodus does not possess exemplary value as a paradigm and archetype. The Exodus is not a norm-giving memory, it is an example-giving memory. While evocation of that event does not create obligations, it does nourish Christian consciousness, give inspiration to the imagination of the faith, and prompt people to liberative action.

The same holds true for other facts and events in the Bible. They are not normative; they are sources of inspiration and liberation. They give rise to a possibility, not to a necessary obligation. In presenting certain actions performed by our forefathers in the faith as an integral part of history in which God is a participant, the biblical account authorizes us to take analogous action on the basis of our faith. To put it concretely, the Exodus is a liberative memory with regard to the possibility of insurrection. The biblical narrative of the escape from Egypt liberates people from fear of revolution. It takes away the fear that rises in us when we advert to the illicit nature of disobedience or insurrection against political authority. Should we be afraid that affiliation with a revolution is incompatible with our faith, the example of the Exodus is there to dispel that particular fear. The Exodus certifies that insurrection is a stance or line of action that is possible for one who has faith.

The same basic interpretation holds true for the sayings of the Bible. They are liberative pronouncements, not constraining ones. One cannot rigorously deduce political norms or even general norms of action from them. The belief that the biblical text contains precepts of divine law in the strict sense is bound up with the myth of the Bible as a revealed oracle. But as soon as Scripture ceases to be viewed as such an oracle, the notion that its precepts are the precepts of God himself disappears.[11]

It must also be pointed out that in the Bible we find not one but several different models of political behavior. Smolik, for example, has been able to detect three models of Christian social life in the New Testament: (1) a prepolitical model in the Gospels; (2) a conservative model in the writings of

Paul; and (3) a revolutionary model in the book of Revelation.[12] Which of these would be obligatory? Since there is a variety of political paradigms in the Bible, there is clearly no room for a constrictive interpretation. They cannot all be normative at the very same time; hence none of them is normative. With its doctrinal pronouncements and its historical narratives the Bible offers inspirational models, not prescriptive standards.

In that sense Spaemann is quite correct when he makes the following observation in the course of criticizing political theology: "It is not possible to deduce concrete maxims of political conduct from theological pronouncements."[13] That is true, of course. But political theology definitely does not try to derive political maxims from theological assertions; it does not propose a theologically grounded politics. Spaemann's objection might well apply to the older theologies of the Christendom outlook, but it does not really apply to current political theology. In the latter there is no causal or logical connection between adhesion to the faith and political affiliation, much less between specific dogmatic theses and specific civil attitudes. As Blanquart points out, the believer "is not a revolutionary because he is a Christian; rather, being a revolutionary is his way of being a Christian."[14] François Biot, who also stresses the fact that the road from faith to politics is a complicated one rather than a matter of straightforward deductive reasoning, spells out the deeper reason that rules out any deductive reasoning of such a kind: "People are political beings before being Christians, if they are Christians at all." Thus any such formula as "I am a socialist because I am a Christian" is objectively unacceptable, even though it may sum up the personal path of some people who went on from their faith to discover socialism.[15]

Let us get back to the Exodus for a moment and its potential value as an exemplar. Insofar as it is an event that was prior in time to Jesus Christ, our valuation of it will depend on our valuation of the Old Testament in general. Some time ago Ernst Bloch called attention to the fact that all Christian rebels have appealed to the Old Testament.[16] Thus there is nothing peculiar in the fact that current political theology should do the same thing, since it too is critical and rebellious toward the prevailing social order. The current rehabilitation of politics in theology goes hand in hand with the corresponding rehabilitation of the Old Testament and its earthy realism.[17] On a certain methodological level the current debate over political theology is also a debate over the present-day relevance of the Old Testament. Hans Maier, for example, fears all the current versions of political theology because he sees them bringing back the pagan and Jewish formulations of an ancient day.[18] Such a rehabilitation, however, does not disturb the proponents of political theology at all. Sölle echoes the common feeling when she reproaches Bultmann for having neglected "the primary Jewish form (of hope) with which all political theology must be linked."[19]

Political theology is particularly deserving of a high credit rating if in fact there is not direct access to the faith of the New Testament and if the thrust of the Old Testament, with its tenacious hold on earthly reality and political history, continues to be a factor intrinsic to the adherence of the Christian. But political theology does not draw its models exclusively from the Old Testament. It also finds them in the New Testament, and in particular in the person of Jesus himself.

NOTES

1. Jürgen Moltmann, *The Theology of Hope: The Ground and the Implications of a Christian Eschatology*, trans. James W. Leitch (New York: Harper and Row, 1967), pp. 324, 337-38.

2. Ibid., p. 330.

3. Harvey Cox, *The Secular City* (New York: Macmillan, 1965), pp. 35-36.

4. Ibid., p. 236.

5. Gustavo Gutiérrez, *A Theology of Liberation: History, Politics and Salvation*, trans. and ed. Sister Caridad Inda and John Eagleson (Maryknoll, N.Y.: Orbis Books, 1973), pp. 294-95.

6. Jean Cardonnel, *Dieu est mort en Jésus-Christ* (Bordeaux: G. Ducros, 1968), p. 123.

7. Jean Cardonnel, in *L'homme chrétien et l'homme marxiste*, Marxist-Christian discussions in Lyons and Paris in 1964 (Paris and Geneva: La Palatine, 1964), p. 81.

8. Ibid., p. 80.

9. Julio de Santa Ana, "Notas para una ética de la liberación a partir de la biblia," in *Pueblo oprimido, señor de la historia* (Montevideo: Tierra Nueva, 1972), pp. 118-21.

10. François Biot, *Théologie de la politique* (Paris: Presses Universitaires, 1972), p. 129.

11. Alfredo Fierro, *Teología, punto crítico* (Pamplona: Dinor, 1971), pp. 179-194.

12. Josef Smolik, "Revolution and Desacralization," *Sacralization and Secularization*, ed. Roger Aubert, Concilium 47 (New York: Seabury, 1969), pp. 163-79.

13. Robert Spaemann, "Theologie, Prophetie, Politik: Zur Kritik der politischen Theologie," *Wort und Wahrheit* 24 (1969): 488.

14. P. Blanquart, "Fe cristiana y revolución," in *Teología de la violencia* (Salamanca: Sígueme, 1970), p. 147.

15. Biot, *Théologie de la politique*, pp. 191-212.

16. Ernst Bloch, *Thomas Münzer, teólogo de la revolución*, Span. trans. (Madrid: Ciencia nueva, 1968), p. 47.

17. Alfredo Fierro, *La fe contra el sistema* (Estella: Verbo Divino, 1972), pp. 137-38.

18. Hans Maier, "Politische Theologie," in *Diskussion zur "politischen Theologie,"* ed. H. Peukert (Mainz and Munich: Kaiser and Matthias Grünewald, 1969), p. 6.

19. Dorothee Sölle, *Teología política*, Span. trans. (Salamanca: Sígueme, 1972), p. 62.

27

JUAN LUIS SEGUNDO

Faith and Ideologies
in Biblical Revelation

Faith is basic commitment to liberation, but the options for concretely realizing liberation in history must be learned through specific modes of political analysis and action, namely, by means of ideologies. The debate over whether the New Testament continues or corrects the Old Testament, or gives it a "fuller sense," is best resolved by stressing the continuity of revelation and the coexistence of faith and ideologies in all levels of the Bible.

There is an inescapable "empty space between the conception of God that we receive from our faith and the problems that come to us from an everchanging history." We must bridge the gap by a system of means and ends. Our reading of the Bible on two simultaneous levels may be explained from the communication theory concepts of proto-learning, *which is simple learning, and* deutero-learning, *which is learning to learn. When, for example, we read how faith came to expression at one time in an ideology of fighting one's way out of bondage and at another time in nonviolent resistance to bondage, we are engaged in simple learning. When we reflect on these expressions,*

Reprinted from *Liberation of Theology* (Maryknoll, N.Y.: Orbis Books, 1976), pp. 108–122.

together with other strategies of fighting oppression, in order to determine what we should do about oppression in our situation, we are learning to learn.

Faith and ideologies, simple learning and learning to learn, are different but vitally linked aspects of our relation to the biblical revelation. The fourth Gospel and Paul pointedly express the Christian reality of a fundamental process of learning to learn that works within and beyond the limitations of simple learning about biblical laws and about the historical Jesus.

What, then, does the faith say to me in the concrete? What is its truth *content*? If I remain logically consistent in deducing conclusions from the above principles, then my only response can be: *nothing*. Let me repeat that in another way. If someone were to ask me what I have derived from my faith-inspired encounter as a clear-cut, absolute truth that can validly give orientation to my concrete life, then my honest response should be: nothing.

However, we are carrying the balance of faith to an irrational extreme in talking about *one* encounter with the objective font of absolute truth. If it is in fact a matter of only *one* encounter, then there is no solution to the problem. The absolute truth would remain totally obscured behind the ideology exhibited in that one historical encounter. It is quite clear that in history we can only have historical encounters, that is, encounters bound up with relative contexts.

This *reductio ad absurdum* prompts us to rediscover the decisive importance of the (historical) *density* of the Bible. Over a period of twenty centuries different faith-inspired encounters took place between human beings and the objective font of absolute truth. All of these encounters were historical; hence each one of them was relative, bound up with a specific and changing context. What came to be known or recognized in each of these encounters was an ideology, but that is not what was learned. Through the process people *learned how to learn* with the help of ideologies. This deutero-learning has its own proper content, and when I say that Jesus had two natures, one human and one divine, I am saying something about the *content* of this learning process. But these contentual items cannot be translated into one or another specific ideology because they belong to a secondary stage or level of learning. They are essentially methodological symbols. On the one hand they have no direct ideological translation; on the other hand they have no other function but to be translated into ideologies.

From these remarks it should at least be clear that one pretension of the ecclesiastical hierarchy makes no sense at all in theology. They often attempt, quite openly, to maintain a distinction if not an outright separation between faith and ideologies in order to safeguard the former. But while faith certainly is not an ideology, it has sense and meaning only insofar as it serves as the foundation stone for ideologies.

Regarding the attempt to separate faith from ideologies, I should like to cite the following remarks in an article by Thomas W. Ogletree:

> Man must answer for what he does. Being able to answer cannot be equated with success in "measuring up" to some pre-established standard. The openness of the historical process continually erodes the authority of such standards, unless they are given a highly abstract form, e.g., "loyalty to being," or "doing what love (agape) requires." Since the abstractness of such formulations makes their applicability to concrete situations problematic, it is clear that there is no precise measuring instrument by which human behavior can be tested. . . . There is no way to remove the moral risk from human action, partly because no one can ever adequately grasp the nature of his situation or the possible consequences of his action, but also because the appropriate tack in a given context may be to innovate, to give rise to the new possibility which cannot be comprehended in terms of previous values and understandings.[1]

This passage is not alluding specifically to a Christian reading of the gospel message or to the difference between faith and ideologies. But it is perfectly applicable to those areas. Even though endowed with absolute value, the Christian faith totally lacks any precise instrument for measuring the historical life of Christians by pre-established standards. And since the human sciences also lack any such value standards, Christians cannot evade the necessity of inserting something to fill the void between their faith and their options in history. In short, they cannot avoid the risk of ideologies.

The problem is of course that we are used to picturing our faith as a plane of eternal certitudes which are destined to be professed on the one hand and translated into actions on the other. Rubem Alves comments on this fact in a reference to the thought of Ebeling: "There are elements in the consciousness of the community of faith, however, which suggest that it is not only possible but indeed necessary to understand faith in exactly the opposite sense, as a radically historical mode of being, as 'the acceptance of truly historical existence.' If this is the case, its language consequently must express the spirit of *freedom for history, of taste for the future, of openness for the provisional and relative.*"[2]

It is worth noting, by the way, that certain passages in the documents of Vatican II, particularly in *Gaudium et spes*, can only make sense if they are interpreted in this light. It is one more proof of the powerful ecumenism implicit in the methodology of liberation theology. The first passage deals with the orientation of faith, not toward other-worldly certitudes, but toward historical problems and their solutions: "Faith throws a new light on everything, manifests God's design for man's total vocation, and thus *directs the mind to solutions which are fully human"* (*Gaudium et spes*, no. 11). Are we to assume from this that the faith *possesses* such solutions? Vatican II unexpectedly rejects such an assumption, the standard assumption of classical theology: "In fidelity to conscience, Christians are joined with the rest of men *in the search for truth, and the genuine solution* to the numerous problems which arise in the life of individuals and from social relationships" (ibid., no. 16).

The latter passage by itself, and even more so when combined with the first passage cited, forces us to a different conception of revealed truth. It is not a *final* truth, however absolute it may be. Instead it is a fundamental element in the search for *the truth*. In other words, it helps to support and verify what was said about faith as a process of learning to learn, as a deutero-learning. However lofty it may be, it is ever in the service of historical solutions to human problems—even though the latter solutions will always be provisional and incomplete. Faith, then, is a liberative process. It is converted into freedom for history, which means freedom *for ideologies*.

Our remarks so far suggest that we would do well to take a final look at certain biblical elements which must be considered if we wish to verify the path that has led us to those conclusions. We are particularly interested in one central point: the relationship between the revelation of Jesus and his own particular moment in history. We are interested in elucidating the relationship between faith and ideologies as it is to be found in this central event of Christianity. We want to consider the life and teaching of Jesus in his own moment of history within the overall historical process.

1. Insofar as content is concerned, liberation theology is known to have a preference and a partiality for the Old Testament in general, and for the Exodus event in particular. The reason for this is clear enough. The Old Testament, and the Exodus event in particular, show us two central elements completely fused into one: i.e., God the liberator and the political process of liberation which leads the Israelites from bondage in Egypt to the promised land. In no other portion of Scripture does God the liberator reveal himself in such close connection with the political plane of human existence. Moreover, it is a well-known fact that from the time of the Babylonian exile on, the *sapiential* literature became more individualistic, inner-directed, and apolitical. And at first glance the New Testament would seem to deprecate or even reject any connection between liberation and politics, even though it might talk about the former.

Jesus himself seems to focus his message on liberation at the level of interpersonal relationships, forgetting almost completely, if not actually ruling out, liberation vis-à-vis political oppression.[3] The same would seem to apply to Paul[4] and almost all the other writings in the New Testament.

Here liberation theology is faced with a pastoral problem of the first magnitude. If concern and commitment constitute the elements fundamental to any encounter with the gospel message, then the results can be and often are disastrous. Why? Because the Gospels seem to center Jesus' main interests on another plane entirely, on an apolitical plane. The young Christian is often advised in advance that he must "translate" the language of Jesus into political dimensions. Aside from the fact that such "translation" is not an easy process, the youth's first encounter with the gospel message often proves to be disheartening anyway. That is not one of the least reasons why liberation theology prefers the Old Testament and, in particular, the Exodus account.

In recent years, to be sure, various exegetes in Latin America and Europe[5] have tried to read between the lines of the Gospels and find a close connection between the activity of Jesus and the Zealots of Israel. I personally think that their interpretations are a bit forced, quite aside from the fact that they do not resolve the problem we have just posed in pastoral terms.

Even though it does not solve the latter problem, I think it is more sensible to realize that we are guilty of an anachronism when we assume that the decisive and critical political plane—precisely in political terms—was the opposition between Judea and the Roman Empire. It is quite possible that some contemporary groups such as the Zealots thought it was. But it seems to me that the political reality that really structured the Israel of Jesus' time and determined people's role and relationships in society was not the Roman Empire but the Jewish theocracy grounded on, and controlled by, the religious authorities who had charge of the Mosaic Law. We have already noted how Jesus destroyed the foundation of that oppressive power structure by teaching the people to reject its theological foundations. His teaching was such a political threat that the authorities of Israel made use of Rome's authorities to eliminate this dangerous *political* adversary. That is precisely what Jesus was.

Whether my last hypothesis is correct or not, indeed even assuming that for a variety of sound reasons[6] Jesus had decided not to take an interest in any political sort of liberation, it is important to realize that we must still explain either attitude in terms of an *ideology*. We must explore the problem in terms of the necessity of combining means and ends vis-à-vis a concrete situation. And it cannot be approached in other terms that are not equally concrete.

More interesting in terms of our purpose here is the fact that two theological explanations are usually offered for liberation theology's preference for certain passages of divine revelation—or, if you prefer, for certain *ideologies* expressed in its content. The first, and more naive, explanation maintains that the Exodus event is the key to the interpretation of Scripture as a whole, including the Gospels and the rest of the New Testament.[7] I consider this position naive because it is very easy for a scientific biblical theology to tear apart any such pretension. To begin with, the Book of Exodus is an historical reconstruction. It is very important, of course, but it can hardly compete with the vivid reflections of living people who are facing the prospect and then the reality of the event—to take just one example.[8] Moreover, Exodus is certainly not the central axis of the sapiential literature. The latter relates to an era of foreign domination in which the historical vocation of Israel was either lost from view or projected into eschatological terms. Still less can it be the central axis of the New Testament unless we go in for a terrible process of mutilating the latter. We could maintain that liberation was the only theme of the New Testament, I suppose, but only if we were willing to go in for a great deal of abstraction.

That brings us to the second argument against this naive attempt to suppress the rich variety of biblical experiences and to replace them with an abstract summary. In any such attempt we lose the pedagogical intent of the whole scriptural process. We also cannot explain the why and wherefore of all that concrete content, if a few summary words could have done the job equally well.

The second theological explanation for the preferences of liberation theology is more complicated. At first glance it seems more immune to attack from critical scholarship. The argument in this case is that the pedagogical principle of the Bible as a whole not only justifies but demands partiality. God reveals himself to human beings who are preoccupied with their own concrete situation. We can only understand and appreciate the word of God if we take that fact into account. Only in connection with the problems that are embodied in the questions of the community can we comprehend who exactly this responding God is. If we fail to understand the situation and problems of the community, we cannot possibly come to know that God. At first glance there may seem to be contradictions in God's revelation and his responses, but they are clarified when we uncover the different historical situations and the different questions addressed to him from within those situations.

This more complex explanation does justice to the pedagogical principle of divine revelation. To cite a different example, let us consider the educational process of any child. If we want to understand that process but do not have direct access to the words or methodology of the educator—as is the case with the pedagogy of Scripture—then we must try to infer all that from what the child says about many different things, in different situations, over a long period of time. The first thing we must keep in mind is that the child does not tell us exactly what the educator is thinking. The educator is attentive to the child, and even the latter's mistakes can help in the pedagogical process. But that does presume that the educator is aware at every moment of the child's own situation, for that is and remains the starting point of education. The fact that at a given point in time the child may insist upon the real existence of Red Riding Hood does not indicate anything in the nature of a pedagogical error. Faced with a real-life situation at that point, the educator felt it made no sense to argue with the child over that point, but that it did make sense to try and draw certain lessons from the story, and so forth.

We can assume that in the Scriptures the people of Israel have accumulated and set forth for us an educative process directed by God. But God does not show up on the tape. All that we get are the *results* that flowed from the reflections and responses of the Israelites to that divine instruction.

2. That brings us to a second problem. What is the exact relationship be-

tween, for example, the revelation of Jesus in the New Testament and the revelation of God in the Old Testament? Though it may seem hard to believe, the fact is that this basic and important question has scarcely been given a clear answer over the past twenty centuries of Christian living. And that fact has conditioned the whole of theology.

The usual responses tend to move in two opposite directions. One response stresses the fact that Jesus represents one more link in a chain of revelation, the revelation itself being one basically and all of it being true. Jesus himself lends support to this view when he says: "Do not suppose that I have come to abolish the Law and the prophets; I did not come to abolish but to complete. I tell you this: so long as heaven and earth endure, not a letter, not a stroke, will disappear from the Law until all that must happen has happened" (Matt. 5:17–18). As we all know, "the Law and the prophets" was a common short-hand way of referring to all of Sacred Scripture in Jesus' day; it did not refer solely to the legal or prophetical books. Jesus, therefore, is referring to the whole of what we call the Old Testament; and he seems to be saying that he himself and his message represent an additional element that is directly and positively a continuation of past revelation.

The implication seems to be that the Scriptures are not a body of law in the modern sense of the term. Instead they embody a divine plan of long-term duration. Jesus did not come to alter this plan, but to bring it to its fulfillment and completion. And if we consider that plan as an educational one, then we are forced to conclude that Jesus is making himself a part of that plan rather than upsetting it. Thus when he goes on to say, on several occasions, "But I tell you . . . ," he is simply trying to purify the moral law of the Old Testament of its grosser material features.

But other features of the Gospel accounts point us in the opposite direction.They show us a break in continuity, a qualitative leap in Jesus' revelation beyond the older divine teaching—even though the exact nature of this leap may be hard to spell out. At the very least it looks more like outright correction than mere continuation.

At the end of the Sermon on the Mount, for example, Matthew informs us: "When Jesus had finished this discourse the people were astounded at his teaching; unlike their own teachers he taught *with a note of authority*" (Matt. 7:28–29). Now this special air of authority by contrast with the teaching of the scribes could be viewed as a revival of prophetic authority in Israel after a long period of prophetic silence. There is no doubt that Jesus presented him-self as prophet and was taken as such from the very beginning. But in this connection we must note that it would never have occurred to the prophets to challenge the very content of the Mosaic Law. That is precisely what Jesus did, Matthew's previous remark notwithstanding. Mark certainly saw Jesus in that new light, for he notes that Jesus declared all foods clean when in fact there was a huge corpus of Mosaic Law and related commentaries on the matter of pure foods (Mark 7:19).

Then there are Jesus' authoritative statements on gratuitous love (Luke

6:27–36), which Paul sums up in his letter to the Romans: "Let your aims be such as all men count honourable. If possible, so far as it lies with you, live at peace with all men. My dear friends, do not seek revenge, but leave a place for divine retribution; for there is a text which reads, 'Justice is mine, says the Lord, I will repay.' But there is another text: 'If your enemy is hungry, feed him; if he is thirsty, give him a drink; by doing this you will heap live coals on his head.' Do not let evil conquer you, but use good to defeat evil" (Rom. 12:17–21). Now if we take Jesus' authoritative statements in this vein as authentic moral precepts, then he certainly did *correct* passages which the Old Testament attribute to God himself and which command such things as the slaying of neighboring peoples who might constitute a threat to the freedom and religion of Israel (e.g., Deut. 7:14 ff.).

Some time ago another view was popular, particularly in Catholic circles, which stood somewhere between the *continuation* view and the *correction* view. It was the notion of the *sensus plenior,* the "fuller sense," of Scripture. Jesus' revelation allegedly pointed up the true sense of older revelation, a sense that had not been appreciated even by those who wrote down God's revelation. With this revelation, in other words, Jesus provided people with new light for understanding the real import of persons, doctrines, and events in the Old Testament: e.g., Moses and the law, Adam and sin.

Now in some way or other we will always be compelled to recognize a fuller sense in God's later revelation. But the notion of the *sensus plenior* presents two very serious difficulties to any attempts to explain and resolve the contradictions cited above. The first difficulty is that unless one chooses to appeal to miracles as part of the scientific hermeneutic process, then one must assume that the whole notion of *sensus plenior* extends to all the different stages of the Old Testament as well. But, to take one example, can one really maintain that the authentic import of the Exodus event is more clearly spelled out in the more spiritualistic and subjective interpretation of the sapiential books? Are we to assume that in analogous circumstances the Israelites should henceforth act in a very different manner than they did the first time around? Clearly that is a basic and important question for any liberation theology.

Let us consider another example from the New Testament. Paul can certainly be considered a proponent of the *sensus plenior.* Looking at Moses and his law in the light of Christ, Paul believes he can pinpoint the true significance of that early legislation. The Mosaic Law was not a restrictive condition imposed by God on the unconditional promise made to Abraham. Rather, it was a preparation for Christ insofar as it revealed the reality and enslaving power of sin. This logically leads Paul to assert that with Christ human beings cease to be subject to the Law. It no longer makes any sense to ask whether some course of action is *licit* or not, when one is faced with some moral doubt. The new meaning brought by Christ serves to correct old, outmoded attitudes and approaches. But that brings us back to the critical question: if we do find thoroughgoing correction in divine revelation, can we really say that there is a oneness of faith from past to present? Can we Christians really say that we have faith in the Old Testament, in the Exodus revelation for example? Is it worth going back to the Mosaic Law when its real meaning is spelled out in the New Testament, to the point where the Law itself is abolished? And in such a case what is the point of preferring the Exodus account to the New Testament in our liberation theology?

3. The first response of liberation theology to the problem posed above involves going back to the notion that there is real continuity in the whole of divine revelation and distinguishing two elements in it. One element is permanent and unique: *faith.* The other is changing and bound up with different historical circumstances: *ideologies.*

If God's revelation never comes to us in pure form, if it is always fleshed out in historical ideologies, then we cannot appeal to the historical Jesus in order to throw out the solutions of the Old Testament. If circumstantial conditions and exigencies are decisive, then Jesus' remarks about turning the other cheek in no way correct the command of Deuteronomy to physically exterminate certain foreign peoples.

Our theory, in other words, assumes that there is an empty space between the conception of God that we receive from our faith and the problems that come to us from an ever-changing history. So we must build a bridge between our conception of God and the real-life problems of history. This bridge, this provisional but necessary system of means and ends is what we are calling *ideology* here. Obviously each and every ideology presented in Scripture is a human element even though in the intensely unified psychological processes of human beings it may seem to be a direct and straightforward translation of the proper conception of the God who has been revealed.

Consider the Israelites who arrived in the promised land. For them the extermination of their enemies was concretely the most clear-cut way of conceiving who God was and what he was commanding in the face of specific historical circumstances. Thus the extermination of enemies was the ideology that faith adopted, with or without critical thought, at that moment in history. And to be logical here, we must say the same thing with regard to the gospel message. When Jesus talked about freely profferred love and nonresistance to evil, he was facing the same problem of filling the void between his conception of God (or perhaps that of the first Christian community) and the problems existing in his age. In short, we are dealing here with another ideology, not with the content of faith itself.

This view of the matter gives liberation theology greater freedom to move, in principle, through the Scriptures and to work with the faith. Moreover, it is actually the scientific approach used by exegesis in dealing with the content of both the Old and the New Testaments. For exegesis regards that content as a succession of religious ideologies, each one being bound up with its historical context and being comprehensible only in terms of that context. As a scholarly science, biblical exegesis is much less concerned about the oneness or unity of the whole complex. It does not decide, for example, whether a specific orientation or line of thinking is incompatible with the rest or not, is heretical or not. Of course it assumes some sort of unity between the Exodus and Jesus, since it is dealing with a process going on in the same cultural world, a world that differs from other cultural worlds of the same era. But it refuses to make a theological value judgment as to whether one of those ideologies is superior to another or not. Each ideology has its historical function to carry out.

Needless to say, liberation theology cannot accept or adopt that impartiality. Its concern is not to describe what happened in the past but to make a decision vis-à-vis new problems that either were not dealt with in Scripture or were dealt with in a very different context.

In this situation theology has two ways open to it in trying to relate the faith to new historical situations—e.g., to the situation of socio-political oppression that prevails in Latin America. One way is to seek out the biblical situations most akin to those of the present day and to accept the ideology that Scripture presents in those situations as the correct response of faith. If, for example, the relationship between the Exodus situation and our own today seems closer than the situation of the Hebrews in the time of Christ and ours today, then the Exodus rather than the Gospels should serve as our source of inspiration in trying to find a present-day ideology that will dovetail with the faith.

The other possible approach is to invent an ideology that we might regard as the one which would be constructed by a gospel message contemporary with us. What would the Christ of the Gospels say if he were confronting our problems today? If the faith is one amid the diversity of history, then there must be some ideology that can build a bridge between that faith and our present-day situation even as there were such ideologies in the past.

These would seem to be the only two approaches open to us. The problem is that the first approach becomes more unrealistic and anti-scientific as time goes on. There seems to be less and less sense in trying to look for similar situations in cultural milieus dating back thirty-five centuries, particularly since the pace of history seems to be accelerating every day. The second approach does call for creativity here and now. But if we must try to imagine what the gospel message would be if it were formulated today, it is becoming more and more obvious to Christians that *secular* inventiveness and creativity is more appropriate and fruitful.

4. These difficulties prompt us to take a further step and to ask a further question: Can the content of faith offer us the precision we so far lack? Here we run into a serious problem. For while ideologies are defined by their content, we run into problems when we try to do the same thing with our faith. What is the faith in *objective* terms, in terms of information rather than merely subjective attitudes? Is there anything left in Scripture once we have discarded the ideological element?

It is too easy to say that what remains is precisely the conception of God that runs through the centuries and that the various ideologies attempt to relate to specific historical circumstances. It is too easy because that conception of God is never found separated from the ideologies that attempt to interpret God by applying his demands to a specific historical situation. Both processes are inextricably linked. You cannot get rid of one without emptying the other of content.

In other words the idea of a liberating God cannot be separated from historical situations and actions, such as the slaying of the firstborn, because no liberating God is revealed outside of such historical situations. As James Cone noted, there are no universal truths in the process of liberation; the only truth is liberation itself.[9] Though some people may feel disappointed, there is no "universal God" in the ordinary sense of the word "universal."[10]

Now this view frees us from the necessity of *reducing* the whole Bible to one singular conception of reality for the sake of maintaining the oneness of our faith. But it does not offer us much help in trying to use our faith as the orientation we need to solve our problems in history. But is it possible that we are confusing the issue for ourselves? When we talk about some objective content of faith and try to dissociate it from the content of various ideologies as if the two were disputing the same ground, may we not be confusing *two simultaneous but different levels of learning?* To borrow the terminology that communication theory uses with reference to such fields as cybernetics, biology, and psychology, may we not be confusing a *proto-learning* with a *deutero-learning,* a first level learning with a second-level learning?[11] The former is *simple learning,* the latter is *learning to learn.*

Consider Pavlov's experiments, for example. His dogs learned that the sound of a bell signified food, and their salivary glands began to secrete as soon as the bell sounded. Here we clearly have a process of *simple learning.* The dogs learned to react to a specific stimulus, and that is all. They could be taught in the same way to react to a second stimulus. Now the characteristic feature of learning at that stage is that information is *added* or *subtracted.* Information about two stimuli tells the dogs nothing about a possible third stimulus, and a mistake represents a subtraction. Thus if a dog were given food one hundred times after a bell was rung and not given food one hundred times after a bell was rung, the sum of information at the end of the experiment would be exactly zero.

On the human level, however, we repeatedly experience a second-level learning, a process of *learning to learn.* The main characteristic of this process is that new information *multiplies* or *divides* the balance of previous information. Let us take mathematics as a case in point. After a certain period of learning, a child is able to solve a certain set of problems. But suddenly we notice that he or she is solving a problem that is not a mere copy of, or addition to, the previous problems. We have reason to assume that in the process of learning mathematics the child did more than merely learn isolated answers to isolated problems. The child acquired a bibliography, as it were, which it could then consult in order to solve a new problem. The information possessed by the student is not a simple sum of the problems already learned and the bibliography previously acquired. It is the product of a multiplication of those two factors. The student, in other words, possesses objective information that enables him to solve new problems which he has not studied before. An inadequate or jumbled bibliography, on the other hand, does not represent a mere subtraction of information already learned; it represents a division of that information because it wipes out much of what had been previously learned. But when they are part of the overall process and do not disorient the child, even errors are helpful. They do not represent subtraction or addition of information; they represent a multiplication of information.

The important point here is that simple learning and learning to learn do not dispute control of the informational content. The bibliography, for example, is not a mathematical formula. The mathematical formulas that the child may retain or construct are dependent on the bibliography, but they are not in competition with it.

Perhaps this allusion to a bibliography may not be the most satisfactory way to explain or comprehend the relationship between faith and ideologies, since a bibliography always remains external to mathematical knowledge and understanding itself. A student who is truly creative in mathematics might afford us a suitable example. Once introduced to the learning process, such a student not only acquires specific formulas but also the possibility of creating them when faced with new problems. The relationship between simple learning and learning to learn becomes more intimate, and it becomes more difficult to distinguish between the content of the two levels. But even in this case what we said of the bibliography above remains true: on one level information is added or subtracted, on the other it is multiplied and divided.

We can say without fear of error that the ideologies present in Scripture belong to the first level. They are responses learned vis-à-vis specific historical situations. Faith, by contrast, is the total process to which man submits, a process of learning in and through ideologies how to create the ideologies needed to handle new and unforeseen situations in history. The Scriptures can and should be examined and studied from both points of view since both processes are in the sacred writings and do not compete with each other over content. This means that fighting one's way out of bondage in Egypt is one experience and turning the other cheek is another experience. Someone who has gone through both experiences and has reflected on them has learned how to learn; he has multiplied his faith-based information, not subtracted it to zero.

These remarks will help us to better understand two basic problems of liberation theology, even if they will not enable us to fully resolve them. The *first* problem has to do with the continuation of revelation. It seems clear in the thinking of John the Evangelist that divine revelation is destined to continue after the physical disappearance of Jesus. Classical theology, however, talks about revelation as a "deposit" closed at the death of the last apostle, the last eyewitness to the teaching of Jesus.

In the fourth Gospel Jesus has this to say as he is about to bid farewell to his disciples: "There is still much that I could say to you, but the burden would be too great for you *now*. However, when he comes who is the Spirit of truth, he will guide you into all the truth; for he will not speak on his own authority. . . . He will glorify me, for everything that he makes known to you he will draw from what is mine" (John 16:12–14).

Jesus clearly affirms that many things remain to be said and that they will be said, although in a different manner. The *Spirit* of truth will take many things which Jesus himself had not spoken and will make them comprehensible as obviously belonging to the same divine revelation. Jesus' language is very clear. It points not towards a better understanding of what has already been spoken but towards the learning of new things.

Can we, in that case, substitute the word "ideologies" for "things"? We have already seen that the concrete responses of the Israelite community or the Christian community at any given moment necessarily constitute ideologies. Well, we have exactly the same situation here. There are things that Jesus *cannot say* because they do not dovetail with the historical situation in which his disciples are living. They could not bear them *now*. When they are spoken by the Spirit, however, they will automatically be converted into ideologies associated with a specific historical situation that renders them comprehensible and useful.

What will be the relationship between these new ideologies and *faith,* the latter being understood as a divine revelation that entails recognition of its revealer? The logical answer is that the former revealer, Christ, is replaced by the Holy Spirit. But the Spirit is not a visible, identifiable revealer, which would seem to indicate that one can really have faith only in past revelation. The only coherent hypothesis is to have recourse once again to the notion of a *deutero-learning* process, a process of learning to learn. This process is by its very definition the opposite of any sort of deposit, for it involves an unending process of acquiring new pieces of information that multiply the previous store of information. That being the case, the only visible guidepost is the presence or absence of the teacher outside of the pupil. At a certain point, however, the external teacher disappears from the scene; yet the internal process of learning goes on continually, based on external experience.

This seems to be the obvious import of Jesus' promise. The Spirit of truth is not an external teacher as Jesus himself was. Or we might say instead that no external teacher after Christ will add any information to the educational process. The process will go on internally, as the pupil confronts reality with new ideologies. Jesus is saying that one stage of the process is ended, but he is also promising that the process can continue through its own proper means. And those means are nothing else but a succession of ideologies vis-à-vis the concrete problems of history. In short, after Christ history itself is entrusted with the task of carrying on the process. The Spirit of Christ, that is, the dynamic, intrinsic result of the revelatory education process, ensures a process that will lead to the full and complete truth.

The *second* problem is intimately bound up with the first, and it is the same problem with which we have been dealing from the very start of this chapter.

From what we have said so far it seems clear that it makes no Christian sense at all to try to separate ideologies from faith in order to safeguard and preserve the latter. Without ideologies faith is as dead as a doornail, and for the same reason that James offers in his epistle: it is totally impracticable (James 2:17).

From this standpoint it is very instructive to give a brief summary of Paul's interpretation of the Christian's moral obligations in the light of Christ's revelation. Remember that Paul's interpretation antedates the redaction of the four Gospels in their present form. His view can be summarized as follows:

a) Only concrete love gives meaning and value to any kind of law existing in the universe (Rom. 13:8-10).

b) Any and every type of law represents a decisive element for Christian conduct insofar as it points up more or less constant relationships between things and persons. But such laws are not decisive as moral laws (Rom. 14:14). They are decisive as constants in the service of the love-based plans and projects of human beings (1 Cor. 6:12 ff.; 10:23 ff.), since they furnish these projects with criteria for judging what is or is not *expedient* in carrying them out (1 Cor. 10:23-29; Rom. 14:7-9).

c) Since this desacralizes the law as a static inventory of questions concerning the intrinsic morality of a given line of conduct, the conduct of the Christian must undergo a basic change. *Faith* rather than the law must serve as the springboard for launching into a new adventure. One's destiny will depend on this venture, but it possesses no *a priori* criteria established in advance. The Christian must accept the riskiness of projects that ever remain provisional and will often go astray (Gal. 5:6 and *passim:* Rom. 14:1 ff.).

d) Therefore this faith does not consist in intellectual adherence to a certain body of revealed content as the definitive solution to theoretical or practical problems. Nor does it consist in having confidence in one's own salvation, thanks to the merits of Christ. Instead it entails the freedom to accept an educational process that comes to maturity and abandons its teacher to launch out into the provisional and relative depths of history (Gal. 4:1 ff.; Rom. 8:19-23; 1 Cor. 3:11-15).

Faith, then, is not a universal, atemporal, pithy body of content summing up divine revelation once the latter has been divested of ideologies. On the contrary, it is maturity by way of ideologies, the possibility of fully and conscientiously carrying out the ideological task on which the real-life liberation of human beings depends.

NOTES

1. Thomas W. Ogletree, "From Anxiety to Responsibility: The Shifting Focus of Theological Reflection," in *Chicago Theological Seminary Register,* March 1968. Reprinted in *New Theology* 6 (New York: Macmillan, 1969), p. 61.

2. Rubem A. Alves, *A Theology of Human Hope* (Washington, D.C.: Corpus Books, 1969), p. 71.

3. If we agree with Gutiérrez that the realm of politics is the most prevalent and pervasive factor in present-day human life, it is anachronistic to ask what Jesus' attitude might have been toward this *present-day* situation of ours. The discovery of the pervasive influence of politics is our contemporary discovery, not his. Hence Jesus' stance vis-à-vis the Roman Empire or the Zealots, as a political stance, is also relatively beside the point. The fact is that the concrete systematic oppression that Jesus confronted in his day did not appear to him as "political" in our sense of the term; it showed up to him as "religious" oppression. More than officials of the Roman Empire, it was the religious authority of the scribes and Sadducees and Pharisees that determined the sociopolitical structure of Israel. In real life this authority was political, and Jesus really did tear it apart. This is evident from the fact that the concern to get rid of Jesus physically—because he threatened the status quo—was primarily displayed by the supposedly "religious" authorities rather than by the representatives of the Roman Empire.

4. See the passages where Paul exhorts slaves to obey their masters (e.g., Eph. 6:5; Col. 3:22; Titus 2:9; and Philemon), or the passages where he tends to minimize but not reject the fact of slavery in the novel light of Christ (e.g., Col. 3:11; 1 Cor. 7:21–22; 12:13; Gal. 3:28).

5. See Gustavo Gutiérrez, *A Theology of Liberation* (Maryknoll, N.Y.: Orbis Books, 1973), Chapter 11.

6. One reason of utmost importance should be noted. Any liberation process—e.g., political liberation—would have concrete historical limitations of its very nature. That fact would have seriously diminished the universality of Christ's message about total liberation, applicable to all human beings and all phases of human existence. To be sure, it is impossible to *talk* about liberation without implementing some concrete forms of liberation if one wants to be credible to others. Jesus submitted to this basic law. But the obligation of summoning human beings to a universal liberation while bearing real witness to some concrete liberation is what explains the curious dialectic in Jesus' life. He first points up the concrete liberations he is effecting, only to try to draw people's attention away from them later in order to emphasize a broader and more profound message. That, in my opinion, is the proper explanation of the so-called "messianic secret" in Mark. The explanation of liberal exegesis is incorrect.

7. The most profound and scholarly effort in this direction is, in my opinion, that of Severino Croatto, *Exodus: A Hermeneutics of Freedom* (Maryknoll, N.Y.: Orbis Books, 1981).

8. See, for example, Gerhard von Rad, *Old Testament Theology* (New York: Harper & Row, 1965), vol. 2, Part II.

9. James H. Cone, *A Black Theology of Liberation* (Philadelphia: Lippincott, 1970), p. 33.

10. Ibid., p. 156.

11. On this process of *deutero-learning* on different scientific levels, see Gregory Bateson, *Steps to an Ecology of Mind* (New York: Ballantine Books, 1974), especially Parts II, V, and VI.

28

RUDOLF J. SIEBERT

Jacob and Jesus: Recent Marxist Readings of the Bible

Since Ernst Bloch wrote The Spirit of Utopia *in 1918, Marxist philosophers of religion, such as L. Kolakowski and M. Horkheimer, have explored ways in which religion and theology point to the essentially human, not merely as the existing ensemble of social relationships but as the potential and drive for relationships yet to be realized. Two Czech Marxists, Vitězslav Gardavsky and Milan Machoveč, have offered readings of the Bible which stress its principle of radical human subjectivity, i.e., the independent personality of the individual, which is for them detachable from the false transcendence of Jewish and Christian theology. This radical human subjectivity is absolutely necessary to the full realization of socialist society.*

The author suggests that the probes of Marxist philosophers of religion and of Christian political theologians point toward a release of God from the devalued and privatized sphere of feeling into the public and rational realms in what would amount to "a political proof of God" by the Christian practice of qualitative social change toward a new more humane world.

Reprinted from *The Bible and Liberation: Political and Social Hermeneutics*, 1st ed., ed. N. K. Gottwald and A. C. Wire (Berkeley: Community for Religious Research and Education [Radical Religion], 1976), pp. 145–56.

Marxist philosophers of religion have begun to read the sacred writings of the positive religions, mainly of Judaism and Christianity, in a critical spirit. They not only seek to clarify the fundamental representations appearing in those religious texts, but they also search the sacred writings for expressions of the universal interest of the human species in emancipation and solidarity.

The dialectical philosophers of religion read the Old and New Testaments very differently from orthodox Jews or Christians and also differently from the phenomenologists of religion. Most importantly, they no longer approach the two Testaments through the glasses of ecclesiastical editorship or even of the Christian tradition. Of course, since L. Feuerbach, many phenomenologists have also freed themselves from such authorities, at least to a large extent. Contrary to the phenomenologists, however, the critical sociologists of religion read the Bible as a subversive and revolutionary book. For the Marxist philosophers, the Bible no longer agrees or harmonizes with ecclesiastical and state power. The dialectical philosopher of religion reads the sacred writings as documents of the struggles of men and women with that God in the master myths of religion who has been proclaimed for too long a time as heavenly master-power—the mere prolongation of the earthly power structures of despots and oligarchs. After a long tradition of religious and theistic exegesis, the critical sociologist of religion practices a new secular atheistic and revolutionary exegesis of biblical figures and stories. This exegesis develops into a negative hermeneutics. Through it, the dialectical philosopher demythologizes and deideologizes the sacred texts.

This new Marxist style of exegesis of religious texts was prepared by Ernst Bloch's great works *Vom Geist der Utopie* (*The Spirit of Utopia*) in 1918 and *Thomas Münzer als Theologe der Revolution* (*Thomas Münzer as Theologian of Revolution*) in 1922. Leszek Kolakowski continued the new type of exegesis throughout the 1960s in the collected stories of *Der Himmelsschlüessel* (*The Key to Heaven*). In those stories even the old religious element of "edification" returns, which Hegel had rejected from his philosophy of history, but without which for Kierkegaard the Hegelian philosophy of history remains merely a product of curiosity, lacking all existential interest. Vitězslav Gardavsky applies the newest Marxist exegesis to the Old and New Testaments and to the works of outstanding Christian thinkers like Augustine, Thomas Aquinas, and Pascal in his *Gott ist Nicht Ganz Tot* (*God Is Not Yet Dead*). Milan Machoveč uses it in his specifically Marxist search for the historical Jesus in *Jesus für Atheisten* (*Jesus for Atheists*).

DIALECTICAL ANTHROPOLOGY

When today the Marxist philosopher Gardavsky approaches the Old and New Testaments as an atheist, the God who appears in those writings means to him ". . . the gathering-point of all of man's potentialities. The Lord is for the Jew an interpretation of man; in him he knows what he could be, contrary to what he is."[1] "God" or "Lord" are for the Marxist philosopher of religion ciphers of human nature, of the human freedom potential.

The Marxist philosophy of religion has been dialectical anthropology of religion from its very beginning. Marx says in his sixth thesis against Feuerbach:

> Feuerbach dissolves the religious essence into the human essence. But the human essence is not an abstraction inherent to the singular individual. In its reality it is the ensemble of the social relationships.
> Feuerbach, who does not engage himself in the critique of this real essence, is therefore forced:
> 1. To abstract from the historical course and to fix the religious heart for itself and to presuppose an abstract—isolated—human individual.
> 2. The essence can therefore be grasped only as "genus," as interior, dumb universality, connecting the many individuals naturally.[2]

In Hegel's dialectical theism, the religious essence and the human essence had been dialectically identical as well as differentiated. The divine essence held the difference open, so to speak, between itself and the human essence in their identity. The absolute essence guaranteed the integrity, dignity, and freedom of the human precisely by this difference or non-identity in identity. Feuerbach arrested the dialectics between the religious and the human essence. He took back undialectically the divine essence into the human essence. Anthropology was the secret of theology. Marx found the secret of religion in the empirically concrete, real historical human essence as the ensemble of social relationships. For Marx, as for Feuerbach, the dialectics between theology and anthropology collapses into pure anthropology. Contrary to Feuerbach's anthropology, however, that of Marx is in itself dialectical, for it is characterized by the dialectics between the individual and the collective. In civil society, the individual and the social whole stand in an antagonistic relationship to each other. "Individual" as well as "collective" are equally abstract and therefore untrue. Feuerbach's anthropology of religion expresses the real situation in civil society. The goal of Marx's and the Marxist anthropology of religion is the dialectical reconciliation of the individual and the social whole—the reconciled society. Only the reconciled society is a free society and only the free society is reconciled.

POTENTIALITY

Contemporary Marxist philosophers of religion preserve Marx's anthropology of religion as their very basis. They share with Marx the goal of the reconciled, that is, the truly free society. But the present-day Marxists go beyond Marx when Gardavsky and Bloch, for example, determine the real historical human essence not only as the ensemble of social relationships but also as the ensemble of all the potentialities of humanity. Marx does not make it sufficiently clear in his sixth thesis against Feuerbach if for him the real human essence is merely the ensemble of the already realized social relationships, or also of the social relationships still to be realized in the future. In the wider context of all eleven Marxian theses against Feuerbach, we may very well assume the latter.

Nevertheless, today's dialectical anthropologists of religion make it fully explicit and clear that the human essence not only contains what has been and is, but also the potential of what shall be: what humanity is not yet. As Bloch expresses it: S is not yet p. The subject is not yet the predicate. The human being is not fully human. These Marxist thinkers stress emphatically precisely the predicate of the human subject, what has not yet emerged from the person as accomplished humanity. Bloch speaks of the *experimentum* not only *mundi* but also *hominis*.

The divine essence, as it appears in the sacred writings of the Bhagavad-Gita or in the Old and New Testaments, is for the dialectical anthropologist the symbol of the human essence precisely insofar as it has not yet been actualized. God is the hopeful sign of the as yet unrealized freedom potentiality of humanity. Freedom means, as for Hegel, that humanity overcomes all forms of estrangement and comes home into its own essence; that human needs are to be fulfilled and human potentials are to be realized.

HUMANISM

The Marxist philosopher of religion approaches the sacred writings in the light of dialectical or negative anthropology, which is not so much concerned with what people have been and are, but with what they could be and should be. For instance, to read the Old and New Testaments atheistically and humanistically means for Gardavsky and Machoveč nothing else than to look within them for that which people could and should be in the future. Marxist anthropologists, insofar as they are concerned with the Jewish and Christian religions, are searching for some kind of biblical humanism. So, for example, Gardavsky feels atheistically and humanistically attracted by the Old Testament figure of Jacob.

In the story of Jacob's night struggle with God at the river Jabbok (Gen. 32:22–32), Gardavsky sees the key to the understanding of the Old Testament in general. This story tells how the human being becomes a subject. The Adam of the Jewish Genesis, whom God created out of loam, is not yet really subject. Adam is not yet a real human name, no actual proper name. Adam is merely a genus name for man as such; Eve signifies only the difference in sex. In the perspective of human subjectivity, the human pair of the Jewish Genesis is a mere neuter. Adam and Eve are already something definite, but not yet somebody.

Jacob, on the other hand, is for Gardavsky a completely different figure from Adam and Eve. Jacob does not appreciate the "given" around him. He does not trust promises or presents. He knows that everything given, everything present, is something contingent. Jacob transcends everything naturally given, his natural destiny. He appears almost as a modern in terms of the differentiation between religious and secular consciousness in Hegel's philosophy of religion. Jacob is determined to overthrow and to change the given, his own natural destiny, through his own deeds. Contrary to traditionalists, Jacob is consciously and intentionally an agent of change. Jacob chooses and decides. He steps over the Jabbok river and fights with God. As he makes his choice, he reaches beyond his immediately given possibilities. Jacob emerges through his choice and his decision from the indistinguishable universality of his genus. In his struggle with God at the river crossing, he achieved his own individual face and his own proper name—Israel, that is, fighter of God. Jacob's deed—the struggle with God—is the first deed of historical rank, the first authentic human act! Under his new name of Israel, Jacob becomes master over time, over history. The story of Jacob signifies the birth of biblical humanism.

PRACTICE

Gardavsky relates the story of Jacob's struggle with God to that thinker Karl Marx, a Jew like Jacob, who—in his eleven theses against Feuerbach's phenomenology of religion—for the first time in the history of philosophy and theology developed a dialectical philosophy of theory-practice, which proved to be a truly revolutionary deed in the context of Western "perennial philosophy." In Gardavsky's view, Marx certainly was an atheist. But he was in no way a primitive or vulgar atheist, who would have neglected to put the question to himself concerning the specific anthropology in every specific theology or myth. Marx was not a philosopher of nature, for instance, like Schelling. Nor was Marx a classical undialectical bourgeois materialist like Feuerbach. He produced the conception of a philosophy of practice, of the history-making deed. In Marx's view, people through their powerful historical action can transcend the class boundaries which cripple their productive forces. They can become agents of qualitative change. They can put their whole existential weight passionately into each world-changing deed for which time has become ripe. They can truly change the face of the earth.

Gardavsky does not want to shy away, as other Marxists have, from the fact that Marx was indeed born into a Jewish family. Certainly Marx was miles away from any type of orthodox Jewish religiosity. Gardavsky believes, nevertheless, that there are contained in Marx's interior spirit the thousands of years old religious experiences of the Jewish people, particularly their religious and prophetic promises. Gardavsky is convinced after long Marxist studies that Marx himself—as almost nobody else before him—was able to understand and to comprehend the biblical proclamations. Otherwise, Marx could not have produced such a sovereign monistic philosophy of social, political, and historical action.

MONISM

It is precisely the monistic character of Marx's philosophy of society and history that motivates Gardavsky to draw a parallel between Jacob and Marx. Jacob's historical deed was sovereignly monistic, out of one piece, to a large extent free from any dualism. The choice which Jacob makes—to step over the river and to struggle with God—was not already part of God's eternal decree or plan, and therefore predestined. In the Old Testament Gardavsky finds no transhistorical, religious archetypes, models, or paradigms of human existence and action which continually repeat themselves. Even the phenomenologist Mircea Eliade must admit that the prophetic Hebrew Bible is revolutionary from the viewpoint of traditional societies, dominated as they are by the eternal repetition of archetypes. According to Gardavsky, everything is "history" in the Jacob story. The phenomenologist Eliade and the critical theorist Gardavsky agree that the roots of Hegelian and Marxist historicity can be found in the Jacob story as well as in other parts of the Old Testament, particularly in the prophetic writings.

Neither in the Jacob story nor elsewhere in the Old Testament can Gardavsky find that "God" or the "Lord" puts a previously known form upon a still ahistorical material. The philosophy and theology of antiquity—and, under their influence, medieval philosophical theology and even classical natural science of modern times—looked at the world as nature and history in terms of such a hylomorphism or form-material dualism. Such dualism Gardavsky believes to be almost unknown in the Old Testament. Gardavsky de-hellenizes the exegesis of the Old and New Testaments.

In the Old Testament people are elected by God insofar as they make a decision, choose in freedom and confirm this choice with their action. It is what Gardavsky calls "biblical monism." Marx's philosophy of historical practice has inherited this monism of the Old Testament.

DUALISM

Gardavsky must of course admit that in the Old Testament—as well as in the New Testament and other sacred writings—a moment of transcendence remains and that this element of transcendence contributes to the Jewish and Christian religions a measure of dualism. He wants to let this residue of dualism simply stand as it is in the sacred text. For the time being it cannot be dissolved. Gardavsky understands this residual dualism as the expression of a stage in human evolution which as such has long passed. This residual dualism is a fixation of something that is in unceasing motion forward toward the future, directed toward the totality of authentic potentialities which humanity possessed from its beginnings, and which will be fully realized in the future realm of freedom. Gardavsky claims that in Marx's monistic philosophy of historical practice this residue of an archaic religious dualism has already been completely superseded.

DIALECTICS

Here we have reached what may be the weakest point of the Marxist philosophy of religion. Its greatness lies in the attempt to dissolve the dualism between the transcendent and the relativity of history. But why does that have to happen in monistic terms? Why cannot the dialectical anthropologist solve the archaic dualism in dialectical terms? That of course would mean a reconsideration of Hegel's dialectical phenomenology and philosophy of religion. In any case, the monistic solution of religious dualism in Marxist dialectical anthropology means an arrest of dialectical logic, of which Hegel at least was not guilty. This arrest of dialectics in the Marxist anthropology of religion constitutes its untruth despite many new and fascinating insights. Only in a few instances, as in the case of Horkheimer or Adorno—and then only with Hegel's help—is the Marxist dialectical anthropology able to penetrate to the very theological core and glowing fire of religion as well as of art and philosophy. In such instances, Marxist anthropology also transcends itself.

PRINCIPLE OF SUBJECTIVITY

Concerning the Old Testament figure of Jacob, Gardavsky asks himself the question: what does the gospel or good news of Jesus in the New Testament really mean? Gardavsky, unlike Machoveč, is little interested in the question of whether or not Jesus really lived. With respect to the figure of Jesus, Gardavsky is really concerned with the personified short formula for a definite Jewish conception of the world and particularly of humanity. More precisely, Jesus is the personified principle of subjectivity. For Gardavsky, as for Hegel, the principle of subjectivity was historically prepared in the figure of Jacob and in the Jewish religion in general and beyond that in other positive religions of the Near East, e.g., the Persian religion, the Syrian religion, and the Egyptian religion. It announced itself in the Greek and Roman religions. But the full realization of the principle of subjectivity Gardavsky finds alone in the figure of Jesus. The principle of subjectivity, therefore, quite as much for Gardavsky as for Hegel, is *the* Christian principle without rival.

Gardavsky and other contemporary Marxist philosophers of religion are principally interested in carrying the originally Christian principle of subjectivity over into the post-bourgeois philosophy and social formation, but in secular form. They would like to preserve the Christian principle of the independent personality of the individual, but without transcendence. Only a few critical theorists have the insight that the Christian principle of the personality of the individual, infinite in itself, cannot be carried into the new world rising hopefully out of the present world-historical transition period without a theological basis; that without theology this principle will be lost. Many Marxist philosophers—particularly in Western Europe, Yugoslavia, and Czechoslovakia—aim nevertheless at a socialist society which has, in Hegel's terms, the strength to posit the completely secularized Christian principle of subjective freedom in harmony with the socio-ethical unity of the new socialist society with its realization of the common good.

The Christian principle of free subjectivity emerges at the beginning of our Christian era, with or without a historical Jesus, in the world of Judaism and late antiquity. Through its inner universality and necessity, it soon explodes the limitations of the Jewish in-group. It spreads rapidly through the Roman Empire, later on through the Western medieval and modern worlds. In Gardavsky's perspective, if contemporary Marxists have once comprehended Christ as the personified principle of subjectivity, they will become sufficiently free to think about him without embarrassment as a figure of the Gospels—and particularly about his call, which embodies and transmits the call to subjective freedom.

CALL

For Gardavsky, the call of Christ poses questions to us concerning our subjectivity, our projects, our plans, our social, political, and historical practice. The Marxist answer to the call of Christ, in Gardavsky's view, does not come to an end with the simple statement that Marxist philosophers and historians of religion have "refuted" the Christian legend. The Marxist answer to the challenge of the Christian call is also not adequately given by the Marxists' declaration that they do not believe in God or in the divinity of Christ, that they are simply atheists.

According to Gardavsky, the questions which original Christianity poses to our own concrete historical, subjectivity are not at all of a religious nature—in the traditional sense—but of a secular nature. Already Hegel shows that the Christian principle of the independent personality of the individual is only originally religious in the sense that it emerges in the religious dimension of the human spirit. Later on, it must be applied in secular form to the secular world as society and history. The true Marxist answer to the challenge of the Christian principle of subjectivity begins, says Gardavsky, only when Marxists recognize clearly that the Christian questions concerning our subjectivity are historically entirely justified. They are justified since they attempt to express a measure that originates from the activities of men and women as social beings, taking place in the historical process.

To give a satisfactory answer to the Christian questions concerning the principle of subjectivity as a measure of human existence and activity is finally not a matter of theory, consideration, reflection, words, but of social, political, and historical practice. In Gardavsky's perspective as it was in Hegel's, the practical application to the lives of individuals and societies of the secular form of the Christian principle of subjectivity is an issue of the practice of fundamental social change.

ESCHATOLOGY

Against the background of the story of Jacob, Gardavsky sees the characteristic quality of the figure of Jesus in the fact that the "Lord" or the "God" of both Jacob and Jesus becomes once more the call for an eschatological decision penetrating into history. For Gardavsky as for Machoveč, the whole attraction of Jesus—in his own time and for us today—rests in the reality that he projects the total future into the present moment, the here and now, the today, the *kairos*. As in the case of Jacob, so with Jesus the decisive choice can no longer be postponed. Already tomorrow may be too late. The promised land, the kingdom of heaven, has come close. Today the decision must be made; either for God and Jesus, who is his prophet, or against them. Whoever makes the choice, thereby chooses at once the whole future: salvation or damnation! Gardavsky takes this "contemporaneous eschatology" from the Revelation of John, where it appears as most urgent. Like Machoveč, Gardavsky puts Jesus into the horizon of this—his own—contemporaneous eschatology. Jesus is for both Marxists an entirely eschatological figure. This eschatological Christology gains actuality today even in Catholic and Protestant theology, as for example in the thought of Küng and of Moltmann. To be sure, for the Marxists the secret of the Christian eschatology and hope is the Marxist political utopia and hope—the realm of freedom beyond nature and beyond society's necessary production and exchange process.

MIRACLES

As Gardavsky puts Jesus into the eschatological horizon, the latter's miracle-working speaks most powerfully to him. This is amazing, since the bourgeois enlightenment of the eighteenth century seemed to be finished with miracles once and for all. Miracles nevertheless raise their heads once more in the Marxist enlightenment, not only in Gardavsky's but also in Bloch's philosophy of religion. For Gardavsky, the accent in Jesus' miracle-working falls on "working." The miracle-working of Jesus is the deed of the subject without parallel who imposes a new higher order and law on the causal connections of the world as nature and history. In the miracle appears the depth and the power of the principle of subjectivity. In Gardavsky's estimation, we experience more from the miracles of Jesus concerning the nature of history-making deeds than in the boring stories about the deeds of Babylonian, Greek, or Roman heroes.

LOVE

Gardavsky finds the real power of the miracle to be love. Jesus is convinced that people in order to be able to decide for themselves radically—that is, to work a miracle—must be completely imbued with love. Gardavsky shares Hegel's view that love is a deep form of knowledge. It penetrates the whole being of persons. It is at each moment experienced in full actuality. It is the knowledge that we exist fully and authentically only when we reach beyond ourselves in relation to ourselves, our neighbors, and God. People are truly real only when they know in love that their historical decisions, their miraculous deeds, challenge fundamentally their whole spirit, their determination, their strength of purpose, their initiative, the participation of all their senses, and their simultaneously active and passive passionateness and ardor.

When people have this knowledge, this love, they no longer need any pre-scriptions concerning what they are supposed to do concretely in a given situation: to distribute their wealth or to keep it; to leave their mates or to stay with them; to kill their rivals or to let them go. Gardavsky observes that Jesus does not tell us in detail what to do in every single situation of our lives. He merely demands that we always enter completely into every singular situa-tion. Jesus shows us through his own deeds that this is very well possible: people are able to perform miracles! Miracles do happen! In the web of hu-man action out of which history shapes itself, miracles are knotty points at which unique and unrepeatable events happen. Love shows itself as the radi-cal subjectivity of history. Marxists like Gardavsky, Machoveč, and Bloch, who are concerned with Jesus, are themselves an historical miracle, born out of love.

DEATH

Gardavsky further contends that, if one thinks it through radically to its end, the notion Jesus has of love is always a confrontation of persons with death. But if love is present as the passion for a higher human life—and that is the essence of Jesus' call—then death, not only in its physical form but in all its many everyday shapes, cannot be victorious. Therefore love, the most difficult condition to achieve, is also the highest condition of humanity. At the counterpole of love stands always the mortal dread. To transcend this boundary between death and love in the direction of the latter means "resur-rection from the dead," "life as human being." In that movement in and toward love, everything is easy, even that which is entirely impossible. For the one who has transcended the boundary between death and love, it is no longer a wonder but something naturally given. It appears miraculous only to those who have not yet made this decisive step.

METAPHYSICS

In his philosophy of religion Gardavsky tries nothing less than to project a metaphysics of Marxist atheism. This metaphysics again is nothing else than an attempt at a theory of subjectivity which is not subjectivistic, and a tran-scendence, a reaching beyond oneself, which is not objectivistic. Bloch speaks similarly of a transcending without transcendence.

Gardavsky starts from two apparently contradictory certainties. First, a person is conscious of being a social existent able to transcend itself. Second, a person has the undeniable certitude that she or he must die someday. Gar-davsky mediates those two contradictory certitudes through the social nature of selfhood. For Gardavsky the individual person, through social activity, becomes in mortality a hope for the others. A person's social nature is funda-mentally nothing else than love, in the sense in which it becomes manifest in the life of Jesus—as complete activation of subjectivity. This love is the existential precondition for all human relations.

In Gardavsky's metaphysics, love is the composition-key which the subject holds in hand in order to bring into harmony the relationships with others and with self. Love is the key word in that love transforms human work into creativity. Love is limitless in relation to the human potentialities, the cipher of which is the "God" and the "Lord" of the Old and New Testaments. Love is bottomless since one can never say in relation to it that its ground has been reached. Love is the abyss of human subjectivity. Love as it appears in Gardavsky's metaphysics is in a plain and simple sense "miraculous," since it supersedes the causality of the world as nature and history by humanizing it. Finally, in this new metaphysics of Marxist atheism, the deed of love breaks open the womb of the future, since it overcomes mortal dread. Gardavsky's metaphysics is philosophy of the future.

ADVENTURE

Gardavsky is completely aware of the fact that his whole attempt at a Marxist interpretation of sacred writings as it climaxes in a metaphysics of Marxist atheism is outrageously adventurous. Does not Gardavsky's philosophy of religion overthrow radically the fundamental principles of Marxism, particularly its emphatic materialism? Is not his metaphysics of Marxist atheism a completely subjectivistic caricature of the Marxian conception of history? What would Marx, Engels, and Lenin say to all this if they were alive today? Does not the Marxist atheistic philosopher write an all-too-enthusiastic apology for the Old and New Testaments at the very time when Christian theologians speak about the death of God or have even ceased to speak about it?

All these questions are justified. It will certainly be indispensable in the future to increase the plausibility and credibility of Gardavsky's attempt at an atheistic humanistic philosophy of religion for Marxists and non-Marxists alike, and to do this through further investigations in and analysis of the doctrines, cult forms, organizational forms, attitudes, ethical and socioethical norms not only of Christianity but of a variety of positive religions. In the meantime, however, such courageous Marxist intellectual and existential adventures into the dimension of religion deserve to be taken seriously and encouraged.

CHRISTOLOGY FROM BELOW

In his book *Jesus für Atheisten* (*Jesus for Atheists*),[3] the Marxist historian and philosopher Milan Machoveč develops that which in Christian theology since Hegel's time has been called a "Christology from below." It is a presentation of the significance of the total phenomenon of Jesus that does not presuppose the affirmation of the confession of Christ's divinity. The Christology from below begins with the historical Jesus. It starts in the Bible with passages that are open to everybody. It is as such methodologically a-theistic.

As Machoveč develops his Christology from below, he limits himself methodologically to that in the Bible which is in human hands. God and also that which people have experienced of God are not in human hands, but only the human statements about such God-experiences. Insofar as Christian theologians, for instance, H. Gollwitzer, Karl Barth, or Hans Küng, also limit themselves in their exegesis of the Bible to what is human in it, they likewise are methodological "atheists." But Machoveč's Marxist atheism goes deeper.

IMMANENCE

Machoveč's Marxist atheism is based on the modern principle of radical world-immanence. This principle has two aspects. In its first aspect, the principle of immanentism does not allow for any thought of an interference of God into the course of the world as nature or history, any thought of revelation, resurrection, effects of the divine spirit, or God's future, at least in the biblical sense. In its second aspect, the principle of immanence contains the conviction that men and women themselves are the makers of their history. The Marxist Erich Fromm speaks of "man for himself,"[4] and the Marxist Ernst Bloch talks of "man on his own."[5] According to the second aspect of the principle of immanentism, in this second half of the twentieth century, it is high time that modern men and women finally begin to shape their history consciously, in responsibility for the greatest possible well-being of all men and women. The first aspect of the principle of immanentism the Marxist enlightener shares with the bourgeoise and Freudian enlighteners. The second aspect of the principle is specifically Marxist.

The first aspect of the principle of immanentism definitely contradicts the spirit of the New Testament, while the second aspect does not. Machoveč makes this completely clear in his book on Jesus, in which he says that the word of Jesus aims at human actions. Marx's theory-practice dialectics has Christian roots. According to Jesus the truth makes one free, but only if the truth is done (John 3:21; 8:32; Rom. 1:18; 2:8; Gal. 2:14; Eph. 4:15; 1 John 3:18; 2 John 4; 3 John 3:48). Machoveč's critique of the Christian proclamation of divine grace is not directed against grace itself, but against its misunderstanding and abuse. Grace in the sense of the New Testament does not mean passivity. Grace aims at the person who has come of age, who has been enabled to act and is free and active. Machoveč welcomes as allies in the struggle for a more humane future all those Christians who are not put to sleep by the gospel but are awakened by it to action. That is the main meaning of Machoveč's book on Jesus: Jesus is no longer a separating factor between Christians and Marxists. In Jesus' call to new action, Christians and Marxists can meet.

DEMYTHOLOGIZATION

Machoveč not only accepts the second but also the first aspect of the modern principle of immanence. It is disputable whether this first aspect of immanence belongs necessarily to Marxism as such or whether it is merely the tribute that Marxism pays to the early stages of the bourgeois enlightenment from which it after all derives. This will become the more questionable the more Christians and other believers participate in the future socialist struggles on different continents. Machoveč nevertheless shares this first aspect of the principle of immanentism, and not only personally, for he finds himself bound to it by his Marxism. His double immanentism, in the sense of the denial of God's possible interference in history and of the obligation of people to emancipate themselves actively, gives his book on Jesus its earthly realism, but it also imposes serious limitations on its exegesis and hermeneutics.

One of those limitations is that Machoveč is forced by his immanentism to declare as "mythological" and therefore time-conditioned and historically negligible what Jesus and his disciples and all those who are mobilized through centuries to new words and deeds by his message, consider to be most important—namely, that God is. Contrary to Christian demythologizers—as, for instance, the Protestant theologian Gollwitzer or the Catholic theologian Küng—for Machoveč the demythologization process is unlimited. So Machoveč must explain the Easter event by the alleged fact that Peter overcame in himself the tragedy and absurdity of Golgotha and that he was able thereby to explain to himself the crucifixion as a victory of Jesus. Another hypothesis of Machoveč is that Peter's primacy over the other disciples, which is undeniable, has its foundation in his witness to Jesus' resurrection. He also interprets Jesus' cry of abandonment and loneliness on the cross as a call to the prophet Elijah. In spite of these and other fascinating exegetical proposals, Machoveč is led by his immanentism to identify Jesus' hope for God and Jesus' mission obedience as mythological forms of representation. Jesus expresses this hope and this obedience very clearly in respect to the future coming of the "son of man" in all his glory as well as to the redemptive significance of his death. His immanence principle prohibits Machoveč from realizing fully those forms of representation, not only in their mythological mode, but also in their inner intent.

Machoveč does indeed admit to the connection between the post-Easter view of the appearance of Jesus as the saving act of God on one hand and the words and deeds of the historical Jesus on the other hand. But Machoveč considers his explanation of the transition from the *proclaiming* Jesus to the *proclaimed* Jesus through historical circumstances to be as satisfactory as his explanation of the reversal of Peter through the "mortal leap" of an explanation which Peter gives to himself. The method of the Christology from below obviously has its limits! But also it cannot be denied that this method produces astonishing new insights into what is really of concern in the New Testament, namely, the Jesus who actually lived in history.

CHRISTOLOGY FROM ABOVE

Machoveč has deep antipathies against any kind of a Christology from above. This Christology takes into consideration the interference of supernatural factors in the Jesus story. God appears in the representation of the New Testament as an historical factor and not only in the faith of Jesus and his community. The Christology from above presupposes the confession about Jesus' divinity. It is concerned with God and with human God-experiences. The Christology from above shows the way to faith in Jesus as the saving interference of God in world history.

Machoveč considers such Christology from above to be precarious and doubtful, because of the exploitability of the faith it contains by the dominating powers in civil society, which have put the church into their services as an equilibrating and integrative societal factor. The Few use the dogmatized image of Jesus the Christ, which the church cultivates, for the control of the Many. Luckily enough, the ecclesiastical Christology from above was never able completely to replace the Christology from below. The never entirely repressed image of the man Jesus of Nazareth remained always alive and effective in the underground of Christianity as a counterforce against the authoritarian guardians of dead conventions. Again and again, the synoptic image of Jesus gained actuality in the protest of heretical and enlightenment movements against the injustices of the establishment in church, society, and state. Unlike Gardavsky, Machoveč prefers by far the synoptics over John, because of the former's emphasis on the simple man Jesus of Nazareth.

But Macoveč overlooks, as the Protestant theologian Gollwitzer[6] has pointed out quite clearly, that the power which repeatedly mobilizes protest against injustice in the history of Christianity was never only the isolated memory of this man Jesus with his sacrificing and sacrificed life. It was always this memory in unity with the divine affirmation and justification of the man Jesus: the dawn of the insight that Golgotha was not the last word; that this Jesus has the truth, the life, and the future on his side. There can be no doubt that the Easter message of Jesus' resurrection has again and again been ideologically misunderstood and abused by the Few for the purpose of the enslavement of the Many, like everything else in Christianity. But that is no argument against the Easter confession to Christ's resurrection as such.

Even Machoveč must admit that not only the memory of the historical Jesus—the Christology from below, kept alive by sceptical heretics and enlighteners—but also the confession to Jesus' uniqueness as the redemptive act of God—the Christology from above—has a socio-revolutionary tendency and energy. How else could have been possible the sacrificial lives and deaths of religious agents of change, such as M. L. King, Jr. and C. Torres, who not only knew of the historical Jesus but also believed in Jesus as the salvific act of God in history and nevertheless—or better still, exactly because of that belief—died bravely for the liberation of the Many from the yoke of the Few as did the Marxist Che Guevara?

Hegel worked himself up in the power of his dialectical logic, later on inherited by the Marxist movement, from the rather one-sided Kantian Christology from below of his youth not only to a Christology from above, but even to a synthesis of both forms of Christology. After his death, Hegel's synthesis between a heretical Christology from below and an orthodox Christology from above once again broke apart. Machoveč may very well go Hegel's way once more to a new synthesis between the two forms of Christology, if he does not continue to arrest the dialectical logic of his book on Jesus in the name of an unnecessarily abstract immanentism, but instead allows the dialectic to work itself out freely.

TOWARD THE FUTURE

As long ago as 1807 Hegel, philosopher of modernity par excellence, announced in the preface of his *Phäenomenologie des Geistes* (*The Phenomenology of Mind*), the beginning of a world historical transition period from modern European civilization to a new culture.[7] Hegel knew that he lived in a time when a new world was being born out of the womb of the old European world. The spirit of humanity had broken with the order of things hitherto prevailing in Western society and with the old ways of thinking, and let them all sink into the depth of the past. The spirit of humanity was initiating its own transformation toward a more rational and freer future. The spirit of the time, growing slowly and quietly ripening toward the new form it was to assume in the future, disintegrates one fragment after another of the structure of the previous European world. That the old world was tottering to its fall was indicated only by symptoms here and there. Frivolity and boredom were spreading in the established order of things, the undefined forebodings of something unknown—all these betokened to Hegel that something else was approaching, something new.

This world historical transition period, announced by Hegel one and a half centuries ago, continues today and may very well be protracted for another century in spite of—or precisely because of—the present social and cultural stagnation. At this moment of qualitative historical and social change, we can see more clearly than Hegel the alternative forms of the future: humanistic socialism or decline into barbarism and a long dark age. What do recent Marxist "atheistic" readings of the Bible mean in this context?

Hegel, the last Christian philosopher of old Europe and at the same time the most outstanding teacher of Marx, during the last decade of his life stated again and again the impossibility of the complete destruction of religious truth even in the most turbulent world historical transition period. For Hegel an entirely secular humanity and society were unthinkable and impossible.

According to Hegel, people cannot possibly be so estranged from their humanity that they would not have some element of religion in themselves, that is, of the experience of the Absolute Reality: even if it were only that they were afraid of religion or that they were longing for it or that they hated it. Even the person who hates religion is still inwardly preoccupied with it and involved in it. To people as people, religion is essential and inwardly necessary and a feeling not at all foreign to them. Marxists have seldom been afraid of religion. Their hatred toward religion is today receding everywhere. Their longing for religion is growing. The Marxists Gardavsky and Machoveč—as well as Bloch, Horkheimer, Adorno, Marcuse, Fromm, and Garaudy—give witness to this longing for that which is wholly other than the relative world as nature and history.

According to Hegel, in the present transition period, for religion everything depends essentially on the relationship between religion and the rest of a person's worldview. In this relationship lies the source of the disunion in this period between people's original urge toward religion and their secular consciousness, between faith and enlightenment, between salvation and emancipation. In this relationship, the most manifold forms of secular consciousness and the most various relationships between these forms and the religious interest have developed. The new atheistic reading of the Bible by Gardavsky and Machoveč constitutes one of those altered relationships between enlightenment and religious faith.

Hegel foresaw the rise of a materialistic critique of religion in the further progression of the present transition period toward a future society and culture qualitatively different from the old Western civilization. Bourgeois enlighteners had refused to posit the knowledge of God into comprehending reason. In their view, the consciousness of God is suppposed to spring only from feeling. The relationship of humans to God lies altogether in the realm of feeling. It must not be drawn into the dimension of dialectical thinking. In Hegel's perspective, when the bourgeois enlightener excludes God from the region of rational insight—the necessary, substantial subjectivity of humankind—then of course there is no alternative but to assign to God the area of contingent subjectivity, i.e., of feeling. Hegel is amazed that the agnostic bourgeois enlightener still attributes any objectivity to the God-experience at all. Bourgeois agnosticism prepares socialist atheism.

In Hegel's view, the materialist enlighteners—the empiricists, positivists, historicists, naturalists, socialists, etc.—are much more consequential in theological matters than the original subjective-idealist, agnostic bourgeois enlighteners. The materialists, taking spirit and thinking as something material—and being furthermore of the opinion that they have reduced them to mere sensations—identify God also as a mere product of feeling and deny God any objectivity whatsoever. The result is atheism. As Hegel sees them, for the materialists and atheists, God is the historical product of weakness, fear, joy, or also of egoistic hope or of greed and will to power. What is rooted only in my feeling, is merely for me, for my particularity. It is my property. It is not its own property. It is not independent in and for itself.

In order to overcome materialism and atheism, it seems to be necessary to Hegel, first of all, to demonstrate that the God-experience has not only feeling for its roots; that God is not merely my particular God. It must be shown that God is the God of all people and not the private property of this or that individual. Hegel asks for the deprivatization of the Christian faith which the bourgeois enlighteners have made into a private feeling. Hegel demands a political proof to all people that *God is* and not merely that the *feeling* of God exists: the application of the Christian principle of free subjectivity or subjective freedom to the secular family, society, state, history, and culture. Hegel is the first critical political theologian in the present transition period. At present, critical political theologians and theologians of liberation like H. Gollwitzer, J. Moltmann, J. B. Metz, C. Torres, and G. Gutiérrez, have begun to understand what Hegel meant: *that materialism and atheism can only be superseded by a political proof of God, the Christian practice of qualitative social change toward a new more humane world.*

Gardavsky says that he is a materialist and an atheist. That God is not yet completely dead means to him that humanity is not yet completely alive. God must die completely so that humanity may be completely alive. The political theologian Moltmann rightly asks: is Gardavsky really more of an atheist than Jacob, who struggled with the Lord and gained victory? Is Gardavsky more of an atheist than Jesus, who was condemned by the Sanhedrin for blasphemy, because he did not announce the Lord to be distant and beyond—as the priests did—but as close to humanity and history in the power of love which performs miracles? Gardavsky recognizes somehow in Jacob and Jesus, and in the power of love, an element which the traditional dualistic theism—not the dialectical theism of Meister Eckhart and of Hegel—missed, since it objectivated transcendence as beyond. This element is the presence of the Lord in the possibilities of love which cannot be exhausted in its notion, and for which all concepts are only names and signals and ciphers.

The young Hegel speaks in his early theological writings of this love, in which God is present, as a genuine living bond, as a true unity of opposites—the oppositions within a person, between person and person, between humans and nature, between man and woman, etc. For the young Hegel, this is the love which Jesus preaches. He puts this love of Jesus in opposition to the traditional, authoritarian religion of the old European world. Gardavsky continues the young Hegel's teaching on the dialectics of Christian love in secular form.

Moltmann also argues rightly that Gardavsky, through reading the Bible, has discovered an element in that reality of the Lord and of love, characterized by time, history, future, subjectivity, decision, which traditional atheism before and after Hegel missed and which cannot be exhausted in any atheistic conceptualization. Gardavsky goes not only beyond traditional dualistic theism but also beyond traditional atheism. The controversy concerning "God is dead" or "God is not yet completely dead" can be overcome in the future development of the present transition period by Marxists and Christians who, like Gardavsky, ask radically for the experience of that reality of the Lord and of love.

The political theologian Gollwitzer suggests rightly that Christians should not capitulate before the principle of absolute immanentism intrinsic to Marxism on the Left as well as to positivism on the Right, since it is precisely the negation of such an adaptation which is necessary for the preservation of the revolutionary energy of the Christian message of a dangerous freedom. To this revolutionary aspect of Christianity is directed today the interest of socialist humanists and critical theologians. Marxists, who at present expect more from Christians than during the entire century since the death of Marx, should certainly be interested in the fact that Christians do not capitulate before modern immanentism, but like Hegel hold firmly on to the position that God is—and thereby remain Christians. The Christian Hegel, a generation before Marx, was in no way hindered by his theology from comprehending the dialectics between the bourgeois and the proletarian classes which drives European civil society not only beyond itself into world markets, colonialism, and imperialism, but even beyond those developments into a new world of more universal rationality and freedom. Only when Christians do not capitulate before immanentism will the common reading of the Bible by Marxists and Christians become exciting and productive for both of them.

According to Gollwitzer, we live in the time of a new discovery of the historical Jesus by Marxists and Jews. This Jesus has been obscured for Jews and Marxists by traditional Christian theory and practice. The Jew and Marxist Max Horkheimer, founder of the famous critical theory of societal process in the Frankfurt School, sums up the new image of Jesus in his *Notizen* (*Notes*), published posthumously in 1974.[8] According to Horkheimer, Jesus died for all people. He could not keep himself back avariciously for himself. He belonged to whatever is suffering. But the church fathers made out of Jesus' death a religion, that is, a teaching which is a consolation, not only for the innocent victim, but even for the murderer. Since that time, this religion has been so successful in the world that the thought of Jesus has no longer anything at all to do with people's practice, not to speak of their suffering. Whoever reads the Gospels and does not see that Jesus died against his present-day representatives, cannot read at all. Traditional theology—not the new critical theology of the world as society and history—is for Horkheimer the grimest disgrace that has ever happened to any thought. After many inner struggles, the early church finally accepted soldiers into its community. The blessing of the murderous tools of two hostile armies became the sad privilege of the medieval and the modern church. All this could not have happened if Christians had read the Bible, not ideologically in order to justify unjustifiable social conditions, but truly.

In the perspective of Gollwitzer, a time will come in the future development of the present transition period when Marxists and Jews will discover not only the social aspect of the original Christian movement, but also the subversive, anti-positivist, future-producing tendencies and energies of the original Christ confessions of a Paul and of a John. Marxists and Jews will discover this not only for themselves but for Christians as well. The disinterest of the majority of Christians in the revolutionary socialist struggle for justice and peace—which only a minority of Christians has so far concluded from its Christ confession—makes the service of the Marxist exegesis of the Bible absolutely necessary. Machoveč's and Gardavsky's Christologies prove this conclusively by their fire of passion and their important exegetical perspectives.

Analogous Marxist and Christian historical experiences render possible those discoveries and encounters we find in Machoveč's and Gardavsky's writings. The socialist experiences how the Marxist theory—which was supposed to serve as a critical analysis of civil society and as a guide for revolutionary action—is transformed into a state ideology, an apology for unjust policies. The socialist revolutions promised communism and what came about was state socialism. The official world religions, including Christianity, sanctioned the domination of the Many by the One or the Few. As the Catholic modernist A. Loisy put it, Jesus promised the kingdom and all that came was the church—a church in which throne and altar were only too often all too closely connected. In the temptations of such degeneration, Machoveč and Gardavsky read the Bible and wrote about Jesus. They are temptations of people who cannot let matters stand as they are, since they are grasped by the vision of new human possibilities. These temptations are at least analogous to those of the disciples of Jesus. According to Gollwitzer, in the perspective of Jesus, they are even the same temptations for the same cause: the well-being of the people; their true greatness and ultimate freedom and dignity, which after all, is the will of the God of Jesus.

When Christians and Marxists, engaged in the same practice for social justice and peace, read the Bible together, they will see each other in a new way. Christians and Marxists will be close to the kingdom of the God who scattered the proud in the imagination of their hearts; who has put down the mighty from their thrones and exalted those of low degree; who has filled the hungry with good things and who has sent the rich away empty. They will understand the ethical imperatives which lead to the kingdom of God: Blessed are those who hunger and thirst for righteousness, for they shall be satisfied; blessed are the peacemakers, for they shall be called children of God; blessed are those who are persecuted for righteousness' sake, for theirs is the kingdom of Heaven.

Marxists and Christians will find out the things they really have in common. These are, first of all, the most simple and practical things, not the so-called theoretical positions, whether materialism or idealism, atheism or theism. They consist in the simple recognition that in all seriousness, no man or woman or child on earth should any longer be hungry; that in all seriousness, there should no longer be wars and no preparation for war in order to overcome economic depressions; that in all seriousness, nature should no longer be destroyed for private profit; that in all seriousness, people should no longer be dominated or exploited by others inside or outside of concentration camps; and that in all seriousness, human alienation and emptiness should be conquered. If such feeling is the fruit of the common Bible readings of Marxists and Christians and if it informs and motivates their political practice, then we may hope that the developments of the present historical transition period will indeed lead to a new world in which the life of all people will be more beautiful, longer, better, freer from suffering, and ever more favorable to the further unfolding of the spirit of women and men.

NOTES

1. Vitězslav Gardavsky, *Gott ist Nicht Ganz Tot* (1968), p. 39; Eng. trans., *God Is Not Yet Dead* (Baltimore: Penguin, 1973).
2. Karl Marx, *Die Fruehschriften,* 1965, p. 340 (Siebert's trans.). For another English translation see T. B. Bottomore and M. Rubel, eds., *Karl Marx: Selected Writings in Sociology and Social Philosophy* (New York: McGraw-Hill, 1956), pp. 68–69.
3. Milan Machoveč, *Jesus für Atheisten* (Stuttgart: Kreuz, 1972); Eng., *A Marxist Looks at Jesus* (Philadelphia: Fortress Press, 1976).
4. Erich Fromm, *Man for Himself* (Greenwich, Conn.: Fawcett, 1947).
5. Ernst Bloch, *Man on His Own* (New York: Herder and Herder, 1970).
6. Helmut Gollwitzer, *The Demands of Freedom* (New York: Harper & Row, 1965).
7. G. W. F. Hegel, *The Phenomenology of Mind,* trans. J. Baillie (London: Allen and Unwin, 1966).
8. Max Horkheimer, *Notizen, 1950–1969* (Frankfurt: Fischer, 1974).

BIBLIOGRAPHY

In this revised version of a longer paper, we omit the copious notes of the original and append this list of the primary philosophical and theological works to which Siebert refers, citing English translations as available.

Bloch, Ernst. *Atheism in Christianity.* New York: Herder and Herder, 1972.
Eliade, Mircea. *Cosmos and History.* New York: Harper & Row, 1959.
Feuerbach, Ludwig. *The Essence of Christianity.* New York: Harper & Row, 1957.
Gutiérrez, Gustavo. *A Theology of Liberation.* Maryknoll, N.Y.: Orbis Books, 1973.
Hegel, G. W. F. *Lectures on the Philosophy of Religion.* Translated by E. S. Haldane. New York: Humanities Press, 1955.
———. *On Christianity.* New York: Harper, 1961.
Horkheimer, Max. *Die Sehnsucht nach dem ganz Anderen.* Hamburg: Furche Verlag, 1970.
Kolakowski, Leszek. *The Key to Heaven and Conversation with the Devil.* New York: Grove Press, 1973.

Marx, Karl. *Die Fruehschriften*. Stuttgart: Alfred Kroner Verlag, 1966.

———. *Karl Marx: Early Writings*. Translated by T. B. Bottomore. New York: McGraw-Hill, 1964.

Marx and Engels on Religion. Edited by R. Niebuhr. New York: Schocken Books, 1967.

Metz, Johannes. *Theology of the World*. New York: Herder and Herder, 1969.

Moltmann, Jürgen. *The Crucified God*. New York: Harper & Row, 1974.

Voegelin, Eric. *From Enlightenment to Revolution*. Durham, N. C.: Duke University Press, 1975.

Index of Scriptural References

Index of Names

Index of Subjects

Definitions or key explanations of terms are marked with an asterisk following the page number. When the definition or explanation occurs within a spread of cited pages, the specific page number is asterisked and placed within parentheses.

Of related interest . . .

Norman K. Gottwald
THE TRIBES OF YAHWEH (2nd Printing)
A Sociology of the Religion of
Liberated Israel, 1250-1050 B.C.E.

"In this massive work on the sociology of religion in premonarchic ancient Israel, Gottwald meticulously examines the biblical theories of such scholars as Noth, Von Rad, Alt, and Mendenhall and sociological and historical-cultural views of Durkheim, Marx, and Weber to define such concepts as tribalism, social structure, and the cultic-ideological and tradition history in the various books of the Bible. He discusses the social systems and economic modes of the other peoples of the Near East and compares the ancient Israelite social structure to the Greek city states. While his conclusions concerning the formation and emergence of early Israel, the role of religion, and the roots of the sociology of Israel's religion may engender controversy, the comprehensiveness of this work in using primary as well as secondary sources makes it a valuable scholarly contribution to the study of this period."

Library Journal

"May well become a classic." *Journal for the Study of the Old Testament*

"A wealth of learning and keen analysis." *Jewish Chronicle*

ISBN 0-88344-499-2 *944pp. Paper $19.95*

J. Severino Croatto
EXODUS
A Hermeneutics of Freedom

"An excellent example of the innovative work now being done by biblical scholars in Latin America. Drawing on the work of Paul Ricoeur, the author develops a novel hermeneutical approach to the liberation theme, an approach that tries to disclose the 'reservoir-of-meaning' contained in foundational events, such as the Exodus, as they are interpreted by a historical community engaged in the struggle for liberation. His hermeneutic leads us once again into the 'strange new world of the Bible' and demonstrates its power to shape thought and life at a new point in time." *Theology Today*

"This book should be of great value, not only to theologians, scripture scholars, seminarians and religious educators, but also to ordinary Christians who wish to understand how to read the Bible in the light of their own experience." *Worldmission*

ISBN 0-88344-111-X *96pp. Paper $4.95*

José Porfirio Miranda
COMMUNISM IN THE BIBLE

"A scholarly study in biblical teaching—brief, direct, powerful—which puts the burden of proof on those who would deny that original and authentic Christianity is communistic (*not,* to say, Marxist). This is vintage Miranda— erudite, passionate, persuasive, and above all, disturbing."
Prof. Robert T. Osborn, Duke Univ.

ISBN 0-88344-014-8   *96pp. Paper $5.95*

George V. Pixley
GOD'S KINGDOM
A Guide for Biblical Study
Foreword by Harvey Cox

"This is a book that analyzes the vital connections between political economy and religious faith in all the major periods of biblical history. Compactly and clearly written, with abundant biblical references, Pixley's work will be a tremendous asset for study groups that want to grasp the Bible as a resource for social change."   *The College Store Journal*

"This is a thoroughly provocative study of the motif of the Kingdom of God, presented not in an abstract fashion but against the backdrop of the liberation issue in Latin America. Pixley, a professor of Old Testament at a Baptist seminary in Mexico City, is well aware of recent studies on this theme, and he deftly outlines the various stages of Kingdom theology against the political and religious contexts of Israel, Jesus, and the early Church."
The Bible Today

ISBN 0-88344-156-X   *128pp. Paper $5.95*

Elsa Tamez
BIBLE OF THE OPPRESSED

"This book attracts our attention, not only for wrestling with a major biblical theme but also for keeping us in continuous contact with the text of the Bible. She approaches 'oppression' and 'liberation' by means of key Hebrew words and provides new insights and stronger convictions for all readers."
Carroll Stuhlmueller editor of The Bible Today

"For those of us eager to hear the voices of Latin American women, this book is doubly welcome! Writing from a perspective of those oppressed by poverty and sexism, Elsa Tamez has brought us a wealth of analysis of the biblical understanding of oppression." *Prof. Letty M. Russell, Yale Univ.*

ISBN 0-88344-035-0   *80pp. Paper $5.95*

Donald Senior & Carroll Stuhlmueller
BIBLICAL FOUNDATIONS FOR MISSION

Two outstanding scripture scholars trace the notion of mission through the Old and New Testaments, searching out those traditions and dynamics that shaped Israel's consciousness of its destiny in relation to the Gentiles, and that ultimately led Christians to proclaim the Gospel to the Gentiles. This volume is concerned with how the universal mission became an accepted part of the Christian scriptural perspective.

Both authors are scripture scholars currently teaching at the Chicago Theological Union. Carroll Stuhlmueller is editor of *The Bible Today* and he and his colleague have brought their respective expertise together in this volume, offering a complete analysis of the Bible from the perspective of mission. The result benefits students of the Bible, missioners, missiologists, and will prove useful as a basic text for introductory courses on the Bible.

ISBN 0-88344-046-6   *384pp. Cloth $25.00*
ISBN 0-88344-047-4   *Paper $14.95*

John L. Topel
THE WAY TO PEACE (3rd Printing)
Liberation Through the Bible

"*The Way to Peace* is good fare. Topel traces the roots of liberation theology through the Old and New Testaments. The book is scholarly, well footnoted and fascinating reading."   *Today's Parish*

"The success of Topel's method results from his strict adherence to his theme and his profound understanding of the Scriptures. Theological arguments are supported by biblical references. Excellent summaries are helpful; and notes, annotated at great length, add value to the book." *Spirituality Today*

"Uses the most sophisticated current scriptural tools to carve out an excellent reintroduction to the Bible and to argue that our present freedom is the World's ultimate aim."   *America*

ISBN 0-88344-704-5   *199pp. Paper $7.95*

Fernando Belo
A MATERIALIST READING OF THE GOSPEL OF MARK

"On certain occasions in the past, the Gospel narratives about Jesus the Messiah have spoken powerfully to men and women caught in the throes of social change and longing for a new world. I believe they can also speak powerfully to us today—if only we can free ourselves from our social conditions enough to hear what they have to say. Fernando Belo has made an important contribution toward this end. In his book he offers a novel analysis of the text of Mark's Gospel and suggests that we distinguish between the messianic narrative and the theological discourse accompanying it. He sets his reading of the Gospel in the context of the social conditions in the first century—specifically, the economic and political structures and the power relationships expressed by them. And he assumes that the struggle between those who have power and privilege and those who long for liberation from bondage is at the heart of social reality. In fact, he claims that we can understand a narrative only if we take into account its relation to a particular social formation; i.e., the way it functions as a force either to support *or* to subvert and transform the established order. . . . As I read the Gospel of Mark in the light of what he has to say, I find myself looking at the text with new eyes. It addresses me in a more compelling way. I hear and am challenged to respond to a Word I had not heard before."

Prof. Richard Shaull, Princeton University

ISBN 0-88344-323-6   *384pp. Paper $12.95*

Richard J. Cassidy & Philip Scharper, editors
POLITICAL ISSUES IN LUKE-ACTS

"Here we have nine studies which sharply probe aspects of the political Luke and/or Luke's political Jesus, including a study by Cassidy himself as well as studies which take him to task on various counts. All told, *Political Issues in Luke-Acts* is an extremely valuable showcase of the most current research in Luke-Acts and its societal concerns."

Prof. Edward C. Hobbs, Wellesley College

"These lively, provocative, and well-informed essays center around the thesis of Dr. Richard J. Cassidy in his *Jesus, Politics, and Society,* in which he challenges the notion that Luke-Acts was written as a political apologetic. The result is a stimulating debate, as though one were participating in a discussion, at once learned and relevant, on the exegetical issue of Lukan redaction, and of course, on the moral question of Jesus' attitude toward civil authority." *Prof. Howard Clark Kee, Boston University*

ISBN 0-88344-390-2   *192pp. Cloth $16.95*
ISBN 0-88344-385-6   *Paper $9.95*